AFRICANA

Arts and Letters

An A-to-Z Reference of Writers, Musicians, and Artists of the African American Experience

D1533862

William Edward Burghardt Du Bois

Praise for the original *Africana*:

"Attractive and well-designed. . . .It is the first reference work I have encountered that is attractive enough and accessible enough to simply pick up, open to any page and start reading. . . . A major achievement."

—The Los Angeles Times Book Review

"For this accessible, fascinating volume, [Gates and Appiah] have commissioned and condensed more than 3000 articles by more than 400 scholars . . . Bursting with information and enhanced by contributions from its illustrious advisory board . . . this book belongs on every family's reference shelf. Du Bois himself could not have done better."

—Starred Publisher's Weekly Review

"A landmark achievement."

—Publisher's Weekly Best Books 99

"An informational jewel."

—Emerge

The editors have admirably fulfilled the dream of African American scholar and leader W.E.B. Du Bois, who worked for much of his life to create such a monument. Highly recommended reading for all."

—Library Journal

"The best one-volume reference book on Africa and the African diaspora now available . . . Excellent articles . . . remarkably up to date."

—The Philadelphia Inquirer

Africana holds a unique place among reference works by bridging the Atlantic in numerous ways . . . the strength of *Africana's* unique linkage of the African and African-American becomes evident in comparison to other reference works treating one or the other half of that whole . . . *Africana* includes unique entries not found in the African American Almanac (Gale, 1997), An African Biographical Dictionary (ABC-CLIO, 1994), Encyclopedia of African American Culture & History (Macmillan 1996) to cite but a few prominent examples."

—Booklist

"Imposing in its sheer mass, *Africana* . . . is a 2,096-page, single volume 'encyclopedia of the black world.' This is no overstatement, as the range of entries ably demonstrates."

—Vibe

"Complete, balanced, informative, and addictively fun to browse."

—*Boston Magazine*

"A source of information that would surely make Du Bois proud."

—*The Tampa Tribune*

"Editors Henry Louis Gates and Kwame Anthony Appiah fulfilled W.E.B. Du Bois' vision on an encyclopedia of African-based culture throughout the world. The scholarship is unassailable [and] the text is accessible and understandable."

—*The Seattle Times*

"An invaluable resource of the historical, social, and cultural lushness of a scattered and varied people . . . Deserve[s] a place in every library, in every heart."

—*The Miami Herald*

"Belongs in every student's library and school . . . A monumental record of the black experience."

—*The Baltimore Sun*

"As the second millennium ends and a third begins, a new landmark volume brings together the richness and history of African and African-American culture."

—*Beyond the Cover*

"A monumental reference work, brings the richness of African and African American culture out of the shadows and into the living rooms of families across America . . . Destined to have a major effect by filling a cultural void . . . *Africana* presents exacting scholarship in an accessible, entertaining and visually animated style . . . conveys the richness, variety, and sweep of the African and African American experience as no other project before it . . . A reference work of both range and depth that symbolically will reunite the richly varied strands of the African Diaspora."

—*The Portland Skanner*

"A long-awaited overview of the history of the peoples of Africa and the African diaspora."

—*Wall Street Journal*

"*Africana* will be a very useful tool, and may even set new standards and change attitudes about the African and African-American experience."

—*The New York Times Book Review*

AFRICANA

Arts and Letters

An A-to-Z Reference of Writers, Musicians, and Artists of the African American Experience

Editors

Kwame Anthony Appiah, *Princeton University*
Henry Louise Gates, Jr., *Harvard University*

RUNNING PRESS
PHILADELPHIA · LONDON

Arts and Letters Cover Credits:
Top: Skirt, detail, Dyula people, Ivory Coast, early-20th century cotton. The Newark Museum/
Art Resource, NY
Bottom: King Oliver's Creole Jazz Band, Chicago, ca. 1922. © Bettmann/CORBIS
Back cover: Phillis Wheatley, Bettmann/CORBIS

Frontispiece: © Bettmann/CORBIS

9   8   7   6   5   4   3   2   1
Digit on the right indicates the number of this printing

Library of Congress Cataloging-in-Publication Number 2004095748
ISBN 0-7624-2042-1

Cover design by Serrin Bodmer
Interior design by Bob Anderson
Edited by Veronica Mixon, Diana Von Glahn, and Lindsay Powers
Typography: 9.5/11.5 Berling Roman

The entries in *Arts and Letters: An A-to-Z Reference of the Writers, Musicians, and Artists of the
African American Experience* originally appeared in Basic Civitas Books' *Africana: The Encyclo-
pedia of the African and the African American Experience* © 1999 Kwame Anthony Appiah and
Henry Louis Gates, Jr.

This book may be ordered by mail from the publisher.
Please include $2.50 for postage and handling.
But try your bookstore first!

Running Press Book Publishers
125 South Twenty-second Street
Philadelphia, Pennsylvania 19103-4399

Visit us on the web!
www.runningpress.com

*To the memory of William Edward Burghardt Du Bois
and in honor of Nelson Rolihlahla Mandela*

Advisory Board

Table of Contents

Introduction

Editor's Note on this Edition: *Arts and Letters: An A-to-Z Reference of Writers, Musicians, and Artists of the African American Experience* was abridged from *Africana: The Encyclopedia of the African and African American Experience*. Some of the entries are accompanied by all new photographs. Credit goes to Veronica Mixon for distilling the very best of the original *Africana* into this more portable, compact desk reference.

The history of how the original *Africana* came to be is a poignant story of faith, politics, and persistence despite what seemed, at times, like an insurmountable struggle. Kwame Anthony Appiah, and Henry Louis Gates, Jr., editors of that original edition, told the story in its introduction. We've chosen to reprint that introduction in this edition, to help you appreciate the struggle that gave birth to *Africana* and the editorial decisions that shaped it.

May the story hearten you as you advance toward your own dreams.

How the original Africana Came to Be

Between 1909 and his death in 1963, W. E. B. Du Bois, the Harvard-trained historian, sociologist, journalist, and political activist, dreamed of editing an "Encyclopedia Africana." He envisioned a comprehensive compendium of 'scientific' knowledge about the history, cultures, and social institutions of people of African descent: of Africans in the Old World, African Americans in the New World, and persons of African descent who had risen to prominence in Europe, the Middle East, and Asia. Du Bois sought to publish nothing less than the equivalent of a black *Encyclopedia Britannica*, believing that such a broad assemblage of biography, interpretive essays, facts, and figures would do for the much denigrated black world of the twentieth century what *Britannica* and Denis Diderot's Encyclopédie had done for the European world of the eighteenth century.

These publications, which consolidated the scholarly knowledge accumulated by academics and intellectuals in the Age of Reason, served both as a tangible sign of the enlightened skepticism that characterized that era of scholarship, and as a basis upon which further scholarship could be constructed. These encyclopedias became monuments to "scientific" inquiry, bulwarks against superstition, myth, and what their authors viewed as the false solace of religious faith. An encyclopedia of the African diaspora in Du Bois's view would achieve these things for persons of African descent.

But a black encyclopedia would have an additional function. Its publication would, at least symbolically, unite the fragmented world of the African diaspora, a diaspora created by the European slave trade and the turn-of-the-century "scramble for Africa." Moreover, for Du Bois, marshalling the tools of "scientific knowledge," as he would put it in his landmark essay, "The Need for an Encyclopedia of the Negro" (1945), could also serve as a weapon in the war against racism: "There is need for young pupils and for mature students of a statement of the present condition of our knowledge concerning the darker races and especially concerning Negroes, which would make available our present scientific knowledge and set aside the vast accumulation of tradition and prejudice which makes such knowledge difficult now for the layman to obtain: A Vade mecum for American schools, editors, libraries, for Europeans inquiring into the race status here, for South Americans, and Africans."

The publication of such an encyclopedia, Du Bois continued, would establish "a base for further advance and further study" of "questions affecting the Negro race." An encyclopedia of the Negro, he reasoned, would establish both social policy and "social thought and discussion...upon a basis of accepted scientific conclusion."

Du Bois first announced his desire to edit an "Encyclopedia Africana" in a letter to Edward Wilmot Blyden, the Pan-Africanist intellectual, in Sierra Leone in 1909: "I am venturing to address you on the subject of a Negro Encyclopædia. In celebration of the 50th anniversary of the Emancipation of the American Negro, I am proposing to bring out an Encyclopedia Africana covering the chief points in the history and condition of the Negro race." Du Bois sent a similar letter to dozens of other scholars, white and black, including William James, Hugo Munsterberg, George Santayana, Albert Bushnell Hart (his professors at Harvard), President Charles William Eliot of Harvard, Sir Harry Johnston, Sir Flinders Petrie, Giuseppe Sergi, Franz Boas, J. E. Casely-Hayford, John Hope, Kelly Miller, Benjamin Brawley, Anna Jones, Richard Greener, Henry Ossawa Tanner, and several others, all of whom—with the sole exception of President Eliot—agreed to serve on his editorial board. Du Bois sought to create a board of "One Hundred Negro Americans, African and West Indian Scholars," as he put it in a letter, and a second board of white advisors. Du Bois, in other words, sought the collaboration of the very best scholars of what we would call today African Studies and African American Studies, as well as prominent American and European intellectuals such as James and Boas.

Nevertheless, as he put it to Blyden, "the real work I want done by Negroes." Du Bois, admitting that this plan was "still in embryo," created official stationery that projected a publication date of the first volume in 1913—"the Jubilee of Emancipation in America and the Tercentenary of the Landing of the Negro." The remaining four volumes would be published between 1913 and 1919.

Despite the nearly unanimous enthusiasm that greeted Du Bois's call for participation, he could not secure the necessary funding to mount the massive effort necessary to edit an encyclopedia of the black world. But he never abandoned the idea. At the height of the Great Depression, the idea would surface once again.

Anson Phelps Stokes, head of the Phelps-Stokes Association, a foundation dedicated to ameliorating race relations in America, called a meeting of 20 scholars and public figures at Howard University on November 7, 1931, to edit an "Encyclopedia of the Negro," a Pan-African encyclopedia similar to Du Bois's 1909 project. Incredibly, neither Du Bois nor Alain Locke, a Harvard trained Ph.D. in philosophy and the dean of the Harlem Renaissance, nor Carter G. Woodson (like Du Bois, a Harvard Ph.D. in history and the founder of the Association for the Study of Negro Life and History) was invited to attend. Du Bois protested, angrily, to Phelps Stokes. A second meeting was convened on January 9, 1932, at which Du Bois was unanimously elected editor-in-chief. Between 1932 and 1946, Du Bois would serve as "Editor-in-Chief" of the second incarnation of his project, now named "The Encyclopædia of the Negro," and housed at 200 West 135th Street in New York City.

Du Bois planned a four-volume encyclopedia, each volume comprising 500,000 words. Just as he had done in 1909, he secured the cooperation of an impressive array of scholars, including Charles Beard, Franz Boas, John R. Connors, Edith Abbott, Felix Frankfurter, Otto Klineburg, Carl Van Doren, H. L. Mencken, Roscoe Pound, Robert E. Park, Sidney Hook, Harold Laski, Broadus Mitchell, "and scores of others," as Du Bois put it in a letter to the historian Charles Wesley. Du Bois's "Encyclopedia of the Negro" would require a budget of $225,000. It would be written by a staff of between "25 and 100 persons" hired to be "research aides," to be located in editorial offices to be established in New York, Chicago, Atlanta, and New Orleans. They would prepare bibliographies, collect books and manuscripts, and gather and write "special data" and shorter entries. Black and white scholars, primarily located in Europe, America, and Africa, would write longer interpretive entries.

Du Bois tells us that his project was interrupted by the Depression for three years. But by 1935, he was actively engaged in its planning full-time, time made available by his forced resignation from his position as editor of *The Crisis* magazine, the official organ of the National Association for the Advancement of Colored People, which Du Bois had held since its first publication in 1910. Du Bois had written an editorial advocating the development of independent Negro social and economic institutions, since the goal posts of the Civil Rights Movement appeared to be receding. The NAACP's board of directors was outraged and demanded his resignation. Du Bois obliged. Du Bois sought funding virtually everywhere, including the Works Progress Administration and the Federal Writers' Project, to no avail, despite the fact that Phelps Stokes had pledged, on a matching basis, half of the needed funds. He continued to write to hundreds of scholars, soliciting their cooperation. E. Franklin Frazier, the great black sociologist, declined Du Bois's overture, citing in a letter dated November 7, 1936, the presence of too many "politicians," "statesmen," "big Negroes," and "whites of good will" on Du Bois's editorial board. Throw out the table of contents, fire the board of editors, replace them with scholars, Frazier wrote, and he would consider joining the project.

A few months before this exchange, Du Bois was viciously attacked by Carter G. Woodson in the black newspaper the *Baltimore Afro-American*. On May 30, 1936, a page-one headline blared the news that Woodson "Calls Du Bois a Traitor if He Accepts Post," with a subtitle adding for good measure: "He Told Ofays, We'd Write Own History." Woodson charged that Du Bois had stolen the idea of The Encyclopedia of the Negro from him and that his project was doomed to failure because Du Bois was financed by, and his editorial board included, white people. Du Bois was embarrassed and sought to defend himself in letters to potential contributors and board members. Between his enemies at the NAACP and his intellectual rivals such as Woodson and Frazier, Du Bois faced an enormous amount of opposition to his encyclopedia project. In this swirl of controversy, in the midst of the Depression, funding appeared increasingly elusive.

Du Bois's assistant editor, Rayford Logan, like Du Bois, Woodson, and Charles Wesley a Harvard-trained Ph.D. in history, told a poignant story about the failure of this project to receive funding. By 1937, Du Bois had secured a pledge of $125,000 from the Phelps-Stokes Fund to proceed with his project—half of the funds needed to complete it. He applied to the Carnegie Corporation for the remaining half of his budget, with the strong endorsement of Phelps Stokes and the president of the General Education Board, a group of four or five private foundations that included the Rockefeller Foundation. So convinced was Du Bois that his project would finally be funded, that he invited Logan to wait with him for the telephone call that he had been promised immediately following the Carnegie board meeting. A bottle of vintage champagne sat chilling on Du Bois's desk in a silver bucket, two cut crystal champagne flutes resting nearby.

The phone never rang. Persuaded that Du Bois was far too "radical" to serve as a model of disinterested scholarship, and lobbied by Du Bois's intellectual enemies, such as the anthropologist Melville J. Herskovits, the Carnegie Corporation rejected the project.

Nevertheless, Du Bois stubbornly persisted, even publishing two putative "entries" from the Encyclopædia in *Phylon* magazine in 1940, one on Robert Russa Moton, the principal of Tuskegee Institute between 1915 and 1935, the other on Alexander Pushkin. He even was able to publish two editions, in 1945 and 1946, of a Preparatory Volume with Reference Lists and Reports of the Encyclopædia of the Negro. But the project itself never could secure adequate backing.

David Levering Lewis, Du Bois's biographer, tells us what happened to Du Bois's promised funding. The executive committee of the General Education Board rejected the proposal early in May 1937. "In his conference a few days later with Carnegie Corporation president Frederick Keppel, GEB's Jackson Davis paradoxically pleaded for favorable Carnegie consideration of the project. 'Dr. Du Bois is the most influential Negro in the United States,' Davis reminded Keppel. 'This project would keep him busy for the rest of his life.' Predictably, Carnegie declined. Within a remarkably short time, the study of the Negro (generously underwritten by the

Carnegie Corporation) found a quite different direction under a Swedish scholar then unknown in the field of race relations, one whose understanding of American race problems was to be distinctly more psychological and less economic than was Du Bois's.... When the president of the Phelps Stokes Fund wrote Du Bois in 1944 at the time of the publication of *An American Dilemma*: [The Negro Problem and Modern Democracy] that 'there has been no one who has been quite so often quoted by [Gunnar] Myrdal than yourself,' Du Bois must have savored the irony."

Adding insult to injury, in 1948 the General Education Board, along with the Dodd Mead publishing company, approached Frederick Patterson, the president of Tuskegee Institute, to edit a new incarnation of the project, to be entitled *The Negro: An Encyclopedia*. Then in 1950, the historian Charles Wesley wrote to Du Bois, informing him that in the wake of Carter Woodson's death, the Association for the Study of Negro Life and History had decided to resurrect The Encyclopedia Africana project, reminding him of Woodson's claims to have conceived of it in 1921. Du Bois wished him well, but cautioned him in a postscript that "there is no such thing as a cheap encyclopedia." Everyone, it seemed, wanted to claim title to the encyclopedia, but no one wanted Du Bois to serve as its editor. For black scholars, Africana had become the Grail. Its publication, as Du Bois put it "would mark an epoch."

Long after Du Bois had abandoned all hope of realizing his great ambition, an offer of assistance would come quite unexpectedly from Africa. On September 26, 1960, Du Bois announced that Kwame Nkrumah, the president of the newly independent Republic of Ghana, had invited him to repatriate to Ghana, where he would serve as the editor-in-chief of *The Encyclopædia Africana*. Du Bois accepted, moving in 1961. On December 15, 1962, in his last public speech before his death on the eve of the March on Washington in August 1963, Du Bois addressed a conference assembled expressly to launch—at last—his great project.

He wanted to edit "an Encyclopædia Africana based in Africa and compiled by Africans," he announced, an encyclopedia that is "long overdue," referring no doubt to his previously frustrated attempts. "Yet," he continued with a certain grim satisfaction, "it is logical that such a work had to wait for independent Africans to carry it out [because] the encyclopedia is concerned with Africa as a whole." Citing his own introductory essay in the Preparatory Volume of 1945, Du Bois justified this project by railing against "present thought and action" that "are all too often guided by old and discarded theories of race and heredity, by misleading emphasis and silence of former histories." After all of these centuries of slavery and colonialism, on the eve of the independence of the Continent, "it is African scholars themselves who will create the ultimate Encyclopædia Africana." Eight months later Du Bois would be dead, and with him died his 54-year-old dream of shepherding a great black encyclopedia into print. Nevertheless, the Secretariat of the Encyclopædia Africana, based in Accra, Ghana, which Du Bois founded, eventually published three volumes of biographical dictionaries, in the late seventies and early eighties, and has recently announced plans to publish an encyclopedia about the African continent in 2009, which is welcome news.

We first became enamored of this project as students at the University of Cambridge. One of us, Henry Louis Gates, Jr., was a student of Wole Soyinka, the great playwright who in 1986 became the first African to receive the Nobel Prize for Literature. The other, Kwame Anthony Appiah, was an undergraduate studying philosophy. Though we came from very different backgrounds—rural West Virginia and urban Asante, in Ghana—we both already had, like Soyinka, a sense of the worlds of Africa and her diaspora as profoundly interconnected, even if, as we learned ourselves, there were risks of misunderstanding that arose from our different origins and experiences. The three of us represented three different places in the black world, and we vowed in 1973 to edit a Pan-African encyclopedia of the African diaspora, inspired by Du Bois's original objective formulated in 1909. Du Bois's later conception of the project was, we felt, too narrow in its scope, and too parochial in its stated desire to exclude the scholarly work of those who had not had the good fortune, by accident of birth, to have been born on the African continent. (Du Bois himself, had this rule been literally applied, would have been excluded from his own project!) Instead, we sought to edit a project that would produce a genuine compendium of "Africana."

Our own attempts to secure the necessary support were in vain too until four years ago when, first, Quincy Jones and Martin Payson, and then Sonny Mehta and Alberto Vitale at Random House, agreed to fund the preparation of a prototype of a CD-ROM encyclopedia of the African diaspora, to be edited by us, with Soyinka serving as the chair of an international and multiethnic board of editors. Two years later we secured the support for a 2-million-word encyclopedia from Frank Pearl, the CEO of a new publisher called Perseus Books, and from the Microsoft Corporation. Modifying the editorial structure that Du Bois planned to use to complete *The Encyclopædia of the Negro*, we deployed a staff of some three dozen writers and editors, and we solicited about 400 scholars to write longer, interpretive articles.

Du Bois's own idea, although he did not admit this, probably arose at least in part out of the publication of the Encyclopædia Judaica in 1907, as well as black encyclopedia antecedents such as James T. Holly, who published *The Afro-American Encyclopedia* in 1895, Alexander W. Wayman's *Cyclopedia of African Methodism* (1882), Charles O. Boothe's *The Cyclopedia of the Colored Baptists of Alabama* (1895), and Revels Adams's *Cyclopedia of African Methodism in Mississippi* (1902). Other unpublished projects patterned after Du Bois's 1909 proposal included Daniel Murray's monumental "Historical and Biographical Encyclopædia of the Colored Race Throughout the World," which was to have been published in 1912 in six volumes and, later, Edward Garrett's self-written "A Negro Encyclopedia," consisting of 4000 entries, and completed on the eve of World War II. Both encyclopedias exist in manuscript form, but tragically were never published. All told, more than two dozen black encyclopedias have been published in the past century with limited distribution, but none has explored in a single compass both the African continent and the triumphs and the tragedies of Africa's people and their descendants around the globe.

That continent is where human prehistory begins. It was in Africa, as biologists now believe, that our species evolved, and so, in a literal sense, every modern human being is of African descent. Indeed, it was probably only about 100,000 years ago that the first members of our species left Africa, traveled across the Suez Peninsula, and set out on an adventure that would lead to the peopling of the whole earth.

It is important to emphasize that Africa has never been separate from the rest of the human world. There have been long periods and many cultures that knew nothing of life in Africa. For much of African history, even in Africa, most Africans were unaware of other peoples in their own continent, unaware, in fact, that they shared a continent at all (just as most people in Europe, Asia, Australasia, and the Americas would have been astonished to learn that they were Europeans, Asians, Australasians, or Americans!). But the Straits of Gibraltar and the Suez Peninsula were always bridges more than obstacles to travel; the Mediterranean was already a system of trade long before the founding of Rome; the Sahara Desert, which so many people imagine as an impenetrable barrier, has a network of trade routes older than the Roman Empire. Starting some 2,000 or so years ago, in the area of modern day Cameroon, Bantu-speaking migrants fanned out south and east into tropical Africa, taking with them the knowledge of iron smelting and new forms of agriculture. And so, when Greek and Arab travelers explored the East Coast of Africa in the first millennium C.E., or European explorers began to travel down the West African coast toward the equator in the fifteenth century, they were making direct contact with cultures with which their ancestors had very often been in remote and indirect contact all along.

The first European scholars to write about Africa in the modern period, which begins with the European Age of Discovery, knew very little of Africa's history. They did not know that their ancestors thousands of generations ago had also lived in Africa. If they had read Herodotus, they might have noticed his brief discussion of the civilizations of the upper Nile, and so they might have realized that Egypt was in touch with other African societies. However, it would probably not have occurred to them that, since those societies were also in touch with still others, Egypt was in touch with Central Africa as well. So they thought of much of Africa as being outside the human historical narrative they already knew.

These first scholars were also obviously struck by the physical differences between Africans and themselves—especially of skin color and hair—and by the differences between the customs back home and the ones the European explorers found on the Guinea coast. And so they thought of Africans as different in kind from themselves, wondering, sometimes, whether they were really also descendants of Adam and Eve.

Attitudes like these had already distorted Western understandings of Africa from the fifteenth century on. Worse yet, as the transatlantic slave trade developed, so did an increasingly negative set of ideas about African peoples and their capacities. It became normal to think of black Africans as inferior to Europeans, and many Europeans found in that inferiority a rationalization for the enslavement of Africans. As a result, much of the writing about Africans and about people of African descent in the New World was frankly derogatory. Because modern Africans were educated in European colonies, they too inherited a distorted and dismissive attitude toward Africa's past and African capacities, and one of the first tasks of modern African intellectuals has been to try to frame a sense of the world and our place in it that is freed from these sad legacies.

There have been many skirmishes in the battle to find a just representation of Africa and her peoples. But in the course of this century—and more especially in the last 30 or 40 years—a more objective knowledge of Africa has gradually emerged, both in Africa and elsewhere. Anthropologists began to describe the rich religious, artistic, and social life of African peoples. African historians have learned to interpret oral histories, passed down in Africa's many traditions, cross-checking them against archæological and documentary evidence to produce a rich picture of the African past. Economists and political scientists, literary critics and philosophers, scholars of almost every discipline in the social sciences and the humanities have contributed to this new knowledge, as have scholars on every continent, Africans prominent among them. Work in African American Studies has led to new understandings of the culture of slaves and of the role of people of African descent in shaping the New World's language, religion, agriculture, architecture, music, and art. As a result, it is now possible to comb through a great library of material on African history and on the peoples of Africa and her diaspora, and to offer, in a single volume, a compendium of facts and interpretations.

An encyclopedia cannot include everything that is known about its subject matter, even everything that is important. So we have had to make choices. (And, alas, some of the most interesting questions are as yet unanswered.) But we have sought to provide a broad range of information and so to represent the full range of Africa and her diaspora. About two-fifths of the text of the encyclopedia has to do exclusively, or almost so, with the African continent: the history of each of the modern nations of Africa and what happened within their territories before those nations developed; the names of ethnic groups, including some that were formerly empires and nations, and their histories; biographies of eminent African men and women; major cities and geographical features: rivers, mountains, lakes, deserts; forms of culture: art, literature, music, religion; and some of Africa's diverse plant and animal life. Another third deals mostly with Latin America and the Caribbean, focusing on the influence of African cultures and people of African descent in shaping those portions of the New World. Slightly less than a third of the material deals with North America in the same way. And the rest is material of cross-cultural significance or has to do with the African presence in Europe, Asia, or the rest of the world.

Our main focus has been on history—political and social—and on literature and the arts, including music, to which African and African American contributions have been especially notable in modern times. Our aim has been to give a sense of the wide diversity of peoples, cultures, and traditions that we know about in Africa in historical times, a feel for the environment in which that history was lived, and a broad outline of the contributions of people of African descent, especially in the Americas, but, more generally, around the world.

It is natural, faced with a compendium of this sort, to go looking first for what we know already and to be especially pleased with ourselves if we find something missing! But in setting out to make an encyclopedia in a single volume, we had to make choices all the time about what to include, and we did so in the light of our own best judgments, in consultation with many scholars from around the world. It has been one of the great satisfactions of compiling a work with so many colleagues with so many different specialized areas of knowledge, that we have been able to fill in some of our own many areas of ignorance. That, we believe, is the great pleasure of this new encyclopedia: it not only answers many questions that you knew you wanted to ask, it invites you to ask questions that you had not dreamed of asking. We hope you will find, as we have, that the answers to these unfamiliar questions are as amazing and as varied as Africa, her peoples, and their descendants all around the globe.

We mentioned earlier some of the many encyclopedias of various aspects of African and African American life that have been published in the past. The publication of *Africana: The Encyclopedia of the African and African American Experience* as a one-volume print edition aspires to belong in the grand tradition of encyclopedia editing by scholars interested in the black world on both sides of the Atlantic. It also relies upon the work of thousands of scholars who have sought to gather and to analyze, according to the highest scholarly standards, the lives and the worlds of black people everywhere. We acknowledge our indebtedness to these traditions of scholarly endeavor—more than a century old—to which we are heirs, by dedicating our encyclopedia to the monumental contribution of W. E. B. Du Bois.

Kwame Anthony Appiah
Henry Louis Gates, Jr.

Acknowledgments

In addition to the contributors, who are acknowledged elsewhere in this book, the editors wish to express their profound gratitude to the following persons:

Sharon Adams, Rachel Antell, Bennett Ashley, Robbie Bach, Tim Bartlett, Craig Bartholomew, John Blassingame, William G. Bowen, Peggy Cooper Cafritz, Elizabeth Carduff, Albert Carnesale, Jamie Carter, Sheldon Cheek, Chin-lien Chen, Coureton C. Dalton, Karen C. C. Dalton, the late Charles T. Davis, Rafael de la Dehesa, John Donatich, David Du Bois, Joseph Duffy, Olawale Edun, Richard Ekman, Lynn Faitelson, Amy Finch, Henry Finder, Lisa Finder, Kerry Fishback, Susanne Freidberg, Elaine Froehlich, Tony Gleaton, Peter Glenshaw, Lisa Goldberg, Matthew Goldberg, Jaman Greene, Holly Hartman, Pete Higgins, Jessica Hochman, Chihiro Hosoe, Pat Jalbert, Mary Janisch, Quincy Jones, Paul Kahn, Leyla Keough, Jeremy Knowles, Joanne Kendall, Harry Lasker, Todd Lee, Krzysztof Lenk, Erroll McDonald, Jack McKeown, Della R. Mancuso, Nancy Maull, Sonny Mehta, Joel W. Motley III, Richard Newman, Peter Norton, Mark O'Malley, Jennifer Oppenheimer, Francisco Ortega, Martin Payson, Frank Pearl, Ben Penglase, Kevin Rabener, Toni Rosenberg, Daryl Roth, Michael Roy, Neil Rudenstine, Kelefa Sanneh, Carrie Seglin, Keith Senzel, Bill Smith, Wole Soyinka, Patti Stonesifer, Patricia Sullivan, Carol Thompson, Larry Thompson, Lucy Tinkcombe, Kate Tuttle, Charles Van Doren, Robert Vare, Michael Vazquez, Alberto Vitale, Sarah Von Dreele, Philippe Wamba, Carrie Mae Weems, and X Bonnie Woods.

Contributors to the original *AFRICANA: The Encyclopedia of the African and African American Experience*

Rosanne Adderley, *Tulane University*
Marian Aguiar, *Amherst, Massachusetts*
Emmanuel Akyeampong, *Harvard University*
Suzanne Albulak, *Cambridge, Massachusetts*
Samir Amin, *Director of the Forum Tiers Monde, Dakar, Senegal*
George Reid Andrews, *University of Pittsburgh*
Abdullahi Ahmed An-Na'im, *Emory University*
Rachel Antell, *San Francisco, California*
Kwame Anthony Appiah, *Princeton University*
Jorge Arce, *Boston Conservatory of Music*
Alberto Arenas, *University of California at Berkeley*
Paul Austerlitz, *Brown University*
Karen Backstein, *City University of New York, College of Staten Island*
Anthony Badger, *University of Cambridge*
Lawrie Balfour, *Babson College*
Marlyse Baptista, *University of Georgia*
Robert Baum, *Iowa State University*
Stephen Behrendt, *Harvard University*
Patrick Bellegarde-Smith, *University of Wisconsin at Milwaukee*
Eric Bennett, *Iowa City, Iowa*
Suzanne Preston Blier, *Harvard University*
Juan Botero, *Former Executive Director, Instituto de Ciencia Politica, Bogota, Colombia*
Keith Boykin, *Washington, D.C.*
Esperanza Brizvela-Garcia, *London, England*
Diana DeG. Brown, *Bard College*
Eva Stahl Brown, *University of Texas at Austin*
Barbara Browning, *New York University*
Eric Brosch, *Cambridge, Massachusetts*
John Burdick, *Syracuse University*
Andrew Burton, *London, England*
Alida Cagidemetrio, *University of Udine, Italy*
Chloe Campbell, *London, England*
Sophia Cantave, *Tufts University*
Yvonne Captain, *George Washington University*
Judy Carney, *University of California at Los Angeles*
Vincent Carretta, *University of Maryland at College Park*
Clayborne Carson, *Editor, Martin Luther King, Jr., Papers Project, Stanford University*

Odile Cazenave, *University of Tennessee*
Alistair Chisholm, *London, England*
Jace Clayton, *Cambridge, Massachusetts*
Patricia Collins, *University of Cincinnati*
Nicola Cooney, *Harvard University*
Belinda Cooper, *New School for Social Research*
Frederick Cooper, *University of Michigan at Ann Arbor*
Juan Giusti Cordero, *Universidad de Puerto Rico*
Thomas Cripps, *Morgan State University*
Selwyn R. Cudjoe, *Wellesley College*
Carlos Dalmau, *San Juan, Puerto Rico*
Darién J. Davis, *Middlebury College*
James Davis, *Howard University*
Martha Swearington Davis, *University of California at Santa Barbara*
Cristobal Diaz-Ayala, *Independent Scholar*
Rafael Diaz-Diaz, *Pontificia Universidad Javeriana, Bogota, Colombia*
Quinton Dixie, *Indiana University*
Andrew Du Bois, *Cambridge, Massachusetts*
Christopher Dunn, *Tulane University*
Anani Dzidzienyo, *Brown University*
Jonathan Edwards, *Belmont, Massachusetts*
Roanne Edwards, *Arlington, Massachusetts*
Joy Elizondo, *Cambridge, Massachusetts*
Robert Fay, *Medford, Massachusetts*
Martine Fernández, *Berkeley, California*
Paul Finkelman, *Harvard Law School*
Victor Figueroa, *Harvard University*
Gerdes Fleurant, *University of California at Santa Barbara*
Juan Flores, *Hunter College and City College of New York Graduate Center*
Paul Foster, *Chicago, Illinois*
Baltasar Fra-Molinero, *Bates College*
Gregory Freeland, *California Lutheran University*
Susanne Freidberg, *Dartmouth College*
Nina Friedemann, *Pontifica Universidad Javeriana, Bogota, Colombia*
Rob Garrison, *Boston, Massachusetts*
Henry Louis Gates, Jr., *Harvard University*
John Gennari, *University of Virginia*
Danielle Georges, *New York, New York*
Peter Gerhard, *Independent Scholar*
Mark Gevisser, *Editor of Defiant Desire: Gay and Lesbian Lives
    in South Africa*
Patric V. Giesler, *Gustavus Adolphus College*
Peter Glenshaw, *Belmont, Massachusetts*
Matthew Goff, *Chicago, Illinois*
Flora González, *Emerson College*
Mayda Grano de Oro, *San Juan, Puerto Rico*
Sue Grant Lewis, *Harvard University*

Roderick Grierson, *Independent Scholar*
Barbara Grosh, *New York, New York*
Gerard Gryski, *Auburn University*
Betty Gubert, *Former Head of Reference, Schomburg Center for Research in
    Black Culture, New York Public Library*
Michelle Gueraldi, *San José, Costa Rica*
Stuart Hall, *The Open University, London*
Michael Hanchard, *Northwestern University*
Julia Harrington, *Banjul, The Gambia*
Elizabeth Heath, *San Francisco, California*
Andrew Hermann, *Former Literary Associate, Denver Center Theatre
    Company*
Evelyn Brooks Higginbotham, *Harvard University*
Jessica Hochman, *New York, New York*
Cynthia Hoehler-Fatton, *University of Virginia*
Peter Hudson, *Toronto, Canada*
Michelle Hunter, *Cambridge, Massachusetts*
Abiola Irele, *Ohio State University*
David P. Johnson, Jr., *Boston, Massachusetts*
Bill Johnson-González, *Cambridge, Massachusetts*
André Juste, *New York, New York*
Chuck Kapelke, *Boston, Massachusetts*
Ketu Katrak,University of California at Irvine
Robin Kelley, *New York University*
R. K. Kent, *University of California at Berkeley*
Leyla Keough, *Cambridge, Massachusetts*
Muhonjia Khaminwa, *Boston, Massachusetts*
David Kim, *Cambridge, Massachusetts*
Martha King, *New York, New York*
Franklin W. Knight, *Johns Hopkins University*
Peter Kolchin, *University of Delaware*
Corinne Kratz, *Emory University*
Modupe Labode, *Iowa State University*
Peter Lau, *New Brunswick, New Jersey*
Claudia Leal, *Former Assistant Director, Socioeconomic Area of the Biopacific
    Project, Bogota, Colombia*
René Lemarchand,University of Florida
W. T. Lhamon, Jr., *Florida State University*
Margit Liander, *Belmont, Massachusetts*
David Levering Lewis, *Rutgers University*
Marvín Lewis, *University of Missouri at Columbia*
Lorraine Anastasia Lezama, *Boston, Massachusetts*
Kevin MacDonald, *University of London*
Marcos Chor Maio, *Rio de Janeiro, Brazil*
Mahmood Mamdani, *University of Cape Town*
Lawrence Mamiya, *Vassar College*
Patrick Manning, *Northeastern University*

Peter Manuel, *John Jay College of Criminal Justice*
Dellita Martin-Ogunsola, *University of Alabama at Birmingham*
Waldo Martin, *University of California at Berkeley*
J. Lorand Matory, *Harvard University*
Felix V. Matos Rodriguez, *Northeastern University*
Marc Mazique, *Seattle, Washington*
José Mazzotti, *Harvard University*
Elizabeth McHenry, *New York University*
Jim Mendelsohn, *New York, New York*
Gabriel Mendes, *Annandale, New York*
Claudine Michel, *Wellesley College*
Georges Michel, *Military Academy of Haiti, Port-au-Prince, Haiti*
Gwendolyn Mikell, *Georgetown University*
Zebulon Miletsky, *Boston, Massachusetts*
Irene Monroe, *Harvard Divinity School*
Sally Falk Moore, *Harvard University*
Judith Morrison, *Inter-American Foundation at Arlington, Virginia*
Gerardo Mosquera, *Independent Scholar*
Luis Mott, *Federal University of Bahia, Brazil*
Salikoko S. Mufwene, *University of Chicago*
Edward Mullen, *University of Missouri at Columbia*
Kurt Mullen, *Seattle, Washington*
Stuart Munro-Hay, *Independent Scholar*
Aaron Myers, *Cambridge, Massachusetts*
Abdias do Nascimento, *Former Senator, Brazilian National Congress, Brasilia*
Ari Nave, *New York, New York*
Marcos Natalí, *University of Chicago*
Okey Ndibe, *Connecticut College*
Nick Nesbitt, *Miami University (Ohio)*
Richard Newman, *W. E. B. Du Bois Institute for Afro-American Research,
    Harvard University*
Liliana Obregón, *Harvard Law School*
Kathleen O'Connor, *Cambridge, Massachusetts*
Tejumola Olaniyan, *University of Virginia*
Mark O'Malley, *Cambridge, Massachusetts*
Yaa Pokua Afriyie Oppong, *London, England*
Carmen Oquendo-Villar, *Cambridge, Massachusetts*
Kenneth O'Reilly, *University of Alaska at Anchorage*
Carlos L. Orihuela, *University of Alabama at Birmingham*
Francisco Ortega, *Harvard University*
Juan Otero-Garabis, *Universidad de Puerto Rico*
Deborah Pacini Hernandez, *Brown University*
Carlos Parra, *Harvard University*
Ben Penglase, *Cambridge, Massachusetts*
Pedro Pérez-Sarduy, *London, England and Havana, Cuba*
Julio Cesar Pino, *Kent State University*
Donald Pollock, *State University of New York at Buffalo*

Angelina Pollak-Eltz, *Univesidad Catolice A. Bella*
Paulette Poujol-Oriol, *Port-au-Prince, Haiti*
Richard J. Powell, *Duke University*
Jean Muteba Rahier, *Florida International University*
João José Reis, *Federal University of Bahia, Brazil*
Carolyn Richardson Durham, *Texas Christian University*
Alonford James Robinson, Jr., *Washington, D.C.*
Lisa Clayton Robinson, *Washington, D.C.*
Sonia Labrador Rodrigués, *University of Texas at Austin*
Gordon Root, *Cambridge, Massachusetts*
Aninydo Roy, *Colby College*
Sarah Russell, *Cambridge, England*
Marveta Ryan, *Indiana University (Pennsylvania)*
Ali Osman Mohammad Salih, *University of Khartoum*
Lamine Sanneh, *Yale University*
Jalane Schmidt, *Cambridge, Massachusetts*
Charles Schmitz, *Sonoma State University*
Brooke Grundfest Schoepf, *Harvard University*
LaVerne M. Seales-Soley, *Canisius College*
James Clyde Sellman, *University of Massachussetts at Boston*
Thomas Skidmore, *Brown University*
James Smethurst, *University of North Florida*
Paulette Smith, *Tufts University*
Suzanne Smith, *George Mason University*
Barbara Solow, *Associate of the W. E. B. Du Bois Institute for Afro-American
    Research, Harvard University*
Doris Sommer, *Harvard University*
Thomas Stephens, *State University of New Jersey*
Jean Stubbs, *London, England and Havana, Cuba*
Patricia Sullivan, *Harvard University*
Carol Swain, *Princeton University*
Katherine Tate, *Univerity of California at Irvine*
Richard Taub, *University of Chicago*
April Taylor, *Boston, Massachusetts*
Christopher Tiné, *Cambridge, Massachusetts*
Richard Turits, *Princeton University*
Kate Tuttle, *Cambridge, Massachusetts*
Timothy Tyson, *University of Wisconsin*
Charles Van Doren, *Former Vice President/Editorial, Encyclopædia
    Britannica Inc.*
Alexandra Vega-Merino, *Harvard University*
Joëlle Vitiello, *Macalester College*
Peter Wade, *University of Manchester*
James W. St. G. Walker, *University of Waterloo*
Phillipe Wamba, *Cambridge, Massachusetts*
William E. Ward, *Harvard University*
Salim Washington, *Boston, Massachusetts*

Christopher Alan Waterman, *University of California at Los Angeles*
Richard Watts, *Tulane University*
Harold Weaver, *Independent Scholar*
Norman Weinstein, *State University of New York at New Paltz*
Amelia Weir, *New York, New York*
Tim Weiskel, *Harvard University*
Alan West, *Northern Illinois University*
Cornel West, *Princeton University*
Norman Whitten, *University of Illinois at Urbana*
Andre Willis, *Cambridge, Massachusetts*
Deborah Willis, *Center for African American History and Culture,
    Smithsonian Institution*
William Julius Wilson, *Harvard University*
Barbara Worley, *Cambridge, Massachusetts*
Eric Young, *Washington, D.C.*
Gary Zuk, *Auburn University*

Abrahams, Peter

(b. March 19, 1919, Vrededorp, South Africa), expatriate South African novelist.

The son of an Ethiopian father and a mother of French and African descent, Peter Abrahams was considered "Coloured" in the South African racial classification scheme. He grew up outside Johannesburg and began working at the age of nine, never having attended school. He later enrolled, however, after he was inspired by hearing *Othello* read to him by a co-worker. As a teenager Abrahams discovered works by African American writers such as W. E. B. Du Bois, Countee Cullen, Langston Hughes, Claude McKay, and Jean Toomer in the library at the Bantu Men's Social Centre.

Though he never again lived in South Africa, Abrahams wrote six of his seven novels about his home country. *Song of the City* (1945) and *Mine Boy* (1946) explore the racial injustices of a rapidly industrializing and urbanizing South Africa. Abrahams also wrote a historical novel about South Africa's Afrikaners, *Wild Conquest* (1950), and another about African-Indian solidarity, *A Night of Their Own* (1965).

In the 1950s Abrahams wrote for the *London Observer* and the *New York Herald Tribune*; an assignment in Jamaica led him to move his family there in 1956. *This Island Now* (1966) deals with political struggles in a fictional Caribbean setting. Abrahams worked as a radio journalist and eventually became chairman of Radio Jamaica, but he resigned in 1964 to concentrate on writing. By then Abrahams was known as a novelist of ideas whom some critics considered didactic, but in whom many readers found provocative and idealistic theories. Abraham's travel books, which include *Jamaica: An Island Mosaic* (1957), and the two memoirs *Return to Goli* (1953) and *Tell Freedom* (1954) are among his most widely praised works.

Achebe, Chinua

(b. November 16, 1930, Ogidi, Nigeria), Nigerian author whose novel *Things Fall Apart* (1958) is one of the most widely read and discussed works of African fiction.

Chinua Achebe once described his writing as an attempt to set the historical record straight by showing "that African people did not hear of culture for the first time from Europeans; that their societies were not mindless but frequently had a philosophy of great depth and value and beauty; that they had poetry and, above all, they had dignity." Achebe's works portray Nigeria's communities as they pass through the trauma of colonization into a troubled nationhood. In bringing together the political and the literary, he neither romanticizes the culture of the indigenous nor apologizes for the colonial.

Achebe's own upbringing spanned the indigenous and colonial worlds. He was born Albert Chinualumogu Achebe to an Igbo (Ibo) family active in the Christian church, and grew up in the rural village of Ogidi, in eastern Nigeria. At a young age he received a coveted scholarship to Government College in Umuahia, where he studied alongside some of Nigeria's future political and cultural leaders. After receiving a bachelor's degree from University College, Ibadan, he worked for the Nigerian Broadcasting Corporation, ultimately acting as director of the radio program Voice of Nigeria in Lagos.

After moving to London in 1957 to attend the British Broadcasting Corporation staff school, Achebe decided to publish the fiction he had been writing for several years. He was inspired, in part, by a need to respond to the racist portrayals of Africa in the work of prominent European writers. In his first novel, *Things Fall Apart*, Achebe retold the history of colonization from the point of view of the colonized. The novel depicted the first contact between the Igbo people and European missionaries and administrators. Since its publication, *Things Fall Apart* has generated a wealth of literary criticism grappling with Achebe's unsentimental representations of tradition, religion, manhood, and the colonial experience. Immediately successful, the novel secured Achebe's position both in Nigeria and in the West as a preeminent voice among Africans writing in English.

Achebe subsequently wrote several novels that spanned more than a century of African history. Although most of these works deal specifically with Nigeria, they are also emblematic of what Achebe calls the "metaphysical landscape" of Africa, "a view of the world and of the whole cosmos perceived from a particular position." *No Longer at Ease* (1960) tells the story of a young man sent by his village to study overseas, who then returns to a government job in Nigeria only to find himself in a culturally fragmented world. As the young man sinks into materialism and corruption, Achebe represents a new generation caught in a moral and spiritual conflict between the modern and the traditional. *Arrow of God* (1964) returns to the colonial period of 1920s Nigeria. In this novel, Achebe focuses on a theme that underscores all of his work: the wielding of power and its deployment for the good or harm of a community. *A Man of the People* (1966), a work Achebe has characterized as "an indictment of independent Africa," is set in the context of the emerging African nation state. Representing a nation thought to be based on Nigeria, Achebe portrays the vacuum of true leadership left by the destruction of the governance provided by the traditional village. Achebe's critical political commentary continues in *Anthills of the Savannah* (1987), in which he uses a complex mythical structure to depict an African nation passing into the shadow of a military dictatorship.

During the 20-year gap between *A Man of the People* and *Anthills of the Savannah*, Achebe was a prolific writer and speaker. He helped found a publishing company in Nigeria with poet Christopher Okigbo and in 1971 was a founding editor for the prominent African literary magazine *Okike*. In addition, he published award-winning poetry collections and children's books.

Achebe taught literature at the University of Nigeria in the 1970s, a period when Nigeria was shaken by a series of military coups. After the start of the Nigerian Civil War, he traveled throughout Europe and North America on behalf of the Biafra state, which had split off from Nigeria. Many of his lectures and essays from this period have been published in *Morning Yet on Creation Day* (1975), *The Trouble with Nigeria* (1983), and *Hopes and Impediments* (1988). In addition to discussing the contemporary political situation in Nigeria, Achebe's nonfiction works address such topics as the role of the writer in the postcolonial African nation, literary depictions of Africa, and the debate over language choice by African writers. Responding to critics such as Ngugi wa Thiongo, who point to the political and cultural implications of writing in the colonial language, Achebe has defended his use of English, asserting that as a "medium of international exchange," the language is a lingua franca that will connect the communities of Africa.

"Art is man's constant effort to create for himself a different order of reality from that which is given to him," Achebe wrote in his essay "The Truth of Fiction." Achebe, who now teaches in the United States, has used his position as one of the most widely read African writers to comment on the crisis situation in contemporary Nigeria. It is still fiction, however, that provides for Achebe "the weapon for coping with [threats to integrity], whether they are found within our problematic and incoherent selves or in the world around us."

North America

Adderley, Julian Edwin ("Cannonball")

(b. September 15, 1928, Tampa, Fla.; d. August 8, 1975, Gary, Ind.), African American alto saxophonist who explored bebop, modal, and soul-fusion styles.

Adderley was introduced to music by his father, a cornetist, and was performing in bands by the time he was 14. He played in local and army bands (he enlisted in 1950) and taught music before moving to New York to join his brother, Nat, in 1955. He immediately found success on the New York jazz scene, joining the bands of Oscar Pettiford and, later, Miles Davis.

The recordings Adderley made with Davis—which included John Coltrane on tenor saxophone, Paul Chambers on bass, and Wynton Kelly on piano—are some of the most celebrated of the 1950s. In 1959 Adderley and his brother, Nat, formed their own quintet and built on the influence of Davis and Charlie Parker. During its 15 years, the quintet played soul jazz style, fusion, and mainstream post-bop, earning critical and popular acclaim and a reputation for drawing heavily on blues and gospel. Some critics hailed Adderley as the "new Bird," noting his style's debt to Parker. At times, Adderley doubled on soprano saxophone. An important innovator on his horn, Adderley also taught and lectured on jazz. Some of his finest performances appear on *Something Else Cannonball and Coltrane, Miles Davis's Kind of Blue,* and the popular Adderley quintet album *Mercy, Mercy, Mercy! Live at "the Club"* (1966).

Julian Adderley earned the nickname "Cannonball," a corruption of "cannibal," for his huge appetite. He died of a stroke while onstage in 1975.

Aidoo, Ama Ata

(b. 1942?, Abeadzi Kyiakor, Ghana), writer whose plays, novels, and poetry examine the traditional roles assigned to African women.

Christina Ama Aidoo was born into a Fante family she once characterized as "a long line of fighters." Encouraged by her liberal-minded father, Aidoo pursued an English degree at the University of Ghana in Legon. As a student, she won a short story prize, but her interests centered on drama as a means of bringing to life the rich oral traditions of the Fante. She worked closely with Efua Sutherland, a leading Ghanaian dramatist, and became familiar with a Fante dramatic style that blossomed in the 1930s.

Aidoo's first play, *The Dilemma of a Ghost* (1965), was staged in 1964 by the Student's Theatre at the University of Ghana. With this play, Aidoo earned her lasting reputation as a writer who examines the traditional African roles of wife and mother. The play, like many of her later works, also demonstrated her willingness to grapple with complex and controversial issues. *The Dilemma of a Ghost* tells the story of an African man who returns to his village from abroad with his African American wife. While the young wife struggles as an outsider among the village women, her Westernized husband attempts to reconcile his inherited traditions with his adopted views. Ultimately, the wife bears the brunt of the couple's decisions, particularly the decision not to have children. Critics of the play noted Aidoo's compelling portrayal of relationships between women.

After receiving a creative writing fellowship at Stanford University in California, Aidoo spent two years traveling. Her next play, *Anowa* (1970), reworked a traditional legend she had learned as a song from her mother. Set in the late nineteenth century, *Anowa* tells the story of a strong-willed woman who refuses an arranged marriage and instead marries a man of her choice, who later makes her miserable. As Anowa's husband becomes a slaveholder, the play also confronts the fact of African participation in the slave trade. Speaking about *Anowa* in an interview, Aidoo cited the importance of dealing with the uncomfortable history of African slavery as a key to resolving Africa's future.

Aidoo's next work, *No Sweetness Here* (1970), was a collection of short stories that undertook a number of complicated themes, including the divide between men and women and between rural and urban societies. In these stories, Aidoo brought a sense of the oral to the written word through the use of elements such as African idioms.

Aidoo described her *Our Sister Killjoy; or Reflections from a Black-Eyed Squint* (1977) as fiction in four episodes. In this dense work Aidoo used an experimental form, interspersing the prose narrative with poetry. The story follows a young African woman as she travels from Africa to Europe in the late 1960s, reflecting on the different yet intertwined histories of the two continents. In *Our Sister Killjoy*, which examines underdevelopment, racism, and the exoticizing of Africans, and includes a scene in which the main character rejects the sexual advances of a white woman, Aidoo again showed a willingness to deal with controversial issues.

In 1982 Aidoo was appointed Ghana's minister of education. She left the country a year later for Zimbabwe, where she continued to teach as well as write poems, published in the collection *Someone Talking to Sometime* (1985), and two children's books.

The 1991 novel *Changes* explores the possibilities of self-determination for contemporary women. The story narrates a woman's experience of a polygamous marriage, and her ultimate decision to leave her husband. For Aidoo, who once proclaimed that, given the seriousness of Africa's political problems, she could not imagine herself writing something so frivolous as an African love story, the novel was a realization that "love or the workings of love is also political." It later won her the Commonwealth Writers Prize for African writers. She followed this novel with a second volume of poetry, *An Angry Letter in January* (1992), and a short-story collection, *The Girl Who Can and Other Stories* (1997).

In a recent interview, Aidoo cited the development of African literature as a central concern for her work: "I still believe that one day, when Africa comes into her own, the dynamism of orality might be something that Africa can give to the world."

North America

Ailey, Alvin

(b. January 5, 1931, Rogers, Texas; d. December 1, 1989, New York, N.Y.), African American dancer and choreographer who founded the Alvin Ailey American Dance Theater (AAADT) and incorporated African American styles and themes into dance performance.

Alvin Ailey grew up in a single-parent household headed by his mother, Lula Elizabeth Cooper. As a boy, he helped her pick cotton. In 1942 they moved to Los Angeles, where she found employment in the World War II aircraft industry. Ailey attended George Washington Carver Junior High School and Jefferson High School, primarily black schools. He went on to study literature at the University of California at Los Angeles (UCLA).

In 1958 Ailey assembled his own dance company, the Alvin Ailey American Dance Theater. Ailey himself stopped dancing in 1965 and reduced his choreographic assignments during the 1970s in order to seek more funding for his growing dance enterprise. The company toured the United States and the world so extensively that by 1989, the year that Ailey died, they had performed for an estimated 15 million people in 48 states and 45 countries on six continents. Two of the most significant awards Ailey received for his achievements in dance were the National Association for the Advancement of Colored People's prestigious Spingarn Medal (1976) and the Samuel H. Scripps American Dance Festival Award (1987).

The AAADT devotes itself to the performance of modern dance classics as well as the creations of Ailey and younger artists. The Alvin Ailey Dance Center School, founded in 1969, is dedicated to educating dance students in the history and art of both modern dance and ballet. The school's curriculum includes courses in choreography, dance technique, music for dancers, and theatrical design. Pursuing Ailey's goal of preserving and building upon great ballets, both classic and contemporary, the AAADT by 1989 had performed 150 ballets by 50 choreographers. In addition to having created over 50 dances for his own company, Ailey choreographed for others: the American Ballet Theater, the London Festival Ballet, the Robert Joffrey Ballet, the Paris Opera Ballet, and the Royal Danish Ballet.

Ailey's own works, whose style is founded on the techniques of modern dance, ballet, and jazz dance, draw upon African American themes, many of which are rooted in his boyhood experiences. Two of his major pieces, *Blues Suite* (1958) and *Revelations* (1960), for example, were inspired by a bar in Texas named the Dewdrop Inn and the Mount Olive Baptist Church he attended as a boy. *Revelations*, the AAADT's most celebrated number, explores the different facets of black religious worship and is performed to a series of spirituals and gospel music selections. His 1971 ballet *Cry*, a tribute to African American women, is dedicated to his mother.

North America
Ai Ogawa, Florence

(b. October 21, 1947, Albany, Tex.), African American poet and creative writer whose work investigates personal as well as societal questions of ethnicity and class.

In 1973 she published *Cruelty*, her first book of poetry, and her next book, the award-winning *Killing Floor* (1979), received critical acclaim. Her later works include *Sin* (1985) and *Fate* (1991).

Through her poetry, Ai gives people from all walks of life—including prostitutes, killers, poor farmers, and famous leaders—the same moral authority. This desire for equality of perspective also manifests itself in her quest for recognition of her multiethnic identity. Given her mixed race (black, Irish, Dutch, Native American, and Japanese), Ai (a self-chosen name that means "love" in Japanese) was unable to fit into predefined racial categories and social roles, and much of her poetry speaks to this tension.

North America

Aldridge, Ira

(b. 1807, New York, N.Y.; d. 1867, Lodz, Poland), the most highly esteemed African American actor of the nineteenth century.

Ira Aldridge earned international recognition as one of his era's finest actors for his moving theatrical performances throughout England, Scotland, Ireland, Europe, and the United States. Though born free in New York City, the son of a slave turned Calvinist preacher, Aldridge saw limited theatrical opportunities in the United States and, after training at the African Free School in New York City, left the United States for England in 1824. Intent on pursuing an acting career, he studied drama at the University of Glasgow for more than a year.

Debuting onstage at the Royal Coburg in London in 1825, Aldridge won widespread praise for his portrayal of Othello, a role that became his trademark, as well as his renditions of other leading characters during the six-week theatrical run. After this success, he performed in the Theater Royal in Brighton, then went on to tour England, Scotland, and Ireland for the next six years. He mastered both black and white characters throughout dramatic literature and was hailed from city to city as an actor of great genius, best known for his portrayals of Shakespeare's Othello, Thomas Southerne's *Oroonoko*, Thomas Norton's *The Slave*, and characters from Matthew Gregory Lewis's *The Castle Spectre*, Isaac Bickerstaff's *The Padlock*, and Edward Young's *The Revenge*.

For many, the mounting claims that Aldridge was the greatest actor of his day seemed to be confirmed when he filled in as Othello for the renowned English thespian Edmund Kean, who fell ill during a performance at London's Covent Garden in 1833. Though some critics grumbled at Kean's having been eclipsed by the young upstart, the 24-year-old Aldridge received immense public acclaim for his portrayal of the Moor, and his fame spread throughout Europe.

In 1852 Aldridge toured Europe performing Shakespearean tragedies, and was so successful that he was invited to play Othello at the prestigious Lyceum Theater in London in 1858, and was offered the same role by the Haymarket in 1865. In 1867, at the height of his career, he died of respiratory failure while on tour in Lodz, Poland, and was buried in that city.

Amadi, Elechi

(b. May 12, 1934, Aluu, Nigeria), Nigerian novelist whose works describe the folklore and spirituality of traditional village life.

A member of the Igbo ethnic group, Elechi Amadi was born in a small southeastern Nigerian village near Port Harcourt. In 1959 he graduated with a degree in physics and mathematics from the University College of Ibadan, a prestigious college attended by other well-known Nigerian writers, such as Chinua Achebe, John Pepper Clark, Wole Soyinka, and Christopher Okigbo. After working as a land surveyor, Amadi taught science for three years at missionary schools in Ahoada and Oba. In 1963 he joined the Nigerian Army; he taught the Ikwerri dialect of Igbo at a military school in Zaria.

His first book, *The Concubine*, blended acute psychological detail and precise observation to tell the story of a young village woman's battle with spiritual forces. The book's publication in 1966 coincided with the proclamation of an independent state—Biafra—in Igbo-dominated southeastern Nigeria. Amadi's steady allegiance to the Federal side in the conflict put him virtually alone among Igbo writers. Steadfastly refusing to write political novels, which he called "a prostitution of literature," Amadi did not detail his wartime experiences until 1973, when he published *Sunset in Biafra: A Civil War Diary*. His novels *The Great Ponds* (1969) and *The Slave* (1978) completed what is thought of as Amadi's trilogy of the mythical in village life.

After the war, Amadi became dean of arts at the Rivers State College of Education (1985–1986) and, later, commissioner for education for Rivers State (1988–1989). In 1986 he published *Estrangement*, a departure from his earlier work in both its urban setting and its exploration of the effects of war on Nigeria's survivors. In addition, Amadi has published four plays—*Peppersoup* (1973), *Isiburu* (1973), *The Road to Ibadan* (1973), and *Dancer of Johannesburg* (1979)—and a scholarly work, *Ethics in Nigerian Culture* (1982).

American Negro Theatre,

pioneering African American theater company and school in which several hundred black actors, writers, and technicians began their careers.

The Academy Award-winning actor Sidney Poitier, the actor and singer Harry Belafonte, and the actress Ruby Dee are three of the prominent African American actors who were affiliated with the American Negro Theatre (ANT). The theater was founded in Harlem in 1940 by black writer Abram Hill and black actor Frederick O'Neal, who wanted to create a company that would provide opportunities for African American artists and entertainment for African American audiences that were unavailable downtown on Broadway. Over the next nine years, 50,000 people attended American Negro Theatre productions.

ANT was not meant to be a segregated organization, although its members were committed to a theater that would reflect the Harlem community. Most of the original members were African American actors and writers, including Dee. Performances were held in a converted lecture room at Harlem's 135th Street Library, which seated 125 people and had been used by several earlier black theater groups. As the playwright and novelist Alice Childress later said, "We thought we were Harlem's theater."

The company's first major production was Abram Hill's *On Striver's Row*, a satire about African American social climbing. It was well reviewed and well attended, and the new company was described by one critic as "a healthy experimental theater, one that at all costs strives to avoid conventional Broadway-bound clichés . . . It remains firmly on the ground, using themes about everyday people, staged and played with originality and imagination." In 1942 ANT added its Studio Theatre, a training program for young artists. Poitier and Belafonte, two of the Studio Theatre's early graduates, went on to become internationally known actors.

Between 1940 and 1949 ANT produced 19 plays, including 12 original scripts. But its 1944 production of *Anna Lucasta*, by the white author Philip Yordan, proved to be a turning point. The play originally had been written about a Polish-American family, but after white companies rejected it, ANT revised it extensively and made it suitable for a black cast. It was an immediate success, and after five weeks it was moved to Broadway.

What should have been a tremendous achievement for ANT, however, instead brought problems. The production ran for two years on Broadway and eventually spawned a national tour and a movie, but ANT received royalties of less than 2 percent for the Broadway show and none at all for the tour or the film. The unfavorable financial arrangements understandably caused bitterness among company members. More important, however, the production undermined some of ANT's initial conceptions of itself as a community theater.

When *Anna Lucasta* went to Broadway, the new production retained only a few ANT actors. Despite ANT's hope that it would provide an alternative to the professional star system, the Broadway connection revived old grievances: actors who had not been chosen to go to Broadway were bitter, and new actors came to ANT seeking their chance to make it to the Broadway stage. The success of *Anna Lucasta* also brought about a new level of professional attention, and the company felt compelled to respond by changing the aim of its productions. Instead of continuing to encourage community-based writers, ANT after 1945 produced only plays by established white playwrights. As a result of these changes, ANT lost much of the creativity and community support that had sustained it.

The company did send three more productions to Broadway, but none was financially successful. In 1945 ANT became the first black theater company to produce a weekly radio series, but the radio show's success did not lessen the theater's difficulties. By the early 1950s, it stopped production.

Despite its eventual decline, however, ANT had played a crucial role in bringing an awareness of black theater to the rest of the American theater scene. As the actor Lofton Mitchell later put it, "There was a great social revolution underway, the plays of protest, the plays of social meaning, and this was the kind of theater we were trying to develop . . . We were trying to say something. We were trying to say it within the black media, with the rhythm and quality of excitement."

North America

Amos 'n' Andy,

popular American radio and television series based on racist and exaggerated stereotypes of black life. As a radio series, it ran from 1928 to 1960.

The "Sam 'n' Henry" radio show, as it was first called, was created in 1926 in Chicago by two white entertainers, Freeman Gosden and Charles Correll. The show portrayed its two African American characters in full racial stereotype, complete with broken English. In 1928 the characters were renamed Amos and Andy and were crafted to reflect white stereotypes of African American life and culture in Harlem in the years immediately following the Great Migration. While Amos was portrayed as weak and submissive, Andy was lazy and pretentious. Together, they were bumbling fools. When the National Broadcasting Company (NBC) acquired the radio program in 1929, they became a national comic sensation.

Due to its great popularity, the show was played on the radio in many of the country's bars, hotels, and restaurants. Controversy erupted in 1931 when the *Pittsburgh Courier*, an African American weekly newspaper, gathered 750,000 signatures calling for the show's cancellation. Despite protests by the National Association for the Advancement of Colored People (NAACP), the Central Broadcasting System (CBS) purchased the television rights to the show in 1951. Large audiences of both whites and blacks made the first all-black television show a huge hit in its first year. Declining ratings forced the show's cancellation after only two years, but it remained in syndication on local stations until 1966. The "Amos 'n' Andy" show was an essential part of the American minstrel tradition, which served to reaffirm white stereotypes of African American life and culture.

North America

Anderson, Eddie ("Rochester")

(b. September 18, 1905, Oakland, Calif.; d. February 28, 1977, Los Angeles, Calif.), American actor best known for his comic portrayal of the character Rochester on the Jack Benny radio show.

The humor and energy between Jack Benny and Eddie Anderson led to the development of a 20-year collaboration that delighted radio, television, and film audiences. The relationship between Anderson and Benny, for all of its sarcasm, wit, and camaraderie, was typical of the "Uncle Tomism" of the era (Anderson's trademark line to Benny became "What's that, Boss?"), yet blacks not only appreciated the comedy, but were also pleased that the character was played by a black actor instead of a white actor attempting to imitate black expression.

Anderson's parents performed in vaudeville, and he began acting when he was eight. His formal show business career began in 1919 when he appeared in a Negro revue and continued when he and his older brother, Cornelius, toured as a two-man music and dance team. After appearing in his first film, *Green Pastures* (1936), Anderson was invited to play the role of Rochester, a Pullman porter on the Jack Benny radio show. Though it was only intended to be a one-show deal, Anderson struck such a chord with audiences that he was offered a permanent spot in the cast.

In addition to teaming up with Benny in the classic films *Man About Town* (1939), *Buck Benny Rides Again* (1940), and *Love Thy Neighbor* (1940), Anderson also acted in numerous films without Benny, including *Jezebel* (1938), *Gone With the Wind* (1939), *Birth of the Blues* (1941), and the "race" films *Stormy Weather* (1943) and *Cabin in the Sky* (1943), now recognized as Negro "classics." In the 1950s and 1960s, Anderson appeared regularly on television, at times with Benny and in many other small roles.

North America

Anderson, Marian

(b. 1900?, Philadelphia, Pa.; d. 1993), American singer and first African American to perform at the Metropolitan Opera.

Marian Anderson was born in Philadelphia, Pennsylvania, around 1900, the first of three daughters of John Berkeley Anderson, an ice and coal peddler, and Anna D. Anderson, who, though trained as a teacher, took in laundry. Throughout her childhood, Anderson's family was poor. When she was 12, her father died from injuries he received at work, and the family's financial situation worsened further. Anderson had an urge to make music from an early age, and was clearly talented. When she was six years old, she joined the junior choir at the church to which her father belonged, Union Baptist, and became known as the Baby Contralto. In addition, she taught herself to play the piano, eventually playing well enough to accompany herself during her singing concerts.

Anderson joined the church's senior choir at age 13. She began singing professionally and touring during high school to earn money for her family. After graduating from South Philadelphia School for Girls in 1921, she earned enough to help her family purchase a home. In 1924, however, Anderson gave a Town Hall concert in New York that was so poorly received by critics that she temporarily stopped performing. She returned to singing, and in 1925 won the opportunity to appear at Lewisohn Stadium with the New York Philharmonic Orchestra. Between 1925 and 1935, Anderson studied and toured in Europe, and her career began to develop. Her reper-

After the Daughters of the American Revolution refused to allow her to perform in Constitution Hall in Washington, D.C., Marian Anderson was invited by Secretary of the Interior Harold Ickes, Jr., to sing at the Lincoln Memorial. Her performance drew 75,000 people. *CORBIS*

toire expanded to comprise over 100 songs in various languages.

In 1939 the Daughters of the American Revolution (DAR) denied Anderson's request to perform at its Constitution Hall in Washington, D.C., because she was African American. Eleanor Roosevelt, wife of President Franklin D. Roosevelt, resigned from the DAR in protest. Reacting to the outrage the DAR inspired, the secretary of the interior, Harold Ickes, arranged an open-air concert at the Lincoln Memorial on Easter Sunday, which was attended by 75,000 people. Anderson performed once more from the steps of the Lincoln Memorial, as part of the March on Washington in 1963, a key event in the Civil Rights Movement.

In 1955 Anderson became the first African American to perform at the Metropolitan Opera, singing the role of Ulrica in Verde's *Un Ballo in Maschera*. In 1958 President Dwight D. Eisenhower appointed her to the United States delegation to the United Nations, where she spoke on behalf of African independence. Anderson retired in 1965 and spent the bulk of her time on a farm in Danbury, Connecticut, which she and her husband, Orpheus Hodge Fisher, purchased shortly after their marriage in 1943. She received numerous awards, including the Spingarn Medal in 1939, the highest award conferred by the National Association for the Advancement of Colored People; the Bok Award in 1941; and the Page One award. She sang at President Eisenhower's inauguration, and in 1977, President Jimmy Carter presented her with a Congressional gold medal bearing her profile.

North America

Angelou, Maya

(b. April 4, 1928, St. Louis, Mo.), American writer and actress who was the featured poet at President Bill Clinton's 1993 inauguration.

The wit, wisdom, and power of Maya Angelou's work have made her one of the most beloved contemporary American writers. Maya Angelou was born

Marguerite Johnson; the name she chose to use combines her childhood nickname (Maya) with a version of her first husband's last name (Angelos). Her family moved to California soon after her birth, but her parents divorced when she was three, and she was sent to Stamps, Arkansas, to be raised by her paternal grandmother. When Angelou was seven, she was raped by her mother's boyfriend. The trauma of this experience rendered Angelou mute for five years, and it was during this period that she began to read extensively.

Angelou returned to California during high school and took drama and dance lessons. As a teenager, she became San Francisco's first female streetcar conductor. She gave birth at age 16 to her only child, Guy Johnson. To support herself and her son she took a variety of jobs, working as a cook, a waitress, and a madam to two prostitutes. At 22, she married her first husband. After their divorce a few years later, she became a professional dancer and made a 1954 tour of Europe and Africa in *Porgy and Bess*.

Angelou was active in the Civil Rights Movement, and from 1960 to 1961 she served as the Northern coordinator for the Southern Christian Leadership Conference (SCLC). In 1961 she moved to Africa with Vusumzi Make, a South African freedom fighter. She spent the next five years in Egypt and Ghana, working as a journalist and a university professor.

After her return to the United States, Angelou joined the Harlem Writers Guild. James Baldwin's editor at Random House was impressed by her poetry and her life story and asked her to consider writing an autobiography. The result was *I Know Why the Caged Bird Sings*, which was published in 1970 and became a best-seller.

In 1971 Angelou's first published book of poetry, *Just Give Me a Cool Drink of Water 'fore I Diiie*, was nominated for a Pulitzer Prize. Since then she has published five other volumes of poetry. The other volumes of her prose autobiography are *Gather Together in My Name* (1974), *Singin' and Swingin' and Gettin' Merry Like Christmas* (1976), *The Heart of a Woman* (1981), and *All God's Children Need Traveling Shoes* (1986). In 1993 she published a collection of essays, *Wouldn't Take Nothing for My Journey Now*, and *On the Pulse of Morning*, the poem she read at President Bill Clinton's 1993 inauguration.

Angelou has had a distinguished career in film and television as well. In 1971 her screenplay for the film *Georgia* was the first movie screenplay by a black woman to be produced. She was nominated for a Tony Award in 1973 for her performance in *Look Away* and for an Emmy Award in 1977 for her performance in *Roots*. She has received numerous honorary degrees and was named Reynolds Professor of American Studies at Wake Forest University in Winston-Salem, North Carolina.

Throughout her diverse career, Angelou has often broken new ground. In her words, "Humility says that there were people before me who found the path. I'm a road builder. For those who have yet to come, I seem to be finding the path and they will be road builders. That keeps one humble. Love keeps one humble." Yet despite her humility, Maya Angelou's determined road building and her willingness to share herself in her work have earned her widespread admiration, respect, and love.

Apollo Theater,

the most influential African American popular theater.

The Apollo Theatre, located at 253 West 125th Street in central Harlem, was the most important venue in black show business from the 1930s through the 1970s, when waning popularity caused it financial problems. With live broadcasts that featured the Duke Ellington and Count Basie orchestras, the Apollo became a mecca for jazz bands in the 1930s and 1940s. By the 1950s the theater was the nation's top stage for established black artists. Its famous Amateur Night, in which unknown performers had their talent assessed by the notoriously raucous Harlem audience, had become a springboard for numerous careers. Ella Fitzgerald, Sarah Vaughan, and Pearl Bailey, for example, were all early Amateur Night winners, and later acts like the Jackson 5 and Stevie Wonder also enjoyed their first major exposure at the Apollo. As musical styles changed, the theater evolved with the times, booking rhythm and blues, gospel, funk, soul and hip hop acts, and hosting landmark performances by artists like James Brown.

During the 1970s the Apollo steadily lost money, forcing its closure in 1977. Its declaration as a national historic landmark in 1983 secured the building's survival, but efforts to make it a viable performance house throughout the 1980s largely failed. The theater was taken on by a non-profit organization in 1991, which intended to make it a significant part of Harlem's 125th Street renewal.

Armenteros, Alfredo "Chocolate"

(b. April 4, 1928, Ranchuelo, Santa Clara, Las Villas Province, Cuba), Afro-Cuban trumpeter, composer, and arranger, a master of Cuba's brass-led *septeto* and *conjunto* styles who helped shape Afro-Latin jazz and salsa music.

Virtuoso trumpet and flügelhorn player Alfredo "Chocolate" Armenteros is the last surviving master of Cuba's distinctive *septeto* style, performed by a small ensemble featuring a trumpet backed by stringed instruments and percussion. He has played in many Latin American musical genres, including Afro-Latin jazz big bands, small-group Cuban *descargas* (jam sessions), and salsa music. *On Knockdown Calypsoes* (1979), he convincingly recreated the sound of Trinidad's 1930s- and 1940s-era calypso bands. In Latin music, Armenteros's trumpet playing is instantly recognizable. Rather than seeking harmonic complexity or intricate rapid-fire melodies, which have characterized jazz trumpet playing since the bop era, he projects a sound that is bold, brassy, and confident. His playing and arranging feature lyrical melodies, catchy riffs, and, above all, the rhythmic drive that epitomizes Afro-Cuban jazz.

Armenteros began playing trumpet at about the age of ten. In 1949 he made his recording debut as a member of Conjunto Los Astros, a band under the leadership of singer René Alvarez. In the early 1950s he joined innovative bandleader Arsenio Rodríguez, whose expanded Conjunto—which added a second (and sometimes a third) trumpet, piano, and conga drum to the standard *septeto* format—helped lay the foundations for salsa music. From 1953 to 1956 he took charge of the brass section in Beny Moré's big band. He first performed in New York City during the late 1950s and was featured on singer Nat "King" Cole's album *Cole Español* (1958). In 1960, following the Cuban Revolution, he relocated permanently to New York and quickly established himself as one of the city's top-rated Latin musicians.

Armenteros has performed and recorded with many prominent Latin musicians, including Afro-Cuban jazz pioneer Machito, Afro-Cuban conga player Mongo Santamaria, Puerto Rican timbales player Tito Puente, and Dominican flutist Johnny Pacheco. From 1968 to 1978 he appeared regularly on Latin jazz pianist Eddie Palmieri's recordings. In 1994 he was featured on Afro-Cuban bassist Israel "Cachao" López's Grammy Award-winning album *Master Sessions, Vol. I.*

North America

Armstrong, Lillian Hardin (Lil)

(b. Feburary 3, 1898, Memphis, Tenn.; d. August 27, 1971, Chicago, Ill.), American jazz singer, pianist, and composer; worked with her husband, Louis Armstrong, in the bands Hot Five and Hot Seven.

Lillian Hardin's career as a jazz musician began with a job in a Chicago music store. She met Louis Armstrong while they were both with King Oliver's Creole Jazz Band in Chicago; they married in 1924 and divorced in 1938. Armstrong worked with her husband in the Hot Five and Hot Seven bands, and went on to appear in two Broadway shows, record under her own name, work as a house pianist for Decca Records, and sustain a long solo career. She died onstage at a Louis Armstrong memorial concert.

North America

Armstrong, Louis ("Satchmo")

(b. August 4, 1901, New Orleans, La.; d. July 6, 1971, New York, N.Y.), African American trumpet player and vocalist; the most significant soloist in the history of jazz.

Louis Armstrong, Jazz, and American Popular Culture
More than anyone else, Louis Armstrong was responsible for legitimizing and popularizing jazz for a wider public. A much-admired jazz trumpeter and gravel-voiced vocalist, Armstrong was also a consummate entertainer,

steadily expanding his career from instrumentalist to popular singer, to film and television personality, and, ultimately, to cultural icon. He acquired many nicknames throughout his life, including Dippermouth, Pops, and Satchelmouth—the latter often contracted to Satchmo. As Satchmo, he was instantly identifiable around the world, decades before Prince, Madonna, or Sting. The international appeal of his music in effect made Armstrong the American good-will ambassador to the world.

Armstrong transformed jazz in two profoundly important ways. Early jazz was characterized by freewheeling group improvisation, but Armstrong, by his virtuosity and lyricism, almost single-handedly elevated the individual soloist to preeminence. In addition, his relaxed phrasing catalyzed a shift away from the staccato and jerky rhythms of early jazz to the even, four-beat swing that still characterizes most jazz today.

Armstrong was above all a soloist, in much the same sense as tenor saxophonist Coleman Hawkins and alto saxophonist Charlie Parker. Unlike Duke Ellington, the other great jazz figure to emerge in the 1920s, Armstrong revealed little distinction as a composer, arranger, or bandleader. Armstrong's most successful ensembles were small—for example, his Hot Five and Hot Seven, which were strictly studio bands that never made regular public appearances. As was apparent in his big-band recordings of the early 1930s, Armstrong had an astonishing ability to transcend the limits of mediocre and sloppy accompaniment, which was a sign not only of his self-sustaining inspiration, but also of his casual attitude toward the quality of his sidemen.

His Move North and Early Recordings

In 1922 King Oliver, who had moved to Chicago four years earlier, invited Armstrong to join him there to play second cornet in his Creole Jazz Band. Black migrants were then filling Chicago's raucous South Side, and white mobsters were busily opening bars, clubs, and speakeasies that featured the new jazz music. In 1923 the Creole Jazz Band traveled to Richmond, Indiana, and made a number of recordings for Gennett Records that remain profoundly important; jazz scholar James Lincoln Collier views them as "one of the root stocks of jazz." The group played in classic New Orleans jazz style, employing elaborate, collectively improvised polyphony, but a number of the brief instrumental breaks—such as Armstrong's two choruses on "*Chimes Blues*" (1923), his first recorded solo—pointed the way to the future. Armstrong's playing already displayed a loose, easy swing quite at odds with the stiff, ragtime-derived rhythms of many of his contemporaries.

Armstrong remained with Oliver only until 1924, when he left for New York City at the invitation of bandleader Fletcher Henderson and at the urging of his wife, pianist Lil Hardin, who wanted Armstrong to strike out on his own. During his brief stint with the Henderson big band, Armstrong had an impact on every jazz musician who heard him. By late 1925 he returned to Chicago, where he organized his most important band—the Hot Five, later expanded to the Hot Seven—and commenced a memorable series of recordings for Okeh Records. On such songs as *"Cornet Chop Suey"* (1926), *"Struttin' with Some Barbecue"* (1927), and above all *"West End Blues"* (1928), Armstrong played solos of breathtaking beauty and technical brilliance.

"West End Blues," in particular, amazed fellow jazz musicians. Armstrong's bravura open horn projected a bell-toned and brassy assurance. He entered on a high B-flat that he held out for four long, tension-building measures before falling away in a precisely articulated flurry of notes. Although there were general precedents for his *"West End Blues"* solo—most notably Bubber Miley's playing on Duke Ellington's *"Black and Tan Fantasy"* (1927) for Victor Records—no other jazz musician of the day could match Armstrong's technique and spontaneous lyricism.

The Defining Qualities of Armstrong's Trumpet Playing

Armstrong projected a clear tone, whatever his register, and whether he was playing high notes or low. His articulation was clean, and when he held out notes, he concluded by adding a slow vibrato, a slight quaver or alteration of the pitch, that was soon much imitated. It was different from the fast vibrato favored by most of his New Orleans contemporaries, including Bechet. Armstrong's melodic ideas were distinctive, classically balanced, and memorable, so much so that his style of improvising inspired countless imitators, including virtually every trumpet player to emerge during the 1920s and 1930s. He also had what was, for that period, an astonishing range.

Like many other self-taught brass players, Armstrong reached high notes by pulling the cornet or trumpet forcefully against his mouth to raise the pitch of his vibrating lips, rather than using the muscles of his mouth and cheeks to change the pitch. Photographs reveal that by the early 1930s Armstrong had already permanently scarred his lips. Over the years, his reckless and competitive nature—sometimes he played 50 or 100 high Cs in succession, topped by a high F—took an inevitable toll on his trumpet playing. His biographer James Lincoln Collier described the results of an April 26, 1933, recording session: "On the last tune of the day, *'Don't Play Me Cheap,'* toward the end of his final chorus we are brought almost to tears as he writhes up to the climactic high note that he felt he had to give his audience. He was by this point jamming the sharp circle of steel of the mouthpiece deep into the flesh of his lips to give them enough support to reach the high notes." Victor Records and Johnny Collins, then respectively Armstrong's record company and manager, held him to a grueling pace, and Armstrong, always eager to please, did not refuse them.

During this period, however, Armstrong began to change his style by simplifying it. He continued to strive for high notes, but he began playing more slowly, using fewer notes per measure and leaving more open space. He improvised melodies that were more flowing, and he played longer phrases. Collier concluded that these changes were not simply an evolution in Armstrong's style; they were a way of sparing his lips. His need to lessen the wear and tear on his embouchure may also help explain his growing reliance upon vocals.

Armstrong as a Vocalist and Entertainer

By the early 1930s Armstrong's gravelly voice and swinging delivery had gained popularity with audiences regardless of race, and record companies urged him to sing more, and better, material. Armstrong was one of the first vocalists to use the technique known as *scat singing*—that is, singing nonsense syllables and improvised melodies instead of the actual lyrics and written melody. His phrasing had a powerful impact on virtually every jazz and popular vocalist to begin singing after 1930, including Cab Calloway, Billie Holiday, Ella Fitzgerald, Bing Crosby, and Frank Sinatra. Crosby declared categorically that Armstrong was "the beginning and the end of music in America."

Armstrong emerged as a certified star during the 1930s. He helped usher in the swing era as the featured soloist and front man of a number of early 1930s big bands. He traveled widely, including his first journeys abroad, to England in 1932 and to Europe in 1933–1934, which foreshadowed his post-World War II globetrotting. He began to appear in Hollywood films, including *Pennies from Heaven* (1936) and *Cabin in the Sky* (1943).

Although Armstrong developed a great popular following, jazz listeners increasingly viewed him as old-fashioned. Nonetheless, he continued to play music that was successful both commercially and artistically. In the post-World War II years, he enjoyed a series of hit recordings, including "*Blueberry Hill*" (1949), "*Mack the Knife*" (1955), and "*Hello, Dolly*" (1963). "*What a Wonderful World*" (1967) hit the charts—fully 17 years after his death—after its inclusion in the soundtrack of the film *Good Morning, Vietnam* (1988).

Beginning in 1947 Armstrong returned to small-group formats, something he had not done regularly since 1929. He organized the All Stars, which initially included his "*West End Blues*" collaborator Earl Hines on piano and other first-rate jazz musicians. The group continued through various personnel changes until the late 1960s. Armstrong's playing declined after a 1959 heart attack, although he recorded some of his

A New Orleans jazz band, Italian style, welcomes trumpeter Louis Armstrong to Rome in 1949.
CORBIS/Bettmann

finest late-career work in collaboration with the Duke Ellington Orchestra, resulting in two 1961 albums, *Together for the First Time* and *The Great Reunion*.

Social Critic and Ambassador to the World

During the 1950s Armstrong moved easily into his final and almost ubiquitous role as America's goodwill ambassador to the world. Beginning in 1949 he toured regularly over-seas, most memorably including several trips to Africa (1956, 1960, and 1964) and a tour of Eastern Europe (1960). During his 1956 African tour, a crowd of more than 100,000 people turned out for him in Accra, Ghana.

Despite his reputation for "Tomming," Armstrong voiced trenchant criticisms of American racial injustices during the late 1950s and the 1960s. In 1957 he was slated to make a groundbreaking tour of the Soviet Union, but he stirred up controversy with his reaction to the Little Rock crisis, declaring that "the way they are treating my people in the South, the government can go to hell." In response, the United States State Department excluded Armstrong from the upcoming cultural mission, instead sending the less outspoken white clarinetist Benny Goodman.

Similarly, in 1965, after the violent beatings of civil rights demonstrators in Selma, Alabama, Armstrong remarked, "They would beat Jesus if he was black and marched." In 1968 he refused to take part in the Academy Awards telecast after the assassination of Martin Luther King Jr. Significantly, he spoke out not because of any personal affront or conflict, but rather in response to injuries inflicted on others.

During the 1960s jazz fans and the wider public gradually stopped thinking of Armstrong in terms of stylistic categories and musical fashions. He was beloved as a popular entertainer and revered as a jazz giant. In 1969 a second major heart attack virtually halted his trumpet playing, although still, on occasion, he could not resist taking up his horn. Following another hospitalization in 1971, Armstrong died in his sleep shortly before his 70th birthday.

Latin America and the Caribbean

Artel, Jorge

(b. April 27, 1909, Cartagena de Indias, Colombia; d. August 19, 1994, Barranquilla, Colombia), Afro-Colombian poet, lawyer, journalist, and diplomat; Artel, whose real name was Agapito de Arcos, was one of the most representative poets of Négritude in South America.

Jorge Artel was born in Colombia, in the colonial city of Cartagena de Indias, once the major entryway for slaves into the Spanish colonies in South America. He grew up surrounded by the drumbeats of the cumbia music, slavery's violent legacies, and the history of resistance embodied in the many maroon communities that dotted the city's borders. In his poetry he evokes those images, especially, as Lawrence Prescott has noted, using the symbol of the drum as the unifying thread essential to the black experience in the Americas. Like other black poets in Spanish America, such as the Cuban Nicolás Guillén (1902–1989) and the Afro-Peruvian Nicomedes Santa Cruz (1925–1992), Artel did not single out race alone as the defining element that shaped his life and his aesthetic vision. For him as for the others, class and economic exploitation were as important, and this awareness allowed them to express strong feelings of commitment toward the various other struggles faced by their fellow countrymen.

Artel published three books of poetry: *Tambores en la noche* (1940, Drums in the Night); *Poemas con botas y banderas* (1972, Poems with Boots and Flags); and the 1987 *Sinú, riberas de asombro jubiloso* (Sinu, River-banks of Joyful Wonder). In 1979 and again in 1986 he published revised anthologies of his poetry. *Tambores en la noche*, published at a time when other important black Spanish American authors such as Adalberto Ortiz (b. 1914), Pilar Barrios (1899–1974), and Juan Pablo Sojo (1908–1948) were issuing their first publications, was probably written during the 1930s in Cartagena. It is considered to be one of the first poetic interpretations of the modern Afro-Hispanic experience. Drawing on the poetic legacies of Candelario Obeso (1849–1884), Artel sometimes used colloquial speech and often explored themes characteristic of the Négritude movement, such as music and dance, Africa, and the question of identity.

Artel also published a novel, *No es la muerte, es el morir* (1979, It Is Not Death, It Is the Dying), that sympathetically portrays the guerrillas in a civil war that has devastated Colombia. In 1986 Jorge Artel was declared a national poet, but he remains relatively unknown both in Colombia and abroad.

North America

Artis, William Ellisworth

(b. February 2, 1914, Washington, N.C.; d. 1977?), African American sculptor who applied traditional style to African American subjects.

William Ellisworth Artis was born February 2, 1914, in Washington, North Carolina, to Elizabeth Davis and Thomas Migget. In 1926 he went to live with his mother and her husband, George Artis, in New York City. Artis's artistic education took him through a number of institutions, including the Art Students League, Pennsylvania State University, Chadron State College in Nebraska, and Syracuse University. He also studied under the Harlem Renaissance sculptor Augusta Savage. Artis won the Metropolitan Scholarship award for creative sculpture in 1933 and the Out-standing Educator of America and Outstanding Afro-American Artist awards in 1970. His sculptures are singular in their treatment of human life and their vitality of form. Later in his career, Artis taught at Nebraska State Teacher's College and the Harlem Young Men's Christian Association (YMCA).

North America

Atkins, Cholly

(b. September 30, 1913, Birmingham, Ala.), African American choreographer, dancer, and dance coach best known for his team tap dancing with the great Charles "Honi" Coles.

Cholly Atkins was born in Birmingham, Alabama, and raised in Buffalo, New York, where he displayed a talent for the stage early on. He began performing at the age of ten, when he won a Charleston contest, and he learned basic jazz and soft shoe steps while in high school. He began his formal career as a singing waiter in 1929 and soon teamed up with William Porter, a dancing waiter, to form the Rhythm Pals, a vaudeville song and dance team. After ten years with Porter, Atkins left the Rhythm Pals to begin dancing and choreographing for the Cotton Club Boys, a tap troupe that toured with Cab Calloway's band and performed with Bill "Bojangles" Robinson in a swing musical, The Hot Mikado, at the World's Fair in New York City. A partnership with Dotty Saulters followed but was interrupted when Atkins was drafted into the army in 1943.

After serving in the military, Atkins joined forces with Charles "Honi" Coles, and they soon became one of the best known black tap duos of the late 1940s. From 1946 to 1950, they toured Europe and the United States (headlining at venues like Harlem's Apollo Theater) and often performed with the bands of Billy Eckstine, Count Basie, the Mills Brothers, and Louis Armstrong. They also appeared on Broadway in Gentlemen Prefer Blondes (1949–1952).

In 1952 Atkins took a brief respite from live performing and began teaching tap at the Katherine Dunham School of Arts and Research in New York City. From 1955 to 1961 he reunited with Coles, performing dates in Las Vegas and with Pearl Bailey, but the pair never repeated the success of the 1940s. With interest in tap waning, Atkins gave up performance in favor of choreography, creating dance routines for the Supremes, the Temptations, Gladys Knight and the Pips, and the O'Jays as a staff choreographer for Motown Records from 1965 to 1971. He also applied his talents to Broadway musicals, winning a Tony Award for his choreography work on Black and Blue in 1989.

Africa

Awoonor, Kofi,

(b. 1935, Wheta, Ghana), Ghanaian poet and novelist. His works in English focus on life in Ghana following independence from Great Britain in 1957, but they also draw heavily from the traditional literature of the Ewe culture in which he grew up.

Born in the coastal town of Wheta, Kofi Awoonor published his first work under the name George Awoonor-Williams. Since the late 1960s he has used his birth name. After receiving his B.A. in English from the University of Ghana at Legon (near Accra) in 1960, he served as managing editor of the Ghana Film Corporation.

In 1968 Awoonor went to the United States, earning his Ph.D. in comparative literature from the State University of New York at Stony Brook in 1972. He later taught there and at the University of Texas at Austin. Shortly after returning to Ghana in 1975 to teach in the English department at the University of Cape Coast, Awoonor was arrested and imprisoned by the military government, which he opposed. After his pardon and release in 1976, he returned to the university. Beginning in the 1980s he held a number of diplomatic positions, most notably as Ghana's ambassador to the United Nations in the early 1990s.

Awoonor has established himself as one of the most significant contemporary African writers, primarily through his poetry. He is a lyric poet in essence, with a strong sense of engagement with political and cultural concerns. Awoonor's first two books of verse, *Rediscovery* (1964) and *Night of My Blood* (1971), show a progression from fascination with his roots to a synthesis of traditional and Western ideas. His first novel, *This Earth, My Brother . . . : An Allegorical Tale of Africa* (1971), remains his most widely read work. In it he writes of a young lawyer's coming to terms with postcolonial West African society. As in his early poetry, Awoonor employs rhythms and motifs from traditional Ewe dirges to express the alienation and anguish that demand a restructuring, refocusing, and revitalizing of individual and communal order in contemporary Africa.

In his next poetry collection, *Ride Me, Memory* (1973), Awoonor reflects on his sojourn in America, often following the patterns of traditional African praise and abuse poetry. The title of his next collection, *The House by the Sea* (1978), alludes to the place where he was imprisoned, and in the poems he transforms the personal experience of imprisonment into a collective statement about his people. In his second novel, *Comes the Voyager at Last* (1991), Awoonor examines the process of an African American coming to Africa and finding his roots. *The Latin American and Caribbean Notebook, Volume I* (1992) is a collection of poems reflecting on global relations during Awoonor's years as an ambassador.

B

Bailey, Pearl

(b. March 29, 1918, Newport News, Va.; d. August 17, 1990, Philadelphia, Pa.),
African American singer, actress, and entertainer known for her comedic timing
and charm, honored for her service to American troops, and named as special
delegate to the United Nations.

Pearl Bailey was born in Newport News, Virginia on March 29, 1918, but
soon moved to Washington, D.C., and then to Philadelphia, Pennsylvania.
Her stage singing debut came when she was 15 years old. Bailey's brother
Bill was beginning his own career as a tap dancer, and at his suggestion,
she entered an amateur contest at Philadelphia's Pearl Theater, where she
won first prize. Several months later, she won a similar contest at
Harlem's famous Apollo Theater, and she decided to pursue a career in
entertainment.

Bailey began by singing and dancing in Philadelphia's African American
nightclubs in the 1930s, and soon started performing in other parts of the
East Coast. In 1941, during World War II, she toured the country with the
United Service Organizations (USO), performing for American troops.
After the tour, she settled in New York. Her solo successes as a nightclub
performer were followed by acts with such entertainers as Cab Calloway.

In 1946 Bailey made her Broadway debut in *St. Louis Woman* and won
the Donaldson Award for most promising newcomer of the year. As an
actress, she was known for her mix of charm and comedic timing. She
went on to appear onstage in *Arms and the Girl* (1950), *House of Flowers*
(1954), and *Bless You All* (1954). In 1947 Bailey made her film debut in
The Variety Girl. She followed that screen appearance with larger roles in
Isn't It Romantic? (1948), *Carmen Jones* (1955), *That Certain Feeling*
(1956), *St. Louis Blues* (1958), *Porgy and Bess* (1959), and *All the Fine
Young Cannibals* (1960).

In 1967 Bailey returned to Broadway with the title role in an all-black production of *Hello, Dolly!* She won a Tony Award for that role in 1968. That same year, President Richard Nixon named her the Ambassador of Love. In 1969 the USO named her Woman of the Year in recognition of her continuing service to American troops. She was also named a special delegate to the United Nations under the Ford, Reagan, and Bush administrations.

Through all of these honors, Bailey continued to perform. In 1971 she hosted her own ABC-TV variety show. She announced her retirement from show business in 1975 but still continued to appear in film roles and in television sitcoms, commercials, game shows, and specials. In 1975 she received the Britannica Life Achievement Award. While in her sixties, Bailey decided to complete her education, and in 1985 she received a B.A. in Theology from Georgetown University. In 1988 President Reagan awarded her the Presidential Medal of Freedom. Pearl Bailey died in Philadelphia on August 17, 1990.

North America

Baker, Augusta

(b. April 1, 1911, Baltimore, Md.; d. February 23, 1998, Columbia, S.C.), African American librarian, educator, and storyteller, the first black to hold an administrative position in the New York Public Library system.

In her 1970 article "My Years as a Children's Librarian," Augusta Baker summed up what she had learned in her long career: "Library work with children has had a great past and has a still greater future. Young black men and women have an opportunity to be part of this exciting future and for the sake of their children they should be." From her appointment as assistant children's librarian in the New York Public Library system in 1937 to her retirement in 1974, Baker pursued a career of library service to children with enthusiasm, vision, and leadership. During the 1940s, while working at the library's 135th Street branch, she spearheaded the creation of the James Weldon Johnson Memorial Collection, whose purpose, she wrote, was "to bring together books for children that give an unbiased, accurate, well rounded picture of Negro life in all parts of the world."

Like her grandmother, Baker became an artful storyteller. After 16 years as a library assistant in the Countee Cullen Branch of the New York Public Library in Harlem, in 1953 she was promoted to the position of assistant coordinator of children's services and storytelling specialist. She directed the New York Public Library system's storytelling program for eight years, teaching and lecturing on oral narration and gathering folk tales from different cultures, a pursuit that culminated in the notable story collections *The Talking Tree* (1960) and *The Golden Lynx and Other Tales* (1960).

From 1961 until her retirement in 1974, Baker held the position of coordinator of children's services, managing children's services in 82 branch libraries and ensuring that the collections reflected the diversity of their readership. In 1971 she published a bibliography entitled *The Black Experience in Children's Books*, widely considered a benchmark guide for librarians in creating minority representation in their collections. During this period, she also worked as a consultant to Sesame Street, initiated a series of radio broadcasts called *The World of Children's Literature*, lectured at universities across the United States, and held senior positions at the American Library Association, including chair of the Newberry/Caldecott Awards Committee.

In 1974 Baker retired to Columbia, South Carolina, where she became storyteller-in-residence at the University of South Carolina. Baker died in 1998 at the age of 86, five years after the American Library Association cited her for a Distinguished Services Award, its highest tribute to a member.

North America
___

Baker, Josephine

(b. June 3, 1906, St. Louis, Mo; d. April 12, 1975, Paris, France), African American expatriate dancer, singer, and entertainer.

For many people, Josephine Baker's name will always evoke a familiar, controversial image: the "black Venus" naked onstage, except for a string of bananas around her waist, dancing to African drums before her white Parisian audiences. It was this image that first made Baker a star, one whose international fame lasted for five decades. But the picture of the exotic dancer does not fully capture the complexity of the woman who was one of the first black performers to transcend race and appeal to audiences of all colors from around the world.

Baker was born Freda Josephine MacDonald (the name Baker came from her second husband). Her parents were not married; her father was a drummer in a local band, and her mother, a washerwoman, rarely had enough money to support Baker and her three younger half-siblings. At age 8, Baker began working as a maid in white homes, and by age 14 she had left home, married and separated from her first of five husbands, and begun working with a traveling vaudeville troupe. Her first break came when she was featured in *Shuffle Along*, Broadway's first black musical, in 1921.

Originally rejected from the show for being too young, too thin, and too dark, she eventually won the role of the comic "end girl" in the chorus line—the one too confused to keep up with the moves—and wound up stealing the show. Four years later she was offered the opportunity to go to Paris and perform in *La Revue Nègre*. By then her teenaged body had fully matured, and her show-stopping finale, "Danse sauvage"—in which she danced the Charleston wearing nothing but a girdle of feathers—made her an overnight sensation. Baker became the living embodiment of everything European

Josephine Baker opens her first Broadway engagement in 15 years, at the Strand Theater in New York City in 1951. *CORBIS/Bettmann*

audiences found exotic and provocative about black women's sexuality.

In the midst of all this adulation, however, American audiences were still cool. Baker returned to the United States to appear with the *Ziegfeld Follies* in 1936 and received terrible reviews. Her stage show had evolved by then into a more glamorous, refined act, and white America did not seem ready to see a sophisticated black star on stage. In 1937, after returning to Paris, Baker legally became a French citizen. During World War II she served as an intelligence liaison and an ambulance driver for the French Resistance and was awarded the Medal of the Resistance and the Legion of Honor.

Soon after the war Baker toured the United States again, and this time she won respect and praise from African Americans for her support of the Civil Rights Movement. She refused to play to segregated audiences or stay in segregated hotels during a 1951 American tour, and as a result the National Association for the Advancement of Colored People (NAACP) named her its Most Outstanding Woman of the Year. She also participated in the 1963 March on Washington, and later that year gave a benefit concert at Carnegie Hall for the NAACP, the Student Nonviolent Coordinating Committee, and the Congress of Racial Equality.

The last five years of her life were marked by an ironic mix of public adoration and personal poverty. At home in France, she was sometimes reduced to begging on the streets for her children—unrecognizable without her makeup, wig, and costumes. Her health also began to decline, and she suffered two heart attacks and a stroke. But she continued to perform, and onstage she was as glamorous as ever. A 1973 tour of the United States brought widespread acclaim, although some African American audiences were upset by Baker's condemnation of the Black Power Movement (which she saw as too separatist). In 1974 she starred in a Monaco production of *Josephine*, a show based on her life, and the performances were so successful that the show came to Paris in April 1975.

That year marked the fiftieth anniversary of her arrival in Paris, and on April 8 there was a huge gala in a Paris hotel to celebrate both that anniversary and *Josephine*'s opening night. Four days later, however, Baker suffered a fatal cerebral hemorrhage during a nap. Twenty thousand people attended her Paris funeral in a massive show of devotion to an African American performer whose boldness and unconventional style had taken France and the world by storm.

Baldwin, James

(b. August 2, 1924, Harlem, N.Y.; d. December 1, 1987, St.-Paul-de-Vence, France), African American novelist, essayist, playwright, and poet known especially for his astute commentary on American race relations.

"We are responsible for the world in which we find ourselves, if only because we are the only sentient force which can change it." In this statement from his collection of essays, *No Name in the Street*, James Baldwin sums up a philosophy that drove much of his work. Baldwin was continually conscious of the hypocrisies and injustices in the world around him, and as a writer, he strove to make his audiences aware of the possibility that people could do, and be, better. An expatriate most of his adult life, Baldwin nevertheless wrote tirelessly about the contradictions inherent in American identity, and especially about the state of American race relations. He came to be respected as one of the sagest intellectuals in the Civil Rights Movement and as a leading figure in the African American literary tradition.

After his high school graduation in 1942, Baldwin took a series of odd jobs in New Jersey. But when his stepfather's death and the Harlem riots occurred during the same 24-hour period in the summer of 1943, the trauma of the two events spurred him to return to New York, where he settled in Greenwich Village, determined to concentrate on his writing. During the winter of 1944–1945 he met the celebrated black writer Richard Wright, who became a mentor and father figure to him and who recommended him for the Eugene Saxton Fellowship that he received in 1945. Until that time Baldwin had been working only on an unpublished draft of a novel, but in 1946 he published his first essay in the Nation. He soon became well known as an essayist, publishing in the *New Leader, Commentary*, and *Partisan Review*. In 1948 Baldwin was awarded a Rosenwald Fellowship and used the prize money to buy a one-way ticket to Paris. He left New York on November 11, 1948.

As an openly gay African American, Baldwin had long felt stifled by the prevailing racial and sexual prejudices in the United States. The 1948 trip marked the beginning of his career as an expatriate writer, and while his writing often returned to American subjects, he was based abroad for most of the next 40 years. In Paris, though he lived as a struggling artist, his friends included French writers Jean-Paul Sartre and Simone de Beauvoir and fellow American expatriates Saul Bellow, Truman Capote, Beauford Delaney, and Wright. Baldwin's 1949 essay "Everybody's Protest Novel" and 1951 essay "Many Thousands Gone," however, both of which criticized Wright's *Native Son*, created a lasting break in that friendship. But by then Baldwin was well on his way to establishing his own identity as a writer.

Baldwin finished his long-awaited first book, *Go Tell it on the Mountain*, during a stay in his companion's Swiss hometown, and published it in 1953. The novel, a largely autobiographical account of his teenage years, received

James Baldwin, novelist and essayist, who has been elected a member of the National Institute of Arts and Letters, the nation's highest honor society of the arts. *Bettmann/CORBIS*

critical acclaim, but his next two novels caused controversy. *Giovanni's Room* (1956) and *Another Country* (1962) featured characters struggling to define sexual, racial, and national identities, and the matter-of-fact depictions of gay relationships in both books surprised many readers. During the same period, however, Baldwin also published three collections of essays, and it was the nonfiction books—*Notes of a Native Son* (1955), *Nobody Knows My Name* (1961), and *The Fire Next Time* (1963)—that secured his reputation as an important American writer and social critic.

Through his essays, Baldwin developed a reputation for being a shrewd and prophetic commentator on American culture, particularly on racial identity. As one critic explains, these three books—each of which sold more than a million copies at publication—"won Baldwin a popularity and acclaim as the 'conscience of the nation,' who brought to racial discourse a passion and honesty that demanded notice . . . Baldwin's knife-edged criticism of the failed promises of American democracy, and the consequent social injustices, is unrelenting and demonstrates a piercing understanding of the function of blacks in the white racial imagination."

During this period, Baldwin's trips to the United States became more frequent. He visited the American South for the first time in 1957, and during the 1960s was one of the most public intellectuals in the Civil Rights Movement, lecturing and speaking out at such forums as a meeting he arranged between Attorney General Robert Kennedy and black celebrities including Harry Belafonte, Lena Horne, and Lorraine Hansberry. It was *The Fire Next Time*, whose publication coincided with the 1963 March on Washington and the hundredth anniversary of the Emancipation Proclamation, that earned Baldwin his national reputation as a prophet. Baldwin took the book's title from the lines of an old spiritual—"God gave Noah the rainbow sign / No more water, the fire next time"—as he argued that American race relations were in danger of reaching violent conclusions. Many readers interpreted the riots that occurred in American cities throughout the late 1960s as the fulfillment of Baldwin's warnings.

But Baldwin had concluded that essay on a hopeful note, suggesting that "if we [blacks and whites] do not falter in our duty now, we may be able . . .

to end the racial nightmare, and achieve our country, and change the history of the world." This optimism about the possibility of reconciliation in American race relations had been expressed even more strongly in some of his earlier essays, and it created a rift between Baldwin and many younger African Americans—most notably black nationalists such as Eldridge Cleaver and the more militant black writers who were associated with the Black Arts Movement. But even as his politics began to be criticized, Baldwin kept writing.

Baldwin's 1955 play *The Amen Corner* and 1964 play *Blues for Mr. Charlie* were both successfully produced on Broadway. Baldwin's other publications in the 1960s included *Going to Meet the Man* (1965), a collection of short stories, and the novel *Tell Me How Long the Train's Been Gone* (1968). In the 1970s his books included the essay collection *No Name in the Street* (1972) and the novels *If Beale Street Could Talk* (1974) and *Just Above My Head* (1979). By then, Baldwin was again recognized and embraced as a major figure in African American literature, and he lectured and taught at several American colleges and universities between the late 1970s and mid-1980s. In 1985 he published *The Evidence of Things Not Seen*, a collection of essays on the 1980–1981 Atlanta child murders, and *The Price of the Ticket: Collected Nonfiction, 1948–1985.*

When Baldwin died in France of stomach cancer on December 1, 1987, he was at work on a play and a biography of Martin Luther King Jr. Baldwin's memorial service at the Cathedral of St. John the Divine in New York City drew thousands of mourners, and writers from Maya Angelou to Toni Morrison spoke of his profound impact on their own work. As Amiri Baraka said in his eulogy, "This man traveled the earth like history and its biographer. He reported, criticized, made beautiful, analyzed, cajoled, lyricized, attacked, sang, made us think, made us better, made us consciously human."

Latin America and the Caribbean

Barreto, Ray,

(b. 1929), percussionist and bandleader, renowned for his contributions to Latin jazz and salsa. Born in New York of Puerto Rican heritage, Barreto joined Tito Puente's big band in the 1950s. In the 1960s he established the Ray Barreto Orchestra, which recorded under the Fania label. In 1992 he established the jazz band New World Spirit.

North America

Barthé, Richmond

(b. January 28, 1901, Bay Saint Louis, Miss.; d. March 6, 1989, Altadena, Calif.), a sculptor of the Harlem Renaissance era whose sculptures and busts defied universal negative representations of African Americans and other individuals of African descent. Barthé introduced such themes as balance, rhythm, grace, and beauty to the image of his subjects.

Richmond Barthé grew up in Bay Saint Louis, Mississippi, and New Orleans, Louisiana. His father died at the age of 22, one month after Barthé's birth. His mother, Marie Clementine Roboteau, raised him alone, nurturing his interest in the arts. He also received encouragement from fellow townspeople and the nuns at his parochial school. In early childhood, Barthé began drawing and painting watercolor scenes. When he was 12 years old, Barthé's work was exhibited at the Mississippi County Fair.

In 1915 Barthé moved to New Orleans, where he painted and worked as a butler. At the age of 18, he won the blue ribbon for his submission to a parish contest. During the nine years that Barthé spent in New Orleans, he attempted to enter art school but his admission was denied because he was black. Lyle Saxon of the *Times-Picayune* wielded his influence to gain entry for Barthé into a New Orleans art school, but his efforts failed.

Eventually, Barthé focused his interest on schools within the Chicago area. With the help of Father Harry Kane, a Catholic priest who was impressed by Barthé's paintings, Barthé entered the Chicago Art Institute in 1924 with the intention of becoming a painter. As he followed the curriculum for painting majors, two occurrences shaped his interest in sculpting. The first was an assignment for his anatomy professor, Charles Schroeder; the second was his participation in *Negro Week*.

As part of an assignment intended to enhance his understanding of anatomy, Barthé designed two clay heads. The final result of these two pieces showcased his deep understanding of three-dimensional pieces. Barthé viewed the successful reception of these works as an incentive to launch a sculpting career, which he did by participating in the exhibition mounted in Chicago during *Negro Week* in 1927.

Barthé graduated from the Chicago Art Institute in February 1929 and moved to New York City that same year. The time after his relocation to New York proved to be prosperous for him; his work was widely honored and exhibited. For example, in 1932 he sculpted *Blackberry Woman*, and *African Dancer* in 1933. The Whitney Museum of American Art purchased these two pieces in 1935. The Caz Delbo Galleries granted Barthé his first solo show in 1934, and he also gained greater recognition after his 1939 exhibit at the Arden Galleries in New York. As a result, he was nominated for and accepted a Guggenheim Fellowship in 1940 and 1941.

He captured the complexities of movement in *The Boxer* (1943), and in 1946 he commemorated such African American achievers as George Washington Carver and Booker T. Washington. The bust of Booker T. Washington was created for the Hall of Fame of New York University. Barthé also modeled a portrait of Othello after the actor Paul Robeson for the Actors Equity. His other commissions included a bas-relief of Arthur Brisbane for New York's Central Park. He designed a large frieze, *Green Pastures: The Walls of Jericho*, for the Harlem River Housing Project, and the General Toussaint L'Ouverture Monument for Port-au-Prince, Haiti.

In 1947, at the apex of his career, when such phrases as "leading moderns of American art" were used in connection with his name, Barthé relocated to Jamaica, West Indies. He exchanged the accelerated pace of city life for the tranquillity of the Jamaican countryside, where he resided until 1969. After he left Jamaica, Barthé lived in Europe. There, in addition to spending time with friends, he studied the art and culture of the masters of the Italian Renaissance such as Donatello and Michelangelo. He returned to the United States in 1976, stayed for a brief time in Queens, New York, and then settled permanently in Altadena, California.

Richmond Barthé's career spanned more than 60 years. The art world consistently responded to his work with acclaim. It recognized him for his impressive bronzes and immense statues by electing him to the National Academy of Arts and Letters in 1915; he was the first black sculptor to receive this honor. His work has also been incorporated into the collections of the Metropolitan Museum of Art, the Pennsylvania Museum of Art, the Virginia Museum of Fine Arts, and the Museum of the Art Institute of Chicago.

Ironically, despite Barthé's fame, he never achieved the financial success that often complements such visibility. Rather, the hardships of his final days were alleviated by the assistance of actors James Garner and Esther Jones. Upon Barthé's death in 1989, Garner donated Barthé's remaining works to the Museum of African Art in Los Angeles and the Schomburg Center in New York City.

North America

Basie, William James ("Count")

(b. August 21, 1904, Red Bank, N. J.; d. April 26, 1984, Hollywood, Calif.), African American piano player and big-band leader from the mid-1930s to the 1980s, whose band made hard-swinging Kansas City jazz popular across the United States.

Though white clarinetist Benny Goodman was proclaimed the "King of Swing," by all rights the title belonged to Count Basie. For nearly half a century, with the exception of a brief interruption between 1949 and 1952, Basie headed one of the finest big bands in jazz, one that has enjoyed an unrivaled longevity. No other jazz orchestra has continued so long under the same leadership. In fact, Basie led two distinct bands, which some critics designate the Old Testament and New Testament bands. The Old Testament band was Basie's aggregation from the mid-1930s through the 1940s; the New Testament band encompasses the Basie band since the early 1950s.

The earlier band played a hard-swinging, rough-around-the-edges Kansas City jazz and often used head arrangements rather than written charts. It featured brilliant musical stylists, including tenor saxophonist Lester Young, trumpeters Buck Clayton and Harry "Sweets" Edison, vocalist Jimmy "Mr. Five by Five" Rushing, drummer Jo Jones, and Basie himself on piano. Basie's later band—although it featured such soloists as trumpeters Thad Jones and Joe Newman, tenor saxophonists Frank Foster and Frank Wess, and vocalist Joe Williams—was above all an arranger's orchestra, skillfully performing the arrangements of Frank Foster, Neal Hefti, Quincy Jones, and Ernie Wilkins. The one constant in the Basie band was Basie himself.

As a boy, Basie dreamed of becoming a drummer, but watching future Duke Ellington drummer Sonny Greer convinced him that he should choose another instrument. Though always modest about his abilities, he was performing locally from the time he left junior high school. In 1924 he went to New York City to try his luck and fell under the influence of the three great Harlem stride pianists, James P. Johnson, Willie "the Lion" Smith, and Thomas "Fats" Waller. Waller, who also played the organ at the Lincoln Theater in Harlem, gave Basie his first instruction in that instrument while the day's movies were shown, helping to inspire his long-standing interest in organ playing.

Basie is rightly known as a pianist, and his playing remained rooted in the *stride* tradition of 1920s Harlem. Stride piano essentially divides the piano keyboard into three ranges. The pianist's left hand covers the two lower ranges, alternating single bass notes at the bottom with chord clusters struck higher up. The style takes its name from the characteristic bouncing "oom-pah, oom-pah" produced by the pianist's "striding" left hand. While the left hand establishes a propulsive beat and outlines the tune's harmonic structure, the pianist's right hand plays the melody, adds ornamentation, and improvises solo lines.

In 1924 and 1925 Basie toured with *Hippity Hop*, a burlesque show on the Columbia Circuit, which took the young pianist as far afield as Montreal, Canada; Omaha, Nebraska; and Kansas City, Missouri. On his second visit to Kansas City, Basie had more time to take part in the night life. Years later, he remembered the experience vividly: "[E]verywhere you went, there was at least a piano player and somebody singing, if not a combo or maybe a jam session. There was so much going on that I couldn't believe my eyes or my ears . . . . There we were, way out there in the middle of nowhere . . . and wham . . . the action was greater than anything I'd ever heard."

In 1926 and 1927 Basie signed on with a vaudeville show on the Theater Owners Booking Association (TOBA), the nationwide circuit of blacks-only theaters. But when the financially strapped TOBA dissolved, Basie's show was stranded and broke up in Kansas City.

As a jazz musician, Basie could not have asked for a better spot to be marooned. Soon he joined a territory band, Walter Page's Blue Devils, out of Oklahoma City, Oklahoma. After two years he became part of Benny Moten's Kansas City Orchestra. Basie played with Moten from 1929 to 1932, including a famed 1932 Victor recording session highlighted by a classic version of "*Blue Room*" that prefigured the swing sound that Goodman would make famous in 1935. When Moten died in 1935, his band broke up and Basie formed his own, mainly comprising members of the Blue Devils and Moten's band. It was initially known as the Barons of Rhythm.

In 1936 a small group of Basie band members recorded one of the most important sessions in jazz history for producer John Hammond. For legal reasons, the Basie-led group was identified as Jones-Smith Incorporated. It brilliantly captured the smooth sound and subtle interplay of Kansas City jazz. Years later Hammond would recall the date as "one of the only perfect sessions I ever had." It was also noteworthy for being Lester Young's first recording session. All four sides, especially Young's lyrical solos on "*Shoe Shine Boy*" and "*Oh, Lady Be Good*," were superb. According to musicologist Gunther Schuller, Young's two choruses on the latter demonstrate a "harmonic freeing up of the language of jazz" that was essential to all subsequent developments in jazz history.

Between 1937 and 1939 the Basie band made a memorable series of recordings for Decca Records, including "*One O'Clock Jump*," "*Jumpin' at the Woodside*," and "*Sent for You Yesterday*." These recordings clearly demonstrate the unrivaled swing of Basie's rhythm section, which consisted of Basie (piano), Walter Page (bass), Freddie Greene (rhythm guitar), and Jo Jones (drums). That rhythm section propelled the shouting unison passages, cushioned the soloists, and drove the music forward both gently and relentlessly. Indeed it was so strong that Basie began to simplify his piano style, deemphasizing the instrument's timekeeping role and concentrating on brief treble fills and punctuations. In so doing, he prepared the way for the more radical transformations that would be wrought by modern jazz pianists Thelonious Monk and Earl "Bud" Powell.

In 1939 the Basie band began a long association with Columbia Records. By the late 1940s, however, the big-band era was nearly over, and like many other groups, Basie's folded around the end of the decade. Basie spent three years touring with small groups that ranged in size from sextets to nonets, but in 1952, disregarding the conventional wisdom, he decided to reform his big band. He signed his new band with Verve Records (1952–1957) and Roulette (1957–1962) and made some of the most successful recordings of his career, in particular the Verve albums *Count Basie Swings, Joe Williams Sings* (1955), and *April in Paris* (1956).

After a series of less memorable recordings in the 1960s, the band joined Pablo Records in 1972, an association that continued until the leader's death. Although Basie performed and recorded in many musical contexts besides his big band, that band unquestionably constitutes his lasting legacy. It is fitting, then, that since Basie's death, his band has maintained its creativity and financial health. Indeed, it is the only such "ghost" band—one that keeps on performing after the death of its leader—that continues to play new music of undiminished vitality.

North America

Basquiat, Jean-Michel

(b. December 22, 1960, Brooklyn, N.Y.; d. August 12, 1988, Brooklyn, N.Y.), American painter, initially a street artist, whose graffiti-inspired work won international acclaim during the 1980s.

Born to a Haitian father and a first-generation Puerto Rican-American mother, Jean-Michel Basquiat grew up in Brooklyn. As a child, he created drawings inspired by comic books and television cartoons. His early interest in art was nurtured by his mother, who often took him to local art museums.

In May 1968, Basquiat was hit by a car. He suffered a broken arm and his spleen had to be removed. While he was hospitalized, his mother gave him a copy of *Gray's Anatomy*, a book that inspired many of his later works as well as the name of the noise band he co-founded in 1979, *Gray*. After his parents separated in 1968, Basquiat and his two sisters lived with their father, including two years in Puerto Rico. At the age of 17, Basquiat dropped out of high school and lived, by choice, on the streets and with various friends.

Basquiat's career as an artist began in 1977 when he began to spray-paint New York City streets and subways with one of his high school classmates, Al Diaz. The works were signed *SAMO*, an acronym for "same old shit," and consisted of short poetic phrases such as "Plush safe he think; SAMO." They strategically placed these street texts in SoHo and the East Village, where they were more likely to be seen by people in influential artistic circles. In December 1978, the *Village Voice* published an article about the SAMO writings. While working on the SAMO project, which ended in 1979, Basquiat sold hand-painted postcards and T-shirts to make money.

Basquiat's art was publicly exhibited for the first time in the 1980 Times Square Show. Art critics responded positively to his debut and in May 1981, after being included in several group shows, he had his first solo exhibition in Modena, Italy. His first one-man show in the United States took place in March 1982 at the Annina Nosei Gallery. Basquiat's work began to be shown internationally in prominent art galleries. In June 1982, the 21-one-year-old Basquiat was the youngest of 176 artists participating in the international exhibition *Documenta 7* in Germany.

Basquiat was also featured in the 1983 Biennial Exhibition at the Whitney Museum of American Art in New York, becoming the youngest artist ever to be included. Between 1983 and 1985, Basquiat produced 31 works in collaboration with Andy Warhol. Basquiat was devastated by the death in 1987 of Warhol, who had been his close friend and mentor. A year later, at the age of 27, Basquiat died of a drug overdose in his New York apartment.

Within the span of eight years, Jean-Michel Basquiat went from being an anonymous tag-writer to an internationally celebrated artist. His large, colorful works combine graffiti art with abstract expressionism. Some of Basquiat's paintings celebrate African American jazz musicians and boxers, while others address issues such as mortality, racism, and commercialism. The three-pointed crown and the circled c of the copyright symbol are recurrent images in his paintings. Basquiat's work is characterized by the inclusion and canceling out of words, which he explained by saying, "I cross out words so you will see them more; the fact that they are obscured makes you want to read them." Basquiat's rhythmic juxtaposition of words and images constitutes one of his most distinctive contributions to twentieth-century painting.

Bates, Clayton ("Peg Leg")

(b. October 11, 1907, Fountain Inn, S.C.; d. December 6, 1998, Fountain Inn, S.C.), American tap dancer who performed in Harlem nightclubs and appeared on the Ed Sullivan television show.

Clayton Bates was born on October 11, 1907 in Fountain Inn, South Carolina. He lost his leg in a cotton-seed mill accident at age 12, but decided to tour the country with a homemade wooden leg at the age of 15, working as a minstrel in racially integrated vaudeville circuits. He later danced in Harlem nightclubs, and frequently appeared on the Ed Sullivan television show. In 1952 Bates opened the Peg Leg Bates Country Club in New York, the largest black-owned and -operated resort in America until it was sold in the late 1980s.

Battle, Kathleen

(b. August 13, 1948, Portsmouth, Ohio), African American soprano in international opera.

Kathleen Battle began singing in church as a child and received bachelor's and master's degrees in music from the University of Cincinnati College Conservatory of Music. She made her professional debut as an opera singer at the 1972 Spoleto Festival in Italy.

Battle debuted at New York's Metropolitan Opera in 1977 and became internationally known within a few years. In addition to singing soprano roles in opera houses and with symphony orchestras, her repertoire has expanded to include spirituals and the work of George Gershwin and Duke Ellington. Battle has received many honors for her work, including three Grammy Awards and a Candace Award from the National Coalition of 100 Black Women.

Beavers, Louise

(b. March 18, 1902, Cincinnati, Ohio; d. 1962), African American film actor best known for her 1934 portrayal of the mother in *Imitation of Life*.

Born in Cincinnati, Ohio, on March 18, 1902, and raised in Los Angeles, Louise Beavers began her career in the silent film *Uncle Tom's Cabin* (1927). She appeared in over 120 motion pictures, always typecast as a Southern mammy or a source of comic relief. Although her portrayal of the mother in *Imitation of Life* (1934) was called the finest film performance of 1934 and established her career, her acting potential was never allowed to develop. Her notable roles included Pearl, Mae West's sassy maid in *She Done Him Wrong* (1933), Robinson's mother in *The Jackie Robinson Story* (1950), and the title role in the popular ABC television series *Beulah* (1952–1953).

North America

Bechet, Sidney Joseph,

(b. May 14, 1897, New Orleans, La.; d. May 14, 1959, Paris), African American clarinet and soprano saxophone player who was, along with Louis Armstrong, the greatest jazz soloist of the 1920s.

Although well known to jazz listeners and critics, Sidney Bechet has never enjoyed the reputation of his only peer, cornet and trumpet player Louis Armstrong. Yet in recent years Bechet has gained greater recognition, at least from jazz scholars and critics. For example, Barry Singer, in a 1997 *New York Times* article, described him as an "intrepid musical pioneer who was not merely Louis Armstrong's contemporary but in every way his creative equal."

At heart, however, the divergent reputations of the two men reflect profound differences in personality and background. Throughout his long career, from the pinched social world of the Jim Crow South to international acclaim, Armstrong always projected a happy-go-lucky demeanor. Bechet, on the other hand, fought to contain a powerful temper and seething rage toward racial injustice.

Bechet, who was four years Armstrong's senior, repeatedly achieved musical successes, only to be eclipsed by the younger and more charismatic trumpeter. During the 1910s Bechet won acclaim throughout New Orleans as an instrumentalist. He left the South for Chicago in 1917, five years before Armstrong, in the first wave of the Great Migration of blacks out of the South, and quickly dominated the Chicago jazz scene. In 1919 he joined Will Marion Cook's orchestra for a European tour.

Bechet remained in Europe until late in 1922. His playing inspired the first piece of serious jazz criticism, an essay by the Swiss conductor Ernest Ansermet, who praised him as "an extraordinary clarinet virtuoso who is, so it seems, the first of his race to have composed perfectly formed blues on the clarinet . . . . [T]heir form was gripping, abrupt, harsh, with a brusque and pitiless ending like that of Bach's second *Brandenburg Concerto*. I wish to set down the name of this artist of genius; as for myself, I shall never forget it, it is Sidney Bechet." It was by no means the last time that Bechet found himself better appreciated by Europeans than by Americans.

In 1923 Bechet became the first major jazz soloist to record, beating Armstrong by several months. In 1924 he joined Armstrong on several recordings, including *"Texas Moaner Blues"* (1924), recorded by pianist

Clarence Williams's Blue Five, and "*Cake Walkin' Babies*" (1924), by the Red Onion Jazz Babies. These recordings reveal Bechet and Armstrong in the act of transforming jazz from collective improvisation—the essence of the New Orleans style—to a focus on the improvising soloist.

Bechet's next trip abroad, in 1925, included lengthy stays in France and the Soviet Union. While sailing to Cherbourg aboard the Cunard liner Berengaria, Bechet had a shipboard romance with Josephine Baker, the 19-year-old singer and dancer who was just beginning her ascent to stardom.

But while Armstrong found success as a singer, bandleader, and entertainer in films and on radio programs, Bechet remained obscure. In 1932 he teamed up with trumpeter Tommy Ladnier in a recording session for RCA Victor, but work dried up during the Great Depression, and Bechet and Ladnier opened a tailor shop in 1933–1934. During the 1930s, Bechet's fortunes gradually improved. He joined Noble Sissle's band from 1934 to 1938. The French jazz writer and producer Hugues Panassie reunited him with Ladnier for a notable 1938 session that produced the classic "*Really the Blues*." The following year Bechet had his first (though minor) hit, a memorable rendition of "*Summertime*" that gave the fledgling Blue Note Records its first commercial success.

Bechet played with a pronounced vibrato. To produce a vibrato, the musician alters the pitch of a note by slightly changing his or her embouchure—that is, the position and pressure of the mouth on the instrument's mouthpiece—making the note waver above and below its true pitch. During the 1920s most jazz musicians favored a rapid vibrato, but during the 1930s, swing-era musicians preferred a slower vibrato. Since the 1940s jazz musicians have largely dispensed with it altogether, except on held-out notes or phrase endings, especially in slow-tempo ballads.

Bechet, however, never changed his sound or style: he always used a rapid, wide vibrato. He was a confident and inventive improviser, both in individual solos and in the collective improvisation that characterized New Orleans jazz. He was also highly competitive, and vied with the trumpet or cornet player for the lead in collective improvisation.

Some of Bechet's best playing occurred in ensembles with trumpet players who would simply get out of his way and give him the room to improvise freely; for example, in an innovative piano-less quartet that recorded eight selections in 1940. Besides Bechet, the group featured Muggsy Spanier on cornet, Welman Braud on bass, and Carmen Mastren on guitar. The quartet played timeless jazz that was exceptional for its light, driving swing and for giving Bechet ample room in which to solo, exemplified by his superb rendition of "*China Boy*."

During the bop revolution of the 1940s Bechet again fell on hard times, but when he appeared at a 1949 jazz festival in Paris, he met with such a warm reception that he decided to remain in France. He performed for enthusiastic audiences in Europe and made occasional return visits to the United States until shortly before his death from cancer in 1959.

Belafonte, Harold George (Harry)

(b. March 1, 1927, New York, N.Y.), African American singer, actor, producer, and activist who has used his position as an entertainer to promote human rights worldwide.

Harry Belafonte may be best known to American audiences as the singer of the *"Banana Boat Song"* (known popularly as *"Day-O"*), but it is his commitment to political causes that inspired scholar Henry Louis Gates Jr.'s comment that "Harry Belafonte was radical long before it was chic and remained so long after it wasn't."

Harold George Belafonte was born in Harlem, New York, to West Indian parents. The family moved to Jamaica in 1935 but returned five years later. Struggling with dyslexia, Belafonte dropped out of high school after the ninth grade and, at the age of 17, joined the U.S. Navy. Although the work was menial—scrubbing the decks of ships in port during World War II—naval service introduced Belafonte to African Americans who awakened Belafonte's political consciousness and introduced him to the works of radical black intellectual W. E. B. Du Bois.

In 1948 Belafonte settled in New York City and, after working a variety of odd jobs, found a calling in acting. As a member of the American Negro Theatre in Harlem, he earned his first leading role in Juno and the Paycock and met Paul Robeson, his hero, and Sidney Poitier, who became his life-long friend.

Belafonte's performance as the only black member of the cast of John Murray Anderson's *Almanac* earned him a Tony award in 1953. A year later he starred with Dorothy Dandridge in *Carmen Jones*, a movie remake of Bizet's opera that brought widespread attention to Belafonte's sensual good looks. His other early films include *Island in the Sun* (1957) and *The World, the Flesh, and the Devil* (1959). In addition, for his work in "Tonight with Belafonte," in 1960 he became the first African American to receive an Emmy Award.

As Belafonte began to achieve success as an actor, he stumbled into the singing career that made him one of the most popular entertainers of the late 1950s. In 1949 a performance at an amateur night at the Royal Roost nightclub in New York led to an RCA recording contract. Belafonte's 1956 album *Calypso* became the first record to sell more than a million copies and started a craze for his husky voice and for the infectious rhythm of such songs as *"Matilda," "Brown Skin Girl,"* and *"Jamaica Farewell."*

To critics who charged that a singer who had never visited Trinidad could not claim to know calypso, Belafonte offered no apologies. Not only did he make his version of Caribbean music accessible to a mainstream American audience but, in the dozens of albums that followed Calypso, he also performed songs such as *"Cotton Fields"* that conveyed the pain of the black African American experience.

Belafonte's appeal to white audiences did not, however, protect him from racial segregation. As a result, he refused to perform in the South from 1954 until 1961, and he became deeply involved in the Civil Rights Movement. In 1956 Belafonte met Martin Luther King Jr. in Montgomery, Alabama, and they quickly became close friends. Belafonte was also a friend of Attorney General Robert F. Kennedy and frequently served as a liaison between King and policymakers in Washington, D.C.

It was Belafonte who sent the money to bail King out of the Birmingham City Jail and who raised thousands of dollars to release other jailed protesters, financed the Freedom Rides, and supported voter-registration drives. He joined Bayard Rustin in leading the youth march for integrated schools from New York to Washington, D.C., in 1958 and helped to organize the March on Washington five years later.

Harry Belafonte waves to Martin Luther King Jr. after walking in the 1965 Selma-to-Montgomery civil rights march. Actor Tony Perkins, behind Belafonte, was another of the celebrities who participated in the march. *UPI/CORBIS-Bettmann*

Belafonte continues to use his power as an entertainer in the struggle for civil rights. His production company, Harbel, formed in 1959, produces movies and television shows by and about black Americans. Belafonte's idea for the hit song "*We Are the World*" generated more than 70 million dollars to fight famine in Ethiopia in 1985. Two years later he became the second American to be named UNICEF Goodwill Ambassador. A long-time anti-apartheid activist, Belafonte recorded an album of South African music, *Paradise in Gazankulu*, in 1988 and chaired the welcoming committee for Nelson Mandela's visit to the United States in 1990.

North America

Berry, Charles Edward Anderson (Chuck)

(b. October 18, 1926, St. Louis, Mo.), American singer, songwriter, and guitarist, a founding figure of rock 'n' roll.

Few performers have had a more profound effect on American popular music than Chuck Berry. The staccato guitar cadenzas with which he opened songs like "*Johnny B. Goode*" and "*Maybellene*" helped define the new guitar idiom of rock 'n' roll. His lyrics, celebrating teen freedom, music, dancing, and the pleasures of automobiles, gave substance to the rock genre. Berry's influence shaped the work of later musicians from the Beatles and the Rolling Stones to artists of the present.

Rock 'n' roll pioneer Chuck Berry, shown performing in Portsmouth, Virginia, in 1959.
CORBIS/Bettmann

Berry's earliest exposure to music came when the choir of his parents' Baptist church gathered to rehearse in the front room of his childhood home. An avid fan of the blues, Berry took up guitar as a hobby at age 14. He worked in an automobile factory and as a hairdresser before turning to his guitar playing and singing as a source of income.

By 1955 Berry had developed enough confidence in his songwriting abilities to travel to Chicago, where he came to the attention of blues singer Muddy Waters. Waters recommended Berry to the president of Chess Records. Berry's first single on Chess, "*Maybellene*," became a national sensation. A string of hits followed until the end of the 1950s, including "*School Days*" and "*Sweet Little Sixteen*." Berry toured relentlessly. He impressed audiences with his trademark "duck walk," a crouching, locomotive dance step that carried him across stage in time to the picking of his guitar.

Berry's most famous compositions captured the remembered pleasures of his freewheeling youth, as well as his pride in making music. "*Roll Over Beethoven*" and "*Rock 'n' Roll Music*" hailed the triumph of rock over the stodginess of classical music and the complexity of modern jazz. "*Johnny B. Goode*" told the autobiographical story of an ordinary boy who rose to stardom because of his natural talent for playing the guitar. Bands as disparate as the Beatles, the Jimi Hendrix Experience, Living Colour, and the Grateful Dead interpreted Berry's songs on records and in live performances.

The success of Berry's early period was interrupted in 1962 when federal prosecutors convicted him on a morals charge for transporting a 14-year-old girl across state lines. The singer spent two years in a penitentiary in Terre Haute, Indiana. After his release, Berry resumed his recording career and scored successes in both America and England with new hits like "*No Particular Place to Go*." In 1968 he opened an entertainment complex in Wentzville, Missouri. At a performance in Manchester, England, in 1972, he recorded the novelty single "*My Ding-a-Ling*," which became his first number one hit in America.

In the decades that followed, Berry continued to tour and perform. He also continued to encounter trouble from police and prosecutors. He served three months in jail in 1979 for tax evasion. He escaped charges of child abuse and drug possession in 1990 because of the prosecutors' misconduct. In 1986 he became a member of the Rock and Roll Hall of Fame. In 1987 the publication of his autobiography and the release of the concert film *Hail! Hail! Rock 'n' Roll* framed the artist's achievements and imperfections for a new generation of fans.

North America

Berry, Halle

A native of Cleveland, OH, born to an African-American father and white mother on August 14, 1968, Berry was raised by her mother. At 17, she appeared in the spotlight for the first time as the winner of the Miss Teen All-American Pageant, and subsequently became a model.

Berry's interest in show business came courtesy of her participation in a number of beauty pageants throughout her teens, including the 1986 Miss U.S.A. Pageant. Berry won her first professional acting gig on the TV series *Living Dolls*, and then appeared on *Knots Landing* before winning her first big-screen role in Spike Lee's *Jungle Fever*. It was on the set of the film that she first earned her reputation for her full commitment to acting.

After her film debut, Berry was cast opposite Eddie Murphy in *Boomerang* (1992) as the comedian's love interest; not only did she hold her own against Murphy, but the same year she did acclaimed work in the title role of the Alex Haley miniseries *Queen*, playing a young woman struggling against the brutal conditions of slavery.

After a comedic turn in the 1994 live-action version of *The Flintstones*, Berry returned to more serious fare with her role in the adoption drama *Losing Isaiah* (1995), starring opposite Jessica Lange as a former crack addict battling to win custody of her child, who as a baby was adopted by an affluent white couple.

In 1998, she starred as a street smart young woman who comes to the aid of a bumbling politician in Warren Beatty's *Bulworth*. She starred as Storm in Bryan Singer's hugely successful adaptation of *The X-Men*. Working alongside a cast that included Ian McKellen, Hugh Jackman, Famke Janssen, and Anna Paquin, Berry was hailed for her work as the first African-American comic book heroine on the screen. Acclaim was not quite as forthcoming for her work opposite John Travolta in Dominic Sena's *Swordfish*.

In 2001, Berry starred in *Monster's Ball*, a romantic drama directed by Marc Forster about a woman who becomes involved with a racist ex-prison-guard (Billy Bob Thornton) who oversaw the prison execution of her husband (Sean Combs). Berry earned wide critical praise for her work in the film, as well as Golden Globe and Oscar nominations for Best Actress. And though she may have lost out to Sissy Spacek in the Golden Globes, her night at the Oscars found Berry the favored performer as took home a statue for Best Actress. A momentous footnote in Academy Award history, Berry's win marked the first time an African American woman had been bestowed that particular honor.

Halle Berry's recent roles include the James Bond flick *Die Another Day*, *Gothika*, *X2: X-Men United*, and *Catwoman*.

North America

Berry, Leon Brown ("Chu")

(b. September 13, 1908, Wheeling, W. Va.; d. October 30, 1941, Conneaut, Ohio), American tenor saxophonist who played swing music with jazz greats such as Bessie Smith, Count Basie, and Billie Holiday.

Leon "Chu" Berry's family taught him piano as a child, and he learned alto saxophone in high school. After three years at West Virginia State College, Berry left in 1929, when he was hired by Edwards' Collegians in West Virginia. He later worked with Sammy Stewart's orchestra in Columbus, Ohio.

In 1930 Berry moved to New York with the Stewart Orchestra. He made his first recordings with Benny Carter's orchestra in 1932, and he played on the esteemed Spike Hughes 1933 recordings. Other significant connections that year included his work with Charlie Johnson and playing on Bessie Smith's final recording session. Performing with Teddy Hill's orchestra from 1933 to 1935, Berry met Roy Eldridge, who became his close friend. Hired by Cab Calloway in 1937, Berry appeared as featured soloist on recordings such as *"Ghost of a Chance"* (1940). Berry also led his own small group swing sessions, recording with leading swing soloists and singers, including Count Basie. *"Indiana"* (1937), *"46 West 52nd Street"* (1938), *"Oh! Lady Be Good!"* (1939), and *"Blowin' Up a Breeze"* (1941) were produced in some of these sessions.

Berry later played with Lionel Hampton, Billie Holiday, Benny Goodman, Mildred Baitly, Gene Krupa, and Wingy Manone. He is remembered as one of the period's most influential swing soloists, celebrated for his warm tone and energetic sense of swing. Berry died at the height of his musical talents in an automobile accident.

North America

Beulah,

fictional black domestic servant on American radio and television programs from 1940 to 1953, who became famous for her comic wisdom and abiding loyalty to her white employers.

Beulah Brown, a black domestic servant in radio and television comedies, carried on a long tradition of white stereotyping of African Americans. An updated version of the faithful Mammy figure, Beulah subordinated her own life and needs to serve as mother figure, therapist, and problem-solver

to her employers—in the NBC television program, a white New York
lawyer and his family.

Whenever a member of the white upper-middle-class Henderson
family faced a crisis, the maid hurried to the rescue with the cry, "Somebody bawl fo' Beulah?" Beulah also opened each episode by sharing some
observation or bit of folksy wisdom that would frame the evening's story;
for example, "If marriages are made in heaven, my guardian angel's sho'
been loafin' on the job. Ha, ha, ha, ha, ha." Despite the demeaning nature
of such material, the program—along with the televised version of *Amos 'n'
Andy* (1951–1953) on CBS—did give work to a considerable number of
African American actors.

Paradoxically, however, in the first seven years of the character's exis-
tence, she was not even portrayed by an African American actor. *Beulah
Brown* was first heard during 1940 on the NBC radio musical program *Show
Boat*. Four years later *Beulah* joined the popular comedy series *Fibber
McGee and Molly* and in 1945 received a much more prominent role in a
spin-off series, *The Marlin Hunt and Beulah Show*, later shortened to simply
Beulah. Only in 1947, when Academy Award-winner Hattie McDaniel
(1895–1952) took the radio role for several seasons, was Beulah finally
played by an African American. In 1950 Beulah's move to television, for
what would be a three-season run, provided greater opportunities for
African American actors, both in the title role and in several supporting
parts as well.

On television, three distinguished black actors played Beulah. Singer
and Oscar-nominee Ethel Waters (1896–1977) took the part for the first
two seasons. McDaniel was slated to take Waters's place, but, due to ill
health, appeared in only a few episodes. The role then passed to Louise
Beavers (1908–1962), best known for her portrayal of the maternal and
long-suffering Delilah in *Imitation of Life* (1934). Important actors in supporting roles included Butterfly McQueen, forever typecast after taking her
chirping portrayal of Prissy in *Gone With the Wind* (1939), and Dooley
Wilson, most memorable in the role of the piano-playing Sam in
Casablanca (1943).

The program was still earning high ratings when it went off the air in
1953, the same year in which protests by the National Association for the
Advancement of Colored People led CBS to cancel *Amos 'n' Andy*. NBC
denied any connection between the two events, attributing the cancellation
of *Beulah* to Louise Beavers' decision to leave the show.

North America

Biggers, John

(b. April 13, 1924, Gastonia, N.C.), African American artist known for his murals
and community-based visual style.

John Biggers was one of seven children whose father, Paul Biggers, was a
school principal, preacher, and basket maker. Biggers studied at Hampton

Institute in Virginia, where he resolved to become an artist. During his time at Hampton, Biggers served in the United States Navy from 1943 to 1946, and in 1944 he painted a mural for the U.S. Naval Training School at Hampton. He subsequently attended Pennsylvania State University, where he received B.S., M.S., and Ph.D. degrees. He founded and chaired the art department at Texas Southern University, where he implemented progressive art programs that involved local communities.

Biggers is known for his murals, a form he began to master while at Hampton. Many of his early works no longer exist, because they were painted directly on buildings that were later destroyed or altered. His works demonstrate his personal interest in the concrete spiritual symbolism of Africa. This fascination is apparent in his mural, *The Rites of Passage*, which incorporates themes of life cycles and transitions. In his later works Biggers addressed the African American heritage, using iconic, domestic symbols such as a washboard, an anvil, and a three-legged wash pot to suggest the daily lives and heritages of African Americans.

His awards include a UNESCO fellowship in 1957, and his work is exhibited in the collections of the Houston Museum of Fine Arts, the Dallas Museum of Fine Arts, Howard University, and Pennsylvania State University.

North America

Birth of a Nation, The,

American director D. W. Griffith's silent film about the rise of the Ku Klux Klan, one of the most controversial films of all time because of its demeaning portrayal of blacks.

First released on February 8, 1915, *The Birth of a Nation's* depictions of blacks as idling and brutish sparked a massive wave of protests from thousands of African Americans. The explosive controversy set off by the film revealed Hollywood's power to reflect and shape public attitudes about race, while setting the stage for what would be a decades-long struggle to improve the portrayal of blacks on film.

Unprecedentedly long—three hours (and 12 reels of film)—*The Birth of a Nation* chronicles the fall of the South during the Civil War and the reemergence of white political domination over the interracial state governments of the Reconstruction era. In the film's final scenes, the Ku Klux Klan, described in a *New York Times* review as "a company of avenging spectral crusaders sweeping along . . . moonlit roads," takes revenge for the attempted rape of two white women by black men. The film, based on the racist novels of Thomas Dixon, *The Leopard's Spots and The Clansmen*, rushes through visually striking Civil War panoramas and melodramatic episodes about the plight of Southern soldiers and depicts the rise of the Klan as heroic, all the while portraying blacks as lazy and weak or violent and dangerous.

Griffith's innovative filmmaking techniques delighted critics and drew a national audience deeply enmeshed in a culture of lynchings, Jim Crow segregation, and widespread antiblack sentiment. In its first 11 months in New York City alone, the film sold an estimated 3 million tickets. On Thanksgiving night in 1915, 25,000 Klansmen paraded through the streets of Atlanta to celebrate the movie's opening. And when Griffith, the son of a Confederate soldier, presented his work to President Woodrow Wilson (reportedly the first screening of a feature film in the White House), the president allegedly declared, "It is like writing history with lightning. And my only regret is that it is all so terribly true."

Black groups, while aware that a public controversy would only boost ticket sales, were quick to react to the film's blatant racism. The National Association for the Advancement of Colored People (NAACP) sent copies of a scathing *New Republic* review to more than 500 newspapers, issued strong warnings that screening the film could spark rioting, and even managed to have deleted some of the movie's harshest moments, including a scene proposing that blacks be sent back to Africa as a remedy for the nation's ills.

But the efforts of the black organizations were drowned out by the film's runaway box-office success. Perhaps the protesters' biggest victory lay in rallying African Americans around a common cause and in increasing awareness of the recently created NAACP and other black political groups. While the film is still praised by critics as a cinematic masterpiece, it has also become an important object lesson in how the relationship of popular media to public opinion can perpetuate racial stereotypes.

North America

Black Arts Movement

(1965–1975), a Black Nationalist African American arts movement focusing on music, literature, drama, and the visual arts.

The Black Arts Movement was a loose network of Black Nationalist African American artists and intellectuals during the mid-1960s to the mid-1970s. In many respects, the Black Arts Movement was the cultural wing of the Black Power Movement. Like the Black Power Movement, its participants held a variety of political beliefs, ranging from revolutionary Marxism to versions of what was understood as the cultures and ideologies of traditional precolonial Africa. Despite this range of often conflicting beliefs, there was a generally shared concept of African American liberation and of the right of African Americans to determine their own destiny. There was also usually some common notion of the development or recovery of an authentic national black culture that was linked to an existing African American folk or popular culture.

It is difficult to date precisely the beginning of the Black Arts Movement. One possibility is 1965, when Amiri Baraka and other black cultural activists founded the Black Arts Repertory Theatre/School (BARTS) in Harlem. However, a number of important forerunners to BARTS helped make the larger movement possible. For example, Umbra, a seminationalist group of African American writers in the Lower East Side of New York City in the early 1960s, provided a training ground for a number of influential Black Arts activists, including Ishmael Reed, Lorenzo Thomas, David Henderson, Calvin Hernton, and Askia Muhammad Touré. The influence of the Nation of Islam on many African American jazz musicians in the 1950s and early 1960s also helped prepare the way for a Black Nationalist arts movement. The journals *The Liberator* and *Negro Digest* (later *Black World*) offered important outlets and encouragement for emerging literary and artistic nationalists in the early 1960s. Baraka's pre-BARTS drama, particularly *Dutchman* (1964) and *The Slave* (1964), were crucial in shaping the form and direction that African American nationalist drama would take in the late 1960s and early 1970s.

It is after 1965, however, that one can talk about a Black Arts Movement in a cohesive sense. Though there often existed sharp conflict between participants in the movement about politics and aesthetics, there was enough common ground to produce national conferences, journals (such as *Black Dialogue, Journal of Black Poetry*, and *Black World*), organizations, and widely read anthologies (such as Amiri Baraka and Larry Neal's seminal *Black Fire* [1968]). Unlike earlier groupings of African American artistic production, the Black Arts Movement flourished in a wide range of locations. Virtually every sizable African American community and many college campuses saw the rise of new black theaters and organizations of nationalist-minded visual artists, writers, dancers, and musicians. Some of these organizations and institutions are the Association for the Advancement of Creative Music, the Organization of Black American Culture, and the African Commune of Bad Relevant Artists, all in Chicago, Illinois; Spirit House, in Newark, New Jersey; the Black Arts Group, in St. Louis, Missouri; the Watts Writer's Workshop, in Los Angeles, California; and Broadside Press, in Detroit, Michigan.

Music (particularly avant-garde or "free" jazz), poetry, and drama were the artistic genres that dominated the Black Arts Movement. In part this was due to the movement's close connection to the political movement of Black Power: music, poetry, and drama were easily performed at street rallies, demonstrations, political meetings, and other communal events. These genres also lent themselves to the multimedia productions, combining spoken, visual, and musical elements, that characterized the movement. Another important art form of the period was the public wall mural, which engaged whole communities in its creation and viewing.

Amiri Baraka is considered the leading figure of the era. Baraka's Black Arts poetry, drama, music criticism, and social commentary were apocalyptic, antiwhite, and often misogynist, anti-Semitic, and homophobic, projecting a powerful vision of a utopian unity of African Americans that proved tremendously important in defining the discussion of a "black aesthetic." Other significant writers of the Black Arts Movement include poet and essayist Larry Neal, poet Sonia Sanchez, poet Don L. Lee (Haki Madhubuti), poet Nikki Giovanni, playwright Ed Bullins, and novelist Toni Morrison. Such critics, scholars, and editors as Addison Gayle Jr. (editor of the anthology of criticism *The Black Aesthetic* [1971]), Harold Cruse (author of the study *The Crisis of the Negro Intellectual* [1967]), and Hoyt Fuller (editor of the journal *Black World*) played prominent roles in promoting and shaping the conversations and debates that took place among Black Arts artists and intellectuals.

Jazz musicians such as Archie Shepp, Sun Ra, and Richard Muhal Abrams were among the most powerful and most visible artists of the movement. Many African American popular musicians were heavily influenced by Black Power and Black Arts, producing best-selling songs such as Curtis Mayfield and the Impressions's *"Keep On Pushing"* and James Brown's *"Say It Loud (I'm Black and I'm Proud)*," which became anthems of the period.

Like its beginning, the ending of the Black Arts Movement is hard to pinpoint. In general, as the activities and the organizations of the Black Power Movement, such as the Black Panther Party and Maulana Karenga's US Organization, dwindled or disappeared in the early and mid-1970s, the Black Arts Movement did so also. Nonetheless, the impact of the movement lasted far beyond its perceived end. On some writers, such as Alice Walker and Sherley Anne Williams, the influence was largely negative, as they reacted against what they saw as the sexism and homophobia of the movement. Others, notably Amiri Baraka and Sonia Sanchez, who both moved away from nationalism toward a "Third World Marxism," acknowledged a positive Black Arts legacy while critiquing its limitations. Still other artists, such as Toni Morrison, continued to embrace what was essentially a Black Arts stance in their work after 1975. Similarly, present-day editors have assembled anthologies of African American writing, such as Keith Gilyard's *Spirit and Flame* (1996), which look back to the key Black Arts anthologies, particularly *Black Fire*, for inspiration.

Another lasting influence of the Black Arts Movement is found in institutions, such as African American Studies departments (and the field of African American Studies itself) as well as African American-oriented publishers, book imprints, academic book series, art galleries, and theaters, which would not have existed without the explosion of African American nationalist-influenced artistic activity in the 1960s and 1970s. Finally, the movement made a considerable impression on artists and intellectuals too young to remember its events firsthand. For example, much rap music owes a large debt to the militancy, urgent tone, and multimedia aesthetics of the Black Arts Movement.

North America

Black Entertainment Television,

a Washington, D.C.-based entertainment company that primarily targets black consumers through original programming on its three cable television channels and through its magazine, clothing, and cosmetic ventures.

Black Entertainment Television Holdings, Inc. (BET Holdings) was founded in 1979 by former cable industry lobbyist Robert Johnson. The company's primary business is its 24-hour cable channel, Black Entertainment Television Cable Network (BET). The BET Cable Network has an estimated 45 million subscribers nationwide. Its predominantly black viewing audience has transformed this once struggling company into a powerful social and economic force in the media industry.

BET began by broadcasting music videos in 1980 and 11 years later became the first black-controlled company listed on the New York Stock Exchange (NYSE). Since then BET has diversified its holdings by moving into the publishing industry. The company publishes several magazines targeting black readers, including *Emerge, BET Weekend*, and *Heart & Soul*. It has also acquired three other cable channels, including a cable jazz channel (BET on Jazz) and the BET Movies/ Starz!3 channel. In 1994 BET established a radio network to provide news and information to radio stations located in urban markets around the country.

Two years later the company formed a partnership with Microsoft to form MSBET, an online service that offers up-to-date information on concerts, entertainers, movies, and cable programming. BET has continued to expand its cable television programming by offering a public affairs show, a weekly show for teenagers, and broadcasts of town hall meetings that address contemporary is-sues facing the African American community.

North America

Black Mural Movement, The,

an urban movement in which African American artists worked in teams to create large-scale public paintings on the walls of predominantly black neighborhoods.

The Black Mural Movement developed out of the 1960s Black Arts Movement and embraced the political creed of the black aesthetic. The founding work of the Black Mural Movement, *Wall of Respect* (1967), by Chicago-based William Walker and other artists, drew on a long-standing tradition of African American mural painting. In the 1930s the Federal Art Project of the Works Progress Administration helped such African American artists as Aaron Douglas, Charles White, and Hale Woodruff complete murals that documented African American history. These monumental works, done in a style best described as social realism, were executed on the interior walls of public buildings.

Students and professors continued to create murals with black themes throughout the 1940s and 1950s. From the 1930s through the Black Mural Movement, African American muralists drew inspiration from the work of Mexican muralists such as Diego Rivera, Jose Clemente Orozco, and David Alfaro Siquieros, who created murals that portrayed and celebrated Mexican history during the 1920s and 1930s.

Murals done before and during the Black Mural Movement commonly

celebrated black historical figures, promoted black pride and racial solidarity, and emphasized the importance of education. Two things distinguish most of the murals of the 1960s and 1970s from their predecessors:
(1) they were painted on exterior walls, where they could be viewed by a
wider, more varied audience, and (2) they were conceived and funded by
members of the African American community at the grassroots level, as
opposed to large government or corporate organizations outside the
African American community.

The success of *Wall of Respect* led to commissions for Walker and his
team of artists and sparked similar projects in other African American as
well as Hispanic neighborhoods throughout the country. In 1968 Walker
and other Chicago muralists went to Detroit to assist in the painting of
three murals in neighborhoods that had been devastated by the 1967
Detroit riots. At the same time, Dana Chandler and Gary Rickson coordinated the creation of several murals in the Roxbury section of Boston, Massachusetts. The African American citizens of Compton and Oakland,
California, initiated a mural program, although urban California emerged as
the center of Latino mural production. Chicago remained at the center of
the Black Mural Movement.

The emergence of public-art agencies followed the proliferation of com-
munity-initiated murals. These organizations work to secure private, corporate, and government funding for mural projects through which African
American artists continue to portray their past and present experiences.

North America

Black Swan Records,

**the first black-owned recording company specializing in "race records"—pop-
ular music, especially blues, recorded for a black audience.**

In 1921 music publisher Harry Pace founded the Pace Phonographic Corporation. Black Swan Records, the division responsible for releasing Pace's
records, was named for the nineteenth-century opera singer Elizabeth
Taylor Greenfield, who was known as "the black swan." Pace hired up-and-
coming bandleader Fletcher Henderson as recording director and composer
William Grant Still as arranger and music director, and in May 1921 Black
Swan released its first record. The success of Black Swan's early recordings,
most notably "*Down Home Blues*," sung by Ethel Waters, led to the formation of the Black Swan Troubadours, a group led by Henderson and Waters
that toured the South to promote the Black Swan label.

Pace purchased the Olympic Disc Record Corporation in 1922 to
market music by black and white artists. Many African American patrons
were disappointed by Pace's decision because it seemed to contradict his
earlier declaration that Black Swan would have only African American
stockholders, employees, and artists. Outmaneuvered by larger, white-
owned recording companies such as Paramount and Okeh, which recog-

nized the market potential of race records, Black Swan went bankrupt in 1923. In 1924 Paramount took over the Black Swan catalogue.

Black Theatre Alliance,

an association of small African American commercial theaters in New York City.

The Black Theatre Alliance (BTA) was founded in 1971 in New York City to support the artistic and financial development of small commercially owned African American theater companies. The alliance was formed partly as a result of the burgeoning African American commercial theater scene in the late 1960s, which had begun to flourish during the Black Arts Movement. Plays written in this period attempted to capture the frustration and anger felt by many African Americans by depicting whites' exploitation of blacks and seeking to create a strong black aesthetic in American theater.

Founded by playwrights Delano Stewart, Hazel Bryant, and Roger Furman, the Black Theatre Alliance initially comprised seven theater companies. To nurture the growth of these theaters, the alliance provided technical equipment, graphics, funds, resources, information, and touring assistance. The alliance compiled the Black Theatre Resources Directory, listing noncommercial black theater operations in the United States, theater technicians, administrators, artistic directors, and works by black playwrights. In 1972 the BTA began publishing a newsletter titled Black Theatre Alliance to encourage collaboration and to promote the activities of member theaters. In the mid-1970s, the BTA began admitting dance companies as members.

Black World / Negro Digest,

the first successful black-owned general interest magazine and the foundation publication of Johnson Publishing Company.

While working for an insurance company, college student John H. Johnson prepared a summary of news about the African American community for distribution among the company's upper managers. Believing that this same news could be marketed to African Americans, who had been largely ignored by the mainstream press, Johnson began publishing *Negro Digest*. The first issue reached newsstands in 1942.

Similar in format to *Reader's Digest*, *Negro Digest* initially reprinted articles, mostly general-interest pieces about African American life, from other periodicals. Soon, however, the magazine began publishing original articles and essays, including the popular feature "If I Were a Negro," which featured pieces by famous white people, including First Lady Eleanor Roosevelt. By the end of 1943, *Negro Digest* had a weekly circulation of 50,000.

The magazine's success led Johnson, whose initial one-man operation had grown to become the Johnson Publishing Company, to develop other magazines, including the short-lived *Copper Romance, Tan Confessions,* and *Black Stars* and the successful and enduring *Ebony* and *Jet. Negro Digest's* popularity dwindled, however, and the company ceased publishing it in 1951.

Ten years later Johnson resumed publication of *Negro Digest*, hiring Hoyt W. Fuller to serve as managing editor. During the 1960s Fuller gradually changed the publication's editorial focus, transforming it from a general-interest, racially integrationist magazine into a literary periodical that explored Black Nationalism. Editorials examined the connection between literature and politics, and the magazine featured the work of both famous and lesser-known African American writers, making it a major voice in the debate about the direction of African American literature, culture, and politics. But much of this revolutionary attitude among blacks waned during the mid-1970s, and the magazine, which had been renamed Black World in 1970, declined in popularity and profitability. Its last issue was published in April 1976.

North America

Blake, James Hubert ("Eubie")

(b. February 7, 1883, Baltimore, Md.; d. February 12, 1983, New York, N.Y.), African American jazz pianist and composer.

Eubie Blake was the son of John Sumner Black and Emily Johnston Black, both former slaves. He began organ lessons at age six and was playing ragtime piano professionally in Baltimore bordellos and saloons just ten years later. Around this time he composed "*Charleston Rag.*" In his early twenties he began playing in Atlantic City, New Jersey, where he composed another of his popular songs, "*Tricky Fingers.*"

In 1916 James Reese Europe, leader of the popular World War I 369th Infantry Band, advised Blake and singer Noble Sissle to collaborate. They became a piano and vocalist team called the Dixie Duo, performing in vaudeville shows and writing music together. In 1921 they joined with the comedy duo of Flournoy Miller and Aubrey Lyles to write a Broadway show, *Shuffle Along*, which was so popular that three separate companies toured the United States simultaneously performing it. This show ran continuously on Broadway until 1928.

In 1924 Sissle and Blake teamed with Lew Payton to create *In Bamville*, later renamed *The Chocolate Dandies*. The show lasted until 1925, when Sissle and Blake returned to the vaudeville stages of the United States, Great Britain, and France. In 1927 the partnership ended when Blake returned to the United States while Sissle remained in Europe. Though he wrote and produced a number of shows in the 1930s, none ever attained the success of *Shuffle Along* or *Chocolate Dandies*.

Blake also had a successful career as a band leader. In 1919, after James

Reese Europe's death, Blake took over his band. During World War II, Blake and his band performed extensively for United States troops in USO shows. While Harry Truman campaigned for president in 1948, Blake's song, *"I'm Just Wild About Harry,"* which he wrote for *Shuffle Along,* became popular. In 1946 he began to study formal composition in semi-retirement, although he appeared in several ragtime revival shows in the 1950s.

In 1969 Blake released a recording, *The Eighty-Six Years of Eubie Blake,* and was once again in demand. He spent much of his time lecturing at colleges and playing concerts and jazz festivals. To preserve piano rags and the songs of the 1920s, he formed his own recording company in 1972. In all, Blake wrote over 300 songs, among which are the popular *"Tickle the Ivories," "Memories of You," "Chevy Chase," "Loving You the Way I Do,"* and *"Love Will Find a Way."* In 1978 *Eubie!,* a revue-style show based on his life, was performed on Broadway.

In addition to the numerous honorary degrees and awards Blake received throughout his life, he was awarded the Presidential Medal of Freedom in 1981. Eubie Blake died on February 12, 1983, five days after his 100th birthday.

North America

Blakey, Art

(b. October 11, 1919, Pittsburgh, Pa.; d. October 16, 1990, New York, N.Y.), African American jazz musician, innovator of bop drumming, and leader of the Jazz Messengers.

As a drummer and bandleader, Art Blakey had a profound impact on the shape of modern jazz. During the late 1940s, along with Kenny Clarke and Max Roach, he was one of the creators of modern jazz drumming. His longstanding group, the Jazz Messengers (1955–1990)—together with Miles Davis's quintet with John Coltrane, the Max Roach-Clifford Brown quintet, and the Horace Silver quintet—popularized the style known as hard bop. Hard bop draws equally on the harmonic and rhythmic complexity of bebop and on the visceral sounds and simpler rhythms that characterize the blues and gospel music. In an interview published in the *Black Perspective in Music,* Blakey summed up his approach simply, declaring that he wanted to play music that would "wash away the dust of everyday life."

Blakey was also one of the great talent scouts of jazz. During his 35 years as leader of the Jazz Messengers, he nurtured countless young jazz musicians, many of whom later became leaders in their own right. His discoveries included trumpeters Wynton Marsalis, Lee Morgan, and Freddie Hubbard; saxophonists Wayne Shorter, Jackie McLean, and Branford Marsalis; trombonist Curtis Fuller; and pianists Bobby Timmons, Cedar Walton, and Keith Jarrett.

Blakey was working in a Pittsburgh-area steel mill when he first began his musical career, playing the piano in small local clubs. But he gave up the piano after hearing Erroll Garner, who was then a local jazz pianist, and turned instead to playing the drums. In 1939 he briefly toured with Fletcher Henderson's big band, and he rejoined Henderson in 1943–1944. When Blakey arrived in New York City in the early 1940s, pianist Thelonious Monk took him in and introduced him to the city's jazz scene. In 1947 Blakey joined Monk on some of the pianist's early recordings. Blakey first gained notice as a bop innovator during his stint from 1944 to 1947 with singer Billy Eckstine's orchestra, which featured such bop luminaries as saxophonists Charlie Parker and Dexter Gordon and trumpeters Dizzy Gillespie, Miles Davis, and Fats Navarro.

In 1955 Blakey was part of the quintet known as the Jazz Messengers. In addition to Blakey on drums, it featured Horace Silver on piano, Kenny Dorham on trumpet, Hank Mobley on tenor saxophone, and Doug Watkins on bass. The group had many different members over the years; yet despite these changes, it retained its identity through Blakey's constant presence and forceful leadership. Jackie McLean told *New York Times* jazz critic Peter Watrous that of the many leaders he had worked with—including the formidable Miles Davis and Charles Mingus—Blakey had taught him the most, "[n]ot just [about] how to be a musician, but about being a man and keeping a sense of responsibility."

North America

Bland, Bobby ("Blue")

(b. January 27, 1930, Rosemark, Tenn.), African American bluesman and songwriter.

Born in rural Rosemark, Tennessee, Bobby "Blue" Bland gravitated to Memphis as a teen, at a time when rhythm and blues was beginning to gain popularity. Bland sang with the Pilgrim Travelers, a gospel group, before joining the Beale Streeters, a loose ensemble of R&B pioneers that included Johnny Ace and B. B. King. In his early recordings on Modern Records, Bland imitated the sounds of King as well as those of Nat King Cole.

Bland served in the United States Army from 1952 to 1954, a tour of duty that slowed his career. When he returned to Memphis, he found that his old friends were already prospering as musicians. Slowly he returned to the scene, recording his best work between the mid-1950s and the early 1960s on the Duke Records label. Hits from the time included "*Cry Cry Cry*" and "*Turn On Your Lovelight.*" Bland developed a distinctive sound, blending big-band influences, Memphis blues, and smooth vocals redolent of Frank Sinatra.

After scoring 37 R&B hits during the 1960s, Bland was outshone by a new generation of performers, and his incorporation of disco in the 1970s met with limited success. Although he succeeded in refreshing his career with a 1983 release, *Here We Go Again*, his most important contributions to popular music remain the ones that he made 40 years earlier.

Blaxploitation Films,

popular film genre of the 1970s that depicted African American heroes defying an oppressive system.

In the early 1970s an American film genre began to crystallize from different elements in the American political and cultural scene. At the center of the new genre was a new kind of hero: a black, urban, poor male striking back at a system that had denied him basic rights and respect. Set in the dense urban landscape of black America, these films gave a vision of America different from the one typically portrayed by mainstream Hollywood cinema.

The term *blaxploitation* was first coined to describe Gordon Parks Jr.'s *Superfly* (1972). Two earlier films are frequently cited as forerunners of the genre: Melvin Van Peebles's *Sweet Sweetback's Baadasssss Song* (1971), and Gordon Parks Sr.'s *Shaft* (1971). Throughout the 1970s it is estimated that some 150 films were made within the blaxploitation genre.

Drawing upon both the mainstream marketability of action films and the growing Black Power Movement, blaxploitation films were popularly well-received, if not always critically acclaimed. In these films, the black hero fought back and won, often against overwhelming odds. Filled with fast-paced action, the plot usually involved a male hero, or antihero, who found it necessary to renounce the system and resort to violence. These films portrayed a virile black male sexuality that had been missing in both mainstream and African American cinema up to that point. A few films, such as *Coffy* (1973) with Pam Grier, featured female protagonists.

Blaxploitation films drew criticism for resorting to formulas and portraying unrealistic scenarios, and were actively opposed by a coalition that included the National Association for the Advancement of Colored People (NAACP). Many critics felt that the films were too simplistic to offer any kind of viable model for African American resistance to an oppressive system. Others noted that the character development, particularly of women, was limited. Some, such as black psychiatrist Alvin Poussaint, saw the films as dangerous for their glorification of criminal life and machismo, and as ultimately destructive to the black community.

For director Melvin Van Peebles, however, this was not the point. The blaxploitation film's attraction was that "the black audience finally gets a chance to see some of their own fantasies acted out—[it's] about rising out of the mud and kicking ass."

The films were oriented specifically toward black urban audiences, who made the blaxploitation film a lucrative business. Made on low budgets, the films were proven financial successes for the studios, with *Shaft* making more than $16 million for MGM. Inner-city youth imitated the fashions and hairstyles worn in the films, and soundtracks, such as Curtis Mayfield's score for *Superfly*, achieved wide popularity.

Although most critics place the term blaxploitation within the 1970s, the genre had a noted effect on later films. Major film studios continued to produce "against the odds" action-packed films. Later works by John Singleton and Mario Van Peebles, Melvin's son, were influenced by the political concerns of blaxploitation, and continued to portray African American life in the inner city.

Africa

Blondy, Alpha

(b. January 1, 1953, Dimbokro, Côte d'Ivoire), popular African reggae singer.

With his 11 albums and worldwide tours, Alpha Blondy has brought an African flavor to the Jamaican-born musical genre of reggae. Although critics admit that Blondy has not yet fulfilled his early goal of becoming the next Bob Marley (probably the best-known reggae artist), they do hail the Côte d'Ivoire singer's passionate lyrics and charismatic performances.

The man born Seydou Kone was renamed *Blondy*, a variation on the Dioula word for *bandit*, by his grandmother, who raised him. Though little is known of his childhood, Blondy says he chose his new first name, Alpha, himself, and that he learned French from reading the Bible (though his grandmother also introduced him to the Muslim holy book, the Koran). He was expelled from school, reportedly for forming his first reggae band, the Atomic Vibrations. Eventually Blondy moved to New York City, where he studied and worked and continued to learn about reggae, often performing Bob Marley songs at Harlem nightclubs.

When he returned to the Côte d'Ivoire, Blondy began to make a name for himself as one of the boldest contemporary singers, dealing with such controversial subjects as police brutality and race relations. His first album, *Jah Glory* (1983), was a hit throughout West Africa. Blondy also sings in French, English, and Dioula, and with later releases he has extended his popularity worldwide. With his insistence on positive, loving images (he says his songs "are all really love songs") and his commitment to social justice, Blondy is among the world's most popular reggae performers and one of Africa's biggest recording stars.

North America

Blues, The,

an African American music originating in the late nineteenth century that connoted both an emotional state and a musical format. During the twentieth century the blues became the most familiar musical form in the world through its role in rhythm and blues (R&B) and early rock 'n' roll.

The blues is a uniquely African American music and reflects the particular history and culture of black America. It emerged during the troubled times of the post-Reconstruction South, when Southern blacks experienced political disfranchisement, economic subordination, and systematic physical violence. During the twentieth century the blues moved from South to North, accompanying the Great Migration. The music itself shifted from simple rural blues to rhythmic and rollicking urban blues; it also became an important influence in jazz.

As African Americans rose to prominence in popular culture, the blues reshaped the vernacular music of the United States and the entire world. During the late 1940s the blues became an important element in the black popular music known as rhythm and blues (R&B). In the following decades it provided the musical structure—though not the emotional depth or state of mind—for much rock 'n' roll. In addition, bop, hard bop, and free jazz musicians introduced new musical complexities to the blues. Today the blues can be heard all over the world—in Norway and England, Japan and Taiwan, Brazil and Africa. But America is its true home.

The Origin of the Blues

The blues grew out of and reflected the social realities of the American South from the 1880s to the 1910s, the nadir of American race relations since Emancipation. During this time, most blacks lived in the South, where they faced increasing social, political, and economic subordination. There were few safe outlets for their hopes, dreams, and pride, the most important being the Black Church. But the main secular response was the blues.

There is no way to determine when the blues first appeared. It emerged from two earlier forms, field hollers and ballads. Field hollers were work songs, generally extemporized and unaccompanied, that evolved out of the call-and-response work songs that had set the pace for gang labor on antebellum slave plantations. African American ballads were narrative in form and were not meant to set or mesh with work rhythms. Some ballads employed the 4- or 8-line structure typical of white balladry, but another common lyrical form used a couplet and refrain line in a 12-bar form, similar to the 12-bar blues—as in the well-known "*Stack O'Lee*" or "*Stagger Lee*."

Musical Characteristics of the Blues

The blues is, above all, a vocalized music. Blues singers and instrumentalists employ a wide range of musical timbres and inflections that are modeled on the nuances of the human voice. Blues notes are the most distinctive of these musical effects. They are slightly flattened or played lower than their true pitch. The keening, moody dissonance of blue notes gives the blues a quality of loneliness, longing, or sadness. Blues notes also lift the blues from resignation to dissatisfaction and discontent.

The principal blue notes are the third and seventh notes of the scale, although the fifth note is sometimes played as a blue note, especially in the music of the bop era of the 1940s. More recently, free jazz musicians such as alto saxophonist Ornette Coleman and trumpeter Lester Bowie (b. 1941), who play with a strong blues sensibility but without traditional blues

With "Memphis Blues" (1912), arguably the first blues song to be published in sheet music form, composer William Christopher "W.C." Handy (1873–1958) began his long career as a popularizer of African American music. *CORBIS/Robert Dowling*

harmony, have shown that any note can be made a blue note.

The most common form of the blues is the 12-bar blues—standardized in particular through such W. C. Handy compositions as *"Memphis Blues"* (1912) and *"St. Louis Blues"* (1914). The 12-bar blues uses a single repeated stanza made up of three phrases, each 4 measures in length. There are also 8-, 16-, and 24-bar blues, and early recordings reveal that country bluesmen—generally singers who accompanied themselves on the guitar—commonly employed stanzas of odd and uneven lengths.

The blues encompasses a wide range of chord progressions. Early rural or country blues was rudimentary, using only three chords. On the other hand, bop musicians of the 1940s and 1950s often relied on harmonically advanced blues progressions. For example, *"Blues for Alice"* (1951) by alto saxophonist Charlie Parker makes use of numerous altered, substitute, and passing chords. But even the most complex blues progressions are direct extensions of the basic blues structure.

Blues Lyrics

The blues also features a simple lyrical structure. A standard 12-bar blues employs a 3-line stanza in which the first 2 lines are repeated and the final phrase responds to and generally rhymes with the first 2. Many blues lyrics convey sadness, as demonstrated in the following two excerpts, the first from *"Crossroad Blues,"* by Robert Johnson (1936–1937), and the second from *"Matchbox Blues,"* by Blind Lemon Jefferson (1927):

> *Well, the blues is a achin' old heart disease . . .*
> *The blues is a low-down achin' heart disease,*
> *Like consumption, killin' me by degrees.*
> *I'm sittin' here wonderin' will a matchbox*
>   *hold my clothes,*
> *I'm sittin' here wonderin' will a matchbox*
>   *hold my clothes,*
> *I ain't got so many matches, but I got so far*
>   *to go.*

More than a music of sadness, the blues encompasses a wide range of emotions, including humor, sometimes salacious and sometimes ironic, as in *"You Ain't Such a Much,"* by Dizzie Gillespie (1952):

> I wouldn't give a blind sow an acorn, wouldn't
>   give a crippled crab a crutch,
> Say, I wouldn't give a blind sow an acorn,
>   wouldn't give a crippled crab a crutch,
> 'Cause I just found out pretty mama that
>   you ain't so such a much.

Although the blues addresses a broad range of subjects, most commonly its lyrics focus on matters of love and its discontents. Many topical blues memorialize significant events or hardships. Blind Lemon Jefferson's *"Rising High Water Blues"* described the destruction of a 1927 Mississippi River flood, and Charley Patton's *"'34 Blues"* addressed the hard times brought on by the Great Depression. Five days before the Japanese attack on Pearl Harbor, Big Bill Broonzy gave voice to black hopes of joining America's then-segregated air force in his *"In the Army Now"* (1941):

> I got a letter this mornin' from a dear old
>   uncle ["Uncle Sam"] of mine,
> I got a letter this mornin' from a dear old
>   uncle of mine,
> Now, boys, I was walkin' today, but tomorrow I
>   may be flyin'.

In effect, blues musicians were informal chroniclers of African American history, and the blues had an organic relationship to black life. Whether a specific blues spoke strictly in personal terms or broached larger social issues, the genre gave voice to black aspirations and experiences.

Early Regional Blues Styles

The blues also exerted relatively little influence on early New Orleans jazz, which was more a product of ragtime, minstrel music, and circus and marching bands. Although some early jazz musicians—for example, cornetist Buddy Bolden—were well versed in the blues, they commonly looked down on the roughhewn rural bluesmen. In *Aspects of the Blues Tradition* (1968), Paul Oliver suggests that another source of the distance between early jazz and blues might lie in the incompatible keys favored by blues guitarists (E or A) and jazz horn players (B-flat).

There was also a strong piano tradition in the blues, emerging during the early twentieth century out of the pine-country timber camps of Georgia and the Carolinas; from countless jook joints scattered across Florida, Mississippi, and Texas; and from the rent parties and honky-tonks of Chicago. This style of playing, with its repetitive, rolling bass patterns, was popularized in the 1930s as boogie-woogie but its origins were considerably older.

Among the best-known boogie-woogie players are Pete Johnson (1904–1967), Albert Ammons (1907–1949), and Meade "Lux" Lewis—who occasionally performed piano trios together—and Jimmy Yancey (1894–1951), a legendary part-time musician who worked for decades as a groundskeeper at the Chicago White Sox's Comiskey Park. Boogie woogie shaped such subsequent R&B and rock 'n' roll pianists as Amos Milburn (1927–1980), Little Richard, and Fats Domino. Memphis Slim, born Peter Chatman (1915–1988), was

William Hudson Ledbetter (1885-1949), best known as Leadbelly, inspired a generation of black bluesmen and also helped bring the Blues to a white audience. *CORBIS/Bettmann*

the most important of the postwar blues pianists who did not move into rock 'n' roll.

The Great Migration and the Dissemination of the Blues

Traveling bluesmen spread the blues throughout the black South, but for many years the blues remained little known to the rest of the nation. All that changed in the 1910s and 1920s with the rise of the re-cording industry and the start of the Great Migration, in which massive numbers of African Americans left the South for the cities of the North and the West Coast. Between the 1940s and the 1960s, the movement rose to a flood.

In making the move, African Americans carried the blues along, and generally speaking, the musical movement followed regional lines. Piedmont blues musicians generally headed up the eastern seaboard with many, like Josh White, ending up in Harlem. East Texas-style players moved west. The so-called blues shouters, Jimmy Rushing and Big Joe Turner (1911–1985), helped create a distinctly blues-rooted jazz style in 1930s Kansas City. Other musicians, including electric guitarists Aaron "T-Bone" Walker and Clarence "Gatemouth" Brown (b. 1924), settled in Los Angeles, where they contributed to the city's emergence in the 1940s as a leading center of R&B. But the most important line of movement was from the Delta to Chicago, a route taken by such musicians as Broonzy and guitarist Muddy Waters.

During the 1920s the recording industry became an important mode of disseminating blues music. Recording companies established "race records" subsidiaries to produce music specifically for an African American audience, often including recordings of rural bluesmen. The recording industry also promoted a new musical tradition of what has been dubbed the classic blues singers.

Unlike their country blues counterparts, who were almost exclusively male, classic blues singers were generally women. A large number of these singers—including Mamie Smith and Alberta Hunter—came out of vaudeville rather than the blues tradition. But Gertrude "Ma" Rainey and Bessie Smith, the most important classic blues singers, had performed the blues extensively throughout the South.

The classic blues era also featured larger ensembles. Rural blues generally involved individual guitarist-singers or very small groups, mainly using the guitar and the harmonica. Classic blues featured full ensembles and included such early jazz musicians as trumpeter Louis Armstrong and clarinetist and soprano saxophonist Sidney Bechet. Over the years, however, jazz gradually moved away from the blues. When big bands gained national popularity during the swing era of the 1930s, they mainly played dance music and pop tunes rather than the blues, although Count Basie's big band was a notable exception to this trend.

Since the 1940s jazz musicians have generally abandoned the raw directness and simplicity of early blues. Bop musicians such as Charlie Parker, trumpeter Dizzy Gillespie, and pianist Thelonious Monk often wrote and played blues, but their music—and the overall sound of jazz—was more complex and sophisticated than that of contemporaneous blues performers. Trumpeter Miles Davis's album *Kind of Blue* (1959) and tenor saxophonist Oliver Nelson's *Blues and the Abstract Truth* (1961) radically extended the blues tradition. During the 1950s and 1960s Charles Mingus, Art Blakey and the Jazz Messengers, and Cannonball Adderley returned to an earthier form of musical expression, but they were influenced more by bluesy gospel music than by the blues itself.

The Blues Since World War II: Chicago Blues, the Blues Revival, and Its Decline

Within the blues tradition the most important development was the rise of Chicago blues. During the 1940s and 1950s Chicago blues musicians were largely transplants from Mississippi, but they modernized the Delta blues sound by exchanging their acoustic guitars for electrically amplified ones. In Chicago blues a small combo, consisting of one or two electric guitars, an electric bass, drums, and a piano or organ, replaced the solo performer. Sometimes the group included a small horn section—for example, a trumpet and one or more saxophones.

Postwar electric blues relied on the electric guitar's potential for angry and "dirty" playing, in sharp contrast to the pure, clean tone sought by contemporary jazz guitarists. Muddy Waters, with his jagged, edgy guitar lines and his band's driving backbeat, was the first musician to gain fame in the new style. Many others followed, including composer and bassist Willie Dixon; electric guitarists Elmore James (1918–1963), Luther "Guitar Jr." Johnson (b. 1934), and Luther Allison (1939–1997); harmonica players Sonny Boy Williamson, Howlin' Wolf, and Little Walter (1930–1968); and vocalist Koko Taylor.

Chicago blues was a key component of rhythm and blues, particularly as recorded and popularized by both Chess and Vee Jay Records. Through the playing of Chuck Berry and Bo Diddley, Chicago blues had a shaping influence on 1950s rock 'n' roll. Numerous other blues-based performers had a powerful impact on the larger pattern of American popular music, including New Orleans pianists Little Richard and Fats Domino; T-Bone Walker; and B. B. King, the most influential blues guitarist of the post-World War II era.

During the 1960s white rock musicians inspired a blues revival. The Rolling Stones, Eric Clapton, the Allman Brothers, and others recorded versions of earlier electric blues tunes and toured and recorded with Howlin' Wolf, Muddy Waters, guitarist Albert Collins (1932–1993), and other bluesmen. By the 1980s, however, King, Collins, and other African American blues musicians had discovered that their audiences were overwhelmingly white rather than black. As blues writer Paul Oliver noted, the blues had been "absorbed by popular music throughout the world with consequent damage to its identity"; in particular, by drawing upon "the modes of expression of the Church," the blues was transformed (and diluted) into gospel and soul music.

Perhaps even more tellingly, economic and social changes in African American life made the blues less relevant to black culture. During the 1970s the music most popular among inner-city black youth was the rhythmic and danceable music known as funk. In the 1980s rap became the music of choice among young blacks. Some younger blues musicians have continued to bring vitality to the genre. Electric blues guitarist Robert Cray (b. 1953) won a Grammy Award for his hit album *Strong Persuader* (1986), and the acoustic country blues stylist Keb' Mo' (b. 1951) has enjoyed considerable visibility.

But contemporary blues music has atrophied. Chicago bluesman Willie Dixon was sufficiently concerned over this state of affairs that in 1991 he founded the Blues Heaven Foundation, intended, among its various activities, to underwrite programs in blues education. The blues continues to flourish in backcountry jook joints of the Mississippi Delta, South Side Chicago blues bars, and other places. But throughout much of the United States, it stands in danger of becoming a musical pressed flower, well preserved in numerous blues festivals and urban nightclubs, but cut off from its living roots.

Bolden, Charles Joseph ("Buddy")

(b. September 7, 1877, New Orleans, La.; d. November 4, 1931, Jackson, La.),
African American coronet player and bandleader whose improvisational style is
said to embody the first true New Orleans jazz.

Charles "Buddy" Bolden was a pioneering and creative force in the development of pre- and early jazz in turn-of-the-century New Orleans. He began
playing coronet in a professional band in his teens and quickly established a
reputation for a clear, powerful tone. Soon Bolden was leading his own
band, earning the title "King" from an appreciative African American public.
His influence came at a time when New Orleans was alive with bands of
black musicians performing for marches, dances, and saloons.

As a soloist, Bolden had a keen ear and memory, which augmented skills
in improvisation and embellishment. He is reportedly the first to "rag the
blues" for dancing and thus to have essentially created jazz. Popular folklore
has it that his coronet tone was so strong and his music so great that people
could hear him from across the river. Jazz historians believe that Bolden's
playing influenced contemporary and subsequent cornet and trumpet
players such as "King" Oliver, "Bunk" Johnson, and Louis Armstrong.

Bolden was committed to a mental institution in 1906, probably as a
result of alcoholism. Thus ended his musical career decades before his death
in 1931. Tragically, he was never recorded.

Bonner, Marita

(b. June 16, 1899, Brookline, Mass.; d. December 6, 1971, Chicago, Ill.), author
whose autobiographical essay depicted the situation of African American
women in 1925.

One of four children of Mary Noel and Joseph Bonner, Marita Odette
Bonner was educated at Brookline High School and Radcliffe College,
graduating with a B.A. in English and comparative literature in 1922.
After teaching for two years at Bluefield Colored Institute in Bluefield,
West Virginia, she moved to Washington, D.C., where she taught high
school until 1930.

As a member of the literary "S" salon in Washington, Bonner met such
members of the Harlem Renaissance as Langston Hughes, Georgia Douglas
Johnson, and Jean Toomer and published her first story, "The Hands," in
Opportunity (1925). She wrote the autobiographical essay for which she is
best known, "On Being Young—A Woman—and Colored," in the same year.
Although as a member of Washington's Krigwa Players she wrote three
experimental plays—*The Pot Maker* (1927), *The Purple Flower* (1928), and
Exit: An Illusion (1929)—her real focus, until she stopped publishing in
1941, was the short story.

Bonner married William Almy Occomy, an accountant, in 1930, and they moved to Chicago. She taught high school there, brought up her three children, and wrote interconnected short stories about the fictional Frye Street. Her literary preoccupations were intergenerational and interracial, depicting class conflict and the corruptive nature of the urban environment. She also won prizes from the magazines in which her stories most frequently appeared—*Opportunity* (supported by the National Urban League) and *Crisis* (a publication of the National Association for the Advancement of Colored People).

North America

Bontemps, Arna

(b. October 13, 1902, Alexandria, La.; d. June 4, 1973, Nashville, Tenn.), American poet, novelist, historian, playwright, editor, and anthologist of the Harlem Renaissance.

Arna Bontemps was born to parents of Creole descent who eventually converted to the Seventh Day Adventist faith. While Bontemps was young, his family moved to Los Angeles, California. Bontemps was affected deeply by the childhood loss of his mother and by his upbringing by a stern, pragmatic father who hoped, mistakenly, that his son would make the family trade of masonry his life's work. Educated at Seventh Day Adventist institutions, Bontemps graduated from Pacific Union College in 1923. In 1924 he took a teaching job at the Harlem Academy in New York City.

Literary success came early to Bontemps. His creativity and social conscience were stirred by the cultural vitality he found in 1920s New York. By 1926 his poetry had appeared in two of the most important journals of the period, *Crisis*, published by the National Association for the Advancement of Colored People, and *Opportunity*, published by the National Urban League. In fact, Bontemps was honored with the *Crisis*'s poetry prize in 1926 for "A Black Man Talks of Reaping" and with *Opportunity*'s 1926 and 1927 Alexander Pushkin poetry prizes for the poems "Golgotha Is a Mountain" and "The Return." This recognition placed him in the company of other poets seminal to the development of African American poetry, such as Langston Hughes, Countee Cullen, and Claude McKay.

Bontemps left Harlem for Alabama and a teaching position at a junior college in 1931, the same year his first novel, *God Sends Sunday*, was published. The story of Little Augie, the prodigal, fun-loving black jockey of 1890s St. Louis became the basis for his first effort as a playwright, *St. Louis Woman*. Written in 1937 with Countee Cullen, the play had a successful run on Broadway in 1946.

While in Alabama, Bontemps turned his literary prowess in two other directions. Hoping to provide black children with positive role models, he wrote his first children's book, *Popo and Fifina, Children of Haiti* (1932) in collaboration with Langston Hughes. Spurred on by the book's success,

Bontemps wrote 15 other books for children and young adults, among them Frederick Douglass: *Slave, Fighter, Freeman* (1959) and *Young Booker: Booker T. Washington's Early Days* (1972). He also wrote the acclaimed historical novel *Black Thunder* (1936). Like much of his poetry, *Black Thunder* gives a lyrical yet realistic description of a passionate struggle for freedom. The children's and young adult books and the historical novel were innovative in their exploration of new genres for the growing canon of African American literature.

In 1943, after earning an M.L.S. degree, Bontemps became a librarian at Fisk University, where he took advantage of his position to preserve the papers of Hughes, Jean Toomer, James Weldon Johnson, and Cullen. During his time at Fisk, Bontemps edited some of the most important mid-century collections of African American literature. With Hughes, he brought out *The Book of Negro Folklore* (1958) and *American Negro Poetry* (1963). *Great Slave Narratives* (1969) and *The Harlem Renaissance Remembered* (1972) appeared under his own editorship.

After retiring from Fisk in 1966, Bontemps spent the remaining years of his life as a professor at the University of Illinois, Chicago Circle, and Yale University and as a writer-in-residence at Fisk.

North America

Bourne, Saint Claire Cecil

(b. February 16, 1943, Brooklyn, N.Y.), African American writer, activist, and filmmaker dedicated to documenting African American culture.

St. Clair Bourne was the son of St. Clair Bourne Sr., who was an editor of the *Amsterdam News* and a reporter for the *People's Voice* in the 1930s. Although Bourne began his education at Georgetown University in 1961, he was expelled for student activism. In 1967 he received a B.A. from Syracuse University after working with the Peace Corps. Bourne began a degree in filmmaking at Columbia University in 1968 but was again asked to leave on account of his political activities.

From 1968 until 1970 Bourne was a producer, writer, and director for "Black Journal" (NET). He established his own company, Chamba Productions, and produced such African-American documentary films as *Something To Build On* (1971) and *Let the Church Say Amen!* (1973). In 1974 he received the Bronze Award from the New York International Film-TV Festival. In 1976 he acted as film coordinator for the World Black and African Festival of the Arts in Lagos, Nigeria.

Commissioned by the British Broadcasting Corporation (BBC), *The Black and the Green* (1982) documented Bourne's commitment to civil rights activism. He examined literary subjects in films such as *In Motion: Amiri Baraka* (1982) and *Langston Hughes: Keeper of the Dream* (1987). In 1989 the popular *Making "Do the Right Thing"* examined the work of a younger filmmaker, Spike Lee. In 1997 Bourne teamed up with Charles

Fuller on a film about Oliver Law, an African American officer in the Spanish Civil War.

North America
Bradford, Alex
(b. 1926?, Bessemer, Ala.; d. 1978?), African American gospel singer and composer known as "The Singing Rage of the Gospel Age."

Alex Bradford was born in Bessemer, Alabama where he grew up listening to the country blues, gospel quartets, and music in the Holiness Church. He moved to Chicago after serving in the United States Army in World War II and honed his singing and composing skills under the tutelage of gospel singers Mahalia Jackson and Roberta Martin. He composed "*Since I Met Jesus*" and "*Let God Abide*" for Martin. In 1954, Bradford created the Bradford Specials, an all-male gospel group. The Specials were famous for their colorful robes, soaring falsettos, and dramatic body gestures. Their biggest hit was Bradford's "*Too Close to Heaven*," which sold over 1 million records. By 1960 Bradford had moved to New York, where he began to experiment with gospel theater. Langston Hughes wrote the play *Black Nativity* for Bradford and Marion Williams in 1961. Bradford continued to participate in gospel theater, collaborating with Vinette Carroll and Micki Grant on *Don't Bother Me, I Can't Cope* in 1972 and *Your Arm's Too Short to Box With God* in 1976. In the 1970s Bradford formed the Creative Movement Repertory Company. He directed the Greater Abyssinian Baptist Choir of Newark, New Jersey, and served as minister in three churches. His impressive range and powerful voice garnered him the epithet the Singing Rage of the Gospel Age.

North America
Bradley, David Henry, Jr.
(b. September 7, 1950, Bedford, Pa.), African American novelist, essayist, and professor who focuses on the links between history and community.

Author of the award-winning novel *The Chaneysville Incident* (1981), writer David Bradley is profoundly concerned with personal and community history. Born and raised in a rural, coal-mining town, he is the son of a preacher, the late Rev. D. H. Bradley Sr., and Harriet M. Jackson Bradley, a local historian. A National Achievement Scholar in high school and a summa cum laude graduate of the University of Pennsylvania, Bradley began a serious study of nineteenth-century American history while doing post-graduate work in London in 1974.

Having come from a rural background, Bradley was alienated from urban blacks while a student in Philadelphia. He based his first novel, *South Street* (1975), on his own experience as an outsider in the city. The novel centers on the observations and interactions of a young black poet with the local hustlers, prostitutes, and bar patrons. Although *South Street* is now overshadowed by *The Chaneysville Incident*, it nevertheless exhibits Bradley's singular ability to depict convincing characters in the drama of life.

The Chaneysville Incident, Bradley's second novel, was inspired by a local legend verified by the detective work of Bradley's mother. While doing research for Bedford's bicentennial celebrations, she found the unmarked graves of 13 slaves. In danger of capture while traveling the Underground Railroad, the slaves had chosen suicide over reenslavement. Winner of many awards, among them the prestigious PEN/Faulkner Award in 1982, the novel narrates the journey of a history professor as he struggles to under-stand his natural father's suicide. Aided by his own father's journals and manuscripts, his surrogate father's stories from the past, and the support of his girlfriend, a white psychologist, the young professor connects his own history to that of his community.

Stints as an editor and English professor led Bradley to a position as pro-fessor of English and creative writing at Temple University, from which he resigned in 1996. He is a frequent contributor of essays and book reviews for national magazines and newspapers.

North America

Braithwaite, William Stanley Beaumont

(b. December 6, 1878, Boston, Mass.; d. June 8, 1962, New York, N.Y.), African American poet, anthologist, critic, and editor who championed work by both black and white authors.

Although he praised and supported many African American writers, poet and critic W. S. Braithwaite always held the belief that the best writing was never racially or culturally specific, but spoke to universal themes. Braith-waite was born into a genteel Boston family, but after his father's death in 1884, he was eventually forced to leave school and take a job with a pub-lisher to help support his family. He later said that it was while typesetting John Keats's poem "Ode on a Grecian Urn" that he realized he wanted to write poetry. His first pieces appeared in the *Atlantic Monthly* and *Scribner's*, and he published his first book, *Lyrics of Life and Love*, in 1904.

In 1906 Braithwaite began writing a regular column for the *Boston Transcript* in which he reviewed other contemporary poets, and in the same year he edited his first anthology, *The Book of Elizabethan Verse*. These accomplishments established him as a respected literary critic in addition to being a writer. After editing two more anthologies of older poetry, in 1913 he began publishing an annual collection of new poetry, the *Anthology of Magazine Verse and Yearbook*. Inclusion in Braithwaite's anthologies soon became an honor for young writers. He showcased black writers such as Langston Hughes, Countee Cullen, Claude McKay, and James Weldon Johnson and exposed them to a larger audience by including them with white writers such as Robert Frost, Edwin Arlington Robinson, and Amy Lowell. Cullen dedicated his famous Harlem Renaissance anthology, *Caroling Dusk*, to Braithwaite.

In 1918 Braithwaite received the Spingarn Medal, the highest honor of the National Association for the Advancement of Colored People, in recognition of his contributions to literature. He continued to work full-time as an editor and publisher until 1935, when he received an appointment as a professor of creative writing at Atlanta University. Six years later he published his autobiography, *The House Under Arcturus*. After his retirement in 1945, Braithwaite moved to Harlem, New York, where he published his *Selected Poems*, a novel, and a biography of the Brontë sisters before his death in 1962.

North America

Breakdancing,
a form of African American dance that emerged from the hip hop culture of the South Bronx, New York, during the mid-1970s.

Breakdancing developed out of the Bronx, New York, disco scene. When disco DJs changed records, dancers would fill the resulting musical breaks, or "breakbeats," with movements that emphasized the rupture in rhythmic continuity. These highly acrobatic interludes developed into a new genre that mixed Afrodiasporic dance styles, reflecting the influence of the lindy hop, the Charleston, the cakewalk, and the jitterbug as well as the Afro-Brazilian martial-arts dance capoeira and the antics of Kung Fu movies.

Breakdancing included "breaking" (flipping, spinning, pivoting on the head and hands), "up-rock" (a mock-combat style, often directed against an opponent), and "webbo" (fast footwork between other dance moves). When breakdancing spread to Los Angeles, California, dancers added the "electric boogie," automaton-like dance moves that incorporated pantomime. In the beginning, breakdancers adopted a confrontational attitude, as "crews" met each other in fake rumbles that often turned into real fights. Even peaceful displays resembled the competitive toasting of Bronx musicians in concurrently developing rap music.

Like other facets of the hip hop movement, breakdancing met with commercial success and public notoriety in the early 1980s. Paralleling Soho's embrace of Bronx graffiti art, Manhattan dance clubs welcomed breakdancers to their floors. And like rap, breakdancing appeared in a number of popular films, including *Wild Style* (1982), *Breakin'* (1984), and *Beat Street* (1984), which featured the Rock Steady Crew, breakdancing's most renowned posse. This publicity, which deemphasized breakdancing's confrontation-al aspect, turned the dance into a national sensation among white as well as black youths; suburban schoolchildren donned hip hop fashions, and some white teenagers signed up for breakdancing lessons.

Widespread media attention diminished breakdancing's power as a unique voice of self-affirmation for inner-city youth. Its influence, however, set the trajectory of subsequent dance trends. Black performers such as Michael Jackson, MC Hammer, and Missy Elliot draw from breakdance styles that never stop evolving. Even such breakdancing originals as Richard "Crazy Legs" Colón of the Rock Steady Crew continue to innovate and perform.

Europe
___

Bridgetower, George Frederick Polgreen

(b. February 29, 1780, Baila, Poland; d. February 29, 1860, London, England), Afro-British violinist of considerable talent who performed in concerts with Ludwig van Beethoven.

Called the Abyssinian Prince by an admiring public, George Polgreen Bridgetower gained renown throughout nineteenth-century Europe as a violinist of exceptional talent. As a youth, he became the prized violinist of the Prince of Wales, and he is said to have studied with Joseph Haydn. In 1803 he gave the first performance of Beethoven's *Kreutzer Sonata for violin*— written expressly for him—with the great German composer accompanying him at the piano.

Bridgetower grew up in London, England, the son of an African father and a European mother. At the age of ten, he debuted publicly as a violinist in Paris and soon after gave his first London performance, at the Drury Lane Theatre. His violin playing so impressed the Prince of Wales (later King George IV) that he was taken into the royal retinue. He also received extensive musical instruction from such noted violinists as Giovanni Mane Giornovichi and François-Hippolyte Barthélemon. By the late eighteenth century, Bridgetower had established himself as one of England's leading instrumental virtuosos, and in 1802 he began touring Europe.

Bridgetower's musical virtuosity gained him entry into Vienna's highest musical circles, and he soon met Beethoven. In 1803 the two musicians debuted the Kreutzer Sonata in a concert together at the Augarten Theatre. "As usual, Beethoven was late in finishing the sonata," wrote musicologist Gabriel Banat, "and the violinist had to read the first two movements from Beethoven's hardly legible manuscript, while the composer played his unfinished part mostly from memory." Beethoven held Bridgetower in high regard, both as a soloist and as a chamber group player. Wielding his influence among Vienna's leading aristocrats, he promoted Bridgetower in letters as "a master of his instrument, a very skillful virtuoso worthy of recommendation." Yet the two men later grew distant from one another—reputedly because of a quarrel over a woman.

After spending several years in Austria, Bridgetower returned to England, where he married and had one daughter. He received a bachelor of music degree from Cambridge University in 1811, taught music, and performed with the London Philharmonic Society Orchestra. During his later life he lived in Paris and Rome for many years before returning to England. He died in London at the age of 80.

Briggs, Cyril Valentine

(b. May 28, 1888, Nevis, Leeward Islands; d. October 18, 1966, Los Angeles, Calif.), African American newspaper editor and writer; a radical presence in Harlem's New Negro Movement.

Among the individuals who contributed to the political and cultural foment of Harlem's New Negro Movement in the first decades of the twentieth century, Cyril Briggs was one of its most radical. Born in Nevis, Briggs immigrated to New York in 1905 and within a few years had worked for the African American newspapers the *Colored American Review* and the *Amsterdam News*. In 1919 he was forced to resign from the *News* after an editorial he wrote that described the League of Nations as the "League of Thieves" spurred an investigation by the United States Postal Service.

After leaving the *Amsterdam News*, Briggs committed his time to publication of his journal, the *Crusader*. Founded in 1918, the *Crusader's* early editorials advocated black self-government and African independence and lent support to Marcus Garvey's nascent Universal Negro Improvement Association (UNIA). But within a year, the *Crusader* repudiated Garvey and the UNIA. In response to the violence of the Red Summer of 1918, in 1919 Briggs founded the African Blood Brotherhood (ABB), a semisecret organization that advocated black armed self-defense and aligned itself with the Communist Party USA (CPUSA). Briggs's embrace of Bolshevik principles alienated him from the vociferously anticommunist Garvey, and he became one of Garvey's strongest critics. "Is Mr. Garvey really in earnest when he talks about the liberation of Africa?" Briggs wrote in a Crusader editorial. "Or is he too busy resurrecting mediaeval systems and titles and making the glorious U.N.I.A. movement a tinsel show and a laughing stock to give time to real efforts in the liberation struggle." Briggs eventually supplied the U.S. government with information leading to Garvey's imprisonment on charges of postal fraud.

Briggs's involvement with the CPUSA increased during the 1920s and 1930s. He helped organize its black subsidiaries such as the American Negro Labor Congress (ANLC)—becoming the editor of its paper, the Harlem Liberator, in 1929—and the League of Struggle for Negro Rights. In 1938, however, his continued advocacy of Black Nationalism led to his expulsion from the party.

Brindis de Salas, Claudio

(b. August 4, 1852, Havana, Cuba; d. June 2, 1911, Buenos Aires, Argentina), Afro-Cuban violinist virtuoso and composer; sometimes referred to as the Black Paganini.

Born in the bustling city of Havana, a cultural center for the development of classical music in Latin America and the Caribbean, Claudio Brindis de

Salas was already a concert violinist at the age of ten. His father, Claudio Sr., was a well-known musician, teacher, and orchestra leader. Brindis de Salas studied with a Belgian teacher in Havana and later with Danclas, David, Sivori, and others at the Paris Conservatory. He won awards and began traveling widely, earning many accolades in cities like Milan, Florence, Berlin, St. Petersburg, and London. As a violin virtuoso he earned the nicknames "the Black Paganini" and "the King of the Octaves." He toured with great success in Latin America, and in Buenos Aires, Argentina, his admirers gave him an authentic Stradivarius violin.

After his last tour in Cuba, which was a financial disaster, he moved to Buenos Aires. There he suffered from tuberculosis, and died from the disease, in a state of poverty, on June 2, 1911. His corpse was unidentifiable until his passport was found. In 1917 a Buenos Aires newspaper tried to have his remains transferred to Cuba, his homeland, but it was not until 1930 that this final tribute was paid.

Latin America and the Caribbean

Brindis de Salas, Virginia

(b. 1908, Montevideo, Uruguay; d. 1958, Montevideo, Uruguay), Afro-Uruguayan poet, contributor to *Nuestra Raza* (the important black Uruguayan journal), and the first black South American woman to publish in book form and widely distribute her two volumes of poetry.

Poet Gabriela Mistral, the 1945 Chilean Nobel Laureate, praised the poetry of Virginia Brindis de Salas in a letter, claiming that as far away as Los Angeles, her poems were establishing important pan-American links among black people. Despite Mistral's assessment, as literary critic Carroll Young states, there is but one other indication that the work of Brindis de Salas was available outside of Uruguay: a 1954 German translation of her poem "Tango número tres."

Little is known about her life. She claimed to have been the niece of Claudio Brindis de Salas, the famous Cuban violinist who had settled in Buenos Aires. Active in the small but thriving black Uruguayan community, she published a number of poems in *Nuestra Raza* before her first book appeared in 1946, *Pregón de Marimorena* (The Call of Mary Morena). Her second volume of poetry, *Cien cárceles de amor* (One Hundred Prisons of Love), followed shortly after in 1949. In the prologue to this volume she mentioned a third book, *Cantos de lejanía* (Songs from Faraway). This book never materialized, perhaps because the author lacked funds as a result of the economic crisis in Uruguay between 1948 and 1960.

Most of her poetry addresses the social reality of black Uruguayans. Carroll Young notes that the themes of Brindis de Salas's poetry depart significantly from those of her contemporary white female poets, Delmira Agustini, Alfonsina Storni, Juana Ibarbourou, and Gabriela Mistral, who preferred to explore romantic and maternal love or women's roles in Uruguay, Argentina, and Chile. Infused with black consciousness, the verse of Brindis de Salas insists on exposing racial discrimination and the socioe-conomic disadvantages of Afro-Uruguayans.

This radical bent put her at odds with colleagues like Pilar Barrios (1889–1974), who avoided confrontation, hoping to "impress upon the dominant culture the intellectual genius of the black Uruguayan commu-nity." If indeed Brindis de Salas's unflinching sketches of black Uruguayan life alienated her somewhat from leaders like Barrios, it might also help to explain in part why so many of her biographical details remain a mystery and possibly why her third book was never published.

The structure of *Pregón de Marimorena* is of particular interest, as Brindis de Salas did not simply write thematically about black pride but employed oral forms and traditional dances to structure her free verse. The book is divided into four sections, each one pointing to a different kind of African-derived music: "Ballads," "Calls," "Tangos," and "Songs." Pregones, or calls, date back to colonial times when blacks would announce their wares in the streets through distinguishable songs, a custom still observed in Brindis de Salas's day. Tango, the region's most popular dance form, was, however, often identified with white Argentine and Uruguayan culture. Thus, in an attempt to reappropriate the tango for Afro-Uruguayans, Brindis de Salas called it the "Danza que bailaron los esclavos parche y ritmo en su elemental rueda de gallo" (Dance that the slaves danced drum and rhythm in their rudimentary chicken ring) in her "Tango número dos" (Tango Number Two).

Thus, although little is known about her life, her poetry has survived. By the late 1990s her work had been anthologized and she was deservedly receiving more critical attention as Afro-Latin American writers were gaining greater recognition.

Africa

Brink, André Philippus

(b. May 29, 1935, Vrede, South Africa), Afrikaner novelist whose books criti-cizing apartheid were banned by the South African government.

The son of an Afrikaner magistrate, André Brink grew up moving from vil-lage to village in rural South Africa, each characterized, he says, by "conser-vative Protestantism . . . generosity and narrow-mindedness." After receiving master's degrees in English and Afrikaans from Potchefstroom University, he went to Paris in 1959 to study at the Sorbonne. By his own assessment, the 1960 Sharpeville massacre in South Africa (in which the police killed at least 69 innocent protesters) sparked in him a new political awareness and prompted him to return home in 1961.

Brink began to write fiction while lecturing at Rhodes University. Two novels published in the early 1960s were largely apolitical, but his views on writing changed after he spent 1968 in Paris, where he witnessed student uprisings. Brink came to believe that "in a closed society, the writer has a specific social and moral role to fill." In its story of a mixed-race actor convicted of killing his white lover, his next novel, *Looking into Darkness* (1973), dealt directly with apartheid. It was the first Afrikaans novel banned by the South African government. Brink wrote his subsequent novels in both Afrikaans and English.

During the 1970s and 1980s, while enduring constant monitoring and harassment by the authorities, Brink published seven more novels: *An Instant in the Wind* (1976), *Rumours of Rain* (1978), *A Dry White Season* (1979), *A Chain of Voices* (1981), *Mapmakers* (1983), *The Wall of the Plague* (1984), and *States of Emergency* (1988). His novels have been translated into more than 20 languages. *A Dry White Season* won both the Martin Luther King Memorial Prize and the French Prix Medicis Etranger in 1980 and was made into a movie in 1989.

Brink has also written and directed plays, served as president of the Afrikaans Writers' Guild and as a member of South African PEN, and translated Shakespeare, Henry James, Albert Camus, and other authors into Afrikaans. His later books include *An Act of Terror* (1991), *The First Life of Admastor* (1993), *On the Contrary* (1993), *Imaginings of Sand* (1996), *Reinventing a Continent* (1996), and *The Novel: Language and Narrative from Cervantes to Calvino* (1998).

North America

Brooks, Gwendolyn Elizabeth

(b. June 17, 1917, Topeka, Kans.), American poet and novelist, a leading poet of the post-World War II era, and an important figure in the Black Arts Movement of the 1960s and 1970s.

As an infant, Gwendolyn Brooks moved with her parents, David and Keziah Wims Brooks, to Chicago's South Side, where she has resided ever since. Brooks was educated at Chicago public schools and Wilson Junior College. The major early influence on her literary career was her mother, who had Brooks giving dramatic recitals at the age of four. Largely through her mother's urging, the teenage Brooks met the leading black writers James Weldon Johnson and Langston Hughes, who encouraged her to write poetry. By age 16, Brooks had already published poetry in the *Chicago Defender*, the leading African American newspaper of that time.

Brooks's writing further developed as she participated in the vibrant literary scene of the South Side during the late 1930s and early 1940s, which included such important black writers as Richard Wright, Margaret Walker, Theodore Ward, Margaret Danner, Arna Bontemps, and Frank Marshall Davis. Inez Cunningham Stark's poetry workshop at the South Side Community Art Center in the early 1940s was particularly important in the development of Brooks's writing skills. Her poems began to appear in such leading journals and anthologies of the time as *Negro Story* and Edward Seaver's *Cross Section* series. During this period, Brooks also won many prizes and fellowships, including two Guggenheim Fellowships. Brooks's first collection of poetry, *A Street in Bronzeville*, appeared in 1945. A second book of poetry, *Annie Allen*, was published in 1949, earning her the Pulitzer Prize for poetry in 1950, the first time an African American had won the award.

Brooks's early collections are exciting mixtures of modernist treatments of traditional literary forms, such as the sonnet and ballad (heavily influenced by T. S. Eliot) and more popular African American forms after the manner of Langston Hughes. Despite these and other influences, Brooks created a unique poetic voice that grappled with issues of art, identity, race, gender, and the relationship between literature and popular culture more powerfully than that of any other poet in the immediate post-World War II era. Brooks further investigated these concerns in her single novel, *Maud Martha* (1953), a series of loosely connected sketches about a young African American woman from the South Side.

With the upsurge of the Civil Rights Movement in the late 1950s, Brooks's work became increasingly engaged with the events of the African American struggle for freedom. Her 1960 collection of poems, *The Bean Eaters*, contains poems about the 1955 murder of 14-year-old Emmett Till in Mississippi, lynching, and the integration of schools in Little Rock, Arkansas. While retaining much in common with her early style, Brooks's poetry became much more direct during this period. This directness and more overt focus on the immediate conditions and events of the African American community became even more pronounced after Brooks attended a black writer's conference at Fisk University in 1967. There she encountered leading Black Arts Movement writers, such as Amiri Baraka, who greatly influenced her. After the conference, Brooks became the black writer of the earlier generation most prominently identified with the Black Arts Movement. This affiliation was seen almost immediately in the 1968 collection *In the Mecca* ("the Mecca" referring to a South Side apartment building), which included poems to Malcolm X, slain civil rights leader Medgar Evers, and the Blackstone Rangers, a politicized Chicago street gang that became part of the Black Power Movement.

Brooks has retained this political engagement in her work to the present, an engagement seen not only in her poetry, but also in her decision to use African American-run publishing houses rather than larger commercial publishers. In addition to her poetry and her novel, Brooks has written two autobiographical works, *Report from Part One* (1972) *and Report from Part Two* (1997).

North America

Broonzy, William Lee Conley ("Big Bill")

(b. June 26, 1893, Scott, Mississippi; d. August 15, 1958, Chicago, Illinois), prolific country bluesman who played a major role in the introduction of rural Southern music to Chicago.

Big Bill Broonzy was born to sharecropper parents in Mississippi, and in his childhood he moved with his family between Mississippi and Arkansas,

farming in both states. He first played music on homemade fiddles and guitars, and was performing at special occasions by the age of 15. Between the
ages of 15 and 20 he developed his dexterous hollering vocal style, as well
as his characteristically facile guitar technique. Music, however, remained
but an avocation until he resettled in Chicago after serving in the army
during World War I.

Broonzy had begun as a solo performer, but by the 1930s he was
playing with small ensembles. These groups often included a piano,
trumpet, and saxophone, as well as a rhythm section. At this time Broonzy
worked with bluesmen such as Georgia Tom (Thomas A. Dorsey), Little
Walter Jacobs, and Tampa Red (Hudson Whittaker). Dorsey was one
among a number of Chicago blues-men who appealed to emigrants from
the South with songs that combined rural blues sounds with lyrics of an
urban perspective.

After World War II, black audiences turned from the blues toward other
kinds of popular music. Broonzy discerned the change in fashion and began
marketing himself to the white fans who constituted the postwar folk
revival. Although he had played at Carnegie Hall in the "From Spirituals to
Swing" concert in the late 1930s, his popularity among white audiences was
enhanced when he appeared with Sonny Terry, Brownie McGhee, and Pete
Seeger. Broonzy's performances increasingly included protest and folk material as well as anecdotal flourishes, and he began touring extensively. He
played at the London Jazz Club in 1951, gave performances with gospel
superstar Mahalia Jackson, and appeared in Africa, South America, and
Southeast Asia.

While working as a janitor at Iowa State University in the early 1950s,
Broonzy learned to write from students there. In 1953 he finally made
enough money from music to retire from other kinds of work. In 1955 his
letters were published as an autobiography. He died of cancer in 1958.

North America

Brown, Claude

**(b. February 23, 1927, New York, N.Y.), writer best known for his autobiography,
Manchild in the Promised Land.**

Claude Brown, the son of Ossie Brock Brown, a domestic worker, and
Henry Lee, a railroad worker, began *Manchild in the Promised Land* in
1963. Published in 1965, the book told of his troubled childhood in
Harlem, a period during which he ran with a gang and was in and out of
reform schools.

Brown abandoned street life, resumed his education, and was awarded a
grant to study government at Howard University, graduating in 1965. He
studied law at Stanford University and then at Rutgers University, which he
left in 1968 without a degree. In 1976 he published *The Children of Ham*,
about struggling young blacks in Harlem.

North America

Brown, James

(b. May 3, 1933, Augusta, Ga.), American soul and funk singer, known as the Godfather of Soul, Soul Brother Number One, Mr. Dynamite, and the Hardest Working Man in Show Business.

James Brown grew up in Augusta, Georgia, where he did a little of everything: picked cotton, shined shoes, danced, and served time for armed robbery. Brown boxed and played pro baseball before an injury made him turn to music. After dabbling in gospel, he renamed his group, from the Swanees to the Famous Flames. The group's local popularity attracted the attention of Federal Records, which signed them to a contract in 1956. Their first record, "Please Please Please," did well, and "Try Me" topped the rhythm-and-blues charts in 1958.

As his band's fame spread beyond Georgia, Brown became ambitious. He staged elaborate dances, formed the James Brown Revue, and created a Carnival atmosphere at his live shows. An emcee worked the crowd into a frenzy before the singer came onstage, and Brown allegedly lost seven pounds each night through dancing. Soon he had a backup band (the J.B.s) in addition to the Flames, who were largely a vocal group. Although Brown wanted to record with the J.B.s, Federal Records refused. In response, Brown recorded the hit instrumental "Mashed Potatoes" under a pseudonym. This ruse attracted the attention of Federal Record's parent company, King Records, who allowed Brown and the J.B.s to record together. With King this group began a long and fruitful relationship. In 1962 the album Live at the Apollo, Volume 2, sold 1 million copies.

In 1965 Brown achieved artistic control of his records, and the result was unprecedented in popular music. Under Brown's tight direction, he recorded one hit after another. The music was notable for irresistible grooves, precision timing, and Brown's impassioned vocals. Brown specialized in an insistent dance music that was deeply charged with sexual electricity. In many ways, he pioneered the sound that evolved into funk and disco. Starting with "Papa's Got a Brand New Bag," Brown's string of hits continued through the 1960s with such songs as "I Got You," "Cold Sweat," and "Say It Loud, I'm Black and I'm Proud."

Through the late 1960s and into the 1970s, Brown became a spokesman among African American youth, and he targeted more of his songs toward disaffected ghetto youth. Not only did he preach responsibility in songs like "King Heroin," "Funky President," and "Don't Be a Drop-Out," he also invested in black businesses, bought several radio stations, and inspired kids with his tough but uplifting message. Other activities included traveling to Africa and writing music for several films.

Brown's success has been accompanied by personal difficulties. He faced legal trouble for failing to pay taxes and for allegedly assaulting his wife. Despite reorganizing his bands many times, Brown has had relatively few hits since the mid-1970s. Nevertheless, as he nears his fifth decade in music, Brown remains an inspirational performer who has influenced countless younger musicians. Hip hop bands have extensively appropriated funky grooves from his 1970s records in the sampling practices of the 1980s and 1990s.

North America

Brown, Ruth

(b. December 30, 1928, Portsmouth, Va.), African American blues and musical theater singer, one of the pioneers of rhythm and blues (R&B).

Celebrated as Miss Rhythm, Ruth Brown has long been revered for her earthy, innuendo-laden rhythm and blues (R&B) singing. According to music critic Ron Wynn, "Nobody male or female sang with more spirit, sass, and vigor than Brown during the 1950s." She is also noted for her "yelp," which, says *New York Times* writer Ann Powers, "is one of the defining sounds of rock-and-roll, as primary as Little Richard's 'wooo!' or Jerry Lee Lewis's growl." Brown has recorded prolifically and is credited with having laid the foundation for Atlantic Records with such 1950s hits as "*Mama, He Treats Your Daughter Mean*," "*5-10-15 Hours*," and "*Teardrops from My Eyes*." An active performer still, in 1994 she was inducted into the Rock and Roll Hall of Fame.

"All of my childhood was spent singing spirituals," Brown once wrote. The daughter of Leonard Weston, a dockhand, and Martha (Alston) Weston, Brown grew up in a predominantly black community in Portsmouth, Virginia. She received musical training at a local Methodist church, where she sang in the choir her father directed. In the early 1940s she won first prize at the Apollo Theater's Amateur Night in New York City and went on to perform in local nightclubs. She also toured with United Service Organization performers throughout the South and in 1948 sang with the Lucky Millinder Band.

Describing her singing style of the times, Brown wrote, "I was more of a pop torch singer. I preferred the ballads." She soon began to sing R&B, and by the late 1950s had recorded more than 80 songs for Atlanta Records. In 1966, after her third divorce, she scaled back her career to care for her two children. "Until then," she said, "my sons had been like backstage babies, living in a drawer . . . while I performed in and out of train stations." Having received almost no royalties from her recordings, she worked intermittently as a bus driver, housekeeper, and teacher's aide while continuing to record.

In 1989 Brown enjoyed a dramatic comeback. In that year she won a Tony Award for her performance in the Broadway musical *Black and Blue* and recorded *Blues on Broadway*, for which she received a Grammy Award in 1990. In 1991 she began hosting the weekly music program *BluesStage* on National Public Radio. She has recorded more than a dozen albums, including her most recent, *The Songs of My Life* (1993) and *Live in London* (1994).

Brown, Sterling Allen

(b. May 1, 1901, Washington, D.C.; d. January 13, 1989, Takoma Park, Md.);
African American academic, poet, critic, and anthologist known for his
research on black folklore and his poetry written in African American dialect.

Through his long career as a writer anthologist, critic, scholar, and educator,
Sterling Brown became one of the most influential individuals in the field of
African American literary studies. He was born into Washington, D.C.'s
educated black middle class. His father, an ex-slave, was a prominent pastor
and professor of religion at Howard University, and his mother had been
valedictorian of her class at Fisk University. Brown attended the well-known
Dunbar High School, where Jessie Fauset and Angelina Weld Grimké were
among his teachers, and graduated with honors in 1918. He then accepted a
scholarship to Williams College in Williamstown, Massachusetts. There he
was elected to Phi Beta Kappa, earned the distinction of being the only student awarded final honors in English, and graduated with a bachelor's
degree cum laude in 1922. From there, he went to Harvard University to
pursue a master's degree in English, which he received in 1923.

During his studies, Brown was drawn to younger American poets such
as Edwin Arlington Robinson, Robert Frost, and Carl Sandburg, whose
work convinced him that a well-crafted celebration of dialect and of
everyday culture—"the extraordinary in ordinary life"—was possible in
American poetry. But Brown would later acknowledge that his best teachers
were always "the poor black folk of the South," because it was from them
that he came to appreciate the black folklore and language that would form
the basis of most of his own work. Brown's first exposure to this rich culture came just after his graduation from Harvard, when he took a teaching
post at the Virginia Seminary in Lynchburg, Virginia, for three years.

In Virginia he began paying careful attention to the work songs, blues,
and spirituals he heard, calling his visits to jook joints, barbershops, and
rural farms "folklore-collecting trips." He also married Daisy Turnbull, his
wife of more than 50 years, in Lynchburg in 1927. After leaving the Virginia Seminary, Brown taught at Lincoln University in Jefferson City, Missouri, and at Fisk University in Nashville, Tennessee, before accepting a post
as professor of English at Howard University in 1929, a position he would
hold for the next 40 years. During 1931 and 1932 he returned to Harvard
briefly to do doctoral work, and in 1932 he published his first collection of
poetry, *Southern Road*.

Brown's first published poem, "When de Saints Go Ma'ching Home,"
had appeared five years earlier in the National Urban League's journal,
Opportunity. Between 1927 and 1932 several more of his poems appeared
in journals and were included in the Harlem Renaissance anthology *Caroling
Dusk* (1927), edited by Countee Cullen, and *The Book of American Negro
Poetry* (1931), edited by James Weldon Johnson. The poetry in *Southern
Road*, like these earlier pieces, brought to life the ballads and work songs

Brown had collected. Many of his poems were written in African American dialect, imitated folk songs' verse and rhyme patterns, and used black folk heroes as protagonists. Unlike some earlier dialect poetry by black and white writers that had been accused of caricature, Brown's work was praised for realistically portraying black speech and culture.

Southern Road received good reviews, but when Brown could not find a publisher for his second book of poetry, he returned to his scholarly work. In the next decade he published two critical books, *The Negro in American Fiction* (1937) and *Negro Poetry and Drama* (1937), and coedited an anthology, *The Negro Caravan*, which remains one of the most important collections of African American literature. Between 1936 and 1940 he was also national editor of *Negro Affairs for the Federal Writers' Project*, a federally funded program that hired writers to collect American folklore.

In the decades that followed, Brown turned much of his attention to teaching, spending semesters at Vassar College, Atlanta University, and New York University in addition to his post at Howard. He earned a reputation as a much-beloved instructor and was especially celebrated for his willingness to serve as a mentor; his students included Stokely Carmichael, Kwame Nkrumah, Ossie Davis, and Amiri Baraka. After he finally retired from teaching in 1969, Brown enjoyed a revival in his career as a poet.

In 1975 Brown published his second book of poetry, *The Last Ride of Wild Bill and Eleven Narratives*. *Southern Road* was reprinted in the same year. In 1979 he was asked to contribute an autobiographical memoir to the collection *Chant of Saints: A Gathering of Afro-American Literature, Art, and Scholarship*, and in 1980 poet Michael S. Harper edited *The Collected Poems of Sterling A. Brown*, which included the unpublished poems from the volume that had been rejected in the 1930s and which was awarded that year's Lenore Marshall Prize for an outstanding volume of poetry published in the United States.

During the 1970s and 1980s Brown received honorary doctorates from such institutions as Williams and Vassar colleges and Howard, Harvard, and Brown universities; was elected to the Academy of American Poets; and was named poet laureate of the District of Columbia. By the time of his death from leukemia in 1989, Sterling Brown had been confirmed as a key figure in the African American literary tradition.

North America

Brown, William Wells

(b. 1814, near Lexington, Ky.; d. November 6, 1884, Chelsea, Mass.), African American antislavery lecturer and groundbreaking novelist, playwright, and historian.

Scholars have called William Wells Brown the first African American to achieve distinction in writing belles lettres, or "fine letters." Brown's literary career is made up of "firsts": he is considered the first African American to publish works in several literary genres. But Brown was also known for his political activism, particularly in the antislavery movement, and political themes underscored his writing throughout his career.

Brown was born on a plantation outside Lexington, Kentucky, to a white father and a slave mother. He spent most of his childhood and young adulthood as a slave in St. Louis, Missouri, working at a variety of trades, and even traveling to New Orleans three times as a handyman to a slave trader. Brown became free on New Year's Day, 1834, when he was while it was docked in Cincinnati, Ohio, a free state.

Brown's middle and last names honored a white Quaker family, Mr. and Mrs. Wells Brown, who helped him escape. He settled in Cleveland, where he married Elizabeth Schooner. Next, Brown moved to Buffalo, New York, and spent nine years there working simultaneously as a steamboatman on Lake Erie and as a conductor for the Underground Railroad, the secret network of individuals who helped fugitive slaves escape to freedom in the Northern states or Canada.

In 1843 Brown began lecturing on his experiences in slavery for the Western New York Anti-Slavery Society, one of many American abolitionist groups. He eventually became a lecturer on behalf of women's rights and temperance, but it was as a fugitive slave speaking on the evils of slavery that he was best known. This provided the basis for the beginning of his career as a writer. In the wake of Frederick Douglass's successful autobiographical slave narrative in 1845, there was an increased demand for similar narratives. Two years later, Brown wrote his own, and the *Narrative of William W. Brown, a Fugitive Slave, Written by Himself* went through four American and five British editions in its first three years after publication.

Following his autobiography's international success, in 1849 Brown traveled to Europe. The combination of European demand for his antislavery speeches and the passage of the American Fugitive Slave Law in 1850—which put him in danger of being returned to slavery if he were apprehended anywhere on American soil—led Brown to stay in England for the next five years. Between 1849 and 1854 he gave more than a thousand speeches and wrote two books that were important firsts for African American literature. In 1852 Brown published *Three Years in Europe; or, Places I Have Seen and People I Have Met*, the first travel book written by an African American; and in 1853 he published *Clotel, or, the President's Daughter: A Narrative of Slave Life in the United States*, thought by some to be the first novel written by an African American.

The plot of *Clotel*, although fictional, is based on the widespread belief that American president Thomas Jefferson had fathered several slave children. The title character, his beautiful mulatto daughter, is separated from her mother and sister when all three are sold at auction after Jefferson's death. Her new owner falls in love with her and, after fathering her child, promises to marry her but ultimately betrays his promise and sells her to a dealer. Clotel escapes from the dealer and attempts to free her child, but when she realizes she has been discovered, she drowns herself to avoid being returned to slavery.

In later years, *Clotel* has been criticized for its stereotypical portrayal of a "tragic mulatto" and its melodramatic plot and style. At the time of its publication, however, the novel was praised by antislavery groups for its skill in exposing slavery's horrors, and was compared favorably to Harriet Beecher Stowe's antislavery novel *Uncle Tom's Cabin*, which had been a runaway bestseller just a year earlier. *Clotel* was revised and reprinted three times in the United States during Brown's lifetime. It is still honored as one of the landmark texts in the African American literary tradition and is still available in contemporary editions.

In 1854 some of Brown's friends raised enough money to purchase his freedom, allowing him to return to the United States. Once home, Brown continued writing on the same themes in a different genre. In 1858 his play *The Escape; or, a Leap for Freedom* became the first drama published by an African American. Over the next two decades, he focused his efforts on yet another genre: historical works. These included two histories of the black race, another history on blacks and whites in the American South, and a rare military history of African Americans in the American Civil War. Brown's career as an orator slowed down after slavery ended, and he eventually settled in Boston and practiced medicine there until his death from cancer in 1884. But as a pioneering black writer, Brown left a lasting legacy to the generations of African American novelists, dramatists, and historians who would follow him.

North America

Buck and Bubbles,

American piano and tap dance team of Ford Lee "Buck" Washington (b. 1906; d. 1955) and John William "Bubbles" Sublett (b. February 19, 1902, Louisville, Ky.; d. May 18, 1986, New York, N.Y.), who together revolutionized tap dancing and were the first African Americans to perform at Radio City Music Hall.

Buck and Bubbles teamed up in 1912 in Indianapolis. Bubbles, then ten, sang and danced, and Buck, aged six, accompanied on piano. After winning several amateur contests, they played professional engagements in Louisville, Kentucky (often in blackface), Detroit, Michigan, and New York City.

Bubbles developed a style of tap called "jazz tap." Before this, dancers danced on their toes and emphasized flash steps, which were athletic steps with extended leg and body movements. Bubbles changed this style by tapping with his heels and toes and developing complicated moves, such as double over-the-tops (a rough figure-eight that simulates tripping). His new style led tap into the bebop and "cool" jazz eras, and he became known as the "father of rhythm tap."

Audiences delighted in the duo's singing, dancing, and comedy routine, with Buck's variations in tempo that forced Bubbles to quickly adapt. By 1922 they were performing at New York's Palace Theatre, the nation's top vaudeville venue. They broke color barriers by headlining the white vaudeville circuit across the United States, and were featured in several Broadway revues in the 1920s and 1930s. During the 1930s the duo took their vaudeville act to the London Palladium. Their stage success resulted in roles in such movies as *Varsity Show* (1937), *Cabin in the Sky* (1943), *Atlantic City* (1944), and *A Song Is Born* (1948).

Buck and Bubbles performed together until shortly before Buck's death in 1955. Despite suffering a stroke in 1967 that left him partially paralyzed, Bubbles continued to perform. His last performance was in 1980 in the revue *Black Broadway*. John Sublett died May 18, 1986.

Bullins, Edward (Ed)

(b. July 2, 1935, Philadelphia, Pa.), American playwright whose plays reflect the realities of urban life experienced by ordinary African Americans.

Born Edward Artie, Ed Bullins grew up in a tough neighborhood in Philadelphia, where he participated in the violent street life and was nearly fatally stabbed. He dropped out of high school in 1952 to join the United States Navy, returning to Philadelphia in 1955 to complete his secondary education. Philadelphia was still violent, so he moved to Los Angeles in 1958. In 1961 he began attending Los Angeles City College and started writing. Curious about the lives of other African Americans, Bullins traveled throughout the United States. In 1964 he settled in San Francisco, where he began writing plays. He earned a B.A. from Antioch University in San Francisco in 1989.

His early plays draw on the experiences of his youth. Mainstream critics considered Bullins's these plays obscene, and Bullins was unable to find producers for them. This forced him to stage his plays himself where he could, including coffeehouses and pubs. The lack of commercial outlet for his work tempted Bullins to quit writing for the theater, but the work of other playwrights, especially *Dutchman* and *The Slave*, by LeRoi Jones (later Amiri Baraka), inspired him to continue.

In the mid-1960s Bullins became the cultural director of Black House, an African American theater group in Oakland, California, with a militant political and cultural outlook. Its members included Huey Newton, Bobby Seale, and Eldridge Cleaver, founders of the Black Panther Party. Through his association with Black House, Bullins was briefly the Black Panther minister of culture. Black House became divided, however, between members who viewed theater as a spur to political action and those who viewed it mainly as an art form. Committed to artistic vision rather than the political ideology of Black House's revolutionary wing, Bullins left Black House in 1967.

Bullins then became playwright-in-residence at New Lafayette Theatre in New York and eventually its associate director until 1972, when it folded.

Although none of the plays he wrote while at New Lafayette was commercially successful, he received critical praise for his work, including the 1971 Obie Award for *The Fabulous Miss Marie and New England Winter* and the Drama Critics Circle Award for *The Taking of Miss Janie* as best American play of 1974–1975.

Bullins's plays focus on the lives of African Americans who live in ghettos. They contrast the ideal of the American dream with the brutal reality many African Americans face and with their battle to transcend that reality. His plays often reveal his distaste for political rhetoric as a substitute for action. Their unconventional structure allows the audience to interact verbally with the stage characters. To date, his most ambitious undertaking is the Twentieth-Century Cycle, a proposed collection of 20 plays that chart the African American experience and, to a lesser extent, race relations in the twentieth-century United States.

In 1978, after the death of his son, Bullins returned to the West Coast, founding the Bullins Memorial Theatre in California and, with fellow playwright Jonal Woodward, the Bullins/Woodward Theatre Workshop in San Francisco. In 1995 Bullins accepted a teaching position at Northeastern University in Boston, Massachusetts.

North America
Bush, Anita

(b. 1883, New York, N.Y.; d. February 1974), African American actress and the founder of the Lafayette Players, the first major professional, black, nonmusical theater ensemble.

Born in New York City, Anita Bush was introduced to the world of theater by her father, a tailor whose clients included many New York actors and performers. At the age of 16 she joined the Williams and Walker Company as a dancer.

In 1915, determined that blacks should perform serious dramatic works, she formed the Anita Bush Players of Harlem, which later became the Lafayette Players. The company survived until January 1932, and was responsible for training over 300 black performers and introducing serious theater to many cities across the country. Bush left the group in 1920 and went on to costar in *The Crimson Skull* (1921), the first all-black Western movie.

North America
Butler, Octavia Estelle

(b. June 22, 1947, Pasadena, Calif.), American science fiction writer whose work examines representations of race, gender, and systems of enslavement.

Highly regarded for her science fiction novels and short stories, Octavia Butler was born in Pasadena, California, on June 22, 1947. A shy and dyslexic child, she was raised in Pasadena and attended John Muir High

School. She then studied for two years at Pasadena City College before completing additional coursework at California State College and the University of California at Los Angeles (UCLA).

Butler read avidly as a youth and began writing short works of fiction at the age of ten. Her first novel, *Patternmaster*, was published in 1976 as part of a series that includes *Mind of My Mind* (1977), *Survivor* (1978), *Wild Seed* (1980), and *Clay's Ark* (1984). Though best known for her novels, Butler has won awards for her short stories, including a Hugo for "Speech Sounds" (1983) and both a Hugo and a Nebula for "Blood-Child" (1984).

Butler's work often displays her interest in racial themes, particularly the issue of slavery. Set in times ranging from pre-colonial Africa to a distant grim future, many of Butler's stories feature characters who deal with different forms of enslavement and struggle to free themselves from systems of bondage. Butler is also one of the first writers to introduce the black woman's experience in science fiction, as she features many African American and African female protagonists. Her work is celebrated outside science fiction circles for its character development and treatment of human relations and social causes.

C

Cakewalk, The,

an African American dance that was appropriated by the white cultural mainstream it lampooned.

As a product of black folk culture, the cakewalk remains obscure in origin. Perhaps with African roots, it developed on plantations sometime before the Civil War, as slaves imitated the Grand March that concluded the cotillions and fancy balls given by whites. Although plantation owners often mistook the dance for childlike play, the cakewalk in fact had a satirical purpose. Promenading in pairs, dancers crossed their arms, arched their backs, threw back their heads, and strutted with exaggerated kicks. The cakewalk took its name from the cake that was awarded—by the judgment of a boisterous audience—to the couple with the most flair.

In the 1880s and 1890s white black-faced minstrels often ended stage shows with the cakewalk, or "peregrination for the pastry." Thus whites imitated blacks imitating whites, a cultural curiosity that only grew more complex when African Americans began imitating white minstrelsy.

With the advent of ragtime in the 1890s, the cakewalk became a national craze among both blacks and whites. The high-stepping exuberance of the cakewalk meshed perfectly with the march-based yet heavily syncopated new music. Cakewalking contests soon offered prizes bigger than cake, and ragtime pianists, as well as nimble dancers, vied for recognition. Although the cakewalk waned in popularity by the 1920s, its influence was felt in many subsequent dance trends.

Calloway, Cabell (Cab)

(b. December 25, 1907, Rochester, N.Y.; d. November 18, 1994, Hosckessin, Del.), African American singer and bandleader famed for his showmanship and skill at jive.

Cab Calloway was the son of a lawyer who had expected his son to follow in his footsteps. But when Calloway was in his teens he left Baltimore—where his family had moved when he was six—to join an older sister in Chicago. She arranged his first job as a performer, in a vocal harmony quartet. In 1925, the year that Calloway cited as the start of his career, he became the drummer in the Sunset Orchestra; two years later he organized his own band, giving up the drums to focus on singing.

Around 1927 Calloway brought his band, the Alabamians, to New York City for a gig at Harlem's famed Savoy Ballroom, but he found little success and soon disbanded the group. After winning a role in Connie's *Hot Chocolates*, an all-black Broadway revue, Calloway gained acclaim for his rendition of Fats Waller's "*Ain't Misbehavin'*." On the strength of that performance, Irving Mills—Duke Ellington's manager—urged Calloway to return to band-leading, and in 1929 he took over a band, originally from St. Louis, known as the Missourians. In 1930 Calloway's group replaced Ellington's at New York's legendary Cotton Club.

It was at the Cotton Club that Calloway wrote and introduced "*Minnie the Moocher*" (1931), a song that would be forever linked to him. The song combined scat-singing with nonsense syllables and lyrics freighted with the argot of drug use, recounting how Minnie and her cocaine-using lover, Smokey Joe, went to Chinatown, where "he showed her how to kick the gong around"—slang for opium smoking. Calloway became known as a master of jive, the term then applied to African American slang (particularly that used by blacks in the entertainment industry). He wrote *The Hepster's Dictionary* (1938), which sold 2 million copies and became the New York Public Library's standard reference work on the subject.

While at the Cotton Club, Calloway perfected his showmanship, which extended beyond singing to include dancing and comedy. He was the first singer after Louis Armstrong to emphasize scat singing. "*Minnie the Moocher*," for example, featured the memorable call-and-response scat chorus—"Hi de hi de hi de ho." Like Armstrong, he first began using nonsense syllables after forgetting a song's lyrics. Calloway's comic routines, jive patter, and novelty songs often distracted attention from his vocal talents, though his astonishing range encompassed bass, baritone, and tenor; musicologist Gunther Schuller called Calloway the "most unusually and broadly gifted male singer of the thirties."

Calloway maintained the highest standard of musicianship and fronted one of the greatest of the big bands of the 1930s, featuring trumpeters Dizzy Gillespie, Doc Cheatham, and Jonah Jones; saxophonist Chu Berry; drummer Cozy Cole; and bass player Milt Hinton. Musicians recognized, as Gillespie recalled in his autobiography, that playing with Calloway "was the best job that you could possibly have." Nevertheless, Gillespie noted that Calloway "wasn't interested in developing . . . musicians," and Hinton complained of the complacency that he found in the Calloway band. On the other hand, despite his success—and unlike Louis Armstrong, his only counterpart as a black entertainer—Calloway consistently featured his supporting musicians. Although three-minute, 78-rpm records restricted the length of instrumental solos in his recordings, in live performances Calloway shared the spotlight generously.

During the 1940s Calloway appeared in several Hollywood films, most memorably *Stormy Weather* (1943), in which he was featured, resplendent in a white zoot suit, with his band. In the 1950s he had roles in several Broadway productions and won acclaim for his portrayal of Sportin' Life in *Porgy and Bess*, a role that George Gershwin reportedly created with Calloway in mind. In 1980 Calloway's performance in *The Blues Brothers* gained him a worldwide audience and renewed prominence, but from the 1920s to the 1990s he kept up a steady performing schedule. Interviewed for a 1991 article in *Contemporary Musicians*, Calloway scoffed at the notion that he might have musical heroes. "My heroes are the notes, man. The music itself," he declared. "You understand what I'm saying? I love the music. The music is my hero."

North America

Campbell, Luther

(b. 1961, Miami, Fla.), raunchy rapper and First Amendment icon.

Luther Campbell began his career in music in 1979 with Miami's Ghetto Style DJs, but found success with a West Coast group he established called 2 Live Crew. With Campbell at the helm, 2 Live Crew helped create a genre of rap variously known as Bass Music, Booty Music, and Miami Bass. Bass Music features quick beats, exaggerated lowend frequencies, and highly sexualized lyrics reminiscent of black comedians like Richard Pryor, Redd Foxx, and Rudy Ray Moore. Their debut album, *The 2 Live Crew Is What We Are* (1986), featured *"Throw the 'D'"* and *"We Want Some Pussy,"* underground classics that reinvigorated hip hop.

The group's graphic if goofy lyrics and outrageous stage show did not go unnoticed. In June 1990, in the wake of intensive anti-Crew lobbying efforts by Florida governor Bob Martinez and the American Family Association, a Broward County judge ruled obscene the group's third album, *As Nasty As They Wanna Be*. When a record store owner was incarcerated for selling the disc and Campbell himself was arrested for performing at a Florida club, the stage was set for a First Amendment battle that made headlines across the country. The rapper was eventually cleared of all charges, and the publicity of the trial pushed sales of the album past 3 million.

Since the trial, Campbell has continued to perform and produce Bass Music in Florida, earning regional success. He is also the host of *Luke's Peep Show*, a sexually explicit pay-per-view cable television program.

North America

Carr, Wynona

(b. August 23, 1924, Cleveland, Ohio; d. May 12, 1976), gospel singer.

Wynona Carr's first records were *Each Day* and *Lord Jesus* (both 1949), made after she had formed the Carr Singers, a gospel quintet, in 1945. She is best known for *"The Ball Game"* (1952), one of a series of songs that parallel religious and secular themes. Others are *"Dragnet for Jesus," "Fifteen Rounds for Jesus,"* and *"Operator, Operator."* Although she never enjoyed substantial commercial success, even when she tried to switch from sacred to secular songs, she left two impressive recordings: *"Our Father"* (1954)—which probably had an effect on Aretha Franklin—and the rhythm and blues hit *"Should I Ever Love Again"* (1957).

North America

Carroll, Diahann

(b. July 17, 1935, New York, N.Y.), African American singer and actor who starred in the first television series with a black woman as its main character.

Diahann Carroll grew up in a comfortable middle-class home in New York City and began singing in a church choir at age six. She won a music scholarship sponsored by the Metropolitan Opera when she was ten. Encouraged by her mother, who took her to Broadway musicals and other performances, she applied to New York's High School of Music and Art and was accepted.

Born Carol Diahann Johnson, she took her professional name at age 16 when she appeared on Arthur Godfrey's Talent Search, a television showcase for aspiring performers. Despite her parents' wish that she attend Howard University—she had earned money for college by modeling for *Ebony* magazine—she stayed in New York. She left college after one semester at New York University to accept a long-term nightclub engagement. Soon after she went on the road, singing at resorts in the Catskill Mountains and elsewhere, honing her demure, elegant image, a persona that caused one critic to describe her as "Doris Day in blackface."

At age 19 she won her first film role, costarring with Dorothy Dandridge, Harry Belafonte, and Pearl Bailey in *Carmen Jones* (1954), an all-black version of Bizet's opera. Returning to New York, Carroll next appeared in Truman Capote's *House of Flowers* on Broadway, a part that brought her a Tony Award nomination. In 1956 she married Monte Kay, a white casting director. On the set of her next movie, *Porgy and Bess* (1959), she met and fell in love with costar Sidney Poitier; their affair lasted nine years. During a brief reconciliation in 1961, Carroll and Kay had a daughter, Suzanne. Later that year, Carroll appeared again with Poitier in the film *Paris Blues* (1961).

Over the next decade Carroll had a series of successful roles, although she never escaped the racial discrimination that pervaded the entertainment industry. On the day after winning another Tony nomination for *No Strings* (1962), she learned that her role would be played in the movie version by a Eurasian actress. Between acting roles she continued to sing, appearing often in Las Vegas. Starring in *Julia*, a television series launched in 1968, Carroll played a widow who was raising her child alone. Despite the show's success, Carroll was stung by criticism of both the character's single motherhood and her unrealistically affluent lifestyle. In addition, the white press seemed to expect Carroll to act as a spokesperson for black America, an impossible task in a politically fractured era. Carroll quit the show in 1971.

Turning down offers for similar television roles, Carroll could not find anything in film to interest her until *Claudine* (1975), a realistic, gritty survivor's story in which she costarred with James Earl Jones. A series of love affairs (including two more marriages) left her financially and emotionally devastated. It was not until 1982 that she had another significant acting role, this time on Broadway in *Agnes of God*. Carroll then returned to the small screen to play "television's first black bitch" on the hit series *Dynasty*. She has also appeared on *A Different World*, a comedy about students at a historically black university.

North America

Carter, Bennett Lester (Benny)

(b. August 8, 1907, New York, N.Y.; d. July 12, 2003, Los Angeles, Calif.), African American multi-instrumentalist, one of the two great alto saxophonists of the swing era, and a groundbreaking composer and arranger for big bands, films, and television.

Benny Carter, who in his nineties is still performing, stands unrivaled among jazz musicians for the length of his career and the scope of his contributions. There have been other nonagenarians in jazz: pianist and composer Eubie Blake (1883–1983) performed publicly until he was 98; trumpeter Doc Cheatham (1905–1997) played the Blues Alley in Washington, D.C. the weekend before his death at 91; and in his late nineties, Benny Waters (1902–1998) was still playing energetic, jump-style alto saxophone. But none of these musicians can match Carter's more than 70-year musical career. Not only has Carter been continuously active, he has strongly influenced fellow musicians through his improvisations, arrangements, and overall musicianship and professionalism.

Best known—along with Johnny Hodges—as one of the two great alto saxophonists of the swing era, Carter is an exceptionally versatile musician. He is a superb soloist on trumpet, which he occasionally still plays on gigs and recording sessions. He has recorded on tenor, soprano, and C melody saxophones and on clarinet, piano, and trombone. He is also one of the foremost jazz arrangers: as jazz writer Gary Giddins has observed, Carter "is universally celebrated as the leading orchestrator of saxes." In the 1940s Carter was one of the first African American musicians to break Hollywood's color barrier. During the next quarter century, he focused more and more energy on composing and arranging for films and television. In the 1970s, however, he returned with undiminished energy to full-time jazz performance.

Carter grew up in San Juan Hill, a section of Manhattan, then one of the city's toughest neighborhoods and now the site of Lincoln Center for the Performing Arts. Trumpeter Bubber Miley lived in the neighborhood and became one of Carter's early musical idols. Carter began playing C melody saxophone in Harlem's smaller clubs while in his teens. During the mid-1920s, he started playing in larger bands, including those of Earl Hines and Fletcher Henderson. In 1927 Carter began a stint as alto saxophonist and arranger with Charlie Johnson's Paradise Ten, an important but underrated group that included Benny Waters as a sax player and arranger.

By 1930 Carter and Johnny Hodges had laid the foundations of jazz alto saxophone playing, and they reigned unchallenged until the appearance of Charlie Parker and bebop, or modern jazz in the mid-1940s. As a saxophone player, Carter is noted for his pure, rounded tone, harmonic sophistication, and virtuosity. Rather than building his solos out of repeated short phrases, known to jazz musicians as riffs, or by vertical elaboration of the song's underlying chord structure—as was typical of many jazz players during the 1930s—Carter's improvisations featured long melodic lines that prefigured the elliptical playing that characterized bebop.

In 1932 Carter organized his own band, in which Doc Cheatham played lead trumpet. Though a first-rate musician, Carter was not successful in his repeated attempts to form a lasting big band, perhaps because he lacked the requisite flamboyance and showmanship, or because the band's recordings failed to capture the public fancy. "I could never support [a big band]," he explained in 1987, "nor could it support me. I always had to be doing some outside arranging to . . . pay members of the orchestra." During the 1930s Carter also wrote a number of significant jazz compositions, including "*Waltzing the Blues*," one of the earliest jazz waltzes, and the jazz standard "*Blues in My Heart.*"

During the Great Depression, Carter disbanded his own group and joined showman Willie Bryant's orchestra. Soon Carter left the United States and began an extended sojourn in Europe (1935–1938). Initially finding work as featured sax player and arranger for the house band of Chez Florence in Paris, he later led bands and recorded in Denmark, Holland, and England. While in London, he served as staff arranger for the British Broadcasting Corporation dance orchestra (1936–1938). In 1937 he took part in a celebrated recording session in Paris with tenor saxophonist and fellow American expatriate Coleman Hawkins and jazz guitarist Django Reinhardt. Carter's classic, swinging arrangements of "*Crazy Rhythm*" and "*Honeysuckle Rose*" were written for this session.

After his return to the United States, Carter led small groups and again tried to organize a big band. Both his big band and his small combos were important incubators of bebop. In 1941 trumpeter Dizzy Gillespie—soon to emerge alongside Charlie Parker as a co-creator of bebop—was added to Carter's combo for an extended nightclub appearance in New York City. Looking back on the experience in a 1976 interview, Gillespie said, "Playing with him was my best experience next to playing with Charlie Parker . . . . [I]t'll be a long time before people . . . realize what he contributed to our music." During the mid-1940s Carter's big band featured other bebop pioneers such as trumpeter Miles Davis, drummer Max Roach, and trombonist J. J. Johnson.

In the 1940s Carter settled in Los Angeles, the city that would be his home for several decades. The event that precipitated his Hollywood career was the abrupt departure of composer William Grant Still from the set of *Stormy Weather* (1943), an all-black film starring Bill "Bojangles" Robinson and Lena Horne and featuring a wide range of African American performers, including Cab Calloway and his orchestra, pianist Thomas "Fats" Waller, and the Katherine Dunham Dancers. Carter stepped in as an instrumentalist and arranger, and his contributions included the scores for Lena Horne's renditions of *"Stormy Weather"* and *"Good for Nothin' Joe."* Although he received no screen credit, he did gain further film work.

Between 1943 and 1957 Carter played on numerous soundtracks and contributed arrangements for two dozen films, including *Portrait of Jennie* (1948), *Panic in the Streets* (1950), *An American in Paris* (1951), and *The Sun Also Rises* (1957). He also composed for television, beginning in 1958 with the police drama *M Squad*. During the 1960s he aided a number of other jazz musicians who sought work in Hollywood, including J. J. Johnson, tenor saxophonist Oliver Nelson, and Argentinean pianist Lalo Schifrin.

One of the last recordings Carter made before becoming immersed in Hollywood was the jazz classic *Further Definitions* (1961). The album featured Coleman Hawkins in a saxophone ensemble that revisited Carter's arrangements for their renowned 1937 Paris session and included new music as well. Then, after years of curtailed performances and recordings, Carter emerged from Hollywood to record his first small-group album in a decade, *The King* (1976), which marked his active return to jazz.

In recent years Carter has recorded many notable albums. *For Central City Sketches* (1987), he joined the American Jazz Orchestra in playing a number of his arrangements and compositions, including the premiere recording of his six-part *"Central City Suite." My Man Benny, My Man Phil* (1989), with alto saxophonist Phil Woods, highlighted Carter's trumpet playing on two songs. *Harlem Renaissance* (1992) featured Carter, a big band, and the Rutgers University Orchestra, with a full string section, performing two recent Carter suites, *"Tales of the Rising Sun"* and *"Harlem Renaissance."* He died on July 12, 2003 after a brief illness.

North America
_____

Carter, Betty

(b. May 16, 1930, Flint, Mich.; d. September 26, 1998, New York, N.Y.), African American jazz singer credited with integrating bebop into swing jazz style.

Betty Carter, born Lillie Mae Jones, began working as a singer in Detroit clubs when she was in high school. In 1948 she began touring with Lionel

Hampton, who gave her the nickname Betty Bebop. She settled in New York City in 1951, where she sang at the Apollo Theater, the Village Vanguard, and the Blue Note. She toured with Miles Davis (1958–1959) and Sonny Rollins (1963, Japan) and formed her own record company, Bet-Car Productions, in 1971. Carter's work includes *Baby It's Cold Outside* (1966, with Ray Charles) and *Look What I Got* (1988), for which she received a Grammy Award. In 1997 Newsday described her as the "best jazz singer alive"; the same year, she was awarded the National Medal of Arts by President Bill Clinton.

North America
Catlett, Elizabeth

(b. April 15, 1919, Washington, D.C.), African American sculptor and graphic artist whose art combines African and Mexican stylistic elements and who explores the themes of struggle and maternity.

While a student at Howard University in the 1930s, Elizabeth Catlett first encountered African sculptural art and the contemporary work of the Mexican muralists. These two art traditions inform most of Catlett's *oeuvre*. Her sculpted figures have the same voluminous, rounded forms of the people portrayed in the murals of such Mexican artists as Diego Rivera. At the same time, the faces of Catlett's sculpted figures have an owl-like, lunar quality that seems to be derived from African mask design. This stylized facial quality can also be observed in some of Catlett's graphic work, especially in her lithographs. In her linocuts, on the other hand, the faces and bodies of figures are rendered in a more realistic manner; these linocuts are stylistically related to the work of printmakers at the Taller de Gráfica Popular in Mexico City, where Catlett studied in 1946–1947. She combined what she learned in Mexico with what she observed in African art to create a unique idiom for representing the daily struggles of Mexicans and African Americans.

After graduating from Howard University's School of Art with honors in 1937, she pursued an M.F.A. at the University of Iowa, where she changed her concentration from painting to sculpture. Her thesis project, a sculpture entitled *Mother and Child*, was the first of Catlett's many works exploring the theme of maternity. It won the first-place award for sculpture at the 1941 American Negro Exposition in Chicago. This recognition led to a teaching appointment at Dillard University in New Orleans. After two years at Dillard, Catlett married artist Charles White, and the two of them taught briefly at Hampton University in Virginia before settling in New York City. There, Catlett taught art at the George Washington Carver School and studied lithography at the Art Students' League.

In 1946 Catlett was awarded a Rosenwald Fellowship to go to Mexico to execute a series on African American women. During her first year in Mexico, Catlett's marriage to Charles White fell apart. They divorced, and she married Mexican painter Francisco Mora in 1947. Catlett remained in Mexico and continued working at the Taller de Gráfica Popular. Of the Taller she said, "It was a great social experience because I learned how to use art for the service of people, struggling people, to whom only realism is meaningful." Through studies at local art schools, Catlett improved her ability to sculpt in wood, ceramics, and stone. In 1959 she became the first female teacher at the School of Fine Arts at the National Autonomous University of Mexico, serving as the head of the sculpture department. In 1962 she became a Mexican citizen. After her retirement from teaching in 1976, Catlett and her husband moved to Cuernavaca, where they have continued to work in adjacent studios.

Catlett's sculpture and works on paper have won acclaim in Mexico and the United States and can be found in major collections in both countries. She has frequently traveled back and forth between Mexico and the United States to exhibit and speak about her artwork. On April 1, 1961, she delivered a speech titled "The Negro People and American Art at Mid-Century" at the National Conference of Negro Artists. On this occasion, she encouraged artists to look to black people for inspiration and to exhibit in black community spaces. "I have always wanted my art to service my people," she said, "to reflect us, to relate to us, to stimulate us, to make us aware of our potential . . . . We have to create an art for liberation and for life."

North America

Chapman, Tracy
(b. March 20, 1964, Cleveland, Ohio), African American singer and songwriter.

When Tracy Chapman's self-titled debut album was released in 1988, its success—more than 10 million records sold and 3 Grammy nominations—was unprecedented for an artist who had just months before performed only in local coffeehouses and on street corners in the Boston, Massachusetts, area. Her hit singles "Talkin' Bout a Revolution" and "Fast Car," and appearances at such newsworthy concerts as the tribute to African National Congress leader Nelson Mandela on his 70th birthday, helped seal her reputation as the originator of a new wave in politically aware folk music.

Raised by a single mother, often in near poverty, Chapman says she understood "social conditions and political situations" from an early age. When she was in sixth grade she got her first guitar and immediately began writing songs of her own. On scholarship, she attended the Wooster School, a private boarding school in Connecticut, before enrolling in Tufts University in Medford, Massachusetts.

While at Tufts, Chapman became a popular local street musician. After seeing her at a South Africa protest rally, a classmate helped her secure a contract with an agent, who landed her an audition with Elektra Records. Despite what Chapman herself thought was probably an unmarketable style—direct, unadorned, and personal—her first album was an astonishing commercial and critical success. Her subsequent records, *Crossroads* (1989), *Matters of the Heart* (1992), and *New Beginning* (1995), have fared less well but have confirmed her reputation as a perceptive, intelligent, and complex songwriter.

Charles, Ray (Ray Charles Robinson)

(b. September 23, 1930, Albany, Ga., d. June 10, 2004, Beverly Hills, Calif.), African American rhythm and blues (R&B) pianist and singer, known as the father of Soul.

During the 1950s and 1960s Ray Charles was a key figure in the development of rhythm and blues, an African American style that transformed American popular music. Charles and other black R&B musicians gave popular music a broader expressive range and a powerful rhythmic drive, laying the groundwork for rock 'n' roll. In particular, Charles was a leader in incorporating the gospel music of the black church into secular music, investing his compositions with propulsive energy and emotional power.

Born Ray Charles Robinson, he grew up in Greenville, Florida, where his parents, Aretha and Baily Robinson, moved when he was an infant. The United States was experiencing the worst years of the Great Depression, and Charles recalled, "Even compared to other blacks . . . we were on the bottom . . . . Nothing below us except the ground." At the age of four Charles developed glaucoma, and before he turned seven, he lost his sight. His mother secured his admission to the School for the Deaf and Blind in St. Augustine, Florida, where he spent the next eight years, during which time he learned to play the clarinet, piano, and alto saxophone. He also studied composition and learned to arrange music in Braille.

In 1945, following the death of his mother, Charles left the school. He formed a musical combo and played in jook joints. Finding Florida a difficult place to survive as a musician, he asked guitarist Gosady McGee what city in the continental United States was farthest from Florida. McGee's answer—Seattle, Washington—gave the two musicians a destination.

Charles quickly established himself in the small Seattle-area musical community and befriended a young musician named Quincy Jones. With bass player Milt Jarrett, who was also from Seattle, Charles and McGee formed a trio whose style and instrumentation mirrored those of the popular Nat King Cole Trio. Aside from Cole, Charles's early piano style and singing reflected that of blues balladeer Leroy Carr and pianist Charles Brown. In 1949 he traveled to Los Angeles and made his first recordings for the small Swingtime label. "*Baby Let Me Hold Your Hand*" (1950) earned him a following in the black community, and he began touring with bluesman Lowell Fulson. During these years, Charles became addicted to heroin. Although never serving an extended jail sentence, he was arrested for narcotics possession in 1955, 1961, and 1965. After his third arrest, he stopped performing for a year, taking time off to kick his 17-year-old habit.

In 1952 Atlantic Records bought Charles's contract from Swingtime. Charles recorded for Atlantic from 1952 to 1959 and quickly emerged as one of its biggest stars. His recording of "*I Got a Woman*" (1954) spent 19 weeks on the R&B charts and marked the first appearance of his classic style. The song draws on black sacred music—it is based on a gospel song popularized by Alex Bradford—but when Charles sang, "She saves her lovin', early in the mornin', just for me," there was no doubt that his meaning was secular, not sacred. The musical arrangement and delivery reinforce the sexual undertone. Charles begins with a drawn-out, unaccompanied "well," and then the horn section

Ray Charles at Piano, ca. 1960. *Bettmann/CORBIS*

joins in, pushing the beat and acting as an "amen" chorus. He heightens the intensity with intricate vocal ornamentation known as melisma, which conveys a sense of emotional intensity by bending and altering the pitches of notes, and at times his voice soars into a transcendent falsetto.

Charles collaborated with Quincy Jones on two important albums, *The Genius* (1959) for Atlantic and *Genius + Soul=Jazz* (1961) for Impulse! Records, a subsidiary of ABC-Paramount Records. In 1960 he signed with ABC-Paramount and recorded his best-loved hit, a version of Hoagy Carmichael's "*Georgia On My Mind*" (1960) that in 1979 became the official song of the state of Georgia.

During the 1960s Charles branched out into other musical styles, including country and western, such as "*Your Cheatin' Heart*" (1962), and middle-of-the-road pop music, such as "*You Are My Sunshine*" (1962); he even released a rendition of the Beatles' "*Eleanor Rigby*" (1968). He won a following that crossed racial lines, but his long-time fans lamented that some of this later work lacked the inspiration and edge of his Atlantic recordings. In 1961 he organized a successful big band that included such blues-grounded jazz players as David "Fathead" Newman.

During the 1980s Charles achieved the status of popular-culture icon. In 1986 he was one of the first inductees in the Rock and Roll Hall of Fame. Two years later, he provided the voiceover for a television commercial for the California Raisin Advisory Board, and in 1990 he appeared in a series of Diet Coke commercials that won accolades from the advertising industry and an enthusiastic response from the American public.

Checker, Chubby

(b. October 3, 1941, South Carolina), singer best known for his hit song "The Twist."

Born Ernest Evans, Chubby Checker grew up in Philadelphia, Pennsylvania, and worked plucking chickens in a poultry market. He first gained attention singing with the Quantrells on street corners in the evenings. His supervisor at work was impressed with his voice and introduced him to producers at the Cameo-Parkway label, where he was signed in 1959. One of his first songs, *"The Class,"* reached the Top 40 later that year and led to an appearance on the Philadelphia dance show *American Bandstand*, hosted by Dick Clark. Clark's wife suggested that Evans change his name to Chubby Checker to model Fats Domino, a popular blues singer.

Renamed, Checker got a break when Hank Ballard failed to appear for the American Bandstand session and Checker played Ballard's song *"The Twist."* The song quickly reached number one on the pop charts, and sold over 3 million records. This television appearance started a nationwide dance craze. Checker went on to record 20 Top 40 hits by 1964, including *"Pony Time," "Slow Twisting,"* and *"Limbo Rock."* His song *"Let's Twist Again"* was also a hit in Great Britain and sold even more copies there than the original.

Although he was never able to achieve that level of success again, Checker broadened his music to include rhythm and blues, disco, and rap. He also made several appearances on television and in movies demonstrating the twist. He continues to perform with his band, the Wildcats.

Chesnutt, Charles Waddell

(b. June 20, 1858, Cleveland, Ohio; d. November 15, 1932, Cleveland, Ohio), pioneering African American writer known especially for his short stories, which realistically depicted black life.

Charles W. Chesnutt was one of the first African American writers to become a mainstream success by portraying realistically the complexities of African American experience. In the process, he was unusually honest about the problems inherent in that experience, and his stories remain valuable for their descriptions of nineteenth-century black culture and attitudes.

Chesnutt's parents were mixed-race free blacks who had emigrated to Ohio but moved back south to Fayetteville, North Carolina, shortly after his birth. Chesnutt grew up during Reconstruction in relative privilege for an African American, and although he had a reputation for being largely self-taught, he attended a school founded by the Freedmen's Bureau. After working as a schoolteacher and then a principal in Southern schools during his late teens and early twenties, Chesnutt decided that he was too stifled by Southern racism and returned to the North to expand his opportunities.

In 1884 he settled back in Cleveland and began studying law, ultimately passing the bar exam and beginning a career as a legal stenographer. But Chesnutt had already begun writing short fiction, which was published in several local magazines and newspapers. In 1887 his first major story, "The Goophered Grapevine," was published in the *Atlantic Monthly*. It featured Uncle Julius McAdoo, a North Carolina exslave, telling stories about plantation life, and was rich in the descriptions of African American folk culture and "voudou" beliefs that came to characterize many of Chesnutt's works. "The Goophered Grapevine" was praised by both black and white critics and brought the author to a national audience.

Chesnutt continued to publish individual stories, and in the late 1890s the mainstream Boston publisher Houghton Mifflin decided to collect his works in two volumes. *The Conjure Woman* appeared in March 1899, followed that fall by *The Wife of His Youth and Other Stories of the Color Line*. The stories in these books continue the exploration of hoodoo and magic begun in "The Goophered Grapevine," but they also deal with some of the phenomena peculiar to American race relations, especially the tangled family lines that were a result of slavery and miscegenation. Chesnutt's tales attacked white prejudice and racism in their varied forms. But they also explored the "color line" drawn not only between whites and blacks, but also within the black race. His stories include serious considerations of skin color prejudice and the impulse to "pass," unusual subjects in the literature of the time. Both books were successful, and they made Chesnutt the best-known African American fiction writer of his time.

Encouraged by this success, Chesnutt began writing full-time, which gave him the opportunity to write longer works. His biography of Frederick Douglass (1899) was well received, but he then began writing novels, which never found the widespread audience that his stories had. Three novels published between 1900 and 1905 sold poorly, and eventually Chesnutt resumed his full-time career as a stenographer. But his black audience did not forget his influence on African American literature. In 1928 the National Association for the Advancement of Colored People gave him the Spingarn Medal, its highest honor, for his "pioneer work as a literary artist depicting the life and struggles of Americans of Negro descent." Chesnutt's work remains in print, and *The Norton Anthology of African American Literature* calls him "the first writer to make the broad range of African American experience his artistic province and to consider practically every issue and problem endemic to the American color line worthy of literary attention."

North America

Chess Records,

an influential record company that recorded African American rhythm and blues (R&B) and Chicago blues.

Chess Records had a profound impact on American popular culture, popularizing the Chicago blues of Muddy Waters and Howlin' Wolf, and—through the infectious music of Chuck Berry—providing a major catalyst for the rise of rock 'n' roll. Phillip and Leonard Chess were Polish Jews who settled in Chicago, Illinois, and became involved in recording as an adjunct to their Macomba Lounge, a nightclub on Chicago's south side, the heart of the city's black community. They founded Chess in 1949–1950 as a successor to Aristocrat Records (1946–1949), which released the first recordings of Muddy Waters as a leader. For Chess, Waters produced several R&B hits, including *"I'm Your Hoochie Coochie Man"* (1953) and *"I'm Ready"* (1954). He also recommended a young Chuck Berry to the Chess brothers, and Berry's first release, *"Maybelline"* (1955), helped make rock 'n' roll the new youth music.

The Chess offices were in a street-level storefront. Music writer Arnold Shaw noted that the unassuming quarters made it easier for black musicians simply to walk in, as Bo Diddley, Sonny Boy Williamson, and Willie Mabon did. Chess recordings, notorious for their muffled, boxy sound, were produced in the back room of the office. To add echo, the Chess brothers hung a microphone in the bathroom. The poor sound quality of Chess recordings— and the prospect of a stronger national distribution—led the Flamingos, a successful vocal harmony group, to leave Chess in 1956 for Decca.

Besides Chicago blues and rock 'n' roll, Chess released hit recordings by vocal groups, such as the Moonglows' *"Sincerely"* (1954) and the Flamingos' *"I'll Be Home"* (1956), and, between 1960 and 1963, a string of ten Top 10 R&B singles by Etta James. In 1969, when Leonard Chess died, his brother sold Chess Records. By the 1990s the massive Music Corporation of America (MCA) owned the label and its catalogue.

North America

Childress, Alice

(b. October 12, 1920, Charleston, S.C.; d. August 14, 1994, Long Island, N.Y.), African American playwright and novelist and the first black woman to win an Obie.

Alice Childress was the award-winning author of over a dozen plays and novels focusing on the plight of the poor, the role of community, and the struggle of blacks against racism, sexism, and classism. Born in South Carolina, she was raised in Harlem by her grandmother, Eliza Campbell, who inspired her early love of art and concern for the poor. Childress attended Public School 81, Julia Ward Howe Elementary School, and Wadleigh High School, which she left after three years.

Her playwriting career began in 1943 with the start of her 11-year association with the American Negro Theatre, where she was instrumental in the organization's development. Her plays include *Florence* (1949), *Wine in The Wilderness* (1966), and *Moms* (1987). She was the first black woman to win an Obie Award, which she received for *Trouble in Mind* (1955). Although best known for her plays, she also produced a number of novels and children's books, including *Short Walk* (1979) and *Those Other People* (1990). Her numerous awards included a Rockefeller Grant, Writer-in-Residence at the MacDowell Colony, and a Harvard University appointment at the Bunting Institute. On July 17, 1957, she married Nathan Woodward, an artist and musician, with whom she lived until her death on Long Island, New York, in 1994.

Clarke, John Henrik

(b. January 1, 1915, Union Springs, Ala.; d. July 16, 1998, New York, N.Y.), African American writer, educator, and Pan-African nationalist.

John Henrik Clarke was a central figure in late-twentieth-century vernacular American Black Nationalism. As a teacher, writer, and popular public speaker, he emphasized black pride, African heritage—especially communalism—and black solidarity. From the rural South he rode a freight train to New York, where he actively participated in the literary and political life of Harlem in the 1930s. Arthur Schomburg, the black bibliophile, was a major intellectual influence. Largely self-educated, Clarke became professor of Africana and Puerto Rican Studies at New York's Hunter College and president of Sankofa University, an online Internet school.

Born to sharecropping parents, Clarke grew up in Columbus, Georgia, and aspired to be a writer. He produced poetry, short stories (notably "The Boy Who Painted Christ Black"), and books on African history (*The Lives of Great African Chiefs*) and on Africans in the diaspora (*Harlem U.S.A.*). An original member of the Harlem Writers Guild and a founding editor of *Freedomways* magazine, he is perhaps best known as the editor of William Styron's *Nat Turner: Ten Black Writers Respond* (1970), a critique of Styron's fictionalized version of Turner and the Southampton slave revolt.

Clarke served in the United States Air Force and attended New York University and the New School for Social Research. Beginning in 1964 he headed a federal antipoverty program. An active supporter of Pan-African political movements, he was on a first-name basis with many African leaders, and his Harlem home was a way station for visiting Africans. Clarke joined the faculty of Hunter College in 1969 and established the black studies program there and at Cornell. He was professor emeritus at Hunter and a highly sought-after speaker until his death at age 83. The following statement perhaps best summarizes his philosophy: "Wherever we are on the face of the earth, we are an African people."

Cleaver, Eldridge Leroy

(b. August 31, 1935, Wabbaseka, Ark.; d. May 1, 1998, Pomona, Calif.), African American writer, political activist, and former minister of information for the Black Panther Party.

After growing up in Wabbaseka, Arkansas, and Los Angeles, California, Eldridge Cleaver spent much of his young adulthood in the California state penitentiary system. Convicted on drug and rape charges in 1953 and 1958, he used his prison time to broaden his education. During this time, Cleaver studied the teachings of the Nation of Islam and became a devoted supporter of Malcolm X. With the assassination of Malcolm X in 1965, Cleaver broke his ties to the Nation of Islam and sought to carry on the mission of Malcolm X's Organization of Afro-American Unity.

Paroled in 1966, Cleaver went to work as an editor and writer for *Ramparts* magazine. Soon after his introduction to Huey Newton and Bobby Seale, cofounders of the Black Panther Party, in Oakland, California, Cleaver joined the Panthers and became the party's minister of information. In this role, he called on black men to "pick up the gun" against the United States government.

The year 1968 was one of turning points for Cleaver. He established himself as a gifted essayist and cultural critic with the publication of *Soul on Ice*, a collection of prison writings that earned him the Martin Luther King Memorial Prize in 1970. Also in 1968, Cleaver was selected as the presidential candidate of the Peace and Freedom Party. After a shoot-out in Oakland that left Cleaver and a police officer wounded and 17-year-old Bobby Hutton dead, Cleaver was charged with assault and attempted murder. His parole was revoked. Believing his life was in danger, Cleaver fled the country in November 1968.

He spent the next seven years in Cuba, France, and Algeria with his wife, Kathleen Neal Cleaver. Still actively involved with the Panthers, Cleaver published essays in *Black Scholar, Ramparts,* and the *Black Panther,* and served as the head of the International Section of the Black Panther Party in Algeria. After visits to North Korea, North Vietnam, and the People's Republic of China, however, Cleaver became increasingly critical of Marxist governments. A deal with the FBI allowed him to return to the United States in 1975 with a sentence of more than one thousand hours of community service.

After returning to the United States, his commitments shifted toward conservative politics and fundamentalist Christianity. He describes this transformation in *Soul on Fire,* which appeared in 1978. Cleaver lectured on religion and politics in the 1980s and ran as an independent candidate for Ronald Dellums's seat in the House of Representatives in 1984. After dropping out of the congressional race, Cleaver ran for a seat on the Berkeley, California, City Council. His ongoing struggle with drugs became public in 1994, when Cleaver was arrested in Berkeley.

A varied and prolific writer, Cleaver authored numerous political pamphlets, short stories, and poetry. His books *Eldridge Cleaver: Post-Prison Writings and Speeches* and *Eldridge Cleaver's Black Papers* both appeared in 1969. *The Black Panther Leaders Speak: Huey P. Newton, Bobby Seale, Eldridge Cleaver, and Company Speak Out Through the Black Panther Party's Official Newspaper* was published seven years later.

North America

Cleveland, James Edward

(b. December 3, 1931, Chicago, Ill.; d. February 9, 1991, Los Angeles, Calif.), African American gospel singer and composer known as the Crown Prince of Gospel.

A child prodigy, James Edward Cleveland began playing the piano when he was five years old. His family was too poor to afford a piano, so Cleveland practiced on the windowsill, painting the ledge with black and white keys. Growing up in Chicago, he was surrounded by the legends of the first generation of gospel music. At the age of eight, he sang as a soloist for the Junior Gospel Choir at Pilgrim Baptist Church directed by the father of gospel music, Thomas A. Dorsey. Cleveland was also influenced by the Roberta Martin Singers, particularly Roberta Martin's piano playing.

By the time he was 15, Cleveland had joined the Thorne Crusaders, with whom he sang around Chicago until 1954. During this time he began composing, and wrote "*Grace Is Sufficient*" for his idols, the Roberta Martin Singers, when he was 16. The song has now become a gospel standard. In 1950 he joined Norsalus McKissick and Bessie Folk, two former Roberta Martin Singers, to form the trio the Gospelaires. After he left the Thorne Crusaders, Cleveland played piano and arranged for Albertina Walker's Caravans. His work with the Caravans solidified his reputation as an emerging star among the second generation of gospel performers.

During the latter half of the 1950s he composed, arranged, and performed with several groups, including the Meditations in Detroit, Michigan, the Gospel All-Stars in Brooklyn, and the Gospel Chimes in Chicago. Cleveland recorded with the Voices of Tabernacle Choir of Detroit in 1960. Together they performed the Soul Stirrers' song "*The Love of God*," which became a popular hit. According to scholar Tony Heilbut, with this recording "Cleveland simultaneously ushered in the decade and the modern gospel sound."

Capitalizing on this recent success, he signed a contract with Savoy Records to make several recordings with the Angelic Choir of Nutley, New Jersey. Their first recording, "*Peace Be Still*," sold over 800,000 copies and set the standard for modern gospel choir recordings. Cleveland's style moved between singing and preaching, alternating his gruff shouting with sweet falsetto. He used the choir as a response to his call and always recorded with a live congregation, a technique that combined the traditions of the Baptist and Holiness churches. Cleveland often claimed to be "part Baptist, part Sanctified."

During the 1950s and 1960s, his most prolific decades, Cleveland composed over 500 songs. His most popular included "*Oh, Lord, Stand By Me*," "*He's Using Me*," and "*Walk On by Faith*." Cleveland wrote in a colloquial style about everyday trials of the poor. Lyrics such as "One day I woke up, I had no food on the table/ But the God I serve, I know he's able," earned him the moniker "Knife and Fork King."

In 1968 Cleveland founded the Gospel Music Workshop of America to serve as an alternative for young performers to Dorsey's National Convention of Gospel Choirs and Choruses. By the mid-1980s the Workshop boasted several hundred thousand members. Cleveland trained and inspired many performers, most notably Aretha Franklin. In 1970 he founded the Cornerstone Institutional Baptist Church in Los Angeles, which held 7,000 charter members at his death in 1991.

Cliff, Jimmy

(b. James Chambers) (b. April 1, 1948, Somerton, Jamaica), Jamaican musician whose film career introduced many Americans and Europeans to reggae.

Like many Jamaicans, Jimmy Cliff migrated from the countryside to Kingston, the country's capital, during the political upheaval that accompanied Jamaica's independence in 1962. At the time of the move, Cliff was 14 and already had been singing and playing music for years. He sought opportunity and adventure in Kingston, finding both when his improvised rendition of "*Dearest Beverley*" inspired a partnership between himself and a Chinese storeowner, Leslie Kong, who agreed to record and produce his music. By the age of 15 Cliff had become a Kingston celebrity. In the early 1960s he toured with a ska band, appeared in the promotional video *This Is Ska*, and recorded early hits such as "*Hurricane Hattie*," "*King of Kings*," and "*Miss Jamaica*."

In 1964 Cliff appeared at the New York World's Fair and soon after moved to England to record for Island Records. He achieved widespread popularity in the Caribbean and Europe by 1965 but did not win a significant American following until "*Wonderful World, Beautiful People*" became a hit in 1970. Also popular were his protest song "*Vietnam*" (lauded by Bob Dylan) and his cover of Cat Stevens's "*Wild World*."

Cliff appeared in a semi-autobiographical film, *The Harder They Come* in 1970. Released in the United States in 1973, the movie introduced many Americans to Jamaica's new music. *The Harder They Come* tells the story of a gun-slinging pop star who has risen from rural origins to achieve urban notoriety. Despite the success of the film's soundtrack, which featured Cliff's hit "*Many Rivers to Cross*," the film propelled his own career less than he had expected. Instead, it primed American audiences for the music of Bob Marley, the first global superstar of reggae. Ironically, Cliff himself introduced Marley to Kong, aiding a career that would eventually eclipse his own.

Although conditions were ripe for Cliff to follow Marley's lead, he opted instead to explore new directions with his music, releasing *Another Cycle* (1980), an album of soul and rhythm and blues songs recorded in the United States. In the records that followed, Cliff moved toward a pop music sound that never won him popularity. Indeed, since *The Harder They Come*, Cliff's career has been characterized by sporadic and limited success. He released albums throughout the 1980s and 1990s, appeared in the 1986 movie *Club Paradise* alongside Robin Williams, and continues to tour. His crowning accomplishment, however, remains his hep personification of the reggae scene in *The Harder They Come*.

Clinton, George

(b. July 22, 1940, Kannapolis, N.C.), African American musician, pioneer of funk style.

George Clinton grew up in Plainfield, New Jersey, where he worked in a barbershop straightening hair and formed a musical group, the Parliaments. After moving to Detroit, Clinton and the Parliaments had a minor hit, *"(I Just Wanna) Testify,"* in 1967.

Following a lawsuit over the band's name, Clinton formed not one but two new groups, with many overlapping players: the legendary Parliament and Funkadelic (known collectively as P-Funk). Parliament was more commercial; Funkadelic was outlandish, with musicians wearing diapers, Clinton emerging from a coffin, and plenty of references to sex and drugs. The bands merged in the 1970s, and their concerts, featuring such spectacles as giant spaceships landing onstage, became a major attraction.

For all his eccentricity, Clinton was an influential spokesman for African Americans; his song *"Chocolate City"* expresses, in terms both witty and poignant, the dream of an all-black government. Clinton and his many sidemen have swayed post-1970 musical styles. With Bootsy Collins playing bass and Bernie Worrell playing keyboards, P-Funk helped define funk, then helped push this genre into unpredictable new territory. Although Clinton has had little commercial success, he has vitally influenced both African American and white audiences.

North America

Cole, Nat ("King")

(b. March 17, 1919, Montgomery, Ala., as Nathaniel Adams Cole; d. February 15, 1965, Santa Monica, Calif.), African American pianist and singer; one of the most stylistically advanced jazz pianists of the 1940s and a leading popular singer of the 1950s and 1960s.

With a preaching father and musical brothers, Nat King Cole grew up amid performance and music. As a child he lived in Chicago, playing the organ in his father's church and performing in his brother Eddie's ensemble, the Solid Swingers. Cole began his career as a pianist in 1936 when he joined Eubie Blake's traveling revue *Shuffle Along*.

In 1937 Cole settled in Los Angeles and formed a trio with guitarist Oscar Moore and bassist Wesley Prince. In the early recordings of the combo, Cole displayed harmonic and melodic innovation that only his finest contemporaries—Art Tatum and Duke Ellington—could rival. Despite the extraordinary talents of both Moore and Cole, the combo met with limited success, due largely to the era's nearly exclusive demand for the music of big bands. The group achieved its first major success in 1944 with *"Straighten Up and Fly Right,"* which featured a stellar three-part vocal arrangement.

In 1946 his version of Mel Torme's *"The Christmas Song"* became Cole's first mainstream hit. In this and many subsequent recordings, Cole showcased his sultry voice, singing highly orchestrated pop ballads. In 1948 he sold a million records with *"Nature Boy"*; other hits included *"Route 66"*

(1946), "*Unforgettable*" (1950), and "*Mona Lisa*" (1950). Although Cole continued to record jazz, he shifted his focus from piano to voice, and his pop ballads soon wooed white as well as black audiences. In the late 1940s Cole's combo became the first black group to have its own radio program. In 1956 Cole landed a weekly television show, which was canceled, however, when producers failed to attract companies that would sponsor a black artist.

Although he achieved great popularity as a singer, Cole received little recognition for his innovations as a pianist, and many fans had no knowledge of his early career. Yet by the age of 21 Cole had established advanced chord voicings and harmonic substitutions that bebop innovators such as Charlie Parker were just beginning to discover. Cole's melodic style can be seen as an important link between swing and bebop.

Cole died of lung cancer in 1965, just as his financial and popular success seemed to be peaking. In 1991, however, he experienced an uncanny flourish of posthumous success when his daughter, Natalie Cole, released an album of technologically contrived duets in which she sang atop her father's original recordings.

Europe

Coleridge-Taylor, Samuel

(b. August 15, 1875, Holborn, England; d. September 1, 1912, Croydon, England), Afro-English composer and conductor, one of the most important late nineteenth century composers of African descent.

In the late 1890s Samuel Coleridge-Taylor gained worldwide recognition as a composer and conductor who successfully brought West African and black American influences into the realm of classical music. He was a leading exponent of Pan-Africanism, which emphasized the importance of a shared African heritage as the touchstone of black cultural identity. According to music scholar Jewel Taylor Thompson, Coleridge-Taylor endeavored to produce "compositions which would do for Negro music what Brahms, Dvořák, and Grieg had done respectively with folk music of Hungary, Bohemia, and Norway."

Coleridge-Taylor grew up in Holborn, England, the son of an Englishwoman and an African physician from Sierra Leone. He began violin study at age seven with a local orchestral conductor who tutored him for seven years. In 1890 he entered London's Royal College of Music, where he soon revealed his talent for composition and conducted his works in college concerts. In the mid-1890s he began to incorporate African American idioms into his music—an innovation inspired by his friendship with the black American poet Paul Laurence Dunbar and London performances of the Fisk Jubilee Singers. He composed African Romances, seven vocal pieces set to Dunbar's poems, and performed with the poet in a joint recital in London. In 1898 he collaborated with Dunbar on the operetta *Dream Lovers* and composed *Danse nègre*, his first large-scale orchestral work to embrace black American folk themes.

The year 1898 proved critical for Coleridge-Taylor's career as a composer: thanks to the recommendation of British composer Sir Edward Elgar, he was commissioned to write an orchestral piece—his *Ballade in A-Minor*—for England's Three Choirs Festival. Two months later he premiered his widely popular *Hiawatha's Wedding Feast*, the first part of a trilogy based on Longfellow's *The Song of Hiawatha*. Both works received rave reviews in the London papers, and the Hiawatha piece, whose overture theme was drawn from the African American spiritual "*Nobody Knows the Trouble I've Seen*," secured his fame in England and abroad.

During the following decade Coleridge-Taylor composed several works with African and black American-derived rhythms and melodies, such as *Twenty-Four Negro Melodies Transcribed for the Piano* (1905), *Symphonic Variations on an African Air* (1906), and the orchestral rhapsody *Bamboula* (1910), named after a West Indian dance. He toured the United States three times, conducting concerts of his music and performing with such musicians as Harry T. Burleigh and Will Marion Cook.

In August 1912, at the age of 37, Coleridge-Taylor died of acute pneumonia. His music and Pan-Africanist ideas continued to exert considerable influence on African American composers, several of whom became leading figures of New York City's Harlem Renaissance. According to musicologist Samuel A. Floyd Jr., "Societies bearing [Coleridge-Taylor's] name sprang up in cities across the United States in the early years of the twentieth century . . . , [and he] probably served as a model for composers such as Robert Nathaniel Dett, William Grant Still, and Florence Price."

North America

Colescott, Robert H.

(b. August 26, 1925, Oakland, Calif.), African American painter whose raucous, colorful works deal with racial themes.

Robert H. Colescott parodies traditional paintings of historical events with an ironic wit and a lushly expressive style. Since the 1970s he has painted reinterpretations of many of the most famous paintings of Western art, substituting African Americans for white figures in these well-known works. In *George Washington Carver Crossing the Delaware: Page from an American History Textbook* (1975, Robert H. Orchard Collection, Cincinnati, Ohio), Colescott recast the characters from a well-known work by the American painter Emanuel Leutze, Washington Crossing the Delaware (1851, Metropolitan Museum of Art, New York City), as caricatures of early twentieth-century black minstrels. Colescott's borrowings honor great paintings even as they criticize them. *Les Demoiselles d'Alabama (Des Nudas)* (1985, Greenville County Museum of Art, South Carolina), for example, is a tribute to the Spanish artist Pablo Picasso's *Demoiselles d'Avignon* (1907,

Museum of Modern Art, New York City); at the same time, Colescott ironically alludes to Picasso's use of art forms then considered primitive, such as African masks. More recently Colescott's paintings have addressed current racial issues such as urban violence (*Emergency Room*, 1989, Museum of Modern Art, New York City), the subjugation of black women, and the complexities of racial mixing.

Colescott earned both his B.A. (1949) and his M.A. (1952) from the University of California at Berkeley. He studied in Paris in 1949 and 1950 with the French artist Fernand Léger, who urged him to avoid abstraction, a form of art that Léger considered too remote from the interests of most people. Nevertheless, in his early career Colescott explored both abstract and representational painting and was strongly influenced by the figurative paintings of artists of the San Francisco Bay Area, such as Richard Diebenkorn and Joan Brown.

North America

Coltrane, John William

(b. September 23, 1926, Hamlet, N.C.; d. July 17, 1967, Long Island, N.Y.), African American jazz saxophonist, composer, band leader, and stylistic and compositional innovator, widely recognized as the leader of the New Thing or Free Jazz avant-garde movement of the 1960s.

Shortly after John Coltrane was born, his family moved to a lower-middle-class neighborhood in High Point, North Carolina. The Coltranes lived within an extended family headed by Rev. William Blair, John's maternal grandfather, and they followed him to High Point when he accepted a pastorate there. John's father was a tailor and an amateur musician who sang and played the ukulele for his own enjoyment. His mother, Alice Coltrane (not to be confused with Coltrane's second wife of the same name), was a seamstress who sang and played piano in her father's gospel choir, and at one point wanted to be a concert pianist. Also included in Rev. Blair's household were his daughter, Betty; her husband, Goler; and their daughter, Mary. Cousin Mary (who was immortalized by a song with the same title on Coltrane's first album as a leader) was an only child like John, and the two of them grew up as siblings. While not well-to-do by black middle-class standards of today, Coltrane was protected from the poverty that many of his jazz colleagues experienced and seems to have had a reasonably happy childhood. Though shy, he did well in school, had a few close friends, and participated in social activities such as the Boy Scouts of America and neighborhood bands. In grade school he was an honor student, but his studies suffered in high school as his life grew more singularly focused on music.

Adolescence brought events that disturbed the stability of Coltrane's emotional life. Within the space of a few years, all three adult males in the household died, starting with the death of his father in 1939, when John was 13 years old. His grandfather died a few months later, and within three years both his aunt and uncle died. During this period of intense change Coltrane began his lifelong study of music. Playing in a community band first on alto horn, then on clarinet, he eventually switched to alto saxophone, the instrument that he would play throughout most of his apprenticeship as a musician. No one knows for sure how much of Coltrane's absorption into music was therapeutic, but almost from the beginning he practiced for many hours daily (at times till 3:00 or 4:00 in the morning), a habit that would prove legendary after he became a professional musician.

Mastery

The year 1955 was a momentous one for Coltrane both personally and professionally: he married Juanita Grubbs (Naima) and joined the Miles Davis quintet. Coltrane's tenure with Davis lasted off and on through 1960, when he left Davis to form his own quartet. During these years, Coltrane's playing became more personal. He introduced a hard tone that struck some listeners as "hauntingly beautiful" and others as "harsh." Coltrane became a favorite among recording musicians; with Sonny Rollins he was now one of the leading hard bop voices on tenor saxophone.

In Davis's band, Coltrane's playing reached the limelight through club and concert appearances throughout the country, a few television appearances, and commercial recordings. Coltrane began to attract critical attention through such recordings as 'Round About Midnight (on the Columbia label), Steamin', Relaxin', Cookin', and Workin' (all on the Prestige label). In 1957 he was fired from Davis's band and traded places with Sonny Rollins, who left Thelonious Monk's quartet. Monk hired Coltrane for his famous Five Spot Café engagement, which lasted for several months. This engagement is legendary in jazz history for three reasons: first, it launched the Five Spot as the premiere club in New York for experimental jazz (other artists who similarly served the Five Spot were Cecil Taylor and Ornette Coleman); second, it marked the "rediscovery" of Thelonious Monk, who had been barred from playing in New York clubs through alleged police harassment; and third, during this engagement Coltrane came into maturity as a musician. In this band, he combined his astonishing technique with a set of innovative harmonic devices, developing what critic Ira Gitler famously termed "sheets of sound." Coltrane regarded Monk as a master teacher who was "a musical architect of the highest order."

Coltrane then returned to Davis's band, which became the most influential jazz combo of the late 1950s with recordings like Kind of Blue and Milestones (both on Columbia). This period marked a turning point in Coltrane's spiritual life. In 1957 he experienced a spiritual awakening that led him to tell his mother and his friend Eric Dolphy that he had seen God. Dedicating his life, and especially his music, to God, he found the strength to quit his heroin and alcohol addictions. A third phase of Coltrane's artistry emerged as he recorded under his own name and featured his original compositions. His study of Eastern religions and the music of India and Africa led him to pursue lengthy improvisations utilizing a set of pitches, or modes, rather than functional harmony as in bebop. At the same time he devised a set of harmonic formulas known today as "Coltrane substitutions." Coltrane also introduced the soprano saxophone as a viable jazz instrument, the first man to do so since Sidney Bechet over four decades earlier. Coltrane's music of this period can be heard on recordings such as *Giant Steps* (Atlantic), *Blue Train* (Blue Note), and his first "hit record," *My Favorite Things* (Atlantic).

Coltrane's fourth phase began in 1961 when he formed what became known as his classic quartet, featuring himself on tenor and soprano saxophones, McCoy Tyner on piano, either Jimmy Garrison or Reggie Workman on bass, and Elvin Jones on drums. Eric Dolphy also performed with the group periodically until his death in 1964. Coltrane had always divided jazz fans and critics into two camps, one praising and the other denouncing his music. During this stage, as his artistry developed, the distance between these two camps widened, with the fringes of each group shading toward excess. His extreme followers progressed from the adulation of fans to the reverence of devotees, while his extreme detractors not only disparaged his musical vision, but questioned his basic competence. The attacks were brutal enough for Coltrane and Dolphy to write an article with Don Demichael in *Down Beat* titled "Coltrane and Dolphy Answer the Jazz Critics." *Down Beat* solved its problem in an innovative fashion by assigning two reviewers for Coltrane records, one favorable and the other condemnatory.

The music made with his classic quartet is widely considered the high point of Coltrane's oeuvre. The quartet toured throughout the United States and Europe. Starting in 1961 Coltrane won the *Down Beat* Poll in at least one category every year. He was inducted in the *Down Beat* Hall of Fame in 1965 as Jazz Man of the Year when his landmark recording, *A Love Supreme*, was declared Record of the Year. Coltrane's work with the quartet was daringly innovative and has made him, after Charlie Parker, the most imitated saxophonist in jazz history. Also widely influential was the ensemble playing of the quartet. Coltrane was admired not only for being a musical innovator, but for the spiritual qualities of his music and persona. The music of the quartet can be heard on such recordings as *Africa Brass, Live at the Village Vanguard, Crescent, A Love Supreme, First Meditations,* and *Sun Ship* (all on Impulse).

The fifth and final stage of Coltrane's career is sometimes labeled as his avant-garde period. It began in 1966, after Tyner and Jones had both left the band, and were replaced with his wife Alice Coltrane (née Alice McCleod) on piano and Rashied Ali on drums. Pharoah Sanders (née Farrell Sanders) also joined the band on tenor and soprano saxophones. With this group Coltrane continued his explorations of sound, texture, and group improvisation, stretching the parameters of Western music. Due to Coltrane's untreated illness this band canceled its European tours, but did tour Japan in 1966. Recordings of this period include *Live at the Village Vanguard, Again, Interstellar Space, Live in Japan, Expression,* and *Stellar Regions* (all on Impulse).

Tapes found at his widow's house suggest that Coltrane was entering yet another phase of artistic development that was cut short by his death from liver cancer. The National Academy of Recording Arts and Sciences awarded him a Grammy Award for Lifetime Achievement posthumously in 1991.

North America

Combs, Sean ("Puffy")

(b. 1970, Harlem, New York), African American entrepreneur and rap impresario responsible for a string of hit records in the 1990s.

Born in Harlem and raised in Mount Vernon, New York, Combs attended Howard Univesity and started working in the music industry as an intern at Andre Harrell's Uptown Records. He moved quickly through the ranks, producing hits for Uptown artists such as Jodeci and Mary J. Blige. At the age of 22 he was made a company vice president.

In 1993 Combs left Uptown to found Bad Boy Entertainment, where he began to assemble a crew of hip hop and R&B talent. Combs served as executive producer for both albums by Bad Boy's biggest star, Notorious B.I.G. After the 1997 shooting death of Notorious B.I.G., Combs (who raps as Puff Daddy) recorded a tribute song titled "*I'll Be Missing You.*" The single was a smash hit, and it sent Puff Daddy's solo debut album, *No Way Out*, to the top of the charts. *No Way Out* picked up two Grammy Awards, including Best Rap Album, and Combs was named *Soul Train*'s entertainer of the year.

Sean "Puffy" Combs's undistinguished, monotonous rapping style has come under fire in some hip hop circles, but his remarkable success as a producer is incontrovertible. His instantly recognizable rewrites of hit songs (culled from artists as diverse as David Bowie, The Temptations, and Led Zeppelin) have made multiplatinum stars out of rappers such as Lil' Kim and Mase, as well as Notorious B.I.G. and Combs himself. Indeed, as producer and performer, Sean "Puffy" Combs held the Number-One spot on the *Billboard* singles chart for an astonishing 22 weeks in 1997.

North America

Conwell, Kathleen

(b. March 18, 1942, N.J.; d. September 1988), African American playwright and screenwriter whose films have been shown on the Learning Channel and the Public Broadcasting Service.

Kathleen Conwell was born and raised in New Jersey. After receiving a B.A. in philosophy and religion from Skidmore College, she became a member of the Student Nonviolent Coordinating Committee (SNCC). In 1966 she graduated from the Sorbonne in Paris with an M.A. in film. She started her writing career working for radio station WNET in New York City. She began teaching film history and screenwriting at the City University of New York in 1974.

Conwell wrote her first screenplay, an adaptation of a Henry Roth short story, in 1980. That same year she produced and directed *The Cruz Brothers and Mrs. Malloy*, which won first prize in the Sinking Creek Film Festival. She wrote and directed *Losing Ground* (1982), which won first prize at the Figueroa da Foz International Film Festival in Portugal, as well as *Madame Flor* (1987) and *Conversations with Julie* (1988). Her films have been shown on the Learning Channel and the Public Broadcasting Station.

Conwell has written several plays, including *In the Midnight Hour* (1981) and *The Reading* (1984). Theatre Communications Group named Conwell's play *The Brothers* one of 12 outstanding plays of the 1982 season. In addition to *Begin the Beguine* (1985) and *Only the Sky Is Free* (1985), a play about Bessie Coleman, she wrote *While Older Men Speak* (1986) and *Looking for Jane*. In 1988 she wrote a novel, *Lollie: A Suburban Tale*; in September of that year she died of cancer.

North America

Cooke, Samuel (Sam)

(b. January 22, 1931, Clarksdale, Miss., as Sam Cook; d. December 11, 1964, Los Angeles, Calif.), soul music pioneer, among the first African Americans to achieve pop stardom through gospel roots.

As a child, Sam Cooke performed in gospel ensembles in churches in Chicago, where his father was a minister. In his teenage years he joined the Highway QC's, a local group that emulated the renowned Soul Stirrers. Cooke's natural talent and magnetic personality soon drew the attention of singer and manager J. W. Alexander, who landed him a job as lead singer for the Soul Stirrers. Cooke began recording gospel classics with the quintet while honing his smooth vocals and writing music of his own.

In the mid-1950s Alexander, who had noted the success of gospel-gone-rhythm and blues acts such as Ray Charles, convinced Cooke to switch to secular pop music. Alexander's vision of Cooke as a pop sensation among young African American women came true in 1957 when he scored a number one hit on both pop and R&B charts with *"You Send Me."* Cooke recorded with Keen records until 1960, when he signed a deal with RCA, launching the most prolific leg of his career. During his RCA years he sent numerous songs up the charts, including *"Chain Gang"* and *"Twistin' the Night Away."*

Meanwhile Cooke entered into a business partnership with Alexander, who had begun his own music publishing company—a rare enterprise for an African American in the early 1960s. Cooke began producing performers on the Star label and took an interest in developing new talent. He also served as a role model in the black music world, inspiring singers such as Aretha

Franklin to move from gospel to pop. Many consider Cooke a founding father of the hybrid soul, which blended gospel and R&B. Cooke's influence resounds in the works of such artists as Al Green, Wilson Pickett, Smokey Robinson, Marvin Gaye, and Otis Redding.

In 1964 a Los Angeles motel manager shot Cooke dead, allegedly in self-defense. Although some gospel devotees and religious fans—who felt betrayed by Cooke's break with the church—considered his death providential, musicians across genre and race took it as a tremendous loss. A crowd of 200,000 attended his funeral.

North America
_____

Cosby, Bill

(b. July 12, 1937, Germantown, Pa.), African American comedian whose multifarious talent, friendliness, and commitment to positive values led him to become a preeminent television celebrity in the 1980s and a performer admired by both whites and blacks.

Born in a poor section of Philadelphia, Pennsylvania, Bill Cosby left home for a stint in the United States Navy that lasted from 1956 to 1960. He studied at Temple University but dropped out to devote his time to stand-up comedy. After establishing his name on the night-club circuit in 1963, he auditioned successfully to fill a guest spot on Johnny Carson's *Tonight Show*. An instant success, Cosby became the first African American to host the program regularly. In 1965 he became the first black person to have a starring role on a predominantly white television drama, appearing with Robert Culp on the program *I Spy*. Because of his Emmy Award-winning success on *I Spy*, many fans considered Cosby "the Jackie Robinson of television."

As a rising television celebrity, Cosby starred in his own program, *The Bill Cosby Show* (1969–1971), in which he played a high school basketball coach, Chet Kincaid. The Kincaid character neither pandered to white stereotypes nor expressed a black militant doctrine. In the mid-1970s Cosby returned to school, earning a doctorate in education at the University of Massachusetts in Amherst. Meanwhile he continued his television career with *The New Bill Cosby Show* (1972–1973), a comedy and variety program, and *Cos* (1976). An animated Saturday morning feature, *Fat Albert and the Cosby Kids* (1972–1977), delivered messages of rectitude and personal responsibility. Both Fat Albert and Cosby's frequent cameos on *The Electric Company*, a presentation of the Public Broadcasting Service (PBS), reflected his interest in children and education.

In the 1980s Cosby combined his paternal interests with the sophisticated humor of his prime-time career on the hit program *The Cosby Show* (19841992). *The Cosby Show* ranked third in Nielsen ratings its first season and held the number-one slot for three years. It created a glowing embodiment of the American middle-class dream and drew the attention of 38 million people. Cosby's vision of Dr. Cliff Huxtable, his beautiful lawyer wife, and their five handsome, successful children included jokes and conflicts that transcended race. While some critics claimed that *The Cosby Show* failed to address the reality of black America—or, worse, depicted successful blacks as assimilated blacks—others lauded its positive presentation of family values.

While *The Cosby Show* debunked racial stereotypes on screen, Cosby fought discrimination within the television industry. He took advantage of the show's tremendous success, demanding a large role in its production. He hired black writers and directors and invited black celebrities, such as Dizzy Gillespie and Judith Jamison, to make guest appearances; he contracted Professor Alvin Poussaint, an African American professor of psychiatry from Harvard University, as an adviser; and he hung the artwork of black artist Varnette Honeywood on the walls of the set.

The Cosby Show marked the apex of Cosby's public celebrity and financial success, but his accomplishments extend beyond it. In addition to his numerous television ventures, Cosby has continued to perform live and has released more than two dozen comedy albums, many of which have won him Grammy Awards. He also has written a number of books, including the best-selling *Fatherhood* (1986) and *Love and Marriage* (1989), and several children's books in the *Little Bill* series for early readers. Throughout his career Cosby has endorsed the products of Fortune 500 companies such as Coca-Cola, Eastman Kodak, E. F. Hutton, and Jell-O.

Cosby's commitment to education has been persistent. In the 1980s he and his wife made frequent donations to African American colleges. In 1989 they gave their biggest gift, of $20 million, to Spelman College. Cosby's philanthropy has benefited many other African American organizations, including the National Association for the Advancement of Colored People, the United Negro College Fund, the National Sickle-Cell Foundation, and the National Council of Negro Women.

North America

Cotton Club,

a prestigious white-owned Harlem nightclub of the 1920s and 1930s that featured prominent African American musicians, singers, and dancers performing for a white clientele.

The Cotton Club was one of Harlem's premier nightclubs, renowned for its superb jazz music and the exotic routines of its female dancers. The club was also a constant reminder of the reality of segregation in the North as well as the South. Although its performers and waiters were all black and it was located for many years in the heart of Harlem in New York City, the Cotton Club had a whites-only policy, and it only hired female dancers who were light-skinned and who emulated white standards of beauty.

The Cotton Club had its beginnings in 1920, when the controversial

African American boxing champion Jack Johnson opened the Club Deluxe on Lenox Avenue and 142nd Street in Harlem. Johnson sold the club to white gangster Owney Madden, who reopened it in the fall of 1923 as the Cotton Club. Under Madden, the Cotton Club's floor shows and decoration highlighted black primitivism and sensuality. Decorated inside and out in the style of a log cabin and featuring pseudo-jungle décor, the club's appearance starkly revealed prevailing white stereotypes of African Americans.

Madden's timing was fortuitous, for during the 1920s New York City's elite displayed a sudden interest in black life and culture. In 1924 white bandleader Paul Whiteman premiered George Gershwin's jazz-influenced composition *Rhapsody in Blue* at New York City's Aeolian Hall, featuring the composer on piano. During the 1920s white author Carl Van Vechten published *Nigger Heaven* (1926), a popular novel about black life in Harlem, and hosted intimate soirées that featured such African American guests as blues singer Bessie Smith. The smart set considered it fashionable to journey into Harlem to visit the Cotton Club. "Join the crowds after theater," a 1929 advertisement declared. "All Broadway comes to Harlem."

The club's entertainment was certainly first-rate. Perhaps the most significant musician connected with the Cotton Club was Duke Ellington, whose orchestra played there from 1927 to 1931. Singer Cab Calloway first performed at the club in 1930, and in the following year his orchestra took over from Ellington's as the club's house band. During Ellington's tenure, the club was wired for radio broadcasts, which helped Ellington build a national audience for his music. Among the club's featured entertainers were singers Ethel Waters and Billie Holiday and dancers Bill "Bojangles" Robinson and Earl "Snake Hips" Tucker; in the chorus line was a young Lena Horne.

The 1929 stock market crash and the onset of the Great Depression put a damper on the Cotton Club's freewheeling entertainment, but the club did not shut down. The Harlem Riot of 1935 had a more serious impact. In the aftermath of the riots, Madden moved the club out of Harlem, reopening in 1936 in a supposedly safer downtown location on Broadway and 48th Street. The club continued in operation until 1940.

North America
___

Cruse, Harold Wright

(b. March 18, 1916, Petersburg, Va.), African American author of *The Crisis of the Negro Intellectual*, which provided a theoretical basis for black separation.

After his parents' separation, Harold Cruse moved with his father to New York City, where he completed high school. After serving in the quartermaster division of the United States Army from 1941 to 1945, he enrolled at City College of New York on the G.I. Bill, although he dropped out in his first year. During the 1950s and early 1960s, Cruse worked at various part-time jobs and became an active participant in left-wing politics in

Harlem. It was during this period that he joined the Communist Party, which he later rejected. He also wrote two plays and a musical during this period, and, with Amiri Baraka (LeRoi Jones), established the Black Arts Repertory Theater and School in 1965.

In 1967 the *New York Times* hailed *The Crisis of the Negro Intellectual: A Historical Analysis of the Failure of Black Leadership* as "a mind-blowing experience". Cruse's influential book, which remains a controversial critique of racial integration, attacked black leaders for failing to develop a nationalist program for the political, economic, and cultural autonomy of black Americans. Cruse followed *Crisis* in 1968 with a collection of essays titled *Rebellion or Revolution?*

In 1968 he also joined the faculty of the University of Michigan as a visiting professor. At Michigan Cruse helped establish the Center for Afro-American and African Studies and, in 1977, became the first black professor without a college degree to be appointed full professor at an American university. His book *Plural but Equal* was published in 1982. In 1987 he became professor emeritus at Michigan.

Latin America and the Caribbean

Cruz, Celia

(b. October 21, c. 1929, Havana, Cuba, July 17, 2003, New York, N.Y.), Cuban-born, African American vocalist, one of the most recognizable singers of the popular Latin dance music known as salsa.

Nicknamed the Queen of Salsa, Celia Cruz has recorded more than 50 albums, collaborating with many of the leading figures of Latin popular music. During a career that has spanned more than four decades, Cruz has gained a reputation for her tireless work, warm personality, and emotive style of singing. In performance she is known for her skillful improvisation of lyrics. She is one of a few successful female vocalists in a genre dominated by men.

Born in a poor section of Havana, Cruz demonstrated her singing talents at a very young age, but she studied to be an elementary school teacher because her father did not consider singing to be a suitable career for a woman. Encouraged by her mother and a teacher, however, she nevertheless pursued a singing career.

Cruz began her musical career performing for prizes in contests held on the radio or at local venues. In 1950 she became lead vocalist for Sonora Matancera, one of the most popular *conjuntos* (ensembles) in Cuba. Although the group was criticized for hiring a black singer, Cruz's hard work and talent eventually won her popular acclaim. In 1960, following the Cuban Revolution, Cruz left Cuba for Mexico. In 1961 she moved to the United States and a year later married Pedro Knight, a trumpeter for Sonora Matancera, who subsequently became her manager.

In the United States Cruz made a series of recordings for popular bandleader Ernesto "Tito" Puente from 1966 through 1972. Bandleader Johnny Pacheco and Fania Records owner Jerry Masucci took an interest in her, leading to her portrayal of Gracia Divina in the concert production and musical recording of *Hommy, A Latin Opera* (1973). *Hommy* gave further impetus to Cruz's career by bringing her a new generation of fans. In the mid- and late 1970s she collaborated with many of the best-known salsa performers, including Pacheco, Ray Barretto, Willie Colón, Bobby Valentín, and the Fania All Stars.

Cruz continued to perform actively through the 1980s and appeared in several celebrated reunion concerts with Sonora Matancera. In 1990 she shared a Grammy Award with Ray Barretto for their 1988 recording *Ritmo en el Corazón*. She was also recognized with an honorary doctorate from Yale University and, in 1994, with a National Medal of the Arts from President Bill Clinton. Cruz appeared in several motion pictures, most notably the 1992 film *The Mambo Kings*.

Cruz died on July 17, 2003, in New York, after battling cancer.

North America

Cullen, Countee

(b. March 30, 1903, Louisville, Ky.; d. January 9, 1946, New York, N.Y.), African American poet, novelist, and playwright; the best-known black writer of the Harlem Renaissance.

> *Yet do I marvel at this curious thing:*
> *To make a poet black, and bid him sing!*

In these last two lines of his poem "Yet Do I Marvel," Countee Cullen sums up the irony that he saw not only for himself but for all African American writers—the question of what happens when God makes a poet black in a world that discourages black creativity yet still bids him sing. Cullen was part of the generation of authors who emerged during the Harlem Renaissance and answered that question with their own writing.

Cullen's early history remained a mystery for decades, by his own choice. He was adopted as a teenager, and from that point on was always reticent about his birthplace and former family. But recent scholarship indicates that he was born to Elizabeth Lucas in Louisville, Kentucky, in 1903, and raised in New York by Elizabeth Porter, who may have been his maternal grandmother. His original surname was Porter, but sometime around Elizabeth Porter's death in 1918 he was taken in by the Reverend Frederick Cullen, pastor of Harlem's prominent Salem Methodist Episcopal Church, and his wife, Carolyn. Countee Cullen considered them to be his parents, and he readily absorbed their conservative values.

The Cullens sent their son to the predominantly white DeWitt Clinton High School. He was an excellent student and was editor of the school newspaper and literary magazine. He won a citywide poetry contest while still in high school, and wrote much of the material for his first two volumes of poetry as an undergraduate at New York University. His poetry received prizes in three national contests while he was still in college. In 1925 he graduated Phi Beta Kappa and published his first book, *Color*. He went on to receive a master's degree in English and French from Harvard University. In the meantime, poems from *Color* had received prizes from *Crisis*, *Opportunity*, and *Poetry* magazines.

At Harvard, Cullen studied poetry under Robert Hillyard, who emphasized composing in conventional poetic forms. Cullen graduated from Harvard in 1927 and returned to New York, where he became an assistant editor at *Opportunity*. In that same year he published his next two volumes of poetry, *Copper Sun* and *The Ballad of the Brown Girl: An Old Ballad Retold*, and edited *Caroling Dusk: An Anthology of Verse by Negro Poets*, one of the most important collections to emerge from the Harlem Renaissance.

Cullen was better educated in classical literary forms than many of the black writers who were his peers. His poetry was characterized by a use of traditional European verse patterns. He explained that he chose forms and ideas that he believed transcended race because he wanted to be regarded simply as a poet, not a black poet. In his allegiance to ballads, sonnets, and standard English poetic language, Cullen stood apart from other Harlem Renaissance poets who were experimenting with new literary forms based on jazz and blues. As a result, Cullen enjoyed more crossover success than other African American poets at the time, because white scholars and audiences recognized and applauded his technical skills.

Black audiences also praised his work, and his best-known and most powerful poems were often ones with racial themes. For example, in the sonnet "From the Dark Tower," Cullen prophesies an eventual redemption for a race that has learned:

> to hide the heart that bleeds,
> And wait, and tend our agonizing seeds
> We shall not always plant while others reap . . .
> We were not made eternally to weep.

In "Heritage," a longer poem, Cullen expresses longing for Africa along with doubt about what meaning it could hold for a twentieth-century African American:

> One three centuries removed
> From the scenes his father loved.
> Spicy grove, cinnamon tree,
> What is Africa to me?

Later in the same poem, Cullen reflects on what African Americans lost in terms of traditional beliefs and customs:

> Quaint, outlandish heathen gods
> Black men fashion out of rods,
> Clay, and brittle bits of stone,
> In a likeness of their own,
> My conversion came high-priced;
> I belong to Jesus Christ,
> Preacher of humility;
> Heathen gods are naught to me.

"Heritage" ends with a confession, of sorts:

> Lord, I fashion dark gods, too,
> Daring even to give You
> Dark despairing features where,
> Crowned with dark rebellious hair,
> Patience wavers just so much as
> Mortal grief compels, while touches
> Quick and hot, of anger, rise
> To smitten cheek and weary eyes.
> Lord, forgive me if my need
> Sometimes shapes a human creed.

By the late 1920s Cullen had become the most popular black poet in the United States, and had won more major literary prizes—from both black and white sources—than any other black writer.

Cullen's celebrity was reinforced when, on April 9, 1928, he married Yolande Du Bois, the only child of the black intellectual and activist W. E. B. Du Bois. Their lavish wedding, at the Reverend Cullen's church, was attended by 1,000 guests and was one of the major social events of the Harlem Renaissance. It also appeared literally to place Cullen, and his generation of African American intellectuals, in the position of being heir to Du Bois. But Cullen had been involved for years with Harlem schoolteacher Harold Jackman. When Cullen and Jackman sailed for Paris two months after the wedding, leaving Cullen's wife behind, it became clear the marriage was not meant to be. Cullen and Du Bois were divorced in 1930.

Cullen's career took a turn at about the same time. In 1929 he had published *The Black Christ and Other Poems*. He had worked on the title poem for two years and considered it his masterpiece, but the book was not well received. He took a position as a French teacher at Frederick Douglass Junior High (where James Baldwin was among his students), and while he continued writing poetry, he began to experiment with other forms as well. These included *One Way to Heaven* (1934), his only novel, and *The Lost Zoo* (1940) and *My Lives and How I Lost Them* (1942), books of children's verse. In 1936, with his translation of *Medea*, Cullen also became the first twentieth-century African American writer to publish a major translation of a classical work.

Just before his death, Cullen collaborated with the black writer Arna Bontemps on a dramatization of Bontemps's novel *God Sends Sunday* as a musical, *St. Louis Blues*. The production had been criticized by some African American for its portrayal of lower-class black life, but it opened on Broadway two months after Cullen's sudden death from high blood pressure and uremic poisoning on January 9, 1946.

Cullen had remarried in 1940, and his second wife, Ida, survived him. After Cullen's death, Langston Hughes eclipsed him as the best-known poet of the Harlem Renaissance. The extraordinary degree of fame and recognition that Cullen enjoyed during his lifetime has been forgotten, but a contemporary scholar describes his achievements in this way: "Some of his poems are utterly unforgettable, so capable was he of setting down in precise language the subtle feelings that made him one of the most intriguing writers in African American literature."

Damas, Léon-Gontran

(b. March 28, 1912, Cayenne, French Guiana; d. January 22, 1978, Washington, D.C.), the least known of the three principal founders and proponents of the Négritude movement, and the first to illustrate it through poetry.

Léon-Gontran Damas was born into the mulatto bourgeoisie of Cayenne, the capital of French Guiana, a territory vilified in Damas's day as a penal colony. The area contained significant Native American and *nègres bosh* (descended from fugitive African slaves) populations. Damas lost his mother in early childhood and received a bourgeois upbringing from his aunt; he would later reject the values of his youth, together with all forms of political and cultural assimilation. As an adolescent he attended the Victor Schoelcher High School in Martinique, where he first became friends with Aimé Césaire. After graduating he moved to Paris, where he studied literature, Asian languages, and law. He also collaborated in the production of the now-famous black publications *La revue du monde noir, Légitime Défense,* and *L'Etudiant noir.*

With the support of French anthropologist Paul Rivet, Damas returned to French Guiana in 1934 to investigate African cultural crossover among the nègres bosh. His account of the trip appeared in the form of *Retour de Guyane* (Return from Guiana), published less than a year after his book of poems *Pigments* (1937) appeared. Both works denounce the assimilationist policies of the colonial administration, and both were censured by the French colonial government. Police seized the remaining copies of *Pigments* in 1939, after poems from the collection that had been translated into Baule incited Africans in Côte d'Ivoire to resist conscription into the French army. The French also quietly attempted to buy up the print run of *Retour de Guyane.*

After World War II Damas traveled to the United States and began to solidify the connections he had made earlier in Paris among the American black intelligentsia: Countee Cullen, Claude McKay, and especially Mercer Cook and Langston Hughes. He returned to his country and in 1948 was elected to the French Parliament to represent the new department of French Guiana (whose creation he had opposed). Until his electoral defeat in 1951 Damas proposed commonsense reforms and improvements in the colony; after leaving Parliament he broadened his activities and became a sort of roving ambassador of black consciousness. He began to travel extensively in Africa, giving lectures and recruiting and training African radio journalists in the context of his work as consultant and broadcaster for the French overseas radio service. He was eventually fired from that position.

Damas also served as editor of an early French series of the works of African writers; his role was comparable to that of Nigerian Chinua Achebe in the Heinemann *African Writers* series. Damas later traveled to virtually all the countries of the diaspora for the United Nations Educational, Scientific, and Cultural Organization (UNESCO), returning more and more often to speak on campuses in the United States. He finally settled there in 1970, after the publication of two other volumes of poems: *Black-Label* (1956) and *Névralgies* (1966). By this time his contacts in the literary and political worlds of Africa, Europe, and the Americas made him uniquely able to serve as a bridge between the continents and language groups of the diaspora. In the United States he taught at Federal City College (now the University of the District of Columbia) and at Howard University, where he held a position at the time of his death in 1978.

Damas's literary output was rather limited, and his work remained difficult to find until the definitive edition of *Pigments* was published by the Paris publishing house *Présence Africaine* in 1962. At several points in his career Damas had the misfortune of publishing at the same time that seminal works by Césaire and Léopold Sédar Senghor appeared. Césaire's *Cahier d'un retour au pays natal* (Return to My Native Land) was released in 1939, and Senghor's *Anthologie de la nouvelle poésie africaine et malgache de langue française* (Anthology of the New Black and Malagasy Poetry in the French Language) came to the attention of the public in 1948; these coincided, respectively, with Damas's *Pigments* and *Poètes noirs d'expression française* (Black Poets in the French Language). Although Césaire's *Cahier and Senghor's Anthologie* quickly overshadowed the works of Damas, the publication dates reveal the anticipatory quality of his literary products.

Both Senghor and Césaire have credited Damas with exerting a formative influence on their literary output. Although Damas was less prominent a politician and less prolific a publisher than either of his literary successors, he may have been more effective than either in coupling political activity with literary production and in representing the rising international black consciousness after World War II. Senghor felt that Damas was "the most *nègre* of us all," and the first to find the rhythm of the true *poésie nègre*. Most of the conclusions drawn by Senghor and Césaire reflect characteristics of Damas's work in *Pigments* and the long single poem *Black-Label*. Their insights focus on the incantatory repetitions of Damas's verse and the ideology of African revalorization for which Damas's rhythms provided a vehicle. For most of his critics, Damas became the poet of black anger's direct expression. His poem *Pour Sûr* illustrates the raw quality of the poet's sentiment:

> *Sure enough I'll get*
> *fed up*
> *and not even wait*
> *for things*
> *to reach*
> *the state*
> *of a ripe camembert*
>
> *Then I'll put my foot in it*
> *or else simply put*
> *my hand around the neck*
> *of everything that pisses me off in capital letters*
> *colonization*
> *civilization*
> *assimilation*
> *and all the rest*
> *Until then*
> *you will often hear me*
> *slam the door*

Damas and the other members of the Négritude movement were acutely aware of the rise of European fascism and the concurrent decline of colonial regimes. Some of Damas's lapidary pronouncements, however, were not popular with the critics of Négritude's essentialism, who began to accuse the author of making racist diatribes. Gerald Moore's introduction to *Seven African Writers* (1962) cites Damas's work as an example of Négritude "degenerating into a racialism as intolerant and arrogant as any other." To rescue Damas from such attacks, critics during the 1970s and 1980s tended to emphasize less political aspects of his writing. While such defenses recall and extol the very personal poems of *Névralgies*, Damas's most vigorous, satisfying, and freshest works are still his most politically and historically engaged: *Pigments* and *Black-Label*, as well as *Retour de Guyane*.

The poems in these collections do considerably more than act as a manifesto for a version of Négritude quickly dominated by Senghor's political and racialist ideology. In "Nuit Blanche," Damas shows an acute awareness of the historical and situational alienation of which Négritude was both an the expression and the cure:

My friends I've waltzed
waltzed like my ancestors
the Gauls never did
until my blood turned to viennese cream [. . .]

My friends I've waltzed
waltzed
waltzed crazily
often
I thought I was holding the waist of Uncle Gobineau
or of Cousin Hitler
or of some good Aryan chewing over his old age
on some park bench

Despite, or perhaps because of, his experience of cultural alienation, the poet succeeds in rewriting histories; with Damas writing the calypso, we have no doubt who will come off better in his dance with Uncle Gobineau (referring to Joseph-Arthur, Compte de Gobineau, a nineteenth-century French ethnologist who developed a theory of scientific racism, arguing the superiority of the white race) or Cousin Hitler. Perhaps even more than his fellow Caribbean Négritude poet Césaire, Damas feels at home anywhere in the history of the diaspora. Bridging the Anglophone and Francophone Atlantic worlds, and with an enormous personal experience on four continents, Damas was in a unique position to personify the new black historical consciousness of his day. In dancing the Viennese waltz, as he might a Caribbean mazurka, he proves himself, in scholar Mercer Cook's words, "the man of the diaspora par excellence."

North America

Dance Theater of Harlem,

multiracial American dance troupe that was the world's first professional all-black classical ballet company.

Established just months after the assassination of Dr. Martin Luther King Jr., the Dance Theater of Harlem (DTH) has evolved into one of the world's most respected dance companies and a treasured artistic resource in the black community. As its founder and long-time director Arthur Mitchell has said, the group's goal is not only to present dynamic classical dance performances but also "to ignite some sort of passion in young people." To that end, in addition to its professional troupe of more than 30 dancers, the DTH sponsors a dance school in its New York home as well as Dancing Through Barriers, a program designed to nurture young artists in several other cities, including Detroit, Michigan, and Washington, D.C.

After its creation in 1969 the DTH grew quickly, its original 30 students burgeoning to 400 within months. DTH was originally conceived as a dance school, but Mitchell and his partner, the white teacher Karel Shook, expanded the school to include a dance troupe, which debuted at New York's Guggenheim Museum in 1971. A year later, the group moved from its original Greenwich Village headquarters to West 152nd Street in Harlem. The DTH has toured in England, Russia, and South Africa. During the 1992 South Africa visit, Mitchell encouraged his dancers to learn from as well as teach the dancers there. This was a typical gesture from a man renowned for pushing his students to visit libraries and museums, both to widen their artistic horizons and to teach them to act as role models.

Another aspect of the DTH's mission is to disprove the once-popular notion that black people are anatomically unable to dance ballet. (No longer exclusively African American, the DTH retains its commitment to dancers of all skin tones by dyeing costumes and shoes in varying shades of brown and beige.) When he joined the New York City Ballet in 1955, Mitchell himself was the first African American man to dance for a major company. In the works he pioneered with the DTH, Mitchell continued to build on the artistic legacy of his mentor, George Balanchine, while drawing from cultures not usually represented in classical dance. Some of the DTH's best-known ballets include *Dougla*, a work based on Afro-Caribbean history and art, and *Giselle*, a reworking that sets the classic ballet in the Creole community of New Orleans.

North America

Dandridge, Dorothy

(b. November 9, 1922, Cleveland, Ohio; d. September 8, 1965, Hollywood, Calif.), actress who was the first African American woman to receive an Academy Award nomination.

The daughter of a minister and an aspiring actress, Dorothy Dandridge began her career as a singer in 1951, performing at the Cotton Club in New York with the Dandridge Sisters (1951) and as a soloist with the Desi Arnaz Band.

As a child, Dandridge appeared in bit parts in several films. She moved quickly from playing small roles in films such as *Flamingo* (1947) to lead roles in a number of low-budget films, including *Tarzan's Perils* (1951), *The Harlem Globe-Trotters* (1951), and *Jungle Queen* (1951). Her breakthrough role was *Carmen Jones* (1954), for which she became the first black woman to receive an Academy Award nomination for Best Actress. Her next film, *Island in the Sun* (1957), which was the first mainstream film to portray an interracial romance, was not received as well. In 1959 she regained critical recognition for her role as Bess in *Porgy and Bess* (1959).

Despite her appearance on the cover of *Life* magazine after *Carmen Jones*, Dandridge still had difficulty finding suitable lead roles. There were few opportunities for an African American woman attempting to break into the glamorous roles dominated by white actresses, and Dandridge rejected the stock character roles available to black actresses. With fewer singing engagements, her career as a performer began to decline. Dandridge's professional crises were coupled with personal ones. After her divorce, she declared bankruptcy and lost her home. A short time later, she died of an overdose of antidepressants.

North America
Dash, Julie

(b. October 22, 1952, Long Island City, N.Y.), American filmmaker best known for *Daughters of the Dust*, the first full-length general release film by an African American woman.

Born and raised in the Queensbridge Housing Projects in Long Island City, Julie Dash stumbled into filmmaking at age 17, enrolling with a friend in a workshop at the Studio Museum in Harlem. By 19 she had made her first film, shot with a Super 8 camera using pictures from *Jet* magazine attached to pipe cleaners. Dash majored in psychology at the City College of New York but graduated in film production. In 1973 she wrote and produced a documentary, *Working Models of Success*.

Dash moved to Los Angeles after graduation, gaining experience working on many film crews. In Los Angeles, she became the youngest fellow ever at the Center for Advanced Film Studies. During her two-year fellowship, Dash adapted an Alice Walker short story, *Diary of an African Nun* (1977). An experimental dance film that she conceived and directed, *Four Women*, won the Gold Medal for Women in Film at the 1978 Miami International Film Festival. While working for the Motion Picture Association of America in Los Angeles in 1980, she attended the Cannes International Film Festival in France and cosponsored a session on several short films by black Americans.

In 1981 Dash won a grant from the National Endowment for the Humanities (NEH), which was awarded again in 1983 and 1985, and began making her most acclaimed films. *Illusions* (1983), shot in 10 days for under $30,000, explores the roles of black women in film. Set in 1942 Hollywood, the 34-minute film portrays two women, one a studio executive who passes for white, another a singer who dubs the voices of white starlets, who are both made invisible and voiceless as black women by the film industry and society at large. *Illusions* won the 1989 Jury Prize for Best Film of the Decade by the Black Filmmakers Foundation and the 1985 Black Cinema Society Award, among other honors.

Dash moved to Atlanta, Georgia, in 1986, where she formed Geechee Girl Productions, Inc., her own film company. She directed two projects for the National Black Women's Health Project in 1987, *Breaking the Silence: On Reproductive Rights* and *Preventing Cancer*. Two television productions followed: *Relatives* (1990) and *Praise House* (1991).

In 1981 Dash received a Guggenheim grant to study the Gullah culture of the South Carolina coast, which resulted in *Daughters of the Dust* (1992), making her the first African American woman to create a full-length general release film. The film is set during 1902 in the South Carolina Sea Islands, where a family meets for the last time before migrating to the North to seek better opportunities, a migration that puts at risk their African communal values. *Daughters* won first prize in cinematography at the 1991 Sundance Film Festival in Utah, where it premiered, and was televised nationally in 1992 on PBS's *American Playhouse*.

In the mid-1990s, Dash filmed two music videos (1992 and 1994), as well as a documentary about the life of Zora Neale Hurston. She received a Fulbright fellowship to work in London on a screenplay about the black British film collective Sankofa. She lives in Atlanta with her daughter, N'Zinga.

North America

Davis, Anthony

(b. Paterson, N.J., February 20, 1951), African American composer and pianist whose innovations in modern classical music conflate jazz styles and global rhythms.

The son of the first African American professor at Princeton University, Anthony Davis studied classical music as a child in New York, and as an undergraduate at Yale University he played free-jazz with Anthony Braxton. After earning his B.A. at Yale in 1975, Davis moved to New York City, where he supported himself as a jazz pianist. As he developed musically, his compositions deviated from traditional jazz. He often abandoned improvisation and drew elements from Western classical music and African and South Asian rhythms. His recordings from this period include *Hidden Voices* (1979) and *Lady of the Mirrors* (1981). In 1981 he formed an eight-piece ensemble, Episteme, whose repertoire included a combination of improvised and scored music, blurring the distinction between jazz and classical music.

In the 1980s Davis began focusing much of his work on historical subjects. *Middle Passage* (1984) examined the degradation and despair of the slave ships and was performed both by pianist Ursula Oppens and Davis himself. From 1981 to 1985 Davis collaborated with his brother Christopher and cousin Thulani Davis on an opera about black nationalist leader Malcolm X. *X: The Life and Times of Malcolm X* premiered in Philadelphia in 1985 and was performed by the New York City Opera in 1986. Davis's second opera, *Under the Double Moon* (1989), included a science fiction libretto written by Deborah Atherton, his ex-wife. Two subsequent operas, *Tania* (1992) and *Amistad* (1997), dramatized historical events.

Davis has taught at Yale and Columbia Universities, composed scores for numerous dance companies, and written music for several films. His symphonic works have been performed by the New York Philharmonic, the Brooklyn Philharmonic, and the San Francisco Symphony. He won a Pulitzer Prize for his piano concerto *Wayang no. 5* (1984).

Davis, Miles Dewey, III

(b. May 25, 1926, Alton, Ill.; d. September 25, 1991, Santa Monica, Calif.),
African American trumpet player and band leader who contributed significantly
to bebop, cool jazz, modal jazz, and fusion or jazz-rock.

The role of Miles Davis is unparalleled in the history of jazz. Many great
jazz musicians—including Louis Armstrong, Coleman Hawkins, Charlie
Parker, and Dizzy Gillespie—gained renown for their technical mastery and
their distinctive approaches to improvisation. Others, such as Duke
Ellington, Count Basie, Thelonious Monk, Charles Mingus, and Ornette
Coleman, achieved greatness less through instrumental prowess than
through compositions and performances in a distinctive style. Davis is
unique in having made his mark through neither technical mastery nor a
single identifiable style, but rather through his constant evolution and stylistic innovation. Jazz scholar Joachim Berendt has observed that Davis three
times altered the history of jazz, by introducing cool jazz, modal jazz, and
fusion. Since his death, his influence has continued to be greater than that
of any other jazz musician, including tenor saxophonist John Coltrane.

The son of a prosperous dentist who once ran for the state legislature,
Davis grew up in a middle-class home in East St. Louis, Illinois. His mother,
Cleota Henry Davis, was a classically trained musician who could, Davis
recalled, "play a mean blues on the piano." He received his first trumpet at
age 13 and by his mid-teens was playing in the St. Louis area, in the process
befriending St. Louis jazz trumpeter Clark Terry. Shortly after graduating
from high school in 1944, Davis substituted for a sick third trumpet player
in Billy Eckstine's orchestra during its two-week gig in St. Louis.

The Eckstine band was then the most innovative group in jazz. It featured a number of the young lions of bebop, most notably Dizzy Gillespie
on trumpet and Charlie Parker—Bird—on alto sax, but also tenor players
Gene Ammons and Lucky Thompson, drummer Art Blakey, and vocalists
Eckstine and Sarah Vaughan. "B's band changed my life," Davis recalled. "I
decided right then and there that I had to leave St. Louis and live in New
York City where all these bad musicians were." He was accepted by the Juilliard School of Music, which provided Davis with a pretext for moving that
his parents would enthusiastically support.

Davis did attend Juilliard but never graduated; he gained far more of his
musical education in the jazz clubs of 52nd Street. He quickly established
himself in the jazz community, playing with tenor saxophonist Coleman
Hawkins, pianist and composer Tadd Dameron, and pianists Bud Powell and
Thelonious Monk. During 1946 and 1947 he became a regular member of
the Eckstine band.

Davis had his first encounter with cocaine during his stint with Eckstine,
and tenor player Gene Ammons introduced him to heroin. At the time,
heroin use was rampant among younger jazz musicians. Davis recalled that
"the idea was going around that to use heroin might make you play as great

as Bird," who was known to be an addict. "A lot of musicians did it for that. I guess I might have been just waiting for his genius to hit me."

Davis soon had the chance to work with his musical idol on a steady basis. In 1947 he joined Parker's great quintet—which also featured Duke Jordan (piano), Tommy Potter (bass), and Max Roach (drums). During his stint with Parker, Davis perfected his bebop style. By 1949, however, he had acquired a heroin addiction that increasingly hindered his ability to play. In 1953 Davis returned to Illinois and, alone on a farm owned by his father, kicked his habit by sheer force of will. In part, that steely resolve reflected Davis's lifelong struggle to control a tightly coiled rage. Davis was never one to refuse a challenge, whether it was overcoming addiction or meeting a personal insult. He had a number of unpleasant encounters with white authorities, including a notorious police beating in 1959 outside Birdland, the New York City jazz club.

Over the course of 45 years, Davis's playing fell into five distinct, sometimes overlapping phases: bebop (1945–1948), cool jazz (1948–1958), hard bop (1952–1963), modal (1959, 1964–1968), and electric or fusion (1969–1991). After journeyman beginnings in bebop, Davis led the way for all of jazz music. His pathbreaking *Birth of the Cool* recordings of 1949–1950 established the conventions of cool jazz. A series of recordings in the early 1950s with trombonist J. J. Johnson, alto player Jackie McLean, and pianist Horace Silver heralded the hard bop movement, which simplified the musical universe of bebop and gave it harder rhythmic underpinnings.

In the mid-1950s Davis organized the first of his two classic quintets, featuring John Coltrane (tenor sax), Red Garland (piano), Paul Chambers (bass), and Philly Joe Jones (drums). This group alternately played blazing up-tempo hard bop numbers and ballads that featured Davis's pensive trumpet. In his ballad playing, Davis often used a harmon mute to achieve a distinctly poignant sound. During these years, he simplified his playing. On ballads, in particular, he made deliberate use of space, increasing the emotional depth of his solos by the silences that he left between notes and phrases.

Davis's quintet also inaugurated the next major phase of jazz with its increasingly modal playing. Modal jazz replaces standard diatonic scales and chords with other note sequences played in more open, harmonically indeterminate settings. In 1959, with white pianist Bill Evans replacing Garland and with the addition of alto player Cannonball Adderley, Davis's band recorded *Kind of Blue*, one of the most influential and most popular recordings in jazz history. The album, the first significant example of modal jazz, continues to exert a profound influence on young jazz musicians.

Further exploring the cool side of jazz, Davis collaborated with composer and arranger Gil Evans—who had first worked with the trumpeter on the Birth of the Cool sessions—on a series of memorable recordings that epitomize modern orchestral jazz, including *Miles Ahead* (1957), *Porgy and Bess* (1958), and most notably *Sketches of Spain* (1959–1960). During the same period, Davis's small group continued to play hard bop with blazing intensity. In 1964 Davis formed the second of his great quintets, this one featuring Wayne Shorter (tenor), Herbie Hancock (piano), Ron Carter (bass), and Tony Williams (drums).

The creative achievements of Davis's 1960s quintet quickly placed it at the musical forefront. The group's probing modal music drew jazz ever further in the direction of harmonic, melodic, and rhythmic freedom. On the other hand, Davis resisted what he saw as the anarchy of free jazz. "Look," he said, "you don't need to think to play weird. That ain't no freedom. You need controlled freedom." From 1964 to the end of his life, the trumpet player continually, if not always successfully, pursued his ideal of "controlled freedom." In the late 1960s he began experimenting with electric instruments and rock-based rhythms, as foreshadowed on his albums *Filles de Kilimanjaro* (1968) and *In a Silent Way* (1969).

Davis shook the jazz world with his sub-sequent album, *Bitches Brew* (1969), which introduced fusion or jazz-rock, a style that layered jazz improvisation over rock rhythms. Davis's new direction—and the playing of such sidemen as drummers Jack DeJohnette and Billy Cobham, electric keyboard players Chick Corea and Keith Jarrett, and electric guitarist John McLaughlin—alienated many of his old fans but attracted a large following among younger listeners. In the late 1970s Davis ceased performing, mainly because he was debilitated by a cocaine dependency. Yet in the early 1980s he again overcame drug problems and resumed his musical career.

In his autobiography, which appeared two years before his death, Davis declared, "I have to always be on the cutting edge of things because that's just the way I am and always have been." But in his final years Davis twice returned to his past style of playing. In 1990 he appeared as a sideman and featured soloist—playing once again in his 1950s harmon-muted ballad style—on the title song of singer-pianist Shirley Horn's *You Won't Forget Me*. A year later, and only a few weeks before his death, Davis revisited his classic orchestral collaborations with Gil Evans at a Montreux Jazz Festival concert organized and conducted by Quincy Jones.

Of the many posthumous tributes to Davis, none was more astute than an editorial that appeared in the *Boston Globe*. "There were better players," it declared, "[and] certainly better people, but only Miles had that aura: a compound of danger, beauty, and arrogance. With the grace of a dancer, and [the] menace of a gun, Miles exuded a princely hauteur."

North America

Davis, Ossie

(b. December 18, 1917, Cogdell, Ga.), widely acclaimed African American actor, playwright, producer, and director who has long been an activist and leader within the black community.

The son of a railway engineer, Ossie Davis grew up in Waycross, Georgia. The harassment of his parents by the Ku Klux Klan impelled him early on to become a writer so that he could "truthfully portray the black man's experience." At Howard University, under the tutelage of drama critic Alain Locke, Davis developed his theatrical talent, performing in a 1941 production of *Joy Exceeding Glory* with Harlem's Rose McClendon Players. Following his theater debut, however, he received few job offers and for nearly a year found himself living on the street.

Davis never lost his sense of purpose. After serving in the United States Army during World War II, he returned to New York, where he won the title role in Robert Ardrey's play *Jeb* (1946). In 1948 he married fellow performer Ruby Dee, who became his lifelong collaborator on stage, on screen, and as a political activist. During the 1950s Davis and Dee were blacklisted for taking a radical stance in their work against the hard-line anticommunists of the McCarthy era. In an attempt to elude government agents assigned to tail them, Davis and Dee once hid for hours in a costume hamper following a performance of Chekhov's *The Cherry Orchard*. They also organized fundraisers within the theater to pay for the legal defense of black victims of racially based assaults. When in the 1960s Davis had attained celebrity status as an actor, he lent his artistic stature to advance the cause of civil rights by eulogizing both Malcolm X and Martin Luther King Jr. at their funerals. In 1972 he chaired the Angela Davis Defense Fund.

Davis is best known for his roles in Lorraine Hansberry's award-winning Broadway play *A Raisin in the Sun* (1959) and its 1961 film version, as well as for his own satirical play *Purlie Victorious* (1961), in which a black preacher outwits the local landowner to secure an inheritance and finance the building of a church. The play was well received by critics, who praised its mockery of racial stereotypes by blowing them out of proportion. He has since written and directed numerous films, including *Cotton Comes to Harlem* (1970) and *Countdown at Kusini* (coproduced with Dee, 1976), the first American feature film to be shot entirely in Africa by black professionals. Davis has also starred in numerous films that address issues critical to African Americans, such as Spike Lee's *Do The Right Thing* (1989), *Jungle Fever* (1991), and *Malcolm X* (1994).

Among the many awards Davis has received are the Hall of Fame Award for outstanding artistic achievement in 1989 and the U.S. National Medal for the Arts in 1995.

North America
___

Davis, Sammy, Jr.

(b. December 8, 1925, New York, N.Y.; d. May 16, 1990, Los Angeles, Calif.), African American singer, dancer, and actor who starred on the vaudeville stage, Broadway, television, and in motion pictures.

Sammy Davis Jr., the son of vaudeville performers Elvera Sanchez Davis and Sammy Davis Sr., began a life-long career of entertaining at the age of

Sammy Davis Jr. talks with President
Richard M. Nixon at the 1972
Republican National Convention.
CORBIS/Bettmann

three, appearing in the vaudeville group in
which his parents danced, Will Mastin's
Holiday in Dixieland. Two years later, after
his parents' divorce, he stayed with his
father and officially joined the group. Davis
made his movie debut with Ethel Waters in
Rufus Jones for President (1933), and then
filmed *Seasons Greetings.* Throughout the
1930s he toured with the Will Mastin Trio,
becoming the central figure in the group,
singing, dancing, and playing several instruments.

In 1943 Davis joined the army. He
served for two years directing shows and
touring military installations. After leaving
the army he returned to the Will Mastin
Trio, which became an established part of
the club circuit playing bills with Euro-
pean-American entertainers Jack Benny,
Bob Hope, and Frank Sinatra.

Davis's recording career began to take
off in 1946, when he signed with Capitol Records. The song *"The Way You
Look Tonight"* was selected by Metronome as record of the year and Davis
was chosen as Most Outstanding New Personality. Decca Records signed
him in 1954 and released Starring Sammy Davis Jr., which reached number
one on the charts. Later that year, Davis was in a near fatal car accident, lost
his left eye and spent several months in the hospital. It was there that he
converted to Judaism.

In 1956 he made his Broadway debut, starring in *Mr. Wonderful*, which
included his father and adopted uncle from the Will Mastin Trio. He moved
back to film with *The Benny Goodman Story* (1956), *Anna Lucasta* (1958),
and *Porgy and Bess* (1959). In 1959 he married dancer Loray White, but
soon left her for Swedish actress Mai Britt, whom he married in 1960. They
had one child, and he adopted her two children.

In the 1960s Davis socialized and made films with the Rat Pack, a Hol-
lywood group led by Frank Sinatra and Dean Martin. These films included
Oceans Eleven (1960), *Sergeants Three* (1962), and *Robin and the Seven
Hoods* (1964). Also during the 1960s Davis starred on Broadway in *Golden
Boy*, which ran for 568 performances. His 1965 autobiography, *Yes I Can*,
earned him the Spingarn Medal from the National Association for the
Advancement of Colored People.

In 1970 Davis married Altovise Gore, while continuing with his
recording career. He was criticized in 1972 for supporting Republican president Richard Nixon and for being photographed with him at the Republican National Convention. He abandoned his support of Nixon after the
Watergate scandal of 1972. In 1974 Davis was hospitalized for liver and
kidney problems resulting from alcoholism, a product of his days with the

Rat Pack. He was back on stage later that year singing in *Sammy on Broadway*, and from 1975 to 1977 he starred in the television show *Sammy and Company*.

In the 1980s Davis published two more autobiographies, entertained U.S. troops in Lebanon (1983), and toured with Sinatra and Liza Minelli in 1988. In 1989 he filmed *Tap*, a tribute to the great tap dancers, with Gregory Hines. Davis died of throat cancer the following year.

Dee, Ruby

(b. October 27, 1924, Cleveland, Ohio) African American actress, writer, and social activist; the first black woman to play major parts in the American Shakespeare Festival at Stratford, Connecticut; and a major American film and television performer.

Ruby Dee, whose "frail sparrow figure, . . . bright, unsubdued eyes . . . [and] entire being, have a quality of wholeness that is rarely encountered in the theatre," was born Ruby Ann Wallace in Cleveland, Ohio. Her father, Marshall Edward Wallace, was a porter and waiter on the Pennsylvania Railroad; her mother, Emma Wallace, was a schoolteacher. They moved to Harlem while Ruby was a baby. Her education at Public School 119 was supplemented by classical literature and music at home. Although asked to leave Hunter College when her activities at the American Negro Theatre—a Harlem group that also included Hilda Simms, Harry Belafonte, and Sidney Poitier—took up too much of her energy and time, Dee graduated in 1945 with a B.A. in French and Spanish. She worked briefly as a translator for an import company, but her extracurricular activities soon became her career.

Dee's work has run the gamut of entertainment media; she has acted on stage and in film, television, and radio, and she has recorded poetry. Her Broadway debut, a walk-on part in *South Pacific* (a play about World War II that appeared before the Rogers and Hammerstein musical) came in 1943, while she was still at college. Only three years later, she appeared on Broadway in *Jeb* (1946), opposite her husband-to-be, Ossie Davis. They married in 1948, and have collaborated closely ever since. She achieved national recognition in the title role of *Anna Lucasta* (tour, 1946–1947) and went on to principal roles in *A Raisin in the Sun* (1959); *Purlie Victorious* (1961), subsequently filmed in 1963; and Athol Fugard's *Boesman and Lena* (1970), with James Earl Jones, for which she won an Obie in 1971. As Kate in *The Taming of the Shrew* (1965), and Cordelia in *King Lear*, she became the first black woman to play major parts in the American Shakespeare Festival. Most recently, she has appeared in *Two Hah Hahs and a Homeboy* (1995) with her husband and her son, Guy Davis.

Dee has appeared in over 20 films, most importantly as the baseball player's wife in *The Jackie Robinson Story* (1950), with Sidney Poitier in *Edge of the City* (1957), and in Spike Lee's *Do the Right Thing* (1989). Her television work is more extensive, including many guest appearances, the series *With Ossie and Ruby* (PBS, 1981), and dramas such as *Long Day's Journey into Night* (PBS, 1983). She has received numerous awards, including an Emmy for *Decoration Day* (NBC) in 1991, and a Literary Guild Award (1989) in recognition of her plays, poems and children's stories. She has been inducted into both the Black Filmmakers Hall of Fame (1975) and the Theater Hall of Fame (1988).

A well-known social activist and a member of the National Association for the Advancement of Colored People (NAACP) and the Southern Christian Leadership Conference, Dee speaks at many high-profile benefits. Having experienced firsthand the difficulties encountered by minorities in her profession, she established the Ruby Dee Scholarship in Dramatic Art for talented young black women.

North America

Delaney, Beauford

(b. 1902, Knoxville, Tenn.; d. March 26, 1979, Paris, France), African American artist admired for his exquisite use of light and who painted portraits of many of the great figures of jazz.

Even as a young child growing up in Tennessee, Beauford Delaney was preoccupied with art, according to his younger brother, painter Joseph Delaney. Beauford Delaney received his first formal art training from Lloyd Branson, a white artist living in Knoxville. With Branson's encouragement, in 1924 Delaney went to Boston, where he studied painting at the Massachusetts Normal School, the South Boston School of Art, and the Copley Society.

In 1929 Delaney moved to New York City and held a variety of jobs while he established himself as a painter. Twelve of his portraits were displayed in a 1930 group show at the Whitney Studio Galleries (later the Whitney Museum of American Art). In exchange for working at the Whitney as a guard, telephone operator, and gallery attendant Delaney received studio space and a place to live. He had his first one-man exhibition in 1932 at the 135th Street Branch of the New York Public Library.

A music lover throughout his life, Delaney met and painted many of the great figures of jazz. W. C. Handy, Louis Armstrong, Duke Ellington, and Ethel Waters were among the musicians and singers who went to Delaney for their portraits. Additionally, he developed friendships with a wide range of writers and other artists in New York in the 1930s and 1940s. One of Delaney's closest friends was the novelist James Baldwin, who first visited Delaney's Greene Street studio (in the area now known as SoHo) when he was a teenager and always gave Delaney credit for showing him that a black American could make a living as an artist. Other admirers included James Jones and Henry Miller, who published an essay titled "The Amazing and Invariable Beauford Delaney." Artist Georgia O'Keeffe painted a portrait of Delaney and composed a tribute to him for his 1973 one-man show in Paris.

Delaney is also remembered for his paintings of street scenes. Critics admired his use of color in these paintings and his efforts to convey the variations of light through more abstract paintings. "I learned about light from Beauford Delaney," Baldwin wrote in a 1965 issue of *Transition* magazine. In 1978 the Studio Museum in Harlem dedicated the first show of its *Black Masters* series to Delaney's work. His art was also exhibited in a one-man show at the Philippe Briet Gallery in 1991.

Delaney left New York for Paris in 1953 and remained there until his death. Because of his generosity to friends, Delaney struggled financially even after he became a successful artist. In 1961 he suffered a nervous breakdown. Although he continued to paint, he never fully recovered. He entered St. Anne's, a psychiatric hospital in Paris, in 1975, and died there four years later.

North America

Delany, Samuel R.

(b. April 1, 1942, New York, N.Y.), African American science fiction writer, literary critic, and nonfiction author known as an important voice in African American literature and gay literature.

Samuel R. Delany's early work played a major role in the development of a more literary "new wave" in science fiction during the 1960s. In a genre known previously for its ideas rather than stylistic innovation, Delany's fist novels were heavily influenced by the formal experimentation of modernist and postmodernist writers such as James Joyce, Ralph Ellison, and Djuna Barnes, as well as the work of such leading science fiction writers as Isaac Asimov and Theodore Sturgeon.

Delany's writing was largely concerned with technology and the development of artistic and outlaw subcultures on the margins of society, anticipating the later "cyberpunk" trend in video, film, fiction, and graphic art. Delany's fiction may have been influenced by his being one of the very few African American science fiction writers of his generation, and by his open homosexuality (though he also had significant heterosexual relationships); from the beginning his work took up the issues of race and sexuality with a seriousness never before seen in mainstream science fiction. Since the 1970s his fiction and nonfiction work have increasingly been concerned with the investigation of race and sexuality, establishing him as one of the most powerful chroniclers of an African American gay sensibility.

Delany was born April 1, 1942, in New York City to Samuel R. Delany Sr., a successful funeral director, and Margaret Carey, a staff member of the New York Public Library. He grew up in Harlem, graduated from Bronx High School of Science, and attended the City College of New York. He married the poet Marilyn Hacker in 1961. They were divorced in 1980 and have one daughter.

Delany's first novel, *The Jewels of Aptor*, appeared in 1962. He won the first of his five Nebula Awards (the major award in science fiction) for his 1966 novel *Babel-17*. He has also won other major science fiction accolades such as the Hugo Award and the Pilgrim Award. The postmodern epic *Dhalgren* (1975) is considered by some critics to be Delany's most intriguing novel. Its protagonist is a bisexual African American named Kid who comes to a largely abandoned American city after an unnamed disaster. The novel describes Kid's experiences with the subcultures of the desperate, deviant, and/or voyeuristic people who remain in the city.

More recently Delany has focused on nonfiction writing. *The Motion of Life in Water* (1988), his autobiographical account of the intersection of the 1960s counterculture and the gay subculture of New York, has been widely acclaimed. His academic work as a teacher and literary critic has also become more prominent. He has been a member of the faculty of the University of Massachusetts at Amherst since 1988.

North America

Diddley, Bo

(b. December 30, 1928, McComb, Miss.), African American singer, guitarist, and songwriter; member of the Rock and Roll Hall of Fame.

Bo Diddley, born Otha Elias Bates, was sent as a baby by his family to live with cousins in Chicago, Illinois, where he took the name McDaniel. He learned to play the guitar in his teens. At 23, he took a regular job at the 708 Club in Chicago, playing blues and rhythm and blues. He toured the Midwest with rhythm and blues groups and as a solo artist.

As rock 'n' roll began its rise to popularity in the mid-1950s, he began to write songs in the new style. He came to the attention of Chess Records in Chicago and took the name Bo Diddley in his first recordings for the label. Sources differ on the name's origin. It may have been a childhood nickname for a mischievous boy, a slang term for a witty storyteller, or the name under which he had boxed in his youth.

He gave his first single the same name. The song *"Bo Diddley"* became a nationwide hit in 1955. Diddley produced more Top 10 singles during the next five years. He established himself as a major concert attraction, known for his distinctive cigar-box shaped guitar as well as his vital performances.

Diddley's music owed much to the blues. Songs like *"I'm a Man"* and *"Who Do You Love"* emphasized his persona of powerful independence and manhood. The distinctive stuttering rhythm of many of his compositions became a hallmark of early rock 'n' roll.

Diddley continued to tour and record in the four decades that followed his early fame. He was inducted into the Rock and Roll Hall of Fame in 1987.

Africa

Diop, Alioune

(b. January 20, 1910, Saint-Louis, Senegal; d. May 2, 1980, Paris, France),
Senegalese writer and editor who became a central figure in the Négritude
movement.

Alioune Diop was born in Saint-Louis, Senegal, whose inhabitants enjoyed
automatic French citizenship during the colonial period. He obtained his
secondary education at the Lycée Faidherbe in Saint-Louis, then studied in
Algeria and at the Sorbonne in Paris. He took a position as professor of classical literature in Paris and represented Senegal in the French senate after
World War II. In 1947 Diop founded *Présence Africaine*, perhaps the most
influential intellectual journal of its time on anticolonial and emancipatory
culture and politics among Africans and peoples of African descent. With
frequent contributions from his friend and associate Léopold Sédar Senghor,
Diop's journal helped foster the *Négritude* movement, which aimed to promote an African cultural identity and the liberation of the people of Africa
and the African diaspora. In 1949 Diop founded *Présence Africaine Editions*,
a leading publishing house for African authors.

Diop's journal, though anticolonial in spirit, published the work of
notable black politicians, poets, fiction writers, and essayists from Africa, the
Caribbean, Europe, and the United States from a variety of ideological perspectives. Although the journal became increasingly political, Diop's own
work often focused on the significance of the arts in African culture. A
devout Catholic, he also wrote essays critical of the colonial tendencies of
some church organizations.

The energetic Diop's contributions to the Négritude movement
extended beyond his own publishing ventures. He founded the Société
Africaine de Culture (1956) and helped organize several conferences for
black writers and artists, including the first and second International Congress of Black Writers and Artists in Paris (1956) and Rome (1959); the first
World Festival of Negro Arts in Dakar (1966); and the second Festival of
Black and African Arts and Culture in Lagos (1977).

Diop left a cultural legacy that has continued since his death in 1980.
Cultural ministers from the sub-Saharan states established a literary prize in
his honor in 1982; the 50th anniversary celebration of *Présence Africaine* was
held in Paris in 1997; and *Présence Africaine Editions* remains active under
the direction of Yandé Christian Diop, his widow.

North America

Dixon, Willie

(b. July 1, 1915, Vicksburg, Miss.; d. January 29, 1992, Burbank, Calif.), prolific
African American blues musician who composed, produced, and recorded
both his own and his contemporaries' music.

Willie Dixon performed in a gospel quartet as a youth and was greatly influenced by the blues piano of Little Brother Montgomery. Dixon initially decided, however, to capitalize on his massive frame and make his fortune as a heavyweight boxer. In the 1930s he moved from Mississippi to Chicago and in 1937 won the Illinois State Golden Gloves heavyweight championship. He switched to music later that year, after a dispute with his manager over money.

Dixon played bass for a number of groups in the 1940s but his career was interrupted by a jail sentence when he refused to honor the draft. In 1946 he joined Leonard Caston and Bernardo Dennis in the Big Three Trio, a group that played blues, pop, boogie woogie, and novelty music. The Big Three Trio toured the Midwest and recorded with Columbia Records until they disbanded in 1952. By that time Dixon had secured a part-time job with Chess Records, for which he worked until 1971.

Through Chess Records, Dixon collaborated with star after star. He was soon serving the company full-time, working as A&R (artist and repertory) man, composer, arranger, session musician, and talent scout. Bluesmen such as Muddy Waters, Howlin' Wolf, and Little Walter & His Jukes recorded Dixon originals; Dixon himself recorded with Waters, Chuck Berry, Bo Diddley, and many more. During his two decades with Chess, Dixon helped pioneer the new Chicago Blues that transformed languid, rural, acoustic songs into hard-edged electric numbers. When Dixon temporarily left Chess for Cobra Records in 1957, he helped develop Chicago's West Side sound by producing the music of Buddy Guy, Otis Rush, and Magic Sam.

During the 1960s Dixon performed with Memphis Slim in American and European concerts that sparked widespread interest in blues and folk among young white listeners. British bands of the late 1960s such as Led Zeppelin and Cream reflected Dixon's influence, scoring smash hits with psychedelic versions of his old blues songs. Such bands covered—and in some cases stole—Dixon's compositions.

Dixon continued to record throughout the 1980s and 1990s. In his old age he became a blues activist, founding, in 1991, the Blues Heaven Foundation. The organization contributed funds to music education programs and helped old blues musicians win royalties for songs others had plagiarized. In 1989 he published his autobiography, boldly yet not inaccurately titled *I Am the Blues*. Dixon died in 1992 of heart failure. He was inducted into the Rock and Roll Hall of Fame in 1994.

North America

Dobbs, Mattiwilda

(b. 1925, Atlanta, Ga.), American opera singer; first black person to sing at La Scala in Milan, Italy, and second black woman to sing at the Metropolitan Opera House in New York City.

Mattiwilda Dobbs, a coloratura soprano, was born in Atlanta, Georgia, to Irene Thompson Dobbs and John Wesley Dobbs, a mail clerk who later organized the Georgia Voters League. Dobbs attended Spelman College (1946) and Columbia University (1948). She studied with Lotte Leonard (1946–1950), a lieder and Wagner specialist, and won the Marian Anderson Award in 1947.

A John Hay Whitney Fellowship (1950–1952) allowed her to study in Paris under Pierre Bernac and Lola Rodriguez de Aragon. Her professional career began when she won first prize at the International Music Competition in Geneva in 1950. In 1953, at the request of Herbert von Karajan, she became the first black person to sing at La Scala in Milan. Success at Glyndebourne in the same year led to a command performance for Queen Elizabeth II and the king and queen of Sweden at Covent Garden; the latter awarded her the Order of the North Star, and she sang at Covent Garden from 1953 until 1958.

Following a positive critical reception at the New York Town Hall in 1954, Dobbs made her American opera debut at the San Francisco Opera House, in Rimsky-Korsakov's *Le Coq d'Or* (1955). In 1956 she became the second black woman to appear at the Metropolitan Opera House in New York City, as Gilda in Verdi's *Rigoletto*. She married a Swedish journalist, Bengt Jansen (1957), and although she has taught at Howard University (1976–1991) and other U.S. establishments, her career has been centered in Europe. She was elected to the Metropolitan Opera Association National Board in 1989.

North America

Domino, Antoine ("Fats"), Jr.

(b. February 26, 1928, New Orleans, La.), African American singer, pianist, and songwriter whose songs topped both rhythm and blues and rock 'n' roll charts during the 1950s.

Fats Domino was one of the few black musicians of the 1950s to successfully span rhythm and blues (R&B) and rock 'n' roll, appealing to young white audiences while maintaining his popularity with black audiences. His formula for success was a driving, boogie-woogie style of piano playing and a New Orleans Creole style of singing.

Domino was born and raised in New Orleans, where French Creole was his first language. He learned to play the piano by the age of nine and was performing at local music venues by the time he was a teenager. His musical career took off in the late 1940s after he teamed up with Dave Bartholomew, a former Duke Ellington trumpet player, and his band. After signing a contract with New Orleans-based Imperial Records, Domino collaborated with Bartholomew to record *"The Fat Man"* (1950), his first R&B hit. His *"Goin' Home"* reached the number one slot on the R&B charts in 1952.

Domino's songs began to storm *Billboard*'s rock 'n' roll charts in the mid-1950s. *"Ain't That a Shame"* (1955) marked the beginning of a string of hits in 1956 that included *"I'm in Love Again," "My Blue Heaven,"* and *"Blue-*

berry Hill." Domino continued to record hits with Bartholomew, who served as his arranger, conductor, and producer, and even made some movie appearances before leaving Imperial Records in 1962.

Even though some of his songs were stolen and quickly marketed by such white artists as Pat Boone and Ricky Nelson, Domino put more than a dozen songs in the Top 10 and sold more than 65 million records between 1950 and 1962. With the exception of Elvis Presley, no other artist was more popular than Fats Domino during the 1950s. In 1986 he was inducted into the Rock and Roll Hall of Fame.

Dorsey, Thomas Andrew

(b. July 1, 1899, Villa Rica, Ga.; d. January 23, 1993, Chicago, Ill.), African American pianist, arranger, and composer, known as the "Father of Gospel Music."

Thomas A. Dorsey's name is synonymous with modern gospel music. Dorsey composed over 1,000 songs in his lifetime, half of which were published. With creative genius and business savvy, Dorsey popularized songs that combined the rhythm and tonality of blues with lyrics about personal spiritual salvation. Countless gospel performers achieved their first success singing Dorsey's music. His most famous song, *"Precious Lord, Take My Hand,"* is one of the most popular gospel songs in America.

Dorsey was born to Etta and Thomas Madison Dorsey. Thomas Madison was an itinerant preacher, and Etta played the organ in church. As a child, Dorsey was regularly exposed to spirituals and Baptist hymns. Extended family members introduced Dorsey to rural blues and shaped-note singing. In 1908 the family moved to Atlanta, where Dorsey learned to play the piano by watching pianists at a vaudeville theater on Decatur Street. Dorsey also saw Ma Rainey and Bessie Smith perform at this theater. By age 12 Dorsey had become a proficient piano player, honing his improvisational skills at dances and rent-parties around Atlanta. After teaching himself to read music, Dorsey left Atlanta and traveled to Chicago in 1916.

In Chicago Dorsey continued his musical training and learned the skills of composing and arranging. He copyrighted his first blues composition, *"If You Don't Believe I'm Leaving, You Can Count the Days I'm Gone,"* on October 9, 1920. During the 1921 National Baptist Convention, Dorsey heard W. M. Nix sing "*I Do, Don't You*" and became convinced that his mission in life was to evangelize through music. In 1922 Dorsey wrote his first two sacred songs, *"If I Don't Get There"* and *"We Will Meet Him in the Sweet By and By."* Dorsey's evangelical efforts did not last long, and he returned to secular music, joining Will Walker's "The Whispering Syncopators" a few months after being saved at the Convention. While playing with the "Syncopators" Dorsey began composing blues in the style of W. C. Handy for the Chicago record companies. Dorsey's first hit came when King Oliver's

Creole Jazz Band recorded his composition *"Riverside Blues"* in December 1923. The success of Bessie Smith's recording of *"Downhearted Blues"* in 1923, however, soon made Dorsey's vaudevillian blues obsolete. Almost singlehandedly, Smith swayed the blues recording industry to her "downhome" style. Fortunately for Dorsey, he was well versed in this style from his days playing in Atlanta.

In April 1924 Dorsey became piano player and director of Ma Rainey's Wild Cat Jazz Band. For the next two years Dorsey served as composer, arranger, and conductor for this touring band. (During that time, Ma Rainey's only rival among popular downhome blues singers was Bessie Smith.) After suffering from incapacitating depression starting in 1926, Dorsey underwent a second conversion in 1928. This conversion and the death of a close friend inspired Dorsey to compose his first gospel blues song *"If You See My Savior, Tell Him That You Saw Me."*

Again, however, the financial lure of commercial secular music convinced Dorsey to begin composing and playing the blues. This time his partner was guitar player Hudson Whitaker. Together they recorded over 60 songs as Georgia Tom and Tampa Red between 1928 and 1932. Dorsey and Whitaker are credited with creating the "hokum" blues style. "Hokum" consisted of guitar and piano instrumentation, up-tempo rhythms, strong bass, and usually included sexually suggestive lyrics. Popularizing this style with their seminal double entendre blues, *"It's Tight Like That,"* Dorsey and Whitaker went on to write and record such songs as *"Pat That Bread," "You Got That Stuff," "Where Did You Stay Last Night?" "It's All Worn Out,"* and *"Somebody's Been Using That Thing."*

At this point in his career Dorsey was straddling the fence between sacred and profane music. He continued recording blues with Whitaker as well as selling sheet music of his gospel songs and organizing a gospel choir at Ebenezer Baptist Church. After Dorsey's wife Nettie and their child died in August 1932, Dorsey forsook the blues. While in St. Louis to promote his gospel songs, Dorsey was called home to find that Nettie had fallen ill. When he returned Nettie had died and their child was on the verge of death. Stricken with grief, Dorsey sat at his piano to console himself and composed *"Precious Lord, Take My Hand."*

Dorsey met Sallie Martin, the "Mother of Gospel Music," in 1932, and they collaborated until 1939 organizing gospel choruses and publishing gospel songs. Together they founded the National Convention of Gospel Choirs and Choruses in August of 1933. The 1930s were Dorsey's most prolific years. Mahalia Jackson replaced Sallie Martin as Dorsey's singer in 1939, and they toured together until 1944. The Jackson-Dorsey combination ushered in the golden age of gospel music, during which many artists achieved their first success with a Dorsey song. Singers such as Sister Rosetta Tharpe (*"Rock Me"*), Marion Williams (*"Standing Here Wondering Which Way To Go"*), The Soul Stirrers (*"Never Turn Back"*), Dixie Hummingbirds (*"When the Gates Swing Open"*), and Bessie Griffin (*"Shake My Mother's Hand"*) had popular hits with Dorsey's songs. Elvis Presley and Red Foley garnered gold records from singing Dorsey's song *"Peace in the Valley."*

Dorsey continued promoting gospel music as the head of the National Convention of Gospel Choirs and Choruses until his death in 1993.

North America

Douglas, Aaron

(b. May 26, 1899, Topeka, Kans.; d. February 2, 1979, Nashville, Tenn.), African American artist closely associated with the Harlem Renaissance; Douglas synthesized formal and symbolic elements of African art with a modern European aesthetic.

Aaron Douglas came to Harlem from Topeka, Kansas, in 1925, the year in which the cultural critic and philosopher Alain Locke launched the "New Negro" Movement. This movement expressed African Americans' new pride in their African heritage, which manifested itself in literature, song, dance, and, most significantly for Douglas, art.

Shortly after his arrival in Harlem, Douglas made the acquaintance of the German American portrait artist Winold Reiss, who illustrated the March 1925 *New Negro* issue of *Survey Graphic* for Locke. Both Reiss and Locke encouraged Douglas to develop his own American black aesthetic from design motifs in African art. Douglas followed their suggestions and sought examples of African art, which in the 1920s were beginning to be purchased by the collections of American museums and galleries. Locke recognized that the sculptural art of Africa had inspired the art of such leading modernists as Pablo Picasso and Constantin Brancusi and that it could lead to the creation of great art by African Americans.

Douglas developed a unique aesthetic that linked black Americans with their African past by using imagery derived from African sculptural and ancestral art to express aspects of the black experience in the United States. The two principal types of works he executed were drawings and murals. His drawings were characterized by bold, sharply delineated designs in black and white. On the other hand, softer outlines, superimposed forms, and a subdued color scheme in the red-green range characterized his murals. Douglas's murals focus on African American history and religious practices.

Though he had been instructed in the academic mode of painting at the University of Nebraska, Douglas rejected realism in favor of a geometric painting style that he developed while studying under Reiss during the late 1920s. Douglas reduced forms to their fundamental shapes, such as circles, triangles, and rectangles. He tended to represent both objects and black people as silhouettes. Most of these forms are hard-edged and angular, reminiscent of the Art Deco designs popular in the United States during the early twentieth century. Some figures, however, have a curvilinear character, apparently influenced by the contemporary Art Nouveau trend in France that endows them with a sense of movement. One critic compared the rhythmic quality and arrangement of Douglas's figures to those of Greek vase paintings.

Douglas began his artistic career as an illustrator, working in black and white with an occasional touch of gray. He burst onto the art scene in 1925 with a cover illustration for *Opportunity* magazine and a first-place award from the *Crisis* magazine for his drawing *The African Chieftain*. Douglas became a regular contributor to each of these publications. In that same year, he collaborated with Reiss to illustrate Locke's *The New Negro*, a landmark anthology of black writers.

Douglas's visual exploration of African motifs and his use of black subjects commanded the attention of the black intellectual and writer James Weldon Johnson, who commissioned Douglas to illustrate his *God's Trombones: Seven Negro Sermons in Verse* (1927). Douglas considered his work for this book to be his most important and most mature set of illustrations. *God's Trombones* attempts to capture the rhetoric of the black preacher, and in illustrating its pages, Douglas said, "I tried to keep my forms very stark and geometric with my main emphasis on the human body. I tried to portray everything not in a realistic, but in [an] abstract way—simplified and abstract as . . . in the spirituals."

In *God's Trombones*, Douglas offered an unconventional interpretation of traditional biblical themes. In *Go Down Death*, for example, death is depicted not as an evil force, but as a swift rescuer that many slaves welcomed as a means of deliverance from the hardships of bondage. In another illustration, *The Crucifixion*, Douglas challenges traditional representations of this event by focusing on the benevolence of Simon, the dark-skinned man who took up the cross for Christ on his way to Mount Calvary, rather than exclusively on the suffering of Christ. Throughout the series, Douglas depicts blacks as central to biblical history.

In the same year that Douglas completed the illustrations for *God's Trombones*, he executed for Club Ebony a mural series inspired by Harlem's nightlife. Like his illustrations, it was done in black and white. Art collector and historian Albert C. Barnes was impressed with the murals and remarked that Douglas should try doing them in color. He offered Douglas a year-long scholarship to study color at his art school outside Philadelphia, and Douglas, who had very little experience in mixing colors, accepted. As a result of this study, Douglas came to incorporate color in his murals.

The mural series for which Douglas is best known is *Aspects of Negro Life* (1934), now at the Countee Cullen Branch of the New York Public Library. It consists of four chronological compositions. The first, *The Negro in an African Setting*, highlights the African heritage of African Americans through representations of African dance and music. The second spans three stages of African American history: slavery, emancipation, and Reconstruction. *The Idyll of the Deep South*, the third composition, portrays the problem of lynching and how African Americans, in spite of this omnipresent threat, continued to work, sing, and dance. The final mural, *Song of the Towers*, charts three events: the mass migration of blacks to Northern industrial centers during the 1910s, the flowering of black artistic expression in 1920s New York City known as the Harlem Renaissance, and the onset of the Great Depression in the 1930s.

In *Aspects of Negro Life*, Douglas used a technique that became his signature mural style. First he arranged a series of concentric circles that expanded from a fixed point. Then he imposed figurative elements on this circular background. While layering the composition, Douglas maintained the continuity of the circular design by altering a person's or object's shade of color in the places where it intersected with a circle. As a result, a person or object would bear several diffused shades of the same color. This procedure lent to Douglas's murals a mystical, dreamlike quality. The chromatic complexity and sophisticated design of *Aspects of Negro Life* is unparalleled by other murals done during the Works Progress Administration's Federal Art Project (WPA/FAP), a New Deal program that supported unemployed artists.

Douglas was not exclusively an illustrator and a muralist, although these two mediums occupied most of his career. Influenced by a year of independent study at the Académie Scandinave in Paris, he occasionally painted portraits and landscapes, which were more naturalistic than his other work. He was also a social activist who, as the first elected president of the Harlem Artists Guild (1935), worked to obtain WPA recognition and support for African American artists. Finally, Douglas was an educator. After graduating from the University of Nebraska, he taught art at Lincoln High School in Topeka, Kansas, from 1923 to 1925. Beginning in 1939, he occasionally taught drawing and painting at Fisk University in Nashville, Tennessee. After earning a master's degree in art education from Columbia University in 1944, he became a permanent member of the Fisk University faculty, serving as a professor in and as chair of the art department until his retirement in 1966. He continued to lecture and paint until his death in 1979. He was one of the first African American artists to affirm the value of the black experience, and his artistic vision was permeated by his refusal "to compromise and see blacks as anything other than a proud and majestic people."

North America

Dove, Rita

(b. August 28, 1952, Akron, Ohio), African American poet and writer, who became the second African American woman to win the Pulitzer Prize for her collection of poetry Thomas and Beulah in 1987; served as United States Poet Laureate from 1993 to 1995.

Rita Dove was born August 28, 1952, in Akron, Ohio, to Ray and Elvira Hord Dove. After graduating with a B.A. summa cum laude from Miami University in Ohio in 1973, she received a Fulbright award to study at the University of Tübingen in West Germany. From there she went to the Iowa Writers Workshop, where she completed an M.F.A. in creative writing in 1977.

Dove joined the faculty of Arizona State University in 1981 and spent 1982 as writer-in-residence at the Tuskegee Institute. While at Arizona State she participated in several literary panels for the National Endowment for the Arts (1984–1986), served on the board of the Associate Writing Programs from 1985 to 1988, and was the organization's president in

1986–1987. In 1987 she became a member of the Commission for the Preservation of Black Culture of the Schomburg Center for Research in Black Culture. She also held several editorial positions on such journals as *Callaloo, Gettysburg Review* and *TriQuarterly*. She received a Guggenheim fellowship in 1983 and the Lavan Younger Poets Award from the Academy of American Poets in 1986. She then wrote *Thomas and Beulah* (1986), a collection of poems based on her grandparents' lives for which she won the Pulitzer Prize for Poetry in 1987. Dove was the first African American woman to achieve this award since Gwendolyn Brooks received it in 1950.

In addition to several chapbooks, including *Ten Poems* (1977) and *The Only Dark Spot in the Sky* (1980), Dove's early works of poetry include *The Yellow House on the Corner* (1980) and *Museum* (1983). These works "won praise from reviewers for their technical excellence and unusual breadth of subject matter." Her other poetry collections include *Grace Notes* (1989), *Selected Poems* (1993), *Mother Love* (1995), and most recently, *On the Bus with Rosa Parks* (1999). She also wrote a novel, *Through the Ivory Gate* (1992), a play titled *The Darker Face of the Earth* (1994), a book of short stories titled *Fifth Sunday* (1995), and a collection of essays, *The Poet's World* (1995). Critics praise her poetry, in which she "gathers the various facts of this life and presents them in ways that jar our lazy assumptions. She gives voice to many positions and many characters." Critic Emily Grosholz declares that, "Dove can turn her poetic sights on just about anything and make the language shimmer."

At age 40 Dove became the youngest person and first African American to be honored as U.S. Poet Laureate, a title she held from 1993 through 1995. In addition to honorary doctorates from numerous colleges and universities, including Dart-mouth College and Columbia University, she has received, among other awards, the NAACP Great American Artist Award (1993), the Renaissance Forum Award for Leadership in the Literary Arts from the Folger Shakespeare Library (1994), the Chrales Frankel prize National Medal in the Humanities (1996), and the Levinson Prize from *Poetry* magazine (1998). In 1993 she received an endowed chair at the University of Virginia as the Commonwealth Professor of English. She lives in Charlottesville with her husband, Fred Viebahn, a German novelist, and their daughter, Aviva.

North America

Drifters, The,

an African American rhythm and blues band that scored hit after hit in the 1950s and 1960s.

The Drifters is a group name under which numerous musicians have performed. The group began in 1953 when Atlantic Records cofounder Ahmet Ertegun learned that tenor Clyde McPhatter had been fired from his position with Billy Ward & His Dominoes. That night, the story goes, Ertegun searched for McPhatter in Harlem and immediately got him to agree to form a new band. The two then recruited singers to back McPhatter's superb lead vocals, hiring Bill Pinkney and Andrew and Gerhart Thrasher. By the end of that year *"Money Honey"* had become the first of the group's many smash pop and R&B hits. But late in 1954 the Drifters were forced to reorganize when McPhatter was drafted by the United States Army.

The remaining members continued without him, adopting in turn David Baugh, Johnny Moore, and Bobby Hendricks as front men. When McPhatter returned from the service, he pursued a solo career instead of rejoining the group, and in 1958 manager George Treadwell fired the rest of the original members. In their place he hired the Crowns to assume the Drifters' name. Singer Ben E. King was the new leader, while the prolific white songwriting team of Jerry Leiber and Mike Stoller composed most of the group's material. The new Drifters rivaled the old in sending songs up the charts; their hits included *"There Goes My Baby,"* which popularized the use of strings in traditional R&B arrangements.

Although King left the group in 1960 to record as a solo act, the Drifters, led by Rudy Lewis and later Johnny Moore, continued to release hit songs, including *"Up on the Roof"* (1963) and *"Under the Boardwalk"* (1964). By the end of the 1960s, however, their albums were receiving less play; in the 1970s their releases were successful only in Europe. In 1977 they represented the United States in Russia. In the late 1970s and the 1980s and 1990s, the Drifters persisted as a nostalgia act, its members gaining weight and losing fans. They appeared at the 1998 Sportours Superbowl Gala for Superbowl XXXII and were inducted into the Rock and Roll Hall of Fame in 1988.

North America

Du Bois, Shirley Graham

(b. November 11, 1896?, Indianapolis, Ind.; d. March 27, 1977, Beijing, China), African American author, musical director, composer, playwright, and political activist; second wife of the prominent black scholar and activist W. E. B. Du Bois.

The oldest of five children of Rev. David A. Graham and Etta (Bell) Graham, Shirley Graham Du Bois moved with her family to various locations throughout the United States. As a teenager in Colorado Springs, she first met W. E. B. Du Bois when he came to lecture at the local African Methodist Episcopal (AME) Church. Soon after high school, she married a local man, Shadrack T. McCanns; the marriage soon ended, leaving her to support two small children. "In quick succession I knew the glory of motherhood and the pain of deep sorrow," she wrote later. "For the years immediately following, everything I did . . . was motivated by my passionate desire to make a good life for my sons."

The nomadic quality of Graham's early life carried over into her educational experiences, just as it would in her later years. After attending classes at Howard University's School of Music, in 1930 she spent time in Paris, France, where she studied music and French at the Sorbonne. In that same year she entered Oberlin College in Ohio, earning a bachelor's degree in music (1934) and a master's degree in music history (1935), with an emphasis on Africa. In addition to her studies as a vocalist and composer, she wrote plays and in 1932 became the first African American woman to produce an all-black opera based on her one-act play *Tom-Tom*, a portrayal of black Americans and their music from the seventeenth century to the present.

During the late 1930s Du Bois worked for the Federal Theater Project designing sets and composing musical scores for all-black stage productions, including an adaptation of Eugene O'Neill's *The Hairy Ape* and Theodore Ward's *Big White Fog*. The recipient of a Julius Rosenwald grant in 1938, she attended the Yale School of Drama, where she focused on writing and directing plays, including the comedy *Elijah's Ravens* (1941) and the tragedy *Dust to Earth* (1941). Between 1944 and 1964 she turned her talent to writing critical biographies on noted African Americans, including Frederick Douglass, Phillis Wheatley, and Booker T. Washington.

Du Bois's artistic and scholarly endeavors were deeply motivated by a desire to convey the struggles and achievements of blacks. She actively protested racial injustice and in 1943 became the New York field secretary for the National Association for the Advancement of Colored People (NAACP), where she worked alongside W. E. B. Du Bois. In him she found a kindred soul, and in 1951 the two married. After spending several years with her new husband in Brooklyn, New York—where he was surveyed by government agents for his political radicalism—she took refuge with him in Ghana in 1961, returning briefly to the United States in 1971 and 1975. She died on March 27, 1977, in Beijing, China, where she was undergoing treatment for cancer.

Europe

Dumas, Alexandre, Père

(b. July 24, 1802, Villers-Cotterêts, France; d. December 5, 1870, Puys, France), French novelist, dramatist, and essayist of African descent, a central figure in nineteenth-century French Romantic literature.

In 1893 the playwright George Bernard Shaw described Alexandre Dumas père (senior) as "a summit of art," comparing him to Mozart: "you get nothing above Dumas on his own mountain . . . . If you pass him you come down on the other side instead of getting higher." Dumas's literary work is striking in its breadth and originality, and is accessible to all lovers of adventure regardless of their social or educational background. In theater, Dumas created two new genres, the prose historical drama and the *drame moderne*, and, although dated today, his plays enjoyed unprecedented success in their time. His greatest novels, rich in passionate characters, lively dialogue, and gripping plots, have lasting appeal, and many, such as *Les trois mousquetaires* (The Three Musketeers), have become household names.

The story of how young Dumas—a provincial, light-skinned boy, whose tightly curled hair revealed his African ancestry—rose to become the supreme literary entertainer of his time is as intriguing as his novels. His father, Thomas-Alexandre Dumas Davy de la Pailleterie, was the son of the French Marquis Antoine-Alexandre Davy de la Pailleterie and a black slave woman named Marie-Cessette Dumas. Thomas-Alexandre was born in the French colony of Saint-Domingue (later Haiti), where he remained until he was brought to France at age 18. On enlisting in the French army, he dropped the name Davy de la Pailleterie, because his father disapproved of his enlistment, and took instead the name of his black mother. He rose to the rank of general but quarreled with Napoleon while on campaign with him in Egypt. On his way back to France, he stopped in the kingdom of Naples, which, unbeknownst to him, had recently declared war on France. He was imprisoned for two years in wretched conditions that ruined his health. He returned to France in 1801 and died five years later, leaving his widow and children in relative poverty in the rural town of Villers-Cotterêts.

Were it not for a Swedish aristocrat, Adolphe de Leuven, who began vacationing at Villers-Cotterêts when Dumas was 16, Dumas would probably never have pursued a literary career. De Leuven convinced Dumas to collaborate with him on a number of light theatrical pieces, and also introduced Dumas to the historical romances of Sir Walter Scott. Dumas moved to Paris in 1823, continued to write vaudeville plays with de Leuven, and supported himself by working as a copyist for the duke of Orleans. There he found another mentor in the literary-minded assistant director, E. H. Lassagne, who guided him to the authors who would most aid the development of his literary gifts.

The next major step forward came in 1828, when a friend, Charles Nodier, invited Dumas to become a member of his literary salon, which included such leaders of the French Romantic movement as Victor Hugo, Alfred de Vigny, and Alphonse de Lamartine. In the following year, Dumas premiered to great success his historical drama *Henri III et sa cour* (Henry III and His Court) at the prestigious Comédie-Française theater. This triumph secured his financial position and reputation in Paris as a dramatist of verve and substance. From 1829 until 1851 he brought out a new play in Paris almost every year; in some years he premiered four or five. His most original and critically acclaimed plays, such as the psychological drama *Antony*, the melodrama *La tour de Nesle* (The Tower of Nesle), and his comedy *Mademoiselle de Belle-Isle*, date from the 1830s. Most of his plays were received with enthusiasm. In his plays and novels he wrote for the widest possible audience, and although some elite writers faulted his literary style, they envied his popularity.

Dumas's career as a novelist began between 1837 and 1843. During this period, after some disappointing reactions to some of his plays, he sought a new audience among the readers of *romans-feuilletons* (serial novels published in newspapers and journals). In 1838 he published four novels, including two romans-feuilletons, but it was not until the publication of *Le chevalier d'Harmental* in 1842 that he became established as a novelist. During the next 13 years, he produced a wealth of novels. His most important historically inspired works are the D'Artagnan trilogy, which includes his most famous work, *Les trois mousquetaires*; the Valois cycle, which includes *La reine* Margot (Marguerite de Valois) and draws on the bloody religious wars in France in the 1570s and 1580s; and the five Marie-Antoinette romances, which span the reign of Louis XVI and the French Revolution. His *Le comte de Monte-Cristo* (1846, The Count of Monte-Cristo), which enjoyed instantaneous and enduring success and which has a more contemporary setting, is described by literary scholar F. W. J. Hemmings as "an epic fantasy of vengeance."

The standard edition of Dumas's complete works runs to 301 volumes, and some scholars have raised doubts about the authenticity of some of his work. As French writer André Maurois observed in his biography of Dumas, "no one has read all of Dumas; that would be as impossible as for him to have written it all." It is true that Dumas collaborated with friends on some of his novels and plays. His most important collaborator was Auguste Maquet, who helped with many of his historical novels, sketching out plots and characters. However, as literary scholar Richard Stowe concludes, "while Dumas might not have been able to write certain of his novels without his collaborators, without him none of the best ones could have been written at all."

Dumas's nonfiction works—travel writings and a 3,000-page memoir—present a portrait of an energetic and curious adventurer. Indeed, Dumas often found himself personally caught up in the political upheavals of mid-nineteenth-century Europe. In 1832, shortly after *La tour de Nesle* had begun its highly successful first run, he was present at a violent clash between French troops and republican insurrectionists in Paris. He took the revolutionaries to a nearby theater that was running one of his plays, *Napoléon Bonaparte*, broke down the door, and distributed the props from the play—a cache of weapons—to the delighted republicans. He then went home to rest. The next day he learned that the uprising had been crushed and all the revolutionaries massacred. He also read an account in a Paris newspaper of his own capture and execution by firing squad. The author of the account deplored the premature termination of such a promising literary career, and Dumas wrote to thank him for the kind obituary.

In 1860 Dumas became a close friend and collaborator of Giuseppe Garibaldi, the unifier of Italy, accompanying Garibaldi's "redshirts" during their invasion of Sicily. Dumas subsequently went to Naples to rouse opposition to the monarchy of Francis II, whose grandfather had been responsible for the imprisonment of Dumas's father. Dumas organized a team of tailors to sew and distribute red shirts, and set off fireworks to encourage Garibaldi's supporters in the city. After the king fled Naples and Garibaldi arrived and took control, he publicly embraced Dumas as a sign of gratitude.

Of Dumas's many trips through Europe, his longest and most eventful was a nine-month journey across the Russian Empire, beginning in June 1858. He was astonished to find people across the country who knew his books: monks in a remote monastery on Lake Ladoga in the north; administrators in Astrakhan on the Caspian Sea; and Persians in the Caucasus, who had retranslated his books from Russian into Persian. He also took many sea voyages in the Mediterranean—one of the few pursuits that gave him rest from a life of intense work and activity: "As soon as my sight is lost in immensity . . . there falls on my senses a delightful twilight, something that smokers of opium and eaters of hashish can alone understand—that voluptuous absence of the will."

Dumas had many mistresses throughout his life and fathered a number of children, including Alexandre Dumas fils (junior), who in later years became a conservative moralist and writer. Earlier, however, Dumas and his son went out dancing together, and they shared mistresses. As the young Alexandre once remarked to a disapproving middle-aged woman, "At least, if he doesn't set me a good example, he provides me with an excellent excuse." One of Dumas's last mistresses was Adah Menken, an actress, ballet dancer, and minor poet from New Orleans, who was widely believed to be an African American Creole, and who first performed in Paris in 1866. Known as the Naked Lady, she specialized in riding horses bareback across stage seminude. She described Dumas as "the King of Romance, the child of Gentleness and Love."

A few days before he died, Dumas recounted a dream to his son Alexandre. In the dream he had been standing on the peak of a mountain made up of all his books. Gradually, the ground beneath his feet had given way, leaving only a small heap of pumice stones and ashes. Deeply troubled, he asked his son if he believed that his work would survive after his death. To his son's reassurance, contemporary scholars and readers can add their own affirmation: the mountain of Dumas's life and work still towers.

North America

Dunbar-Nelson, Alice

(b. July 19, 1875, New Orleans, La.; d. September 18, 1935, Philadelphia, Pa.), African American writer, journalist, and activist whose work focused on the multiracial experience, women's rights, and race relations.

Alice Dunbar-Nelson was born into a mixed Creole, African American, and Native American family. She graduated from the two-year teacher training program at Straight College (now Dillard University) in 1892, and taught school at various times throughout her life.

Dunbar-Nelson published her first book, a collection of poetry, short stories, essays, and reviews called *Violets and Other Tales*, in 1895. Paul Laurence Dunbar, the famous poet, began to correspond with her after admiring her poetry (as well as her picture) in a Boston magazine. They married on March 8, 1898.

The Dunbars moved to Washington, D.C., where they were lionized as a literary couple. Dunbar-Nelson's second collection of short fiction, *The Goodness of St. Rocque*, was published in 1899 as a companion to her husband's *Poems of Cabin and Field*. While Dunbar was known for his dialect poetry, Dunbar-Nelson's stories explored the Creole and multiracial experience. The couple separated after four years of marriage, and Paul Laurence Dunbar died four years later, in 1906. But Dunbar-Nelson continued to be honored for the rest of her life as the widow of the famous poet.

After her marriage had ended, Dunbar-Nelson moved to Wilmington, Delaware, where she taught school. Her mother, sister, and four nieces and nephews joined her there, and her extended family continued to live with her throughout most of her life. During this period Dunbar-Nelson continued her education with courses at Cornell University, Columbia University, and the University of Pennsylvania. She also edited such works as *Masterpieces of Negro Eloquence* (1914) and *The Dunbar Speaker and Entertainer* (1920). She was involved in several relationships with both men and women during this period, and in 1916 she married journalist Robert Nelson.

Together with Nelson, Dunbar-Nelson published the *Wilmington Advocate* newspaper from 1920 to 1922. She went on to write regular columns for several newspapers over the next decade. She also continued her work as a political and social activist. A few years earlier she had participated in World War I relief efforts and the fight for women's suffrage. During the 1920s she served on the Delaware Republican Committee, headed the Delaware Crusaders for the Dyer Antilynching Bill, and was executive secretary of the Inter-Racial Peace Committee.

Dunbar-Nelson remained active in the African American literary community, and her poems were included in Harlem Renaissance journals and anthologies. Her circle of friends included such renowned African Americans as Langston Hughes, W. E. B. Du Bois, Carter G. Woodson, and Mary McLeod Bethune. Dunbar-Nelson kept a diary in 1921 and from 1926 to 1931, which describes many of these friendships and mentions romantic relationships with several women during this period. In 1932 she and her husband moved to Philadelphia, where she became an influential member of African American social and literary circles. She died of heart disease three years later.

North America

Dunbar, Paul Laurence

(b. June 27, 1872, Dayton, Ohio; d. February 9, 1906, Dayton, Ohio), African American poet, often remembered for his Dialect Poetry.

Three years before his death in 1906 at the age of 34, Paul Laurence Dunbar wrote these lines in his poem, "The Poet":

He sang of life, serenely sweet,
With, now and then, a deeper note,
From some high peak, nigh yet remote,
He voiced the world's absorbing beat.
He sang of love when earth was young,
And Love, itself, was in his lays.
But ah, the world, it turned to praise
A jingle in a broken tongue.

Its words may express his own regrets about the direction of his literary career. Dunbar was the most famous African American poet and one of the most famous American poets of his time. His career brought him international fame and by any measure was a tremendous success. Although Dunbar felt his best work was his poetry in standard English, he was celebrated almost exclusively for his folk poetry about African Americans written in dialect—the "jingle in a broken tongue." This identification of Dunbar with dialect poetry disappointed him during his lifetime and alienated some later African American readers. But Dunbar's poetry has also been praised by readers from W. E. B. Du Bois to Nikki Giovanni, who recognized the challenges Dunbar faced as a turn-of-the-century black poet trying to sound the "deeper note."

Dunbar's parents had both been slaves on plantations in Kentucky. Although Dunbar was born in Ohio during Reconstruction, his parents' stories about slavery were the basis for some of his folk poetry. He attended Dayton public schools and was the only student of color at Dayton High School, where he was class president, editor of the school paper, president of the literary society, and class poet. After graduating in 1891 Dunbar tried to pursue a career in journalism; when he could not find a writing job because of his race, he became an elevator operator. He earned the nickname "the elevator boy poet," however, when he continued writing.

Dunbar took out a loan to publish his first book, *Oak and Ivy*, in 1893. Later that year, he read his poetry at the World's Columbian Exposition in Chicago, where he was praised by Frederick Douglass and other prominent African Americans. Dunbar became a cross-over literary sensation in 1896, when his second book, *Majors and Minors*, was noticed by the well-known white critic and writer William Dean Howells. Howells arranged for an expanded version of the book, titled *Lyrics of Lowly Life*, to be published by the mainstream white firm of Dodd, Mead. The national publication, and the speaking tour that followed, made Dunbar famous among black and white audiences. His reputation soon spread overseas.

William Dean Howells was also among the first critics to reserve his praise for Dunbar's dialect poetry, and from that time, poems and short stories in dialect became the basis for most of Dunbar's popularity. Although there was a handful of other African Americans who had published works in dialect before Dunbar, most of his direct literary inspiration in that genre seemed to come from white authors in the sentimental "plantation tradition" of American literature. This literature, which was extremely popular in the decades following the Civil War, was often written by Southerners who romanticized black slaves and scenes of plantation life. Dunbar used dialect that resembled the words of these authors more closely than it resembled actual African American speech, and he also tended to portray the folk simplicity of slaves' lives rather than the injustice and oppression of slavery itself.

Dunbar's dialect poetry is often about courtship, folk traditions, and other benign aspects of the slave experience. Its neutral tone on slavery added to its popularity with white audiences but was often criticized by black readers. "When De C'on Pone's Hot," for example, is a nostalgic tribute to slave cooking, and its narrator clearly states that any troubles slaves had were instantly erased by the good feeling experienced when dinnertime came:

> [G]loom tu'ns into gladness . . . joy drives out de doubt
> When de oven do' is opened,
> An' de smell comes po'in out.

In some of his dialect poetry, however, Dunbar does include an awareness and irony missing from white plantation literature. In "An Ante-Bellum Sermon," for example, he quotes a slave preacher's speech, a familiar topic for parody. But within this sermon, the preacher's message is about Moses delivering his people from slavery, and the wrath God then brought to bear on the slaveholders. And the preacher makes very plain that even though his text is ostensibly "judgin' Bible people by deir ac's," it has a special relevance to his audience:

> So you see de Lawd's intention,
> Evah sence de worl' began,
> Was dat His almighty freedom
> Should belong to evah man.

Dunbar's poetry in standard English takes his feelings on race even further. Poems such as "Douglass," "The Colored Soldiers," and "Black Sampson at Brandywine" are specific tributes to black individuals. And several of his best-known poems appear to speak powerfully about race without ever mentioning it as such. In "Sympathy," for example, Dunbar creates the powerful image of empathy with the caged bird who still sings—an image that poet Maya Angelou recalled in the title of her autobiography. And in "We Wear the Mask"—which begins with the line "We wear the mask that grins and lies"—he speaks of the necessity of presenting a contented face to the world to mask the deep pain and anger within. Many readers see this poem as Dunbar's explanation for the minstrel role he himself played by writing dialect poems that pandered to white audiences.

Dodd, Mead published four volumes of Dunbar's poetry during his lifetime. Although his audiences always favored his dialect poetry and short stories, Dunbar also wrote standard poetry, four novels, and several essays. In 1895 he began to correspond with another black poet whose work he admired, Alice Moore. The correspondence led to marriage in 1898, and although the marriage ended amicably just four years later, while it lasted Dunbar and Alice Dunbar-Nelson were a celebrated literary couple. Dunbar's literary fame, great as it was, came to a premature end. Near the beginning of his marriage, Dunbar contracted tuberculosis, and eventually developed a dependency on the alcohol prescribed as a painkiller. Within a few years, he was limited by both the disease and the alcoholism, and he died on February 9, 1906.

In the last several decades, scholars and readers have started to reconsider Dunbar's life and work. He remains a key figure in the African American literary tradition not only because he was one of the first black authors to create a sensation on the mainstream American literary scene, but also because his writing—even in dialect—contains powerful nuances that still move readers.

E

Eckstine, William Clarence (Billy)

(b. July 8, 1914, Pittsburgh, Pa.; d. March 8, 1993, Pittsburgh, Pa.), African American jazz singer and bandleader.

Billy Eckstine became famous in the 1950s as the smooth-voiced baritone singer of such hits as *"Fools Rush In"* and *"Skylark,"* but music critics and serious jazz fans know him as the man whose big band launched such renowned performers as Dizzy Gillespie, Miles Davis, Charlie Parker, Dexter Gordon, and Sarah Vaughan. Eckstine (born Eckstein) began his musical career on a piano his father had bought for his two sisters. A star athlete, Eckstine soon joined his Washington, D.C., high school choir and found himself more compelled by his musical talents. After attending Howard University, he began singing with various groups, touring in the Midwest before settling in Chicago in 1939, where he joined the band led by Earl "Fatha" Hines.

It was with Hines that Eckstine had his first hit, the blues song *"Jelly Jelly,"* which he wrote and sang. In 1944 he formed his own big band. Always a favorite with other musicians, the band helped pioneer the then-new bebop sound. Its avant-garde musicianship often overshadowed Eckstine's more traditional vocals, and the band suffered from being badly re corded. Though it left behind no notable recordings, music historians consider it one of the most influential big bands of its era.

Eckstine's solo career took off after the band dissolved in 1947. With his deep, romantic voice, elegant presence, and good looks, he became a popular performer. Often referred to as "Mr. B," he garnered several film roles in the following decades, and many have called him the first black sex symbol. He continued to perform until he suffered a stroke in 1992. Eckstine died in 1993.

Edwards, Melvin

(b. May 4, 1937, Houston, Tex.), African American sculptor known for his works of welded steel and other metals.

Melvin Edwards was born in Houston, Texas. He studied painting at the University of Southern California (USC) and began sculpting in 1960. He received his B.F.A. from USC in 1965. He first gained critical attention with a series of sculptures titled *Lynch Fragments*, which by 1997 totaled more than 150 individual works constructed since 1963. The sculptures in this series are made using both forged and welded parts of knife sheaths, automotive gears, chains, ball bearings, horseshoes, and other metal. The works, which are each about the size of a human head and hang on a wall, explore themes of violence and incorporate both American and African symbolism.

In 1967 Edwards moved from California to New Jersey and his work shifted away from the manipulated, unpainted metal. A solo exhibition at the Walker Art Center in Minneapolis, Minnesota, in 1968 included geometric shapes painted in red, blue, and yellow. *Homage to My Father and the Spirit* (1969, Ithaca, New York), an outdoor sculpture at Cornell University, is a large-scale work that incorporates discs and triangles in painted steel. In a 1970 solo exhibition at the Whitney Museum of American Art in New York City, Edwards suspended barbed wire and chains from the ceiling to confront the viewer with the brutality of these materials.

Since the 1970s Edwards has spent time in several African countries studying their art and architecture. One result of his studies is a monumental sculpture at Morgan State University titled *Holiday at Soweto* (1976–1977, Baltimore, Maryland). The work is constructed out of steel and consists primarily of three circles, each 2.44 m (8 ft) in diameter. Cutouts in two of the circles are large enough for a person to walk through. According to Edwards, the piece was inspired by the incomparable singing of Billie Holiday, who grew up in Baltimore, and by a 1976 protest against the use of the Afrikaans language in black schools in Soweto, South Africa. Edwards wanted the work to express the great possibilities open to young black people living in Africa and the United States. A later piece, *Gate of Ogun* (1983, The Neuberger Museum, Purchase, New York), takes its name from the god of metalwork in Nigeria's Yoruba culture. It, too, combines African and American elements and allows the viewer to walk in and around it. Edwards has also created smaller wall-hung sculptures of brushed stainless steel, which are dedicated to Ogun.

Ekwensi, Cyprian

(b. Sept. 26, 1921, Minna, Nigeria), Nigerian novelist, short-story writer, and children's author who has portrayed the moral and material problems besetting rural West Africans as they migrate to the city. A prolific and popular writer, he owes his great success to his ability to write realistically about current issues affecting ordinary people.

Born Cyprian Duaka Odiatu Ekwensi in Minna, Nigeria, he began his secondary education at Government College in Ibadan and completed it at Achimota College in present-day Ghana (then the Gold Coast) in 1943. In the early 1950s he studied pharmacy at the Chelsea School of Pharmacy in London, England. While working at various jobs—forestry official, teacher, journalist, and broadcasting executive—Ekwensi pursued his writing career. He got his start as a writer by reading his work on a West African radio program. His first published success came with the novella *When Love Whispers* (1948). *People of the City* (1954), a collection of short stories tied together almost as a novel, chronicles the frantic pace of life in modern Lagos, Nigeria's commercial capital. The book introduced the critical view of urban existence that won Ekwensi national as well as international attention.

From 1957 to 1961 Ekwensi was head of features at the Nigerian Broadcasting Company, and from 1961 to 1967 he was federal director of Information Services. During this period he wrote his most successful novel, *Jagua Nana* (1961), the story of a vibrant middle-aged prostitute who moves between the corrupt, pleasure-seeking life of the city and the pastoral life of her rural origins. He continued exploring the contrast between the appeal of city life and its corruption in his collection *Lokotown and Other Stories* (1966). During the Nigerian Civil War (1967–1970) Ekwensi was director of the Broadcasting Corporation of Biafra, and in 1968 he won the Dag Hammarskjöld International Prize for Literary Merit.

After the war Ekwensi continued his career as a writer, reflecting on the war and its aftermath in the novels *Survive the Peace* (1976) and *Divided We Stand* (1980). In 1986 he published a sequel to *Jagua Nana* called *Jagua Nana's Daughter*. His children's books include *The Passport of Mallam Ilia* (1960), *The Drummer Boy* (1960), and *Juju Rock* (1966).

North America

Ellington, Edward Kennedy ("Duke")

(b. April 29, 1899, Washing ton, D.C.; d. May 24, 1974, New York, N.Y.), African American jazz pianist and bandleader, and the greatest composer in the history of jazz.

For nearly half a century Duke Ellington led the premier American big band, and through his compositions and performances he brought artistic credibility to African American jazz. Ellington played the piano, but his orchestra was his true instrument. In the late 1920s he perfected an exotic style that was later termed jungle music. During the 1930s Ellington developed a lush approach to orchestration that introduced new complexity to the simplistic conventions of swing-era jazz. Throughout the 1930s and 1940s he struggled against the limitations of the three-minute 78 rpm recording and the general adherence to 12- and 32-bar song forms, in the process vastly extending the scope of jazz. Personally and politically, he preferred to avoid direct confrontation; yet he was active as far back as the early 1940s in the cause of racial equality.

Ellington took what had begun as a vernacular dance music and created larger and more artistically challenging musical forms, exemplified in his three-movement composition *Black, Brown, and Beige* (1943). Due to his fame as a bandleader, Ellington, the pianist, is often overlooked. Yet particularly during the 1960s some of his most creative playing took place in small groups and demonstrated his willingness to engage such younger musicians as tenor saxophonist John Coltrane.

Ellington's Musical Beginnings and His Move to New York City

Ellington was born to a middle-class black family in Washington, D.C., at a time when Washington was the nation's preeminent black community. He began studying piano at age seven and quickly exhibited a gift for music. He began playing professionally as a teenager in a style derived from ragtime, which had a particularly strong influence in the vicinity of Baltimore and Washington. By 1919 he had emerged as a leader of small groups that played for local parties and dances. Although ragtime pianists led most of these bands, the other musicians were mainly reading musicians who played in a sweet style and did not improvise.

In 1922 Ellington moved to New York City, which was then emerging as the nation's jazz capital. He played with various theater orchestras and with jazz-oriented bands like the one led by Elmer Snowden (1900–1973). He also made his first foray into musical theater, writing the music for an ill-fated Broadway comedy, *Chocolate Kiddies* of 1924. In 1924 he took over the Snowden band, and that six-man group became the nucleus of the Ellington Orchestra. By 1926 the group had grown to 11 members; the most important additions were cornetist Bubber Miley and trombonist "Tricky Sam" Nanton (1904–1946). Through their influence the orchestra moved away from its sweet style and embraced a bluesy and improvisational jazz.

Like many jazz pianists of the day, Ellington came under the sway of the Harlem "stride" piano style, exemplified in the playing of James P. Johnson (1894–1955) and Willie "the Lion" Smith. The stride style essentially divides the piano keyboard into three ranges. The pianist's left hand covers the two lower ranges, alternating single bass notes at the bottom with chord clusters struck higher up. The style takes its name from the characteristic, bouncing "oom-pah, oom-pah" produced by the pianist's striding left hand. The pianist's left hand thus establishes a propulsive beat and outlines the tune's harmonic structure; the right hand plays melody, adds ornamentation, and improvises solo lines. Ellington evolved from this rather florid piano style, in part, by simplifying it and by adding harmonic complexities and dissonance that at times foreshadowed the playing of bop pioneer Thelonious Monk and free-jazz pianist Cecil Taylor (b. 1929).

Ellington at the Cotton Club, 1927–1931

In the fall of 1927 the Ellington Orchestra secured a long-term gig at the Cotton Club, New York City's most prestigious nightclub, which was wired to permit "live" remote radio broadcasts that gave Ellington nationwide recognition. The demanding stint at the Cotton Club also gave him a crash course in composing and arranging. Many of his early orchestrations involved little more than transposing note for note what he composed at the piano to the instruments of the band. While at the Cotton Club he became more adventuresome in his harmonies and voicings, and he began to experiment with changes in tempo and meter. By 1928 his orchestra had emerged as the nation's foremost jazz ensemble, surpassing the bands of Fletcher Henderson and King Oliver.

During 1927–1928 Ellington made a series of recordings that epitomized the orchestra's first classic style. They featured the growling, plunger-muted solos of Miley and Nanton, who virtually defined the orchestra's jungle style. Miley also composed or cowrote several key songs, including the masterpieces *"East St. Louis Toodle-Oo"* (1926) and *"Black and Tan Fantasie"* (1927). These songs and Ellington's lyrical *"Black Beauty"* (1928) were staples in the band's repertoire for years to come.

Moving Beyond the Boundaries of Dance Music

Ellington gained further exposure during the 1930s. The orchestra was featured in RKO's popular Amos 'n' Andy film *Check and Double Check* (1930). In 1931 Ellington wrote his first extended work, "Creole Rhapsody." The Victor version of the song, recorded in June 1931, filled two sides of a 12-inch 78 rmp record and was eight and a half minutes long. In the mid-

American composer, bandleader, and pianist Duke Ellington poses in 1931 with members of his band Nuf Said. *CORBIS/Bettmann*

1930s Ellington wrote the score for a nine-minute musical film, Symphony in Black (1935), which featured a young Billie Holiday and foreshadowed Black, Brown, and Beige.

Devastated by the death of his mother in 1935, Ellington wrote *Reminiscing in Tempo* (1935) as his tribute to her. His most ambitious work to date, it was a unified composition that filled four album sides. None of Ellington's contemporaries in jazz had attempted such large-scale works. Among his important shorter compositions of this period were *"Mood Indigo"* (1930), *"It Don't Mean a Thing If It Ain't Got That Swing"* (1932), *"Sophisticated Lady"* (1933), and the haunting ballad *"In a Sentimental Mood"* (1935).

During the mid-1930s new swing bands—under the leadership of Count Basie, Jimmie Lunceford, and such white bandleaders as Benny Goodman and Artie Shaw—threatened to eclipse the Ellington Orchestra. Although Ellington's *"In a Sentimental Mood"* never became a hit, Goodman's simplified 1936 rendition did. Moreover, the personnel of the Ellington Orchestra, normally quite stable, underwent considerable turnover during the mid-1930s.

Despite these difficulties, the Ellington Orchestra had many strengths, in particular its many talented soloists. Most swing big bands got by with two or three prominent soloists. During the mid-1930s Ellington's Orchestra featured nine significant solo talents: alto saxophonist Johnny Hodges; clarinetist Barney Bigard (1906–1980); baritone saxophonist Harry Carney (1910–1974); trumpeter Cootie Williams (1910–1985); cornetist Rex Stewart (1907–1967); trombonists Nanton and Lawrence Brown (1907–1988); vocalist Ivie Anderson (1905–1949); and Ellington himself on piano. Despite setbacks, the Ellington Orchestra toured constantly during the Great Depression and made successful visits to Europe in 1933 and 1939.

The Great Ellington Band: The Early 1940s

By 1940 Ellington and his orchestra had overcome the difficulties of the mid-1930s. In 1938 Billy Strayhorn began his nearly 30-year stint as Ellington's closest collaborator; he composed such memorable works as the orchestra's longtime theme, *"Take the A Train"* (1941). Ellington himself had a burst of creativity during which he produced some of his most enduring compositions. He benefited from an outstanding group of musicians, including two vital new additions—tenor saxophonist Ben Webster (1909–1973) and virtuoso bassist Jimmy Blanton (1918–1942). Among the orchestra's most important recordings of this period were *"Ko-Ko"* (1940), *"Cotton Tail"* (1940), and *"I Got It Bad and That Ain't Good"* (1941).

In 1943 Ellington appeared at New York City's prestigious Carnegie Hall. The first African American bandleader to be so honored, he responded with the 44-minute-long *Black, Brown, and Beige: A Tone Parallel to the History of the American Negro*, a path-breaking work in twentieth-century American music. Unfortunately, the ambitious piece broke the conventions of both jazz and classical music, satisfying neither audience. The critical response deeply disappointed Ellington; following his Carnegie Hall appearance (and an earlier run-through in Boston), he never performed the work in its entirety again.

Later Large-Scale Works and Ellington's Social Activism

Neither Ellington nor Strayhorn was dissuaded from creating other large-scale jazz suites, including the *Liberian Suite* (1947); *Harlem* (1951); the *Festival Suite* (1956); *Such Sweet Thunder* (1957), a musical tribute to Shakespeare; *Suite Thursday* (1960), which paid tribute to author John Steinbeck; and the *Far East Suite* (1966). Ellington also composed film scores for *Anatomy of a Murder* (1959) and *Paris Blues* (1961).

In 1965 Ellington broke new ground with his first *Concert of Sacred Music*, commissioned by San Francisco's Grace Episcopal Church. In the concert the Ellington Orchestra was joined by the Grace Cathedral Choir; the Herman McCoy Choir; singers Jon Hendricks (b. 1921), Esther Marrow, and Jimmy McPhail; and tap dancer Bunny Briggs. *"In the Beginning, God,"* Ellington's opening movement, won a 1966 Grammy Award for best original jazz composition. In 1968 Ellington composed a *Second Sacred Concert*. At the time of his death he was preparing a third.

From the early 1940s Ellington was active in the emergent Civil Rights Movement, although his role has largely been overlooked. In 1941 he wrote the score for the groundbreaking musical *Jump for Joy*, which challenged the demeaning stereotypes of African Americans in Hollywood films and throughout American popular culture. *Jump for Joy* had a buoyant sense of optimism that is suggested in such numbers as *"Uncle Tom's Cabin Is a Drive-In Now."*

Ellington's speaking voice, like his musical one, was eloquent and complex. He disliked head-on confrontation. As Ellington biographer John Edward Hasse has observed, *Music Is My Mistress*, the composer's 1973 autobiography, contains "hardly a negative word," passing in silence over various personal conflicts and his negative encounters with Jim Crow segregation. This indirection was equally evident in his political activism. During the Carnegie Hall premiere of *Black, Brown, and Beige*, Ellington looked out on the formally attired ranks of New York's elite and declared: "[W]e find ourselves today struggling for solidarity, but just as we are about to get our teeth into it, our country is at war, [so, of course], we . . . find the black, brown, and beige right in there for the red, white, and blue."

Though stressing African American patriotism, Ellington—in his distinctly oblique way—voiced black aspirations for racial equality and integration.

In 1951 Ellington premiered Harlem, which he regarded as his most successful extended work, at a benefit concert for the National Association for the Advancement of Colored People (NAACP). Two months before the concert he wrote to President Harry S. Truman, stating that concert proceeds would "help fight for your civil rights program—to stamp out segregation, discrimination, [and] bigotry." He suggested that Truman's daughter, Margaret Truman, serve as honorary chair for the event. Ellington biographer Hasse notes that Truman or someone on his staff wrote on the letter "an emphatic 'NO!' in inch-high letters, underlined twice."

Ellington's Later Career

During the 1950s and 1960s Ellington and his orchestra led a split existence. They debuted substantial extended works in concerts and recordings, but they also endured a grueling schedule of one-night stands in which the orchestra reprised old hits with what bordered on formulaic playing. An inspiring performance at the 1956 Newport Jazz Festival helped draw the orchestra out of a creative slump. Ellington also found inspiration in a series of small-group recordings, such as *Money Jungle* (1962), featuring bassist Charles Mingus and drummer Max Roach, and *Duke Ellington and John Coltrane* (1962), a classic collaboration between two of the seminal figures in jazz.

In these years Ellington faced the loss of several long-term orchestra members, including the irreplaceable Johnny Hodges, who died in 1970. But the greatest loss was that of Billy Strayhorn, who died of throat cancer in 1967. In *And His Mother Called Him Bill* (1967), Ellington paid tribute to his long-time collaborator with a set of Strayhorn compositions; the emotional recording sessions yielded one of the orchestra's last great albums. In 1969 President Richard Nixon presented Ellington with the Medal of Freedom at a gala 70th birthday party.

Ellington gave little sign of slowing down in the early 1970s, but in 1973 he learned that he had lung cancer. Even after he was hospitalized in the spring of 1974, he continued to work on new compositions. Following his death, some 65,000 people came to view his body, and more than 10,000 turned out for his funeral. In subsequent years Ellington's reputation has continued to grow. He is rightly acclaimed as one of America's greatest composers.

North America
***

Ellison, Ralph

(b. March 1, 1914, Oklahoma City, Okla.; d. April 16, 1994, New York, N.Y.), African American writer; author of *Invisible Man* (1952), one of the most famous twentieth-century American novels.

The great irony of the career of Ralph Ellison, one of the most acclaimed and influential of all-American novelists, may be that when he died at the age of 80, he had only published one novel. His second, on which he had been working for almost 40 years, was still unfinished. But with that extraordinary first work, *Invisible Man*, Ellison changed the standards for the American novel. As the *Norton Anthology of African American Literature* says, with *Invisible Man* Ellison simultaneously "defined the historic moment of mid-twentieth century America" and "single-handedly re[wrote] the American novel as an African American adventure in fiction."

Ellison was born in 1914 in Oklahoma City. His parents had migrated to Oklahoma from the South because they hoped the West might offer better opportunities for African Americans. Ellison's father, an avid reader, named his son Ralph Waldo after the nineteenth-century white American writer Ralph Waldo Emerson. His father died when Ellison was only three, and his mother worked at a variety of jobs to raise Ralph and his brother. Ellison attended segregated public schools in Oklahoma City and excelled in music. When he graduated, local officials—afraid he would try to integrate a white Oklahoma college—gave him a scholarship to Tuskegee Institute in Alabama, and he arrived there by hitching a ride on a freight train in 1933.

Ellison had been encouraged to read widely since childhood, but a sophomore English class introduced him to a new variety of authors. He was especially captivated by the way he felt T. S. Eliot's poem "The Waste Land" captured the rhythms of jazz. Ellison later said that discovery of the potential connections between music and literature was what led him to consider writing instead of music as a career. In 1936, when his scholarship ran out, he took what he thought would be a short break in New York, planning to save enough money to return in the fall. Instead, Ellison met the great writers Langston Hughes and Arna Bontemps, who in turn introduced him to novelist Richard Wright. Once he had been exposed to the black New York literary scene, he essentially remained in it, and in New York, for the rest of his life.

Ellison took a series of odd jobs to support himself and studied writers Ernest Hemingway, James Joyce, and Fyodor Dostoyevsky. In 1938 he took a position with the Federal Writers' Project collecting black folklore and oral histories through interviews with older African Americans, which provided him with stories and insights that ultimately found their way into his later writings. Meanwhile, Wright, who was already known in New York as a writer and a Communist Party activist, became Ellison's mentor. Ellison's first published work was a 1937 book review in *New Challenge*, a radical journal that Wright edited. More reviews and essays in similar journals followed over the next few years. Ellison's first short stories, "Slick Gonna Learn" (1939) and "The Birthmark" (1940), explored the political and social constraints on black life in a narrative mode similar to the novel Wright was working on, *Native Son* (1940). When even Wright criticized Ellison's style for being too derivative of his own, their relationship deteriorated. Ellison gradually rejected Wright's aesthetics and his politics, and matured into a style that was indisputably his own.

In 1940 and 1941 Ellison published two essays that praised the use of African American folklore in African American fiction. Black folklore, language, and customs figured prominently in several of his subsequent stories, including "Flying Home" (1944), which most closely prefigured *Invisible Man*. "Flying Home" was initially meant to be part of a novel about a black American World War II pilot captured by the Nazis. But in 1945, while still at work on that project, Ellison wrote a single sentence on a piece of paper: "I am an invisible man." He later recalled that at the time, he had no idea what that line meant, but he became consumed by trying to imagine what kind of character would say such a thing. Over the next seven years the line turned into a story of its own, and became the opening sentence of *Invisible Man*.

Invisible Man follows its unnamed black protagonist from South to North, from youth to adulthood, and from innocence and naiveté to experience and awareness. At the novel's beginning, the protagonist is just about to graduate from high school with a scholarship to attend a prestigious Southern black college. He is ambitious and optimistic that the world will be full of promise for a smart black boy who works hard. But shortly before leaving home he has a dream in which his dead grandfather appears to him and, in a parody of a high school graduation, presents him an engraved plaque that reads "To Whom It May Concern: Keep This Nigger Boy Running."

The protagonist is kept running for the rest of the novel—by the patronizing white trustees and accommodationist black founder of his college; by the white men he hopes will hire him when he is forced to leave school and seek work in New York; by the boss at the paint factory where he does find a job; and by the leaders of the Brotherhood, an organization much like the Communist Party, who recruit and train him to be a leader but reject him when he becomes more powerful than they would like. At the novel's end, the protagonist finally realizes that he has suffered because he has allowed his identity to be defined by others who do not really know him, who see him as indistinguishable from other black people, who do not value his individuality. He has been defined by people to whom he is invisible.

Invisible Man was immediately celebrated not only as a key exploration of the contemporary African American psyche, but also for its very modern depiction of the fragmentation, invisibility, and lack of self-knowledge many people experienced in the larger American society. In 1965 a poll of 200 critics called *Invisible Man* "the most distinguished American novel written since World War II." Ellison followed the book with two successful collections of his essays, interviews, and speeches on the African American experience, *Shadow and Act* (1964) and *Going to the Territory* (1987). In the late 1950s he began work on his much-awaited second novel.

During the 1960s many black writers were critical of Ellison's belief that African Americans are fundamentally American, shaped by the United States more than by Africa. But within several years, public opinion had swayed to affirm Ellison's point of view, and readers once again held high hopes for the next novel, which Ellison hinted would be a multi-volume magnum opus. He apparently kept going even after a fire at his summer home destroyed a year's worth of manuscript, but he died of cancer in 1994 without having completed it. Several of Ellison's unpublished short stories were posthumously collected along with his earlier stories in the 1996 volume *Flying Home*. In 1999 Random House published *Juneteenth*, a 400-page novel that Ellison's literary executor crafted from the thousands of pages Ellison left when he died.

In his creation of a new style that embraced black folk tradition and emphasized the importance of self-knowledge and self-awareness for African Americans, Ellison broke new ground for the generation of black authors who followed him. And his sharp observations on the problem of black "invisibility" in white culture gave new insights on the American racial scene to a generation of black and white readers.

Africa

Emecheta, Buchi

(b. July 21, 1944, Yaba, Nigeria), Nigerian writer whose novels have focused on the lives of women.

Florence Onye Buchi Emecheta was born near the city of Lagos, Nigeria. At a young age, she lost both her mother and her father, who was killed while serving the British army in Burma. After completing a degree at the Methodist girls' high school in Lagos, she married Sylvester Onwordi at age 16. The couple moved to London, and during the next six years, Emecheta bore five children while supporting the family financially. She began to write during this time, but, as she later said in an interview, "The first book I wrote, my husband burnt, and then I found I couldn't write with him around."

Emecheta left her husband in 1966, supporting herself for the next few years by working at the library in the British Museum. She enrolled at the University of London, where she received a sociology degree in 1974. In her first literary works she represented her own experiences of poverty, racism, and motherhood, "the cumulative oppression resulting from being alien, black and female," as she described it. These reflective, semi-fictional accounts were first published in *New Statesman* and later collected into her first novel *In the Ditch* (1972). She followed this with *Second-Class Citizen* (1974), which drew on the earlier years of her life and her experience of immigration. Both *In the Ditch* and *Second-Class Citizen* dealt with the socioeconomic problems of Africans in both Africa and the diaspora, and particularly highlighted the multiple oppressions of women.

Emecheta's next novel, *The Bride Price* (1976), was set in Nigeria in the early 1950s. She told the story of a young Ibo woman who defies tradition by running away with a man descended from a slave caste. The novel portrays a woman constrained by Ibo social hierarchies and beliefs, including the belief that if the bride price is not paid, the bride will die in childbirth. The story ends without resolution: Emecheta leaves the reader to imagine whether the traditional prophecy is fulfilled. In *The Slave Girl* (1977), set in early twentieth-century Nigeria, a young girl is forced into domestic slavery by her brother, then bought from her master by a suitor. Emecheta uses the narrative to illustrate a parallel between slavery and marriage.

Emecheta published her best-known work, *The Joys of Motherhood*, in 1979. This story, depicting the migrant rural Ibo community in Lagos, spans the time in Nigeria between the 1930s and independence in 1960. Emecheta focuses on the lives of women who can achieve status only through motherhood—specifically, their ability to bear sons.

Emecheta's early portrayals of oppressive gender relations created a great deal of controversy, especially among her African readership. Some critics accused her of portraying African men unfairly. Others, especially in the West, held her up as one of Africa's most eloquent feminists. Yet Emecheta herself has consistently rejected the title "feminist." In an interview, she clarified her position: "I do believe in the African kind of feminism. They call it womanism, because, you see, you Europeans don't worry about water, you don't worry about schooling, you are so well off. Now, I buy land, and I say, 'OK, I can't build on it, I have no money, so I give it to some women to start planting.' That is my brand of feminism."

In her later novels, Emecheta addressed a range of sociopolitical issues. *Destination Biafra* (1982) was, in the words of Emecheta, a novel that "needed to be written" about the civil war that wracked Nigeria from 1967 to 1970. *Double Yoke* (1982) dealt with the moral deterioration of postcolonial Nigeria. *The Rape of Shavi* (1983), an experimental departure from Emecheta's realist style, was a slightly disguised tale of colonization. Emecheta returned to the theme of the immigrant experience with the novel *Gwendolen* (1989) (published in the United States as *The Family*), about a Caribbean immigrant girl who experiences rape and incest.

Throughout much of her writing career, Emecheta has taught at various universities. In addition, she founded the publishing company Ogwugwu Afor, which specializes in African literature. She has also published an autobiography, two children's books, and several books for young adults, amassing an impressive total of 16 works published in 14 years.

Europe

Equiano, Olaudah

(b. 1745, Nigeria; d. April 31, 1797, England), African ex-slave and abolitionist who wrote the first autobiographical slave narrative.

First published in Great Britain in 1789, *The Interesting Narrative of the Life of Olaudah Equiano*, or *Gustavus Vassa the African*, written by himself, became a bestseller within Olaudah Equiano's lifetime, with nine English editions and one American as well as translations in Dutch, German, and Russian. Though Ottobah Cugoano, an African abolitionist in England, had published an autobiographical account in 1787, it was probably heavily edited, and thus *The Interesting Narrative* is considered the first autobiography of an African slave written entirely by his own hand. This makes Equiano the founder of the slave narrative, a form central to African American literature.

Equiano describes his abduction in Africa, his enslavement in the West Indies, and his manumission in Britain, as well as the legal insecurity and terror faced by both enslaved and free West Indian blacks. His autobiography greatly influenced the rhetorical strategies, content, and presentation of later nineteenth-century slave narratives, such as Frederick Douglass's *The Life and Times of Frederick Douglass* (1845).

Equiano was born the son of an Ibo chief in present-day Nigeria. When he was 11 years old, he and his sister were captured by African traders and sold to Europeans. He was transported to the West Indies, where Michael Pascal, an Englishman, bought Equiano and named him after the Swedish hero Gustavus Vassa. Though Equiano at first detested the name, he later used it in most of his writings and became known by it. Equiano served as a seaman with Pascal in the Seven Years War (1756–1763) in Canada and the Mediterranean. In 1757 Pascal took Equiano to England, where his honesty and trustworthiness won him friendship and support from many English people. During this formative period, Equiano was educated and converted to Christianity.

To Equiano's dismay, in 1763 Pascal sold him to an American, Robert King. By this time, Equiano knew seamanship, hairdressing, wine making, and arithmetic and had become fully literate in the English language. He worked for King as a seaman and trader, once again coming in close contact with the atrocities of the transatlantic slave trade. Even after he bought his freedom in 1766, Equiano elected to remain at sea for several years. He voyaged to the Arctic as a surgeon's assistant and to the Mediterranean as a gentleman's valet, and for a time lived among the Moskito Indians of Nicaragua.

Equiano returned to England in 1777 and became active in the abolitionist movement. He brought the massacre of 130 slaves on the ship Zong to the attention of the white abolitionist lawyer Granville Sharp, thereby greatly influencing public support for abolition of the slave trade. He also wrote on behalf of abolition and interracial marriages. In 1792 he married Susannah Cullen, a white Englishwoman, with whom he had two daughters.

In 1787 Equiano was appointed Commissary for Stores to the Expedition for Freed Slaves, and settled in Sierra Leone. Though at first he was "agreeably surprised that the benevolence of government had adopted the plan of some philanthropic individuals," he soon discovered fraudulence among the organizers. Equiano invited outsiders to view the negligent conditions under which the blacks lived on board the ship set to sail to Sierra Leone and described corrupt procedures to a friend in a letter that was later published. He was later dismissed from his post as a "troublemaker."

Though demoralized, Equiano returned to England and published his autobiography. He fought unceasingly for abolition as a member of the Sons of Africa and in his letter-writing and public-speaking campaigns until his death in 1797.

North America

Eric B. and Rakim

(b. Eric Barrier and William Griffin) (New York, N.Y.), hip hop duo who revolutionized the art of rapping.

Eric B. and Rakim's debut album, *Paid in Full* (1987), amply displayed DJ Eric B.'s danceable beats and restrained turntable technique, but the real revelation was Rakim—generally regarded as one of the most skilled MCs in hip hop history. "To me, MC means move the crowd," he rapped, in a deadpan voice simultaneously inviting, threatening, and cool. Rakim's rhymes were peppered with witty analogies ("I draw a crowd like an architect") and distinguished by careful construction: on *"My Melody,"* Rakim declaims, "I'm not a regular competitor / first rhyme editor / Melody arranger / poet et cetera."

The duo returned in 1988 with *Follow the Leader*, an innovative album that won similar acclaim. Eric B. created increasingly sophisticated beats, over which Rakim further shattered rap's conventions of rhyme and meter. Rakim, an adherent of the gnostic Nation of Islam, wove intricate allegories about rap itself, presenting an image of a man with a microphone defending his art. Tracks like *"Follow the Leader"* and *"Lyrics of Fury"* (later covered by the black British musician Tricky) never achieved huge crossover success, but the album's creative beats and rhymes sent the hip hop world running to catch up.

Let the Rhythm Hit 'Em (1990) was the duo's third and final gold record; they finally split up after *Don't Sweat the Technique* (1992). After four years of relative silence, Rakim received a hero's welcome—along with mild critical and commercial success—when he reemerged with his solo debut, *The 18th Letter*, in 1997.

North America

Evans, Mari E.
(b. July 16, 1923, Toledo, Ohio), African American poet and teacher.

Mari Evans lost her mother at age seven and was raised by her father, an upholsterer, whom she credits with nurturing her love of writing. She attended the University of Toledo. Langston Hughes's works influenced her considerably from an early age, and Hughes himself later became a friend and mentor.

A "blues philosopher" who believes that a poet must be politically engaged, Evans became a respected figure in the Black Arts Movement. Her work focuses on such wide-ranging themes as black enslavement and poverty in the United States, the oppression blacks share with other Third World peoples, and failed relationships between black men and women. In addition, it celebrates blackness, Africa, and the struggles of the Civil Rights Movement. Her work has been published in more than 200 anthologies, and among her best-known works are *I Am a Black Woman* (1970) and an edition of collected essays, *Black Women Writers* (1950–1980): *A Critical Evaluation* (1984). She has also authored several works for children.

From 1968 to 1973 Evans created and hosted a weekly television program, *The Black Experience*, in Indianapolis. She also adapted Zora Neale Hurston's *Their Eyes Were Watching God* as a musical, *Eyes* (1979). Evans has held numerous teaching posts at universities, including Purdue, Northwestern, Cornell, and Indiana. Among many honors and awards, she received an honorary doctorate in 1979 from Marian College and won a National Endowment for the Arts Creative Writing Award in 1981. Evans is divorced and has two sons, and lives in Indianapolis.

North America

Eyes on the Prize,
award-winning PBS television series documenting the Civil Rights Movement from 1954 to 1965.

Following its release in 1987, *Eyes on the Prize* became the most celebrated documentary series in the history of public television. Many reviewers hailed the documentary as the finest depiction to date of the civil rights era. Carolyn Fluehr-Lobban of American Anthropologist wrote that what distinguishes the series from its predecessors "is not only its comprehensive grasp of the civil rights period, but its fair and equal representation of all of the signal events and the heroes and heroines of the Civil Rights Movement." The series won more than 20 awards, including the Peabody Award and the DuPont-Columbia Award, and has become a standard reference source in American libraries and schools.

Produced by African American Henry Hampton of Blackside, Inc., *Eyes on the Prize* comprises six one-hour television programs. It covers the 11 years between the landmark 1954 Supreme Court ruling to desegregate schools and, in 1965, the march from Selma to Montgomery and passage of the Voting Rights Act. Narrated by civil rights activist Julian Bond, the series combines archival films, newsreels, photographs, and interviews with those involved in the events. To accompany the series, Viking/Penguin published two guides for instructional use: *Eyes on the Prize: America's Civil Rights Years* by Juan Williams and *A Reader and Guide: Eyes on the Prize* edited by Clayborne Carson.

In 1990 Hampton produced *Eyes on the Prize II*, which chronicles the continuing civil rights struggles of African Americans from 1965 to 1985.

Fauset, Jessie Redmon

(b. April 27, 1882, Camden County, N.J.; d. April 30, 1961, Philadelphia, Pa.),
influential African American novelist and editor during the Harlem Renaissance.

Poet Langston Hughes referred to Jessie Fauset as one of "the three people
who mid-wifed the so-called New Negro literature into being," a statement
that reveals how influential Fauset was as an editor during the Harlem
Renaissance of the 1920s and 1930s. But Fauset was also the era's most prolific black novelist, publishing four books between 1924 and 1933. In both
capacities, Fauset helped shape one of the most important movements in
African American literature.

Fauset was born in what is now Lawnside, New Jersey, and grew up in
Philadelphia. She hoped to attend Bryn Mawr College, but instead of
admitting a black student, Bryn Mawr arranged for Fauset to receive a
scholarship to Cornell University. There, Fauset became the first black
woman in the country to be elected to Phi Beta Kappa, the academic honorary society. She also began corresponding with the noted black intellectual
W. E. B. Du Bois, whose work she admired, forming an association that
would become the cornerstone of her literary career.

After graduation Fauset moved to Washington, D.C., where she taught
at the prestigious all-black M Street (later Dunbar) High School from 1905
to 1919 while taking courses toward a master's degree in French from the
University of Pennsylvania. But beginning in 1912, Fauset was also a literary
contributor to the *Crisis*, the journal of the National Association for the
Advancement of Colored People (NAACP), which Du Bois edited. When
the *Crisis* created the position of literary editor at its New York office in
1919, Du Bois offered it to Fauset, and she accepted.

It was at the *Crisis* that Fauset cultivated the talents of many younger
Harlem Renaissance writers, including Langston Hughes, Jean Toomer,
Countee Cullen, and Claude McKay. Under her tenure, the *Crisis* became

one of the major publishing outlets for black writers at the time. But Fauset also published short stories, essays, reviews, and poems of her own in both the *Crisis* and its short-lived children's magazine, the *Brownies' Book*. In 1924 she published her first novel, *There Is Confusion*. Many of her stories and all four of her novels feature light-skinned, middle-class black protagonists. Fauset stated that one of her goals was to present normally "the home-life of the colored American," without the melodrama or caricature that she often saw in white writers. But her fiction did explore the ways in which race and gender affect characters, even in their domestic lives.

Fauset left her position at the *Crisis* in 1926—perhaps because of a falling out with Du Bois—and took another teaching job, this time in New York. Although *There Is Confusion* had been well received by black critics, she still had difficulty securing publishers for her later novels—perhaps because she was a novelist at a time when black poets were in vogue. But she continued to write, publishing *Plum Bun* in 1929, *The Chinaberry Tree* in 1931, and *Comedy: American Style* in 1933. In 1929 Fauset married insurance broker Herbert Harris, and in the early 1940s they moved to Montclair, New Jersey, signaling her formal retirement from the New York scene. After Harris's death in 1958, Fauset lived with her stepbrother in Philadelphia until her death on April 30, 1961. Jessie Fauset left a lasting impression on the African American literary tradition at a formative period through her profound influence on the authors she nurtured, and through the merits of her own work.

Africa

Faye, Safi

(b. 1943, near Dakar, Senegal), Senegalese film director, one of the few independent women filmmakers in Africa.

Safi Faye is not only one of the few independent African women film directors, but also one of the few making ethnographic films. The daughter of a village chief and businessman of Serer origin, Faye moved to Dakar at age 19 to become a teacher. While in Dakar she became interested in the educational and ethnographic uses of film and upon meeting Jean Rouch, the French filmmaker and ethnologist, she embarked on a film career.

Faye acted in Rouch's *Petit à petit ou Les Lettres persanes* (1968). She also learned about Rouch's style of cinéma-vérité, characterized by an unobtrusive camera and spontaneous nonprofessional acting, which would later influence her own film work. With Rouch's encouragement she moved to Paris in 1972 and enrolled in the Ecole Pratique des Hautes Etudes to study ethnology, and the Louis Lumière Film School to study film. She completed film school in 1974, and began using film as a way to publish her ongoing research on the Serer. By the time she received her Ph.D. she had produced three films—*Kaddu beykat* (1975); *Fad'jal* (1979); and *Goob na na* (1979).

Faye has since held a number of academic positions in Europe, while continuing to make ethnographic films. Although much of her work focuses on the Serer, she has also produced documentaries for the United Nations and German and French television stations, filmed in both Europe and Africa. In a 1970s interview she described her methods: "I go talk to the farmers in their village. We discuss their problems and I take notes. Even though I may write a script for my films, I basically leave the peasants free to express themselves in front of a camera and I listen. My films are collective works in which everybody takes an active part." Because the messages communicated by peasants through Faye's work are, as she intends, clearly political, government censorship in Africa has prevented most of them from being shown.

North America

Film, Blacks in American,

a historical overview of black filmmaking and the portrayal of blacks in American film.

The thread of African American history is spun from two sources: the struggle to define a place in the wider American life and the effort to maintain an authentic black presence in the larger American culture. This duality has meaning in the realm of filmmaking because the tools of cinema—film and cameras—cost more than the paper and pencil tools of writers. It is the cost of doing business that affects, indeed, threatens the black presence on the screen.

The costly collaborative nature of filmmaking has blurred the definition of a "black" movie. Is it black if it is merely angled toward blacks, or must it be made by blacks, or both? Critics disagree, although a few traits of black films seem characteristic. They might be either pastoral, speaking nostalgically about a rural past, such as Spencer Williams's pious *The Blood of Jesus* (1940), or hip and urbane, in a current jive idiom, such as Oscar Micheaux's *Swing* (1938) or Bessie Smith's *St. Louis Blues* (1929). Some black movies have provided a voice of advocacy, such as the Colored Players' *The Scar of Shame* (1927), in which an old lecher mourns the heroine whose passing reminds him that "our people have much to learn." Others have celebrated small victories, such as Michael Roemer's *Nothing but a Man* (1963), with a lead actor who will fix flat tires for a living but knows that he will never take on the stereotypical role of "picking other people's cotton." This theme is echoed in Ivan Dixon's *The Spook Who Sat by the Door* (1973), in which a cabal of black heroes joyously mounts an all-but-hopeless black insurrection.

Often a black movie provides an anatomy of black cultural life, a glossary of style, patois, and politics, such as Michael Shultz's *Car Wash* (1976). Sometimes a so-called crossover movie finds an audience on both sides of the racial divide by drawing on a black cultural trait that speaks to black and white audiences. King Vidor's *Hallelujah!* (1929), for example, used the metaphor of a railroad train going to hell much as Eloyse Gist, the black evangelist, had done in her own *Hell Bound Train,* each conveying the same sense of pious urgency entwined with an almost erotic sensibility. In much the same way, Spike Lee, in his *Do the Right Thing* (1989), drew a crossover audience into a dramatic debate over what, indeed, the right political thing was. Sometimes a black-angled movie succeeds as a crossover because it successfully mingles cultures. For example, Marcel Camus's *Orfeo Negro* (1959) retold the Greek myth of Orpheus and Eurydice, set in the annual Afro-Brazilian Carnival. In Trevor Rhone's *The Harder They Come* (1973), the reggae singer Jimmy Cliff plays a victim of a sleazy recording-industry boss. Driven to a life of outlawry, Cliff adopts a fantasy life of revenge in the mode of an American cowboy (not unlike Travis Bickle in Martin Scorsese's *Taxi Driver*). And in almost any Paul Robeson or Josephine Baker film of the 1930s, the theme involves a poignant outreach across racial cultures.

In any case, African American movies, whether so-called race movies made for black audiences or crossovers for a wider reach, arise from "the particular cultural conditions" (as the historian Gerald Mast wrote) of black life and history that surely "influence, if not dictate" the imagery and voice of black film. Therefore, the black critic James Snead has argued that a black cinema must "coin unconventional associations for black skin within the reigning film language" to replace well-known stereotypical images.

The Silent Era

African American images first appeared on the screen in 1898, only months after the first theatrical projection of moving images. At first benign in their effect, the earliest films showed black soldiers embarking for the Spanish-Cuban-American War and West Indians at their daily tasks. In 1903 a 14-minute *Uncle Tom's Cabin* appeared. Thereafter, as editing for narrative effect improved, black figures fell more in line with the racial stereotypes of the day, appearing as chicken thieves, venal preachers, and the like. They only rarely turned up in marginally authentic roles in films such as *The Fights of Nations* (1907), which at least depicted black culture, albeit in a warped form. As the 50th anniversary of the Civil War approached in 1910, collective nostalgia for the war inspired maudlin tales of fraternity. Black slaves, once the focus of the combat, were reduced to sentimental figures who often sided with their Southern masters against their Northern libera-tors. The most renowned and artistically the most compelling of the genre was D. W. Griffith's *The Birth of a Nation* (1915).

The first steps toward a specifically black cinema arose out of these rit-uals of white chauvinism. Bill Foster, an African American whose work has been lost, made such films as *The Railroad Porter,* probably a light comedy set in a particularly black milieu in 1912. *The Birth of a Race* (1918), two years in the making and perhaps three hours in length, began as a response to Griffith's film. But its succession of producers and backers, including Booker T. Washington's Tuskegee circle, Universal Pictures, and Julius Rosenwald of Sears, Roebuck, lost touch with the original concept. Nonetheless, it inspired George P. Johnson and his brother, Noble, to found the Lincoln Motion Picture Company to carry forward the quest for a black cinema, only to fail because of a nationwide influenza epidemic that shuttered theaters.

After World War I the American movie industry gradually moved to California—to Hollywood. The ensuing Jazz Age offered little new to African Americans. Few movies offered blacks parts with any authenticity. Such parts included the grizzled hobo in Jim Tully's tale of the lowly, *Beggars of Life* (1928); the seaman boldly played by the boxer George Godfrey in James Cruze's *Old Ironsides* (1926); the faithful renderings of blacks in *Showboat* (1927) and *Uncle Tom's Cabin* (1927); and those in early sound films such as Dudley Murphy's *St. Louis Blues* (1929). However, blacks generally played out conventional roles as chorus girls, convicts, racetrack grooms, boxing trainers, and flippant servants.

The sameness of the images surely led to the first boom of race movies that were made by black, and often white, producers specifically for black audiences. George and Noble Johnson made as many as four such films that were black versions of already defined Hollywood genres—success stories, adventures, and the like—all of them since lost. In Philadelphia the Colored Players crafted a canon, most of which survived in the late 1990s, that included a Paul Laurence Dunbar story, a black *Ten Nights in a Bar Room* (1926), and their masterpiece, *The Scar of Shame* (1927), a melodrama about caste and class in black circles.

Of all African American filmmakers of the era, Oscar Micheaux dominated his age. A sometime Pullman porter, homesteader, and novelist who sold his books door to door, he was also a legendary entrepreneur who both broke with and built on Hollywood genres. More than any other known figure, Micheaux took up themes that Hollywood left untouched: lynching, black success myths, and color-based caste. For years there was scant access to his work: there was only *Body and Soul* (1924), starring the black athlete, singer, and activist Paul Robeson. But his recently rediscovered films of equal stature, among them *Within Our Gates* (1920) and *The Symbol of the Unconquered* (1921), have allowed fuller study.

Sound Film in the Jazz Age

The coming of sound film at the onset of the Great Depression momentarily daunted black filmmakers. On the one hand, Hollywood for the first time could exploit black musical traditions, while, on the other, makers of race movies lacked the capital to invest in sound filmmaking or wiring old ghetto theaters. Fortified by sound, white filmmakers acted with unaccustomed boldness. Al Jolson's "talkie" *The Jazz Singer* (1927) linked the oppression of blacks with that of white immigrants. Several short films attained equal social meaning, among them *The St. Louis Blues* (1929); Duke Ellington's *The Black and Tan Fantasy* (1930) and his allegorical *Symphony in Black* (1934); and Jimmy Mordecai's fable of the black migration from Southern farms to Northern cities, *Yamacraw*. MGM's *Hallelujah!* (1929) and Fox's *Hearts in Dixie* (1929) similarly focused on the tensions of this migration and devoted rare attention to the details of black life. Dudley

Murphy's film version of Eugene O'Neill's *The Emperor Jones* was graced with a charming prologue by the black activist and poet James Weldon Johnson that would have eluded O'Neill. This film closed the brief era of socially engaged films by bringing Paul Robeson to the screen in the title role. Taken together, these films hinted at the "unconventional associations" for which James Snead had called.

However, corporate Hollywood returned to its profit-driven caution. Marc Connelly's Pulitzer Prize-winning musical drama of 1930, *The Green Pastures*, for example, took half a decade to reach the screen in truncated form. Thereafter, black Americans, as usual, waited for small favors, such as Robeson's "Joe" in a 1936 remake of *Showboat*, Clarence Muse's rebellious slave in *So Red the Rose* (1935), Clarence Brook's Haitian doctor in John Ford's *Arrowsmith* (1931), and ten years of Hattie McDaniel's flip servants in films ranging from *Alice Adams* (1933) to *Gone With the Wind* (1939). Other nods at the reality of black life included John M. Stahl's social drama based on Fannie Hurst's novel of the practice known as passing (for white), *Imitation of Life* (1934), and a sprinkling of black proletarians among the outcasts of Depression-ridden America.

Once again, black makers of race movies strained to fill the void, this time in competition with a cadre of white producers. Micheaux recovered from a bankruptcy, remade his autobiography as *The Exile* (1931), broke into talkies with *The Girl from Chicago* (1932) and *Swing* (1938), and survived the Depression. George Randol, a sometime Broadway actor, joined him, as did William Alexander, who would make black newsreels during World War II, and other blacks. A few interracial films swelled their ranks. In Texas, Alfred Sack and Spencer Williams turned out the evocative *The Blood of Jesus* (1940), while Muse joined with B-moviemaker Harry Fraser to make a film biography of the boxer Henry Armstrong (played poignantly by himself).

Perhaps because of these white newcomers, race movies achieved a synthesis of black and Hollywood styles in which gangster movies, westerns, and musicals promoted black concerns. At the height of this movement, from 1937 to 1940, gangster movies linked poverty with the incidence of crime and included celebrations of black aspiration. Ralph Cooper's *Am I Guilty* (1940), for example, obliged a black physician to choose between patching up a crook or ministering to the sick, a version of similar dilemmas in other films of the genre. Some, like Bert and Jack Goldberg's *Paradise in Harlem* (1940), focused on Harlem's communal spirit, in this case revealed in a jazz version of *Othello* mounted as a fundraiser to fight urban crime. Similar themes appeared in a 1939–1940 cycle of all-black westerns and a series of Louis Jordan musicals, including one, *Beware* (1946), in which he saves a black college from closure.

The War Years and Their Aftermath

With the onset of World War II, at a moment when American propaganda embraced brotherhood, tolerance, and equality as war aims, makers of race movies slipped from view—victims of short rations of raw film stock. Yet black activists and their government together pressed filmmakers to address wartime racial injustice. The black railway porter's union, led by A. Philip Randolph, threatened a march on Washington unless the government granted equality of opportunity in war industry; the National Association for the Advancement of Colored People (NAACP) held its annual convention in Los Angeles, partly to lobby Hollywood directly for better roles; and the black Pittsburgh Courier campaigned on its front pages for a Double V: a simultaneous victory over foreign fascism and domestic racism.

In response, federal agencies made several movies of advocacy. First among them in quality and breadth of distribution to both army and civilian theaters was the United States War Department's *The Negro Soldier* (1944), written by Carlton Moss, who also starred in the film. Late in the war, the government commissioned or inspired short civilian films on the theme of equitable race relations, among them *Don't Be a Sucker*, *It Happened in Springfield*, and *The House I Live In* (which won an Oscar in 1947 as the best short film). The studios joined the ranks—partly at the urging of the U.S. Office of War Information—and racially integrated the military years before the armed forces themselves would do so. Among works with an integrated cast were MGM's *Bataan* (1943), Twentieth Century Fox's *Crash Dive* (1943), and Columbia's *Sahara* (1943). Movies set in civilian life, among them *Since You Went Away* (1944) and Alfred Hitchcock's *Lifeboat* (1943), made similar gestures.

Documentaries strove for a similar liberal voice. Gjon Mili's *Jammin' the Blues* (1944) (a *Life* magazine "movie of the week") so evoked the mood of a black jazz club that seasoned newspaper reporters thought it had been done with a hidden camera. Janice Loeb and Helen Levitt's *The Quiet One* (1947) caught the dedication that social workers gave to the plight of black juveniles. And the United Auto Workers sponsored an animated cartoon, *The Brotherhood of Man* (1947), that took up the fate of racism in postwar America.

In the spring of 1949 at least three movies addressed racial issues: MGM's movie version of William Faulkner's *Intruder in the Dust* made racism an issue of conscience rather than politics; Louis DeRochemont's *Lost Boundaries* came from a Reader's Digest report on passing for white in a Vermont village; and, boldly for the times, Darryl Zanuck asked Jane White, daughter of Walter White of the NAACP, to do an uncredited but sweeping job of script doctoring on *Pinky*, yet another story on passing.

Thereafter, in the 20 years following Sidney Poitier's debut in Zanuck's *No Way Out* (1950)—an era that might well be dubbed "the age of Sidney Poitier"—scores of films emerged from Hollywood, each with an obligatory scene, sequence, or subplot involving a small, often painfully obvious victory over racism. Indeed, Poitier won an Oscar for his Christ-like savior of a group of nuns in *Lilies of the Field* (1963) and starred in the culmination of the genre, *Guess Who's Coming to Dinner* (1968). As if warning of the ominous price to pay for not following the liberal path to racial harmony, Harry

Belafonte's *Odds Against Tomorrow* (1959) closed with a scene in which two prejudiced bank robbers, one black and one white, blow themselves to bits rather than team up to pull off a job. By the 1950s such movies played a sort of backbeat to the actual Civil Rights Movement.

Civil Rights and Blaxploitation

During the 1960s, with the full flowering of the Civil Rights Movement, such films began to take on a harsher, more politically demanding edge. At first from abroad, later from sources outside the major studios, they challenged the simplistic optimism of Poitier's heyday. Costa-Gavras's *The Battle of Algiers* (1966) seemed to some black militants a textbook for direct action, while Amiri Baraka spoke of the movie version of his short play *Dutchman* (1967) as a "revolutionary revelation." Even the Hollywood movies hardened: Robert Mulligan's film version of Harper Lee's novel *To Kill a Mockingbird* (1962) ended with the death of its black protagonist, and Sidney Lumet's *The Pawnbroker* (1965) is set in a harsh Harlem dominated by a coldly ominous drug dealer (played by Brock Peters). By way of contrast, more pastoral films such as Martin Ritt's *Sounder* (1972) and Gordon Park's autobiographical *The Learning Tree* (1969) seemed childlike in their remoteness from the coming wave of angry films.

Catalysts for this turn toward rage, the cities of the late 1960s burst into

1973's *Cleopatra Jones* starred Tamara Dobson, pictured here in a fight, in an action-packed spy thriller of the blaxploitation era. *CORBIS/Bettmann*

riots of despair at the assassination of Martin Luther King Jr. and the seeming exhaustion of his movement. Awaiting the arrival of this new wave of films were hundreds of derelict, cavernous downtown theaters, along with thousands of black youths upon whom the Civil Rights Movement had had scant impact. The prototype of the new genre, soon dubbed "blaxploitation" films by the trade paper *Variety*, was Melvin Van Peeble's *Sweet Sweetback's Baad Asssss Song* (1971). More than any other movie, *Sweetback* defined its era. Jangling in its lighting and music track, and heady with contempt for the white social order and its cops, the film's success all but invited Hollywood's major studios to rush forward in pursuit of the new audience. MGM's *Shaft* (1971), for example, played to the crowd by featuring a mouthy, streetwise hero who, in reality, was not an outlaw in *Sweetback's* mold but merely a plainclothes cop. From the outset, the Hollywood studio version of this black, urban, outlaw culture cynically followed a familiar pattern. *Cool Breeze* (1972) was remade from *The Asphalt Jungle*, *The Lost Man* (1969) from Canon Reed's *Odd Man Out*, and *Up Tight* (1968) from John Ford's film of an Irish rebellion, *The Informer*. The Hollywood studios even plundered genres like horror movies in films such as *Blacula* (1972) and *Blackenstein* (1972).

The New Black Cinema

Meanwhile, a younger generation of black filmmakers emerged from academic settings: the film schools of the University of California at Los Angeles (UCLA), the University of Southern California, New York University (NYU), and later from historically black schools such as Howard University. Variously they embraced Van Peebles, Micheaux, and African filmmakers such as Ousmane Sembène of Senegal as their cultural models. For the first time women joined black filmmakers' ranks.

Asserting that black expression could be appreciated on its own terms, this new black cinema aimed to preserve black culture both within the Hollywood system and apart from it. New distributors, including the Black Filmmakers Foundation, California Newsreel, and Women Make Movies, Inc., aimed at select audiences and academic circles rather than mass markets. Yet there were crossovers such as Warrington Hudlin, who made *Black at Yale* (1977) and *Street Corner Stories* for the new distributors, but who also penetrated Hollywood, together with his brother Reginald. St. Clair Bourne's *Let the Church Say Amen* (1972) revealed both a filmmaker and a movement journalist. Women's films ranged from Madeleine Anderson's documentary pieces, Kathleen Collin's *Cruz Brothers* and *Miss Malloy*, and Ayoka Chinzira's satiric *Hair Piece: A Film for Nappy Headed People* (1985) to Julie Dash's commercially distributed, nostalgic *Daughters of the Dust* (1991). Others who crossed the line between the avant-garde and the commercial were Charles Burnett with his *Killer of Sheep* (1977) and Haile Gerima (of Howard University) with, most successfully, his fable of a clash between African and American sensibilities, *Sankofa* (1993).

The best known of the new black filmmakers during the 1980s and

1990s was probably Spike Lee, an NYU alumnus. He managed to win large audiences for almost everything he produced—film school exercises, credit-card-financed early efforts such as *She's Gotta Have It* (1986), television commercials, and promotional pieces. He also directed a string of Hollywood successes, including one of the most politically challenging and commercially successful films of the new black cinema, *Do the Right Thing* (1989).

As black filmmakers became more prolific, black actors in Hollywood—Danny Glover, Halle Berry, Will Smith, Denzel Washington, and Jada Pinkett Smith, among others—got steady, rather than sporadic work. By the late 1990s the steadily expanding black presence in American film seemed to assure a solid future for the new black cinema.

North America

Fishburne, Laurence

(b. July 30, 1961, Augusta, Ga.), African American stage and motion-picture actor whose consistently commanding performances have won widespread critical acclaim.

Laurence Fishburne III began his acting career as Larry Fishburne. Between the ages of 10 and 13 he performed on the television series *"One Life to Live,"* making his film debut at age 12 in *Cornbread, Earl and Me* (1975). He won a role as a jittery young soldier in the motion picture *Apocalypse Now* (1979), an epic drama of the Vietnam War by American director Francis Ford Coppola. He later delivered notable performances in Coppola's films *Rumble Fish* (1983) and *The Cotton Club* (1984).

Fishburne played in a number of strong supporting roles throughout the 1980s, appearing in the films *The Color Purple* (1984), *School Daze* (1988), and *King of New York* (1990) before establishing himself as a powerful leading actor in *Boyz N the Hood* (1991). His role in the film as a wise but embittered father signaled the beginning of a new era for Fishburne, symbolized by his return to using his full first name, Laurence. In 1993 he was nominated for an Academy Award as best actor for his riveting performance as American rhythm-and-blues singer Ike Turner in *What's Love Got to Do With It* (1993). His other films include *Searching for Bobby Fisher* (1993), *Higher Learning* (1994), *Othello* (1995), and *Hoodlum* (1997).

In addition to winning critical praise for his film performances, Fishburne has received acclaim for his work for television and the stage. His television performances include roles in *"A Rumor of War"* (1980), *"Pee-Wee's Playhouse"* (1986–1991), and *"The Tuskegee Airmen"* (1995). In 1992 he was named Best Actor at the Tony Awards for his performance in the world premiere of the stage play *Two Trains Running* (1990), by American playwright August Wilson. He also wrote, directed, and starred in a one-act play, *Riff Raff* (1995).

Fisk Jubilee Singers,

choral group from Fisk University that introduced African American spirituals to a worldwide audience in the 1870s and helped preserve the work songs of the slaves.

The Fisk Jubilee Singers was founded in 1867 by George L. White, the treasurer and vocal-music teacher at Fisk University in Nashville, Tennessee. The university had been established two years earlier to educate newly freed black slaves. Since few students could afford the tuition, the school needed other sources of revenue, and White came up with the idea of a performing choir as a way to raise money.

After several successful local appearances, the reputation of the 11-member choir began to spread, and in 1871 the Jubilee Singers embarked on a tour of the Northeast, performing mainly in churches before all-white audiences. Their repertoire included anthems, popular ballads, and operatic excerpts, but their most popular pieces proved to be African American spirituals and work songs, which many in their audiences were hearing for the first time. Highlights of the tour included a performance before 40,000 people at the World's Peace Jubilee in Boston in 1872 and a concert for President Ulysses S. Grant in Washington, D.C. That first tour was a big hit and spurred widespread interest in plantation hymns and other Southern black music. The Jubilee Singers eventually took their show to several European countries, including a performance for Queen Victoria in England.

With the money they raised, Fisk University was able to complete construction in 1875 of its first permanent building, called Jubilee Hall. Other black schools such as Hampton Institute, Tuskegee Institute, and Howard University soon followed with traveling choirs of their own. To many of the newly freed African American slaves, the spirituals and work songs represented an unwelcome reminder of slavery, and they were eager to discard them. But thanks to the work of the Fisk Jubilee Singers and other groups like them, these songs did not die, and are now celebrated as an indigenous American music.

Fitzgerald, Ella

(b. April 25, 1917, Newport News, Va.; d. June 15, 1996, Beverly Hills, Calif.), African American singer; one of the greatest jazz vocalists of all time, she was known as the First Lady of Song.

Ella Fitzgerald was quite possibly the greatest vocalist in the history of jazz. Only Billie Holiday and Sarah Vaughan offer her any serious competition. Of the three, Holiday came first and profoundly influenced the entire course of jazz singing, but she had a small voice, limited range, and never really moved beyond the 1930s swing jazz style. Vaughan, who emerged in the mid-1940s, was the first to sing with a truly operatic range; she had nearly perfect pitch and superb technique. Both Vaughan and Fitzgerald were blessed with pure voices and exceptionally clear enunciation. But only Fitzgerald melded the headlong swing of the 1930s with the adventurous harmonies of modern jazz.

Fitzgerald was born into poverty in Newport News, Virginia. When she was three years old, her mother moved her to Yonkers, New York, as part of the Great Migration of African Americans out of the South. In 1932 her mother died, and Fitzgerald went to live with an aunt in Harlem. On a dare, she entered herself as a dancer in one of the Apollo Theater's weekly Amateur Night in Harlem contests. But at the last moment, on November 21, 1934, she decided to sing instead, performing *"Judy" and "The Object of My Affection"* in the style of her idol Connee Boswell of the Boswell Sisters. Fitzgerald won the competition and secured a job singing with Tiny Bradshaw's band.

After alto saxophonist Benny Carter brought her to the attention of drummer and band leader Chick Webb, Fitzgerald joined Webb's band, then appearing regularly at Harlem's Savoy Ballroom. Webb became Fitzgerald's mentor and legal guardian, and in 1935 she commenced a recording career that would ultimately span six decades. At first Fitzgerald's singing showed little in the way of jazz improvisation and was closer to a straight pop music sensibility, but she achieved national popularity in 1938 with the hit *"A-Tisket, A-Tasket,"* a medium-tempo novelty number that she recorded with the Webb band. After Webb died in 1939, Fitzgerald fronted the group until mid-1942, when it broke up and she continued as a solo artist.

During the bebop or bop era of the mid-1940s and early 1950s, Fitzgerald honed her jazz abilities and emerged as one of the foremost exponents of scat singing, in which the singer's voice mimicked a soloing horn, using nonsense syllables in place of words or song lyrics. During 1946 she toured with Dizzy Gillespie's big band and in the late 1940s recorded exciting scat versions of *"Oh, Lady Be Good"* and *"How High the Moon."* In 1948 *Downbeat*, the jazz magazine, proclaimed her "as great a master of bop as she has been of swing." Fitzgerald later recalled, "I thought bebop was 'it,' and that all I had to do was go someplace and sing bop." But when many listeners rejected the complex harmonies and challenging angularity of modern jazz, she decided to modify her style.

What she achieved in the 1950s was a remarkable synthesis of accessibility and sophistication. A year after appearing in the film *Pete Kelly's Blues* (1955), Fitzgerald signed with Norman Granz's Verve Records and made some of the greatest recordings of her career. The range of Fitzgerald's mature style is exemplified by her hilarious 1960 rendition of *"Mack the Knife,"* recorded during a concert in Berlin in which she forgot Bertolt Brecht's lyrics and spontaneously invented her own, as well as in a series of Verve *Songbooks*, each offering her classic interpretations of the music of a particular composer, notably Cole Porter (1956), Duke Ellington (1958),

and George and Ira Gershwin
(1959). "I never knew how good
our songs were," Ira Gershwin
remarked, "until I heard Ella
Fitzgerald sing them."

Fitzgerald maintained a busy
schedule into the 1980s, touring
from 40 to 45 weeks a year,
appearing at numerous jazz festivals, and recording prolifically. She
also received countless awards and
honors, including 13 Grammy
Awards, a National Medal of the
Arts, a 1979 Kennedy Center
Award for lifetime achievement,
and honorary degrees from Dart-
mouth College and Yale University. On receiving an honorary
doctorate of music at Yale, she
remarked with characteristic mod-
esty, "Not bad for someone who
only studied music to get that half
credit in high school!"

Jazz vocalist Ella Fitzgerald performs in the
1950s, a decade during which she made classic
recordings in her mature style. *CORBIS/Hulton-
Deutsch Collection*

Fitzgerald's voice began to fade
by the mid-1970s, though her solid professionalism and unerring rhythmic
sense allowed her to continue making creditable music. During the 1980s,
however, diabetes, failing eyesight, and heart trouble increasingly restricted
her concert appearances and in 1991 she retired from active performance.
Yet apart from Sarah Vaughan, Fitzgerald was without peer as a jazz vocalist
for more than a generation, and her compelling sense of swing influenced all
who followed her.

North America

Flack, Roberta

(b. February 10, 1940, Black Mountain, N.C.), African American singer known
for a style that combines jazz, soul, blues, and pop.

Born to Laron and Irene Flack, who both played piano, Roberta Flack began
playing by ear as a toddler. She began taking formal lessons at 9, and at 15,
she received a scholarship to Howard University in Washington, D.C.,
where she majored in music education.

Flack taught music and English in North Carolina and Washington,
D.C., for several years after her graduation in 1958. She began her singing
career at clubs in the evenings. She initially sang opera, but she soon gained
a following by singing popular music that incorporated elements of jazz,

soul, blues, and pop. She released her first album, *First Take*, in 1969. Her second, *Chapter Two* (1970), sold over a million copies. She gained national recognition that year after appearing on many television shows, and *Downbeat* magazine named her 1970's Female Vocalist of the Year.

In 1971 her song *"The First Time Ever I Saw Your Face"* was included on the soundtrack of the movie *Play Misty for Me*; it became a number-one hit and won a Grammy Award for record of the year. She had more number-one songs with *"Killing Me Softly with His Song"* (1973) and *"Feel Like Makin' Love"* (1974). Her other hit songs include two duets, *"The Closer I Get to You"* (1978), with Donny Hathaway, and *"Tonight I Celebrate My Love"* (1983), with Peabo Bryson, and *"Set the Night to Music"* (1991).

North America

Forty Acres and a Mule,

a phrase whose meaning has evolved since its Civil War beginnings. It is also currently the name of filmmaker Spike Lee's film company.

The phrase "40 acres and a mule" probably stems from a field order given in 1865 to former slaves in the Savannah area of Georgia. On January 16, 1865, Gen. William T. Sherman of the Union Army issued Special Field Order 15. This order reserved the Sea Islands and areas of coastal South Carolina, Florida, and Georgia for freed people to own. Each person or family was to receive a 40-acre plot of agriculturally fit land. With Sherman's permission, the army could also loan mules to former slaves. About 40,000 blacks settled 400,000 acres of land (called Sherman Land) within six months. In March 1865 Congress authorized the Freedmen's Bureau to rent 40-acre plots of confiscated and abandoned lands to freed people.

The land reform and redistribution remained crucial to the freed people's demands and very controversial in congressional debates during the Reconstruction period. Land became a widespread expectation of the ex-slaves, both because most thought the land belonged to them, as they had tilled it while enslaved, and because of pervasive rumors. On May 25, 1865, President Andrew Johnson ordered that the 40-acre plots be returned to the former slave owners. Radical land redistribution never took place. "Forty acres and a mule" became a symbol not only of the limitations of Reconstruction but of African Americans' unfulfilled reparations, expectations, and hopes.

North America

Four Tops, The,

African American vocal group that recorded during the Motown label's golden age.

Originating in Detroit, Michigan, in 1953, the Four Tops were one of the most popular and successful of the soul-influenced pop acts that emerged in the 1960s. Motown signed the four singers—Levi Stubbs Jr., Renaldo Benson, Lawrence Payton, and Abdul Fakir—in 1963, and almost immediately they began producing hit after hit. Motown, a black-owned label, is largely credited with creating a highly commercial style that popularized black musical influences such as gospel and blues. The company also boasted the songwriting talents of Brian Holland, Lamont Dozier, and Eddie Holland, who not only penned most of the Four Tops' biggest hits— including *"Baby, I Need Your Loving"* (1964) and *"Reach Out, I'll Be There"* (1966)—but provided the raw material for other Motown hit machines, such as the Supremes and the Temptations.

Four years after Holland, Dozier, and Holland left Motown in 1967, the Four Tops left as well, recording with Dunhill Records a series of rhythm and blues hits, including *"Ain't No Woman (Like the One I Got)"* (1973). During the 1980s and 1990s, the Four Tops toured extensively but recorded little new material.

North America

Foxx, Redd (John Elroy Sanford)

(b. December 9, 1922, St. Louis, Mo.; d. October 11, 1991, Hollywood, Calif.), African American comedian and actor known for his television role on *Sanford and Son*.

Born John Elroy Sanford, Redd Foxx was the second son of Fred Sanford, an electrician, and Mary Alma Hughes Sanford, a minister. Called Redd because of his red hair and light complexion, he added the name Foxx after baseball player Jimmy Foxx. Redd Foxx dropped out of high school to play in a washtub band with friends. In 1939 they went to New York, calling themselves the Bon-Bons, but the group dissolved during World War II.

Rejected by the army, Foxx began to perform standup comedy in nightclubs. He teamed with Slappy White, and the two worked the African American nightclub circuit from 1951 to 1955. After the two broke up, Foxx moved to the West Coast to work. In 1956 he recorded the first of his 50 "party albums," comedy records featuring adult humor. The albums eventually sold over 20 million copies.

Although he had never acted, Foxx accepted a small role as a junkman in the popular movie *Cotton Comes to Harlem*. NBC executives liked the character so much that they developed it into a situation comedy character. In 1972 *Sanford and Son* first appeared on television, with Foxx in the starring role of Fred Sanford, a gruff junk dealer. The show lasted until the 1977 television season and with it, Foxx attained mainstream popularity. He appeared in several other films, including *Norman . . . Is That You?* in 1976 and *Harlem Nights* in 1989. Foxx suffered a fatal heart attack while on the set of a new situation comedy, *The Royal Family*, in 1991.

Franklin, Aretha Louise

(b. March 25, 1942, Memphis, Tenn.), the preeminent black female vocalist of the 1960s and 1970s, who earned, through her secular and gospel master-pieces, the title Queen of Soul.

As a daughter of the renowned Baptist preacher C. L. Franklin and his wife, Barbara Siggers Franklin—whose singing won the laurels of Mahalia Jackson—Aretha Franklin was born into gospel. As a child she began to sing in her father's New Bethel Baptist Church in Detroit, Michigan, which he had built up to a congregation of 4,500. C. L. Franklin recognized his daughter's talent and had her performing in New Bethel's choir by the age of 8. She sang solos at age 12, and at age 14 made her first recordings, including a version of Thomas A. Dorsey's gospel classic *"Precious Lord, Take My Hand."* She also began touring with her father, singing wherever he served as an itinerant preacher.

From Franklin's earliest days, something more than pure vocal bravura ignited her performances. Profound emotion infused her singing. Music historian Peter Guralnick writes, " . . . her voice and phrasing worked on even the most familiar sentiments and material . . . as to suggest a whole other subtext of experience." For Franklin this subtext was real and tragic. Her mother had left the family when Franklin was 6 and died a few years later. Franklin's subsequent childhood years, characterized by shyness, despondency, and extreme dependence on her father, ended with a pregnancy at age 15. Jo King, who managed Franklin's early gospel career, said of her, "I realized I had a real woman here, one who knew more than I did when it came to men, alcohol and everything. She had tremendous depth."

Although childhood difficulties influenced Franklin's development, she also had positive role models. Mother figures included American gospel singers Mahalia Jackson, Marion Williams, and Clara Ward, whose rendition of *"Peace in the Valley"* at the funeral of Franklin's aunt apparently inspired her resolve to sing professionally. One of her father's parishioners, James Cleveland, moved in with the family and helped Franklin with her piano playing. Most important, Franklin's friendship with gospel-gone-soul singer Sam Cooke inspired her to leave the church for a professional career in music.

At age 18 Franklin went to New York, cut demos, took voice lessons, and signed a five-year recording contract with Columbia Records. Supervised by John Hammond – who had "discovered" such musicians as Count Basie, Charlie Christian, Lionel Hampton, and Billie Holiday – Franklin recorded pop standards, Broadway tunes, and jazz ballads. Due to overwrought, often saccharine arrangements, Franklin's recordings with Columbia met with limited success. Although some historians attribute her early mediocrity to Columbia's mismanagement, Franklin often chose such arrangements for herself.

By 1966 Columbia Records had incurred approximately $80,000 in debt from Franklin's nine-album stint. They terminated her contract, but Jerry Wexler of Atlantic Records swiftly signed her to his company. He encouraged Franklin to drop her Columbia sound, thereby initiating her career in soul. Wexler claims that he "urged Aretha to be Aretha"—and indeed her Atlantic recordings of the late 1960s pulsed with an authenticity that attracted millions of fans. Although Franklin was not known as an innovator, she expressed a level of sincerity unprecedented in pop music. A 1967 article in *Time* magazine stated, "She does not seem to be performing so much as bearing witness to a reality so simple and compelling that she could not possibly fake it."

Franklin's first release with Atlantic, *"I Never Loved a Man (The Way I Love You),"* sold a million copies and was followed by four other million-selling records that same year. Between 1967 and 1969 she won four Grammy Awards. In addition, Franklin became politically engaged, singing a soulful rendition of *"The Star Spangled Banner"* at the 1968 Democratic convention. Her cover of *"Respect"* by Otis Redding transformed the song into an anthem of black feminist pride. Franklin also became associated with the Civil Rights Movement by singing at the funeral of Martin Luther King Jr., a friend and colleague of her father.

During the 1970s Franklin won six more Grammy Awards, sending song after song up the R&B charts. Although she continued to release secular soul, Franklin returned to her gospel roots in 1972 with a double-album collection titled *Amazing Grace* that featured her former mentor, James Cleveland. In 1980 Franklin left Atlantic Records for Arista and that same year made her film debut in *The Blues Brothers*. Through the 1980s and 1990s she continued to release new work and began donating large sums of money to the United Negro College Fund, the National Association for the Advancement of Colored People, and sickle cell anemia research.

By the end of the century, Franklin had recorded almost 50 albums. Her popular recognition as the Queen of Soul extended to include the esteem of white politicians: in 1986 the state of Michigan declared her voice a natural resource, and in 1989 state senator Carl Levin honored Franklin for her financial support of the fight against drunk driving. Displaying her ongoing affiliation with the Democratic Party in 1997, she performed at President Clinton's second inaugural celebration.

North America

Freeman, Morgan

(b. June 1, 1937, Memphis, Tenn.), African American stage, television, and motion-picture actor best known for his critically acclaimed character roles.

Morgan Freeman began acting as a child, enlisted in the United States Air Force at 18, and later returned to acting while enrolled at Los Angeles City College. He then moved to New York City, where he perfected his craft in minor stage plays and appeared on the television soap opera *Another World*.

He made his Broadway debut in 1968 in an all-black production of *Hello Dolly!* and went on to win a Tony Award nomination for his performance in *The Mighty Gents* (1978) and Obie Awards (given for off-Broadway work) for his roles in *Coriolanus* (1979), *Mother Courage and Her Children* (1980), and *The Gospel at Colonus* (1983).

Freeman's film debut, in the low-budget children's feature *Who Says I Can't Ride a Rainbow?* (1971), led to a recurring role on the educational television series The Electric Company broadcast by the Public Broadcasting Service from 1971 to 1977. In his first Hollywood movie, *Brubaker* (1980), a prison reform drama directed by Robert Redford, Freeman made a strong impression in a small but important part as a death-row inmate. His breakthrough came in 1987, when his chilling performance as a pimp in *Street Smart* earned Best Supporting Actor Awards from the New York Film Critics Circle, the Los Angeles Film Critics Association, and the National Society of Film Critics, in addition to an Academy Award nomination for Best Supporting Actor.

Freeman was nominated for Academy Awards as Best Actor for his performances as a long-suffering chauffeur in the sentimental drama *Driving Miss Daisy* (1989) and as a prison inmate in *The Shawshank Redemption* (1994). In 1993 he made his directing debut with *Bopha!*, a drama set in South Africa under the country's policy of strict racial segregation known as apartheid. His performance as a world-weary police detective in the 1995 thriller *Seven* won wide critical praise. Freeman's other films include *Clean and Sober* (1988), *Glory* (1989), *Unforgiven* (1992), *Kiss the Girls* (1997), and *Amistad* (1997).

Africa

Fugard, Athol

(b. June 11, 1932, near Middleburg, South Africa), South African playwright whose dramatic works deal with the personal wounds inflicted by apartheid.

Best known for his plays *Blood Knot* and *Master Harold . . . and the Boys*, Athol Fugard has brought to a wide audience images of life in South Africa under apartheid. The child of an English father and Afrikaner mother, Fugard grew up in Port Elizabeth, the Cape Province city where most of his plays are set. He studied philosophy and anthropology at the University of Cape Town, then left just before graduating and hitchhiked the length of the continent to Port Sudan, where he spent the next two years working on a steam ship.

Returning to South Africa in 1956, Fugard married Sheila Meiring, an actress whom he credits for developing his interest in theater. In 1958 he became a clerk for the Fordsburg Native Commissioner's Court. The court handled cases of people accused of violating the pass laws, which were among the many laws restricting Africans' right to live and work where they pleased. Fugard called the job "the ugliest thing I have ever been part of," but it also inspired the intimate view of apartheid's cruelty that became an ever-present element in his work.

By 1959 Fugard had written and produced two plays, *No-Good Friday* and *Nongogo*, and he and his wife moved to London to gain theatrical experience. They stayed only a year, returning to South Africa after the Sharpeville massacre in 1960. Fugard's next play, *The Blood Knot*, opened in 1961 with Fugard and an African actor, Zakes Mokae, playing two mixed-race half-brothers confronting the psychic toll of institutionalized racism. At the same time Fugard began protesting the official segregation of theater audiences.

In 1967 the South African government seized Fugard's passport and placed him under surveillance. But the harassment did not stop Fugard from collaborating in 1972 with black actor-playwrights John Kani and Winston Ntshona on *Sizwe Banzi Is Dead* and *The Island*, each of which was nominated for three Tony Awards. His 1982 play *Master Harold . . . and the Boys* concerns the relationships between a privileged white boy and his family's black servants. Considered one of the best playwrights in the English-speaking world, Fugard continues to write and produce plays.

North America

Fuller, Meta Vaux Warrick

(b. June 9, 1877, Philadelphia, Pa.; d. March 18, 1968, Framingham, Mass.), African American sculptor, one of the earliest studio artists to depict black themes.

"Art must be the quintessence of meaning. Creative art means you create for yourself. Inspirations can come from most anything. Tell the world how you feel . . . take the chance . . . try, try!" This statement by Meta Vaux Warrick Fuller reflects the spirit of a woman who created bold, dramatic work that took new chances in African American art. Fuller was born in Philadelphia in 1877, the daughter of two successful entrepreneurs. Her father owned a catering business and a barbershop, and her mother was a hairdresser. She grew up in a privileged home, receiving lessons in art, music, dance, and horseback riding. When one of her high school projects at the J. Liberty Tadd Industrial Art School was selected to be part of Tadd's exhibit at the 1893 World's Columbian Exposition in Chicago, her public career as an artist began.

In 1894 Fuller received a three-year scholarship to the Pennsylvania School of Industrial Art, followed by a one-year postgraduate fellowship in 1897. As a student she received several awards and prizes for her sculpture. Her work had a signature bold, sensational style that her instructors felt would be especially successful overseas, so in September 1899, Fuller sailed for Paris. During the next four years she studied at the Académie Colarossi and the Ecole des Beaux-Arts and received private guidance from such prominent sculptors as Auguste Rodin and Augustus Saint-Gaudens. Rodin was an especially significant early supporter, and after he praised her 1901 sculpture *Secret Sorrow (Man Eating His Heart)*, her work was exhibited at several important galleries.

In Paris Fuller drew inspiration for her sculptures from Greek myths, French literature, and the Bible as well as various European traditions. Her works often portrayed dramatic and even grotesque figures—other titles included *Medusa, The Wretched*, and *Man Carrying a Dead Comrade*—and were praised for their force and power; the French press called Fuller "the delicate sculptor of horrors." But even as she was developing a reputation based on this genre of work, new influences began to present themselves.

One of her earliest friends in Paris was the African American painter Henry O. Tanner. In 1900, during a trip to Paris, W. E. B. Du Bois saw Fuller's work at the Paris Universal Exposition, and both Tanner and Du Bois began encouraging her to explore African American subjects. Fuller initially resisted these suggestions, content with the images that had made her a success in Paris. But when she decided to return to the United States in October 1902, she found the art world in her hometown unwilling to accept her. After the cold reception she received from mainstream Philadelphia critics and dealers, Fuller began constructing new pieces that appealed to the black Philadelphia audience. In the process, she became one of the first African American studio artists to depict African American faces and themes.

In 1907 Fuller became the first black woman artist to receive a federal commission for her work when she was asked to contribute a set of tableaux on African American history for the Jamestown Tercentennial Exposition. The finished work was awarded a gold medal and brought her national attention, but over the next few years, several events temporarily slowed Fuller's art. In 1909 she married Liberian neurologist Solomon Fuller and moved with him to Framingham, Massachusetts; within two years she had two infant sons (a third was born in 1916). In 1910 a fire in the Philadelphia warehouse where Fuller had stored her pieces destroyed 16 years' worth of work, including everything she had created in Paris. The fire devastated Fuller and caused her to stop sculpting altogether for three years. But in 1913 she accepted a commission from Du Bois to create a sculpture for New York's state celebration of the 50th anniversary of the Emancipation Proclamation, and the second phase of her career began.

Over the next few decades, Fuller became known for pieces that celebrated African and African American history, struggle, and heritage. These included the 1914 work *Ethiopia Awakening*, which portrayed an African woman removing mummy bandages from her eyes; the 1919 work *Mary Turner: A Silent Protest Against Mob Violence*, which commemorated the much-publicized 1917 lynching of a pregnant woman; and the 1937 piece *The Talking Skull*, which dramatized an African fable. Fuller is sometimes remembered as a Harlem Renaissance artist because her work from this period coincided with the flowering of art by other black writers, musicians, and artists that began in New York in the 1920s.

In 1950 Fuller again temporarily retired from sculpting, this time to care for her ill husband and to recover from her own tuberculosis. But by the late 1950s she had returned to her art, creating a bust of educator Charlotte Hawkins Brown in 1956 and a series of works depicting notable black women for the National Council of Negro Women in 1957. In the 1960s Fuller sculpted works that reflected her support of the Civil Rights Movement: *The Crucifixion*, which commemorated the four girls killed in the 1963 Sixteenth Street Baptist Church bombing in Birmingham, Alabama, and *The Good Shepherd*, which celebrated the clergymen who had marched to Selma, Alabama, with Martin Luther King Jr. By the time she passed away in 1968 at age 90, Fuller had spent more than 70 years creating art that "[took] a chance" and "[told] the world" how she felt, in the process becoming one of the most innovative black artists of the twentieth century.

North America

Funk,

a musical style pioneered by James Brown and Sly and the Family Stone during the late 1960s and 1970s; funk evolved from soul music, deepening its rhythms and incorporating psychedelic elements inspired by late 1960s rock 'n' roll.

Funk evolved from soul music during the late 1960s, much as Black Power grew out of the Civil Rights Movement. During the 1960s rhythm and blues (R&B) performers drew upon the harmonies and vocal style of gospel music to create the distinctive style that became known as soul music. Soul music voiced the pride and optimism that many blacks shared during the Civil Rights Movement. By the late 1960s, the political climate had deteriorated. The Vietnam War displaced President Lyndon Johnson's War on Poverty, and between 1965 and 1968 violence erupted in many black urban neighborhoods. The civil rights coalition was increasingly divided as the Black Power Movement brought a new militancy to African American politics.

Popular music could not help reflecting such influences, and for African Americans the result was funk. Funk was a heavily rhythmic, dance-oriented music with lyrics that mostly focused on sex, drugs, and partying. Surprisingly often, however, funk lyrics spoke to contemporary black pride and anger. In *"Say It Loud (I'm Black and I'm Proud)"* (1968), James Brown sang, "We'd rather die on our feet, than be livin' on our knees." Sly and the Family Stone recorded equally militant lyrics in such songs as *"Don't Call Me Nigger, Whitey"* (1969) and on the album *There's a Riot Going On* (1971). Parliament's *"Chocolate City"* (1975) envisioned the possibilities of an all-black American government.

Ultimately, funk music was not about political commentary; it was about the beat. Trombonist Fred Wesley—who in the 1970s worked with such leading funk performers as Brown, George Clinton, and bassist Bootsy Collins—explained the essential elements of a funk song: "If you have a syncopated bass line, a strong, strong, heavy back beat from the drummer, a counterline from the guitar, or the keyboard, and someone soul-singing on top of that in a gospel style, then you have funk."

Funk music deepened the heavy rhythms of soul music, and it followed the lead of guitarist Jimi Hendrix in bringing the beat and performing style of psychedelic rock 'n' roll into African American popular music.

The key funk innovator was the "godfather of soul," James Brown. His bands featured tightly riffing horn sections coupled to an underlying rhythm that turned decades of black music topsy-turvy by putting the accent on one and three, rather than on the back beats (two and four). Brown's albums *Out of Sight* (1964) and *Papa's Got a Brand New Bag* (1965) predated the stylistic label funk, but they clearly foreshadowed the style.

Although Brown set the stage for funk, Sly Stone completed the funk synthesis. Stone formed Sly and the Family Stone in 1967 in San Francisco, a hotbed of counterculture activity that was home to the psychedelic rock bands Jefferson Airplane and the Grateful Dead. Sly and the Family Stone was the first interracial rock band, and it included women and men as well as blacks and whites.

The band had its greatest success between 1968 and 1971, including an appearance at the 1969 Woodstock Festival. Sly and the Family Stone's early hits, *"Every day People"* (1968) and *"Hot Fun in the Summertime"* (1969), suggested a pop-music innocence, but in concert the group's punchy horn riffs and frenzied guitar solos merged a strong funk beat with intense, psychedelic rock-style guitar solos.

More than any other musician, George Clinton has kept funk music alive. Through the 1970s and 1980s Clinton and his related and overlapping groups Parliament and Funkadelic, which during the 1970s began performing together as P-Funk, kept the funk beat alive during an era dominated by disco and punk rock. Other popular funk bands included Earth, Wind, and Fire; the Ohio Players; the Commodores; and the Bar-Kays. In the 1980s, funk—especially the recordings of Clinton and Brown—provided the music for many early rappers.

G

Gaines, Ernest J.

(b. January 15, 1933, Oscar, La.), African American novelist and short story writer best known for his 1971 novel *The Autobiography of Miss Jane Pittman*.

Although Ernest Gaines has spent much of his adult life in the San Francisco Bay Area, all of his work returns to the setting of his southern Louisiana childhood, with its complicated intersections of African American, Creole, Cajun, and white culture. Gaines was born on the River Lake Plantation in Point Coupée Parish County, Louisiana, and raised largely by a disabled great-aunt who later provided the model for his powerful fictional character Miss Jane Pittman. The parish had no black high school, and when Gaines was 15 his mother and stepfather sent for him to join them in Vallejo, California, where he could continue his education. After graduating from high school, he attended a junior college and served in the military before receiving a bachelor's degree in English from San Francisco State College in 1957.

In college Gaines began to read voraciously and write his own stories. He was never exposed to black writers. His literary models were such white American writers as Ernest Hemingway and William Faulkner and European writers such as Russian novelist Leo Tolstoy. He decided early, however, to focus his own writing on what he knew—which meant portraying African American culture and language. Gaines published his first short stories in a college literary magazine, where they were noticed by the white literary agent Dorothea Oppenheimer. Oppenheimer helped Gaines obtain a fellowship to Stanford University to study creative writing and a contract with Dial Press that led to his first novel, *Catherine Carmier* (1964).

Catherine Carmier and Gaines's second novel, *Of Love and Dust* (1967), both use interracial relationships as a means of exploring the complexities of racial intolerance and injustice in Louisiana. He explored similar themes in the short story collection *Bloodline* (1968). Each of these books bolstered his literary reputation, but it was *The Autobiography of Miss Jane Pittman* (1971) that brought Gaines widespread recognition. In this novel the eponymous 108-year-old heroine tells her life story in her own words—a life story that follows Miss Jane and her community through slavery, Reconstruction, Jim Crow, and the Civil Rights Movement. The compelling narrative that resulted—still considered Gaines's masterpiece—became a best-selling book and a successful made-for-television movie.

Gaines followed that novel with *In My Father's House* (1978), *A Gathering of Old Men* (1983), and *A Lesson Before Dying* (1993). Throughout his career one of Gaines's hallmarks has been his ability to capture authentic African American voices. Most of his novels and short stories are first-person narratives, and his skill in portraying black speech is felt in every line. Gaines is also applauded for his gift of evoking the Louisiana community he describes—a process he calls "knowing the place, knowing the people." By doing both successfully, he is able to write about them so convincingly that his readers feel as if they know the place and people too.

This talent proved especially important in *The Autobiography of Miss Jane Pittman*, which reached an audience of unprecedented breadth. Said one critic, "More than any other single book, this novel helped white Americans understand the personal emotions and the historical events that had produced the civil rights revolution." Gaines lives in California, but since 1983 has spent part of each year as a professor of English at the University of Southwestern Louisiana in Lafayette.

North America
___

Gaye, Marvin

(b. April 2, 1939, Washington, D.C.; d. April 1, 1984, Los Angeles, Calif.), African American singer and songwriter, a recording artist for Motown Records, and one of the most popular and influential singers of rhythm and blues (R&B) music in the 1960s and 1970s, whose songs were notable for their brooding, introspective qualities.

Marvin Gaye began singing in church as a child. The son of a poor Pentecostal minister, he grew up listening to the music of American blues singer Ray Charles, which became a major influence on his work. In 1958 Gaye joined an R&B vocal group called the Moonglows. Three years later he signed a recording contract with Tamla, one of the Motown record companies, serving as a drummer for studio sessions and, later, as a singer. Influenced by American singers Frank Sinatra and Nat "King" Cole, Gaye had hoped to sing in the popular style known as crooning, but after his first album—a series of jazz standards—received little attention, Motown had him record up-tempo soul music material. The result was a series of songs that became classics, beginning with "*Stubborn Kind of Fellow*" (1963) and culminating in "*I Heard It Through the Grapevine*" (1968).

Gaye's other popular records from this 1960s Motown era include "*Can*

I Get a Witness" (1963), a song with traits of gospel music and a strong influence on British rock groups such as the Rolling Stones (the group recorded the song in 1964); *"How Sweet It Is"* (1964), a song with jazz influences; and *"Ain't That Peculiar"* and *"I'll Be Doggone"* (both 1965), pensive songs written and produced by American Motown artist Smokey Robinson. Later in the decade Gaye recorded a series of romantic duets with Motown singer Tammi Terrell, including *"Ain't No Mountain High Enough"* (1967), *"If This World Were Mine"* (1967), *"You're All I Need to Get By"* (1968), and *"What You Gave Me"* (1969).

Shortly after Terrell's death in 1970, Gaye established a new style of soul music with the album *What's Going On* (1971), a deeply personal and spiritual reflection on family and social issues and particularly on the Vietnam War (1959–1975). A work that blended styles of soul, jazz, and rock music, the album marked one of the first times Motown had given an artist nearly complete creative control.

During the next ten years Gaye recorded and produced a series of brooding, erotic songs, including *"Trouble Man"* (1972), *"Let's Get It On"* (1973), and *"I Want You"* (1976). By the end of the 1970s his career was in decline and his personal problems were mounting. He retreated to Europe, where he recorded the hit song *"Sexual Healing"* (1982). He then returned to the United States and, after a disappointing musical tour, moved in with his parents. In 1984, in the midst of a heated quarrel, he was shot to death by his father.

In 1982 Gaye won two Grammy Awards for *"Sexual Healing."* In 1987 he was inducted into the Rock and Roll Hall of Fame.

North America

Gillespie, John Birks ("Dizzy")

(b. October 21, 1917, Cheraw, S.C.; d. January 7, 1993, Englewood, N.J.), African American trumpet player, the co-creator with alto saxophonist Charlie Parker of bebop or modern jazz, and an Afro-Cuban jazz innovator.

John Birks "Dizzy" Gillespie may have been the greatest trumpeter in the history of jazz. His bravura trumpet playing featured a brilliant but sensitive tone, a wide range, and mind-boggling speed and articulation. To the wider public, Gillespie's name also conjured up images of his distinctive trumpet with its upswept bell, the way his cheeks bulged out when he played, and his penchant for clowning that included a seriocomic campaign for president in 1964. But Gillespie was extremely serious about his music and was a leader in two major developments in jazz. Beginning in the 1940s he played a key role in bringing Afro-Cuban music into American jazz. More significant, during the mid-1940s Gillespie was a primary force, along with alto saxophonist Charlie Parker, in the development of bebop or modern jazz.

Although Gillespie's role in this movement is well known, he has generally received less attention than Parker, in part because Gillespie did not fit the stereotype of the ill-fated and misunderstood musician. Jazz has a long tradition of mythologizing its troubled geniuses. Gillespie was in many respects closer to being the counterpart in modern jazz of Louis Armstrong in traditional jazz. As Armstrong had done in the 1920s, Gillespie redirected the course of jazz and expanded its improvisational possibilities. Both men played with a technical facility that astonished their peers. And like Armstrong, Gillespie had a winning personality and a gift for comedy.

John Birks Gillespie was born in Cheraw, South Carolina, the youngest of James and Lottie Gillespie's nine children. His father, a brickmason who led a band on the weekends, died not long before John's tenth birthday. During the Great Depression, the fatherless family survived by dint of hard work and struggle. Lottie Gillespie did laundry for white families, and John and his siblings picked cotton. Gillespie showed an early interest in music and took his first piano lessons from a neighbor. He was also influenced by the sanctified church. "I first learned the meaning of rhythm there," he recalled in his autobiography *To BE, or not . . . to BOP*, "and all about how music could transport people spiritually."

In 1929 Gillespie joined the school band, playing trombone and, later, trumpet. His first public performances were in accompaniment to amateur minstrels in school minstrel shows. Gillespie and several other members of the band formed a small group that played at local dances, white and black. In 1933 Gillespie received a scholarship to Laurinburg Technical Institute, a black high school in North Carolina, which he attended until his family moved to Philadelphia, Pennsylvania, in 1935. There Gillespie joined the big band of prominent local bandleader Frankie Fairfax, and members of the Fairfax band soon dubbed the antic young trumpeter "Dizzy."

After two years of playing in Philadelphia, Gillespie decided to move to New York City, the nation's jazz capital. He lived with older brother James P. Gillespie, played in jam sessions, and sat in with various groups, including Chick Webb's big band at the Savoy Ballroom. During these years Gillespie's major influence was the dynamic swing trumpeter Roy Eldridge. Gillespie played many of Eldridge's "licks" or characteristic phrases and memorized entire solos that his idol had recorded. Gillespie made his recording debut in 1937, soon after joining Teddy Hill's big band, and then joined the band on a European tour.

After returning from Europe, Gillespie discovered that the regulations of New York City's musicians' union made it difficult for him to find work. The only regular gig he found was with Cass Carr, "a West Indian guy who played the musical saw." Gillespie said that Carr "played for all the ethnic things" and "for all the communist dances," including a gig at the Communist Party of the United States of America's Camp Unity. "White-black relationships were very close among the communists," Gillespie recounted. Gillespie himself became a "card-carrying communist," although he later downplayed the significance of this decision.

After resolving his problems with the musicians' union, Gillespie played with some of the most prominent big bands of the day, including those of

Cab Calloway, Ella Fitzgerald, Benny Carter, Lucky Millinder, Earl Hines, and Billy Eckstine. In 1937 Gillespie had met dancer Lorraine Willis, and three years later the two were married. During these years Gillespie began moving beyond Roy Eldridge's trumpet playing and the musical conventions of the swing era. Dissatisfied with the clichés and constraints of swing-era jazz, he began to explore new harmonic directions.

Gillespie faced considerable resistance from older jazz musicians. Bandleaders Les Hite and Lucky Millinder each fired the young trumpeter, and Cab Calloway disparagingly referred to Gillespie's trumpet solos as "Chinese music." Rather than tempering his style, Gillespie began to proselytize. When the Calloway band was playing its regular gig at the Cotton Club, Gillespie took bass player Milt Hinton up to the roof during band breaks to teach him bass parts that fit Gillespie's harmonically challenging solos.

After-hours jam sessions proved far more important than the musically regimented big bands in creating the bebop or bop revolution. The key gathering places for creative young musicians were two Harlem nightspots, Minton's Playhouse and Monroe's Uptown House. Gillespie explained: "What we were doing . . . was playing, seriously . . . blending our ideas into a new style of music . . . . We had some fundamental background training in European harmony and music theory superimposed on our own knowledge of Afro-American musical tradition . . . . Musically, we were changing the way that we spoke, to reflect the way that we felt."

The house band at Minton's was especially significant and included pianist Thelonious Monk and drummer Kenny Clarke. Guitar player Charlie Christian, a member of the Benny Goodman Sextet, kept a spare amplifier at Minton's so that he could sit in whenever he was in town.

During these years Gillespie met an alto player from Kansas City named Charlie Parker. Parker had independently achieved harmonic breakthroughs comparable to those of Gillespie. Indeed, Parker alone had the technical mastery and creativity to make him Gillespie's musical peer. The two men became better acquainted during stints in two important incubators of modern jazz, the big bands of Earl Hines (1943) and Billy Eckstine (1944). Later in 1944, when Gillespie and bass player Oscar Pettiford formed the first true bop group—a quintet that debuted at the Onyx Club on 52nd Street—Parker was out of town, and tenor saxophonist Don Byas became the second frontline instrument. The Gillespie-Pettiford quintet marked the full emergence of modern jazz.

Shortly afterward, however, came the group that in Gillespie's opinion achieved the "height of the perfection of our music." This quintet included Parker and commenced a long stint at the New York nightclub the Three Deuces. During 1945 Gillespie and Parker also recorded a series of bebop classics, often taken at blistering tempos, including "*Dizzy Atmosphere*," "*Salt Peanuts*," and "*Shaw Nuff*." Playing some of the tightest unison lines in the history of jazz, the two seemed to breathe and think as one. In the late 1980s, more than 30 years after Parker's death, *New York Times* columnist Bob Herbert asked Gillespie how close he and Parker had been. "How close are those two coats of paint?" the trumpeter replied.

Gillespie, far more than Parker, retained an interest in big bands, and he led several during the late 1940s and mid- to late 1950s. In 1946 he recorded the blazing and apocalyptic *"Things to Come,"* a classic example of big band bop. And in the following year, his big band introduced Afro-Cuban music to jazz audiences. When Gillespie played in Cab Calloway's orchestra, Cuban trumpet player Mario Bauza had introduced him to the rhythms and harmonies of Afro-Cuban music.

In 1947 Gillespie turned to his old friend Bauza for advice on hiring a percussionist who could bring a Latin flavor to his big band. Bauza recommended Cuban percussionist Luciano "Chano" Pozo, whom Gillespie featured prominently on several memorable Latin jazz recordings, including *"Manteca"* (1947) and *"Guarachi Guaro"* (1948). After economic difficulties forced him to break up his big band in 1950, Gillespie retained his interest in Afro-Cuban music. In 1951 he recorded what would become his best-known Latin composition, the moody *"Tin Tin Deo."*

At a party in 1953, Gillespie's trumpet was accidentally knocked over and its bell bent upward. When Gillespie tried to play it, he found that he actually preferred the bent shape because the upturned bell made it easier to play softly and improved his ability to hear his own playing. Soon after, he had the Martin Company build him a trumpet designed with an upswept bell, and he played similar instruments for the rest of his life. Also in 1953, at Toronto's Massey Hall, Gillespie played with Parker in one of their rare reunions. A recording of that performance made by bass player Charles Mingus reveals the continued brilliance of Parker and Gillespie's collaborations. Yet by the mid-1950s, when Parker died, the musical innovations of the two men were so thoroughly integrated into jazz that many listeners and critics had begun to take them for granted. Gillespie, however, continued to play vital and challenging music, mostly in small-group settings but occasionally in larger ensembles.

In 1956 Gillespie was invited by the United States State Department to organize a big band and act as a musical goodwill ambassador on a world tour. It was the first time the American government had recognized the most distinctly American art form—jazz. The new Gillespie band included the young trumpeter Quincy Jones and featured a number of Jones's compositions and arrangements. The tour was a resounding success, and the band continued to play together until 1958. Gillespie also performed a number of large-scale works, including pianist Lalo Schifrin's *"Gillespiana"* (1960) and *"The New Continent"* (1962); trombonist J. J. Johnson's *"Perceptions"* (1961); and, as the featured soloist with Machito and his orchestra, composer Arturo "Chico" O'Farrill's *"Afro-Cuban Jazz Moods"* (1975).

In 1971 Gillespie toured with an all-star group known as the Giants of Jazz that included Thelonious Monk, drummer Art Blakey, and saxophonist Sonny Stitt. The response of audiences and critics was overwhelmingly positive, and for the rest of his life Gillespie was regarded as one of the giants of jazz. He well understood his own musical influence, particularly on jazz trumpeters. "If he's younger than me and playing trumpet," Gillespie declared, "then he's following in my footsteps." Even in his mid-seventies, he kept up a grueling schedule of appearances at nightclubs and jazz festivals. During the 1980s Gillespie's embouchure weakened and his playing became more erratic, but his live performances remained dynamic and musically challenging. He continued to play actively until early 1992.

North America

Gilpin, Charles Sidney

(b. November 20, 1878, Richmond, Va.; d. May 6, 1930), African American actor and singer, best known for his title role in Eugene O'Neill's Pulitzer Prize-winning Broadway play, *Emperor Jones*.

Charles Gilpin, the youngest of 14 children, was born in Richmond, Virginia, to Caroline Gilpin, a nurse, and Peter Gilpin, a laborer in a steel-rolling mill. Gilpin's first job, as a printer's assistant at the Richmond Planet, taught him skills that would later be useful between theatrical engagements, but by age 18 he had begun touring nationally with minstrel groups such as the Perkus and Davis Great Southern Minstrel Barn Storming Aggregation (1896) and the Smart Set (1905).

Gilpin's first dramatic appearances were at the Pekin Theater in Chicago (1907–1911)—the first legitimate Negro theater—and with various touring companies. In 1915 he joined the Anita Bush Players at the Lincoln Theater in New York; the group soon combined with the Lafayette Theater Company, also in Harlem. Here, Gilpin was both star performer and director.

Gilpin made his Broadway debut as William Custis in John Drinkwater's *Abraham Lincoln* (1919), a performance that impressed Eugene O'Neill so much that he cast Gilpin in the title role of his Pulitzer Prize-winning Broadway play, *Emperor Jones*. This was the pinnacle of Gilpin's career, and marked the first time a black actor had played a role of such magnitude. The National Association for the Advancement of Colored People awarded him the Spingarn Medal for his "notable performance" in 1921; the Drama League elected him one of the ten persons who had contributed the most to American theater, and President Warren G. Harding received him privately at the White House. Gilpin suffered a breakdown in 1929 and died in Eldridge Park, New Jersey, on May 6, 1930.

North America

Giovanni, Yolande Cornelia ("Nikki")

(b. June 7, 1943, Knoxville, Tenn.), groundbreaking African American poet who began writing during the Black Arts Movement and who continues to celebrate black culture in her work.

Nikki Giovanni, one of the best-known contemporary black poets, rose to prominence in the 1960s as part of the generation of young black poets of the Black Arts and Black Power movements whose work reflected their radical political views. A typical poem of hers from that era, "My Poem," begins:

> *i am 25 years old*
> *black female poet*
> *wrote a poem asking*
> *nigger can you kill*
> *if they kill me*
> *it won't stop*
> *the revolution*

While Giovanni's Black Arts Movement poetry is still often anthologized, her range has expanded over the decades to reflect other facets of the African American experience.

Giovanni, originally named Yolande Cornelia after her mother, was raised in Wyoming, Ohio, but spent summers and her junior and senior years of high school with her grandmother in Knoxville, Tennessee. Intelligent, bold, and outspoken since childhood, she entered Fisk University at age 17 but was asked to withdraw later that fall for "attitudes [which] did not fit those of a Fisk woman." Giovanni returned four years later and eventually graduated with an honors degree in history in 1967. As an undergraduate, she helped reinstate Fisk's chapter of the Student Nonviolent Coordinating Committee (SNCC) and was part of a writing workshop led by black author John O. Killens.

The year she graduated, Giovanni published her first poetry collection, *Black Feeling*. She followed it with *Black Talk* (1968) and *Black Judgment* (1970). These books secured her reputation as one of the most accessible of the young writers whose poems encouraged black solidarity and revolution, and she soon became the most prominent woman writer of the Black Arts Movement. Giovanni was also well-known for dynamic readings of her poetry, and she recorded several albums of her readings set to gospel and other black music, including *Truth Is on Its Way*, which became a bestseller in 1971. That same year she published a collection of autobiographical essays, *Gemini: An Extended Autobiographical Statement on My First Twenty-Five Years at Being a Black Poet.*

At about the same time, her poetry became less aggressively political and more reflectively personal. As Giovanni explained the transition, "I like to think I've grown and changed . . . How else can I ask people to read my work or listen to me?" In 1969 she gave birth to a son, and she has since written several books of poetry meant for black children. Giovanni's poetry for adults in collections such as *My House* (1972), *The Women and the Men* (1972), and *Cotton Candy on a Rainy Day* (1978) explored relationships between black men and black women, connections between families, and simple questions of identity and purpose for the African American women who found themselves, as she said:

black female and bright
in a white male mediocre world.

In the 1980s and 1990s Giovanni published two more books of essays, which address both personal and larger social issues. The recipient of numerous honorary degrees and awards, in 1989 she became professor of English at Virginia Polytechnic Institute and State University, and continues to write and lecture around the country. In 1996 she published *The Selected Poems of Nikki Giovanni*, a comprehensive volume that reflects her artistic and personal evolution during her first three decades as a writer. Above all, in her poetry, essays, and speeches she still celebrates black identity, which she sees as the defining characteristic of African American poets, who "see love and beauty in the blooming of the Black community; power in a people whose only power has been the truth."

North America

Glover, Danny

(b. July 22, 1947, San Francisco, Calif.), African American actor whose career has spanned television, theater, and film.

Danny Glover was born in San Francisco to politically active parents, and as a youth participated in the student activism of the Haight-Ashbury district, a center of 1960s counterculture activity. He studied economics at San Francisco State University and, after graduating, took a job as an economic planner for the city of San Francisco. While in his twenties he began participating in the American Conservatory Theater's Black Actors' Workshop but kept his job in the mayor's office until 1975. When he was nearly 30 years old, he began acting professionally, landing television roles on *"Gimme A Break," "Chiefs," "Lou Grant,"* and *"Palmerstown, USA,"* an Alex Haley production.

Glover distinguished himself as an actor of great promise in the early 1980s when he appeared in two plays by South African playwright Athol Fugard in New York: with *The Blood Knot* (1980) Glover made his off-Broadway debut, and for his performance in *Master Harold . . . and the Boys* (1982) he garnered high acclaim. He also appeared in *The Island, Sizwe Banzi Is Dead, Macbeth,* and *Suicide in B Flat.*

Impressed by Glover's performance in *Master Harold*, Hollywood director Robert Benson cast him as a sharecropper in *Places in the Heart* (1984), Glover's first leading role in a big-budget production. Glover's watershed came in 1985, however, when he appeared in three of the year's most successful movies: *Silverado, Witness,* and *The Color Purple.* Thereafter, lead roles in numerous top-grossing films, including *Lethal Weapon* (1987), its two sequels, and other action films, indicated Glover's mainstream acceptance.

Glover continued to appear on television, most notably in *Mandela* (1987) and *Queen* (1993), another Alex Haley project. Although Glover has at times been attacked for role choices, especially his clichéd character in *Lethal Weapon 3*, he considers acting a political vocation. His serious dramatic work—such as *The Color Purple* and *Mandela*—and awards from the National Association for the Advancement of Colored People (NAACP) and the TransAfrica Forum, reflect his interest in race and politics.

North America

Goldberg, Whoopi

(b. November 13, 1954, Chelsea, N.Y.), comedian, film star, and the first African American woman to win an Oscar (1990) since Hattie McDaniel (1939).

Whoopi Goldberg was born in New York City, where she exhibited early talent as a performer. She struggled with her studies and was later diagnosed as dyslexic. Dropping out of high school, she spent her teen years amid the fashions, credos, and drugs of the hippie movement. She maintained involvement in theater through chorus roles in the Broadway productions *Hair*, *Jesus Christ Superstar*, and *Pippin*.

In 1974 Goldberg moved to California and worked a variety of jobs as she tried to launch her acting career. She helped found the San Diego Repertory Theater and began performing one-woman shows, including *Moms*, which showcased the life of black comedian Jackie "Moms" Mabley. Goldberg's satiric bite, as well as her talent for playing numerous character types, attracted the attention of producer Mike Nichols, who helped her stage an eponymous show of skits on Broadway.

Goldberg's success in New York caught the attention of Hollywood, and in 1985 Steven Spielberg cast her in his adaptation of Alice Walker's *The Color Purple*. After Goldberg received an Academy Award nomination for her portrayal of Celie, a poor young black woman who overcomes the limitations of her life in the segregated South, her status as a film actor was ensured. Since 1985 she has appeared in over two dozen movies, including *Sister Act* (1992), *The Lion King* (1994), *Boys on the Side* (1995), and *Ghost* (1990), for which she won an Oscar as Best Supporting Actor.

Goldberg also has appeared extensively on television, making regular cameos on *Star Trek: The Next Generation* and *Moonlighting*. In 1992 she cofounded Comic Relief, an annual fundraiser to help the homeless. In addition to her Oscar, Goldberg has won a Grammy, a Golden Globe, and several Emmy nominations. She hosted the Oscar Award ceremonies in 1994, 1996, and 1999.

Africa

Gordimer, Nadine

(b. November 20, 1923, Springs, South Africa), South African novelist and Nobel Prize winner who was a vocal opponent of the system of apartheid.

"I have come to the abstractions of politics through the flesh and blood of individual behavior. I didn't know what politics was about until I saw it all happening to people." In this 1965 interview, Nadine Gordimer assessed her political consciousness with a self-scrutiny that characterized much of her political writing. In her novels and short stories, she has captured the "flesh and blood of individual behavior" in minute and sentient detail, chronicling daily life in South Africa under apartheid and portraying the human face of resistance.

Gordimer grew up in a small gold-mining town near Johannesburg, the daughter of a Lithuanian Jewish father and an English mother. Although she read voraciously during her early years, she was taken out of school at age 10 because of a perceived heart ailment; she had little formal schooling. Trailing her mother to afternoon teas, the lively Gordimer spent her time observing and mimicking the people she would later portray so astutely— the "well-meaning" members of white South African society. By age 15, when her first story appeared in an adult journal in 1939, Gordimer was already a seasoned writer of children's stories.

A new world opened to Gordimer in 1949 when she began taking courses in Johannesburg at the University of Witwatersrand. There she mixed with musicians, journalists, and writers, crossing for the first time the color line that segregated blacks from whites. As she read the philosophies of Marxism, nationalism, and existentialism, she began to question the social structure of apartheid. She also became involved in the political and cultural movement of the Sophiatown renaissance, which produced the literary journal *Drum*.

During the same year in which she started classes in Johannesburg, Gordimer published her first book of short stories, *Face to Face*. Her first novel, *The Lying Days* (1953), was a loosely autobiographical coming-of-age story. She gained international recognition when her stories were published in the *New Yorker* magazine during the 1950s. A prominent critic of apartheid and an open supporter of the African National Congress, she continued to live in South Africa under apartheid despite the repeated banning of her books. The remarkably prolific Gordimer has published 12 novels and 13 short story collections.

In the words of critic Stephen Clingman, her writing has represented "the rise to power of the National Party in 1948; the life under apartheid; the political, social and cultural world of the 1950s; the sabotage and resistance of the 1960s, as well as their defeat by the state; the rise of the Black consciousness movement in the 1970s and the Soweto Revolt; the revolution which seemed to have begun by the 1980s." In her well-known novel *Burger's Daughter* (1979), Gordimer examines the political choices made necessary by the heroine Rosa Burger, the daughter of two communist revolutionaries, who finds herself ultimately unable to opt out of political commitment. Like two of her earlier books, *Burger's Daughter* was initially banned.

Without compromising her realistic portrayal of the political world, Gordimer also explores the realm of sexuality in works such as the *Late Bourgeois World* (1966), *July's People* (1981), and *Sport of Nature* (1987). Under a political system where the body—skin color, hair texture, facial features—defines identity, she has argued that the political and sexual are inextricable. Her narrative style, influenced by such Russian authors as Turgenev, links the social, political, and personal. Using the gestures, words, and thoughts of her characters, she portrays "a society whirling, stamping, swaying with the force of revolutionary change."

A self-proclaimed political radical, Gordimer was one of the most visible opponents of apartheid for those outside South Africa. With a long-established readership abroad, her words have reached a broader audience than those of most black authors writing on similar issues. Her international reputation, particularly after she won the Nobel Prize for literature in 1991, has protected her from some of the reprisals that faced other South African radicals. After receiving the Nobel, Gordimer spoke about the responsibility that she felt attended such international prestige: "I have two roles in my life—one as a writer and another one, my commitment to the cause of freedom in South Africa and creating a new post-apartheid culture in South Africa." In her most recent novel, *House of Gun* (1998), Gordimer highlights the interpersonal relationships that have always been a major part of her work, setting the story within the climate of violence that continues to mark post-apartheid South Africa.

North America

Gordon, Dexter Keith

(b. February 27, 1923, Los Angeles, Calif.; d. April 25, 1990, Philadelphia, Pa.), African American jazz musician.

Dexter Gordon was one of the most influential tenor saxophone players of the 1940s movement known as bebop. He also played a major role in the development of saxophone styles after the big-band era of the 1930s and 1940s.

Gordon began playing the clarinet at age 13. By age 17 he had switched to tenor saxophone. An important early influence was tenor saxophonist Lester Young, whose smooth phrasing prefigured that of the bebop style. In 1940 Gordon left high school, began playing in a local band, and was invited to tour with the big band of vibraphonist Lionel Hampton. Gordon remained with Hampton for three years.

In 1943, after working briefly with bandleader Fletcher Henderson, Gordon recorded with a quintet that featured pianist Nat "King" Cole. The following year Gordon played with the big band of trumpeter Louis Armstrong before joining the orchestra of singer Billy Eckstine. In Eckstine's band, Gordon met up with trumpeters Dizzy Gillespie, Fats Navarro, and other musicians central to bebop, a style that featured elaborate improvised melodies over rapid chord progressions. During 1945, having relocated to New York City, Gordon recorded "*Groovin' High*" and "*Blue 'n' Boogie*" with Gillespie's quintet and played frequently with musicians Charlie Parker, Miles Davis, Bud Powell, and Max Roach. In 1946 Gordon returned to California, although he continued to perform on both the East and West Coasts for a number of years. Between 1947 and 1952 he made a series of highly popular recordings with tenor saxophonist Wardell Gray.

In 1960 Gordon acted in the play *The Connection* by Jack Gelber. Gordon also composed and performed music for the play. Following a successful tour of Europe in 1962, he moved to Copenhagen, Denmark. For the next 15 years he remained in Europe, where he appeared at major jazz festivals, taught music, and recorded frequently. He returned permanently to the United States in 1977.

Gordon has influenced numerous American jazz musicians, including tenor saxophonists Sonny Rollins and John Coltrane. He was named Musician of the Year by *Downbeat* magazine in 1978 and 1980, and was elected to the *Downbeat* Hall of Fame in 1980. In 1986 he acted in and performed music for the motion picture *Round Midnight*, earning an Academy Award nomination for best actor. Also in 1986 he received a Jazz Masters Award from the National Endowment for the Arts. Shortly before his death, he acted in the film *Awakenings* (1990).

North America

Gossett, Louis, Jr.

(b. May 27, 1936, Brooklyn, N.Y.), African American film and stage actor known for his portrayal of compassionate authority figures.

A stage actor from age 17, Louis Gossett Jr. gained national recognition for his Emmy Award-winning role as Fiddler in the popular television adaptation of Alex Haley's *Roots* (1977). In 1982 he became the third African American to win an Academy Award, as Best Supporting Actor for his role as Sergeant Emil Foley in *An Officer and a Gentleman*.

Gossett grew up in a predominantly Jewish neighborhood in Brooklyn, New York. He was the only child of Louis Gossett Sr., a porter, and Helen (Wray) Gossett, a domestic and community activist. Inspired by his mother's activism, he ran for and was elected president of his high school senior class. He was voted best all-around athlete and acted in a school play—a success that led Gustave Blum, a former Broadway director, to encourage him to audition for the Broadway play *Take a Giant Step* (1953). Gossett won the role of Spencer Scott, a black boy coming of age, and subsequently received the Donaldson Award as Best Newcomer of the Year.

Gossett went to New York University (NYU) on an athletic-drama scholarship and majored in dramatic arts while aspiring to become a professional basketball player. He also continued his acting career, appearing on television and in several Broadway and off-Broadway productions, including Kurt Weill's musical *Lost in the Stars* (1957). After graduating from NYU in 1959, he was drafted by the professional basketball team the New York Knickerbockers. Soon after, he won a role in Lorraine Hansberry's award-winning Broadway play, *A Raisin in the Sun* (1959), and decided to focus on acting.

During the 1960s and 1970s Gossett appeared in numerous stage performances, including the musical *Tambourines to Glory* (1963), based on Langston Hughes's novel, and Conor Cruise O'Brien's *Murderous Angels* (1971), in which he played the Congolese political leader Patrice Lumumba—a role for which he received the Los Angeles Drama Critics Circle Award. He also debuted in his first film, a screen adaptation of *A Raisin in the Sun* (1961), and in the mid-1960s created an acting school in New York's Lower East Side for disadvantaged black youth.

Despite Gossett's considerable talent, he received few substantive film offers after his appearance in *An Officer and a Gentleman* in 1982. For several years he struggled with depression and drug addiction while appearing in such films as *Enemy Mine* (1985) and *Iron Eagle* (1986), in which he starred as the tough-talking airforce colonel Chappy Sinclair. During this time, he adopted an abandoned boy whom he had seen on an ABC news segment about homeless children. "My life wasn't working for me," he told *People Weekly* writer Mark Goodman. "Let me help somebody else and get out of myself."

Gossett continues to pursue an active film and television career. In 1989 he starred as a crime-fighting professor in the short-lived television series *Gideon Oliver*, and in 1992 played the retired boxer Honey Palmer in *Diggstown* (1992). In addition to acting, Gossett has lent his voice to a variety of historical figures in documentaries, such as the BBC's critically acclaimed series *The Great War* and the *Shaping of the Twentieth Century* (1996).

North America

Graffiti Art,

a New York City folk-art phenomenon among African American and Hispanic urban youth, characterized by brilliant color and cryptic intricacy.

In the late 1960s a Greek American teenager from Washington Heights, New York, achieved notoriety by painting his nickname, or "tag," Taki 183, throughout New York City. Taki 183's fame sparked the envy and imagination of hundreds of black and Hispanic teens, who began leaving tags of their own. Graffiti soon became a competitive sport, as numerous artists vied to be the most prolific. As competition grew, stylistic prowess replaced sheer ubiquity as the coveted distinction, and enormous, three-dimensional murals superceded unembellished tags. Because graffiti artists wished to display their tags before as large an audience as possible, they selected subway cars—which traversed the entire city—as their canvas.

While New York officials tried to eradicate graffiti, the Manhattan art scene gobbled it up. In the late 1970s the artist Fab Five Freddy (later the host of the television program "*Yo! MTV Raps*") established a connection between the uptown graffiti artists and the downtown galleries. Soon numerous artists painted on real canvases and earned large sums of money for their work. Subject to art-world caprice, however, the trend was short-lived.

Although its daring practitioners have declined in numbers, graffiti persists as an art and an aesthetic. Hip hop periodicals chronicle the innovations of new graffiti artists, while T-shirts, music videos, and the fashions of famous rap artists reflect their influence.

North America

Grandmaster Flash, Melle Mel, and the Furious Five,

an African American musical group that was important in the creation of rap music.

Now regarded as one of the founding groups—along with Afrika Bambaataa and Kool Herc—of what hip hop and rap fans call "old school" rap, Grandmaster Flash and the Furious Five was formed in 1977. Flash, born Joseph Saddler, began acting as a disc jockey (DJ) at local parties in the early 1970s while still in high school in the Bronx. Like some other DJs of the time, he began making a kind of musical collage by playing two or more records at once and experimenting with *scratching*—manually moving the needle across the disc to create a new, rhythmic sound. Flash teamed up with fellow DJs Cowboy (Keith Wiggins), Melle Mel (Melvin Glover), Kid Creole (Nathaniel Glover, brother to Melle Mel), Mr. Ness (Eddie Morris), and Rahiem (Guy Williams)—the Furious Five.

The group became the most popular rap act in New York City, playing parties, balls, and nightclubs. Soon after the Sugarhill Gang released the first rap hit single, *"Rapper's Delight,"* in 1979, Grandmaster Flash and his band signed with Sugar Hill Records, the first company to market rap to a national audience. The group's 1982 hit single, *"The Message,"* a starkly poetic look at the nightmares of urban poverty, is credited by critics with changing rap's focus from buoyant dance music to a forum for social commentary.

By 1984 the original band had split up, reforming into two separate groups—one led by Flash, the other by Melle Mel. In 1987 they reunited, and have since toured along with other old school rap artists.

North America

Green, Al

(b. April 13, 1946, Forrest City, Ark.), African American singer and minister, pioneer of 1960s soul music.

Al Green (originally spelled "Greene") was born into a large family of sharecroppers. At age nine he formed a gospel quartet with three of his brothers, the Green Brothers. Green always enjoyed non-religious music, however, and at age 16 formed his first pop group in Michigan, where his family had moved. In 1967 he released *"Back Up Train,"* which became a minor hit.

Green's career gained momentum in 1969 when he met producer Willie Mitchell, who signed him to Hi Records in Memphis, Tennessee. Their partnership resulted in an innovative new soul sound featuring spare instrumentation (simple horns and backbeats, muted guitar) accompanied by Green's quiet but insistent vocals pleading lyrically for the possibilities of love and often taking off into wild falsettos. Though quieter than the Stax sound, Green's music was nonetheless complex, and it was a popularly welcomed change from the heavily produced records of the late 1960s. A string of hits followed in the early 1970s, including "Let's Stay Together," "I'm Still in Love With You," "Here I Am (Come and Take Me)."

Despite popular success, Green was pulled by the tug of his gospel origins, especially after a girlfriend's suicide in 1974. In 1976 he became the pastor of the Full Gospel Tabernacle in Memphis. His musical output since then has been primarily gospel, but it remains as intensely personal as his songs about romantic love.

North America

Green Pastures, The,

an all-black Broadway musical and Hollywood film that, despite its racial stereotyping, gained widespread appeal among blacks during the late 1930s.

First produced as a Broadway musical in 1930, The Green Pastures featured an all-black cast and starred Shakespearean actor Richard B. Harrison in the lead role of De Lawd. The show garnered a Pulitzer Prize for its white author Marc Connelly, who based his story on white writer Roark Bradford's book of tales, Ole Man Adam and His Chillun. African American poet Langston Hughes characterized the musical as "a naïve dialect play about a quaint funny heaven full of niggers."

In 1936 the film studio Warner Brothers, in collaboration with Connelly, turned the musical into a motion picture. The cast of the movie version of The Green Pastures was also all black, and included the popular Hall Johnson Choir—founded in 1925 by the African American violinist and choral conductor Hall Johnson—and such notable actors as Rex Ingram, Ossie Davis, and Eddie Anderson. African American film historian Thomas Cripps says that the film "rose above the common ruck, averted the worst taints of Southern metaphor, and brought black Southern folk religion to a wide and appreciative audience. Blacks, except for a few intellectuals, enjoyed it and lionized the players."

The Green Pastures was produced at a time when Hollywood film roles for African Americans were scarce, and often limited to portrayals of chauffeurs, butlers, and housemaids. Even independent black filmmakers depended largely on white capital and distributors and were thus compelled to accommodate the preferences of white audiences. That The Green Pastures had an appealing story and provided jobs for 95 black actors and singers suggested to many a hopeful future for blacks in the film industry.

Yet the film, like the original Broadway musical, also stereotyped rural blacks: in depicting a black folk version of the Bible's Book of Genesis, for example, it portrayed heaven as a grand fish fry with mammies for angels. Some critics claimed that *The Green Pastures* merely created an illusion of black success that diverted blacks from the principal goal of independent black cinema—to empower and affirm the black community through positive, realistic media representations.

The Green Pastures, like the earlier Hollywood black musical films *Hearts in Dixie* and *Hallelujah!* (both 1929), grossed far less income than Warner Brothers had anticipated. Consequently, major film studios became reluctant to take on all-black musical films, and black actors and film producers returned to musical shorts. More than a decade passed before the prospects of blacks in film began to change significantly.

North America

Gregory, Richard Claxton "Dick"

(b. October 12, 1932, St. Louis, Mo.), African American comedian and civil rights activist whose social satire changed the way white Americans perceived African American comedians.

Dick Gregory entered the national comedy scene in 1961 when Chicago's Playboy Club booked him as a replacement for white comedian "Professor" Irwin Corey. Until then Gregory had worked mostly at small clubs with predominantly black audiences (he met his wife, Lillian Smith, at one such club). Such clubs paid comedians an average of $5 dollars per night; thus Gregory also held a day job as a postal employee. His tenure as a replacement for Corey was so successful—at one performance he won over an audience that included Southern white convention goers—that the Playboy Club offered him a contract extension from several weeks to three years. By 1962 Gregory had become a nationally known headline performer, selling out nightclubs, making numerous national television appearances, and recording popular comedy albums.

Gregory began performing comedy in the mid-1950s while serving in the army. Drafted in 1954 while attending Southern Illinois University at Carbondale on a track scholarship, he briefly returned to the university after his discharge in 1956, but left without a degree because he felt that the university "didn't want me to study, they wanted me to run." In the hopes of performing comedy professionally, he moved to Chicago, where he became part of a new generation of black comedians that included Nipsey Russell, Bill Cosby, and Godfrey Cambridge. These comedians broke with the minstrel tradition, which presented stereotypical black characters. Gregory, whose style was detached, ironic, and satirical, came to be called the "Black Mort Sahl" after the popular white social satirist. He drew on current events, especially racial issues, for much of his material: "Segregation is not all bad. Have you ever heard of a collision where the people in the back of the bus got hurt?"

From an early age Gregory demonstrated a strong sense of social justice. While a student at Sumner High School in St. Louis he led a march protesting segregated schools. Later, inspired by the work of leaders such as Dr. Martin Luther King Jr. and organizations such as the Student Nonviolent Coordinating Committee (SNCC), Gregory took part in the Civil Rights Movement and used his celebrity status to draw attention to such issues as segregation and disfranchisement. When local Mississippi governments stopped distributing federal food surpluses to poor blacks in areas where SNCC was encouraging voter registration, Gregory chartered a plane to bring in seven tons of food. He participated in SNCC's voter registration drives and in sit-ins to protest segregation, most notably at a restaurant franchise in downtown Atlanta, Georgia. Only later did Gregory disclose that he held stock in the chain.

Through the 1960s Gregory spent more time on social issues and less time on performing. He participated in marches and parades to support a range of causes, including opposition to the Vietnam War, world hunger, and drug abuse. In addition he fasted in protest more than 60 times, once in Iran, where he fasted and prayed in an effort to urge the Ayatollah Khomeini to release American embassy staff who had been taken hostage. The Iranian refusal to release the hostages did not decrease the depth of Gregory's commitment; he weighed only 44 kg (97 lbs) when he left Iran.

Gregory demonstrated his commitment to confronting the entrenched political powers by opposing Richard J. Daley in Chicago's 1966 mayoral election. He ran for president in 1968 as a write-in candidate for the Freedom and Peace Party, a splinter group of the Peace and Freedom Party, and received 1.5 million votes. Democratic candidate Hubert Humphrey lost the election to Republican Richard Nixon by 510,000 votes, and many believe Humphrey would have won had Gregory not run. After the assassinations of King, President John F. Kennedy, and Robert Kennedy, Gregory became increasingly convinced of the existence of political conspiracies. He wrote books such as *Code Name Zoro: The Murder of Martin Luther King Jr.* (1971) with Mark Lane, a conspiracy theorist whose ideas Gregory shared and espoused in numerous lectures.

Gregory's activism continued into the 1990s. In response to published allegations that the Central Intelligence Agency (CIA) had supplied cocaine to predominantly African American areas in Los Angeles, thus spurring the crack epidemic, Gregory protested at CIA headquarters and was arrested. In 1992 he began a program called Campaign for Human Dignity to fight crime in St. Louis neighborhoods.

In 1973, the year he released his comedy album *Caught in the Act*, Gregory moved with his family to Plymouth, Massachusetts, where he developed an interest in vegetarianism and became a nutritional consultant. In 1984 he founded Health Enterprises, Inc., a company that distributed weight loss products. In 1987 Gregory introduced the Slim-Safe Bahamian Diet, a powdered diet mix, which was immensely profitable. Economic losses caused in part by conflicts with his business partners led to his eviction from his home in 1992. Gregory remained active, however, and in 1996 returned to the stage in his critically acclaimed one-man show, *Dick Gregory Live!*

Grimké, Angelina Weld

(b. February 27, 1880, Boston, Mass.; d. June 10, 1958, New York, N.Y.), African American poet, playwright, author of first staged play in the United States by an African American.

Angelina Weld Grimké was born to Archibald and Sarah Grimké. Her father, the son of a slave, was a lawyer and the executive director of the National Association for the Advancement of Colored People (NAACP). He was also the nephew of white abolitionists Sarah and Angelina Grimké and the brother-in-law of African American poet and essayist Charlotte Forten Grimké. Grimké's mother was white. Sarah Grimké left her husband when Angelina was 3, taking her daughter with her; she returned Angelina to her father when she was 7, and never visited her again.

Grimké attended several elite private schools and graduated from the Boston Normal School of Gymnastics in 1902. Most of her writing was done over the next 25 years, which she spent teaching English in Washington, D.C. Her best-known work, the play *Rachel*, was produced by the NAACP in March 1916. *Rachel* was the first play by an African American that was meant to be staged (in contrast to earlier costume dramas, such as William Wells Brown's, which were simply read aloud). Both *Rachel* and Grimké's second play deal with themes of racial injustice.

Grimké's poetry was included in such works as Alain Locke's *The New Negro* (1925) and Countee Cullen's *Caroling Dusk* (1927). Her poetry dealt with more conventional romantic themes, often marked with frequent images of frustration and isolation. Recent scholarship has revealed Grimké's unpublished lesbian poems and letters; she did not feel free to live openly as a gay woman during her lifetime. She spent the end of her life living alone in New York City.

Gronniosaw, James Albert Ukawsaw

(b. 1710, Nigeria; d. 1775, Great Britain), African prince sold into slavery whose life story became an influential book.

Ukawsaw Gronniosaw's idyllic childhood as a prince in the area that is now Nigeria came to an abrupt end when a merchant persuaded the teenaged Gronniosaw to travel to the Gold Coast (present-day Ghana) and then sold him into American slavery. Years later, in Great Britain, Gronniosaw related his story to a Dutch woman, who wrote and published *A Narrative of the Remarkable Particulars in the Life of James Albert Ukawsaw Gronniosaw, An African Prince, as Related by Himself* (1770). Class-conscious British readers were sympathetic to the story of the victimized African prince; the book was widely read and later influenced the British slave narratives of the authors and abolitionists Olaudah Equiano and Ottobah Cugoano.

Gronniosaw was a slave to several Dutch families in colonial New England. His last owner was Theodorus Jacobus Frelinghuysen, a Dutch Reformed minister in New Jersey, who bought Gronniosaw in 1730, taught him Dutch, and presided over his conversion to Christianity. On his deathbed in 1748, Frelinghuysen granted freedom to Gronniosaw. Gronniosaw left to serve in the British Navy and then moved to London, where he became known as James Albert Ukawsaw Gronniosaw.

After spending the year of 1762 in Netherlands, Gronniosaw returned to London to marry a white weaver he had met previously. His minister and friends objected to the marriage not because of the difference in race, but, according to Gronniosaw, "because the person I had fixed on was poor."

The Gronniosaw family moved frequently, finding work where they could but suffering long periods of poverty and deprivation. Shortly after moving his family to Kidderminster, a town whose inhabitants were known for their religiosity, Gronniosaw narrated his life story to a young local woman. She published it in the hope that the sales would profit the Gronniosaws; little is known of their lives after this. The document, however, helped enable the abolitionist battle in England and remains one of the most compelling slave narratives.

North America

Guardian, The,

Boston-based, African American newspaper, edited by William Monroe Trotter, that challenged Booker T. Washington's philosophy of accommodation in the first half of the twentieth century.

The Guardian was founded in November 1901 by William Monroe Trotter, a Harvard-educated, African American businessman, and George Washington Forbes, an Amherst-educated, African American librarian. Trotter and Monroe founded the newspaper in part because racially discriminatory Jim Crow laws, which were prevalent in the South, were spreading to parts of the Northeast. Soon after its founding the *Guardian* targeted black leader Booker T. Washington as a chief obstacle to racial equality. Washington was immensely popular among whites and many blacks for his views that African Americans should set aside goals such as political equality, which he claimed were out of reach, and focus instead on modest economic gain through industrial education and hard work.

The *Guardian*'s editorials sharply attacked Washington for ignoring the link between economic and political growth; for claiming that race relations were improving, when in fact they were worsening; for enjoying his political influence at the White House while urging other blacks to ignore politics; and for disregarding liberal arts education—and, indeed, all higher learning—while building his educational empire at the Tuskegee Institute on the strength of liberal-arts-educated Guardian had a circulation of more than 2,500.

The conflict with Washington was not without cost. Forbes, facing a libel suit by Washington and vulnerable because of his employment at a city library, left the paper within a few years of its founding. Washington also wielded his influence with businessmen and other newspapers in an attempt to silence and condemn the *Guardian*. Although Trotter's was initially a lone voice, the *Guardian* gained prominence after Washington spoke in Boston in July 1903. A confrontation between the two men, later called the Boston Riot, led to a one-month jail term for Trotter and—when it became clear that Washington's lawyers were pursuing the case to its end—growing support for Trotter's cause. *The Guardian* played a significant role in energizing W. E. B. Du Bois, the Niagara Movement, and other anti-Washington forces.

When Trotter supplemented the *Guardian*'s political reporting with news and gossip from cities across the country, its national readership grew markedly. After Forbes left, Trotter's wife, Geraldine Pindell Trotter, became instrumental in supporting and editing the newspaper, and Trotter's sister Maude Stewart and brother-in-law Charles Stewart provided financial and editorial help. In its later years the newspaper prominently protested the racist 1915 film *The Birth of a Nation* and succeeded in having it banned in Boston. *The Guardian* also protested the segregation of blacks in the armed forces during World War I and came to the defense of the Scottsboro defendants in the 1931 Scottsboro Case. After Geraldine's death in 1918 and William's death in 1934, Maude Stewart continued publication of the newspaper until she died in 1957. *The Guardian* ceased operations in 1960.

North America

Guillory, Ida Lewis ("Queen Ida")
(b. January 15, 1929, Lake Charles, La.), African American accordionist and leader of a popular zydeco band.

Despite a musical childhood, the Grammy Award-winning accordionist Ida Lewis "Queen Ida" Guillory started her performing career relatively late in life. After growing up along the Louisiana and Texas Gulf Coast, she and her family moved to San Francisco, California. There Guillory married and raised three children while working part-time as a school bus driver. It was not until her children were nearly grown that she took up the accordion, an integral part of both cajun and zydeco music and an instrument that two of her uncles also played. Returning to *zydeco*, a rhythmic, dance-oriented music with both African and French influences (a style Guillory calls "earthy—simple, but happy"), she began playing at home and at parties and in 1975 made her debut at a San Francisco Mardi Gras party, where she was dubbed "Queen Ida."

Along with her Bon Temps Zydeco Band, Guillory has toured extensively throughout the United States and abroad, including a trip to Africa in 1989. Her energy, charisma, and talent have made her a popular performer at music festivals, and she has appeared on television (on *Saturday Night Live* and *Austin City Limits*) as well as in such films as the documentary *J'ai été au bal*. In 1983 she won a Grammy Award for her live album, *On Tour*. Guillory also co-authored a cookbook, *Cookin' with Queen Ida* (1990), which features Creole recipes. Of her late-blooming fame, Guillory says, "I believe it's never too late to expand your human potential."

North America

Gumbel, Bryant Charles

(b. September 29, 1948, New Orleans, La.), African American journalist, sportswriter, and TV personality.

A member of the post-World War II baby boom, Bryant Gumbel was reared in Chicago, where his parents, Rhea LeCesne and Richard Dunbar Gumbel, were active in the Democratic Party. Graduating from Bates College in Maine in 1970, Gumbel began his career in 1971, writing freelance articles for *Black Sports* magazine, where he was quickly brought onto the staff. After working as a staff writer for eight months, his journalistic career accelerated and he became editor in chief.

Moving into television broadcasting in 1972, Gumbel appeared as a weekend sportscaster at KNBC-TV in Los Angeles. In 1976 he became the station's sports director, a position he held until 1980. During this time, NBC also utilized his talents as a pre-game host for football, baseball, and other sports events. This work was awarded two Emmys, one in 1976, the other in 1978.

In 1981 the *Today* show promoted Gumbel from regular sports contributor to co-anchor with Jane Pauley. With this position, Gumbel achieved nationwide fame as a television personality. Among other projects, he created the teen-oriented magazine show *Mainstreet* in 1986. Gumbel's *Today* show broadcasts from the Soviet Union were honored in 1984 with the Edward R. Murrow Award for Outstanding Foreign Affairs Work. In 1993 he was recognized for his broadcasts from sub-Saharan Africa by TransAfrica, UNICEF, and the National Association of Black Journalists.

Having achieved both fame and professional respect by his forties, Gumbel left NBC for CBS in 1997, where he signed a five-year contract that includes his own primetime news magazine show, several entertainment specials each year, and co-ownership in a production company.

Guy, Rosa Cuthbert

(b. September 1, 1925, Trinidad, West Indies), Caribbean American author and cofounder of the Harlem Writers Guild, known especially for her young adult fiction.

Over the last five decades, Rosa Guy has written books for children, teenagers, and adults, but she is best known for her novels for young adult readers. Guy places great importance on the power of communicating to teenagers through literature, and she has said of her books, "If I have proven to be popular with young people, it is because when they have finished one of my books, they not only have a satisfying experience—they have also had an education."

Guy was born in Trinidad but her parents emigrated to the United States when she was two, and she and her sister joined them five years later in Harlem. As a child, Guy found that her West Indian heritage made her an outsider in the African American community at the same time that her black skin made her an outsider in the larger society. After her parents' early deaths, Guy lived in an orphanage, and at age 14 she left school and took a job at a factory. Two years later, in 1941, she married Warner Guy, and the following year gave birth to a son, Warner Jr.

Although busy as a young working wife and mother, Guy began to study writing and drama in her free time. In the early 1940s she became part of the American Negro Theatre, a community theater group based in Harlem. A few years later she, John O. Killens, and two other black authors formed the writers' collaborative that became the Harlem Writers Guild. The guild provided an informal setting for aspiring Harlem writers to critique one another's work, and as its membership grew and its reputation spread, it became the most influential black literary organization of its time.

Guy's marriage ended in 1950, but throughout the next two decades, even as she took a variety of jobs to support herself and her son, she continued to write. Her one-act play *Venetian Blinds* was produced off-Broadway in 1954, and her first novel, *Bird at My Window*, was published in 1966. But Guy was inspired to write for teenagers after the assassinations of Malcolm X and Martin Luther King Jr., which left her concerned about how the violence and racism in American society affected young people's lives. As a young adult writer, she is especially known for two award-winning trilogies. The first, which was published in the 1970s and begins with *The Friends* (1973), charts the friendship between a Caribbean American and an African American girl as they come of age. *The Imamu Jones series,* published in the 1980s, follows the title character, an African American teenage male detective.

Guy has also received acclaim for two adult novels, *A Measure of Time* (1983), set in Harlem during the Harlem Renaissance, and *My Love, My Love; or, the Peasant Girl* (1985), which was made into the 1990 Broadway musical *Once on This Island*. Her other books include several for younger children. Guy's books are popular not only in the United States but also with the large Caribbean population in Great Britain. Her work with the Harlem Writers Guild and her own fiction for adults and children have allowed her to influence several generations of black authors and readers.

Hackley, Emma Azalia Smith

(b. June 29, 1867, Murfreesboro, Tenn.; d. December 13, 1922, Detroit, Mich.), African American educator and singer who worked to promote African American musicians and performers.

Azalia Smith, the daughter of Corilla Beard and Henry Smith, was raised in Detroit, Michigan, after her mother's school was closed due to opposition from the white community and the family moved. She started taking piano lessons at age three, later studying violin and voice, and played professionally after school.

In 1883 Hackley became the first African American to attend Washington Normal School, taking education classes and supporting herself by teaching music lessons. After her graduation, she taught second grade until 1894, when she eloped with journalist Edwin Henry. They moved to Denver, where Hackley organized a branch of the Colored Women's League and earned a music degree from the University of Denver (1900). In 1901 she separated from her husband and left Denver.

Hackley gave her farewell performance in 1911 and embarked on a lecture tour of universities. *The Colored Girl Beautiful* (1916), a book of her lectures, was published, complementing her self-published *A Guide in Voice Culture* (1909). In 1915 Hackley founded the Normal Voice Institute, designed to train music teachers. She left soon after to organize Folk Song Festivals across the country. The school failed, but she continued organizing choruses until her death.

Haley, Alexander Palmer (Alex)

(b. August 11, 1921, Ithaca, N.Y.; d. February 10, 1992, Seattle, Wash.), African American writer and journalist who authored two of the most influential books in the history of African American scholarship.

Alex Haley grew up in Henning, Tennessee, with maternal relatives who spent many hours telling family stories, some of which extended back to Africa. This exposure directed the course of much of Haley's work as an adult. Haley completed high school at age 15 and attended two years of college, but was uninspired by his studies and left school to join the United States Coast Guard, where he began writing to counteract the tedium of life at sea. When Haley retired from the service in 1959, he disembarked a mature, self-taught writer.

Haley settled in Greenwich Village, New York, determined to make his name as a journalist. After a period of hard work and obscurity, he broke into mainstream publications such as *Readers' Digest, Harper's,* and the *New York Times Magazine.* In 1962 he sold a Miles Davis interview to *Playboy* that began the magazine's famous interview series. Later that year *Playboy* commissioned Haley to interview Malcolm X, an assignment that led to Haley's first book, his ghost-written *Autobiography of Malcolm X.*

The Autobiography of Malcolm X (1965) sold more than 5 million copies and changed the nation's opinion of the black nationalist leader. The book, which concludes with Malcolm X's reevaluation of the Nation of Islam, highlights the complexity, compassion, and humanity of a figure whose public image might otherwise have remained monolithic and negative. The assassination of Malcolm X in 1965 increased public interest, and Haley's book became required reading in many college courses.

Soon after the publication of *The Autobiography of Malcolm X,* Haley began research for a second contribution to African American literature. The half-fictive, half-factual epic *Roots* (1977), which traces Haley's own maternal lineage back to an enslaved West African named Kunta Kinte, captured the attention of the nation. Haley took 12 years to write and research *Roots,* consulting relatives, archives, and libraries as well as a tribal historian from Kunta Kinte's village. At one point Haley even attempted to relive the Middle Passage experience of enslaved Africans by sleeping in the hold of a transatlantic ship.

Roots sold more than 8.5 million copies, was translated into 26 languages, and won 271 different awards. The Pulitzer Prize and National Book Award committees honored its contribution to American history, and ABC turned it into an eight-part television series, of which 130 million Americans watched at least one episode. *Roots* not only touched blacks whose histories resembled Haley's but also whites who were confronted by America's tragic past.

In the wake of the *Roots* phenomenon, two different plaintiffs accused Haley of plagiarism. Haley disproved one of the claims but settled the other out of court, conceding that, given his extensive and often unannotated notetaking, he had accidentally used material from Harold Courlander's book *The African* (1968). Critics also questioned Haley's method of presenting fiction as fact. Haley, however, repeatedly defended his methods as a necessary way of tapping the emotional poignancy of his subject.

Haley's career peaked with *Roots*—despite a television sequel (*Roots: The Next Generation,* 1979), a second, similar book-and-television project

(*Queen: The Story of an American Family*, 1992), and a television drama about race and childhood in the American South (*Palmerstown U.S.A.*, 1980). These projects, along with a record called *Alex Haley Speaks*, which gave tips on constructing family genealogies, never achieved the success of Haley's second book. Haley worked on a long-delayed biography of Madam C. J. Walker that remained unfinished when he died from a heart attack in 1992.

Hall, Arsenio

(b. February 12, 1955, Cleveland, Ohio), African American comedian, producer, and star of the first successful African American late-night television talk show.

Arsenio Hall is a member of the influential Black Pack, a group of highly successful African Americans in the entertainment industry whose other members include Eddie Murphy, Robert Townsend, Damon and Keenan Ivory Wayans, and Paul Mooney. In the mid- to late 1980s, Hall and his syndicated television program revitalized late-night talk shows.

Arsenio Hall was born in the projects of Cleveland, Ohio, to Annie and Fred Hall. His father, a strict disciplinarian, was minister of Elizabeth Baptist Church. His parents divorced when Hall was five years old, and he cites their acrimonious relationship as the catalyst for his early attempts at entertainment. In the fall of 1973 he entered Ohio University in Athens, but soon transferred to Kent State University, where he subsequently received an undergraduate degree.

After garnering moderate success on the stand-up comedian circuit in Chicago, Hall moved to Los Angeles in early 1980. His break arrived in 1987 with his appearance on the *Tonight Show*, hosted by Joan Rivers. In late 1987 he was named host of the *Late Show*. After the cancellation of that show in 1989, Hall went on to star opposite Eddie Murphy in the film *Coming to America*. In January of that same year he began hosting the *Arsenio Hall Show*. The show popularized the barking chant ("woof, woof") in substitution for applause, and ushered in the casual, hip, urban talk show.

Hammer, MC

(Stanley Kirk Burrell b. 1962, Oakland, Calif.), African American rap artist whose flashy dance moves catapulted him to fame in the early 1990s.

MC Hammer debuted in 1988 with the self-produced *Let's Get It Started*. His style—frenetic beats and chanted lyrics—did not impress the hip hop cognoscenti, but the album sold more than a million copies and the stage was set for one of hip hop's biggest surprises. Buoyed by the genial dance floor anthem "*U Can't Touch This*" (based on Rick James's 1981 classic,

"*Super-freak*"), *Please Hammer Don't Hurt 'Em* held the top spot on the charts for 21 weeks, becoming the biggest-selling rap album in history.

Hammer was a better entertainer than a rapper: his live shows were energetic spectacles, intricately choreographed events that highlighted the hugely popular dance routines of Hammer and his massive entourage. The artist's videos distilled the live experience into simple but effective blasts that found heavy rotation on MTV.

Hammer's good-natured dance music earned him continued—if diminished—success with *Too Legit to Quit* (1991). But *The Funky Headhunter* (1994) was an unexpected commercial failure: reacting to the current popularity of gangsta rap, Hammer abandoned his cheerful, energetic music and persona in a wholly unsuccessful effort to secure street credibility.

With his professional and financial life in disarray, the rapper filed for bankruptcy in 1996, claiming almost $14 million in debt. Although his career ended abruptly, Hammer's success paved the way for hip hop entertainment moguls like Bad Boy's Sean "Puffy" Combs.

North America

Hammon, Jupiter

(b. October 17, 1711, Oyster Bay, N.Y.; d. 1806?, Oyster Bay, N.Y.?), African American poet and the first published African American writer.

The following stanza is from Jupiter Hammon's poem "A Dialogue Entitled the Kind Master and the Dutiful Servant," published in 1786, when Hammon was in his seventies.

> *Dear Master, I will follow thee,*
> *According to thy word,*
> *And pray that God may be with me,*
> *And save thee in the Lord.*

Hammon had been a slave his entire life, and had served several generations of the Lloyd family on Long Island, New York. Many of his writings neither condemn nor even mention slavery; instead, they praise Christianity in the same manner as the evangelical hymns that were his models. But even when his words were not deliberately radical, they represented a radical act—Hammon became the first known African American to publish a piece of literature.

Hammon's owners were wealthy, and the few records of his life with them indicate that he was a favorite servant who worked as a clerk in their family business and was trained both as a farmhand and as an artisan. He was also allowed to attend school, and his formal education influenced his development as a poet. Like his masters, Hammon was a devout Christian, and was influenced by the religious revivals taking place in eighteenth-century New England. His extant writing reflects his deep spirituality, and his first published poem was written on Christmas Day, 1760.

"An Evening Thought. Salvation by Christ with Penitential Cries: Composed by Jupiter Hammon, a Negro belonging to Mr. Lloyd of Queen's Village, on Long Island, the 25th of December, 1760" was published as a broadside in early 1761, making it the first piece of literature published in the United States by a person of African descent. His second extant piece of poetry, published 17 years after the first, honors Phillis Wheatley, his contemporary and another African American slave poet. This poem, "An Address to Miss Phillis Wheatly [sic], Ethiopian Poetess, in Boston, who came from Africa at eight years of age, and soon became acquainted with the gospel of Jesus Christ" (1778), praises and encourages the younger poet. Hammon never mentions himself in the poem, but it appears that in choosing Wheatley as a subject, he was acknowledging their common and unlikely bond.

His other known writings include two more poems, three sermon essays, and a speech, *An Address to the Negroes of the State of New York*, which he gave before the African Society in New York on September 24, 1786. In this speech Hammon expressed his opinions on slavery most clearly. As an individual, he claimed he did "not wish to be free"—as one critic has observed, he felt "it was his personal duty to bear slavery with patience." But Hammon did add that he believed slavery was unjust, and would be "glad if others, especially the young negroes, were free." The speech was reprinted twice for a Pennsylvania Abolitionist society.

Hammon apparently remained a slave until his death. During the Revolutionary War he lived with his owners in Hartford, Connecticut; the family later returned to Oyster Bay, which is probably where Hammon died. His poetry is still often anthologized, in recognition of his role as a founder of the African American literary tradition.

North America

Hancock, Herbert Jeffrey (Herbie)

(b. April 12, 1940, Chicago, Ill.), piano and keyboard player, composer, and group leader who has contributed to modal, free, and fusion jazz.

Since the 1960s Herbie Hancock has been, along with trumpet player Miles Davis, one of the most popular jazz musicians in the United States. As did Davis, he has played effectively in a wide range of styles, including modal, free jazz, and, most controversially, fusion or jazz-rock. Hancock first gained national acclaim in Davis's mid-1960s quintet along with Wayne Shorter (tenor saxophone), Tony Williams (drums), and Ron Carter (bass), but his talent was evident at an early age. He began studying piano at age 7 and performed with the Chicago Symphony Orchestra in a young people's concert when he was 11 years old.

After graduating from college in 1960, Hancock played piano professionally, including stints with tenor saxophonist Coleman Hawkins and trumpeter Donald Byrd. He moved to New York City in 1962 and later that year recorded his debut album, *Takin' Off*, which included the gospel-tinged soul jazz hit *"Watermelon Man."* Hancock recorded a series of classic Blue Note albums, including *Empyrean Isles* (1964), *Maiden Voyage* (1965), and *Speak Like a Child* (1968). His light touch and modal approach reflected the influence of white pianist Bill Evans. Several Hancock compositions, including *"Maiden Voyage"* and *"Dolphin Dance,"* have become jazz standards.

Hancock joined the Miles Davis Quintet in 1963, and his distinctive piano stylings became an integral part of Davis's classic 1960s group. Although playing in a harmonically advanced modal style, Hancock and other members of the quintet moved steadily in the direction of greater harmonic freedom and rhythmic openness, reflected in classic recordings that include *E.S.P.* (1965), *Miles Smiles* (1966), and *Nefertiti* (1967). Hancock began playing electric keyboards with Davis in the late 1960s and, after leaving the Davis Quintet in 1971, continued to explore the possibilities of the electric piano and various synthesizers in his own band, Sextant.

In 1973 Hancock formed Headhunters, his most popular group, which merged the danceable rhythms of funk and rock with jazz. *Headhunters* (1973), the new group's first album, became a huge pop music success, especially the hit single *"Chameleon."* But many critics and fans of his earlier playing complained that Hancock had compromised his music to gain commercial success, views that the pianist dismissed as elitist.

In any case, Hancock never altogether left acoustic jazz. His later career has included the late 1970s V.S.O.P. (Very Special One-time Performance) tour—a reunion of the 1960s Davis Quintet with trumpeter Freddie Hubbard taking Davis's place—and piano duets with Chick Corea during the 1980s. His acoustic jazz score for the film *Round Midnight* won an Academy Award in 1986, and in the following year he toured as part of an all-star acoustic trio and quartet. In 1997 he released a well-received duet album with Wayne Shorter.

North America

Handy, William Christopher (W.C.)

(b. November 16, 1873, Florence, Ala.; d. March 28, 1958, New York, N.Y.), composer, cornet and trumpet player, bandleader, and self-described "father of the blues."

Although personally soft-spoken and unprepossessing, W. C. Handy titled his autobiography with a bold phrase that had long been associated with him, *Father of the Blues* (1941). But as Handy well knew, the blues, an African American musical genre of incalculable significance, was in no sense the creation of any one individual. More accurately, Handy's importance lay in his success as a promoter of African American music: popularizing the blues was his greatest accomplishment.

Handy took a loosely structured folk idiom performed by unschooled musicians and formalized it, in particular regularizing its most common 12-

bar form. Handy explained that he took a music "already used by Negro roustabouts, honky-tonk piano players, wanderers, and others . . . from Missouri to the Gulf [of Mexico] . . . . [and] introduce[d] this, the 'blues' form, to the general public."

His "*Memphis Blues*," published in 1912, is commonly regarded as the first blues to appear in sheet music. In fact, two other composers had published blues earlier that same year. Furthermore, musicologist Gunther Schuller argued that despite featuring two 12-bar blues-style strains, "*Memphis Blues*" was "not a blues at all" but rather "was closer to the cakewalk."

Handy was likewise not a jazz player. Record producer John Hammond observed that there "wasn't a note of improvisation" in Handy's recordings of "*Memphis Blues*" and "*St. Louis Blues*." Handy's early training was in European art music, and his formative professional experience came in brass bands and in African American minstrelsy. Handy first studied music with Y. A. Wallace, a Fisk University graduate who, despite the fame of the Fisk Jubilee Singers, "had no interest in the spirituals" and "made no attempt to instruct us in this remarkable folk music." Another influence was violinist Jim Turner, who came to Florence from Memphis, Tennessee, and organized a band. About this time Handy took up the cornet. He played with a number of brass bands, sang tenor in vocal quartets, and toured briefly with an amateur minstrel company.

But Handy's key professional experience was with Mahara's Minstrels. He was invited to join the troupe in 1896 as a cornet player earning $6 a week, which was good money during a severe national depression. After one season Handy was made leader of an orchestra of 42 musicians. However, his career choice brought criticism from friends and family. Minstrels, he explained, "were a disreputable lot in the eyes of a large section of upper-crust Negroes," although minstrel shows employed "the best talent of that generation."

Handy then moved to Memphis and organized another band. Mayoral candidate Edward H. Crump hired the group in 1909, and Handy's campaign song, known as "*Mr. Crump*," later became "*Memphis Blues*." This song also led to Handy's involvement in the business side of music. After selling the rights to the song for $100, Handy realized that he had been cheated, and he resolved never to be cheated again. In partnership with lyricist and bank cashier Harry H. Pace, he formed Pace and Handy Music Company to publish sheet music. Pace and Handy had a lucrative hit with "*St. Louis Blues*" (1914), which became Handy's best-known composition and an American musical standard.

In 1918 Handy and Pace moved their company to New York City, and it became the leading publisher of music by black composers. The principals dissolved their partnership in 1920 but continued in the music business separately, Pace establishing Black Swan Records, the first black-owned record company, and Handy organizing Handy Brothers, Inc., a music publishing business, and the short-lived Handy Record Company. Although he continued to perform and compose, over the years Handy became increasingly active as a businessman and impresario.

Handy was forced to curtail his activities in the 1940s and 1950s as the result of blindness and a debilitating stroke, but throughout his long career he was a tireless ambassador for African American music. He organized concerts of black music for the Chicago World's Fair, the New York World's Fair, and the Golden Gate Exposition in San Francisco. He also published two musical collections, *Blues: An Anthology* (1926) and *Book of Negro Spirituals* (1938). Most of all, he understood music's healing power in a racially divided society. "Nothing," he wrote in his autobiography, "made me glow so much as seeing the softening effect of music on racial antagonisms."

Hansberry, Lorraine

(b. May 19, 1930, Chicago, Ill.; d. January 12, 1965, New York, N.Y.), playwright whose award-winning play, *A Raisin in the Sun*, was the first by an African American woman to be produced on Broadway.

Lorraine Vivian Hansberry's parents were Carl Augustus Hansberry, a prominent real-estate broker in Chicago, and Nannie Perry, a schoolteacher who later devoted her life to activism. Hansberry was the youngest of four. Her father's victory in the Supreme Court case *Hansberry v. Lee* (1940) resulted in the repeal of restricted covenants (laws which prevented blacks from buying property in white areas), but enforcement did not follow the change in law, and her disappointed father left the United States and emigrated to Mexico, where he later died.

Frustrated by her education at the University of Wisconsin, Hansberry only stayed for two years—long enough, however, to take courses in drama and stage design and to fall under the spell of Sean O'Casey's *Juno and the Paycock*: "The melody was one I had known for a very long while," she said. "I did not think then of writing the melody as I knew it—in a different key; but I believe it entered my consciousness and stayed there" (*To Be Young, Gifted and Black*, 1969). After briefly studying painting, she went to Harlem to work as a reporter and then as an associate editor at *Freedom*, a monthly headed by Paul Robeson. In 1953 she married Robert Nemiroff. He remained her active literary executor after she died of pancreatic cancer in 1965, despite their earlier, quiet divorce (1964).

Hansberry set *A Raisin in the Sun*, her most famous play, in familiar territory—the terrible living conditions produced for blacks by restricted covenants. It opened at the Ethel Barrymore Theatre on Broadway on March 11, 1959. Directed by Lloyd Richards and starring Sidney Poitier and Ruby Dee, it ran for 583 performances. *A Raisin in the Sun* was the first Broadway play directed by a black person in 50 years, and the first written by a black woman. Hansberry was the first black woman to receive the New York Drama Critics Circle Award (beating out Tennessee Williams, Eugene O'Neill, and Archibald MacLeish), and the youngest ever recipient. When it became a Columbia movie in 1961, the film received a nomination for

Best Screenplay of the Year from the Screenwriters Guild and a special award at the Cannes Film Festival (1961); the musical, *Raisin* (1973), won a Tony Award. The play is widely anthologized and often revived. A second Broadway play, *The Sign in Sidney Brustein's Window* (1964), received mixed reviews, but private donations kept it running until the night Hansberry died. Posthumous productions orchestrated by Robert Nemiroff include *To Be Young, Gifted and Black* (1969) and *Les Blancs* (1970).

Hansberry was prolific: *The Movement: Documentary of a Struggle for Equality*; *To Be Young, Gifted and Black: Lorraine Hansberry in Her Own Words*; and articles in the *Village Voice*, *Freedomways*, the *National Guardian*, and the *Black Scholar* are among her published work. In addition to the protests that her work embodied, she was a committed activist for black and gay rights, involved in the Student Nonviolent Coordinating Committee (SNCC), and a critic of the House Un-American Activities Committee.

North America

Harlem, New York,

political and cultural center of black America in the twentieth century, best known as the major site of the literary and artistic "renaissance" of the 1920s and 1930s.

Slaves to the Dutch West India Company, Africans built the first wagon road into Harlem in the seventeenth century, and in the next 200 years African slaves worked the Dutch and then English farms in Harlem. In 1790, 115 slaves were listed for the "Harlem Division," equal to one-third the population of the area.

But the evolution of Harlem into the political and cultural capital of black America is a twentieth-century phenomenon. Housing in Harlem, which was once a wealthy suburb of New York City, soared in value at the turn of the century, only to collapse beneath excessive real estate speculation in 1904 and 1905. Those years coincided with the completion of the Lenox Avenue subway line to lower Manhattan, facilitating the settlement of African Americans migrating from the South and the Caribbean in Harlem. Philip Payton's Afro-Am Realty Company leased large numbers of Harlem apartment houses from white owners and rented them to black tenants in neighborhoods that began at 135th Street east of Eighth Avenue and over the decades expanded east-west from Park to Amsterdam avenues and north-south from 155th Street to Central Park.

By 1930 the black population of New York had more than tripled, to 328,000 persons, 180,000 of whom lived in Harlem—two-thirds of all African Americans in New York City and 12 percent of the entire population. Between 1920 and 1930 the black population of Harlem increased by nearly 100,000 persons, developing middle- and upper-middle-class neighborhoods such as Striver's Row on West 139th Street.

Not only the cultural and intellectual center of black life in the United States, Harlem has also served as a safe haven, a black community with strong connections among its inhabitants.
CORBIS/Bettmann

The migration led to a political, cultural, and social community that was unprecedented in scope. The African Methodist Episcopal Zion Church, St. Philips' Protestant Episcopal Church, and Abyssinian Baptist Church moved north to Harlem. *The Amsterdam News* was founded in Harlem in 1919. The community also supported a vital literary and political life: by 1920 the trade union newspaper the *Messenger*, edited by A. Philip Randolph and Chandler Owen, was published in Harlem, as were the National Association for the Advancement of Colored People's (NAACP's) magazine the *Crisis*, edited by W. E. B. Du Bois and Jessie Fauset, and the National Urban League's magazine *Opportunity*, edited by Charles S. Johnson. Incipient political movements followed the establishment of a branch of the NAACP in 1910 and Marcus Garvey's Universal Negro Improvement Association in 1916. Flamboyant and charismatic, Garvey promoted both a back-to-Africa drive and the first popular Black Nationalist Movement. Harlem also nurtured a socialist movement led by H. H. Harrison, W. A. Domingo, and A. Philip Randolph.

Especially in the 1920s Harlem fostered pioneering black intellectual and popular movements as well as a dynamic nightlife centered on nightclubs, impromptu apartment "buffet parties," and speakeasies. Many of Harlem's cultural venues developed at this time, ranging from the Lincoln and Apollo theaters to the Cotton Club, Smalls Paradise, and Savoy Ballroom. In popular dance Florence Mills was one of the most celebrated entertainers of the 1920s, while in tap, Bill "Bojangles" Robinson was called "the Mayor of Harlem." In vaudeville Bert Williams broke the color line. In drama Paul Robeson was an honored figure for both his acting and singing.

In 1925 Alain Locke filled an issue of *Survey Graphic* magazine with black literature, folklore, and art, declaring a "New Negro" renaissance to be guided by "forces and motives of [cultural] self determination." The renaissance was led by writers such as Jean Toomer, Langston Hughes, Countee Cullen, Claude McKay, Nella Larsen, and Zora Neale Hurston, and Harlem became its symbol. In art Aaron Douglas, Richmond Barthé, and (later) Jacob Lawrence launched their careers.

In music Harlem pianists such as Fats Waller and Willie "the Lion" Smith began one of the most storied traditions of jazz in the world. In the 1920s it included big bands led by Fletcher Henderson, Duke Ellington, and Chick Webb and individual virtuosos such as Eubie Blake. Later, it

HARLEM

MAJOR SITES OF BLACK CULTURE
IN THE 1920S

included Charlie Parker, Bud Powell, Ornette Coleman, Thelonious Monk, and Miles Davis.

In the 1920s Harlem gained some political power and institutions. Arthur Schomburg's renowned collection of black literature and historical documents became a branch of the New York Public Library. Three years later Charles Fillmore was elected the first black district leader in New York City, and black physicians were admitted to the permanent staff of Harlem Hospital.

But such advances were modest. Harlem blacks owned less than 20 percent of Harlem's businesses in 1929, and the onset of the Depression quadrupled relief applications within two years. Blacks continued to be excluded from jobs, even in Harlem. The Communist Party and the Citizens' League for Fair Play organized a boycott of Harlem businesses that refused to hire blacks, but the boycott collapsed in 1934. A year later frustration erupted into a riot in which millions of dollars of property was damaged and 75 were arrested. By 1937 four African American district leaders were elected, and the Greater New York City Coordinating Committee for the Employment of Negroes was formed.

From Marcus Garvey's Universal Negro Improvement Association to the National Memorial African Bookstore, pictured here in 1964, Harlem has long served as home to movements and ideas stressing African American self-reliance and self-esteem. *UPI/CORBIS-Bettmann*

During World War II migration from the South and the Caribbean increased enormously, the direct result of the opening of defense industry jobs to blacks, for which the 1941 March on Washington—organized by A. Philip Randolph—was instrumental. But racism persisted, and an incident of police brutality in 1943 precipitated a riot in which 6 African Americans were killed and 185 were injured. In 1944, on the heels of widespread efforts to improve race relations, Adam Clayton Powell Jr. was elected to the United States Congress and Benjamin Davis replaced him on the City Council.

The 1940s and 1950s brought further political cohesion and literary expression. Hulan Jack was elected the first black borough president in 1953. Through the 1970s Harlem was home to heralded writers such as novelist Ralph Ellison, essayist James Baldwin, playwright Lorraine Hansberry, and poets Audre Lorde and Maya Angelou—many of them associated with the Harlem Writers Guild. Yet by 1960 middle-class flight from Harlem produced a ghetto in large sections of the community. Half of all housing units were unsound, and the infant mortality rate was nearly double that in the rest of the city. Under the leadership of Harlem Youth Opportunities Unlimited (HARYOU), organized by Kenneth B. Clark, Harlem tried to draw federal funding into the area to rebuild the community and create jobs. The effort was largely unsuccessful, and in 1964, when an off-duty police officer shot a black youth, a riot ensued. One person was killed, and 144 were injured; stores were looted for several days.

In the 1950s Malcolm X arrived to head the Harlem Mosque and soon created an independent religious and Black Nationalist Movement that declared itself ready to fight—"by any means necessary"—against white racism and violence toward African Americans. In 1965, however, Malcolm X was assassinated. His death made him a martyr for Black Nationalists even as his religious movement dissipated.

Percy Sutton was Manhattan borough president for 11 years beginning in 1966. In 1970 Charles Rangel was elected to the congressional seat vacated by Adam Clayton Powell Jr. By the late 1970s, however, de-industrialization and inflation led to widespread unemployment, while poverty, drugs, crime, and a deteriorating school system plagued the community for the next decade.

When, in 1989, Harlem's David Dinkins was elected mayor of New York, racial divisions briefly lessened and some parts of Harlem were revitalized. But Dinkins's defeat in the 1993 election cut short those efforts. In the more mercantilist environment of the late 1990s Harlem has turned to private development efforts by African Americans, such as the mall planned for 125th Street, as a means for rehabilitating an impoverished community.

North America

Harlem Renaissance
The "Talented Tenth"

The Harlem Renaissance was a somewhat forced phenomenon, a cultural nationalism of the parlor, institutionally encouraged and directed by leaders of the national civil rights establishment for the paramount purpose of improving race relations in a time of extreme national backlash, caused in large part by economic gains won by African Americans during the Great War. W. E. B. Du Bois labeled this mobilizing elite the "Talented Tenth" in a seminal 1903 essay. He fleshed out the concept that same year in "The Advance Guard of the Race," a piece in *Booklover's Magazine* in which he identified the poet Paul Laurence Dunbar, the novelist Charles W. Chesnutt, and the painter Henry O. Tanner, among a small number of other well-educated professionals, as representatives of this class. The Talented Tenth formulated and propagated a new ideology of racial assertiveness that was to be embraced by the physicians, dentists, educators, preachers, businesspeople, lawyers, and morticians who comprised the bulk of the African American affluent and influential—some 10,000 men and women out of a total population in 1920 of more than 10 million. (In 1917, traditionally cited as the natal year of the Harlem Renaissance, there were 2132 African Americans in colleges and universities, probably no more than 50 of them attending "white" institutions. This minuscule vanguard of a minority—a fraction of 0.1 percent of the racial total—jump-started the New Negro Arts Movement, using as its vehicles the National Association for the Advancement of Colored People [NAACP] and the National Urban League [NUL], and their respective publications, the *Crisis* and *Opportunity* magazine.)

The Harlem Renaissance was not all-inclusive of the early twentieth-century African American urban experience. The potent mass movement founded and led by the charismatic Marcus Garvey was a parallel but socially different force related primarily through dialectical confrontation. Equally different from the institutional ethos and purpose of the Renaissance was the Black Church. An occasional minister (such as the father of poet Countee Cullen) or exceptional Garveyites (such as Yale-Harvard man William H. Ferris) might move in both worlds, but black evangelism and its cultist manifestations, such as Black Zionism, represented emotional and cultural retrogression in the eyes of the principal actors in the Renaissance.

When Du Bois wrote a few years after the beginning of the New Negro

Movement in arts and letters that "until the art of the black folk compels recognition they will not be rated as human," he, like most of his Renaissance peers, fully intended to exclude the blues of Bessie Smith and the jazz of "King" Oliver. As board members of the Pace Phonograph Company, Du Bois, James Weldon Johnson, and others banned "funky" artists from the Black Swan list of recordings, thereby contributing to the demise of the African American-owned firm. But the wild Broadway success of Miller and Lyles's musical *Shuffle Along* (which helped to popularize the Charleston) and Florence Mill's *Blackbirds* revue flouted such artistic fastidiousness. The very centrality of music in black life, as well as of black musical stereotypes in white minds, caused popular musical forms to impinge inescapably on Renaissance high culture. Eventually, the Renaissance deans made a virtue out of necessity; they applauded the concert-hall ragtime of "Big Jim" Europe and the "educated" jazz of Atlanta University graduate and big-band leader Fletcher Henderson, and took to hiring Duke Ellington or Cab Calloway as drawing cards for fundraising socials. Still, their relationship to music remained beset by paradox. New York ragtime, with its "Jelly Roll" Morton strifes and Joplinesque elegance, had as much in common with Chicago jazz as Mozart did with "Fats" Waller.

Although the emergence of the Harlem Renaissance seems much more sudden and dramatic in retrospect than the historical reality, its institutional elaboration was, in fact, relatively quick. Because so little fiction or poetry had been produced by African Americans in the years immediately prior to the Harlem Renaissance, the appearance of a dozen or more poets and novelists and essayists seemed all the more striking and improbable. Death from tuberculosis had silenced poet-novelist Dunbar in 1906, and poor royalties had done the same for novelist Chesnutt after publication the previous year of *The Colonel's Dream*. Since then, no more than five African Americans had published significant works of fiction and verse. This relative silence was finally to be broken in 1922 by Claude McKay's *Harlem Shadows*, the first book of poetry since Dunbar.

North America

Harlem Writers Guild,

influential African American writers' group based in Harlem, New York City.

Poet and essayist Maya Angelou, mystery writer Walter Mosley, and *Waiting to Exhale* author Terry McMillan are only three of the dozens of writers who have been part of the Harlem Writers Guild over the last five decades. Its first members, Rosa Guy, John O. Killens, Walter Christmas, and John Henrik Clarke, began meeting in a Harlem storefront in the late 1940s to critique one another's stories. At that time, the mainstream American literary world had just started to take notice of black authors. Richard Wright's novel *Native Son* had been a bestseller a few years earlier, and many young African American writers who wanted to follow his lead created their own forums to discuss their work. The Harlem Writers

Guild became one of these forums, and the membership soon outgrew the first storefront.

The Guild's members also shared a commitment to social change, and many of them were interested in incorporating political ideas into their art. The first novel published by a Guild member, Killens's *Youngblood* (1954), depicted four characters fighting for dignity in the segregated American South. Other novelists, like Paule Marshall, wrote about the black experience in the West Indies and other parts of the African diaspora. Guild writers also identified with other political organizations and causes that were not focused only on race—for example, Christmas and Clarke both wrote for Communist periodicals, and other members were union organizers and Progressive Party supporters.

In 1965 the Guild and the New School for Social Research in New York City cosponsored a conference called "The Negro Writer's Vision of America," which more than a thousand people attended. The conference's widely publicized highlight was a debate between Guild founders Killens and Clarke and white scholar Herbert Aptheker and artist Walter Lowenfels on what role, if any, artists should play in the fight against racism. This was the exact question that Guild members and writers like them were trying to answer in their own careers, and they believed that artists did have a responsibility to include social issues in their work. Members during the 1960s included Maya Angelou, whose first published book, the autobiography *I Know Why the Caged Bird Sings*, became a bestseller in 1970; novelist Chester Himes, known for his detective fiction set in Harlem; and Walter Dean Myers, an award-winning writer for children and young adults.

The Black Arts Movement declined in the 1970s, but the Guild continued as a forum for yet another generation of writers. Since 1988 Guild workshops have met at the Schomburg Center for Research in Black Culture of the New York Public Library. In 1991 Guild director William H. Banks Jr. began hosting "In Our Own Words," a weekly show featuring Guild members, for New York television station WNYE. The show was carried in six viewing areas in the United States and Canada, and this gave the Guild's latest writers a new forum. Former members Terry McMillan and Walter Mosley both became best-selling authors in the 1980s and 1990s, and in 1993 Maya Angelou was asked to compose and read a poem, *On the Pulse of Morning*, for the inauguration of United States President Bill Clinton.

North America
Harper, Frances Ellen Watkins

(b. September 24, 1825, Baltimore, Md.; d. February 20, 1911, Philadelphia, Pa.), African American writer and antislavery, women's rights, and temperance activist.

At her death in 1911, one memorial tribute said that Frances Ellen Watkins Harper "had acquired the title of 'Empress of Peace and Poet Laureate.'" As a lecturer, activist, poet, and novelist, Harper dedicated her life to promoting social uplift—of women, of African Americans, and of African American women in particular—in as many forums as she could find. In the process, she became one of the best-known and most respected black women of the nineteenth century.

Harper was born into a free black family in Baltimore. She was orphaned at the age of two and then raised by her uncle, Rev. William Watkins, director of Baltimore's prestigious Academy for Negro Youth. Harper herself attended the school, where she studied Greek, Latin, and the Bible. As a result, she was better educated than most other American women of her day, black or white. She began writing poetry as a teenager and started her career as a writer in 1845, when she reportedly published the poetry collection *Forest Leaves*. Her second career, as an activist, began almost a decade later.

Audiences were often surprised by the petite black woman, nicknamed the "Bronze Muse," whom they encountered. Some complimented the fact that her speeches were "fiery" yet still "marked by dignity and composure" and "without the slightest violation of good taste." Others—unwilling to believe that a black woman could carry herself with intelligence and grace— accused her of being either a black man dressed as a woman or a white woman painted black. But her composure and bearing were precisely what made her a powerful symbol of black woman-hood for much of the nineteenth century.

Harper often quoted original poetry in her lectures, and consequently her reputation as a poet spread as far as her speaking tours. Her second volume of poetry, *Poems on Miscellaneous Subjects* (1854), sold 10,000 copies between 1854 and 1857, and was then enlarged and reprinted. She published several more volumes of poetry and reprinted new editions of her poems many times. In the process, she became the most famous black poet of her time.

Many of Harper's lectures were to women's clubs and associations, and some of her most popular speeches were on the rights and roles of women in general, and black women in particular. She worked in the American Equal Rights Association with white activists Elizabeth Cady Stanton and Susan B. Anthony. But when they began to criticize the Fifteenth Amendment, which gave black men the vote, because they felt that white women should have received it first, Harper's loyalty was to her race over her gender.

Harper continued speaking out in favor of women's rights, however, and was a member of the American Woman Suffrage Association and the National Council of Women. She also spoke at the International Council of Women in Washington, D.C., in 1888, and gave a lecture titled "Women's Political Future" at the Columbian Exposition in Chicago. But she remained committed to arguing for the particular needs of African American women. In 1893 Harper, Fannie Barrier Williams, Anna Julia Cooper, Fannie Jackson Coppin, Sarah J. Early, and Hallie Q. Brown together charged the World's Congress of Representative Women with overlooking black women. Harper belonged to the National Federation of Afro-American Women and helped found the National Association of Colored Women.

Throughout all of her political activism, Harper continued to write, and in the twentieth century she is best remembered as one of the earliest black women writers. Her story "The Two Offers" (1859) is considered the first published short story by an African American woman. In addition to short stories and poetry, Harper wrote three short novels that were serialized by church presses, and in all of these works, as one scholar points out, the major themes "are those that [Harper herself] expounded throughout her career: personal integrity, Christian service, and social equality."

MRS. FRANCIS E. W. HARPER.
See p. 755.

This engraved portrait from *The Underground Railroad* (1872) by William Still shows poet and antislavery activist Frances Ellen Watkins Harper. *CORBIS*

These themes are all also present in Harper's best-known work, the 1892 novel *Iola Leroy*, which tells the story of a light-skinned African American woman who is raised believing she is white. She learns the truth under dramatically tragic circumstances but accepts and eventually welcomes the news, and devotes the rest of her life to racial uplift, working to improve the status of African Americans.

Iola Leroy has been criticized for its melodrama and its stereotypical portrayal of the Tragic Mulatto, but the novel can also be read as a blueprint for the intelligent, independent black woman activist that Harper encouraged others to become—and that she herself was. Contemporary reviewers called *Iola Leroy* the crowning effort of Harper's life. *Iola Leroy* was published when Harper was nearly 70, and she continued writing until a few years before her death in 1911.

Even during her lifetime, Harper was commemorated through F. E. W. Harper Leagues, Frances E. Harper Woman's Christian Temperance Unions, and chapters of other organizations that bore her name. Harper was also recognized by the Daughters of America and Patriots of the American Revolution. But her title as a Woman of Our Race Most Worthy of Imitation may have come closest to recognizing her signature achievement. Harper provided a model for the best of what any nineteenth-century woman could be—and as a black woman, who made a point of writing about and speaking to other black women, she set the standard for a generation of African American women's activism.

North America

Harrington, Oliver Wendell (Ollie)

(b. February 14, 1912, Valhalla, N.Y.; d. November 7, 1995, Berlin, Germany), African American cartoonist and expatriate best known for creating the character Bootsie.

Known to friends as Ollie, Oliver Harrington was the eldest of five children born to Herbert Harrington and Eugenia Tarat. He graduated from high school in 1929 and moved to New York City during the Harlem Renaissance.

Harrington attended the National Academy of Design, where he studied painting and drawing. By 1932 his comic strips were being featured in black newspapers, including the *Pittsburgh Courier, New York Amsterdam News*, and *Baltimore Afro-American*. Bootsie, a cartoon character who mimicked the styles and trends in the urban black community, and who would become Harrington's most famous creation, first appeared in a comic strip called "Dark Laughter." In 1958 a collection of Bootsie comic strips was published as *Bootsie and Others*.

In 1940 Harrington received his bachelor's degree in fine arts from the Yale University School of Fine Arts. Two years later he became art director for the *People's Voice*, a weekly published by Adam Clayton Powell Jr. In 1943 he designed another comic strip, this one chronicling the adventurous life of a fictitious African American aviator named Jive Gray.

In 1944 Harrington traveled to Italy and France as a war correspondent. After the war he took jobs as a journalist and book illustrator, and in 1946 created the public relations department for the National Association for the Advancement of Colored People (NAACP). In 1951 he moved to Paris, where he met Richard Wright, another African American expatriate. After Wright's death in 1962, Harrington accepted a job illustrating classic novels and moved to East Berlin, where he met his wife, Helma Richter. He resided there for 13 years until his death.

North America

Hawkins, Coleman Randolph

(b. November 21, 1904?, St. Joseph, Mo.; d. May 19, 1969, New York, N.Y.), jazz musician, called the "father of the tenor saxophone," whose career spanned the years from early swing to post-bop jazz.

Famous for his landmark 1939 recording *"Body and Soul"* and as sideman in the big bands of Mamie Smith and Fletcher Henderson, Coleman Hawkins is credited with bringing the tenor saxophone into the jazz ensemble. When he began his long musical career in the early 1920s, the saxophone was, according to jazz historian Joachim Berendt, in "the category of strange noise makers." No previous player had explored the instrument's potential for carrying a song's melody, for mimicking the human voice, or for use in tonal experimentation.

Hawkins, known to his contemporaries as "Hawk" or "Bean," changed all that. Born in St. Joseph, Missouri, to a musically talented mother, Hawkins began piano lessons when he was five, studied cello at age seven, and started playing the saxophone by the time he was nine. His formal training also included classes at Washburn College in Topeka, Kansas. Hawkins played at weekend dances in Kansas City, Missouri, as a young teenager, and at 17 joined the big band fronted by blues singer Mamie Smith. Two years later, in 1923, he followed her to New York City.

Hawkins left Smith to join the city's premier big band, led by Fletcher Henderson, the legendary bandleader considered by many to be the leading architect of the swing era in jazz. From 1923 to 1934 Hawkins played with Henderson's band, during which time he pioneered the saxophone as a solo instrument within the jazz ensemble. Especially on romantic ballads, his solos influenced scores of other musicians. "When I heard Hawk," the trumpeter Miles Davis once said, "I learned to play ballads." In addition to playing with Henderson, Hawkins recorded with fellow saxophonist Benny Webster in a smaller ensemble called the Chocolate Dandies.

In 1934 Hawkins left Henderson and New York for an extended European tour. He stayed for five years, playing throughout England, France, and the Netherlands. Only when World War II loomed in 1939 did he come back to the United States. Shortly after his return he recorded what would become his trademark song, *Body and Soul,* a standard in which Hawkins's solo established him as the preeminent saxophonist of jazz. It was a best-selling record, his first in 20 years as a musician. From 1939 to 1940 Hawkins briefly fronted his own big band, but for the rest of his career he mostly worked solo, backed up by house musicians or playing in impromptu groups.

A lifelong innovator, Hawkins worked with musicians who were pioneering the new style known as bebop. He recorded *Woody 'n' You* in 1944 with Dizzy Gillespie and Max Roach, and later played with both Thelonious Monk and Miles Davis. In the last two decades of his life Hawkins recorded prolifically, toured Europe often, and continued to play in and around New York. He died in 1969 of liver disease. More than 500 people, including numerous jazz luminaries, attended his funeral.

North America

Hayden, Robert Earl

(b. August 4, 1913, Detroit, Mich.; d. February 25, 1980, Ann Arbor, Mich.), African American poet and educator.

Born Asa Bundy Sheffey, Robert Earl Hayden was adopted by William and Sue Ellen Hayden, who changed his name. Hayden spent a difficult childhood in the Paradise Valley ghetto of Detroit. He suffered from very poor eyesight and was in frequent conflict with his extremely strict and religious foster parents, who imbued in him the sense of sinfulness—particularly about his homosexual inclination, which would inform much of his poetry.

After graduating from Detroit City College (now Wayne State University) in 1936, Hayden worked on the Federal Writers' Project and as an editor and critic for the *Michigan Chronicle*, Detroit's leading African American newspaper. He became involved in Detroit's lively left-wing arts scene, reading his poetry at political demonstrations and union rallies. With help from Louis Martin, editor in chief of the *Michigan Chronicle*, in 1940 Hayden published a collection of his radical poetry, *Heart-Shape in the Dust*.

In 1946 Hayden joined the English Department at Fisk University. After teaching there for 23 years, he took a job at the University of Michigan, where he taught for the rest of his life. He published eight books of poetry, but it was not until the publication of his *Selected Poems* in 1966 that he received national recognition.

Although Hayden would, like many African American poets before him, sometimes use traditional forms such as the ballad and the sonnet, more often he wrote a sort of modernist collage, juxtaposing images, phrases, and rhythms. This ornate diction and combination of abstract but suggestive metaphors with homely local detail contributed to his reputation as a difficult and intellectual poet influenced by the modernism of T. S. Eliot and Auden.

The influence of Euro-American modernism on Hayden's poetry as well as Hayden's frequent declarations that he wanted to be considered an "American poet" rather than a "black poet" led to much criticism of him as a literary Uncle Tom by African American critics during the 1960s. Ironically, African American history, contemporary black figures such as Malcolm X, and African American communities, particularly Hayden's native Paradise Valley, were the subjects of many of his poems.

During the 1960s and 1970s Hayden adopted a simpler and more directly personal style, as in his "Elegies for Paradise Valley." In 1976 he became the first African American to be appointed Consultant in Poetry at the Library of Congress, an equivalent at the time to being named national poet laureate.

North America

Hayes, Roland Willsie

(b. June 3, 1887, Curryville, Ga.; d. December 31, 1976, Boston, Mass.), African American tenor whose pioneering recitals of German lieder and other classical music opened the concert stage for black singers.

Born on the plantation where his mother had been enslaved, Roland Hayes grew up in extreme poverty, but sang in the local church choir and managed to complete the eighth grade. An Oberlin College student heard him sing, and urged him to pursue vocal training. Hayes was, he claimed, "born again" one evening when he heard recordings of opera singer Enrico Caruso and other classical artists.

Hayes attended Fisk University and was working as a waiter in

Louisville, Kentucky, when the president of Fisk invited him to join the famous Fisk Jubilee Singers on a concert tour to Boston, Massachusetts. In Boston a benefactor arranged for voice lessons, and Hayes began studying with Arthur Hubbard in 1911. Hayes worked as a messenger for the John Hancock Insurance Company and sang in black churches. In 1920 he toured Europe, where he received positive reviews.

On December 2, 1923, Hayes presented a self-financed concert at Boston's Symphony Hall that won favorable attention and established him in a successful life-long career as an international recital artist. He sang French, Italian, and German songs around the world and was considered a master of German leider. Hayes had deep affection for African American folk music, and he introduced Negro spirituals to much of the world. He received many honors and awards, including the prestigious Spingarn Medal, the highest recognition of the National Association for the Advancement of Colored People (NAACP).

Africa

Head, Bessie

(b. July 6, 1937, Pietermaritzburg, South Africa; d. April 17, 1986, Serowe, Botswana).

South African author and teacher Bessie Head was one of the great postwar African novelists. Her writings sound existential themes in unfamiliar terrain, treating such topics as personal and societal alienation, political exile, racial identity, and sexual oppression. She was particularly concerned with describing the institutionalization of evil.

Head was effectively an orphan. The child of a white woman and a black man, she was born in the mental institution in which her mother had been placed. Adopted by a white Afrikaner family when she was very young, she was later returned when her black features revealed themselves. She then lived with a black family, until she moved into an orphanage at age 13. In a few years she acquired a teaching degree, and taught school in Durban for two years, later leaving that position to work as a journalist for Drum Publications in Johannesburg.

Head became active in politics in the 1960s, eventually joining the Pan-Africanist Congress (PAC). She married Harold Head in 1961, and had a son. Following several arrests and continual harassment by Afrikaner authorities, Head moved with her son to Botswana, where she lived in the village of Serowe, working both as a schoolteacher and unpaid agricultural worker. Her experiences in political exile were extremely traumatic, provoking a nervous breakdown.

Head's first novel, *When Rain Clouds Gather* (1969), is the only work set in and developed from her experiences in South Africa. Her second novel, *Maru* (1971), addresses the issue of racism among blacks. Head focuses on the abuse of the Masarwa or Bushmen, considered slaves and outcasts within

African society, by Serowe tribal people. As in Head's other novels, the antiracist sentiments expressed in *Maru* are not intended as a condemnation of the village of Serowe, but more as a broader reflection on the racial prejudices found throughout the world in many different societies. Head's third novel, the largely autobiographical *A Question of Power* (1973), is a portrait of her nervous breakdown, a condition she believes resulted from the ongoing psychological struggles she faced as both a woman and a political exile. This novel is often considered a milestone in the development and evolution of African literature, as it is one of the first African novels written from a largely personal and introspective point of view, focusing on the individual as opposed to broader societal issues. Furthermore, as a story written from a woman's perspective, *A Question of Power* gained the attention of feminists and established Head's reputation as a woman's author, although Head hesitated to embrace the feminist label for herself.

Head further established herself as a feminist with her short nonfiction piece, *The Collector of Treasures and Other Botswana Village Tales*, a collection of Botswana village stories told from a woman's perspective. These stories are decidedly optimistic and positive in tone, and serve to emphasize the inherent personal and communal strength of women in overcoming male oppressors. Head's major nonfiction work, *Serowe: Village of the Rainwind* (1981), is a history of Serowe, recorded as a series of interviews conducted by Head herself.

North America

Henderson, Fletcher Hamilton, Jr.

[sometimes identified as James Fletcher Henderson] (b. December 18, 1897, Cuthbert, Ga.; d. December 28, 1952, New York, N.Y.), African American jazz pianist, composer, and arranger whose orchestra is considered the first true big band of the swing era.

Fletcher Henderson is regarded by most music historians as the architect of the big-band movement in jazz music. In his 30-year career he saw, and helped, jazz evolve from its ragtime and Dixieland roots to a polished, streamlined sound that hinted at the bebop and cool jazz styles that would follow. Though he began as a pianist, it was as a bandleader and arranger that Henderson's impact was most significant. His bands nurtured such influential talents as Coleman Hawkins, Louis Armstrong, Ben Webster, and Lester Young; his arrangements and compositions became the basis for hit records by Count Basie and the white bandleader Benny Goodman.

Born in Cuthbert, Georgia, Henderson's parents—his father was a school principal and his mother a pianist and music teacher—encouraged their son's talents, giving him piano lessons starting at the age of six. A good student, Henderson graduated from Atlanta University with a degree in chemistry in 1920, after which he traveled to New York City for graduate study. To support himself, he took a job with a music publishing and recording company run by African American musicians Harry Pace and W. C. Handy. Henderson led the house band, the Black Swan Troubadours, in accompanying the blues singer Ethel Waters. When Waters planned a tour in 1921, she took Henderson along as pianist, bandleader, and tour manager.

When Henderson returned to New York (having had his academic musical style loosened up by Waters, according to his biographers), he again worked as an accompanist for various artists, including the blues singer Bessie Smith. Henderson also began leading loose collaborations of musicians in nightly jam sessions. By 1923 a group of players had jelled into Henderson's first recognizable big band, which was based at the Club Alabam and later the Roseland Ballroom. Coleman Hawkins, the pioneering tenor saxophonist from Kansas City, joined Henderson when he moved to New York, and the coronetist and singer Louis Armstrong brought New Orleans style to the band.

In recordings such as "*Sugar Foot Stomp*," arranged by Don Redman and featuring Armstrong's searing solos, Henderson's band established the sound and feel that defined the era. Brass, wind (or reed), and rhythm instruments worked together in sections, often in a call-and-response pattern, and the syncopated, stomping beat made pop standards swing. As the big-band movement grew, however, Henderson's knack for attracting innovative talent began to break down. Known as a kind and friendly employer, he lacked the ambition and organizational drive of his burgeoning competition, which included Duke Ellington and Cab Calloway. By the mid-1930s Henderson's band began to dissolve.

Having fallen on hard times, Henderson sought a second career as an arranger. Always generous with other bandleaders—sharing, for instance, most of his musical library with the up-and-coming Count Basie—Henderson began selling compositions and arrangements to the white bandleader Benny Goodman. In 1939 and 1940, Henderson worked as Goodman's house arranger, and briefly as his pianist. Semi-retired after 1940 due to declining health, Henderson scored a musical, "*Jazz Train*," and briefly led a sextet at a small bar in New York's Greenwich Village. He suffered a stroke in 1950, never fully recovered, and died in 1952.

North America

Hendrix, Jimi

(b. November 27, 1942, Seattle, Wash.; d. September 18, 1970, London, England), African American musician, rock 'n' roll singer, and guitar virtuoso.

Jimi Hendrix taught himself guitar by listening to Muddy Waters, B. B. King, and Chuck Berry. After serving as a paratrooper in the army, he began his music career. Under the name Jimmy James, he played as a backup guitarist for many top rock 'n' roll and rhythm and blues artists, including Little Richard, Sam Cooke, B. B. King, Wilson Pickett, Ike and Tina Turner, and the Isley Brothers. Between 1962 and 1964 Hendrix began to captivate audiences with such guitar tricks as playing with his teeth, behind his back, and between his legs.

Aspiring to move out of the background, Hendrix formed a band called Jimmy James and the Blue Flames in 1965, and played coffeehouses in New

York's Greenwich Village, where he was influenced by Bob Dylan. Chas Chandler, bassist for the popular group the Animals, discovered Hendrix in New York. In 1966, Chandler, who would later become Hendrix's manager, convinced him to accompany him to London by promising to introduce Hendrix to Eric Clapton. In London, Hendrix formed a band, a power trio called the Jimi Hendrix Experience, with drummer Mitch Mitchell and bassist Noel Redding.

The London rock world, hungry for a new trend, was consumed by Hendrix. His style of playing fascinated even such elite guitarists as Pete Townsend and Eric Clapton, who placed Hendrix's musicianship on a level above their own. Considered a true virtuoso, the left-handed Hendrix played a right-handed Fender Stratocaster strung upside down. He used new techniques, including distortion, "wah-wah," and feedback to add an electrifying sonic architecture to already accomplished songs. The Experience was one of the first integrated big-time rock bands that was led by an African American.

In 1967 the Experience released its first album, *Are You Experienced?*, which contained the hits "*Hey Joe*" and "*Purple Haze*," and featured Hendrix's famously expansive lyrics ("Scuze me while I kiss the sky"). In June 1967 the Experience made a dramatic debut in the American music scene at the Monterey Pop Festival. Because Hendrix and the Experience had not yet released *Are You Experienced?* in the United States, festival promoters were unwilling to book them until Paul McCartney of the Beatles persuaded them to do so. During their performance, Hendrix tore through a set of original compositions and eclectic covers, and closed the set by setting fire to his guitar.

On the strength of the Monterey performance Hendrix became a superstar. He began spending more and more time recording and founded his own studio, Electric Ladyland, in New York, where he associated with fellow musicians, including admirer Miles Davis. The Experience slowly unraveled as Hendrix pursued side projects. In 1969 he appeared at Woodstock, performing an unorthodox, distortion-filled guitar version of "*The Star-Spangled Banner*" that had fans raving and had "middle America," which saw his version as blasphemous, enraged. Following Woodstock, Hendrix formed the Band of Gypsies, an all-black band with Buddy Miles, a friend from the army, on drums and Billy Cox on bass. They released one album, a self-titled recording of a live performance. At age 27, Hendrix died in London of complications following barbiturate intoxication.

North America

Herriman, George

(b. August 22, 1880, New Orleans, La.; d. April 24, 1944, Los Angeles, Calif.), African American cartoonist whose strip Krazy Kat has been lauded by many as the greatest American cartoon.

George Herriman was born in New Orleans in 1880, but his family soon moved to California, perhaps because his light-skinned Creole parents hoped to pass as white and start life anew. Indeed, Herriman himself obscured his African descent all his life, earning the nickname "the Greek" from speculating coworkers. As a teenager Herriman contributed drawings to local newspapers. In his early twenties he moved to New York City and freelanced until white newspaper mogul William Randolph Hearst saw his cartoons and hired him for the *New York Evening Journal*.

During the first decade of the twentieth century, Herriman explored a number of characters and settings before developing *Krazy Kat*. The strip's main characters emerged from a cat and mouse he drew in the margins of his first success, *The Family Upstairs*. *Krazy Kat* gained independence on October 28, 1913, and ran until Herriman died in 1944.

Krazy Kat's title character, an androgynous cat, loves Ignatz, a married male mouse. Ignatz despises Krazy's affection and hurls bricks at him/her to make him/her go away. Krazy, however, has descended from Kleopatra Kat—an Egyptian for whom bricks were missives of love—and finds encouragement in the violence of Ignatz. Officer B. Pupp, a diligent and well-meaning dog who loves Krazy, attempts to curtail Ignatz's brickthrowing, but seldom succeeds.

The drama transpires in Coconino County, Arizona, a shifting, surreal desert landscape that was inspired by Herriman's own trip to Monument Valley. In addition to Krazy, Ignatz, and Pupp, Herriman introduced Mr. Wough Wuph Wuff, Don Kiyote, Osker Wildcat, Uncle Tomm Katt, and numerous other cleverly named characters.

Krazy Kat never achieved wide popularity among newspaper readers, though it attracted a highbrow following. Fans included Pablo Picasso, Charlie Chaplin, Walt Disney, F. Scott Fitzgerald, Frank Capra, H. L. Mencken, and Ernest Hemingway, and *Krazy Kat*'s lengthy tenure owed much to Hearst's personal love of the strip. Acceptance by the cultural mainstream grew after Herriman's death, as *Krazy* appeared in an animated series by Paramount Studios, in the tattoos and lyrics of rock 'n' roll stars, in a *Star Trek* episode, on T-shirts and postage stamps, in gallery shows and stage productions, and even in a novel. Throughout the twentieth century, cartoonists have considered *Krazy Kat* the founding father (or mother) of sophisticated comic strips.

North America

Hines, Earl Kenneth ("Fatha")
(b. December 28, 1903, Duquesne, Pa.; d. April 22, 1983, Oakland, Calif.), African American pianist and bandleader known as "the father of jazz piano."

Born to musical parents—his father played trumpet, his mother piano— Earl "Fatha" Hines has been largely credited with bringing piano from its solo ragtime roots into the jazz ensemble. He studied trumpet as a very young child and began piano lessons at the age of nine. After dropping out of high school, he played professionally around Pittsburgh, backing up singer Lois B. Deppe.

In 1923 Hines followed Deppe to Chicago, Illinois, where a vibrant African American music scene was flourishing. Hines played with various big bands, including those led by Sammy Stewart, Jimmie Noone, and Carroll Dickerson. In 1927 Dickerson left his orchestra and was replaced by Louis Armstrong, who appointed Hines musical director. The ensemble, based at Chicago's Savoy Ballroom, became one of the city's most popular throughout the late 1920s. Hines also recorded with Armstrong's Hot Seven and other small groups; "*Weather Bird*" and "*West End Blues*" are his best-known numbers from this era.

In 1928 Hines founded his own orchestra, which played regularly at the Grand Terrace nightclub in Chicago. From there, his music was broadcast on radio nightly—whenever the band was not on tour—for more than ten years. While in residence, Hines fostered the careers of singers Billy Eckstine and Sarah Vaughan as well as bebop originators Dizzy Gillespie and Charlie Parker. In the 1930s he acquired the nickname "Fatha," according to most sources because he was the "father of jazz piano." (Hines told *DownBeat* magazine, however, that the nickname came from a drunken radio announcer in response to a lecture on sobriety from the pianist.) Hines continued to lead his own band well into the 1940s, producing such records as *Harlem Laments and Rosetta*.

Hines originated what was called a "trumpet style" on the piano. Influenced by the great New Orleans pianist Jelly Roll Morton, his work combined a strong rhythmic beat with active, idiosyncratic melodies. Hines was a continuous innovator, at one point hiring an all-female string section, and his band is consistently cited as an influence by his fellow musicians. Due to the wartime ban on pressing records during the years that his band included Gillespie and Parker, along with Freddie Webster and other key players, no recordings remain.

In 1948 Hines's orchestra disbanded and he joined Armstrong's All-Stars, which included trombonist Jack Teagarden. After touring worldwide with Armstrong for three years, Hines moved to the West Coast in 1951, where he played in small venues such as the Hangover Club in San Francisco, California. Although he never again led a large swing band, Hines continued to tour with small ensembles in Europe and played a series of solo concerts in New York City during the 1960s and 1970s. He never ceased performing, appearing in New York in 1982 and playing a gig in San Francisco the week before his death in 1983.

North America

Hines, Gregory
(b. February 14, 1946, New York, N.Y.; d. August 9, 2003, Los Angeles, CA.), award-winning African American dancer and actor who reinvigorated tap dancing in the 1970s and 1980s.

Two years after beginning to dance at age three, Gregory Hines teamed with his brother Maurice to perform professionally. The brothers toured nightclubs and theaters nationwide as the Hines Kids. Hines studied tap dancing with Henry LeTang in New York City, and while touring he also learned from such dance legends as Honi Coles, Howard "Sandman" Sims, the Nicholas Brothers, and Teddy Hale.

In 1964 the brothers were joined onstage by their father, Gregory Hines Sr., who played drums. As Hines, Hines & Dad, they toured internationally and appeared on the *Tonight Show*. Tired from almost two decades of intermittent touring, however, Hines moved to California to pursue a career as a guitarist. In 1973 he formed Severance, a jazz-rock band, and released an album.

Returning to New York City, Hines debuted on Broadway in *Eubie* (1978), based on the life of pianist Eubie Blake. He was a major draw on Broadway and earned three Tony nominations for his lead role in *Sophisticated Ladies* (1980–1981). On television, he appeared on *Motown Returns to the Apollo* (for which he earned a Tony nomination) and hosted *Tap: Dance in America* (1989).

Hines combined his dramatic and dance experience in several movies, including *The Cotton Club* (1984), *White Knights* (with Mikhail Baryshnikov, 1985), *Running Scared* (1986), *Tap* (1989), and *A Rage in Harlem* (1991). In the late 1980s he also toured as a solo musical act and released his own album, *Gregory Hines*, produced by Luther Vandross. "*There's Nothing Better than Love*," Hines's duet with Vandross, reached the top of the rhythm and blues (R&B) charts in 1987. In 1992 he won a Tony Award for his role as jazz pianist and arranger Jelly Roll Morton in *Jelly's Last Jam*.

Maurice Hines, *left*, joins his brother Gregory in the finale of the smash Broadway musical "Sophisticated Ladies," at the Lunt Fontanne Theatre. *Bettmann/CORBIS*

Hip Hop in the United States,

an umbrella term for the youth culture that originated in the South Bronx, New York, in the 1970s.

Although *hip hop* includes graffiti art, break-dancing, and rap music, the name connotes more than the sum of these parts. Hip hop is a means of creative expression that gives voice to young, ethnic, urban populations. Says historian Tricia Rose, "Hip hop is a cultural form that attempts to negotiate the experiences of marginalization, brutally truncated opportunity, and oppression within the cultural imperatives of African American and Caribbean history, identity, and community."

A power outage in New York in 1977 and the looting and disorder that followed turned public attention toward the Bronx, and the borough became a national symbol of the inner city crisis. Bronx residents, primarily African and Caribbean Americans, received little external support as they attempted to live amid an economic wasteland. Hip hop culture emerged as a new, creative, and flexible value system in a landscape stripped of value. Although neighborhoods were ugly and neglected, fashion and art could embody pride, beauty, and self-respect.

Teenagers improvised. Black and Hispanic youths who had no dance halls and community spaces began dancing in the streets—first to disco, then to Jamaican-influenced DJ remixes, then to rap. DJs tapped into street lights to drive their booming sound systems. Young musicians, whose underfunded schools could provide no instruments, used stereo technology to make new sounds. Young artists painted on walls and subway cars instead of canvases. Break-dancing, rap, and graffiti art were all, in a sense, need-induced innovations, and each enriched the others. Graffiti artists designed posters, stage sets, and fashions for local DJs and rap musicians; break-dancers followed the rhythms of rap.

Many of hip hop's progenitors were trained in skills such as printing and radio repair, which quickly became obsolete in postindustrial New York. Unable to secure the kinds of jobs that had abounded ten years before, these craftspersons found artistic outlets for their workplace skills; graffiti replaced letterpress printing, rap replaced radio repair. Hip hop helped to ameliorate the archaic conditions of the inner city as the world approached the computer age.

Hip hop culture emphasized the new social allegiances of "crews" or "posses." Often interethnic, always panfamilial, crews and posses resembled gangs. Although a premium was placed on musical and artistic activities, gang-like rivalries characterized intergroup relations. Dancers and rappers held showdowns, competing against opponent performers, and graffiti artists sometimes defaced the murals of rivals. Hip hop culture included ongoing battles for local status, and creative conflicts often erupted into physical fights.

In the early 1980s hip hop culture exploded into the American mainstream. Break-dancing and rap gained nationwide popularity through movies, documentaries, music videos, and albums. The rampant merchandising that followed led some observers to suggest that the social and political power of hip hop died with commercialization.

As rap artists accrued wealth and notoriety, the political impact of the hip hop ethos increased. Some rappers, such as Public Enemy and NWA (Niggaz with Attitude), penetrated public consciousness with aggressive dissent that unnerved many members of the white establishment. Writer Kristal Brent Zook suggests that "there are persistent elements of Black Nationalist ideology which underlie and inform both rap music and a larger 'hip hop' culture. These elements include a desire for cultural pride, economic self-sufficiency, racial solidarity, and collective survival."

At the end of the twentieth century hip hop continues to represent the cultural movement that originally developed in the Bronx. Hip hop sensibilities, however, prevail across the nation and around the globe, comprising social conscience as well as artistic innovation.

North America

Hodges, Johnny

(b. July 25, 1906, Cambridge, Mass.; d. May 11, 1970, New York, N.Y.), African American jazz saxophonist who played for nearly 40 years with Duke Ellington's band.

A part of jazz's most celebrated band for nearly 40 years, Johnny Hodges became known as Duke Ellington's premiere soloist. Hodges's musical range included soaring, sensuous tones that one jazz critic described as being "draped over the notes like a lap rag" as well as snarling, blues-inflected tones inspired by his mentor, Sidney Bechet. Despite the variety of his creative expression, Hodges was also lauded for his consistent musical personality: he was considered the very model of a resourceful, self-assured, virtuosic jazz soloist.

As a child Hodges was given piano lessons, which he reputedly tried to avoid, turning instead to the drums. At age 13 or 14, he began teaching himself the soprano saxophone. When the great reed man Sidney Bechet played in Boston soon thereafter, Hodges's sister arranged for the two to meet. According to legend, Bechet promptly gave Hodges not only his first alto saxophone but also a series of lessons and a lifelong apprenticeship.

By his mid-teens Hodges was spending his weekends playing jazz in New York City. Through Bechet he had met Willie "the Lion" Smith, whose quartet he joined in 1924, and within four years Hodges had played in bands led by Smith, Bechet, and Chick Webb. In 1928 he left Webb to join Duke Ellington's band. For Ellington, Hodges played both alto and soprano saxophone as well as clarinet. He quickly became Ellington's most beloved soloist; his virtuosic range of expression inspired an English critic to say that "he seems to have an inexhaustible supply of ravishing melodic phrases in all moods and tempos."

Except for a four-year hiatus in the mid-1950s during which he led his own band, Hodges stayed with Ellington until his death. He also continued to record with smaller units, often with Ellington, as in the record "*Hodge Podge*." Hodges's work earned him recognition within the industry, and he was chosen best reed player ten times in a poll sponsored by *Down Beat* magazine. In addition to influencing the dozens of saxophonists who worked with him in Ellington's band, Hodges earned the admiration of bebop innovator Charlie Parker, who called him "the Poet." When Hodges died in 1970 Ellington, noting his "unique tonal personality," called the great saxophonist one of "the ever so few inimitables" of jazz.

Holiday, Billie

(b. April 17, 1915, Baltimore, Md.; d. July 17, 1959, New York, N.Y.), African American jazz singer who influenced the course of American popular singing.

Billie Holiday lived two irreconcilably different lives: one as a consummate jazz artist, one as an emotionally traumatized victim of abuse. Her singing has inspired generations of musicians, and she is one of a few women— along with Bessie Smith, Ella Fitzgerald, and Sarah Vaughan—to have attained the status of jazz legend. Jazz scholars treat her no less seriously than they do Louis Armstrong or Duke Ellington. Although Holiday had limited popular appeal during her lifetime, her impact on other singers was profound. In 1958 Frank Sinatra cited Holiday as "the greatest single musical influence on me" and "the most important influence on American popular singing in the last 20 years." On the other hand, Holiday's life story partakes of myth, for example, in the inaccuracies and exaggerations of her autobiography, *Lady Sings the Blues* (1959).

Holiday was also a profoundly tragic figure. Abandoned by her father, raised in poverty, and abused as a child, she claimed that she had become a prostitute by age 11. Throughout her life she remained barely literate, and she lacked self-esteem. Many of the men in her life victimized her and, when she was in her mid-twenties, one—trumpeter Joe Guy—introduced her to heroin. Holiday became addicted, and in 1947 she was imprisoned on narcotics charges.

In attempting to explain the power of Holiday's singing, musicologist Gunther Schuller bordered on the mystical. Her art, he wrote, "transcends the usual categorizations of style, content, and technique" and reaches "a realm that is not only beyond criticism but in the deepest sense inexplicable." Schuller underscored her "uncanny ability to go . . . beyond the song material [and to] . . . characterize it in whatever mood she happened to be in." Holiday linked her life and her singing. She said that it was easy to sing songs like "*The Man I Love*" or "*Porgy*" because, in her own words, "I've lived songs like that." Yet this sort of observation reinforces an unfortunate stereotype of jazz musicians as intuitive performers whose music simply mirrors their lives. Such an image—and the related theme of jazz artists as tortured and tragic figures—discounts the hard work and creative choices that go into jazz.

Although Holiday had no formal musical training, she pursued a far more demanding course of study in the late 1920s and early 1930s in such Harlem speakeasies as the Log Cabin, the Yeah Man, and the Hotcha. She worked hard to perfect her singing. Her 1933 recording debut—a novelty number titled "*Your Mother's Son-in-law*"—reveals a vocalist still not in command of her art, but two years later she secured a long-term contract with Columbia Records.

Between 1935 and 1942 Holiday recorded her greatest work, including "*I Must Have That Man*," "*I Cried for You*," and "*I'll Get By*." She also recorded her best-known original, "*God Bless the Child*." Swing-era stars such as pianist Teddy Wilson and alto saxophonists Benny Carter and Johnny Hodges supported her performances, but her key collaborators were Teddy Wilson and tenor saxophonist Lester Young. Wilson's elegant style contributes to the classic quality of these recordings, and Young was Holiday's musical soul mate. He was renowned for his lyrical improvisations, and together the two achieved a rare musical intimacy. Young gave Billie Holiday her nickname, Lady Day, and she dubbed him Prez, the president of the tenor saxophone, a nickname that also stuck.

Holiday gained a reputation as a racial activist, although she never sought that role. In 1938 she joined clarinetist Artie Shaw's white big band for several months, which placed her in the forefront of those who were challenging racial segregation in popular music. Her most political act was singing the anti-lynching ballad "*Strange Fruit*" (1939), which became her signature piece. Columbia Records refused to record the song because the company feared alienating white record buyers, but at last permitted her to record it for tiny Commodore Records.

Holiday's style was simple and finely crafted. It was partly dictated by the nature of her voice. She had a limited range, and she compressed her singing into little more than an octave. Unlike Bessie Smith, she could not fill a hall with her voice, so she perfected the art of singing with a microphone. Her small voice conveyed an intimacy that more powerful singers could rarely approach. She was also highly improvisational. Even in stating a theme, Holiday reinvented and simplified the song's melody. Unlike most singers of the day, she used very little vibrato, but she employed other vocal embellishments—shifts in rhythm, especially singing behind the beat, and variations in pitch, including dips, scoops, and fall-offs.

During her lifetime these qualities worked against her. She rarely got to record the most popular songs of the day. She sang with a subtlety that did not win her great popularity, and record companies reserved the best material for their best-selling singers. In addition, music publishers and successful songwriters opposed having her record their best songs because she changed the written melodies.

Throughout her life Holiday resented the limitations of the "blues singer" label, and she was greatly disappointed when Doubleday published her autobiography under the title *Lady Sings the Blues*. She had wanted to name it *Bitter Crop*, from the final words of *"Strange Fruit."* Holiday—like her musical alter ego Lester Young—faced serious difficulties during the 1950s. Although she and Young did not collaborate regularly in these years, their lives remained linked. Personal problems hampered their performing abilities, and Holiday's voice, in particular, revealed the ravages of her personal life. In 1957—on *The Sound of Jazz*, a television special—the two performed together in a moving rendition of *"Fine and Mellow"* that perfectly captured their vulnerability and their profound musical empathy. Holiday and Young died within four months of each other in 1959.

North America

Hooker, John Lee

(b. August 22, 1917, Clarksdale, Miss.), African American blues singer and guitarist.

John Lee Hooker's long blues career began at home, where he was influenced by his stepfather, a friend of such legendary bluesmen as Blind Lemon Jefferson and Charley Patton. Born in Mississippi, Hooker was playing and singing in Memphis nightclubs by the time he was a teenager.

In 1943 Hooker moved to Detroit, Michigan, where he worked in a factory and continued performing in clubs. Throughout the 1940s he made dozens of pseudonymous recordings for various small record labels. Influenced by the passionately expressive vocalists of the Mississippi Delta blues style, he integrated moans, groans, and howls into his more driving, electrified, urban blues sound.

Always a popular performer, Hooker sold a million records with *"Boogie Chillun"* (1948), and in the 1950s began working with a band, a departure from the traditional blues structure of one person with a guitar. In 1961 his song *"Boom Boom"* became a hit among teenagers—black and white—and helped bring a new audience to Hooker's urban blues. As the music historian Charles Kiel points out, Hooker helped popularize the blues by playing in settings—college campuses, jazz and folk festivals, and overseas venues—that were not usually frequented by bluesmen. As a result of his popularity and influence, Hooker was inducted into the Rock and Roll Hall of Fame in 1991.

North America

hooks, bell

(b. September 25, 1952, Hopkinsville, Ky.), African American feminist, critic, social activist, writer, and educator; one of the foremost African American public intellectuals.

Cited in *Booklist* as a "formidable feminist social and cultural critic," bell hooks is widely known for her pioneering and provocative scholarship on racism and sexism in the United States. A prolific essayist and the author of nearly 20 books, she has written on a range of issues, including feminist politics and the representation of race in film, television, and advertising.

In a 1995 interview with Carl Posey of *Essence* magazine, hooks affirmed that "fundamentally, my life is committed to revolutionary Black liberation struggle, and I don't ever see Black liberation and feminism as being separate." She has criticized both white, middle-class feminists and black liberation activists for neglecting women of color, and has encouraged African American women to "claim a critique of sexism" based on the black experience. Seeing class divisions among blacks as a principal obstacle to racial justice, in her 1996 book *Killing Rage: Ending Racism*, she wrote, "The ethic of liberal individualism has so deeply permeated the psyches of blacks . . . of all classes that we have little support for a political ethic of communalism that promotes the sharing of resources." She advocates coalitions between antiracist individuals, regardless of color and class, to counter what she has termed the "white supremacist capitalist patriarchy" of the United States.

Born Gloria Jean Watkins, bell hooks was one of seven children of Veodis Watkins, a janitor, and Rosa Bell Watkins, a domestic worker. hooks grew up in Hopkinsville, Kentucky, where her black schoolteachers approved of segregation and her family subscribed to rigid patriarchal values. Pivotal to her life was a violent quarrel she witnessed between her parents as a teenager, during which her father threatened her mother with a gun and temporarily forced her out of the family home. "When her heart broke, I felt mine breaking," wrote hooks of her mother in her memoir *Wounds of Passion* (1997). "Only unlike her I could not cry, I felt one of us had to be strong." An avid reader, hooks took refuge in poetry, learning to "enter these words as though they are flesh, a body of burning desire that can take me . . . through the pain and beyond." She also derived strength from the church women she knew, healers and preachers who, as she wrote in *Sisters of the Yam: Black Women and Self-Recovery* (1993), "worked with as much skill, power, and second sight as their black male comrades."

After high school, hooks left the South in search of a racially integrated environment where she could pursue her intellectual interests. In 1973 she graduated from Stanford University with a B.A. in English, and in 1983 she received her Ph.D., also in English, from the University of California at Santa Cruz. In 1981 she completed her first book—begun at age 19—*Ain't I a Woman: Black Women and Feminism*, a groundbreaking polemic on the dual impact of racism and sexism on African American women. For her writing projects she adopted the pseudonym bell hooks—using the lowercase spelling in an effort to emphasize the substance of her books rather than their author—after her maternal great grandmother, a Native American named Bell Hooks.

Although hooks has been critical of the "conservatizing function" of academia, she has taught at Yale University, Oberlin College, and, since 1994, the City College of New York. In 1996 she published her first memoir, *Bone Black: Memories of Girlhood*, praised by Donna Seaman of *Booklist* as a "lyrical, deeply moving, and brilliantly structured autobiography of perceptions and ideas."

Hopkins, ("Lightnin'") Sam

(b. March 15, 1912, Centerville, Texas; d. January 30, 1982), African American blues musician whose musical simplicity, lyrical originality, and colorful biography place him among the most respected and celebrated of his contemporaries.

As a child, Sam Hopkins met bluesman Blind Lemon Jefferson, whose talent as a performer inspired Hopkins to become a musician. During an adolescence that included cotton picking, gambling, and bootlegging, the young Hopkins developed his guitar playing by performing at parties, picnics, and saloons throughout Texas. Although he first collaborated with his cousin Alger "Texas" Alexander, he formed a duo with Wilson "Thunder" Smith in the mid-1940s after a talent scout directed Hopkins to Los Angeles. Hopkins became the "Lightnin'" to Smith's "Thunder" as the two recorded numerous sides on Aladdin Records.

Hopkins's lyrically improvisational music lent itself to solo performances, and he soon broke with Smith to develop further his freeform style. In the late 1940s and early 1950s he bounced from one label to the next, recording for whoever provided him money to support his wayward lifestyle. In the 1950s the ascendance of Chicago blues, which popularized electric ensembles, began to eclipse his career until white fans of folk discovered his apparently "authentic" share-cropper's sound. In 1959 he signed with Folkways Records and from then on held a position of high prestige with folk music audiences. He toured with white rock bands such as the Grateful Dead and appeared at Carnegie Hall in New York with folksingers Pete Seeger and Joan Baez.

In 1968 Hopkins became the subject of a documentary film, *The Blues According to Lightnin' Hopkins*, and in the next couple of years he recorded soundtrack music for the films *Blue Like Showers of Rain* and *Sounder*. Hopkins toured extensively throughout the 1970s and also recorded new albums. He again appeared at Carnegie Hall in 1979, was inducted into the Blues Foundation's Hall of Fame in 1980, and hardly slowed until his death from cancer in 1982.

Horne, Lena

(b. June 17, 1917, Brooklyn, N.Y.), African American singer and actress whose refusal to be cast in stereotypical roles helped transform the popular image of black women.

Lena Horne's father left home when she was only three, and her mother departed to pursue an acting career, leaving the child in the care of her paternal grandmother, a civil rights activist and suffragist in Brooklyn.

Horne's mother did return to take her daughter on tour with her. Eventually, her mother remarried and the family returned to New York, where Horne attended high school. But financial difficulties forced her to quit school and obtain a position as a chorus dancer at the Cotton Club in Harlem, New York. She was hired for her beauty, but she worked diligently to improve her singing by taking lessons, and she became known for her sultry voice. Horne then accepted a role on Broadway in *Dance with Your Gods* (1934) and afterward left the Cotton Club to sing with Noble Sissle's Society Orchestra in Philadelphia.

In Philadelphia she was reunited with her father, who subsequently played an important role in her life and career until his death in 1970. It was through her father that Horne met Louis Jones, whom she married in 1937. The couple had two children, Gail and Teddy, but divorced in 1941. Horne performed on Broadway in *Blackbirds* of 1939 and became lead singer in Charlie Barnett's band in 1940. In 1941 she was a featured performer at the Café Society Downtown, where she became acquainted with both the singer and civil rights activist Paul Robeson and Walter White, an important figure in the National Association for the Advancement of Colored People (NAACP).

Horne left New York to perform at the Trocadero Club in California. Within a short time, she signed a Hollywood movie contract with Metro-Goldwyn-Mayer. She insisted her contract stipulate that she would not be cast in stereotypical black roles, and with her elegance and glamour, she became known for transforming the image of the black woman in film. Her first role in 1942, like many that followed, was only a guest spot number in *Panama Hattie*, but the same year she played a leading part in *Cabin in the Sky*. In 1943 she was in three films: *I Dood It, Thousands Cheer*, and *Stormy Weather*, the title song of which became her trademark. It was on the set of *Stormy Weather* that Horne met Lennie Hayton. Though the couple married in 1947, the controversial interracial marriage was not publicly announced until 1950. She appeared in *Two Girls and a Sailor* (1944), *Broadway Rhythm* (1944), *Ziegfeld Follies* of 1945 and 1946, *The Duchess of Idaho* (1950) and *Meet Me in Las Vegas* (1956), her first speaking part. She also starred in the Broadway show *Jamaica* (1957) and appeared on several television shows in the 1950s.

Horne has won many honors for her performances. She won a Grammy for the album based on her award-winning show *Lena Horne: The Lady and Her Music*, which began in 1981 and became the longest running one-woman show in Broadway history. In addition to the Kennedy Center Award for Lifetime Achievement in the Arts (1984), Horne received an honorary doctorate from Howard University as well as an Image Award and Spingarn Medal from the NAACP.

North America

Houston, Whitney

(b. August 9, 1963, Newark, N.J.), African American singer, model, and film actress; one of the most successful musical performers in the United States.

Since the release of her debut album in 1985, Whitney Houston has enjoyed a meteoric musical career that has carried her into film stardom and made her an internationally recognized celebrity. With six albums, including three film soundtrack recordings, she continues to stun audiences with the power, range, and resilience of her voice. New York Times writer Stephen Holden has called her "the pop gospel equivalent of an Olympic athlete."

The youngest of three children, Houston grew up in East Orange, New Jersey, where her family settled after the Newark riots of 1967. Her mother, Emily "Cissy" Drinkard Houston, the lead singer of the soul group Sweet Inspirations, frequently brought young Whitney to the recording studios of some of the era's leading female gospel-turned-pop vocalists—Aretha Franklin and Whitney's cousins, Dee Dee and Dionne Warwick. Houston was particularly inspired by the emotional appeal of Franklin's voice and vowed early to do the same in her own singing. At age 12 Houston gave her first solo performance at Newark's New Hope Baptist Church. While in high school, she often performed with her mother in New York clubs and backed such singers as Lou Rawls and Chaka Khan. She also modeled for women's magazines such as *Vogue*, *Cosmopolitan*, and *Seventeen*.

In 1983 Houston met Arista Records founder Clive Davis, who signed her with Arista and proved instrumental in promoting her career. Houston's talent, coupled with a dynamic songwriting team that included Jermaine Jackson and composer Michael Masser, culminated in the record-setting 1985 album *Whitney Houston*, the sales of which topped all albums previously recorded by a black female vocalist. By 1995 Houston's first four albums had sold 66 million copies and won her myriad awards, including 12 American Music awards and five Grammy awards, three of which she received for the film soundtrack *The Bodyguard* in 1992.

In addition to singing, Houston has starred in several films, including *The Bodyguard* (1992), *Waiting to Exhale* (1995), and the *Preacher's Wife* (1996), in which she starred, opposite Denzel Washington, as a church gospel choir director.

North America

Howlin' Wolf (Chester Arthur Burnett)

(b. June 10, 1910, near West Point, Miss.; d. January 10, 1976, Hines, Ill.), blues musician who helped to import the rural music of the Mississippi River Delta to Chicago in the 1950s, thus making possible the creation of the new Chicago blues sound.

Howlin' Wolf was born Chester Arthur Burnett to plantation workers in Mississippi and as a youth worked in the fields himself. Throughout his childhood he was exposed to music from the Baptist church but did not take up the guitar until his teenage years. When Wolf was 18 he met bluesman Charley Patton, who instructed him in the rudiments of the genre. Another blues musician, Sonny Boy Williamson, whom Wolf knew as the husband of his half-sister, completed Wolf's education by teaching him to play the harmonica. During the 1920s and 1930s Wolf traveled the South, sometimes performing with blues veterans such as Robert Johnson, sometimes farming to support himself.

During World War II Wolf was drafted by the United States Army. When he returned from the service in 1945, he settled in West Memphis, Arkansas, where he started a band and secured work with local radio station KWEM. Wolf established himself as a charismatic disc jockey as well as a burgeoning blues star and caught the attention of promoter and musician Ike Turner, who encouraged producer Sam Phillips (later the owner of Sun Records) to record him. Phillips did, and sold the recordings to two different labels, Chicago-based Chess Records and the Bihari Brothers in California. The tremendous popularity of these recordings set the two companies at odds, and after legal negotiations, Wolf signed with Chess and moved to Chicago in 1953.

At Chess Records Wolf met bluesman and songwriter Willie Dixon, who composed many of Wolf's hits, including "*Back Door Man*," "*Little Red Rooster*," and "*I Ain't Superstitious*." Dixon meanwhile provided material for bluesman Muddy Waters, also of Chess Records, who became Wolf's local rival. Waters and Wolf—with the help of Dixon—at this time defined the Chicago Blues sound, each trying to outdo the other with rawness, intensity, and electric bravura. Wolf's performance style, which had always emulated Charley Patton's dramatic approach, became fully realized. He sang a harsh blend of gravelly bellows and falsetto howls, writhing on stage in the spirit of his music. In addition to Dixon's songs, Wolf popularized a number of his own compositions, including "*Smoke-stack Lightning*" and "*Killing Floor*."

Wolf's great popularity sustained him through the blues industry's lull during the late 1950s, and when British rock 'n' rollers such as the Rolling Stones and the Yardbirds began to popularize blues music among white listeners, Wolf experienced a resurgence of fame. He appeared with the Rolling Stones on the television show "*Shindig*," and toured Europe and America with the white groups who had appropriated his music. In the late 1960s he recorded *The London Howlin' Wolf Sessions*, joined by white guitarist Eric Clapton as well as members of the Rolling Stones and Ringo Starr of the Beatles.

In the 1970s Wolf scaled down his demanding tour schedule due to poor health. In the early 1970s he survived a heart attack and a car accident but kidney damage from the latter killed him in 1976. Wolf gave his last performance with bluesman B. B. King in November 1975. He was inducted into the Blues Foundation's Hall of Fame in 1980 and the Rock and Roll Hall of Fame in 1991.

North America

Hughes, Langston

(b. February 1, 1902, Joplin, Mo.; d. May 22, 1967, New York, N.Y.), African American writer known especially for his poetry and for his use of Black Vernacular English, black cultural references, and black musical rhythms in his writing.

The following passage from "Harlem," a poem by Langston Hughes, has been described as a "virtual anthem of black America":

What happens to a dream deferred?

> *Does it dry up*
> *like a raisin in the sun?*
> *Or fester like a sore—*
> *And then run?*
> *. . . Maybe it just sags*
> *like a heavy load.*
> *Or does it explode?*

As a poet, playwright, fiction writer, autobiographer, and anthologist, Hughes captured the moods and rhythms of the black communities he knew and loved—and translated those rhythms to the printed page. Hughes has been called "the literary explicator and interpreter of the social, cultural, spiritual, and emotional experiences of Black America," and this grand description is accurate for the role his writings have played in twentieth-century American literature.

Hughes was born in Joplin, Missouri, in 1902. His father, a lawyer frustrated by American racism, emigrated to Mexico when Hughes was a year old, and Hughes spent most of his childhood at his maternal grandmother's home in Lawrence, Kansas. His grandmother had been an activist for decades. Her first husband had been killed in the slave rebellion at Harpers Ferry; her second, Hughes's grandfather, was the brother of abolitionist John Mercer Langston and a participant in Kansas politics during Reconstruction. In his grandmother's home, Hughes was part of a close-knit black community, and he was always encouraged to read.

As a teenager Hughes lived with his mother in Lincoln, Illinois, and Cleveland, Ohio. In Cleveland he contributed to his high school literary magazine, was elected class poet his senior year, and graduated from high school in 1920. Hughes then spent a year in Mexico with his father. A poem he wrote on the train ride there, "The Negro Speaks of Rivers," was published in the June 1921 issue of *Crisis*, the official publication of the National Association for the Advancement of Colored People (NAACP). It is still perhaps his best-known poem, and it instantly confirmed his potential as a serious writer.

At his father's wish Hughes enrolled at Columbia University in New York in the fall of 1927, but he stayed only one year and spent most of his time in Harlem, in upper Manhattan. He took a series of jobs that included traveling down the West Coast of Africa and then to Europe as a crew member on a merchant steamer. Hughes continued writing poetry during his travels, publishing much of it back home in black journals such as *Crisis* and the National Urban League's *Opportunity*. By the time he returned to the United States in 1924, his reputation was already established. He won first prize in *Opportunity*'s 1925 poetry contest for his poem "The Weary Blues," and the following year Alfred A. Knopf published *The Weary Blues*, Hughes's first volume of poetry.

By this time Hughes was recognized as one of the leading figures in the constellation of black writers, artists, and musicians in New York who created the Harlem Renaissance. Hughes's poetry was greatly influenced by the people and culture around him. He admired the narrative style of poets Carl Sandburg and Walt Whitman, but was also influenced by Paul Laurence Dunbar's poems written in black dialect, and he incorporated the rhythms of black speech into many of his poems. Above all, Hughes was influenced by black music, especially jazz and blues.

Hughes's poems are often "lyrical" in the musical sense of the word—many of them could easily be set to a rhythmic beat. They also incorporate some of the same subject matter found in many blues lyrics, and portray nuances of black life—including sexuality—missing in earlier black literature. In a 1926 essay titled "The Negro Artist and the Racial Mountain," Hughes eloquently defended the honest representations of black culture and the use of jazz, dialect, and other influences from the black vernacular that had become a trademark in the work of many Harlem Renaissance writers. As Hughes put it, "We younger Negro artists who create now intend to express our individual dark-skinned selves without fear or shame."

Hughes enrolled in Lincoln University in Lincoln, Pennsylvania, in 1927, and graduated in 1929. The next year he published his first novel, *Not Without Laughter*. After an argument with a white patron who had been supporting him financially, Hughes spent time traveling, making extended visits to Haiti, Russia, and Carmel, California. He had begun publishing in the Communist Party-sponsored journal *New Masses* even before he left the United States and wrote some of his most politically radical poetry while in Russia.

In Carmel Hughes wrote his first collection of short stories, *The Ways of White Folks* (1934). He finished the decade with several successful plays, including *Mulatto*, loosely based on his grandfather's family, which opened on Broadway in 1935 and became the longest running Broadway play by an African American until Lorraine Hansberry's *A Raisin in the Sun* 25 years later.

In 1940 Hughes published his first autobiography, *The Big Sea*. In it he discusses his childhood, his estrangement from his father, and other personal topics, but readers especially value its insider's portrayal of the Harlem Renaissance. Two years later he began writing a weekly column for the *Chicago Defender* that unexpectedly spawned his most popular literary character, Jesse B. Semple. "Simple," as he was called, was a fictional Harlem resident who had little education but many street-smart opinions on everything from World War II to American race relations. Simple became a representative for the black Everyman, and over the next 20 years, in addition to his column, Hughes published five books and an off-Broadway play that featured Simple, who has been called "one of the more original comic creations in American journalism."

Hughes also published more poetry and plays in the 1940s, and as lyricist for the 1947 Broadway musical *Street Scene* he earned enough money to buy the Harlem home where he lived for the rest of his life. In 1951

Hughes published one of his most important poetry collections, *Montage of a Dream Deferred*, which contained such well-known works as "Harlem" and "Dream Boogie." During the 1950s Hughes published two more collections of short stories, another novel, several nonfiction works of children's literature, and his second autobiography, *I Wonder as I Wander* (1956).

In the 1960s Hughes wrote several successful Gospel plays, including *Black Nativity* (1961), which remains a holiday tradition in several cities, and *Jericho-Jim Crow* (1964), based on the Civil Rights Movement. He also published anthologies of poetry, short stories, and humor, and the book-length poem *Ask Your Mama* (1962). When he died on May 22, 1967, he was at work on a new collection of poetry celebrating the Civil Rights and Black Power movements, which was published later that year as *The Panther and the Lash*.

As a writer Hughes was prolific both in the genres he covered and the amount he produced, and he became the first African American author able to support himself completely by his writing. But his work was remarkable for much more than its quantity; Hughes's writing captured the essence of black America in a way black Americans felt it had not been captured before. As his biographer Arnold Rampersad said, "From the start, Hughes's art was responsive to the needs and emotions of the black world . . . . Arguably, Langston Hughes was black America's most original poet. Certainly he was black America's most representative writer and a significant figure in world literature in the twentieth century."

North America

Hunter, Alberta

(b. April 1, 1895, Memphis, Tenn.; d. October 17, 1984, New York, N.Y.), African American blues and cabaret singer, an early and enduring black recording star.

Alberta Hunter adapted her large and supple voice to a variety of musical styles and had one of the longest careers of any of the early female blues singers. She ran away from Memphis at age 11 to Chicago, hoping to work as a singer and send money to her mother. She became an immediate success, and as her reputation grew she appeared in nightclubs with such American jazz musicians as cornetist King Oliver and trumpet player Louis Armstrong. She also performed on Broadway, and in 1921 she made her first record. Hunter's best-known song was *"Down-hearted Blues"* (1922), which she wrote. In 1923 African American blues singer Bessie Smith recorded the song, which then became widely known.

In 1927 Hunter traveled to London, where she sang opposite African American singer Paul Robeson in the British premiere of the musical *Showboat*, by American composer Jerome Kern. Hunter subsequently sang in Holland, Denmark, and France, becoming the first singer to perform American blues music in Europe. During World War II (1939–1945) and the Korean War (1950–1953), she toured the world in military entertainment shows. In 1955, when her mother died, she retired from singing. She studied to be a nurse and later worked in hospitals in New York City. In

1977 Hunter's singing talent was rediscovered, and at age 82 she renewed her singing career and became famous once again.

North America

Hunter, Clementine Clemence Rubin

(b. December 1886, Clourtierville, La.; d. January 1, 1988, Melrose, La.), African American folk artist celebrated as the "Black Grandma Moses."

Clementine Hunter was born on a cotton plantation to Mary Antoinette Adams, a woman of Virginia slave ancestry, and Janvier (John) Reuben, a man of Native American and Irish descent. She moved with her family from Hidden Hill to Melrose Plantation (formerly Yucca), near Natchitoches, Louisiana, while she was in her early teens. She remained at Melrose, first as a cotton picker, then as the plantation cook until 1970.

Hunter had two children, Joseph and Cora, with Charles Dupree. Dupree died in 1914, and Hunter married Emanuel Hunter in 1924. She bore five more children: Mary, Agnes, King, and two who died at birth. A widow by 1944, Hunter died at age 101 a few miles from Melrose, having outlived all of her children.

Hunter became a folk artist celebrated for her paintings of familiar scenes of Southern life when she was already well into her fifties. Although she received very little formal education and remained illiterate throughout her life, she became known as the "Black Grandma Moses" for her depiction of black rural Southern life, specifically that of Cane River Settlement on Isle Breville, Louisiana. Her art, quilts, and paintings depicted religious themes, scenes of plantation work and relaxation, wildlife, and abstracts. Hunter was prolific up until her death, having completed approximately 5,000 paintings.

Hunter's first artistic medium was quilt making. Her earliest piece is a quilt from 1938 depicting the rigors of plantation life. Her first painting dates from 1939. Her work began to draw positive attention in the late 1940s and greater admiration still in the 1950s. In 1955 she became the first African American artist to have a solo exhibition at the Delgado Museum (now the New Orleans Museum of Art). By 1973 her work was being shown at the Museum of American Folk Art in New York, and by the time of her death, she was considered one of the century's leading folk artists.

North America

Hurston, Zora Neale

(b. January 7, 1891, Notasulga, Ala.; d. January 28, 1960, Fort Pierce, Fla.), African American writer and folklorist; author of *Their Eyes Were Watching God*, considered the first black feminist novel.

"I do not belong to the sobbing school of Negrohood who hold that nature somehow has given them a lowdown dirty deal and whose feelings are all hurt about it. Even in the helter-skelter skirmish that is my life, I have seen that the world is to the strong regardless of a little pigmentation more or less. No, I do not weep at the world—I am too busy sharpening my oyster knife."

This quotation from her essay "How It Feels to Be Colored Me" (1928) portrays Hurston's joyfully contrary view of herself in a world where being black was often perceived as a "problem" and portrayed that way even by black writers. Hurston considered her own blackness a gift and an opportunity. As an anthropologist and writer, she savored the richness of black culture and made a career out of writing about that culture in all its color and fullness. In the process she became a vibrant figure in the Harlem Renaissance and is now considered one of the defining authors of the African American literary tradition.

Hurston claimed to have been born in Eatonville, Florida, in either 1901 or 1910, but recent scholarship indicates that she was probably born in Alabama in 1891. She did, however, grow up in Eatonville, the first incorporated black town in the United States. Unlike many Southern towns, where African Americans lived under the constant specter of racial harassment or discrimination from their white neighbors, in Eatonville whites only passed through on the road to Orlando. Growing up in a town where she was surrounded by black culture and self-sufficient black people was fundamental to Hurston's work. It was to this organic African American community that she kept returning as an adult—literally, for her anthropological research on black folklore, and figuratively, in her novels and stories.

In her 1942 autobiography, *Dust Tracks on a Road*, Hurston recalled that in her family, her mother, who died when Hurston was 13, was the one who encouraged her to "jump at de sun." After her mother's death Hurston left home and school to work as a maid for a traveling theater company. Her further education came slowly and sporadically, and embarrassment over this probably led her to lie about her age. Hurston received a high school degree from Morgan Academy in Baltimore in 1918 and then took courses at Howard University intermittently until 1924. What was most likely her first published story, "John Redding Goes to Sea," appeared in *Stylus*, Howard's literary magazine, in 1921.

In 1925 Hurston moved to New York and soon became part of the convergence of African American writers, artists, and musicians in Harlem known as the Harlem Renaissance. She was an immediate success in Harlem literary circles: Alain Locke chose her short story "Spunk" for inclusion in his landmark 1925 anthology, *The New Negro*, and two of her pieces received awards from *Opportunity* magazine in May 1925.

Hurston received a scholarship to study anthropology at Barnard College, under then well-known Columbia University scholar Franz Boas. The only black student at Barnard, she received a B.A. in 1928 for research that focused on black folklore. She continued to write fiction, but in 1929 she also began a series of fieldwork trips to the American South, Haiti, and Jamaica to collect black folklore that formed the basis for much of her later writing. Hurston received Rosenwald and Guggenheim fellowships and private funding from a white patron to support her research. She wrote at least three books that focused exclusively on her findings: *Mules and Men* (1935), the first collection of black folklore by a black American; *Tell My Horse* (1938), materials on the religion Vodou gathered during travels to the Caribbean; and *The Florida Negro* (1938), which was funded by the Federal Writers' Project but never published.

Hurston's interest in black culture was also reflected in her fiction, which was often set in all-black communities and attempted to capture dialect and local life. She published four novels between 1934 and 1948, including what became her most famous work, *Their Eyes Were Watching God* (1938). But in the 1930s and 1940s Hurston's works were often considered anachronistic or offensive even by black audiences. Author Richard Wright accused her of portraying a "minstrel image" of African Americans—in contrast to more politically oriented books like his own *Native Son*.

Hurston also came under criticism from the African American community for some of her political beliefs. For example, her own positive experience within all-black communities made her an outspoken critic of integration. Many other African Americans have since come to agree with that view, but during Hurston's lifetime, black segregationists ran against the grain. And when she portrayed black characters not as victims of society, but as individuals who were as capable of succeeding and living and loving as anyone else, she was accused of being naïve and ignoring social realities.

By the 1940s Hurston's style was considered *passé* in the current literary scene, and she was no longer able to support herself as a writer. Largely forgotten, she returned to the South, and during the 1950s took a series of menial jobs while trying fruitlessly to find a publisher for several new works that she hoped to produce. On January 28, 1960, she died of a stroke in a Florida welfare home. She was buried in an unmarked grave.

In the 1970s Hurston's works underwent a dramatic literary renaissance, based largely on the power of *Their Eyes Were Watching God*. The story follows a black woman, Janie, through several black communities and several love rela-

Folklorist, anthropologist, and writer Zora Neale Hurston (1891-1960) is perhaps best known for her book *Their Eyes Were Watching God* (1938). *CORBIS*

tionships. Over the course of the novel, Janie comes to recognize and embrace her own identity. Long after *Their Eyes* had gone out of print, black women continued to circulate old paperback and xeroxed copies, and in the early 1970s Alice Walker published a widely read essay about Hurston and her work. *Their Eyes* was reprinted at the height of the women's movement, and black and white scholars alike embraced it as the first black feminist novel.

Since its rediscovery, *Their Eyes* has become one of the most frequently assigned novels on college campuses and one of the best-known works of African American literature. Moreover, Hurston's other books have been reprinted; scholar Robert Hemenway has written her biography; and Walker and other contemporary black women novelists freely acknowledge her influence on their work. A new generation of readers has been exposed to a writer who celebrated black culture and refused to portray blacks as victims; who saw the world as her oyster, and sharpened her knife.

I

Ice Cube (O'Shea Jackson)

(b. June 1969, Los Angeles, Calif.), African American rap artist, actor, and
music producer.

Musical artist Ice Cube was born and raised in South Central Los Angeles,
one of the nation's toughest inner-city neighborhoods; both of his parents
held jobs at the University of California at Los Angeles. Cube, as he is
known, composed his first rap, or metered, rhyming lyrics, in ninth-grade
typing class, and found that his music, which combined violent fantasies and
bawdy humor, was well received by peers. Within a few years he was rapping with a group, CIA, that performed at parties around South Central Los
Angeles. In the mid-1980s, along with fellow rappers Eazy E., Dr. Dre,
M.C. Ren, and DJ Yella, Cube formed the now-legendary group N.W.A.
(usually spelled out as Niggaz with Attitude), whose gritty messages of
anger and violence set them apart from the more politically minded East
Coast hip hop artists.

Cube left N.W.A. in 1987 to pursue a degree in architectural drafting at
the Phoenix Institute of Technology. After completing the one-year program, he returned to help with the production of N.W.A.'s seminal album,
Straight Outta Compton, which marked the explosive emergence of
"gangsta" rap, in which themes drew from life on the streets. After a bitter
falling-out with band manager Jerry Heller, Cube left the group, this time
heading to New York to collaborate with the Bomb Squad, producers for
Public Enemy.

The resulting album, *AmeriKKKa's Most Wanted* (1990), established
Cube as a menacing solo force. His lyrics, although more articulate and
intelligent than those of many rappers, were loaded with misogyny and
nihilism, and the album was sharply criticized by the press. Despite limited
radio and video play, the record went gold within its first two weeks of
release. Cube defended his own words, and the genre, by saying, "Rap is

the most positive thing for black kids because it gives information and talks about society, about black history." Cube used profits from his first album to form a multimedia corporation, through which he began producing records for other artists. In the same year, he received critical acclaim for his acting debut as a South Central gang leader in John Singleton's film *Boyz N the Hood*.

Cube's next album, *Death Certificate* (1991), expressed even more of his venomous rage, earning him the reputation of "America's angriest black man." His song *"No Vaseline"* lashed out against N.W.A.'s manager Heller as Cube defended himself against the group's accusations that he had betrayed them; the song was regarded as anti-Semitic. Another track, *"Black Korea,"* was interpreted as a call to Los Angeles blacks to burn Korean-owned grocery stores. In an unprecedented criticism, *Billboard Magazine* suggested that music stores "protest the sentiments" of the album. *Death Certificate* went platinum, and a year later, in the wake of the 1992 Los Angeles riots (in which many Korean-owned grocery stores were burned), Cube claimed to have delivered a prophetic message.

Following his conversion to the Nation of Islam, Cube released his most popular album, *The Predator* (1992), in which he aimed his lilting, aggressive rhymes at crumbling school systems and corrupt police. His next album, *Lethal Injection* (1993), was less popular, and he took a break from rapping to produce debut recordings by Da Lench Mob and Kam. In 1995 he reemerged, forming the group the Westside Connection.

Cube continued his acting career, appearing in 1995 in Singleton's *Higher Learning*. He also starred in the 1997 blockbuster thriller *Anaconda*, and he wrote, produced, and starred in *Friday*, a lighthearted look at two men spending a day in South Central Los Angeles.

North America

Ice-T (Morrow, Tracey)

(b. February 16, 1958, Newark, N.J.), African American rap singer, music producer, and actor.

One of the nation's most prolific and outspoken rap artists, Ice-T helped to pioneer the "gangsta" musical style, in which the turmoil of urban street life is exposed through blunt, explicit lyrics and a bass-heavy, fluid musical style.

Following the death of his parents in a car accident in 1968, Ice-T moved to South Central Los Angeles, where he attended high school. During this time he reportedly stole cars and wrote rhyming slogans for local street gangs. Ice-T took his name from Iceberg Slim, a local pimp who wrote novels and poetry and with whom Ice-T was personally acquainted. After high school Ice-T joined the army but returned to Los Angeles four years later, at which point he recorded *"The Coldest Rap"* on a local label to launch his musical career.

In 1984 Ice-T's first recording on a major label appeared, on the sound-tracks for the low-budget hip hop films *Breakin'* and *Breakin' 2: Electric Boogaloo*, in which he also acted. A year later he formed his own record company, Rhyme Syndicate Productions, before signing with Warner Brothers in 1986. His first album, *Rhyme Pays* (1987), was the first ever to be voluntarily labeled with a warning about potentially offensive lyrics, but neither the warning nor mixed reviews hindered the success of the album, which sold more than 500,000 copies. Ice-T wrote and performed the title song for the film *Colors* (1987), which ensured his long-term popularity.

Ice-T's next album, *Power* (1988), included themes about death and street life, and thus anticipated the emergence of "gangsta" rap. The following year, he released the album *The Iceberg/Freedom of Speech . . . Just Watch What You Say* as a political commentary on hip hop censorship. In 1992 Ice-T released *Body Count*, recorded with his heavy-metal band of the same name. It featured the song *"Cop Killer,"* which was cited by President George Bush and Vice President Dan Quayle as an incendiary threat to law-enforcement officials. While no police were harmed as a result of the song, Ice-T voluntarily pulled *"Cop Killer"* from the album.

Despite these sporadic "bad boy" episodes, Ice-T has become a major spokesperson for rap music. He has worked to change the problems he sings about: in 1988 he released an anti-gang video, and he later testified before a United States Congressional Committee about the gang problem in South Central Los Angeles. He has toured the nation's college campuses speaking about censorship and promoting anti-drug and anti-violence campaigns.

Other highlights from Ice-T's musical career include his collaboration with Quincy Jones on the album *Back on the Block* (1990), which earned him a Grammy Award; and the release of *OG: Original Gangster* (1991), which is frequently hailed as his finest album. His later efforts, including *Return of the Real* (1996), have received mixed popular and critical acclaim.

In addition to his music career, Ice-T has appeared in several films, including *New Jack City* (1991), *Ricochet* (1991), *Trespass* (1993), and *Tank Girl* (1995). He has also written a book, *The Ice Opinion* (1994), in which he expresses his views on music, love, religion, and politics.

North America

Ink Spots, The,

African American quartet famous for vocal harmonies that helped lay the foundations for doo-wop, rhythm and blues, and rock 'n' roll music.

Four porters at New York's Paramount Theater formed the Ink Spots in 1934. The group's career peaked in the 1940s but continued, with changes in membership, until the 1970s. The original lineup consisted of bass Orville "Hoppy" Jones, baritone Ivory "Deek" Watson, and tenors Slim Greene and Charlie Fuqua. Greene died shortly after the group's debut and tenor Jerry Daniels replaced him. The Ink Spots' first recording, *"Swingin' on the Strings"* (Victor Records, 1935), featured upbeat, walking-bass, scat-rich music reminiscent of the Mills Brothers. Bill Kenny succeeded Jerry Daniels in 1939 and it was then that the Ink Spots developed their ground-breaking sound. Kenny's sterling tenor lead vocal was backed by sparse and languid arrangements. Watson added lyricless lower-register harmonies and Jones provided spoken, bassy recapitulations of the lyrics of the song. A whole lineage of popular musicians, most notably Elvis Presley, imitated this effect. Many more imitated the Ink Spots' innovation of a guitar-riff intro-duction to a song.

Success for the group started in England, and transatlantic broadcasts of their concerts in Great Britain bolstered their following back home. The Ink Spots' first big hit in the United States was their recording *"If I Didn't Care."* Other songs that gained wide popularity included *"We Three (My Echo, My Shadow, and Me),"* *"Maybe,"* *"Java Jive,"* and *"I Don't Want to Set the World on Fire."* The group recorded with Ella Fitzgerald in the mid-1940s, appeared in the films *The Great American Radio Broadcast* (1941) and *Pardon My Sarong* (1942), and entertained American forces at home and in Europe during World War II. In 1952 Fuqua and Kenny split, each taking the Ink Spots name for his new ensemble. A third group, led by Stanley Morgan, also adopted the name, which led to a number of pro-tracted lawsuits.

The Ink Spots remained active as a nostalgia act for more than two decades. Kenny, the last original member, died in 1978, and the charter group was inducted into the Rock and Roll Hall of Fame in 1989.

North America
Isley Brothers,
an African American pop music group whose career has spanned five decades, evolving from 1960s soul to 1970s funk to 1980s pop.

As teenagers, O'Kelly, Ronald, and Rudolf Isley sang gospel music with another brother, Vernon, until he died in a car accident in 1954. In 1956 the three remaining brothers moved from their home in Cincinnati, Ohio, to New York City and struggled to establish themselves as an act. They released a series of unsuccessful singles on small New York labels before appearing at the Apollo Theater in Harlem and signing a contract with RCA Victor Records.

The Isley Brothers first reached a large audience in 1959 with *"Shout,"* a soul music single that reflected the call-and-response style of gospel music as well as the Isleys' signature vocal style—O'Kelly and Rudolf backing Ronald's tenor lead. After an album with RCA the Isley Brothers switched to Atlantic and then Wand Records, a subsidiary of Scepter, with whom they released their second big hit, *"Twist and Shout"* (1962).

"Twist and Shout" was pure rhythm and blues (R&B), and for the rest of the 1960s the Isleys recorded in this vein. Under pressure from Wand

Records, they released insipid rewrites of *"Twist and Shout"* (such as *"Surf and Shout"*) until they started their own label, T-Neck, in 1964. At that time few African American musicians controlled the production of their own music, and in the face of the high-budget competition of white companies, the venture floundered financially. T-Neck records was precocious in another way, capturing the early guitar innovations of Jimi Hendrix, who backed the Isleys during the mid-1960s.

The Isley Brothers signed with Motown Records in 1965 and quickly sent *"This Old Heart of Mine"* up the R&B charts. By the end of the decade, however, they were prepared to change with the times. They replaced mole-hair suits with hipper fashions, and began writing songs that reflected the influence of James Brown and funk. The change in style was coupled with a change in roster when younger brothers Ernie and Marvin and cousin Chris Jasper joined the group. During the 1970s the Isley Brothers achieved the height of their success, combining dance rhythms with politically charged lyrics in songs such as *"Fight the Power"* (1975) and *"Harvest for the World"* (1976).

As the group's success waned in the early 1980s, the latecomers left to form their own group, Isley, Jasper, Isley. The charter members continued to record and perform until O'Kelly died of a heart attack in 1986. Thereafter Angela Wimbush, who later married Ronald, wrote and produced most of the duo's music. The Isley Brothers continued recording into the 1990s, having influenced popular music throughout the previous four decades. In 1992 they were inducted into the Rock and Roll Hall of Fame.

J

Jack and Jill of America,

an American nonprofit philanthropic organization founded in 1938 as a play group for the children of Philadelphia's African American professional elite.

Jack and Jill was born during the Great Depression and grew out of the voluntary community work of upper-class African American women in Philadelphia, Pennsylvania, who wanted their children to have cultural opportunities, develop leadership skills, and form social networks in the midst of segregation.

By 1968 Jack and Jill had become a full-fledged national organization, and the first founded by African American women. It continues to sponsor educational, health, and cultural projects in inner-city neighborhoods. Jack and Jill publishes a national journal, *Up the Hill*, and has 187 local chapters in the United States.

Jackson, George Lester

(b. September 23, 1941, Chicago, Ill.; d. August 21, 1971, San Quentin Prison, Calif.), African American anti-capitalist revolutionary whose prison writings served as a manifesto for New Left activists in the 1970s.

George Jackson grew up on the West Side of Chicago, the son of Lester Jackson, a postal worker, and Georgia Jackson. He was the second oldest of five children. Street smart and rebellious, Jackson had several run-ins with the law for petty crimes by the time he was ten. In 1956 his family moved to Los Angeles, where Jackson's troubles with the law continued, including several arrests for robbery. Paroled in June 1960 after serving time for a gas station holdup, Jackson was arrested later that year for a gas station robbery that netted $71. Due to his previous convictions, he received an indeterminate sentence of one year to life. He was 19 and remained in prison for the rest of his life.

While in prison, Jackson studied the writings of Karl Marx, Frantz Fanon, Mao Zedong, Fidel Castro, and others. He developed a critique of capitalism and racism that enabled him to see his criminal activity and his imprisonment within a political context. Jackson and several others organized study groups to help raise the political consciousness of African American prisoners. Jackson, who worked as a prison organizer for the Black Panther Party, aimed to channel the anger and rebellious spirit of African Americans toward political activism. His revolutionary philosophy cohered around a program of armed struggle directed at overthrowing the racist and imperialist establishment in the United States.

Over the years Jackson was repeatedly denied parole. Prison officials said that it was because of Jackson's disruptive behavior; Jackson and his supporters argued that it was due to his political activism.

On January 16, 1970, in response to the death of three black inmates, a white guard, John Mills, was killed in Soledad Prison. Jackson and two other black men, John Clutchette and Fleeta Drumgo, were accused of the murder. The facts of their alleged involvement have never been satisfactorily established. The three accused men became known as the Soledad Brothers and attracted international attention. *Soledad Brother: The Prison Letters of George Jackson* was published during this time and became a national bestseller. Many people protested that the Soledad Brothers were being framed due to their political activities. Angela Davis played a leading role in organizing support for their defense.

The trial dissolved into complete chaos on August 7, 1970, when Jonathon Jackson, younger brother of George, attempted to take over the courthouse and free the three accused. During the melee, Jonathon was shot to death, along with the judge and two of the inmates. A little more than a year later, on August 21, 1971, prison guards killed George Jackson. The official report said that Jackson was armed, that he had participated in a revolt, killing two white prisoners and three guards, and that he was attempting to escape. Supporters have noted several inconsistencies in the report and believe that prison authorities, fearful that Jackson had grown too powerful, set him up and murdered him.

North America

Jackson, Mahalia

(b. October 26, 1911, New Orleans, La.; d. January 27, 1972, Chicago, Ill.), African American gospel singer who fused the varied musical traditions of New Orleans to become known as the "World's Greatest Gospel Singer."

Mahalia Jackson's father, John Jackson, worked on the New Orleans docks during the week and preached the gospel on Sundays. Her mother, Charity Clark, died at 25, four years after Jackson's birth. At her mother's death, Jackson moved in with her mother's sisters and began singing at Plymouth

Rock Baptist Church. Later, she sang in Mount Moriah Baptist Church and in several other neighborhood churches.

In addition to singing traditional church hymns on Sundays, Jackson was exposed to the blues and jazz heard constantly in the streets of New Orleans. Musicians like Joseph "King" Oliver played on the bandwagons in her neighborhood and in the dance halls she frequented as a child. Although jazz bands were ever present, the two most profound influences on the young woman were blues singer Bessie Smith and the music of the sanctified church. She heard Smith's "*Careless Love*" and was instantly impressed by the down-home moans and shouts. Although Jackson refused to sing the blues because it was "the devil's music," Smith's contribution to Jackson's gospel style is unmistakable.

As a child Jackson lived next door to a sanctified church. She never converted to the Holiness Movement, but she was inspired by the joyous and spirited singing. The beat and bodily expression of the sanctified congregation stayed with Jackson throughout her career. She was frequently criticized for being crude and unsophisticated because of her hand-clapping and swaying, but she would always respond with Scripture. "As David said in the Bible, 'Make a joyful noise unto the Lord.'"

In 1927 Jackson moved to Chicago to live with her aunt, Hannah Robinson. She supported herself by working as a maid and laundress but continued singing in the choir at the Greater Salem Baptist Church. Jackson also studied beauty culture at C.J. Walker's and at the Scott Institute of Beauty Culture, eventually opening Mahalia's Beauty Salon. This was the first of several independent business ventures, which also included a florist shop and a chain of fried chicken restaurants. It did not take long for the choir director to recognize Jackson's talent, and she soon became the church's primary soloist. Together with the sons of the pastor of Greater Salem, Robert, Prince, and Wilbur Johnson, along with Louise Barry Lemon, Jackson formed the gospel quintet the Johnson Gospel Singers. At the time their style was very modern, with Prince Johnson playing a boogie-woogie piano patterned after Thomas A. Dorsey. The group supported itself by touring the local storefront churches and asking for donations at the end of its performances. By 1935 the group had broken up and its members were pursuing solo careers.

Jackson married Isaac Hackenhull in 1936. The marriage was strained from the beginning because Hackenhull, a graduate of Fisk and Tuskegee universities, wanted Jackson to take advantage of the financial opportunities available to jazz and blues singers. He convinced her to audition for *The Hot Mikado*, a jazz version of the Gilbert and Sullivan operetta. Although she got the lead by singing "*Sometimes I Feel like a Motherless Child*," she refused to participate in the show. Hackenhull did not understand Jackson's religious commitments, and Jackson did not approve of Hackenhull's gambling. These conflicts led to their divorce.

By the late 1930s Jackson had begun to garner some regional popularity. In 1937 she recorded her first 78 for Decca Records, which included "*God's Gonna Separate the Wheat from the Tares*," an adaptation of a New Orleans funeral song; the Baptist hymn "*Keep Me Every Day*"; and a modern gospel piece, "*God Shall Wipe All the Tears Away*." The record was a minor hit in the South and demonstrated Jackson's potential, but she did not record again until 1946. In the meantime she teamed up with Thomas A. Dorsey, the pianist, composer, and "father of Gospel Revival." Together they toured the country, Jackson's powerful contralto convincing congregations to purchase Dorsey's musical compositions. Jackson brought her enormous range of expression to Dorsey's gospel blues, providing the perfect medium for Dorsey's combination of Baptist hymns and gutbucket blues. As collaborators, they ushered in the era of modern African American gospel music.

A testament to the promotion of Jackson and Dorsey was her first recording for the Apollo label. The song, "*Move On Up a Little Higher*," sold more than 8 million copies. At once, Jackson's commercial viability and that of gospel music in general were established. From this point on she was the superstar of gospel music. Her talent and versatility were unequaled; her voice was comfortable and powerful whether singing a raucous blues growl or a sweet soulful ballad. Jackson recorded more than 30 albums in her career, including 12 million-selling singles.

By the early 1950s Jackson began to appeal to white fans with the help of Studs Terkel, who featured her music on his radio program. In 1951 she headlined a night of gospel stars that sold out New York's Carnegie Hall. She received the French Academy Award in 1953, prompting a European tour that established her as an international musical celebrity. She also appeared on the television shows of Dinah Shore and Ed Sullivan and hosted her own show on CBS from 1954 to 1955. At the 1958 Newport Jazz Festival, she received a standing ovation from the audience of jazz enthusiasts.

During the 1960s Jackson supported Martin Luther King Jr. and the Civil Rights Movement by singing "*We Shall Overcome*" during her performances. She also preceded King at the March on Washington in 1963 with a rendition of "*I've Been 'Buked and I've Been Scorned*." At King's funeral in 1968 Mahalia sang his last request, the Dorsey standard "*Precious Lord, Take My Hand*." Politically, Jackson became close to Mayor Richard Daley of Chicago and the Kennedy family. She sang at John F. Kennedy's inauguration in 1961. After the assassinations of King and John and Robert Kennedy, Jackson no longer took part in politics. Her philanthropy continued and she established the Mahalia Jackson Scholarship Fund. She died of a heart attack in 1972.

North America

Jackson, Michael, and the Jackson Family,
superstar singer and his musical siblings, who together form the preeminent family of pop music in the 1970s, 1980s, and 1990s.

Joseph and Katherine Jackson, a working-class couple from Gary, Indiana, produced nine children, all of whom displayed considerable musical talent.

Joseph encouraged his three eldest sons, Sigmund "Jackie" (b. May 4, 1951), Toriano "Tito" (b. October 15, 1953), and Jermaine (b. December 11, 1954) to practice the guitar and write songs. In the early 1960s the boys formed a trio that precocious youngsters Marlon (b. March 12, 1957) and Michael (b. August 29, 1958) joined, creating the Jackson Five. Although he was the youngest, Michael quickly became the focus of the act, deftly imitating the mannerisms of James Brown while singing with a sophistication and maturity that belied his young age.

The brothers won a talent contest in 1965 that led to a recording contract with the Indiana-based Steeltown Records. Then the Jackson Five toured regionally, opening for larger-name rhythm and blues (R&B) groups. In 1967 the brothers took first place at an amateur night at Harlem's legendary Apollo Theater, and in 1969 they signed a recording contract with Motown Records.

That year the Jackson family moved to Los Angeles, where Motown founder Berry Gordy carefully cultivated the image of the Jackson Five. Motown Records dressed the group in extravagant, hip outfits, choreographed their elaborate dance numbers, and provided them with musical material. The Jackson Five achieved success almost instantly, scoring number-one hit-singles with their first four releases: "I Want You Back" (1969), "ABC" (1970), "The Love You Save" (1970), and "I'll Be There" (1970).

In 1971, in response to MGM Records' solo recordings of 13-year-old Donny Osmond, Motown launched solo careers for Michael, Jermaine, and Jackie. Although Jermaine scored a Top Ten hit with "Daddy's Home" (1972), Michael was far and away the most successful of the three. His early solo hits include "Got to Be There" (1971) and "Rockin' Robin" (1972), as well as "Ben" (1972), an unlikely number-one soundtrack hit about a boy and his pet rat.

Meanwhile, the Jackson Five continued recording and performing as a group, and by the mid-1970s they had forsaken Motown's songwriters to produce and record hits of their own. They also covered classic pop and R&B songs from the 1950s and abandoned their earlier soul arrangements for the harder sounds of funk. In 1975, when their contract expired with Motown, four of the five brothers switched to Epic Records. Jermaine, who had married Berry Gordy's daughter, stayed with the old label to pursue a solo career. Steven "Randy" Jackson (b. October 29, 1962) replaced Jermaine, and the new group assumed a new name, the Jacksons. In 1976 and 1977 they starred in a self-titled CBS variety show, which introduced the Jackson girls Maureen "Rebbie" (b. May 29, 1950), LaToya (b. May 29, 1956), and Janet (b. May 16, 1966) to popular audiences. In 1978 the Jacksons released the album Destiny, which many fans and critics consider the best of the Jackson brothers' later work.

Michael's success as a solo performer continued with his appearance as the Scarecrow in The Wiz (1978), an African American remake of The Wizard of Oz. The movie led to his partnership with Quincy Jones, who composed the soundtrack, including Jackson's duet with Diana Ross, "Ease

On Down the Road." Later that year Jones and Jackson collaborated on *Off the Wall* (1979), the solo album that established Michael as a sophisticated adult pop star. *Off the Wall* sold more than 7 million copies and included four Top Ten songs, including the number-one hits *"Don't Stop 'til You Get Enough,"* and *"Rock With You."* Although Michael continued to perform with his brothers, this album signaled the beginning of a solo career that eclipsed the celebrity of the other Jackson children.

In 1982 Michael released another Jones-produced album, *Thriller,* which became the best-selling pop album of all time. *Thriller* incorporated the hoary oration of Vincent Price, the hard-rock licks of Eddie Van Halen, and the cooing of Paul McCartney, as well as the R&B, soul, and disco influences of Jackson himself. More than 40 million people bought the album, whose seven chart-topping singles included the number-one hits *"The Girl Is Mine,"* *"Billie Jean,"* and *"Beat It."* *Thriller* was a black landmark in the white-dominated market because Jackson's videos were the first by an African American to receive regularly scheduled rotation on MTV. The success of the album was bolstered by a well-planned marketing campaign that highlighted Jackson's dancing, fashion, musicianship, and commercial endorsement of Pepsi-Cola.

Although Jackson achieved this success as a solo performer, he continued to perform with his family throughout the 1980s. He also collaborated with Lionel Richie on the humanitarian hit *"We Are the World"* (1985), though he did not release a follow-up to *Thriller* until *Bad* (1987). Both *Bad* and Jackson's subsequent release, *Dangerous* (1991), sold well by standards of the industry, yet poorly in comparison to the global success of Thriller.

In the late 1980s and the 1990s Michael appeared to have increasing difficulty coping with celebrity, often withdrawing from the public eye. Numerous bouts of plastic surgery, allegations of pedophilia, and a secret marriage and publicized divorce with Lisa Marie Presley all exacerbated his public image as a troubled person. Despite high-visibility appearances on the *Oprah Winfrey Show* in 1993 (estimated 90 million viewers) and *Prime Time Live* in 1995 (estimated 60 million viewers), Jackson's career was considered in decline. His poorly selling 1995 album *HIStory—Past, Present and Future, Book I,* which anthologized old hits with new material, only seemed to underscore his waning popularity.

Michael's sister Janet achieved greater celebrity as Michael lost popularity. Although she had appeared in television programs in the 1970s and released her first solo album in 1982, Janet Jackson did not win considerable public attention until her quadruple-platinum album *Control* (1986). With Janet Jackson's *Rhythm Nation 1814* (1989), she topped the charts, won a Grammy, and sold more than 8 million records. She persevered as a major name in 1990s pop, scoring hit albums with *Janet* (1993) and *The Velvet Rope* (1997).

None of the other Jacksons approached Michael's or Janet's level of success, although LaToya released solo albums in the early 1980s and appeared in *Playboy* magazine, and Jermaine recorded throughout the 1980s, working with Pia Zadora as well as with Whitney Houston. Taken collectively, however, the Jackson family's career, spanning three decades, was the biggest pop-music phenomenon of the late twentieth century.

Jacobs, Harriet Ann

(b. 1813?, Edenton, N.C.; d. March 7, 1897, Washington, D.C.), African American writer known especially for her autobiography, which is the most significant African American slave narrative by a woman.

Harriet Jacobs states in the preface to her autobiography, *Incidents in the Life of a Slave Girl, Written by Herself,* published under the pseudonym Linda Brent in 1861, that she wanted her story to "arouse the women of the North to a realizing sense of the condition of millions of women at the South, still in bondage, suffering what I suffered." In this statement, which stresses her appeal to a female audience, Jacobs touches on one of her autobiography's most important features: Jacobs is the only African American woman slave to leave a long and detailed record of the particular ways in which slavery affected women, from sexual abuse to constraints on motherhood. For most of the twentieth century, however, scholars thought her narrative was a novel by a white author and ignored the book. It was not until the 1980s, when literary historian Jean Fagan Yellin used letters and manuscripts to prove that Jacobs had indeed written her autobiography "by herself," that readers rediscovered Jacobs as a key early African American writer.

Jacobs lived with her parents and younger brother until her mother's death, when Jacobs was six. She then was sent to live with her mother's owner, Margaret Horniblow, who treated her well and taught her to read and write. At her death, however, she willed Jacobs to her three-year-old niece, Mary Matilda Norcom, and at age 12 Jacobs was sent to live with the Norcom family. Her time with the Norcoms is a large part of her autobiography—especially the sexual harrassment she received from Dr. Norcom, the evil "Dr. Flint" in her narrative. Jacobs's narrative is very frank about Norcom's frequent sexual advances and threats, and makes explicit the particular hazards slave women faced, which are often only alluded to in men's slave narratives.

In 1829 and 1833 Jacobs gave birth to Joseph and Louisa Matilda, whose father was a white neighbor. This relationship only angered Norcom, and when he began to use her children, who were legally his property, as another means of controlling her, Jacobs decided to take a chance on running away. She hoped that if she was gone Norcom might sell her children to their father, and so in 1835 she ran away from the Norcom household.

Jacobs was first hidden in several Edenton homes by sympathetic black and white neighbors. But when it became apparent that it was going to be difficult for her to leave Edenton undetected, family members constructed a secret crawlspace in the house that belonged to her grandmother, who was free. The crawlspace was nine feet long, seven feet wide, and at its tallest, three feet high—but Jacobs hid in the tiny enclosure for the next seven years, a fact so harrowing that it may have been what led historians to suspect her autobiography was fictional.

In 1842 Jacobs was finally able to escape to New York. There she was reunited with her children, who had indeed been purchased by their father and sent to the North. In New York Jacobs worked as a nursemaid for a white family and became active in the antislavery movement. In 1850 her freedom was threatened when the Fugitive Slave Law stated that runaway slaves could and must be returned to their owners if apprehended in any part of the United States. The Norcom family sent agents to New York who attempted to kidnap her from her employers' home. Her employer finally secured her legal freedom by purchasing her from the Norcoms and emancipating her in 1853. That same year Jacobs began writing her autobiography, which she worked on at night after her childcare duties were done. The book was edited by white abolitionist Lydia Maria Child and received good reviews in the antislavery press when it was published in March 1861. But the outbreak of the Civil War one month later quickly stole readers' attention away.

During the war Jacobs and her daughter, Louisa, worked in the relief efforts for African American soldiers and newly freed slaves, first in Alexandria, Virginia, then in Savannah, Georgia. Increased violence and racial tension in the postwar South led them to Cambridge, Massachusetts, where Jacobs served as clerk of the New England Women's Club and ran a boarding house for Harvard University students and faculty. But by 1877, Jacobs and Louisa had returned to Washington, D.C., where Jacobs continued to work among the freed slaves while Louisa taught at several schools, including Howard University. Jacobs lived with her daughter in Washington, D.C., until her death on March 7, 1897.

Since its rediscovery, Jacobs's autobiography has become required reading in English, history, African American studies, and women's studies courses around the country. In her narrative, Jacobs stated that she hoped to "add [her] testimony to that of abler pens to convince the people of the Free States what Slavery really is." The book she wrote is now recognized as one of the most valuable testimonies on what slavery really was, especially for the black women who endured it.

North America

James, Etta (Jamesetta Hawkins)

(b. January 5, 1938, Los Angeles, Calif.), African American soul and rhythm and blues (R&B) singer.

Raised in California, Etta James—Jamesetta Hawkins at birth—began her singing career early. At age 5, she was the star of her church choir; by 14 she was singing professionally with a rhythm and blues band. In 1954 James recorded her first song, *"Roll with Me Henry,"* a joking response to Hank Ballard and the Midnighters' ribald hit *"Work with Me Annie."* *"Henry"* was itself sexually suggestive enough to be banned by radio disc jockeys.

Throughout the late 1950s James recorded for Modern Records, producing the 1955 hit *"Good Rockin' Daddy"* and a series of less successful songs. In 1960 she signed with Chess Records, where she blossomed into a fully formed talent. Songs like *"All I Could Do Was Cry"* (1960) showed how her passionate, powerful voice could caress a ballad. Lighter, more pop-oriented numbers like *"Pushover"* (1963) also became hits.

James's drug addiction caused her to quit and resume recording periodically in the 1960s and 1970s, but she produced some of her best work during her healthy intervals in these decades. In 1967 she scored another series of hits, recorded at the legendary Muscle Shoals studio, which included *"Tell Mama"* and a remake of Otis Redding's *"Security."* After beating her heroin addiction in the mid-1970s, James returned to the music scene, recording and touring steadily. In 1993 she was elected to the Rock and Roll Hall of Fame.

North America

Jazz,

a twentieth-century African American music characterized by improvisation, a rhythmic conception termed swing, and the high value placed on each musician achieving a uniquely identifiable sound. Jazz musicians have consistently challenged musical boundaries and played leading roles in challenging racial discrimination.

Jazz is one of the crowning achievements of African American culture. It is a profoundly integrative genre, both musically and socially. Drawing on earlier traditions of New Orleans marching bands and ragtime-influenced society orchestras, jazz has continued to incorporate new musical influences, including the blues, gospel music, Latin American music, European art music, and rock 'n' roll. African Americans have accounted for every significant musical advance in jazz, but the music has been open to all, regardless of race or nationality. During the first half of the twentieth century—a time of pervasive racial discrimination in the United States—jazz was strikingly democratic. Although far from perfect, the jazz world was remarkably successful in challenging racial segregation.

Jazz also reflects a continuing tension between individual freedom and group structure, as seen in the shifting emphasis between the spontaneously improvising soloist, on the one hand, and composed and arranged ensemble music, on the other. Successive jazz styles—including New Orleans, swing, bop, cool, hard bop, free jazz, jazz-rock, and neo-traditionalism—have, to a considerable extent, reflected an increase in musical complexity, both in the playing of individual soloists and in the work of composers and arrangers. Jazz historians often liken the twentieth-century evolution of jazz to the changes that took place in European classical music—from eighteenth-century Bach inventions to Schönberg's 12-tone music of the twentieth century.

Although the historical development of jazz is often seen as a straight-forward evolutionary process, it was complex and was powerfully influenced by the unique contributions of major innovators. A small number of creative and charismatic individuals were responsible for profound transformations in the music, most notably Louis Armstrong, Duke Ellington, Charlie Parker, Dizzy Gillespie, Miles Davis, John Coltrane, and Wynton Marsalis. The rapid dissemination of their new musical ideas suggests that, to a large extent, jazz musicians share a common artistic conception.

Over the course of the century jazz remained a dynamic tradition that profoundly influenced America and the world. Three characteristics have distinguished jazz throughout its history: (1) improvisation; (2) a distinctive rhythmic approach known as swing; and (3) an expectation that each jazz musician should attain a unique, individual sound through his or her distinctive improvisational approach to harmony, melody, and rhythm, and often through intentional variations or distortions of tone and timbre. The instrumental colorings and complex harmonies of jazz are evident in popular music and film scores heard by millions of people. Perhaps even more than African American literature or popular music—including the recent and pervasive genre of rap—jazz has changed the cultural inflections of a great portion of the world.

New Orleans and the Origins of Jazz

Jazz emerged in New Orleans around the turn of the twentieth century. New Orleans is distinctive among American cities for its French and

Jazz trumpeter Papa Celestin plays for his young grandson on the front porch of his house in New Orleans, Louisiana. *CORBIS/Bradley Smith*

Spanish colonial origins. As jazz historian James Lincoln Collier noted, it was "the most musical American city." Until the mid-1850s African-derived drum playing and dancing took place regularly in New Orleans's Congo Square. The city's population was diverse, combining French, Spanish, Caribbean, Anglo-American, Irish, German, and African elements.

Among African Americans the most significant division was between the poorer blacks and the more privileged, mixed-race Creoles. Creoles lived downtown, in the French Quarter; blacks lived uptown, beyond Canal Street.

Creole children generally received formal training in music. Creole musicians such as trumpeter Oscar "Papa" Celestin (1884–1954), clarinetist and soprano saxophonist Sidney Bechet, and saxophonist Barney Bigard (1906–1980) were able to read music and were expected to take part in well-established Creole musical traditions, including society dance bands for elegant Quadroon Balls. Black musicians—like cornetists Buddy Bolden, Joseph "King" Oliver, and Louis Armstrong—were less well schooled and emphasized playing by ear rather than reading music.

One primary catalyst for jazz was the growing contact among black and Creole musicians around the turn of the twentieth century, as Jim Crow segregation reduced the distinctions between blacks and Creoles. But jazz, which was commonly played in black honky-tonks and the bawdy houses, remained an outlaw music for relatively prosperous and upright Creoles. When Sidney Bechet cast his lot with jazz, he crossed a social as well as a musical divide.

The Musical Roots of Jazz

Jazz evolved from earlier forms of music, including minstrel show bands—such as the band led by African American cornetist and composer W.C. Handy—and ensembles on Mississippi River steamboats, like the one headed by African American pianist Fate Marable (1890–1947). Black and Creole marching bands—such as the Excelsior Brass Band, the Olympia Brass Band, and the Algiers Brass Band—were another source of jazz. In addition, many pianists played in the honky-tonks and brothels of Storyville, New Orleans's red-light district. Creole pianist Jelly Roll Morton recounted, "New Orleans was the stomping ground for all the greatest pianists in the country. We had Spanish, we had colored, we had white, we had Frenchmans, we had Americans, we had them from all parts of the world."

The blues, which has come to be closely connected with jazz, had little impact on jazz in its early years. At that time the blues was primarily a rural music. Jazz emerged in New Orleans and other urban areas. Blues musicians were mainly self-taught and self-accompanied performers. Some black jazz musicians, such as Buddy Bolden or King Oliver, were familiar with the idiom, but generally speaking the blues was seen as separate from jazz. "What's called jazz today," bassist Pops Foster (1892–1969) recounted, "was called ragtime back then . . . . From about 1900 on, there were three types of bands around New Orleans. You had bands that played ragtime, ones that played sweet music, and the ones that played nothin' but blues."

Ragtime, the main precursor to jazz, derived its name from its syncopated, or "ragged," time. Although now usually thought of as piano music, it was also performed by vocal ensembles and by instrumental groups. Until about 1920 the terms *ragtime* and *jazz* were used more or less interchangeably. Cornetist Buddy Bolden is said to have been the first musician to "rag the blues" for dancing around the turn of the century, thus creating jazz. Jelly Roll Morton, however, claimed to have invented both ragtime and, in 1902, jazz. In truth, no single musician created jazz; it was a collective effort of various black and Creole musicians.

The Role of Improvisation in Jazz

What separated jazz from ragtime was its emphasis on improvisation. Such ragtime composers as Scott Joplin saw ragtime as written music that should be played as it was written. Jazz was more freewheeling. Such jazz musicians as cornetist King Oliver made use of "freak" effects through the use of mutes, changes in embouchure, and unusual fingerings. As the influence of the blues gradually increased, New Orleans musicians adopted the blue notes and vocalized the instrumental sound of the blues. Almost from the start, however, jazz solos were more than just aural effects and ornamentation; they involved the creation of new melodic ideas.

Early jazz was characterized by collective, not individual, improvisation. Each instrument in the ensemble had a specific responsibility. The cornetist played mid-range variations on the melody. The clarinetist performed more intricate ornamentation in a higher register. The trombonist filled in punchy, rhythmic lines in a lower register, often punctuated by long descending slurs or smears created by rapidly extending the trombone's slide while playing, which gave rise to the term tailgate trombone. The drummer, pianist, and perhaps a banjo player or a tuba or bass player supplied the rhythmic underpinnings. New Orleans jazz maximized individual latitude, but, in the absence of extended individual solos, it also subsumed the individual within the group.

The two greatest exemplars of the New Orleans style were Oliver's Creole Jazz Band and Morton's Red Hot Peppers. The Creole Jazz Band made a series of classic recordings in 1923. The group included Oliver and his young protégé Louis Armstrong on cornets, clarinetist Johnny Dodds (1892–1940), trombonist Honore Dutrey (d. 1935), pianist Lil Hardin Armstrong, Warren "Baby" Dodds (1898–1959) on drums, and bassist Bill Johnson (1872–1972). The Red Hot Peppers recorded during the years 1926 to 1928 and featured Morton on piano and a shifting personnel that included such New Orleans musicians as trumpeter George Mitchell (d. 1942), clarinetist Omer Simeon (1902–1959), and trombonist Kid Ory. Morton's recordings reveal a deft balancing of textural variety and structural cohesiveness that earned him recognition as the first great composer in jazz.

The Transformation and Dissemination of Jazz

During the first quarter of the twentieth century, jazz moved out of New Orleans and reached much of the United States and Europe. Many prominent jazz musicians left New Orleans during the first two decades of the twentieth century and played a key role in disseminating jazz. In 1904 Jelly Roll Morton became an itinerant performer, playing with minstrel shows and vaudeville troupes in St. Louis and New York City as well as throughout the South. From 1911 to 1915 he lived in Chicago, where he performed with a small ensemble.

In 1918 King Oliver and clarinetist and soprano saxophonist Sidney Bechet left New Orleans for Chicago. Bechet traveled on to New York City, and in the following year he journeyed to Europe with an orchestra led by

African American composer Will Marion Cook (1869–1944). In 1919 Kid Ory moved to California and in 1925 to Chicago. In 1922 Louis Armstrong left New Orleans for Chicago, where he joined Oliver's Creole Jazz Band. In 1924–1925 he moved to New York City, where he was featured in bandleader Fletcher Henderson's big band.

That New Orleans jazz musicians moved to Northern cities in these years is hardly surprising. In the 1890s and early 1900s Jim Crow segregation had tightened throughout the South. The first two decades of the twentieth century had witnessed the beginnings of the Great Migration, a vast movement of African Americans who left the South for greater opportunities in the urban North and West. Although jazz musicians were part of this larger movement, their wide-ranging travels reflect the popularity of jazz among blacks and whites in the United States and a growing audience abroad.

By the 1920s jazz bands and jazz-flavored dance bands were appearing in many cities. The 1912 recordings of New York City bandleader James Reese Europe (1881–1919) capture a bouncy, ragtime-influenced precursor to jazz. By 1919, several years before he moved to New York, Duke Ellington established a reputation in Washington, D.C., as a pianist and a leader of pickup bands that played at various dances and social functions. In 1922 he relocated to New York City and two years later took over a six-man band that became the nucleus of the Duke Ellington Orchestra. In 1923 Fletcher Henderson organized his first big band in New York City and a year later convinced Armstrong to join the group.

Two New Orleans musicians, Armstrong and Bechet, were central in transforming jazz from its focus on the collectively improvising ensemble to the individual soloist. Armstrong's and Bechet's lyrical extended solos established a new ideal for jazz and inspired countless musicians. Virtually every jazz trumpeter of the 1920s and 1930s was indebted to Armstrong. Bechet's influence, though less evident, was clear in the perform ances of clarinetist and tenor saxophonist Barney Bigard and alto saxophonist Johnny Hodges, who filled key roles in the 1930s Ellington Orchestra.

During the 1920s Armstrong and blues singer Bessie Smith established a tradition of jazz singing. During the 1930s Smith and Armstrong would be the two strongest influences on Billie Holiday, the greatest jazz singer of the swing era. In addition, Armstrong and bandleader Cab Calloway helped to popularize what came to be known as scat singing, in which the vocalist improvised by stringing together nonsense syllables.

The Emergence of Duke Ellington and the Ellington Orchestra

Duke Ellington's role in jazz history is, to use one of his favorite phrases, "beyond category." For almost half a century, from the 1920s to the 1970s, Ellington was the most significant composer and bandleader in jazz. At first his potential was less clear, but during a 1927–1931 stint at the Cotton Club, he evolved from a derivative pianist and pedestrian arranger into the preeminent composer in jazz. Ellington was initially inspired by Bubber

Miley, a trumpet player who composed or co-composed some of the band's greatest early works, including *"East St. Louis Toodle-oo"* (1926) and *"Black and Tan Fantasy"* (1927).

At the Cotton Club, Ellington's creative abilities expanded steadily. He began to employ adventurous harmonies and voicings and experimented with radical changes in tempo and meter. He quickly recognized the importance of Hollywood in reaching a wider audience. The Ellington Orchestra appeared in such motion pictures as the Amos 'n' Andy film *Check and Double Check* (1930) and the all-black *Cabin in the Sky* (1943). Ellington also challenged the creative limitations imposed by the three-minute 78 rpm recording and the notion that jazz was merely dance music. Ellington's most significant compositions were not his individual songs, but such ambitious suites as *Reminiscing in Tempo* (1935), the nine-minute film *Symphony in Black* (1935), and *Black, Brown, and Beige* (1943).

The Bop Era, 1945–1955

In the 1940s a number of younger musicians, especially in Harlem, began pressing at the boundaries of swing-era jazz. These musicians usually played in small combos at obscure nightclubs. They made no radio broadcasts and, due to a wartime shortage of the shellac used in pressing records, as well as a long strike by the American Federation of Musicians, they made almost no recordings before 1945. With the nation's attention fixed on World War II, few outside Harlem were aware of the new style known as bop.

Bop, as played by its greatest exemplars, alto saxophonist Charlie Parker and trumpeter Dizzy Gillespie, was a challenging music. Bop solos typically involved swirling cascades of notes, and bop tunes often used complex chord progressions—for instance, Parker's *"Blues for Alice"* (1951)—and tempos that were much faster than swing-era jazz—as in Gillespie's *"Salt Peanuts"* (1945) and *"Shaw Nuff"* (1945). Unlike big-band swing, bop was

Widely credited as the architect of bop in the 1940s, trumpeter Dizzy Gillespie performs at the Monterery Jazz Festival in Monterey, California in the 1980s. *CORBIS/Craig Lovell*

emphatically not for dancing.
There were bop big bands,
including those of singer Billy Eckstine, white clarinetist Woody
Herman, and, above all, Gillespie,
but only virtuoso dancers could
negotiate their frantic tempos.

Gillespie's big band was also
instrumental in introducing Afro-
Latin jazz to an American audi-
ence. In 1948 Gillespie added
Cuban conga drummer Chano
Pozo to his orchestra and began
playing such fiery pieces as "Man-
teca" (1947) and "Guarachi Guaro"
(1948). Two other Cubans—
Machito and his brother-in-law,
arranger and trumpet player Mario
Bauza—led the most important
Afro-Latin jazz band of the 1940s,
Machito and His Afro-Cubans.
Machito's band made such influen-
tial recordings as "Tanga" (1949)
and Chico O'Farrill's classic "Afro-
Cuban Suite" (1950), which fea-

One of the greatest jazz vocalists of any era,
Sarah Vaughan sings at a club in Los Angeles in
1950. *CORBIS/Joseph Schwartz Collection*

tured Charlie Parker as a guest soloist. So strong were the links between
Cuban musicians and bop that many labeled Afro-Latin jazz Cu-bop.

Bop musicians idolized the improvising soloist, above all, the brilliant
Parker and Gillespie. Other top soloists were pianists Thelonious Monk and
Bud Powell, tenor saxophonist Dexter Gordon, drummers Art Blakey and
Max Roach, and vocalists Ella Fitzgerald and Sarah Vaughan. The most
important younger bop-style soloists to emerge in the 1950s were tenor saxophonist Sonny Rollins, pianist Hampton Hawes (1928–1977), and trumpeters Clifford Brown (1930–1956) and Lee Morgan (1938–1972). Bop
musicians generally viewed themselves not as popular entertainers but as
artists. They insisted that their music be taken seriously. But bop dismayed
many listeners and older jazz musicians. In 1948, for instance, Louis Armstrong criticized the new style, referring to it as "that modern malice" of
"young cats playing them weird chords" with "no melody to remember and
no beat to dance to."

Some white record producers and fans sought refuge in the past,
bringing several New Orleans jazz musicians out of retirement to perform
in the old style. The movement, variously termed the New Orleans revival
or the traditionalist revival, brought new attention to Kid Ory, clarinetist
Omer Simeon, and trumpeters Bunk Johnson (1889–1949) and Papa
Celestin. The most visible beneficiary of the New Orleans revival was Armstrong himself, who formed his traditionalist All Stars in 1947 and con-

tinued touring with the group into the 1960s. But as the original New Orleans jazz musicians died, the result was a slick commercial style, performed by and for whites, known as Dixieland.

Cool Jazz, Hard Bop, and Jazz in Hollywood

During the late 1940s the other main response to bop was cool jazz. Cool jazz slowed down bop's tempos and smoothed out its dissonances. Miles Davis's *Birth of the Cool* (1949–1950) and his late-1950s collaborations with arranger Gil Evans epitomized the cool style. Pianist John Lewis (b. 1920), a founding member of the Modern Jazz Quartet (MJQ), was known for bringing elements of European classical music into such compositions as *"The Queen's Fancy"* (1953) and *"Fontessa"* (1956). The attempt to combine jazz and classical music came to be termed third-stream music, partly on the basis of the MJQ's album *Third Stream Music* (1960). Like Dixieland, however, cool was dominated by such white musicians as trumpeter Chet Baker, tenor saxophonist Stan Getz, and arranger Gil Evans.

Young black jazz musicians of the late 1950s preferred the raw-edged and dynamic style known as hard bop, the antithesis of cool. Hard bop embraced the harmonic innovations of bop but incorporated earthier harmonies inspired by the blues and gospel music. Cool jazz was an arranger's music, often played by large ensembles or orchestras. Hard bop was played in small groups, especially quintets. The key hard-bop groups were the Max Roach-Clifford Brown Quintet, the Horace Silver (b. 1928) Quintet, Art Blakey and the Jazz Messengers, and the Cannonball Adderly Quintet.

Beginning in the 1940s a number of jazz musicians sought to break through Hollywood's racial barriers. When composer William Grant Still departed from the set of the all-black *Stormy Weather* (1943), Benny Carter stepped in. Carter served as an instrumentalist and arranger but received no screen credit. He worked on many films of the 1940s and 1950s and in 1958 began composing for television. He also aided other jazz musicians seeking careers in Hollywood, including trombonist J. J. Johnson (b. 1924) and tenor saxophonist Oliver Nelson (1932–1975). In the late 1950s Duke Ellington made his debut as a feature-film composer with *Anatomy of a Murder* (1959) and *Paris Blues* (1961). In the 1960s and 1970s Hollywood's most ubiquitous jazz musician was Quincy Jones, who composed music for such films as *In the Heat of the Night* (1967) and *The Wiz* (1978) as well as for television.

Jazz Experimentalists: Charles Mingus, Ornette Coleman, and John Coltrane

Jazz in the 1950s set the foundations for the free jazz—sometimes termed avant-garde jazz—of the 1960s. An important precursor of this atonal style, which dispensed with traditional chord progressions and melodies, can be found in the music of bassist and composer Charles Mingus. Mingus was iconoclastic, and his hard-to-label music attracted few disciples or imitators. Mingus avoided written scores; he sang the various parts to his musicians to

achieve a looser, more spontaneous sound. In such compositions as
"*Wednesday Night Prayer Meeting*" (1959), Mingus goaded his musicians into
impassioned performances that joined basic gospel and blues harmonies
with high-energy bop improvising. Although Mingus did not play free jazz,
many of his sidemen did, most notably alto saxophonist Eric Dolphy
(1928–1964).

Free jazz had its real beginnings in the work of alto saxophonist Ornette
Coleman and pianist Cecil Taylor (b. 1929), and the experimental and often
dissonant style takes its name from *Coleman's Free Jazz: A Collective Improvisation* (1960). Other significant free-jazz musicians were bandleader and
arranger Sun Ra; trumpeters Don Cherry (1936–1995) and Lester Bowie (b.
1941); pianist Marilyn Crispell; and tenor saxophonists Albert Ayler
(1936–1970), Archie Shepp (b. 1937), and—after 1965—John Coltrane. Of
these, Coltrane had by far the greatest impact on jazz. Coltrane's sound on
tenor was rather thin, and his improvisations were both meditative and
impassioned. He became the greatest influence on tenor saxophonists since
Coleman Hawkins and Lester Young.

Coltrane's music evolved out of hard bop. His hard-bop style, which
jazz critic Ira Gitler characterized as "sheets of sound," can be heard on his
albums *Blue Train* (1957) and *Giant Steps* (1959). During the late 1950s
Coltrane and Miles Davis were instrumental in developing a new modal
style of jazz playing. Modal jazz replaced the complex chord changes of bop
with modes or tone rows, often played over extended two-chord vamps.
Coltrane pioneered the style as a sideman on Miles Davis's *Kind of Blue*
(1959) and on his own *My Favorite Things* (1960). In 1965 he embraced
free jazz, adding two free-jazz musicians—drummer Rashied Ali (b. 1935)
and tenor saxophonist Pharaoh Sanders (b. 1940)—to his group. Coltrane
probed the outer reaches of tonality as part of a larger spiritual quest. In the
notes for his album *A Love Supreme* (1964), he wrote that in 1957 he had
experienced "a spiritual awakening, which was to lead me to a richer, fuller,
more productive life . . . . I feel this has been granted through His grace.
ALL PRAISE BE TO GOD . . . . This album is a humble offering to Him."
Coltrane continued playing spiritually grounded free jazz until his death in
1967 of liver cancer.

Miles Davis: Modal Jazz and Jazz-Rock

Despite the importance of Coltrane's influence, the single most significant
jazz musician from the late 1940s to the 1970s was trumpeter Miles
Davis. Davis was a leader in cool jazz, and from 1952 to 1954 he led a
number of seminal hard-bop sessions. In the late 1950s he pioneered
modal jazz with *Kind of Blue* and a decade later ushered in the jazz-rock
era with the album *Bitches Brew* (1969). Jazz-rock—sometimes termed
fusion—combines jazz improvisation with the hard rhythms and electric
instruments of rock music.

Bitches Brew exemplified the jazz-rock style, and it featured many musicians who would be significant in the 1970s, including saxophonist Wayne

Shorter (b. 1933), guitarist John McLaughlin, keyboardists Chick Corea and Joe Zawinul, and drummer Jack DeJohnette (b. 1942). Former Davis sidemen went on to found several important jazz-rock units, including Shorter and Zawinul's *Weather Report*, Corea's *Return to Forever*, keyboardist Herbie Hancock's *Headhunters*, and *Lifetime*, led by drummer Tony Williams (1945–1997).

During his long career Davis led two bands, known as his classic quintets, which played particularly timeless music. In 1955–1956 Davis's first classic quintet featured Coltrane, pianist Red Garland (1923–1984), bassist Paul Chambers (1935–1969), and drummer Philly Joe Jones (1923–1985). From 1965 to 1968 his second classic quintet included Shorter, Hancock, Williams, and bassist Ron Carter (b. 1937). The latter group perfected an elliptical and rhythmically fluid style of modal jazz that inspired many jazz musicians in the 1980s and 1990s, most notably trumpeter Wynton Marsalis.

Wynton Marsalis and Neotraditionalism Since 1980

Since the early 1980s Marsalis has been the most prominent figure in jazz. A talented trumpeter and promising composer, Marsalis is also an outspoken defender of jazz. He has become the most articulate spokesperson for a younger generation of jazz musicians known as the Young Lions—so named because of their relative youth and vociferous pronouncements on jazz. Their music has been variously termed modern mainstream, post bop, and classicism. Perhaps a better label would be neo-traditionalism. Just as the traditionalists of the 1940s harked back to the music of the first two decades of the twentieth century, so the neo-traditionalists of the 1980s and 1990s embraced the hard bop and modal jazz of the late 1950s and early 1960s.

The Young Lions play acoustic jazz and condemn the electronic instruments and rock rhythms of jazz-rock. Where free jazz is abstract and often dissonant, the music of the neo-traditionalists is tonal, often featuring familiar chord progressions and well-known jazz standards. Besides Marsalis, important neo-traditionalists are trumpeters Terence Blanchard and Roy Hargrove (b. 1969); pianists Mulgrew Miller (b. 1955) and Marcus Roberts (b. 1963); drummers Jeff "Tain" Watts (b. 1960) and Marvin "Smitty" Smith (b. 1961); and bass player Christian McBride (b. 1972). A second group of young jazz musicians has taken a strikingly different approach, open to a wider range of music, from free jazz to R&B. Such performers as pianist Geri Allen, alto saxophonist Donald Harrison (b. 1960), and tenor saxophonists David Murray b. 1955) and Joshua Redman (b. 1969) combine a respect for past jazz styles with an active probing of musical boundaries.

In 1987 Marsalis was named the head of a new jazz program at New York City's Lincoln Center for the Performing Arts, giving him a visible pulpit from which to preach his version of the jazz gospel. Under his leadership Lincoln Center presented major retrospectives of such jazz masters as Armstrong, Bechet, and, above all, Ellington. Marsalis also composed a series of major works that call to mind Ellington's suites, including *In This House, On This Morning* (1993) and *Blood on the Fields* (1995), which in 1997 became the first non-classical work to receive a Pulitzer Prize in music. The Lincoln Center jazz program and a comparable program instituted at Carnegie Hall in 1993 under trumpeter Jon Faddis (b. 1953) reveal the full acceptance of jazz as part of American high culture.

Jazz Today

Jazz musicians can be heard playing today in almost every style from the earliest beginnings of jazz. Because jazz has had such a short history, listeners can still hear, in person, many of the musicians who created the core traditions of jazz. During the 1970s several New Orleans musicians remained active who had recorded in the 1920s with King Oliver and Jelly Roll Morton. Pianist Eubie Blake—who composed *"The Charleston Rag"* (1899)—was a living link to the ragtime era who continued performing into the early 1980s, when he was 98 years old.

In the 1990s most of the older musicians of jazz derived from the swing or bop eras, although trumpeter Doc Cheatham (1905–1997), saxophonist Benny Waters (1902–1998), and Benny Carter all began recording in the 1920s. One could also hear leading cool, hard bop, modal, and free-jazz players. Because of its rapid evolution, jazz is not so much a linear sequence of styles as a crazy quilt. The creative improvisations and swinging music of several generations of jazz musicians, and their sharply contrasting juxtapositions, reveal both the continuity and the change that characterize jazz.

In defining their music, today's Young Lions invoke the conventions of hard bop and modal jazz. Their stylistic conservatism reflects, in part, a need for consolidation after the sweeping discontinuities of free jazz and jazz-rock. But neo-traditionalism is by no means the final word in the evolution of jazz. Throughout its history, jazz has undergone profound and unexpected transformations in style, approach, and technique. As jazz critic Whitney Balliett has observed, jazz is the "sound of surprise," and, above all, that capacity to surprise underscores the continued vitality of the jazz tradition.

North America
___

Jefferson, ("Blind") Lemon

(b. 1897, near Couchman, Tex.; d. 1930?, Chicago, Ill.), country bluesman who made some of the earliest blues recordings and profoundly influenced numerous subsequent blues musicians.

Blind Lemon Jefferson was born on a farm in Freestone County, Texas, where he spent his childhood. Although his mature songwriting suggests a familiarity with the visual world, Jefferson seems to have lost his sight at least by the time he was a teenager. Thereafter he devoted himself to music, a vocation that suffered little from his handicap. Jefferson began his career close to home, singing in the Shiloh Baptist Church in Kirvin, Texas, and playing his guitar in Wortham, Texas, at parties and on the street.

Sometime around 1915 Jefferson moved to Dallas and began performing full-time in the Deep Ellum neighborhood, mostly as a street musician. Some critics suggest that Jefferson's stentorian singing style arose to out-clamor the noise of the street. Jefferson did sing loudly, but he also sang with great mastery. He commanded a broad vocal range and sometimes performed gospel songs in addition to the blues. The intricacy and staggered rhythms of his guitar accompaniments also showed his superior musical skill. A body of lore grew about Jefferson's life as a blind performer, including the claim that he could recognize the clink of pennies in his tin cup and reject them as inadequate payment.

Jefferson earned enough money from his street performances to support a family; he reportedly married in the early 1920s and had a son. During these years he played throughout Mississippi and Alabama, as well as in Texas. Despite his blindness, he lived a rambler's life, likely carrying a gun and boot-legging liquor. He kept company with Leadbelly (William "Huddie" Ledbetter), who also lived the rough life of his songs.

In 1925 Jefferson caught the attention of Sammy Price, a music store owner who recorded a demo for him and sent it to Paramount Records. Paramount invited Jefferson to Chicago in 1925 or 1926 and began to record his extensive repertoire of original and folk material. His first Paramount recordings were gospel songs, released under the pseudonym Deacon L. J. Bates, but soon Jefferson was a premier name in secular race records.

Jefferson created a niche for male blues artists in an industry hitherto dominated by female performers such as Ma Rainey, Ida Cox, and Bessie Smith. Although he recorded only from 1926 to his death in 1929, he cut approximately a hundred sides and left a legacy of songs that later became standards of folk and blues, including *"That Black Snake Moan"* (1926), *"See That My Grave Is Kept Clean"* (1928), *"Corrina Blues"* (1926), and *"Match Box Blues"* (1927).

During this phase of his life Jefferson became wealthy and well known. He could afford to own cars and hire chauffeurs, and at times employed young blues musicians, such as Leadbelly and T-Bone Walker. Within three or four years, however, near the end of his life, his celebrity had begun to wane.

Although uncertainty surrounds the date and details of Jefferson's death, the most common story is that he froze to death in March 1930 on the streets of Chicago. Allegedly, he got drunk and then lost, and his body was found in the snow the next morning. He was buried in Texas in a family plot next to his mother.

The Blues Foundation Hall of Fame inducted Jefferson in 1980. His music has influenced generations of performers, including Sonny Terry, Muddy Waters, Joe Turner, T-Bone Walker, and Josh White. Even the music of performers outside the blues genre, from Bob Dylan's to Louis

Armstrong's, has reflected the influence of Jefferson's singing style and repertoire.

North America

Jessye, Eva

(b. January 20, 1895, Coffeyville, Kans.; d. February 21, 1992, Ypsilanti, Mich.), African American choral director, composer, and educator, the first African American woman to gain international renown as a professional choral director.

A woman of many talents, Eva Jessye pursued a music career that spanned more than half a century and won her a reputation as "the dean of black female musicians." During the 1930s she gained international attention as director of the Eva Jessye Choir, which toured the United States and Europe and sang in the first production of George Gershwin's folk opera *Porgy and Bess* (1935). During the next three decades she led the choir in numerous revivals of the opera and in 1963 directed the choir for the historic March on Washington led by Martin Luther King Jr.

Jessye grew up in Coffeyville, Kansas, where, after the separation of her parents in 1898, she was reared by her grandmother and her mother's sisters. As a child she began singing, organized a girls' quartet, and, at age 12, helped composer Will Marion Cook copy music for his orchestra when he toured her hometown. At age 13 she began musical studies at Western University in Quindaro, Kansas. After earning a teaching certificate from Langston University in Oklahoma, she spent several years teaching music in Oklahoma schools, and in 1920 became the head of the music department at Morgan State College in Baltimore.

In 1922 Jessye moved to New York, where she studied privately with Will Marion Cook and the music theorist Percy Goetschius. Four years later she had established herself as director of the Original Dixie Jubilee Singers, later renamed the Eva Jessye Choir. In 1929 she went to Hollywood to train a choir to perform in the first black musical film, *Hallelujah* (1929, Metro-Goldwyn-Mayer), written and directed by King Vidor, and in 1934 she became choral director of Virgil Thompson's opera *Four Saints in Three Acts*. Achieving international fame as choral director of Gershwin's *Porgy and Bess*, she continued to tour with her choir for more than 40 years. A respected composer, she conducted her own music in both radio and stage performances and in 1972 directed her critically acclaimed folk oratorio Paradise Lost and Regained (composed in 1934) at the Washington Cathedral.

Jessye exerted considerable influence as a teacher. She held several teaching posts, lectured widely, and played an important role in the careers of such concert artists as Muriel Rahn, Andrew Frierson, and Lawrence Winters. In 1974 she established the Eva Jessye Collection of Afro-American Music at the University of Michigan in Ann Arbor, where she spent the last ten years of her life. She died of natural causes in Ypsilanti, Michigan, at age 97.

Johnson, "Blind" Willie

(b. 1902, near Marlin, Tex.; d. 1947, Beaumont, Tex.), African American gospel bluesman who recorded best-selling religious race records in the late 1920s.

Willie Johnson's date of birth remains uncertain, as do the circumstances of the accident that took his sight at age seven. Allegedly, his stepmother threw lye water in his face during a domestic fracas. Johnson's blindness probably led him to cultivate his musical talent, as the handicap interfered less with this than with his interest in the ministry. By his teens Johnson was supporting himself as a musician, playing guitar, singing religious songs, and preaching on the streets of Waco and Dallas as well as in the Baptist churches of nearby towns.

Johnson married late in the 1920s, settled permanently in Dallas, and began to record with Columbia Records. All his best-known works have religious themes, and he is lauded as a major progenitor of gospel blues. It is believed that he also recorded at least two secular blues songs under the name of Blind Texas Marlin.

Most of Johnson's Columbia recordings are characterized by gravelly bass vocals—apparently affected—and artful slide-guitar, although some reveal his natural tenor voice and his aptitude as a fingerpicker. His basslike singing is often backed by a female vocalist, possibly his wife, Angeline. His most famous recordings include "*Motherless Children Have a Hard Time*," "*Jesus Make Up My Dying Bed*," and "*Dark Was the Night and Cold Was the Ground*," which was featured on the soundtrack of *The Gospel According to Saint Mark* and was interpreted by white guitarist and folk musician Ry Cooder for the film *Paris, Texas*. All of Johnson's records proved commercially successful.

Johnson ceased to record after the onset of the Great Depression in 1929. But he continued to perform until his death in 1947, the details of which are as obscure as those surrounding much of his life. According to his wife, Johnson died of pneumonia contracted by having slept in the wet ashes of his burnt-down house.

Jones, Bill T.

(b. February 15, 1952, Bunnell, Fla.), internationally acclaimed African American dancer, one of the foremost choreographers of contemporary dance theater.

In the mid-1980s Bill T. Jones emerged as one of America's preeminent dancers and avant-garde choreographers. Rooted in the postmodern experimentation of the 1960s, his work often combines speech, song, dance, and mime as well as spontaneous movement. He infuses his art with candid autobiographical details in an effort to challenge audiences' ideas about tolerance, sexuality, death, and interracial romance, issues he has dealt with as a gay black man diagnosed in 1985 as HIV-positive. Jones "has a reputation for doing anything he wants, on and offstage," wrote dance critic Gus Solomons Jr. "Movement spills out of [his] powerful, instinctual body, driven by a fecund imagination."

The tenth of 12 children, Jones was reared and educated in Wayland, New York, a predominantly white agricultural community where his parents, then migrant farm workers, settled after moving from the Southeast. In 1970 he entered the State University of New York at Binghamton, where he excelled in track and theater and enrolled in movement classes with Trinidadian choreographer Percival Borde. Encouraged by his friend Arnie Zane, he began to study modern dance, particularly the pioneering techniques of choreographers Martha Graham, Merce Cunningham, and Alvin Ailey.

Jones and Zane, a white photographer and theater student, soon began a personal as well as professional partnership. In 1979, after successfully choreographing a variety of pieces for the American Dance Asylum, they settled in New York City. Influenced by postmodern choreographer and filmmaker Yvonne Rainer, Jones often incorporated spontaneous monologues into his solo pieces. When he and Zane performed in duets, they creatively emphasized their differences in race, size, and character and elaborated on each other's movements as a form of commentary, dialogue, or argument.

In 1982 Jones and Zane founded the Bill T. Jones/Arnie Zane Dance Company, a diverse troupe of dancers of all shapes, sizes, and ethnicities. Dance critic Tobi Tobias said, "Jones has always been addicted to unusual physical types; everyone in the company looks picked for body as well as for soul and technique." In 1983 the company debuted at the Brooklyn Academy of Music with the critically acclaimed Intuitive Momentum, a series of pieces set to the music of famed drummer Max Roach and pianist Connie Crothers. Attentive to stage design, Jones and Zane collaborated with such innovators as graffiti artist Keith Haring and fashion designer Willi Smith and soon gained recognition for work that was profoundly expressive and visually dazzling. In 1986 Jones and Zane received the coveted New York Dance and Performance (Bessie) Award.

With the death of Zane from AIDS in 1988, Jones focused his work on the themes of loss and mortality, producing and performing such celebrated solo pieces as *Absence* (1989) and the *Last Night on Earth* (1992). He also created pieces that affirm life and community, including *D-Man in the Waters* (1992), which earned him a second Bessie Award, and *Last Supper at Uncle Tom's Cabin/The Promised Land* (1990), a multimedia work that employs nudity as a metaphor for the common human condition and features, along with dance and music, the taped voice of Martin Luther King Jr.

In 1994 Jones and his dance company premiered *Still/Here*, a multimedia work about death and dying that ignited sharp controversy among journalists and cultural critics. Opening at the Brooklyn Academy of Music's Next Wave Festival, *Still/Here* incorporated videotaped testimonies of terminally ill people, including AIDS patients, whom Jones had been interviewing since 1992. Although the New Yorker dance critic Arlene Croce censured *Still/Here* as "victim art," *New York Times* columnist Frank Rich, who noted that AIDS is "part of art because it is part of life," wrote that Jones's *Still/Here* had captured "the story of our time." *Newsweek*'s Laura Shapiro considered the piece "so original and profound that its place among the landmarks of twentieth-century dance seems ensured."

No less complex than Jones's relationship to contemporary dance is his relationship to black culture. Since the early 1980s some black artists have openly questioned Jones's racial allegiances. Jones, who considers himself first and foremost an artist, has had to defend his 17-year partnership with Zane as well as his dance innovations, which have attracted mainly white avant-garde audiences. Still, over the years Jones has won the respect of many black artists and intellectuals, including Maya Angelou, Dance Theater of Harlem founder Arthur Mitchell, and Jessye Norman, who considers him "the most soulful dancer I know."

In addition to creating works for his own company, Jones has choreographed for such companies as the Alvin Ailey American Dance Theater and the Boston Ballet and has applied his talents to opera and musical comedy. The recipient of a MacArthur Fellowship in 1994, Jones continues to perform throughout the United States and Europe, and in March 1997 premiered his *Ballets Mozart* with the Lyons Opera Ballet in France.

North America

Jones, James Earl

(b. January 17, 1931, Arkabutla, Mississippi), African American stage, film, and television actor whose resonant bass voice is instantly recognizable.

In a long and successful career James Earl Jones has portrayed a wide range of characters in stage productions, motion pictures, and television. He transcended the limitations of his rural Mississippi childhood and became a much-loved actor with one of the most recognizable voices in the United States. His beginnings were far from auspicious. Not long after his birth, his actor father Robert Earl Jones abandoned the family. Young James was adopted and raised by his maternal grandparents. When he was five years old, his family moved to Michigan.

Jones's deep, resonant voice has reached countless millions of people, in particular as Darth Vader in the original *Star Wars* trilogy (1977, 1980, 1983), as father lion Mustafa in *The Lion King* (1994), and as the official voice of the telephone company Bell Atlantic. During his youth, however, Jones avoided speaking altogether for several years because of a pronounced stutter. "I was unable to talk from the age of eight to the age of 15," he recalled in a 1979 *Jet* magazine interview. " . . . I thought, if I can't say it, I just won't make an ass of myself . . . so I didn't talk." But while he was in high school, his English teacher discovered that Jones wrote poetry and took an interest in him, giving him the incentive to overcome his speech impediment.

Actor James Earl Jones, portraying singer and activist Paul Robeson in a one-man play, stands with a bust of Robeson. *CORBIS/Hulton-Deutsch Collection*

In 1949 he entered the University of Michigan in Ann Arbor and majored in drama, although he had initially intended to study medicine. He graduated magna cum laude in 1953 and, after a stint in the military, moved to New York City. In 1957 he made his professional debut in New York City. During the 1960s he had a long association with Joseph Papp's New York Shakespeare Festival. Jones also gained prominence as part of an all-black production of Jean Genet's *The Blacks*. Over the years he tackled a wide range of Shakespearean roles, including Othello, King Lear, and Oberon in *A Midsummer Night's Dream*. In 1960 he won his first leading role, in Lionel Abel's *The Pretender*.

Jones found success in motion pictures as well as on stage. In 1966 he played the fictional boxer Jack Jefferson, who is closely modeled on Jack Johnson (1878–1946), in Howard Sackler's *The Great White Hope*. In 1968 the play moved to Broadway, and a year later Jones's portrayal earned him a Tony Award. Reprising the role in the 1970 movie version, Jones was nominated for an Academy Award as Best Actor and won a Golden Globe for best new male talent. In 1966 he made his television debut in the daytime drama *As the World Turns*. During the 1970s he pursued a busy schedule of film and stage acting with occasional television appearances.

In 1977 and 1978 Jones encountered controversy while playing the title role in *Paul Robeson*, a dramatic recounting of the singer-activist's life. The play unintentionally sparked widespread opposition from the black intellectual community. Picketers appeared outside theaters during the production's tour, insisting that the play misrepresented Robeson's life, and prominent African Americans—including actor Ossie Davis, civil rights activist Coretta Scott King, and writers James Baldwin and Maya Angelou—publicly criticized the production. In retrospect, the film has been credited with helping to reawaken interest in Robeson's life and accomplishments. In his 1993 autobiography, *James Earl Jones: Voices and Silences*, Jones noted that in recent years the play, under the sponsorship of Malcolm X's daughter, Attilah Shabazz, has been "performed all over the country, without any form of protest."

Jones's long career has produced many finely honed performances. During 1985–1987 he won critical praise and a second Tony Award for his lead role in August Wilson's drama *Fences*. On television, he portrayed Alex Haley in *Roots: The Next Generations* (1979), the sequel to the 1977 miniseries *Roots*. Jones also appeared in such memorable films as John Sayles's *Matewan* (1987), Phil Alden Robinson's *Field of Dreams* (1989), and Darrel James Roodt's *Cry the Beloved Country* (1995). Since the late 1950s Jones has had a prolific and busy acting career. "I might cry for great dramas being written for me," he remarked in a 1980 interview, "but until one is, I'll take a crack at almost anything."

North America

Jones, M. Sissieretta ("Black Patti")

(b. January 5, 1869, Portsmouth, Va.; d. June 24, 1933, Providence, R.I.), African American singer, a gifted soprano who rose to fame as a soloist and troupe leader during the last decades of the nineteenth century.

Sissieretta Jones came early to music. Her father was the pastor and choir director of their Portsmouth, Virginia, African Methodist Episcopal Church, and her mother was a soprano in the choir. She married at age 14 and began voice training the next year in Providence, Rhode Island. She continued her studies at the New England Conservatory in Boston, making her performance debut in that city in 1887. She acquired the nickname "Black Patti" from a newspaper review that praised her as an African American match for the renowned Italian soprano Adelina Patti.

National fame arrived with Jones's performance at the 1892 Grand Negro Jubilee at Madison Square Garden in New York City. Before an audience of 75,000, she sang selections from the opera *La Traviata* as well as the song "*Swanee River*." This combination of high opera and a popular repertoire continued throughout Jones's career. Racism kept Jones from ensemble roles in established white opera.

Jones toured the West Indies, South America, Europe, and North America as a soloist. She performed for the English royal family and four American presidents and appeared in New York with composer and conductor Antonin Dvořák in 1894.

In 1896 she formed her own troupe of African American entertainers, Black Patti's Troubadours. The group's performances drew on elements of vaudeville and minstrelsy, integrating opera selections into a musical comedy format. After 1916 she retired to Providence to care for her aging mother. She died there, penniless, in 1933.

Jones, Quincy Delight, Jr.

(b. March 14, 1933, Chicago, Ill.), African American arranger, composer, and entertainment industry executive who has worked in music, film, and television.

Quincy Jones has had several careers in popular entertainment, including roles as a big-band musician, composer-arranger, record company executive, producer of films and music videos, and partner in a television production company. He has emerged as one of the most influential figures in Hollywood. He commenced his music career in Seattle, Washington, where his family moved during the mid-1940s from Chicago, Illinois. He sang in a vocal harmony group directed by Joseph Powe, who had once been with Wings Over Jordan. After trying various instruments in his high school band, Jones settled on the trumpet.

As a teenager Jones played in local jazz and rhythm and blues (R&B) groups. He became acquainted with Ray Charles, an early musical influence, who moved to the Seattle area in 1950. Besides leading his own trio, Charles wrote and arranged for the five-member R&B vocal group in which Jones sang. Before he was 16, Jones had written his first suite, *From the Four Winds*, which later earned him a scholarship to Seattle University. Dissatisfied with the university's offerings, he moved to Boston, Massachusetts, and studied at Berklee School of Music.

Jones also found work in the big bands of Jay McShann (1949) and Lionel Hampton (1951–1953). While with Hampton, Jones played in a trumpet section that featured two superb jazz stylists, Clifford Brown and Art Farmer. Jones made his mark not by his playing but through his skilled arrangements. After leaving Hampton, he freelanced as an arranger and with his own big band led various recording dates, most memorably the sessions that produced *This Is How I Feel about Jazz* (1956). He provided arrangements for Count Basie, Billy Eckstine, Sarah Vaughan, Ella Fitzgerald, Dinah Washington, Tommy Dorsey, and others. In 1956 Jones helped organize and wrote many of the arrangements for a new big band for Dizzy Gillespie, touring Africa, Asia, and the Middle East under the auspices of the United States State Department—the first time a jazz group was chosen for such cultural diplomacy.

Jones settled in Paris for several years, where he studied arranging, organized a big band, and worked for Barclay Records as an arranger and producer. He also studied arranging with Nadia Boulanger. In 1961 he returned to the United States and became head of artists and repertoire (A&R) at Mercury Records. Three years later he became Mercury's first African American vice president. During this period Jones stopped playing the trumpet in order to devote his energies to composing and arranging. His music increasingly employed R&B and pop elements, including dance rhythms and electric instruments.

In the 1960s Jones moved to Los Angeles, California, and soon became one of the most successful composers and arrangers in the film industry. He followed in the footsteps of Benny Carter, the alto saxophonist, composer, and arranger who played a key role in challenging the color barrier in Hollywood during the 1940s and 1950s. According to Jones's biographer Raymond Horricks, white composer Henry Mancini aided Jones in his move into film music. Jones provided scores for many films, including *The Pawnbroker* (1965), *In the Heat of the Night* (1967), *The New Centurions* (1972), and *The Wiz* (1978). In 1974 he suffered a cerebral hemorrhage and underwent brain surgery. Upon recovering, he returned to work with undiminished vigor. He arranged and wrote music for numerous television programs of the 1970s, including *The Bill Cosby Show, Ironside, Sanford and Son*, and the miniseries *Roots*.

During these years, Jones further extended his role in the entertainment industry. In 1980 he established his own record label, Qwest. Later in the decade he expanded into movie producing. In addition to composing the film score, Jones served as one of the co-producers for the 1985 movie version of Alice Walker's novel *The Color Purple*. He also showed his ability to master popular musical styles and media, as in the hit albums and music videos that resulted from collaborations with Michael Jackson, including *Off the Wall* (1979), *Thriller* (1982), and *Bad* (1987).

Jones became a highly visible figure in American popular culture. In the mid-1980s he was one of the driving forces behind USA for Africa, producing the *We Are the World* (1985) album and video. In the 1990s his production company developed a number of television programs, including the hit series *Fresh Prince of Bel Air*, which debuted in 1990. Jones received his first Grammy Award from the National Academy of Recording Arts and Sciences (NARAS) in 1963, and by the mid-1990s he had received nearly two dozen Grammys, making him the most honored musician in the award's history. In 1997 he produced the televised Motion Picture Academy Awards ceremony.

Periodically, however, Jones has returned to his jazz roots. In 1964 he arranged and conducted *It Might As Well Be Swing*, an album that featured Frank Sinatra with the Count Basie Orchestra, and 20 years later he conducted and produced Sinatra's *L.A. Is My Lady*. In 1983 Jones conducted a big-band tribute to trumpeter Miles Davis, and in 1991 he appeared with Davis in one of the trumpeter's final public performances—a concert highlighting the collaborations between Davis and arranger Gil Evans—which was released on video and compact disc as *Miles and Quincy Live at Montreux* (1993).

More representative of Jones's musical vision, however, is the Grammy Award-winning *Q's Jook Joint* (1995), which pays tribute to the jook joint, a distinctly African American place for music, dancing, and socializing. Like Jones, this album—which features an eclectic mix of instrumental jazz riffs,

R&B ballads, pop music and hip hop rhythms, and rap vocals—is hard to categorize. "I'm all for de-categorizing the different musical pigeonholes," Jones has said. "Basically, they are all related anyway—blues, jazz, and gospel music, it's all the same thing."

North America

Joplin, Scott

(b. November 24, 1868, rural eastern Texas; d. April 1, 1917, New York, N.Y.), African American composer and pianist properly known as the "King of Ragtime Writers."

Scott Joplin led the black musicians who, at the turn of the twentieth century, melded African American folk music with classical and Romantic European traditions to form ragtime, a march-based yet heavily syncopated style of popular music. His compositions fueled the ragtime craze that led thousands of middle-class whites to buy pianos, collect sheet music, and enjoy, for the first time, the pulse of black vernacular culture. While Joplin's energetic rags created a sensation in middle-class parlors, he also wrote more conventional classical music. He composed waltzes, tangos, operas, and ballet, yet, due to his tremendous success as a sheet-music scribe—and due to his race—he died with a reputation far smaller than the body of his work deserved.

Joplin spent his first years in the lawless Reconstruction countryside of East Texas's Red River Valley. His father was a laborer and former slave and his mother a free black from Kentucky. Both parents played musical instruments, and Joplin and his five siblings grew up amid fiddles, banjos, and song. When the family moved to Texarkana, Arkansas, in the mid-1870s, the city environment benefited Joplin's musical development. His mother worked as a domestic servant, and her white employers allowed her son to play their piano. Joplin's father, who had come to Texarkana for the good wage of railroad work, bought his son a used piano as soon as he could afford one.

Joplin earned a reputation throughout Texarkana's black community for his precocious musical skill. At age 11 he attracted the attention of a classically trained German musician who introduced him to the rudiments of music theory. As a teenager Joplin left home, probably to ride the new rail lines and play as an itinerant pianist in St. Louis, Memphis, and Dallas sporting houses and at the whistle-stop bars between.

In 1893 Joplin emerged as a well-practiced musician at the World's Columbian Exposition in Chicago, Illinois, where he probably played along the Midway Plaisance. Although white management excluded African Americans from the official program of concerts, black pianists entertained fairgoers along the exposition's bustling periphery. These Midway performances afforded a rare opportunity for middle-class whites to experience the lively music of African Americans. Although the ragtime craze was a

few years away, the 1893 exposition—and fairs like it—sowed the seeds.
While Joplin may have contributed some of the unofficial entertainment, he
also listened to it, absorbing the influences of such great performers as
"Plunk" Henry Johnson and Johnny Seymour.

At the same time Joplin met lifelong friend Otis Saunders, with whom
he spent the next two years traveling the Midwest in a quartet that played
many of Joplin's early compositions. By 1895 the two men were convinced
that Joplin had composed songs that the public would buy. Joplin and Saunders settled in Sedalia, Missouri, and joined its local black music scene. In
Sedalia, Joplin married Belle Jones, wrote pieces for the Queen City Band,
took a course in composition at the George R. Smith College for Negroes,
and, most important, began to peddle his compositions.

Joplin sold "*Maple Leaf Rag*" to white Sedalia businessman John Stark.
Allegedly Stark doubted the salability of the tune but liked it so much that
he took a chance and published it in 1899. "*Maple Leaf Rag*" was an instant
hit, selling all of its 10,000-copy run and, by 1909, more than 500,000
copies. After the success of "*Maple Leaf Rag*," Stark moved his business to
St. Louis, and Joplin, who had signed a contract with him, soon followed.
Ironically the success of "*Maple Leaf Rag*" crippled the music scene from
which it was born, as a number of influential Sedalia musicians followed
Joplin to the city.

While Joplin's music deserved the enthusiasm it inspired, Stark's business savvy contributed significantly to the Joplin craze. Long before Joplin
was well known, or even very prolific, Stark dubbed him the "King of Ragtime Writers." In addition to printing high-flown promotional rhetoric, Stark
marketed Joplin's sheet music with covers that would appeal to the values
of middle-class whites. While much contemporary music bore bawdy, racist
caricatures, Stark opted for elegant line drawings. Nevertheless, racial
ambivalence characterized even Stark's view of ragtime. The ragtime craze
both celebrated and questioned the "otherness" of African Americans; Stark
himself proclaimed that Joplin combined "the skill of a Beethoven with the
sentiment of a Black Mamma's croon."

In the first years of the new century Joplin published numerous rags
with Stark, including "*Peacherine Rag*" (1901) and "*The Entertainer*" (1902).
Joplin also embarked on more ambitious ventures, such as a folk ballet, *The
Ragtime Dance* (1902), and his first opera, *A Guest of Honor* (1903), the
text of which does not survive. Although these works demonstrated Joplin's
growing maturity as a musician, they were rarely performed. Even Stark,
whose money-making priorities often slackened for Joplin, dragged his heels
when it came to publishing more complex music.

By 1906 both Stark and Joplin were facing new difficulties: Stark suffered economically as phonographs and player pianos usurped sheet music's
appeal, while Joplin endured personal as well as financial loss. His first child
died a few months after birth, and his marriage was in a state of deterioration. Belle died shortly thereafter, and Joplin decided to leave St. Louis.

After a period of meager productivity, during which he traveled to
Chicago and Texarkana, Joplin relocated in New York, where the publishers

of Tin Pan Alley provided a ready market for ragtime writers. While Joplin continued to write piano music, including the experimental "*Wall Street Rag*" and "*Magnetic Rag*," he devoted much of his time to larger projects. He wrote a study guide for up-and-coming ragtime pianists called *School of Ragtime* (1908), and in 1911 he began work on another opera, *Treemonisha*.

Joplin set *Treemonisha* in rural Arkansas during Reconstruction. Its moralistic plot contrasts the evil of ignorance with the hope of education, indicting the rural superstition that Joplin remembered from his childhood. *Treemonisha* contains some of Joplin's most beautiful music, but he never did see its full production. In 1913 a theater that had promised to stage *Treemonisha* backed out on him, and in 1915 he produced the show himself without costumes, sets, or even an orchestra in the Lincoln Theater in Harlem.

In 1916 Joplin began to exhibit advanced signs of syphilis, and in 1917 he died in a psychiatric ward, diagnosed with dementia. He worked through his final days and left behind several unfinished compositions. His last years in New York were marked by diminished popular recognition and the grand frustration of *Treemonisha*. His second wife, Lottie Stokes Joplin, organized a small funeral, and her deceased husband sank from popular consciousness over the following decades.

In 1950, however, scholars Rudi Blesh and Harriet Janis revived public interest in Joplin with their book *They All Played Ragtime: The True Story of an American Music*. In addition, pianist Joshua Rifkin made recordings of Joplin's rags that were released in 1970, introducing many people to the music. In 1973 the Hollywood blockbuster *The Sting* featured Joplin's music on its soundtrack, launching "*The Entertainer*" into frequent radio play. At the same time, interest in his later work grew, and in the 1970s three different productions of *Treemonisha* were staged. In 1976 Joplin was awarded a posthumous Pulitzer Prize.

Killens, John Oliver

(b. January 14, 1916, Macon, Ga.; d. October 27, 1987, New York, N.Y.), African American writer and scholar whose politically engaged novels, essays, and screenplays exposed the racism of America in the decades after World War II and argued for new forms of African American independence and identity.

John Oliver Killens was born in Macon, Georgia, in 1916 to Charles Myles Sr. and Willie Lee Killens. He heard fanciful folktales as well as stories of the harsh realities of slavery from his great-grandmother. Between 1934 and 1936 he attended Edward Waters College in Jacksonville, Florida, and Morris Brown College in Atlanta. He moved to Washington, D.C., where he worked for the National Labor Relations Board and finished his B.A. at Howard University. He studied to be a lawyer, then entered the army in 1942 and was stationed in the South Pacific.

After 1948, when Killens moved to New York City, his political work brought him into contact with a broader world of African American scholarship and art. He met Paul Robeson, and W. E. B. Du Bois and Langston Hughes, whose editorials he had admired as a boy. While studying at Columbia University and New York University, he wrote for the socialist newspaper *Freedom*. He founded the Harlem Writers Guild in the early 1950s and produced his first novel, *Youngblood*, in 1954.

Youngblood told the story of a contemporary African American family's hardships in segregated Georgia. Later novels *And Then We Heard the Thunder* (1963) and *'Sippi* (1967) dramatized racism in the armed forces and in the South. *The Cotillion; or, One Good Bull Is Half the Herd* (1971), a satire, addressed internal strife within the black community.

In 1964 Killens founded the Organization for Afro-American Unity with Malcolm X. Black Nationalism influenced much of his later work. Two of his novels received nominations for the Pulitzer Prize. Killens taught in universities and continued to write for national magazines until his death in 1987.

King, Riley B. ("B. B.")

(b. September 16, 1925), one of the most successful bluesmen to emerge from the Memphis scene.

B. B. King has served as the prime ambassador of American blues. Although others may exceed his talent, King did more than anyone else to popularize the genre. After distinguishing himself on the rhythm and blues (R&B) charts during the 1950s, he broke into the pop mainstream in the 1960s, touring with top-name rock bands. His success can be attributed to longevity as much as skill, something he himself admits: "I was 63 when my career hit its hottest stride." Having avoided the substance abuse and violence that took the lives of many of his peers, he continues to record and perform.

Born a sharecropper's son and raised on a plantation in Mississippi, King first found music through the church. After singing in a number of gospel groups, he left to play the blues in Memphis. He soon secured work at the famed WDIA radio station and began performing in bars and night-clubs. King the disc jockey was known as "the Blues Boy from Beale Street," then "Blues Boy," and then simply "B. B."

Photographed at a 1991 concert in the Netherlands, the blues guitarist B. B. King is pictured here with his guitar, nicknamed "Lucille." *CORBIS/Derick A. Thomas; Dat's Jazz*

King's distinctive sound includes a robust vocal style and abbreviated, melodic guitar playing. In the tradition of call and response, King sings a line and follows it with a flourish of guitar. His riffs mimic patterns of speech, giving his performances an air of autonomous duet. Both his harmony, which uses abundant sixths, and his phrasing, which often subverts the beat, demonstrate the influence of jazz musicians such as Charlie Christian and Lester Young. King's lyrics depart from the popular blues themes of violence and sexual braggadocio. Instead, he emphasizes love, fidelity, security, reflecting his early days in gospel as well as his connection with soul.

After a series of hits on a Memphis record label in 1949, King attracted the attention of Ike

Turner, who signed him to Los Angeles-based Modern Records. In 1952 King scored a number-one hit on the R&B charts with *"Three O'Clock Blues."* For the next ten years, he toured the circuit of small black clubs. In the mid-1960s, just as his career seemed to be winding down, the sounds of "British Invasion" bands, particularly Cream and the Rolling Stones, introduced blues to young white Americans and renewed King's popularity. He began recording and touring with these musicians, inspiring a comeback that culminated in his 1970 release *"The Thrill Is Gone."*

In the 1970s King toured the Las Vegas and dinner-club circuits, appeared in films, lectured at universities, received an honorary degree from Yale, and won awards for his prison-charity work. He also collaborated with musicians such as Stevie Wonder, Steve Winwood, and Ringo Starr, though often with marginal results.

Although his recordings grew less reliably outstanding, his mainstream success persevered. Indeed, through both his television endorsements for companies such as Wendy's Hamburgers and Northwest Airlines as well as through his collaborative recordings, King gave the Memphis blues something hitherto unheard of—commercial importance. As an archetype, he paved the way for other blues musicians to become icons of mainstream culture. In 1987 he was inducted into the Rock and Roll Hall of Fame.

North America
Kitt, Eartha Mae
(b. January 26, 1928, North, S.C.), cabaret singer and stage and screen performer known for her seductive stage presence and her "sex kitten" style.

Born on a farm to poverty-stricken sharecroppers, William Kitt and Anna Mae Riley, Eartha Mae and her sister, Pearl, were abandoned by their mother at a young age. The two sisters were raised by a foster family until 1936, when they moved to New York City to live with their aunt. In New York Kitt attended Metropolitan High School (now the New York School of Performing Arts), and at age 16 was invited by Katherine Dunham to join her dance troupe. The group toured Europe and South America from 1946 to 1950, and while they were in Paris, Kitt was discovered by Orson Welles, who cast her in his 1951 production of Marlowe's *Dr. Faustus*. She returned to New York and performed at La Vie en Rose and the Village Vanguard, where she developed a sexy and sensual stage style. In 1952 she appeared in the Broadway show *New Faces of 1952* and in 1954 in the film version. She sang in nightclubs and cabarets from the mid-1950s through the 1960s.

During this period Kitt also worked in film, television, and the theater, as well as recording music. Her stage work included *Mrs. Patterson* (1954) and *Shinbone Alley* (1957). She appeared in the films *The Accused* (1957), *St. Louis Blues* (1958), and *Anna Lucasta* (1959). During this time she recorded two albums, *Bad But Beautiful* (1961) and *At the Plaza* (1965). In the 1960s she also had a stint as Catwoman in the TV series *Batman*.

Some reviewers focused on her haughtiness and sophistication, while others gossiped about her alleged preference for white men and disdain for her rural past.

In 1968, while at a luncheon at the White House hosted by Lady Bird Johnson, Kitt publicly criticized American involvement in the Vietnam War by saying that juvenile delinquency and street crime were direct results of the war. She subsequently experienced a major loss of popularity and underwent personal investigations by the FBI and CIA. After that she performed mostly in Europe until the late 1970s. In 1978 she returned to Broadway to perform in Timbuktu and made an album, *I Love Men* (1984). She produced two autobiographies, *I'm Still Here* (1989) and *Confessions of a Sex Kitten* (1991). In 1993 a five-compact-disc retrospective of her work titled *Eartha Quake* was produced.

Kitt married William McDonald on June 6, 1960. They were divorced in 1965 and have a daughter, Kitt McDonald.

North America

Knight, Gladys

(b. May 28, 1944, Atlanta, Ga.), African American soul and rhythm and blues (R&B) vocalist whose career spans more than 45 years.

Gladys Knight's parents sang in the famous Wings Over Jordan Choir and raised their daughter on the music of the black church. Knight joined the choir at the Mount Moriah Baptist Church in Atlanta at age four, toured with the Morris Brown Choir when she was five, and won the $2,000 grand prize on the Ted Mack Amateur Hour at age eight. She also sang with family members, first informally but soon as an opening act for such big-name performers as Jackie Wilson and Sam Cooke. In addition to superlative singing, the Knight family displayed strong stage presence and savvy dance steps.

In 1961 Gladys Knight and "the Pips" (two cousins and a brother) released a version of Johnny Otis's ballad *"Every Beat of My Heart"* that attracted Atlanta-based Huntom records as well as Fury Records in New York. Following a legal fracas between the two labels, Knight and the Pips began to record singles with Fury, slowly establishing themselves on the R&B charts. They recorded and performed throughout the mid-1960s but did not meet with great success until they switched labels to a Motown subsidiary, Soul Records, in 1965. Their 1967 version of *"I Heard It Through the Grapevine"* reached number two on the pop charts and introduced them to mainstream audiences. Other hits included half a dozen albums and the hit single *"Neither One of Us (Wants to Be the First to Say Goodbye)"* (1972).

Despite their growing popularity, Gladys Knight and the Pips felt relegated by Soul Records to an undeserved second-tier status. When Motown moved from Detroit to Hollywood, the group opted to drop its affiliation, signing a contract with Buddah Records in 1973. After this change they hit their stride, releasing *Imagination*, a Grammy Award-winning album that included the smash single *"Midnight Train to Georgia."* By 1975 they had landed four more singles on the pop charts, and in 1976 Knight made her film debut in *Pipedream*.

Legal debacles with Motown in the late 1970s prevented Knight from recording with the Pips, and although she signed a solo contract with Columbia Records, her career seemed to be in decline. When the group reunited in 1980, however, they regained a name on the R&B charts with *About Love*. Likewise, Knight's 1985 collaboration with Stevie Wonder, Dionne Warwick, and Elton John on the number-one single *"That's What Friends Are For"* evinced an enduring vitality. In 1985 she starred with Flip Wilson in the situation comedy *Charlie and Company*; in 1986 she appeared on an HBO special with Warwick and Patti Labelle; and in 1987 she and the Pips scored another major pop hit with *"Love Overboard."* Knight released a new album of solo material in 1995, called *Just for You*, and in 1996 was inducted into the Rock and Roll Hall of Fame.

North America

KRS One (Laurence Kris Parker)

(b. 1965, Brooklyn, New York), African American rap artist, self-styled "Teacher" of the hip hop nation.

KRS One was born Laurence Kris Parker and grew up in the South Bronx section of New York City. A graffiti artist turned rapper, he founded the seminal rap group Boogie Down Productions (BDP) in 1986 with the disc jockey (DJ) Scott LaRock (Scott Sterling). Their first album, *Criminal Minded* (1987), combined LaRock's harsh, spare, reggae-influenced beats with KRS One's long-winded rhyme style on underground classics such as *"9 MM Goes Bang"* and *"South Bronx."* The album's gritty portrait of life on the streets (as well as the firearms that adorned its cover) influenced the gangsta rap movement that began in earnest two years later.

LaRock was fatally shot soon after Criminal Minded was released, but KRS One recruited a new production team for the second BDP album, *By All Means Necessary* (1988). The album retained some of the thuggish imagery of *Criminal Minded* but also explored the black radicalism suggested by its title, a riff on the words of Malcolm X: "by any means necessary." In tracks like *"My Philosophy,"* *"Stop the Violence,"* and *"Illegal Business,"* KRS One affirmed his new persona—"The Teacher"—with scathing diatribes against institutionalized racism and black-on-black crime. Soon after, KRS One joined other rappers to form the Stop the Violence Movement, which addressed many of the same issues. *By All Means Necessary* stands as the most convincing political hip hop album to date.

In 1989 BDP's third album, *Ghetto Music: Blueprint of Hip Hop*, was released, and KRS One expressed his increasing Afrocentrism on a lecture tour of colleges and universities. BDP's fourth effort, *Edutainment* (1990), contained the hit *"Love's Gonna Get 'Cha (Material Love),"* but some critics complained that the group was running low on inspiration. After two more albums, KRS One dissolved BDP and embarked on a solo career, beginning with the highly acclaimed *Return of the Boom Bap* (1995). Since then, KRS One has maintained his status as hip hop's most committed voice. He has continued to release fairly successful solo albums, and in 1996 he founded the world's first school for hip hop culture, the Temple of Hip Hop.

L

LaBelle, Patti

(b. October 4, 1944, Philadelphia, Pa.), African American singer whose career followed trends in popular music from soul music "girl-groups" in the 1960s through extravagant stage shows in the 1970s to synthesizer pop in the 1980s and 1990s.

Born Patricia Louise Holt, Patti LaBelle first performed for audiences as a teenager at Beulah Baptist Church in Philadelphia. In high school she formed a singing group, the Ordettes, with Cynthia "Cindy" Birdsong; later the two joined with Wynona Hendryx and Sarah Dash of the Del Capris to form the Bluebelles. The Bluebelles' music resembled that of many of their black female pop-singing contemporaries in terms of both repertoire and style. In fact the controversy over whether LaBelle actually recorded "*I Sold My Heart to the Junkman*"—attributed as her first hit—is unresolved. Some contend that the 1962 hit was cut by the Starlets.

Shortly after getting started, the Bluebelles changed their name to Patti LaBelle & the Bluebelles. In the mid-1960s they toured theaters throughout the East and Midwest, landing a number of songs on the R&B charts but failing to become superstars. In 1965 producer Jerry Wexler signed them with Atlantic Records, but even this breakthrough did not launch them onto pop charts. Soulful recordings of such standards as "*Over the Rainbow*" and "*Danny Boy*" earned LaBelle a steady following, yet the high quality of new compositions such as "*Groovy Kind of Love*" was often overlooked by mass audiences. In 1967 Cindy Birdsong left the Bluebelles and took Florence Ballard's place with the Supremes.

At the beginning of the 1970s LaBelle, persuaded by others, decided to change the group's look. She recruited Vicki Wickham, producer of Britain's hip television program "*Ready, Steady, Go!*," to oversee the rebirth of her career with the Bluebelles. Under Wickham's supervision, the group changed its name to the simpler, sleeker LaBelle and donned outrageous

339

stage costumes with silver, feathers, leather, and much exposed flesh. The group's music followed their change in fashion, as they fused new hard rock sounds with old strains of R&B.

Despite its new look LaBelle remained on a low rung of stardom for the next two years. Although the flamboyant and defiant sexuality of its stage shows attracted a following among the gay male community, it remained a second-tier feature in the mainstream. Labelle nevertheless landed a gig at New York's Metropolitan Opera House in 1974, a first for a female African American group. And in 1975 the success of *"Lady Marmalade"*—which reached number one on the pop charts—caused sales of the album *Nightbirds* to break a million, propelling LaBelle to international fame. LaBelle flaunted its extravagant fashion and enjoyed its notoriety until 1977, when the group broke up over musical differences.

Patti LaBelle's career since the group's breakup has shown her ability to change with the times. In the 1980s and 1990s her solo albums sold as well as her group recordings ever had; meanwhile, she courted other media. She broke into television with appearances on *A Different World* and *Out All Night*, as well as on a special of her own. She appeared on Broadway with Al Green in *Your Arm's Too Short to Box with God*. She contributed hit songs to the soundtrack of the film *Beverly Hills Cop* and started her own line of perfume and cosmetics. In 1996 she released her autobiography, *Don't Block the Blessings: Revelations of a Lifetime*, and in 1997 won the Image Award of the National Association for the Advancement of Colored People (NAACP).

Patti LaBelle has employed her celebrity to social ends, sponsoring and speaking for the United Negro College Fund, civic programs in Philadelphia, and medical school scholarships for African Americans.

Africa

Ladysmith Black Mambazo,
a renowned South African musical group.

By improvising on traditional Zulu singing styles, the all-male a cappella choir Ladysmith Black Mambazo became an international sensation after a series of critically acclaimed albums in the 1980s and 1990s. Choral singer Joseph Shabalala formed the ten-member group with friends and relatives in 1962. With Shabalala as lead singer and composer, Mambazo includes seven bass singers, one alto, and one tenor. Since its formation, Mambazo has recorded some 40 albums, with songs in both Zulu and English.

The group's name reflects the Zulu roots of its members. "Ladysmith" is the Shabalala family's hometown in KwaZulu-Natal Province. "Black" refers to black oxen, the strongest animals on the farm, while "mambazo" is the Zulu word for ax, implying that the group could chop down rivals during singing competitions. Their artistic roots lie in a type of performance called *iscathamiya*—Zulu for "walking like a cat"—that combines dancing and call-and-response singing. Iscathamiya originated in the mines, where workers learned to "walk like a cat" and not bother the guards. At home on Saturdays, men would sing and dance late into the evening. Today teams of roughly ten men perform iscathamiya without instrumental accompaniment in competitions before judges.

After converting to Christianity in his youth, Shabalala blended church choral and Zulu singing, a style known as *mbube*. Mambazo generated a following through competitions and appearances on Radio Zulu. Their first release, *Amabutho* (1973), became the first African album to achieve Gold Medal status, with sales of over 25,000 copies.

Popular in South Africa, Mambazo remained largely unknown elsewhere until 1986, when American singer Paul Simon performed with them on his *Graceland* album, which fused African and Western pop music. With sales of more than 7 million, *Graceland* became one of the top-selling LPs of the decade and turned Mambazo into a musical phenomenon.

In 1988 Mambazo won the Grammy Award for Best World Music Recording with *Shaka Zulu*. Five other Mambazo albums have received Grammy nominations, including *How the Leopard Got His Spots* (1989), a collaboration with Danny Glover; *Gift of the Tortoise* (1993); *Liph' Iqiniso* (1994); and *Thuthukani Ngoxolo* (1996).

Mambazo has appeared in several films, including two 1990 documentaries, *Spike Lee & Company—Do It A Cappella* and *Mandela in America*. They were also featured in *Waati*, a 1995 political drama. The group recorded soundtracks for various other movies, including *Moonwalker, A Dry White Season, Coming to America*, and *Cry the Beloved Country*.

In 1991 Mambazo began collaborating with Chicago's Steppenwolf Theatre Company in the production of two musicals, *Song of Jacob Zulu*, which opened on Broadway in 1993 and received six Tony Award nominations, and *Nomathemba*, based on Shabalala's first composition. Mambazo sang at the ceremony when Nelson Mandela and F. W. De Klerk, then president of South Africa, won the Nobel Peace Prize in 1993; at Mandela's inauguration as South African president in 1994; and before Queen Elizabeth during Mandela's 1996 state visit. Their 1997 album, *Heavenly*, broke new ground with gospel and rhythm and blues numbers, as well as collaborations with Lou Rawls, Dolly Parton, and Bonnie Raitt.

North America

Lafayette Theatre,

pioneering African American theater in Harlem that staged both serious drama and light entertainment.

Like many Harlem theaters, the Lafayette Theatre originally opened in 1912 for all-white audiences. A few years later black drama critic Lester Walton leased the theater and created a black stock company to bring meaningful dramatic theater to New York's black audiences. By 1916 the Lafayette Players, led by Anita Bush, had successfully produced plays by Shakespeare, Dumas, and Molière.

Eventually, the Lafayette adapted to its audience's taste for musical comedies and more lighthearted theater. The theater remained a center for black entertainment through the 1930s, when the Federal Theater Project brought more serious works back to the Lafayette stage. In 1967, at the height of the Black Arts Movement, the New Lafayette Theatre opened in Harlem, honoring its namesake's commitment to producing theater with African American performers for African American audiences.

North America

Larsen, Nella

(b. April 13, 1891, Chicago, Ill.; d. March 30, 1964, New York, N.Y.), African American novelist of the Harlem Renaissance; landmark figure in the black women's literary tradition.

Nella Larsen's celebrity has followed an unusual trajectory. She was one of the most celebrated black novelists during the Harlem Renaissance and received several major awards for her writing, including the first Guggenheim Fellowship ever given to a black woman. She and her husband were also notable members of the Harlem social scene, and she was friends with most of the prominent Harlem writers of her time. After a public accusation of plagiarism and an equally public divorce, Larsen removed herself from the public eye and was effectively forgotten by acquaintances and audiences until after her death. But renewed interest in both the Harlem Renaissance and black women writers has brought her back to prominence, and Larsen is again celebrated as a key figure in the African American literary tradition.

Larsen was born Nellie Walker to a Danish mother and a West Indian father in Chicago. After her father's death when she was two, her mother married a Danish man and had a second daughter, making Larsen the only black member of her family. As a result, she always felt estranged from them, and in 1909 she left home to attend Fisk University. A year later she traveled to Denmark and spent the next two years living with relatives and studying at the University of Copenhagen. Larsen next studied nursing in New York, and in 1916 she returned south to Tuskegee Institute to become assistant superintendent of nurses there. But while she had come to feel most comfortable in all-black environments, she was still unhappy in the South, and in 1916 she returned to New York.

Larsen worked as a nurse and a children's librarian in New York over the next ten years. In 1919 she married Dr. Elmer Imes, a prominent physicist, and her marriage brought her into contact with the upper classes of New York's black society, including many of the writers who were already active in Harlem. She published her first two essays, both on Danish children's games, in 1920 in *The Brownies' Book*, a children's magazine that was an offshoot of the *Crisis*, the monthly magazine of the National Association for the Advancement of Colored People (NAACP). Encouraged by writers and artists around her, especially black writer Walter White and white patron Carl Van Vechten, in 1926 she began writing full-time.

Larsen's two novels, *Quicksand* and *Passing*, were published by the mainstream publisher Alfred A. Knopf in 1928 and 1929. Both novels deal with upper-class, mixed-race black women protagonists, reflecting the world Larsen found herself in, but they go beyond simply painting that world. Instead, they are complicated explorations of the ways in which race, gender, class, and sexuality all constrict the women's lives to varying degrees. In *Quicksand* the main character is a biracial Danish and black woman, like Larsen, who finds that she is not entirely at home in either Danish or African American society but who cannot find an alternative. And in *Passing*, the protagonists are two childhood friends who meet as adults and find that while one has settled into a safe life in the black bourgeoisie, the other has chosen to pass as white. That novel's tensions rise as the women find themselves drawn to one another yet jealous of one another's lives.

Quicksand and *Passing* were both well received. Larsen was awarded the Harmon Foundation's Bronze Medal for Literature in 1929 and the Guggenheim Fellowship in 1930, which she used to travel to Spain and France to research a third novel. But the charge of plagiarism came that same year, over the short story "Sanctuary" that Larsen had published in January 1930 in the prominent mainstream journal the *Forum*. Larsen's publisher supported her assertion that any resemblance between the plot of her story and one published in another magazine several years earlier was purely coincidental, as is probably true. But the damage still hurt Larsen's reputation and her confidence.

This was followed by the humiliation of her 1933 divorce, which stemmed from her husband's alleged affair with a white woman. Newspapers covering the story accused Larsen of being too preoccupied with her writing to be a good wife, and claimed that she had tried to commit suicide over the affair. While Larsen did not literally kill herself, she did close herself off from all contact with her former life. Spreading a rumor that she was moving to South America, she moved instead to New York's Lower East Side, where she lived alone and worked quietly as a nurse for the next 30 years. She was found dead in her apartment in 1964.

Despite the obscurity of the end of her life, Larsen's reputation and writings have been resurrected. Contemporary critics now regard her as one of the most sophisticated and modern novelists to emerge from the Harlem Renaissance, and her two books are regarded as landmark examples of black women's attempts to explain their complex identities—and the complicated forces circumscribing them—in fiction.

North America

Lawrence, Jacob Armstead

(b. September 7, 1917, Atlantic City, N.J.), the most acclaimed African American artist at the end of the twentieth century.

Jacob Lawrence has painted figurative and narrative pictures of the black community and black history for more than 60 years in a consistent modernist style, using expressive, strong design and flat areas of color. His parents, Jacob Armstead Lawrence of South Carolina and Rose Lee of Virginia, were part of the Great Migration, the movement of African Americans from the South to the promise of jobs in Northern industry during the two decades following the onset of World War I.

When Lawrence was two years old, his family moved to Easton, Pennsylvania. A few years later they moved to Philadelphia, where his father became a part-time dining-car cook on the railroads. After his parents separated in 1924, Lawrence, his mother, and his younger brother and sister moved to Harlem, where they joined relatives who had also relocated in the North.

During Lawrence's youth in Harlem his mother enrolled him in after-school arts and crafts classes held at the 135th Street Branch of the New York Public Library. Charles Alston, who taught art there, later moved to the Utopia Neighborhood Center, where Lawrence also enrolled. Using a variety of techniques, including collage and *papier-mâché*, the young Lawrence made colorful masks and cityscapes on the insides of cardboard shoe-boxes. He was introduced to African American history in his classes, and he visited the exhibition of African sculpture held at the Museum of Modern Art in 1935.

Lawrence took classes at the Harlem Art Center and the American Artists School from 1936 through 1938, and in 1936 he also worked briefly for the Civilian Conservation Corps, one of the relief agencies set up by the Roosevelt administration to create employment for youth during the Great Depression. Among the older artists, Augusta Savage was probably the most influential on Lawrence's work. A dynamic sculptor, she believed her mission was to teach art to children and young people in Harlem, and she spearheaded the establishment of the Harlem Community Art Center in 1937, financed by the Federal Art Project (FAP) of the national Works Progress Administration (WPA). She arranged to have Lawrence hired as a professional artist in 1938 in the easel section of the FAP.

Although he was still young as an artist, in his late teens and early twenties Lawrence participated fully in the activities at art centers and at Alston's studio at 306 West 141st Street. At this time Lawrence met his future wife, fellow artist Gwendolyn Knight. The intellectuals, writers, and artists who gave talks and readings at art centers were crucial to the development of Lawrence and other young Harlem artists such as Knight, Romare Bearden, and Bob Blackburn. Lawrence was particularly influenced by Claude McKay and Alain Locke, but Katherine Dunham, Countee Cullen, and Langston Hughes also stand out in his memory.

In 1936 Lawrence was painting scenes of Harlem interiors and street life, using the flat style that was to become his lifelong trademark. During the next year he began his first narrative series with texts: 41 panels on the life of Toussaint L'Ouverture, the liberator of Haiti. Some of Lawrence's Harlem scenes were included in a 1937 group exhibition of the Harlem Artists Guild and then featured in his first solo exhibition, which was held in the next year at the Harlem YMCA. After a New York showing at the De Porres Interracial Center, his *Toussaint* series traveled to the Baltimore Museum of Art in 1939 for the exhibition *Contemporary Negro Art*.

During the late 1930s and the 1940s Lawrence worked on two other narrative series: *Frederick Douglass* (1938–1939), comprising 32 paintings, and *Harriet Tubman* (1939–1949), comprising 31 paintings. For both he received support from the Harmon Foundation. There was support from the Julius Rosenwald Fund for *Migration* (1940–1941), a series of 60 paintings; and *John Brown* (1941–1942), a series of 22 paintings. Alain Locke, who had included Lawrence in his influential book *The Negro in Art* (1940), brought him to the attention of Edith Halpert, the prominent New York art dealer, who agreed to give Lawrence a show at her Downtown Gallery.

Halpert alerted publisher Henry Luce, who reproduced 26 pictures from the *Migration Series* in the November 1941 issue of *Fortune* magazine. The 60 panels were subsequently divided between the Phillips Collection in Washington, D.C., and the Museum of Modern Art in New York City. In 1942 Lawrence received another grant from the Rosenwald Fund to create a *Harlem* series of 30 genre paintings.

Lawrence and Gwendolyn Knight had married in 1941, but with the country at war, Lawrence was drafted into the United States Coast Guard in 1943, where he served until 1945. Even when he was in the service, he continued painting. After his discharge he used a Guggenheim Fellowship to paint a *War* series of 14 panels. In 1947 *Fortune* commissioned him to produce a series on rural life in the postwar South. In 1948 he illustrated *One Way Ticket* by Langston Hughes.

During the 1950s Lawrence continued to paint pictures in series. Even though he spent a year at Hillside Hospital in Queens for psychiatric treatment, he used the opportunity to paint a *Hospital* series of 11 panels, exhibited at the Downtown Gallery in 1950. In 1952 he painted his *Theater* series. During the Civil Rights Movement of the mid-1950s, he turned again to black history and painted 30 panels of a projected 60-panel series entitled *Struggle: From the History of the American People*, which highlighted the contributions of African Americans.

Lawrence's first teaching job came in the summer of 1946 when Joseph Albers persuaded him to join the Summer Institute of his experimental arts school, Black Mountain College, in Asheville, North Carolina. In the summer of 1954 Lawrence taught at the Skowhegan School of Painting and Sculpture in Maine, and in the fall of 1955 he became an instructor at Pratt Institute in Brooklyn, where he stayed until 1970. In that year he was appointed visiting artist at the University of Washington in Seattle and in 1971 he became a full professor there, a position that he held until his retirement in 1986. He also held several visiting positions: Skowhegan in the summers, 1968–1972; Brandeis University as artist-in-residence in the spring of 1965; the New School for Social Research as part-time instructor, 1966–1969; the Art Students League, 1967–1969; and California State College at Hayward, 1969–1970.

In 1961 Lawrence began reworking earlier themes as prints. When he and Knight lived in Nigeria in 1954, he painted scenes of the local market. He increasingly received commissions to design posters and prints. He designed two *Time* magazine covers, one of Jesse Jackson and one of Colonel Ojukwu, military governor of Biafra. He did a poster for the 1972 Olympic Games, and he completed the *George Washington Bush* series for the state of Washington in 1973. During the 1970s he began making paintings with the theme of building and carpenters, which to Lawrence symbolized the goal of constructing strong, integrated communities.

Major retrospective exhibitions of Lawrence's paintings have had national tours organized by the American Federation of Art in 1960, the Whitney Museum of American Art in 1974, and the Seattle Art Museum in 1986. The 60-panel *Migration Series*, organized by the Phillips Collection, circulated between 1993 and 1995. Murals on the themes of sports and work are on the walls of Kingdome Stadium in Seattle and the New York City subway system. Lawrence was honored by President Jimmy Carter in 1980, and he was inducted into the American Academy of Arts and Letters in 1994. In 1990 he received the National Medal of Arts from President George Bush.

North America

Ledbetter, Hudson William ("Leadbelly")

(b. January 21, 1885, near Mooringsport, La.; d. December 6, 1949, New York, N.Y.), African American itinerant musician who played from a wide repertoire that centered on blues but included folk ballads, popular songs, and music from the American West.

As a child Leadbelly picked cotton with his parents, first as a sharecropper in Louisiana and then on land that his parents bought in Leigh, Texas. During his youth in Leigh, he demonstrated substantial musical talent. He played the accordion, mastered the 12-string guitar, and soon frequented the red-light district of neighboring Shreveport as a musician.

In his early twenties Leadbelly left home and was married, though not to the woman who mothered his two children. At this age he was already an inveterate rambling man, versed in violence, drink, and promiscuity. He settled in Harris County, Texas, and then moved to Dallas, where he met and formed a musical relationship with the great bluesman Blind Lemon Jefferson. When possible, Leadbelly supported himself with his music; otherwise he worked on farms and at other manual labor.

Throughout the next two decades Leadbelly had frequent skirmishes with the law. He was jailed in 1915 but escaped; he served a prison sentence from 1918 to 1925 for murder; and he returned to prison in 1930 until 1934 for attempted homicide. Both his stints in prison ended by means of his music. In 1925 he improvised a song that successfully begged the pardon of Gov. Pat Neff, who was visiting the penitentiary; and in 1934 Leadbelly shortened his sentence by impressing white folklorist John A. Lomax, who requested Leadbelly's release.

With the help of his son, Alan, John Lomax compiled folk recordings for the Library of Congress, traveling the south with new technology to capture America's oral traditions. In Leadbelly they found an immense repository of folk and original music, which they recorded and promoted in the East. John Lomax transformed Leadbelly's life, hiring him as a chauffeur and introducing him to white audiences.

Leadbelly cut commercial recordings and released "race records" but achieved his largest following on college campuses, at political rallies, and in the folk scene of Greenwich Village in the early 1940s. He collaborated with both white and black members of this crowd, including Woody Guthrie, Brownie McGhee, Sonny Terry, and Big Bill Broonzy. Like these musicians, Leadbelly became associated with left-wing politics and wrote such overtly political tunes as "Scottsboro Boys" (1938) and "Bourgeois Blues" (1938). In the 1940s he achieved greater celebrity by appearing on radio and in film. In 1949 he toured in Europe but returned to New York, where he died later that year.

Leadbelly had a rough and powerful voice, yet he could perform with subtle and surprising delicacy. He was a master of the 12-string guitar and accomplished on mandolin, accordion, piano, and harmonica. His work as a musician yielded approximately 70 original or highly reworked compositions in addition to scores of children's songs, Southern ballads, blues tunes, field hollers, and popular songs. In Europe Leadbelly influenced the skiffle bands that later culminated in the Beatles and the Rolling Stones. In the United States he inspired a generation of black bluesmen as well as white folk singers such as Joan Baez and Bob Dylan. In 1976 Gordon Parks Sr. made a biographical film about his life. In 1988 Leadbelly was inducted into the Rock and Roll Hall of Fame.

North America

Lee, Canada

(b. May 3, 1907, New York, N.Y.; d. May 10, 1952, England), African American prizefighter and actor noted for performing strong, non-stereotypical roles in the 1930s and 1940s.

As an African American actor, Canada Lee played non-stereotypical roles during the late 1930s and 1940s, when black actors and actresses were relegated to demeaning roles. Originally a boxer, he entered theater after being blinded in one eye in a fight in 1933. He began his acting career when he was cast in the role of Banquo in a black production of *Macbeth* funded by the Works Progress Administration (WPA) Negro Federal Theatre Project in

1936. The play was directed by Orson Welles and marked the beginning of Lee's casting in nontraditional roles.

Although *Macbeth* received some negative reviews (due more to the fact that a black cast was performing Shakespeare than to the acting), it gave Lee the needed exposure to continue in such roles. Through the WPA Negro Federal Theatre Project, he continued to experiment with the nontraditional, performing in Eugene O'Neill's *One Act Plays of the Sea* in 1937 and *Haiti*, by W. E. B. Du Bois, in 1938. Due to the "communist leanings" of the play *Haiti* and *Big White Fog* in 1940, the Negro Federal Theatre Project was halted by the House Committee on Un-American Activities (HUAC).

Nevertheless, Lee had gained enough exposure to be cast in the part of Drayton in *Mamba's Daughters* on Broadway in 1939. Further, the experience he gained with the Negro Federal Theatre Project led to his role as Bigger Thomas in *Native Son* in 1940 and 1941. Critics cite his portrayal of Bigger as the best role of his career. Because the play had an interracial cast, it became highly controversial.

Lee's visibility as a black actor doing unconventional roles inspired him to speak out against the limited casting of black actors and actresses in Hollywood and Broadway. Determined not to take stereotypical "handkerchief head roles," he decided to produce *On Whitman Avenue* to achieve that end. In 1947 the HUAC cited Lee's play as "left-wing."

Lee garnered even greater visibility when he portrayed Stephen Kumalo, a father whose son kills a white man, in the play *Cry, the Beloved Country*, produced by Zoltan Korda. Despite worldwide attention for his acting, Lee could not escape being blacklisted and pursued by HUAC as well as by the Federal Bureau of Investigation for speaking out against stereotyping. He died in 1952, 45 years old and penniless.

North America

Lee, Shelton Jackson ("Spike")

(b. March 20, 1957, Atlanta, Ga.), African American film director, writer, and actor.

Starting with the phenomenal popularity of *She's Gotta Have It*, Spike Lee has emerged as one of America's most successful filmmakers, garnering both good reviews and healthy box-office receipts for his movies. He has also attracted criticism; detractors have called him arrogant and paranoid and his movies incendiary, even racist. But controversy has not kept Lee from becoming a media icon, famous for his acting, fashion sense, and provocative public pronouncements on a variety of subjects.

Raised in the Fort Greene neighborhood of Brooklyn, New York, Lee is the eldest of five children born to Bill Lee, a jazz musician and composer, and Jacquelyn Lee, a schoolteacher. Both of his parents came from well-educated families, and Lee's childhood was rich in art, music, and literature. Like his father and grandfather before him, Lee attended Morehouse College in Atlanta, Georgia. It was at Morehouse that he first began to "dib and dab in super-8 filmmaking." These early experiments led to his enrollment at the Institute of Film and Television at New York University (NYU).

One of the few black students at NYU's film school, Lee attracted controversy with his short film *The Answer* (1980), a response to D. W. Griffith's classic silent film *Birth of a Nation*, which has become famous as much for its racist politics as for its cinematic excellence. Later student works included *Sarah* (1981), a loving depiction of Thanksgiving in Harlem, and Lee's last student film, *Joe's Bed-Stuy Barbershop: We Cut Heads* (1982), which garnered an award from the Academy of Motion Picture Arts and Sciences as well as screenings at prestigious film festivals.

Despite this early recognition, Lee received no offers from Hollywood after graduating from NYU, a situation he attributed to the systemic racism in the entertainment industry. While working at a film distribution company, he raised money to finance an independent film. In 1986, following the collapse of his plans for a movie about a bike messenger, Lee released his first feature film, *She's Gotta Have It*, a romantic comedy about a single black woman dating three men simultaneously. Critics praised the movie's style, intelligence, humor, and realistic portrayal of African Americans—something seldom seen in Hollywood productions—and it received the coveted New Film Award at the Cannes Film Festival.

For his next project Lee returned to a script he had written while at Morehouse. *School Daze* (1988) focused on conflicts between fair-skinned, upwardly mobile African American "wannabes" and darker, more Afrocentric "jigaboos" at a historically black university. Lee, who has appeared in nearly all of his films, costarred with Laurence Fishburne and Giancarlo Esposito in *School Daze*, which received mixed reviews but was financially successful.

It was Lee's third feature that received the most attention. *Do the Right Thing* (1989), set in the Bedford-Stuyvesant and Bensonhurst sections of Brooklyn, came in the wake of a series of racially motivated attacks against African Americans. Ending with a scene in which white police officers kill a black teenager, *Do the Right Thing* was met with alarm by many white critics and commentators who feared that it would incite rioting among African Americans. It did not. The movie, widely considered Lee's best film artistically, was a box-office success.

Attention from *Do the Right Thing*, combined with Lee's popular commercials for Nike and other products, made him a recognizable celebrity by 1990. With the increased exposure, Lee's comments on race relations, politics, other filmmakers, and even basketball sparked heated responses from many quarters. Despite the occasionally negative press, many credit Lee's visibility and the success of his first three films with inspiring a wave of African American filmmakers. Young directors such as John Singleton (*Boyz N the Hood*, 1991) and Matty Rich (*Straight out of Brooklyn*, 1991) began finding the financial and institutional support that had eluded Lee only a few years earlier.

Lee's next two films—*Mo' Better Blues* (1990) and *Jungle Fever* (1991)—were less well received critically, though each made money. In 1992 he released his most ambitious film, *Malcolm X*, a sweeping biography of the slain civil rights leader. *Malcolm X* attracted at least as much controversy as *Do the Right Thing*, particularly within the black community, some of which saw Lee as co-opting the Black Muslim hero's image. Lee, who had used security personnel from the Nation of Islam to guard the sets on previous films, responded with typical bravado. The film, starring Denzel Washington, received mostly favorable reviews but was criticized for its length and simplistic political message.

After *Malcolm X*, Lee made a number of movies—*Crooklyn* (1994), *Clockers* (1995), *Girl 6* (1996), *Get on the Bus* (1996), and *He Got Game* (1998)—that did not attract the critical or commercial attention that his earlier work did. Lee also continued to film commercials and music videos and command a film studio (40 Acres & A Mule, named for a broken promise the United States government made to former slaves after the Civil War) and a clothing store in his home neighborhood in Brooklyn. Lee's 1998 documentary *Four Little Girls*, about the victims of a 1963 church bombing in Birmingham, Alabama, was nominated for an Academy Award. In 1999 he released *Summer of Sam*, a drama set in the late 1970s.

North America

LeNoire, Rosetta Olive Burton

(b. August 8, 1911, New York, N.Y.), African American actress, theater executive, and social activist.

Encouraged by her godfather, the dancer Bill "Bojangles" Robinson, Rosetta LeNoire began to sing and dance at an early age. Robinson gave her the nickname "Bubbling Brown Sugar in a Crystal Ball," which she carried with her throughout her life. LeNoire began her career playing the First Witch in a Haitian *Macbeth*, a production directed by Orson Welles in 1936. Over much of her career, she played the roles of housemaids with a self-confident grace that inspired pride and respect. For over 50 years she performed on and off-Broadway. In her eighties, LeNoire appeared on television in such roles as Nell Carter's mother on *Gimme a Break* and the grandmother on *Family Matters*.

LeNoire was active in the creation of the Negro Actors Guild (NAG) and the Coordinating Council for Negro Performers (CCNP), both of which strove to aid black actors in financial need, create acting opportunities for blacks, and fight to eliminate demeaning portrayals of African Americans on television and on film. In 1968 LeNoire helped establish the Amas Repertory Theater in New York City. The purpose of Amas has been to encourage racial understanding through theatrical productions. Its most successful show, *Bubbling Brown Sugar*, an award-winning musical tribute to black music and culture, opened on Broadway in 1976.

Lewis, Edmonia

(b. 1845?; d. ?), believed to be the first woman sculptor of African American and Native American heritage.

Edmonia Lewis often drew upon her dual ancestry for inspiration. Her best-known work, *Forever Free* (1867, Howard University Gallery of Art, Washington, D.C.), was inspired by the Emancipation Proclamation. Created in marble, *Forever Free* depicts a man and a woman who have learned of their freedom. In an expression of gratitude, the woman kneels with her hands clasped; the man rests his foot on the ball that held them in bondage, raising his arm to display the broken shackle and chain on his wrist.

Little is known about Lewis's early life. Sources give differing birth dates—1843 and 1845—and birthplaces—Ohio, New York, and New Jersey. Her father was an African American, and her mother was a member of the Ojibwa community. In 1859 Lewis entered Oberlin College in Oberlin, Ohio, where she excelled at drawing. Known as *Wildfire* in the Ojibwa community, Lewis changed her name to Mary Edmonia during her time at Oberlin; she generally signed her sculptures and her correspondence with the name Edmonia. When a teacher at Oberlin missed some paintbrushes, Lewis was accused of the theft; she was also accused of attempted murder when two girls fell ill after drinking mulled wine, which Lewis allegedly served them. Although acquitted of both charges, she was not permitted to graduate.

In 1863 Lewis moved to Boston, where the abolitionist William Lloyd Garrison introduced her to sculptor Edward Brackett, who became her first mentor. Lewis's earliest sculptures were medallions with portraits of white antislavery leaders and Civil War heroes, which she modeled in clay and cast in plaster. Her *Bust of Colonel Robert Gould Shaw* (1865, Museum of Afro-American History, Boston, Massachusetts) depicted the young Bostonian who led an all-black battalion, the Fifty-fourth Massachusetts Volunteer Regiment, in battle against Confederate forces. Sales of replicas of the bust enabled Lewis to travel to Italy in 1865, where she established a studio in Rome.

The high point of Lewis's career was the completion of *The Death of Cleopatra* (1876, National Museum of American Art, Washington, D.C.), which created a sensation at the Philadelphia Centennial Exposition of 1876. Other sculptors generally depicted Cleopatra contemplating death; Lewis showed Cleopatra seated on her throne after death, her head thrown back. In her right hand Cleopatra holds the poisonous snake that has bitten her, while her left arm hangs lifelessly. This realistic portrayal ran contrary to the sentimentality about death that was prevalent at the time.

Lewis was reported as still living in Rome in 1911, but the date and location of her death are not known.

Lewis, Henry

(b. October 16, 1932, Los Angeles, Calif.; d. January 26, 1996, New York, N.Y.), African American double-bass player and orchestra conductor; the first black to become a regular conductor of a major American symphony orchestra.

During a music career that spanned nearly five decades, Henry Lewis gained wide respect as a conductor, instrumentalist, and pioneer in the classical music world. At age 16 he joined the Los Angeles Philharmonic, becoming the first black instrumentalist in a major orchestra. In 1968 he became the first black to head a major American orchestra, the New Jersey Symphony, and in 1972 he debuted at the New York Metropolitan Opera, conducting Puccini's *La Bohème*.

Lewis began studying piano at age five and later learned to play the clarinet as well as several string instruments. After six years as a double-bassist with the Los Angeles Philharmonic Orchestra, he played with and conducted the Seventh Army Symphony while serving in the United States Armed Forces (1955–1956). He gained national recognition in 1961 when he was appointed assistant conductor of the Los Angeles Philharmonic under Zubin Mehta, a post he held until 1965.

After serving as a guest conductor of major symphony orchestras in the United States and abroad, Lewis moved to Newark, New Jersey, where in 1968 he became conductor and music director of the New Jersey Symphony—a small community ensemble. He transformed the ensemble into a nationally recognized orchestra that annually performed more than a hundred concerts, including outreach programs for local communities. From 1960 to 1979 he was married to famed opera singer Marilyn Horne, who considered him her "teacher and right hand." After retiring from the New Jersey Symphony in 1976, Lewis continued to tour as a guest conductor until his death from a heart attack at age 63.

Lewis, Meade ("Lux")

(b. September 3, 1905, Chicago, Ill.; d. February 7, 1964, Minneapolis, Minn.), African American pianist who popularized boogie woogie.

In the 1930s and 1940s Lux Lewis worked alongside fellow boogie-woogie piano players Albert Ammons and Pete Johnson. Bringing this blues piano style to Carnegie Hall in New York City in 1938, Lewis raised the speedy rhythms and energetic solos of boogie woogie to new heights of popularity. His signature tune, *"Honky Tonk Train Blues,"* was recorded in 1927 and was released by Paramount Records in 1929. Lewis's early musical mastery laid the foundation for New York City rhythm and blues and rock and roll. Lewis died in an automobile accident in 1964.

Lincoln, Abbey

(b. August 6, 1930, Chicago, Ill.), African American actress and jazz vocalist, arranger, and composer.

Although she calls herself a "late bloomer," Abbey Lincoln has excelled both musically and dramatically for more than 40 years. Born Anna Marie Wooldridge and raised in a family of 12 children in a small Michigan town, Lincoln began her show business career as a singer. Under the stage name Gaby Lee, she sang in nightclubs in California and Hawaii throughout the early 1950s. Her carefully crafted image as a seductress helped earn her a small role in the 1956 film *The Girl Can't Help It*.

In the late 1950s Lincoln (re-christened Abbey Lincoln by her manager) met the jazz drummer Max Roach, with whom she moved to New York City. There she met Thelonious Monk, John Coltrane, and other avant-garde members of the black musical world. Lincoln married Roach in 1960, the same year she sang in his *Freedom Now Suite*, a musical celebration of the Civil Rights Movement. The 1960s saw Lincoln's return to the screen in groundbreaking roles in such movies as *Nothing But a Man* (1964), with Ivan Dixon, and *For Love of Ivy* (1968), with Sidney Poitier. Critics praised both performances for their stereotype-shattering realism.

In the 1970s, facing the shortage of movie roles available to African American women as well as the end of her marriage to Roach, Lincoln left the United States and toured Asia and Europe as a solo singer. She also visited Africa, where she took the African name Aminata Moseka. Returning to New York in 1981, she joined M-Base, a group of young jazz musicians, and began recording again. Lincoln's 1991 album *You Gotta Pay the Band* won acclaim for both her voice and her songwriting talent.

Lincoln Theatre,

popular African American theater in Harlem from approximately 1910 to 1930 that catered to New York's Southern immigrants.

In the decades before the Harlem Renaissance, when many Harlem theaters admitted only whites, the Lincoln Theatre's open-admissions policy made it the hot spot for Harlem's African American audiences. On 135th Street at Lenox Avenue, the Lincoln catered to the community's working-class Southern immigrants. It was known for its live entertainment and lively audiences, who often participated in the onstage action with loud and witty running commentary. Pianist Thomas "Fats" Waller got his start at the Lincoln, and "Mother of the Blues" Ma Rainey, "Empress of the Blues" Bessie Smith, jazz musician Duke Ellington, and vaudeville entertainer Bert Williams all performed there before it became a movie theater and later a church.

Latin America and the Caribbean

Lisboa, Antônio Francisco ("Aleijadinho")

(b. August 29, 1730, Villa Rica do Ouro Preto, Minas Gerais, Brazil; d. November 18, 1814, Villa Rica do Ouro Preto, Minas Gerais, Brazil), the most famous sculptor and architect of colonial Brazil.

Antônio Francisco Lisboa, better known by his nickname "Aleijadinho" (the Little Cripple), distinguished himself as an artist in Minas Gerais, Brazil, during the baroque and rococo artistic periods. The Minas Gerais variant of the baroque and rococo styles is distinct because, unlike the coastal states of Rio de Janeiro and Bahia, whose frequent contact with Portugal kept the art and architecture of those provinces in tune with European artistic developments, the location of Minas Gerias in the interior largely insulated it from European influences. Minas Gerais was also a more recently settled province, and it had few convents or monasteries of the regular orders, which would have otherwise encouraged the duplication of European architectural designs.

During the colonial era in Latin America, the church was the center of social life and the principal patron of the arts. Virtually all of Aleijadinho's works have religious themes, because they were commissioned by churches in Minas Gerais, whose construction was made possible by the province's lucrative mining industry.

Aleijadinho was the son of a Portuguese architect named Manuel Francisco Lisboa and a

Known as "Aleijadinho" (little cripple), Lisboa created some of his most famous sculptures after losing the use of his hands to a crippling disease. In the later part of his life his assistants strapped tools to his wrists so that he could continue to work. *Corbis/Genevieve Naylor*

slave named Isabel. As a mulatto growing up in colonial Brazil, he faced some restrictions, but otherwise his youth was relatively unburdened. His father recognized Antônio Francisco as his son and instructed him in the fundamentals of architecture. Aleijadinho also learned architecture and design from other artists in Villa Rica, including the painter João Gomes Baptista. He began to carve wood, sculpt in stone, and draft building plans at age 14. Beyond what Aleijadinho was taught by his mentors in Minas Gerais, he was also exposed to European art through book illustrations and engravings of buildings and paintings by European artists. He reinterpreted some of these forms in his own work, giving birth to a uniquely Brazilian version of the rococo style. Some of the distinguishing elements of Aleijadinho's work include the use of soapstone, which until then had rarely been employed; a church plan synthesizing the rectangular, linear forms of the traditional Portuguese designs with a more curvilinear Italian-influenced design; the execution of an ornate, circular relief sculpture on the façade of the church above the central door, a type of ornamentation previously reserved only for the interior; and the unprecedented use of cylindrical towers topped with elegant bulb-shaped forms.

In addition to sculpting statues, pulpits, and altars, Aleijadinho designed churches and decorated their interiors, usually by means of ornamental reliefs. He often worked in collaboration with the painters Francisco Xavier Carneiro and Manoel da Costa Ataíde, also of African descent. In part or whole, Aleijadinho's most famous works are the churches of São Francisco de Assis in Ouro Preto and São João de Rei; Nossa Senhora do Carmo in Sabará; and Bom Jesus de Matosinhos in Congonhas dos Campo, Aleijadinho's masterpiece. Bom Jesus de Matosinhos is a pilgrimage church and houses a set of 66 life-size wooden figures carved by Aleijadinho that represent the scenes from the Last Supper and the Stations of the Cross. The stairway leading to the church features 12 massive yet dynamic statues of the Old Testament prophets executed by Aleijadinho.

Many of Aleijadinho's best-known works, including his *Prophets*, were done after he contracted a debilitating and painful disease in his forties. The disease, which has frequently been labeled as leprosy, caused severe scarring, atrophy, and disfigurement. His appendages shriveled, he lost fingers and toes, and eventually he had to have his three assistants strap the chisel and mallet to the stumps of his gnarled hands. His appearance became so deformed that he hid himself from public view, traveling and working behind curtains. Although in a state of physical deterioration, he worked with increasing intensity during the last three decades of his life. He died in 1814 at age 84, never having traveled or worked beyond the state of Minas Gerais.

In an artistic career lasting more than half a century, Aleijadinho produced a vast oeuvre that includes some 80 sculptures as well as the design and decoration of numerous churches. In addition, a number of works are believed to have been executed by Aleijadinho, most notably the church of Santa Ifigênia for Chico Rei, but there is no documentation or signature to verify these attributions. Most of Aleijadinho's work is concentrated in the city of Ouro Preto (formerly Villa Rica), which is today a Brazilian national monument. In the words of art historian Pál Kelemen, "Aleijadinho carried Brazilian rococo to its fullest flowering . . . . A rare human story lives in his masterpieces; his gift was genius."

North America

Little Richard (Richard Wayne Penniman)

(b. December 25, 1932 or 1935, Macon, Ga.), African American musician; rock and roll pioneer.

Born Richard Penniman, Little Richard was one of 12 children in a family divided by the religious concerns of some—many were Seventh Day Adventist preachers—and the more secular interests of others—his father was a bootlegger. Richard was kicked out of the house at age 13 for reasons that remain unclear but that probably relate to his precocious and adventurous sexuality. He was taken in by a white family who owned the Tick Tock Club in Macon, where he began his musical career.

Little Richard in concert at Wembley Arena in London, 1995 *Matthew Polak /CORBIS SYGMA*

After several years of playing around the South and recording in Atlanta and Houston, Little Richard sent a demonstration tape in 1955 to Specialty Records, a rhythm and blues label based in Los Angeles. Specialty found the tapes promising and arranged a recording session in New Orleans. This turned out to be one of the germinal sessions of rock and roll. Little Richard's explosive vocal energy heralded a new style, far removed from the conventional jump blues he had been playing.

Most of these songs were filled with barely concealed sexual imagery (even after cleaning up the lyrics), made more outrageous by Little Richard's falsetto squeals. One of them was "*Tutti Frutti*," featuring the immortal introduction: "A-wop-bop-a-lu-bop, a-wop-bam-boom." Other hits quickly followed, including "*Long Tall Sally*," "*Rip It Up*," "*Lucille*," and

"*Good Golly Miss Molly.*" Little Richard became a sensation, touring nationally and appearing in Hollywood movies about rock and roll, of which the most popular was *The Girl Can't Help It* (1956), named after one of his compositions.

In retrospect, Little Richard's popularity is startling. He may have modeled his outrageous stage persona in the tradition of effeminate black male entertainers wearing makeup, such as Billy Wright. While the sight of an African American man wearing makeup and singing about barnyard sex unnerved some, both black and white teenagers loved it. Almost as soon as Little Richard created a new hit, Pat Boone would produce a less soulful cover rendition of it. But American youth preferred and respected the Originator, as Little Richard sometimes calls himself.

In 1957, while performing successfully at the top of the American music industry, Little Richard quit rock and roll after a trip to Australia, following a religious conversion that he believed alerted him to the immorality of rock 'n' roll. After becoming an ordained Seventh Day Adventist minister, he toiled away in obscurity for several years. Little Richard returned to rock 'n' roll in the mid-sixties and toured in Europe with the Beatles and the Rolling Stones, who were among the artists directly influenced by his work. Since that time, he has moved back and forth between his church life and preaching and the world of rock 'n' roll.

In 1986, Little Richard was inducted into the Rock and Roll Hall of Fame; that same year he appeared in the film *Down and Out in Beverly Hills*. He was honored with a Grammy Award for Lifetime Achievement in 1993, and in 1994 he was among the recipients of the Rhythm and Blues Foundation's Pioneer Award.

North America

LL Cool J

(also known as James Todd Smith) (b. January 14, 1968, Queens, New York), African American hip hop pioneer, actor, and sex symbol whose 15 years of success make him rap's longest-running superstar.

LL Cool J—short for Ladies Love Cool James—was raised in Hollis, Queens, a neighborhood that also produced the early rap masters who formed Run-DMC. *Radio*, his 1985 debut album, sported such signature songs as "*Rock the Bells*" and "*I Can't Live Without My Radio.*" It sold more than 1 million copies. The kid in the sneakers, gold chains, and Kangol hat rapped over spare, programmed beats that were sometimes splashed with rock guitar. In an art form founded on cocky sparring, LL Cool J was the king of the boast. Fans admired him for his cherubic looks and smooth style as well as his lyrical skills.

While *Bigger and Deffer* (1987), LL's second release, contained one of the all-time great battle raps, "*I'm Bad*," it also revealed the MC's softer side in "*I Need Love*," the first rap love ballad. His next album, *Walking with a*

Panther (1989), succeeded commercially but not critically; Public Enemy's black nationalist politics were then in vogue, and critics protested LL's conspicuous materialism. The next year, in a furious rebuke to naysayers, he released *Mama Said Knock You Out.* "Don't call it a comeback," he warned on the title track and added: "I've been here for years/ I'm rockin' my peers/ Puttin' suckers in fear." The album, produced by Marley Marl, continued LL's history of hits: chart successes, such as *"Around the Way Girl," "Jingling Baby,"* the bass-heavy *"Boomin' System,"* and the title track, pushed album sales past the 2 million mark.

LL suffered a rare commercial failure with *14 Shots to the Dome* (1993), but as his hip hop credibility started to drop, he branched out. LL Cool J performed at Bill Clinton's 1993 presidential inauguration; starred in the popular television sitcom, *In the House*; and acted in a string of feature films. In 1995 he returned to rap music with *Mr. Smith*, a multi-platinum success that garnered little critical acclaim but earned him two Grammy Awards. With *I Make My Own Rules* (1997), a best-selling autobiography, LL confirmed his status as hip hop's preeminent superstar.

North America

Locke, Alain Leroy

(b. September 13, 1885, Philadelphia, Pa.; d. June 9, 1954, Washington, D.C.), African American philosopher, intellectual, and educator; editor of *The New Negro*, the anthology credited with defining the Harlem Renaissance.

In his introduction to *Alain Locke: Reflections on a Modern Renaissance Man*, Russell J. Linnemann points out that though Locke was trained as a philosopher at Harvard, Oxford, and Berlin Universities, "anthropology, art, music, literature, education, political theory, sociology, and African studies represent only a few of his wide range of intellectual pursuits." Linnemann goes on to hypothesize that this extraordinary breadth of intellectual activity is "the primary reason why a biography of him has not yet been written . . . . Few if any potential biographers who might wish to examine the scope of his thought, assess his often provocative contributions, and place them within the context of the appropriate disciplines, would have the intellectual breadth or depth to fulfill the task properly." The title of Linnemann's edited volume gets to the heart of Alain Locke's legacy: while he is often best remembered for his role in the Harlem Renaissance, the scope of his work makes him a Renaissance man in all senses of the term.

Born into Philadelphia's black elite, Locke was the only child of schoolteacher parents who were both descended from established free black families. By high school he was an accomplished pianist and violinist in addition to being an excellent student. In 1904 Locke became one of the few African American undergraduates at Harvard University, where he was elected to Phi Beta Kappa and received a B.A. in philosophy magna cum laude in 1907. That same year he became the first African American to be awarded a Rhodes Scholarship, which he used to continue studying philosophy at Oxford University and the University of Berlin.

He remained the only African American Rhodes scholar until the 1960s, and the achievement brought him national publicity in both the black and white presses. Locke returned to the United States in 1911, and in 1912 joined the faculty of Howard University as a professor of philosophy and English, a position he held for the rest of his life. He took a sabbatical in 1916–1917 to complete his Ph.D. in philosophy at Harvard, and became the chair of Howard's philosophy department upon his return. As a philosopher Locke was highly respected, and he has been called one of the most important philosophical thinkers of his day. But his best-remembered accomplishments come from his scholarship on literature and art.

In 1923 Locke began contributing essays on a range of subjects to *Opportunity*, the journal of the National Urban League. These essays gained him even wider prominence as a rising black intellectual, and in 1925 he was asked to edit the March issue of the *Survey Graphic*, a national sociology magazine, which was planned as a special issue devoted entirely to race. Locke decided to turn the issue into a showpiece for the gifted young African American writers then gathering in Harlem. The resulting journal, subtitled *Harlem: Mecca of the New Negro*, included poetry, fiction, and essays by W. E. B. Du Bois, James Weldon Johnson, Langston Hughes, Countee Cullen, Jean Toomer, and Anne Spencer—many of them writers who were touted as the new generation in African American art, the best and the brightest black America had yet produced.

The issue was an outstanding success. Locke expanded it into a book, and *The New Negro*, published eight months later, immediately became the definitive anthology of the Harlem Renaissance. In addition to writers featured in the magazine special, *The New Negro* included poetry and fiction by Claude McKay, Zora Neale Hurston, Angelina Grimké, and Jessie Fauset; essays by scholars William Stanley Braithwaite, Kelly Miller, J. A. Rogers, and E. Franklin Frazier; and striking artwork by Aaron Douglas. The book was widely interpreted as a resounding rebuttal to the argument that African Americans were not capable of great literature and art. As Braithwaite later said, *The New Negro* was "a protest against the imposed limitations of the spirit of the Negro artist . . . and [marked] the assumption of his membership in the wide realm of human vision and imagination."

Locke's intellectual interest in African American art and its relationship to black culture remained clear long after *The New Negro*'s publication. Like many black intellectuals of his day, Locke was intrigued by the question of just how much influence Africa had on African America. He believed that one of Africa's clearest legacies came through the visual arts, and argued that even though it was impossible to trace many direct lines of cultural descent to Africa, there were still undeniable artistic connections that should keep the African American from considering himself "a cultural foundling without his own inheritance." In fact, Locke saw defining this artistic connection as an important step in defining African American culture.

As a result, Locke became a leading critic and collector of both African and African American art. In an era when African art was being hailed by whites for being "primitive" and "pure," Locke insisted on documenting its technical artistry. As one of the earliest critics of black art, he was especially vocal in encouraging black colleges to train more scholars in the field, and as a collector he was responsible for greatly enlarging Howard University's art collection. He also became a scholar on black folk music, and even as he pointed out African influences on African American music, he was among the earliest critics to argue for African American music's importance to American music as a whole. Locke called black music "the closest America has to a folk music," and noted that it had become "one of the main sources of America's serious or classical music" and "almost as important for the musical culture of America as it is for the Negro."

Locke documented these interests in several books. In the 1930s he established the Associates in Negro Folk Education, dedicated to publishing scholarly books on African American subjects geared toward interested adult learners. Through it he published *Negro Art: Past and Present* and *The Negro and His Music*, both in 1936, and the comprehensive, illustrated volume *The Negro in Art: A Pictorial Record of the Negro Artists and the Negro Theme in Art* in 1940, which remains his most celebrated work after *The New Negro*.

In 1935, at age 50, Locke published his first article on philosophy. By then, most observers agreed that the Harlem Renaissance was over, and Locke appeared to make a seamless transition from his focus on literary and art criticism to new work that used philosophy to explore larger questions about race and culture. He was especially interested in the concepts of cultural relativism and cultural pluralism, which emphasize both the fundamental equality among different cultures and the usefulness of identifying commonalties among cultures. His philosophy has been described as an effort to "direct the collective energies of all peoples towards a transcendental approach to interactions in which differences of race, culture, values and ideas are respected and appreciated."

In 1942 Locke coedited an anthology on global race relations, *When Peoples Meet: A Study in Race and Culture Contacts*, which is considered the best legacy of his later intellectual work. He planned an even larger volume entirely on African American cultural identity. Called *The Negro in American Culture*, Locke envisioned the work as his magnum opus and worked on it for years between lectures, teaching, and other publications. But when he died from complications from heart disease in June 1954, it was left unfinished. Margaret Just Butcher, a Howard University colleague's daughter, did complete and publish a version of it, but most scholars agree that it cannot be considered Locke's work.

Even without that final volume, the sum of Locke's books, essays, articles, and lectures has been more than enough to establish his place in the history of American and African American arts and letters. Locke made a career of thinking about black culture in innovative ways, and in the process he became one of the most important black intellectual leaders of the twentieth century.

Luca Family Singers,

a troupe of African American musicians who traveled the midwestern and
eastern United States in the mid-nineteenth century performing secular as well
as religious music.

John W. Luca was born in 1805 in Milford, Connecticut. Although his
formal training was in shoemaking, he also acquired a musical education
that, combined with his substantial natural aptitude, won him a job as a
chorister at a Congregational church in New Haven. There he met and
married the equally talented Lisette Lewis, with whom he had four sons. In
the 1840s the Luca parents began performing alongside their children and
Mrs. Luca's sister. Their son Cleveland evinced the most talent; he later
achieved renown as a master pianist. He also sang, as did Alexander, a violinist; Simeon, a violinist; and John Jr., a cellist and bassist. John Sr. eventually gave up performing in order to manage the engagements of his
talented family.

The Luca Family Singers won regional success and then achieved
national attention in May 1853 at an Antislavery Society concert in New
York. Thereafter they toured Pennsylvania, Ohio, and New York, generating
considerable acclaim. In 1854 Simeon died and Jennie Allen, a contralto
from New York, joined the group. In 1859 the Lucas teamed with a white
family troupe, the Hutchinsons, who performed a similar act. Both groups
drew from an eclectic repertoire, combining comic and temperance songs
with classical European arias.

Upon the invitation of the president of Liberia in 1860, Cleveland left
the group and went to Africa, where he composed Liberia's national
anthem. The troupe disbanded, but its members continued to pursue
music individually.

Lunceford, James Melvin (Jimmie)

(b. June 6, 1902, Fulton, Mo.; d. July 12?, 1947, Seaside, Oreg.), jazz bandleader and arranger whose big band helped define the swing era of the 1930s.

Regarded as the most exciting band of its time, Jimmie Lunceford's big
band was known for its precise arrangements and smoothly polished choreography. Light, swinging hits such as "*My Blue Heaven*" reflected the perfec-
tionism and charm of the band and its leader. Raised in Denver, Colorado,
Jimmie Lunceford graduated from Fisk University in Nashville, Tennessee,
in 1926. After doing graduate work in New York City, he taught high
school music and physical education in Memphis. It was there that he put
together his first band, originally called the Chickasaw Syncopators.

Soon renamed the Jimmie Lunceford Orchestra, the band toured the
Upper Midwest and Great Lakes region for several years before making its

first New York appearance at Harlem's fabled Cotton Club. For the next decade the orchestra dominated the city's lively big-band scene. Although Lunceford's group featured talented and dynamic musicians, it became famous more for its playful sound and vibrant stage presence than for its musical virtuosity. Instead of playing any of the several instruments he had studied, Lunceford acted as the band's conductor, head arranger, and business leader, keeping the group together during more than ten years of frequent national and international touring and dozens of recordings for the Decca and Columbia labels.

Despite Lunceford's discipline and leadership, the band lost key members in the early 1940s, including arrangers Sy Oliver and Willie "the Lion" Smith, and began a decline from which it never recovered. Nevertheless, it continued working until 1947, when Lunceford died following a publicity appearance in Oregon. The band soon folded for good, but Lunceford's work has gone on to influence countless jazz ensembles.

M

Mabley, Jackie ("Moms")

(b. March 19, 1897, Brevard, N.C.; d. May 23, 1975, White Plains, N.Y.), African American vaudeville performer and comedian, the first African American woman to establish herself as a single act in standup comedy.

Jackie "Moms" Mabley rose to national recognition as a standup comedian in the early 1960s. A pioneer of social satire, she strongly influenced such contemporary black comedians as Richard Pryor and Whoopi Goldberg. Author Elsie A. Williams said that Mabley "found a unique way to connect herself to her audience . . . often breaking propriety and breaching established lines of decorum, across gender, race, and class." Mabley was also known for her compassion and kindness to others—qualities that earned her the endearing sobriquet "Moms"—and focused her humor on the pain and dissonance of black life.

Born Loretta Mary Aiken, Mabley grew up in a large family in Brevard, North Carolina. Her father ran several businesses while her mother presided over a large household that included boarders. When Loretta was 11 her father, a volunteer firefighter, died when his fire truck overturned and exploded.

Loretta underwent additional trauma when, as an adolescent, she was raped twice: first by an older black man and later by the town's white sheriff. Both rapes resulted in pregnancies. Encouraged by her grandmother to make a life for herself, she left her babies in the care of two women and departed for Cleveland, Ohio, where she lived with a minister's family.

In Cleveland, Mabley befriended a number of local entertainers, including the Canadian Jack Mabley, who became her boyfriend. "He took a lot off me," she would later say, "the least I could do was take his name." After singing and dancing in local shows, she began performing throughout the country on the Theater Owners Booking Association (TOBA), a circuit of white- and black-owned theaters catering to African American audiences.

Traveling the vaudeville circuit she experienced overt racism and demeaning working conditions and deflected her pain through satirical wit that drew heavily from black folk traditions. As black comedian Godfrey Cambridge observed, "The line that leads to Moms Mabley, Nipsey Russell, Bill Cosby, and myself can be traced to the social satire of slave humor, back even through minstrels, through countless attempts to cast off that fantasy."

Mabley's career took off when in 1921 the husband-wife vaudeville team Butterbeans and Susie invited her to perform with them in Pittsburgh, Pennsylvania. She accompanied them to New York and soon began entertaining at nightclubs, including Harlem's Cotton Club, where she appeared on bills with Duke Ellington, Count Basie, Louis Armstrong, and Cab Calloway. Mabley also performed in early black theater, and collaborated with Harlem Renaissance writer Zora Neale Hurston in the Broadway play *Fast and Furious: A Colored Revue in 37 Scenes* (1931).

In her comedy routines Mabley adopted a stage persona based loosely on her own grandmother but with a distinctly cantankerous and sassy edge. She was known for her folksy humor and ribald jokes and affectionately referred to her audience as her "children." Mel Watkins, author of a recent study on African American humor, noted, "The guise [of a granny] provided the buffer or intermediary necessary to quell resistance to a woman doing a single comic routine." It also endeared her to both black and white audiences.

Onstage Mabley became famous for her gaudy housedresses, floppy hats, and oversized clodhoppers. Audiences especially appreciated her spicy, innuendo-laden quips such as "A woman is a woman until the day she dies, but a man's a man only as long as he can"; and "The only thing an old man can do for me is bring a message from a young one."

From 1939 until the 1960s Mabley regularly performed at Harlem's Apollo Theater. She also won roles in the films *Killer Diller* (1947) and *Boarding House Blues* (1948), a social commentary on struggling black entertainers in which she starred as a boardinghouse matron. During the 1960s she recorded more than 20 albums of her comedy routines and appeared on television shows hosted by Harry Belafonte, Mike Douglas, Merv Griffin, and Bill Cosby. A year after starring in the feature film *Amazing Grace* (1974), Mabley died of natural causes at age 78.

North America

Markham, Dewey ("Pigmeat")

(b. April 18, 1906, Durham, N.C.; d. December 13, 1981, New York, N.Y.), African American comedian best known for his famous line "Here Come de Judge."

Dewey Markham ran away from home at age 13 to join the circus, the beginning of a six-decade-long career as a stage performer. After six years with the circus, he became a regular with minstrel shows, singing, dancing, and honing his comedy skills. He gained his nickname "Pigmeat" from a song he performed called "*Sweet Papa Pigmeat.*"

In the 1930s Markham branched out to Broadway and eventually to Hollywood, where he starred in all-black films. During his long career, he also recorded 16 albums, which combined his talents for comedy and singing the blues. In the 1950s and 1960s Markham appeared frequently on television talk and variety shows. It was during an appearance on the hit comedy *Laugh-In* that he unveiled his legendary skit, "Here Come de Judge." The punchline became an overnight sensation.

Latin America and the Caribbean

Marley, Bob

(b. February 6, 1945, Rhoden Hall, Jamaica; d. May 11, 1981, Miami, Fla.), Jamaican singer and songwriter whose name invokes reggae music, the tenets of Rastafarianism, and, more broadly, the struggle of the economically and politically oppressed.

The first global pop star to emerge from a developing nation, Bob Marley has won fans from nations around the globe who share his vision of redemption and freedom and love his innovative blend of American and Caribbean music.

Bob Marley was born Robert Nesta Marley in rural Rhoden Hall in the parish of St. Ann, Jamaica. His mother was a Jamaican teenager and his father a middle-aged captain in the West Indian regiment of the British Army. Marley's parents separated when he was six and soon thereafter he moved with his mother to Kingston, joining the wave of rural immigrants that flooded the capital during the 1950s and 1960s. Marley and his mother settled in Trench Town, a west Kingston slum named for the sewer that ran through it.

There Marley shared quarters with a boy his age named "Bunny" Neville O'Riley Livingston. The two made music together, fashioning a guitar from bamboo, sardine cans, and electrical wire and learning har-monies from local singer Joe Higgs. Like a number of their contemporaries, Marley and Bunny listened to radio from New Orleans; and like their peers they adopted the sounds of rhythm and blues, combined them with strains of a local musical style, mento, and produced a new music called ska. Although encouraged by his mother to learn a craft, Marley soon abandoned an apprenticeship as a welder to devote himself to music.

Peter McIntosh (later Peter Tosh) joined Bunny and Marley's musical sessions, bringing with him a real guitar. In the early 1960s the three formed a harmony group, the Wailing Wailers; meanwhile, Marley recorded a few songs with producer Leslie Kong, to whom local ska celebrity Jimmy Cliff had introduced him. Marley's earliest recordings received little radio play but strengthened his desire to sing.

Joined by Junior Braithwaite and two backup singers, the Wailing

Wailers recorded on the Coxsone label, supervised by local sound-system superstar Clement Dodd. The group became Kingston celebrities in the summer of 1963 with "*Simmer Down*," a song that both indicted and romanticized the lives of Trench Town toughs, known as "rude boys." The Wailing Wailers recorded more than 30 singles in the mid-1960s, reflecting—and sometimes leading—the evolution of reggae, from mento to ska to rocksteady.

In 1963 Marley's mother moved to Delaware, expecting that her son would follow her and begin life anew. Marley did make a prolonged visit in 1966, working jobs for Chrysler and DuPont; yet his heart lay back home, where his new wife, the Jamaican Rita Anderson, and his old passion—the music of the island—both remained. When he returned to Jamaica in 1967, he converted from Christianity to Rastafarianism and began the mature stage of his musical career. Marley reunited with Bunny and Peter Tosh, and together they called themselves the Wailers and began their own record label, Wail 'N' Soul. They abandoned the rude-boy ethos for the spirituality of Rastafarian beliefs and slowed their music under the new rocksteady influence.

Although the Wailers soon cohered as a group, they did not find success beyond Jamaica for a few years. In 1970 bassist Aston "Family Man" Barnett and his drummer—together considered the best rhythm section on Jamaica—joined the Wailers. With this addition the group attracted the attention of Island Records, a company that had started in Jamaica but moved to London. In 1971 they recorded *Catch a Fire*, the first Jamaican reggae album to enjoy the benefits of a large budget and widespread commercial promotion. *Catch a Fire* sold modestly, better in Europe than America, but well enough to sustain Island's interest in the Wailers.

During the early 1970s the band recorded an album each year and toured extensively, slowly breaking into the European and American mainstream. They played shows with American superstars Bruce Springsteen and Sly and the Family Stone, and in 1974 British rocker Eric Clapton scored a hit with "*I Shot the Sheriff*," a Marley composition. In 1975 the Wailers made their first major splash in the United States with "*No Woman No Cry*" as well as an album of live material. At this point, Peter Tosh and Bunny left the band, which took the name Bob Marley & the Wailers.

Although Marley had melded politics and music since the early days of "*Simmer Down*," as his success grew he became increasingly political. His 1976 song "*War*" transcribed a speech of Haile Selassie I, the Ethiopian king upon whom the Rastafarian sect was based. In addition to Rastafarian spirituality and mysticism, his lyrics probed the turmoil in Jamaica. Prior to the 1976 elections, partisanship inspired gang war in Trench Town and divided the people against themselves. By siding with Prime Minister Michael Manley—and by singing songs of a political bent—Marley angered some Jamaicans. After surviving an assassination attempt in December, he fled to London until the following year.

When Marley returned to Jamaica in 1978, he performed in the One Love Peace Concert, which sought to ameliorate existing political conflicts.

During his set Marley orchestrated a handshake between political opponents Manley and Edward Seaga, a highly symbolic moment.

Marley's activism extended beyond Jamaica, and people from developing nations around the world found hope in his music. In 1980 Bob Marley & the Wailers had the honor of performing at the independence ceremony when Rhodesia became Zimbabwe. The group's concerts in the late 1970s attracted enormous crowds in West Africa and Latin America as well as in Europe and the United States.

Bob Marley died at age 36 from a cancer that began in his toe and spread throughout his body. His memory was honored by the Jamaican government and he was given a national funeral. During Marley's lifetime his music became closely associated with the movement toward black political independence that was then prominent in several African and South American countries. His songs have remained popular, and for many they symbolize the hopes of the downtrodden for worldly redemption and spiritual transcendence. The conviction and sincerity of Marley's performances, and his unique, melodic songwriting have influenced many pop artists, including Stevie Wonder and Eric Clapton. He was inducted into the Rock and Roll Hall of Fame in 1994.

North America

Marsalis, Wynton

(b. October 18, 1961, New Orleans, La.), African American trumpeter who excels in both jazz and classical music; a leading advocate of the acoustic, bop-based jazz mainstream and the most prominent figure in contemporary jazz.

Trumpeter Wynton Marsalis is the leading figure in contemporary jazz. He burst onto the jazz scene as part of Art Blakey's 1980 edition of the Jazz Messengers. More than an inventive and talented musician, Marsalis has become the de facto spokesman for the neoclassical movement in jazz that emerged in the early 1980s, drawing inspiration from acoustic jazz styles that antedate the free jazz and jazz-rock of the late 1960s and 1970s. He has also worked effectively as a jazz educator, particularly for his four-part Public Broadcasting System (PBS) series *Marsalis on Music*, which won a Peabody Award in 1996.

Besides achieving acclaim as a musician, Marsalis emerged in the 1980s as an outspoken and controversial figure in America's ongoing dialogue on race and culture. His ideas on jazz and African American culture are indebted to the thinking of Albert Murray and Murray's intellectual disciple, Stanley Crouch. Murray and Crouch share a black-centered social vision, but they reject nationalism and repudiate the separatist legacy of Malcolm X and the radicalism of Amiri Baraka. Crouch, in particular, has become Marsalis's mentor and has contributed liner essays for several of his recordings.

Marsalis is part of a family of active jazz musicians, including his father, pianist Ellis Marsalis (b. 1934); his older brother, saxophonist Branford (b.

1960); and his younger brothers, trombonist Delfeayo (b. 1965) and drummer Jason (b. 1976). He was named for jazz pianist Wynton Kelly (1931–1971). Moreover, he was born in New Orleans, the historic birthplace of jazz. He received his first trumpet when he was 6 years old from white New Orleans trumpeter Al Hirt. At age 12, after hearing a record by legendary jazz trumpeter Clifford Brown (1930–1956), Marsalis began to take his own trumpet playing seriously.

During his high school years Marsalis played in a wide range of ensembles. He joined New Orleans marching bands and, together with his brother Branford, took part in a local funk unit called the Creators. His formal training involved both jazz and classical music. While in high school, he played first trumpet with the New Orleans Civic Orchestra. At age 14 he performed as featured soloist with the New Orleans Philharmonic Orchestra. After high school he attended the Juilliard School of Music in New York.

In 1980 Art Blakey asked Marsalis to join the Jazz Messengers for a summer tour. Soon the young trumpeter became the group's musical director. One year later Marsalis decided to leave Juilliard in order to tour again with Blakey. During 1981 he left Blakey temporarily to join V.S.O.P., pianist Herbie Hancock's acoustic group, featuring bassist Ron Carter (b. 1937) and drummer Tony Williams (1945–1997), all of whom were part of the classic 1960s combo of trumpeter Miles Davis.

Marsalis quickly established a considerable reputation in jazz circles. During his stint with Blakey he emulated past Jazz Messengers' trumpeter Freddie Hubbard (b. 1938), but by 1981 his playing recalled the mid-1960s Miles Davis, albeit with much greater technical virtuosity. By the late 1980s Marsalis had established his own identity by revisiting jazz history, going all the way back to the 1920s. His mature style combines post-bop harmonies with the melodic sensitivity of trumpeter Louis Armstrong and the penchant for mutes and "freak" effects of cornet players Joe Oliver and Bubber Miley.

In 1981 Columbia Records signed Marsalis to an unprecedented contract for both jazz and classical music recordings. Later that year he formed his own band, the Wynton Marsalis Quintet, which included his brother Branford. The group recorded several albums, including the widely praised *Black Codes (from the Underground)* (1985). In 1985 Branford Marsalis and other members of the band quit to tour with the rock singer Sting. But by early 1986 Wynton had organized a new and equally talented group, the Wynton Marsalis Quartet, featuring pianist Marcus Roberts (b. 1963). Over the years it grew into a septet that provided a perfect vehicle for Marsalis's talents as a composer and arranger.

In 1987 Marsalis became cofounder and artistic director of Jazz at Lincoln Center, a program of New York City's prestigious Lincoln Center for the Performing Arts. The new position gave him an unrivaled ability to shape the critical understanding of jazz. He has presented major retrospectives of the music of past jazz masters, including Louis Armstrong and Sidney Bechet, but above all he has emphasized the towering role of

Duke Ellington. Marsalis's position at Lincoln Center also broadened his own writing talents.

Marsalis, as director of the Jazz at Lincoln Center program, agreed not only to direct the Lincoln Center jazz band, but also to compose and present one significant new work per year. These commissioned works suggest that his study of Ellington's music has shaped his own composing and arranging. In 1993 Marsalis introduced the first of these new works, *In This House, On This Morning*, a musical evocation of Sunday services at an African American church. In the following year he debuted *Blood on the Fields*, an oratorio for three singers and a 14-piece orchestra, his most ambitious piece thus far. *Blood on the Fields* recounts the story of two Africans, Leona and Jesse, who are captured and sold into slavery in the American South but who ultimately find love and escape to freedom together. In 1997 *Blood on the Fields* became the first non-classical work to receive a Pulitzer Prize for music.

Marsalis is one of the few jazz musicians whose classical and jazz performances are equally acclaimed. In 1984 he won a Grammy Award from the National Academy of Recording Arts and Sciences (NARAS) for his classical debut album, *Trumpet Concertos* (1983). His widely praised second jazz album, *Think of One* (1983), also received a Grammy Award in 1984 for best jazz recording, making Marsalis the first artist to win Grammy Awards in two different musical categories in a single year. In 1995 he debuted his first string quartet, *(At the) Octoroon Balls*, at the Lincoln Center, and the following year he released In Gabriel's Garden, which he recorded with Anthony Newman on harpsichord and organ and the English Chamber Orchestra.

North America

Martha and the Vandellas,

rhythm and blues group of female vocalists who recorded hits for Motown Records throughout the 1960s.

Martha Reeves (b. July 18, 1941, Alabama) was working as a secretary for the Hitsville Studio of Motown Records in Detroit, Michigan when singer Mary Wells failed to show for a recording session. Reeves, who had sung in area talent shows with a group of friends, the Del-Phis, summoned the other members of the group; they filled in at the scheduled recording of "*There He Is (At My Door).*" In addition to Reeves, Roselind Ashford, Annette Sterling, and Gloria Williams sang at this formative session, although Williams left the group after the single flopped. The three remaining women formed the group called Martha and the Vandellas. They backed other Motown acts (most notably Marvin Gaye) and began recording their own material.

Martha and the Vandellas first achieved pop-chart success in 1963 with the release of "*Come and Get These Memories.*" Thereafter Reeves and Ashford, along with Betty Kelly, who had replaced Annette Sterling, inched their way up the charts with each successive hit, a climb that culminated in 1964 with *"Dancing in the Street."* This upbeat song reached number two of the Top 40, and it took on political significance as an anthem for the decade's urban race riots. Earlier minor hits included *"Heat Wave"* and *"Quick Sand"* (both 1963).

In the late 1960s the group underwent further changes in its roster, but when Reeves became ill, the Vandellas disbanded in 1968. They reunited in 1970 and worked together until Reeves launched a solo career around 1972. Motown had moved to Los Angeles, California, and Reeves, who had stayed behind in Detroit, had little luck on her own. She recorded and performed throughout the 1980s, but the peak of her career seemed to be over.

The Vandellas reunited in 1989 and performed and recorded in the 1990s. Reeves published an autobiography, *Dancing in the Streets* (1994), which describes the Motown milieu in which she began her career.

North America

Martin, Sallie

(b. November 20, 1886; d. June 8, 1988, Pittsfield, Ga.), gospel singer who was an influential proponent of gospel music throughout the twentieth century.

After leaving the eighth grade, Sallie Martin moved to Atlanta, Georgia, and joined the Fire Baptized Holiness Church in 1916, where she learned to sing in the spontaneous and spirited manner of the church's sanctified folk. In 1932 she met Thomas A. Dorsey, the "Father of Gospel Music," at Ebenezer Baptist Church. This meeting spawned an eight-year business relationship, during which Martin traveled the country singing and promoting Dorsey's songs as well as organizing gospel choruses. Together they founded the Gospel Singers Convention, later known as the National Convention of Gospel Choirs and Choruses. Martin and Dorsey severed their relationship in 1940, after which Martin went on to form her own singing groups and publishing company.

For a brief period she teamed with Roberta Martin to form the Martin and Martin Gospel Singers. After that she created the Sallie Martin Singers, one of the first all-female gospel groups. Ruth Jones, later known as Dinah Washington, sang and played piano for the group. Martin toured with the group throughout the 1940s until the mid-1950s to promote the songs of the Martin and Morris Publishing Company, which she co-owned with songwriter Kenneth Morris.

"Just a Closer Walk with Thee" was their most successful song, helping Martin and Morris to become the largest African American-owned gospel publishing company. Martin remained a pillar in the gospel community for over 60 years, always stubbornly representing the old-time gospel music in the face of many new trends. Her raw and rough style of singing influenced

performers such as Willie Mae Ford Smith, Alex Bradford, J. Earl Hines, and Clara Ward.

North America

Mayfield, Curtis

(b. June 3, 1942, Chicago, Ill.), African American singer and composer whose work as a solo artist and with the group the Impressions combined music with political messages.

A self-taught guitarist, Curtis Mayfield led his first group, the Alphatones, at age 14. One year later, his childhood friend Jerry Butler invited him to write music and lyrics for the Roosters, a quintet that later changed its name to the Impressions. In 1958 they recorded their first rhythm and blues hit, *"For Your Precious Love,"* on Vee Jay Records. Their music was influenced by the Civil Rights Movement, as evidenced by some of their most popular songs, including *"People Get Ready"* (1965) and *"We're a Winner"* (1968).

In 1970 Mayfield left the group to become a full-time songwriter and producer. His record *Curtis* was one of the most successful African American music albums of the year, and his compositions for Hollywood's *Superfly* (1972) brought him superstardom. Mayfield then wrote and produced for television and such films as *Claudine* (1974) and *Let's Do It Again* (1975). In 1977 he composed the soundtrack for a film in which he also appeared, titled *Short Eyes*.

Mayfield took part in an Impressions re-union tour in the late 1980s and composed songs for *The Return of Superfly* and *I'm Gonna Get You Sucka* (1989). Popular since his early days with the Impressions in Japan, Mayfield has toured there and in Europe extensively. In August 1990, before opening an outdoor performance in Brooklyn, New York, he was paralyzed from the neck down by a falling lighting rig. He was honored in 1994 at the Grammy Awards show with a Grammy Legend Award.

North America

Maynor, Dorothy Leigh

(b. September 3, 1910, Norfolk, Va.), African American opera singer, choral director, and founder of the Harlem School for the Arts.

Dorothy Leigh Maynor (originally Mainor) was born to John J. Mainor, a pastor, and Alice (Jeffries) Mainor. At age 14 she enrolled at Hampton Institute, where she studied with the goal of becoming a public school teacher. During her college years Maynor's focus increasingly shifted toward vocal training and the study of piano and orchestral instruments.

After graduating, she decided to pursue a second degree in music from Westminster Choir College in New Jersey, and then spent four years in New York continuing her musical studies privately under Wilfried Klamroth and John Alan Houghton.

In 1939 Maynor made her solo singing debut at the Berkshire Musical Festival in Tanglewood, Massachusetts, for which she received widespread acclaim. The performance was soon followed by a New York debut at Town Hall, where reviewers called her "one of the most remarkable soprano voices of [her] generation." She went on to perform in concert halls across the United States, Europe, and Australia, with a repertoire that included lieder, Bach, Handel, spirituals, and opera arias.

In 1964 Maynor retired as a concert artist to fulfill her dream of establishing a school to create opportunities for African American youth. She founded the Harlem School for the Arts, which offered a comprehensive cultural education, and provided instruction in the visual and performing arts of piano, painting, string orchestra, classical and modern dance, and voice.

North America

McClendon, Rose

(b. August 27, 1884, Greenville, S.C.; d. July 12, 1936, New York, N.Y.), African American actor who promoted African American theater, playwrights, and actors.

Rose McClendon, born Rosalie Virginia Scott, moved to New York City with her family around 1890 where, in 1904, she married Henry Pruden McClendon, a chiropractor who also worked as a porter.

McClendon directed and acted in dramatic performances at Saint Mark's African Methodist Episcopal Church, but her professional acting career began with a scholarship to the American Academy of Dramatic Arts in 1916. Her first role was in *Justice* (1919) and she appeared in *Roseanne* (1924) with Charles Gilpin and, later, Paul Robeson. She achieved critical acclaim for her performance in *Deep River* (1926) with Jules Bledsoe. In Paul Green's Pulitzer Prize-winning *In Abraham's Bosom* (1926) she won a *Morning Telegraph* acting award. She also acted in *Porgy* (1927), *House of Connelly* (1931), *Never No More* (1932), *Black Souls* (1932), *Roll Sweet Chariot* (1934), *Brainsweat* (1934), *Panic* (1935), and Langston Hughes's *Mulatto* (1935), the first dramatic play by an African American to appear on Broadway.

McClendon promoted African American theater as a board member of the Theatre Union and as director of the Harlem Experimental Theatre. With Dick Campbell, she organized the Negro People's Theatre and co-headed this project when it was incorporated into the federal relief agency, the Works Progress Administration, in 1935.

McClendon contracted pneumonia and died on July 12, 1936. After her death, Campbell established the Rose McClendon Players community theater group in her honor. In 1946 Carl Van Vechten instituted the Rose McClendon Collection of Photographs of Distinguished Negroes at Yale University.

McCoy, Elijah J.

(b. May 2, 1843, Colchester, Canada; d. October 10, 1929, Eloise, Mich.), African American inventor with whom the saying "the real McCoy" gained popularity.

Elijah McCoy was one of 12 children born to runaway slaves who had used the Underground Railroad to escape slavery in Kentucky. Living in extreme poverty, McCoy's parents emphasized education to their children as the surest means of betterment. When he was 15, McCoy's parents sent him to study mechanical engineering in Edinburgh, Scotland, training that was impossible for blacks to get in the United States. After finishing his schooling in Scotland, McCoy returned to the United States with the hope of obtaining an engineering job.

Although a trained engineer with impressive credentials, McCoy was unable to find work in his field because of his race. He was forced to accept a job as a locomotive fireman with the Michigan Central Railroad, a position that required no engineering knowledge, only that he shovel coal into the engine and apply oil in the moving parts of the machine. McCoy found the work unchallenging and sought other more productive forms of occupation.

It had long been considered a problem that railroad engines were unable to lubricate themselves. When in need of lubrication, the machines had to be shut off entirely, causing a loss in time and money. As this was a regular necessity, the industry found profit nearly impossible to realize. In his free time McCoy began to consider solutions to this problem, and after two years he developed the "lubricating cup" for steam engines. According to McCoy, the cup allowed for the "continuous flow of oil on the gears . . . thereby do[ing] away with the necessity of shutting down the machine."

McCoy received a patent for his lubricating device in 1872. The lubricating cup was essential to industries throughout the world, and those in possession of the valuable cup were said to have "the real McCoy." The lubricating cup was his most successful and best-known invention, although McCoy also obtained patents for an automatic sprinkler and an ironing table, eventually acquiring 58 patents in his lifetime.

McDaniel, Hattie

(b. June 10, 1895, Wichita, Kans.; d. October 26, 1952, Woodland Hills, Calif.), African American singer, actress, and radio performer, the first black ever to win an Oscar for her role as Mammy in Gone With the Wind.

Hattie McDaniel appeared in more than 300 films and, despite her considerable talent, was limited to mainly housemaid roles, as were most black actresses of the 1930s and 1940s, including Louise Beavers, Ethel Waters, and Lillian Randolph. Although McDaniel's housemaid roles often exemplified the stereotypes blacks abhorred, she transformed many of these roles into sassy, independent-minded characters. In a Hollywood that enshrined white stars at the expense of black performers, she became the first black ever to win an Academy Award—as Best Supporting Actress for her "Mammy" role in the 1939 film *Gone With the Wind*.

Hattie McDaniel grew up in Denver, Colorado, the 13th child of Henry McDaniel, a Baptist preacher, and Susan (Holbert) McDaniel, a church singer. Her talents for singing and drama were apparent from an early age. Encouraged by a teacher, she often sang and recited poetry at her predominantly white elementary school. At age 13 she began performing in black minstrel shows—billed as "Denver's favorite soubrette"—and took the lead in high school plays and musical performances. In a contest sponsored by the Woman's Christian Temperance Union, she won a gold medal for her moving rendition of "Convict Joe," an Alexander Murdoch poem about a man ruined by drink. Based on this success, she quit high school to tour full-time with minstrel groups along the West Coast, mainly with her father's Henry McDaniel Minstrel Show. When her father retired from performing in 1916, McDaniel supported herself clerking in a Denver bakery.

In 1920 McDaniel began touring with the Melody Hounds, a musical ensemble led by one of Denver's top black musicians, George Morrison. Traveling from Portland to El Paso, she received popular recognition as a singer and vaudeville performer, and in 1924 made her radio debut with Morrison in Denver. She was also a talented songwriter and recorded many of her own songs on the Okeh and Paramount labels in Chicago.

By the late 1920s McDaniel's theater bookings were dependent on the Theater Owners Booking Association (TOBA), and in 1929, when TOBA went bankrupt, she was left stranded and broke. Seeking work as a performer at the Club Madrid in Milwaukee, she was hired as a ladies' washroom attendant. When finally the club invited her to sing, she won immediate success and soon after set her sights on Hollywood.

Arriving in Los Angeles in 1931, McDaniel visited film studios looking for work while washing "three million dishes on her way to stardom." She also performed weekly on Los Angeles radio, where she became popularly known as Hi-Hat Hattie, a bossy, effervescent maid "who continually forgets her place." In 1932 she won her first, uncredited film role as a Southern house servant in Fox's *The Golden West*. Numerous offers followed and in 1934 she was chosen to play the washerwoman Aunt Dilsey, a lead part in Will Rogers's film *Judge Priest*.

By the late 1930s she had become a widely recognized Hollywood "Mammy" with two distinct film personae. As her biographer Carlton Jackson points out, while "she was much too servile in *The Little Colonel* for the liking of many blacks, she was much too independent in *Alice Adams* for numerous whites." Indeed, with the exception of the 1941 film *In This Our Life*, in which McDaniel's character, Minerva Clay, openly confronts racial issues, her film roles alternated between subservient and cantankerous maids. Although McDaniel relished her success, her film personae weighed heavily on her. During the 1940s she spent much time defending herself before the National Association for the Advancement of Colored People (NAACP), which claimed that she was perpetuating a stereotype. The NAACP particularly criticized her role in *Gone With the Wind*, in which Mammy spoke nostalgically about the Old South.

From 1947 to 1952 McDaniel was the host of *The Beulah Show*, a nationally broadcast radio program later transferred to television. She portrayed Beulah, an ebullient Southern maid, yet this time without using dialect and entirely on her own terms. Beulah was also the first radio program in which a black played the starring role. Praised by the NAACP and the National Urban League, *The Beulah Show* attracted nearly 20,000 listeners weekly and finally provided McDaniel with a role in which she could truly be herself. Suffering from breast cancer, she died in 1952 at age 57.

Latin America and the Caribbean

McKay, Claude

(b. September 15, 1889, Sunny Ville, Jamaica; d. May 22, 1948, Chicago, Ill.), Jamaican poet, essayist, and novelist who was one of the founders of both modern African American literature and modern Jamaican literature.

Claude McKay's work as a poet, novelist, and essayist heralded several of the most significant moments in African American culture. His protest poetry of the second and third decades of the twentieth century was seen by may of his contemporaries as the premier example of the "New Negro" spirit. His novels were sophisticated considerations of the problems and possibilities of Pan-Africanism at the end of the colonial era, influencing writers of African descent throughout the world. His early poetry in Jamaican patois, and his fiction set in Jamaica, are now seen as crucial to the development of a national Jamaican literature.

McKay's Early Life

McKay's parents, Thomas Francis McKay and Hannah Ann McKay, were prosperous farmers by the standards of the town. Through the efforts of his brother Uriah Theodore, a schoolteacher, and Walter Jekyll, an expatriate Englishman who became McKay's patron and who was particularly important in encouraging McKay's literary ambitions, McKay received more formal education than was typical for a child of a farming family. He became a police constable (or "constab") in Kingston in 1911.

McKay's Early Writing

McKay published two collections of poetry, *Songs of Jamaica* and *Constab Ballad*, in 1912. These poems emerged largely out of McKay's experience as a constab, which McKay found, along with urban life in general, to be alienating. He felt uncomfortably located between the Jamaican elite and

Jamaica-born poet and novelist Claude McKay became a pivotal figure in the Harlem Renaissance. *CORBIS*

the great mass of the urban poor. Many of the concerns of McKay's later work, such as the opposition of the city and the country, the problems of exile, and the relation of the black intellectual to the common folk, appear first in these poems.

McKay moved to the United States in 1912 to attend Tuskegee Institute. After brief stints at Tuskegee and Kansas State University, he left for Harlem. There he wrote poetry while holding several menial jobs, including working on a railroad dining car. This period of McKay's work is best remembered for his militant protest sonnets, notably "If We Must Die," considered by such contemporaries of McKay as James Weldon Johnson and Walter White to be the beginning of the Harlem Renaissance. McKay also wrote many poems of exile, such as "Flame-Heart" and "The Tropics in New York," in which he nostalgically invokes a tropical landscape and the desire to return to a remembered community. Even many of the protest sonnets can be considered exile poems, since a break between the poem's speaker and his original community is often at the root of the speaker's anger. Much of McKay's early poetry was collected in the book *Harlem Shadows* (1922).

McKay and Communism

In 1919 McKay moved to Europe, where he became increasingly involved in the new communist movement. McKay saw in communism an alternative to racism, poverty, and colonialism. He worked on Sylvia Pankhurst's pro-communist newspaper *Worker's Dreadnought* in London. On his return to New York in 1921, he became coeditor (with Mike Gold) of the radical journal the *Liberator*. After personal and aesthetic disagreements with Gold and the other members of the *Liberator* editorial board, McKay left the journal in 1922. As a delegate to the Fourth Congress of the Communist International (Comintern) in 1922, McKay declared that the "Negro Question" was central to the world revolutionary movement. He moved again to Europe in 1923 and remained in Europe and North Africa until 1934.

In his two novels of the 1920s, *Home to Harlem* (1928) and *Banjo* (1929), McKay investigated how the concepts of race and class worked in a world dominated by capitalism and colonialism, and how cosmopolitan and rural black communities can be reconciled to each other. Home to Harlem was more commercially successful than any novel by an African American author to that point. Its plot revolves around an intellectual Haitian expatriate, Ray, and an African American longshoreman and World War I veteran, Jake. Ray worries constantly and feels isolated from the African American community as a result of his European education. Jake is spontaneous and direct. Ray and Jake work for a time as dining car workers, becoming close friends. Ray appears again in *Banjo* with another "natural" black character, the African American musician Lincoln Agrippa Daily (or "Banjo"). *Banjo* is set in the old port of Marseilles and features a shifting group of black longshoremen, sailors, and drifters from Africa. In both novels McKay articulates the need for the exiled black intellectual to return to the common black folk. This theme is taken even further in McKay's final novel, *Banana Bottom* (1933). The protagonist of *Banana Bottom* is Bita Plant, a European-educated Jamaican woman who returns to her native village in Jamaica. In the course of the novel, Plant rejects European culture and the Jamaican elite, choosing instead to rejoin the farming folk.

McKay's Later Career

McKay returned to the United States in 1934. During the 1920s and early 1930s he moved further away from the communist movement, becoming at last an active anticommunist. His final books, the autobiographical *A Long Way from Home* (1937) and the sociological *Harlem: Negro Metropolis* (1940), were in large part attacks on the Communist Party of the United States of America (CPUSA). McKay also sharply criticized black intellectuals for either being intimidated or deceived by the CPUSA in the late 1930s and early 1940s. While working as a member of the Works Progress Administration's Federal Writers' Project in New York during the late 1930s, McKay attempted without success to organize an anticommunist writer's group in Harlem. Throughout this work, McKay became increasingly isolated from the mainstream of black artists and intellectuals.

McKay's interest in Roman Catholicism grew significantly during the 1940s, and he officially joined the Catholic Church in 1944. At this time he wrote much new poetry which he failed to get published, a failure he blamed on the influence of the CPUSA.

North America

McMillan, Terry

(b. October 18, 1951, Port Huron, Mich.), African American novelist and short story writer known for realistic portrayals of contemporary black life.

The success of the 1995 film version of her 1992 novel *Waiting to Exhale* established Terry McMillan as one of the most popular contemporary black authors. The story, which portrays four successful black women struggling with their romantic relationships, careers, and families, touches on all of the themes for which McMillan's work is known—and with which her readers readily identify. She is especially liked as an author for her down-to-earth, conversational writing style, which has been described as "tough and sexy."

McMillan grew up in a factory town 100 km (60 mi) northeast of Detroit, Michigan, the oldest of five children. Her mother divorced her alcoholic, abusive husband when McMillan was 13 and supported her family as a factory and domestic worker. The only book in their home was the Bible, and at school McMillan was exposed only to white authors. Then when she was 16, she discovered James Baldwin during a part-time job at a library and realized that "if we [African Americans] did have anything important to say . . . someone would actually publish it."

McMillan graduated with a degree in journalism from the University of California at Berkeley in 1979, then studied screenwriting at Columbia University in New York. She published her first short story in a campus literary magazine as an undergraduate, and in New York joined the Harlem Writers Guild. While working by day as a typist, she wrote the short story that became the first chapter of her first novel, *Mama* (1987). *Mama* was published by the mainstream firm Houghton Mifflin, but McMillan chose to arrange a publicity tour herself, contacting colleges and bookstores and scheduling appearances in areas that would attract black readers. Even Houghton Mifflin agreed that her grassroots approach had a strong impact on sales, and *Mama* was reprinted three times in its first two months of publication. As has been noted in *Black Women in America: An Historical Encyclopedia*, the "conventional wisdom among [commercial publishing houses] had been that black people do not buy books. McMillan proved that when someone reaches out to them, black readers are indeed there." McMillan has become one of the first black authors to achieve large-scale success with a predominantly black audience.

Her subsequent novels—*Disappearing Acts* (1989), *Waiting to Exhale*, and *How Stella Got Her Groove Back* (1996)—each added to her reputation and success. *Waiting to Exhale* became a bestseller in its first week of publication and remained on the *New York Times* Bestseller List for months. McMillan's work has been celebrated and criticized for the same strong feature—its honesty in portraying black people and black relationships, especially between men and women. A frequent complaint when the film *Waiting to Exhale* was released was that it portrayed black men too negatively. Some readers have also objected to her use of profanity. But most of her readers find her semi-autobiographical novels relevant because they identify with the characters. McMillan has avoided stereotypical "problem" novels about African Americans and instead presents middle-class, educated black characters working through common challenges, speaking in familiar language. In the process she has become one of the most successful contemporary black authors, and one the *Norton Anthology of African American Literature* calls "in many ways the apotheosis of the renaissance in writing by African American women." In 1998 *How Stella Got Her Groove Back* was made into another successful film.

North America

McQueen, Thelma ("Butterfly")

(b. January 8, 1911, Tampa, Fla.; d. December 22, 1995, Augusta, Georgia), African American actor and dancer known for her exaggerated roles as a domestic worker.

Thelma McQueen was born in Tampa, the child of a maid and a stevedore. In New York City she developed her interests in ballet and modern dance. Through the "Butterfly Ballet" in *A Midsummer Night's Dream*, McQueen earned her nickname "Butterfly" and her major break as an actress. After this part came others, all with McQueen earning the praise of critics. It was in a Benny Goodman-Louis Armstrong musical, "*Swingin' the Dream*," that she was spotted by David O. Selznick, who cast her as Prissy the maid in *Gone With The Wind* (1939). The role of Prissy immortalized McQueen with her line, "Lawdy, Miz Scarlett . . . I don't know nuthin' 'bout birthin' babies!"

It was her comic role as the flustered maid, or some variation of it, that McQueen would continue to play for most of her career, to uniformly fine reviews. Yet, while her great talent was widely acknowledged, she could not find roles that were not demeaning stereotypes. As one film critic observed, McQueen was fated "to act stereotypes or starve." She soon tired of playing roles that she called "dumb colored maid parts" and, in frustration, walked out of Jack Benny's radio show. For this she was boycotted for more than a year by casting agents. Refusing to play stereotypes, McQueen left acting altogether by the early 1950s.

After leaving acting, she occasionally took small roles in projects but mainly held jobs as a waitress and a factory worker, and finally opened her own restaurant in Augusta, Georgia. In the early 1970s she returned to college to receive a Bachelor of Arts degree in Spanish at age 64. McQueen then dedicated herself to community-based projects in New York City that aid black and Hispanic children in Harlem. Although McQueen appeared occasionally in films in the 1970s and 1980s, such as *The Mosquito Coast* (1986) with Harrison Ford, she preferred to serve in roles that aided her community.

North America

McRae, Carmen

(b. April 8, 1922, New York, N.Y.; d. November 10, 1994, Beverly Hills, Calif.), African American singer internationally known for her jazz and pop repertoire and unique lyrical projection.

Born in Harlem in 1922, Carmen McRae studied classical piano as a youth, although singing was her first passion. When she won an amateur contest at the Apollo Theater, her singing career was launched. McRae was greatly influenced by Billie Holiday, a lifelong friend and mentor. She dedicated her albums and most of her nightclub performances to Lady Day's memory. In her later years McRae's original style similarly influenced singers Betty Carter and Carol Sloane.

In the early 1940s McRae performed with bandleaders Benny Carter, Earl Hines, and Count Basie. While she was married to Kenny Clarke, she made her recording debut as Carmen Clarke with Mercer Ellington's orchestra in 1946–1947. When Ellington's group disbanded in 1948, McRae spent several years in nonmusical jobs. She also performed solo, accompanying herself as an intermission pianist, and met jazz accordionist Matt Mathews. Their association led to McRae's first solo recordings in 1953–1954. In 1955 McRae signed with Decca Records, having achieved popularity at Minton's Playhouse in Harlem.

From the 1950s onward, McRae toured internationally, developing significant popularity in Japan. Her best-known recordings were *Skyliner* (1956) and *Take Five with Dave Brubeck* (1961). McRae also acted in the films *Hotel* (1967) and *Jo Jo Dancer Your Life Is Calling* (1986). Her wide-reaching talents won six Grammy Award nominations and the National Endowment for the Arts' National Jazz Masters Fellowship Award in 1994. She died in 1994.

North America

Miley, James Wesley ("Bubber")

(b. April 3, 1903, Aiken, S.C.; d. May 20, 1932, New York, N.Y.), African American trumpeter who was one of the first great soloists in jazz and who, as a member of the Duke Ellington band, was largely responsible for its early "jungle" sound.

Bubber Miley—along with Louis Armstrong, Sidney Bechet, and Bix Beiderbecke—was one of the great jazz soloists of the 1920s. Miley's career, like that of Bechet, illustrates the importance of professionalism in securing long-term success in jazz, something that Armstrong and Duke Ellington, each in his own way, clearly understood. Ironically, however, much of Ellington's early renown as a composer and bandleader was a direct product of Miley's contributions to the Ellington orchestra.

Born in Aiken, South Carolina, Miley moved with his family to New York City in 1909. He began playing music in public school, initially trombone, then cornet. During 1918 he joined the United States Navy and served for 18 months, including the final months of World War I. In 1920, after his discharge from the navy, he began playing professionally. The following year he joined the Jazz Hounds, the group that had accompanied blues singer Mamie Smith on many of her recordings, including "Crazy Blues" (1920), the song that initiated the blues craze of the 1920s. In the fall of 1923 Miley joined banjo player Elmer Snowden's Washingtonians, which soon came under the leadership of its pianist, Duke Ellington.

The addition of Miley transformed the Washingtonians, giving them an instantly recognizable sound. Prior to Miley's arrival, the group had often played "sweet" dance music. Ellington recalled, "Our band changed character when Bubber came in. He used to growl all night long, playing gut-bucket on his horn. That was when we decided to forget all about the sweet music." In particular, Miley's playing reflected the influence of the great New Orleans cornet player Joe "King" Oliver. Oliver's playing was suffused with a deep blues feeling. He combined his gift for melody with the use of a plunger mute; by variously positioning the rubber cup of a toilet plunger over the bell of his instrument, he could alter the sounds and produce vocal-like growling effects.

Miley adopted this technique—combining the plunger mute with a straight mute inserted directly into the cornet's bell—and raised it to an expressive art. Most important, he did not use the plunger mute strictly for novelty effects; he made it an expressive element of the music, intrinsic to the emotional content of the melody. Miley became the most prominently featured soloist in the early Ellington band. He also taught trombone player Joe "Tricky Sam" Nanton everything that he knew about mutes. During the mid- to late 1920s the two provided a distinctive tonal quality, commonly referred to as the "jungle-music sound," for which the early Ellington band became well known.

Miley and Nanton's musical influence is particularly evident in many of Ellington's recordings between 1926 and 1928—for example, the various renditions of the slow-tempo *Black and Tan Fantasy* (1927), particularly the Victor Records version, on which Miley played what may be his greatest recorded solo. He opened on a keening high b-flat, which he held for four long measures before tumbling downward in a brilliant, bluesy cascade of plunger-muted notes. "It is also a highly dramatic solo," musicologist Gunther Schuller concluded, "equal to anything achieved up to that time by the New Orleans trumpet men. And perhaps none of them ever achieved the extraordinary contrast produced by the intense stillness of the four-bar-long high b-flat, suddenly erupting, as if unable to contain itself any longer, into a magnificently structured melodic creation."

Miley's superb improvisation may even have influenced the great Louis Armstrong. Eight months after Miley recorded this solo on *Black and Tan Fantasy*," Armstrong took a strikingly similar approach in his classic improvisation on *West End Blues* (1928), entering on a high b-flat that he held for four tension-building measures before falling away in a cascade of notes. Armstrong did not directly copy Miley's solo: after the first four measures, their note choices, phrasing, and rhythms were quite different, and Armstrong's bravura open horn sounded completely different from Miley's plunger-muted growl. Yet the two solos share a remarkable similarity in their ways of building and releasing dramatic tension.

Miley also created some of the Ellington band's most memorable melodies. It is difficult to determine who was responsible for many pieces in the band's early repertoire. However, Gunther Schuller and Ellington biographer John Edward Hasse agree in assigning Miley a key role in creating some of the group's signature pieces, including *Black and Tan Fantasy*,"

"East St. Louis Toodle-Oo" (1926), *"Creole Love Call"* (1927), and *"The Mooche"* (1928). Late in 1927 the Ellington band secured a long-term gig at the Cotton Club, New York City's most prestigious nightclub, and by the following year it emerged as the nation's foremost jazz ensemble.

But early in 1929 Ellington forced Miley, his most celebrated soloist, out of the band. Miley's heavy drinking and increasing unpredictability had at last exhausted Ellington's patience. Ellington scholar John Edward Hasse wrote that on occasion Miley did "not show up for several days," missing performances and recording sessions. As his replacement, trumpeter Charles "Cootie" Williams, explained, "[E]very time some big shot come up [to the Cotton Club] to listen to the band, there wasn't no Bubber Miley, and [Ellington] had the whole band built around Bubber Miley."

After leaving Ellington, Miley joined the Noble Sissle band on a 1929 trip to Paris. During the early 1930s he played with several other ensembles and briefly led his own group before succumbing to tuberculosis, aggravated by alcoholism, in the spring of 1932. He was 29 years old.

Miley left an enduring legacy within the Ellington band. Many of his compositions remained an active part of the band's repertoire, and Tricky Sam Nanton showed Cootie Williams the secrets of Miley's plunger mute technique. Through the years Ellington brass players passed on this knowledge to succeeding generations of musicians, maintaining a living link to the band's first famous soloist.

North America

Mills Brothers,

an African American pop vocal quartet that became famous in the 1930s for its ability to imitate jazz instruments.

The four Mills brothers were born to a musical family in Piqua, Ohio. Their paternal grandfather had sung with the Sourbeck Jubilee Singers. As children, John Jr., Herbert, Harry, and Donald performed professionally at local social events. In 1925 the boys—then between ages 10 and 15—auditioned to appear on Cincinnati radio station WLW and won a prolonged broadcasting contract.

During the next few years they became station regulars and adopted stage names in accord with station sponsors—the Tasty Yeast Jesters (Tasty Yeast) and the Steamboat Four (Sohio Motor Oil)—but also achieved renown as Four Boys and a Guitar. Their success caught the attention of talent scouts from New York City, and in 1930 they signed a three-year contract with CBS Records, at the time an unusually long contract for African American musicians. The Mills Brothers' debut album in 1931 won them instant acclaim. Their single *"Tiger Rag"* sold a million copies and in 1932 they performed with Bing Crosby in The Big Broadcast, the first of the numerous films in which the quartet appeared.

Much of the Mills Brothers' popularity originated from arrangements in which they simulated a full instrumental ensemble by singing as horns. The only accompaniment came from John Jr.'s guitar playing; the rest of their rich sound comprised saxophone, trumpet, and tuba imitations, as well as tight, sweet, four-part harmonies. Throughout the 1930s they scored hit after hit with this formula, including "*You Rascal You*," "*Good Bye Blues*," and "*Swing It Sister*." In the 1940s the quartet adopted conventional pop arrangements yet maintained their popularity—their 1942 hit, "*Paper Doll*," sold 6 million copies. Meanwhile, they undertook collaborations with some of the era's top African American musicians, such as Duke Ellington, Cab Calloway, and Ella Fitzgerald.

The Mills Brothers remained together until 1982 but not without changes in their roster. The oldest brother, John Jr., died in 1935; his father then filled his role as bass vocalist, and ex-bandleader Bernard Addison played guitar. At times the three remaining brothers performed as a trio. By the end, the group had recorded almost 2,500 songs.

The Mills Brothers' legacy involved social as well as musical accomplishments. Their vocal styles were a historic first, as were the terms under which they recorded them for white record companies. And their popularity among audiences of different races was unprecedented and influenced the formation, and mainstream acceptance, of doo-wop and rhythm and blues (R&B) groups in the 1950s.

North America

Mills, Florence

(b. January 25, 1896, Washington, D.C.; d. November 1, 1927, New York, N.Y.), African American musical comedy singer and dancer; one of the most celebrated black entertainers of the Jazz Age and the Harlem Renaissance.

Florence Mills, who rose to stardom in the early 1920s, joined performing to a crusade for racial justice. She expressed a profound race consciousness and a conviction that her career could advance the status of African Americans. "The stage is the quickest way to get to the people," she said in an interview with London's *Daily Express* in 1927. "My own success makes people think better of other colored folk."

Rejecting an offer to join the Ziegfeld Follies, America's leading white musical revue, she helped create a rival all-black musical revue in the heart of Broadway. She also broke through Broadway's racial barriers, performing in some of New York City's leading white vaudeville theaters, including the Palace Theater, where she was the first black ever to headline. Yet her principal goal was to foster opportunities for black entertainers and to remain true in her art to her black roots. "Harlem loves Florence Mills," wrote journalist Dudley Nichols in 1926. "She is the melodious, impish spirit of the Afro-American embodied piquantly."

The youngest of three daughters of John and Nellie (Simon) Winfrey, Mills grew up in Washington, D.C.'s poverty-stricken Goat Alley. Her mother and father, former slaves and tobacco workers from Virginia, worked as a laundress and a day laborer to make ends meet. It was the golden age of vaudeville, and Mills, a child prodigy, began singing and dancing at local black theaters at age three.

In 1903, under the guidance of ragtime singer Aida Overton Walker, Mills sang "*Miss Hannah from Savannah*" in a touring production of Bert Williams's and George Walker's musical *Sons of Ham*. Although her talent won her recognition and much-needed family income, she suffered racial exploitation performing as a "pickaninny" with a white vaudeville team. In 1910 she began touring the East Coast with her two sisters and faced the difficult travel conditions imposed on blacks by segregation. Eventually she found herself in Chicago, where gangster-controlled cabarets welcomed black clientele and the new jazz music. She sang with Cora Green and Ada "Bricktop" Smith at the Panama Cafe, a notorious cabaret in the city's red-light district. She also met and married the dancer "Slow Kid" Thompson; they would have a devoted and lifelong relationship.

Mills's career took off in 1921 when she replaced Gertrude Sanders in the black musical comedy *Shuffle Along*, by Noble Sissle and Eubie Blake. Performed off-Broadway in New York, the musical introduced white audiences to the ebullient, fast-paced rhythms of authentic black song and dance and heralded the beginning of the Harlem Renaissance.

Dainty and elfin, Mills dazzled listeners and critics with her "flute-like" voice and quick, frolicking dance steps. Impressed by her talent, the white promoter Lew Leslie hired her as a nightly performer at the Plantation Club (so named to inform would-be patrons that its entertainers were black). The club drew a variety of famed black performers, including Will Vodery and his orchestra, and in 1922 Leslie turned his nightclub show into a Broadway musical group called the Plantation Review. Mills starred in the show and received effusive praise from New York critics.

In 1923 the Plantation Review cast performed in the musical *Dover Street to Dixie* at the Pavilion in London. Hostile to the visiting black Americans, British entertainers threatened to demonstrate in the theater on opening night. However, Mills's poignant rendition of "*The Sleeping Hills of Tennessee*" left the British audience enchanted; their opposition to the Review immediately subsided. For many British critics the Review's performance was nothing short of high art. American Alexander Wollcott described Mills as "a slender streak of genius five feet tall." Another reviewer wrote that she was "by far the most artistic person London had ever had the good fortune to see."

When Mills returned to London in 1926, this time in the widely acclaimed musical *Blackbirds of 1926*, she became the toast of British society. The Prince of Wales saw the revue more than a dozen times, and many artists and intellectuals of the period mentioned Mills in their writings and personal diaries. "Anything she did was super," wrote one critic, "whether spotlighted solo singing . . . or high-stepping in a smashing full-dress suit, her top hat at a rakish angle, jauntily swinging a malacca cane."

For Mills the London visit proved an auspicious time to voice openly her feelings about racial prejudice. British journalist Hannen Swaffer, who heard a speech Mills gave in the Picadilly Cabaret, wrote that "her eloquent plea for tolerance made an impression on many minds." Her title song, *"I'm a little Blackbird, Looking for a Bluebird"*—which for Mills contained a message about the quest for racial equality—became a hit with British and American audiences alike. "Few realized it, but the number was a protest song," noted black American journalist Alvin White. "There were no hidden meanings, no dramatic phrases, just simple words that told of the poignant yearnings of black women everywhere."

Throughout her short life Mills worked relentlessly; eventually she became seriously ill. Unable to continue her British tour, she sailed back to New York, where on November 1, 1927, she died following an operation for appendicitis. Her funeral on November 6 was an elaborately planned public event. More than 5,000 people filled the Mother African Methodist Episcopal Zion Church in Harlem, while 150,000 more lined the streets to witness the funeral cortege and pay homage to the beloved "blackbird," who had never forgotten her heritage.

North America

Milner, Ronald

(b. May 29, 1938, Detroit, Mich.), African American playwright and producer prominent in the Black Theater movement of the 1970s.

With training from Harvey Swando's writing workshop at Columbia University, plus a wealth of creative material from his childhood in inner-city Detroit, Michigan, Ronald Milner produced his first play, *Who's Got His Own*, off-Broadway in 1966. Three years later, as one of four African American playwrights in the production *A Black Quartet*, he helped inaugurate the Black Theater Movement. With connections to the Black Power Movement, the Black Theater Movement promoted plays allowing African Americans to represent their lives on stage.

With *What the Wine-Sellers Buy* (1973) Milner achieved national recognition, and followed with *Jazz Set* (1980), *Checkmates* (1987), and *Don't Get God Started* (1987). He worked closely with fellow playwright Woodie King Jr., co-founding the theater company Concept-East in 1962 and co-editing the *Black Drama Anthology* in 1971.

North America

Mitchell, Loften

(b. April 15, 1919, Columbia, N.C.), African American playwright and novelist who portrayed the court case that ended school segregation in his play *A Land Beyond the River.*

Loften Mitchell grew up in Harlem, where as a young man he began working in theater with the Rose McClendon Players. In 1943 he completed an A.B. at Talladega College in Alabama and studied playwriting with John Glassner at Columbia University.

Mitchell's play *A Land Beyond the River*, which depicted a court case ending school segregation, was met with critical acclaim in 1957. His prolific literary output includes *The Photographer* (1962), *Ballad of Bimshire* (1963), *Ballad for the Winter Soldiers* (1964), *Tell Pharaoh* (1967), and the successful musical co-written with Rosetta LeNoire, *Bubbling Brown Sugar* (1976).

Mitchell also taught at the State University of New York at Binghamton, published the novel *The Stubborn Old Lady Who Resisted Change* (1973), and wrote two histories of drama, *Black Drama: The Story of the American Negro in the Theatre* (1967) and *Voices of the Black Theatre* (1975).

North America

Modern Jazz Quartet (MJQ),

American jazz quartet that was one of the first and most important ensembles to combine group jazz improvisation with elements of classical music.

The Modern Jazz Quartet, also known as the MJQ, was formed in 1952 by John Lewis on piano and director of the ensemble; Milt Jackson on vibraphone; Percy Heath on double bass; and Kenny Clarke on drums. The quartet evolved from the Milt Jackson Quartet (1951), which included Lewis, Clarke, and bassist Ray Brown, veterans of the 1946 big band of trumpeter Dizzy Gillespie. Drummer Connie Kay replaced Clarke in 1955. The quartet's refined ensemble sound, closely aligned with the style known as cool jazz, eventually came to be known as third-stream music.

Lewis's compositions featured his own understated, melodic playing layered against Jackson's freer, more rhythmically complex solos. The group recorded many of Lewis's compositions, including "*Versailles*" (1956), "*Three Windows*" (1957), and "*England's Carol*" (1960), as well as pieces by American composer Gunther Schuller and French composer André Hodeir. The quartet favored dressing in tuxedos and performing in concert halls over the usual nightclub venues.

During its more than 20 years the group annually disbanded during the summer, allowing members to play in other ensembles. Formally dissolved in July 1974, the MJQ reunited for a concert in November of that year and in later years for occasional tours. In the early 1980s the MJQ resumed playing together for several months a year. The group's albums include *Fontessa* (1956), *The Modern Jazz Quartet* (1957), *The Modern Jazz Quartet and Orchestra* (1960), *The Last Concert* (1974), and *Together Again!* (1982). Kay passed away in 1994 and was succeeded by drummer Albert "Tootie" Heath, brother of Percy Heath, in 1995.

North America

Monk, Thelonious Sphere

(b. October 10, 1917, Rocky Mount, N.C.; d. February 17, 1982, Weehawken, N.J.), African American jazz pianist and composer noted for his highly individual compositions and angular and rhythmic style of playing.

Thelonious Monk was one of the great iconoclasts of jazz. He has long been classed among the main creators of bebop or modern jazz in the 1940s, along with alto sax player Charlie Parker, trumpeter Dizzy Gillespie, drummer Kenny Clarke, and guitarist Charlie Christian. Many also emphasize Monk's importance as a precursor of free jazz; jazz scholar Joachim Berendt notes that "what leads to Ornette Coleman, John Coltrane, Eric Dolphy, and all the other avant-gardists of jazz was heard for the first time in his music." Although Monk had some formal instruction, he was essentially self-taught and never really fit within any larger movement or style. Still, in going his own way, he ultimately took much of the jazz world with him.

Monk was born in North Carolina but moved with his family to New York City when he was an infant. He first became interested in playing piano when he was five or six years old. Growing up, he lived near the great Harlem stride pianist James P. Johnson, and Monk himself initially played in the stride style. In effect, the stride piano style divides the piano keyboard into three ranges. The pianist's left hand covers the two lower ranges, alternating single bass notes at the bottom with chord clusters struck higher up. The term "stride" comes from the characteristic bouncing "oom-pah, oom-pah" of the pianist's "striding" left hand. While the left hand sets up a propulsive beat and outlines the tune's harmonic structure, the pianist's right hand plays the melody, adds ornamentation, and improvises solo lines.

Throughout his performing career, Monk continued to display hints of the stride piano style of his youth. But he soon began moving further, not just away from the stride style, but beyond the conventions of swing jazz in general. His explorations coincided with the experiments of a generation of young jazz players who were in the process of creating bebop or modern jazz. Monk himself became a part of these efforts during his 1940–1943 stint in the house band of Minton's, a New York City jazz club and bop incubator. There he played with Charlie Christian, Dizzy Gillespie, and Don Byas, among others. Impromptu recordings made at Minton's reveal a pianist strongly influenced by the stripped-down melodic swing of Teddy Wilson. These early recordings also capture some of the irregular rhythms and jarring harmonies that would characterize Monk's mature playing.

Monk played briefly with Lucky Millinder in 1942 and two years later joined Cootie Williams's short-lived big band, which had recorded two Monk compositions, "*Epistrophy*" and his most famous piece, "*'Round Midnight.*" Monk enjoyed much wider recognition, and had his recording debut, after joining tenor saxophonist Coleman Hawkins, who consistently supported creative younger players. Nonetheless, during a period when other bop musicians found growing acceptance—in fact, near pop-culture celebrity during the short-lived bebop craze of the late 1940s—Monk continued to play in obscurity.

In certain respects, his compositions and solos are forbidding. The chord progressions are unexpected and sometimes jarring, the melodies often agitated and edgy. In an era in which jazz soloists strove to play more and more notes at ever faster tempos, Monk's lines were spare, with open space between the notes and phrases. And the tempos he played in were often remarkably slow. Between 1947 and 1952 he recorded several sessions for Blue Note that were later acclaimed by jazz musicians and listeners alike—featuring such classic Monk compositions as *"Ruby My Dear," "Well You Needn't," "'Round Midnight,"* and *"Straight No Chaser"*—but he remained too "far out" for widespread acceptance until the latter half of the 1950s.

Monk did not alter his style between 1947 and the end of his life. But after 1955, when he began recording for Riverside Records with jazz producer Orrin Keepnews, jazz at last caught up with him. In 1956 Monk recorded his outstanding *Brilliant Corners* album, praised in *Downbeat* magazine by jazz critic Nat Henthoff. Monk's talent was finally recognized in 1957, when he played an extended gig at the Five Spot, then one of New York City's premier jazz clubs. At the Five Spot, Monk performed with a quartet that featured tenor saxophonist John Coltrane. Under the pianist's tutelage, Coltrane began his own rapid growth toward musical greatness.

During the 1960s Monk established a long-standing quartet featuring Charlie Rouse on tenor saxophone, which recorded regularly for Columbia Records. In his later years Monk suffered psychiatric problems that led to his effective retirement in 1973, though he made occasional appearances to the end of the decade. Since his death, jazz musicians have continued to embrace his music. It has become almost *de rigueur* for jazz players to include at least one Monk tune in their recording sessions and nightclub sets.

North America

Moorhead, Scipio

(fl. 1773, Boston, Mass.), African American slave and artist known primarily for his painting of Phillis Wheatley.

Despite Scipio Moorhead's position as a slave in the home of Rev. John Moorhead, a Presbyterian minister in Boston, he managed to develop his artistic talent. Sarah Moorhead, a painter who was the wife of the minister, probably provided some instruction.

Attributed to Moorhead is the painting of African American poet Phillis Wheatley that inspired the engraved frontispiece of her book of poetry. The volume, *Poems on Various Subjects, Religious and Moral*, was published in London in 1773 and provoked public debate concerning the intellectual abilities of those of African descent.

Unfortunately, no signed works by Moorhead are known to exist. It is believed to be Moorhead whom Wheatley immortalized with her 1773 poem "To S.M., A Young African Painter, on Seeing His Work." The poem describes two paintings presumably by Moorhead, *Aurora* and *Damon and Pythia*.

Morrison, Toni

(b. February 18, 1931, Lorain, Ohio), African American writer; one of the most celebrated twentieth-century American writers and the first black woman and first African American to receive the Nobel Prize for Literature.

"I'm interested in how men are educated, how women relate to each other, how we are able to love, how we balance political and personal forces, who survives in certain situations and who doesn't and, specifically, how these and other universal issues relate to African Americans. The search for love and identity runs through most everything I write." In this excerpt from a 1992 interview, Toni Morrison gives one description of the complex range of issues she explores in her work. Morrison is widely recognized as one of the most influential American writers, and her novels are taught in literature and history courses and in women's and African American studies programs across the country and around the world. She has received numerous honorary degrees, prizes, and awards, including the Nobel Prize for Literature. Above all, Morrison is known for her rich, lyrical prose, which fuses the rhythms and imagery of African American speech and music with other literary influences to create a discourse of its own. In a 1977 interview, she said that it "seemed to [her] Black people's grace has been what they do with language." Morrison is unparalleled in her ability to capture that grace on the page.

Toni Morrison was born Chloe Anthony Wofford in Lorain, Ohio, a small, racially mixed steel town. Her grandparents were all originally from the South, and Morrison credits her family with giving her a rich foundation in the language and rhythms of African American culture. She has said she was born into a family of storytellers, and considers her father's folktales, her mother's singing, and her grandmother's numbers games all examples of the uniquely black language she absorbed as a child. After graduating with honors from Lorain public schools, she received a bachelor's degree from Howard University in 1953. In 1955 she earned a master's degree in English Literature from Cornell University, where she wrote her thesis on alienation in the works of William Faulkner and Virginia Woolf. She taught at Texas Southern University for two years before accepting a teaching position at Howard.

While teaching at Howard, Morrison married Jamaican architect Harold Morrison and gave birth to two sons. She later said it was the "powerlessness" she felt during her years as a wife and mother of small children that led her to begin writing. In 1964 Morrison and her husband divorced, and she took a job in Syracuse, New York, as a textbook editor for Random House. In 1968 she moved to Random House's trade division in Manhattan, becoming its first black woman senior editor. There she focused on black authors and edited books by Angela Davis, Toni Cade Bambara, Gayl Jones, and Muhammad Ali. Morrison continued writing her own fiction at night, after her sons were asleep, and in 1970 published her first novel, *The Bluest Eye*.

The Bluest Eye tells the story of a nine-year-old black girl in a 1940s Ohio town who prays for blue eyes, thinking they will stop the emotional, physical, and sexual abuse she receives from her peers and the adults around her. Morrison became part of a new generation of black women writers, including Jones, Bambara, and Alice Walker, who were interested in telling black women's stories and stories set wholly within the black community. *The Bluest Eye* received critical praise, and Morrison became sought-after for book reviews and articles on black literature and culture. Her next novel, *Sula* (1973), was nominated for the 1975 National Book Award in fiction. Set in another Ohio town between World War II and the Korean War, *Sula* is about the classic forces of good and evil, set within the context of a friendship between two black women and the community that surrounds them. Morrison truly rose to prominence as a novelist, however, with her third book, *Song of Solomon* (1977).

Like both of her earlier novels, *Song of Solomon* is set mainly in a Midwestern town—one of Morrison's innovations in African American fiction, which is traditionally set in either the urban North or the rural South. But in contrast to the earlier works, *Song of Solomon*'s main character is male, and the book has been described as incorporating more traditionally Western and male themes of flight, journey, and violence into its narrative of a particular black community and a particular black family. *Song of Solomon* became a Book-of-the-Month Club selection, the first novel by a black author to be so chosen since *Native Son* (1940), by Richard Wright. It also won the National Book Critics Circle Award and secured Morrison appointments to the American Academy of Arts and Letters and the National Council of the Arts. Twenty years after its publication, the book was again featured as a national book club selection—this time, for the popular television feature Oprah Winfrey's Book Club.

Morrison's next novel, *Tar Baby* (1981), received similar acclaim. It is the first of her novels to be set primarily outside the United States (on a Caribbean island) and in the present, and to feature several white main characters. *Tar Baby* was also a bestseller. But Morrison's fifth novel, *Beloved* (1987), is her most celebrated work to date. *Beloved* is loosely based on a news clipping that Morrison had read years earlier while editing a book on black history: the true story of Margaret Garner, a slave who ran away with her four children. When she was captured, she tried to slit her children's throats, and succeeded with one of them, rather than see them returned to slavery. In its fullness, *Beloved* becomes a novel about slavery, history, community, possession—and ultimately love. *Beloved* was another national bestseller, was internationally reviewed, and won the Pulitzer Prize for Literature in 1988.

Morrison has said that *Beloved* is the first novel in a trilogy about love. The second novel in that trilogy, *Jazz*, was published in 1992. Set in New York during the Harlem Renaissance, the novel pieces together the story of a love triangle in a narrative form that imitates the rhythms of jazz music. The third novel, *Paradise*, was published in 1998. It portrays the lives of the townspeople of Ruby, Oklahoma, who believe their community is "the one all-black town worth the pain," and the women who inhabit the abandoned convent just outside town, whom the townspeople wish to exclude from their Eden. In 1993 Morrison received the Nobel Prize for Literature for her six novels. She was the first African American and the first black woman of any nationality ever to receive the prize.

Morrison has taught at several universities and in 1989 was named the Robert F. Goheen Professor in the Council of the Humanities at Princeton University. Her reputation as one of the most influential American writers rests not only on her fiction, but also on her work as a literary and cultural critic. Her essays and speeches have been included in numerous journals and books, and in 1992 she published her first volume of literary criticism, *Playing in the Dark: Whiteness and the Literary Imagination.* That same year she edited *Racing Justice, En-Gendering Power,* a collection of essays on the Hill-Thomas Hearings. In 1996 she co-edited a second essay collection, *Birth of a Nation'hood: Gaze, Script and Spectacle in the O. J. Simpson Case.* Morrison has also written a play, *Dreaming Emmett,* first produced in New York in 1986.

Through all of these works Morrison has had a tremendous impact on both the American and the African American literary landscapes. Her novels are widely accessible to readers and internationally praised for the quality of their prose; yet they remain dedicated to exploring nuances of African American culture and language. In Mari Evans's 1984 book *Black Women Writers,* Morrison states that for her, the best art "is unquestionably political and irrevocably beautiful at the same time," a standard that many readers believe she has met in all of her work.

North America

Morton, Ferdinand Joseph ("Jelly Roll") (Ferdinand Joseph La Menthe)

(b. October 20, 1890, New Orleans, La.; d. July 10, 1941, Los Angeles, Calif.), early jazz pianist and composer who since his death has risen to the highest tier of critical acclaim for his mastery of the piano.

Jelly Roll Morton was born to fair-skinned Creole parents in New Orleans, and all his life he considered himself more white than black. His father, who left the family when Morton was young, played trombone, as did Morton's stepfather, Ed Morton. Morton received guitar lessons by age 6 but soon abandoned guitar for piano. At age 12 he began playing piano in the bordellos of New Orleans's Storyville district, and as a teenager he traveled the gulf coast, mingling with famous regional musicians, including ragtime pianist Tony Jackson. Morton also received some formal musical training at St. Joseph's Seminary College in St. Benedict, Louisiana.

Beginning with his trip to the St. Louis World's Fair in 1904, Morton embarked on a decade of itinerant music making that carried him throughout the South and to New York and Chicago. He played with vaudeville troupes and minstrel shows, supplementing his income with profits from pool hustling, card playing, and pimping. Indeed, his notoriety as a swindler, braggart, and womanizer often preceded his reputation as a musician.

Morton settled in Chicago from around 1911 until 1915, playing music with a small ensemble. He published *"Jelly Roll Blues"* in 1915, an accomplishment that set him apart from other jazz pianists of the time. While his performances evinced high passion and spontaneity, Morton made music with a composer's fastidious mind. Even when fast and improvised, his playing reflected rational, intentional calculations. In 1915 he uprooted once more, traveling up and down the West Coast until he resettled in Chicago in 1923.

In Chicago Morton observed the new and thriving recording industry and decided to cut his own takes. In 1923 and 1924 he recorded as a solo pianist, and from 1926 to 1930 he led the ensemble Red Hot Peppers, featuring such legendary players as clarinetist Johnny Dodds and trombonist Kid Ory. Morton recorded some of his most famous compositions with this group, including *"Kansas City Stomps"* and *"Smokehouse Blues."* Critics often describe Morton's style in these recordings as orchestral; instead of backing the melody with chords and steady rhythm in the bass, he created one or two lines of counterpoint in which his left hand emulated a trombone for the cornet of his right.

Morton moved to New York in 1928 and began running an all-girl revue that doubled as a prostitution racket. He continued to record, but both the advent of big-band music and the onset of the Great Depression diminished his popularity. He moved to Washington, D.C., in 1935, managed a nightclub, and eventually worked with folklorist Alan Lomax on a set of recordings for the Library of Congress. In the hours of collected footage, Morton expounds on his playing style and reconstructs a history of jazz. Although many of his observations have historical and musicological value, his arrogance and hyperbole limit the recording's veracity, as in his claim that he "invented jazz in 1902," the year he turned 12.

Morton moved to Los Angeles, California, toward the end of his life and died in 1941, with the bulk of his popularity seeming to have passed. Throughout his life he had managed his career poorly, often spoiling business relationships with displays of arrogance and pomp. He is now recognized as a musical genius, however, and jazz pianists today cite his direct influence on their style, approach, and repertoire.

North America

Mosley, Walter

(b. January 12, 1952, Los Angeles, Calif.), African American novelist known for his detective fiction.

Walter Mosley was born to an African American father and a Jewish mother in South Central Los Angeles, where he lived until he left for college in

Vermont. After college he worked a series of jobs, including caterer, potter, and computer programmer. In 1981 he moved to New York and began taking graduate writing courses at the City College of New York. There he completed *Gone Fishin'* and *Devil in a Blue Dress*, two novels that centered on the same Los Angeles protagonist, a working-class African American named Easy Rawlins.

Although *Gone Fishin'* did not sell, the rights to *Devil in a Blue Dress* were soon purchased by Norton, which published the book in 1990. *Devil* portrayed the Easy Rawlins character as a private investigator, and Mosley seemed to have found a strong voice as an author of detective fiction. After *Devil* he published four more Easy Rawlins books: *A Red Death* (1991), *White Butterfly* (1992), *Black Betty* (1994), and *A Little Yellow Dog* (1996).

Although Mosley's fiction falls into a category that many consider sub-literary—detective fiction—his depth of character, researched historical details, and realistic dialogue transcend the cliches of the genre. He portrays the complexity of the Los Angeles African American community between the late 1940s and mid-1960s, and does so with nuance and at times painful realism. Mosley's novel outside the series, *R. L.'s Dream*, evinces a similar level of sophistication in its speculative portrayal of bluesman Robert Johnson.

Mosley's books experienced a boom in sales during the 1992 presidential campaign, when Bill Clinton cited them as among his favorites. Mosley has been included in the *Norton Anthology of African American Literature*, compared to renowned detective novelist Raymond Chandler, and praised as a superior writer of his generation. A film version of *Devil in a Blue Dress*, directed by Jonathan Demme and starring Denzel Washington, was released in 1998.

North America

Moten, Benjamin (Bennie)

(b. November 13, 1894, Kansas City, Mo.; d. April 2, 1935, Kansas City, Mo.), African American jazz bandleader who popularized the "Kansas City" sound in big-band jazz.

In his youth Moten played baritone saxophone in Kansas City brass bands. Switching to the piano, he studied ragtime with two of Scott Joplin's students. In 1918 he formed the ragtime trio B.B.&D. Moten's band toured the Midwest through the 1920s, settling in New York near the end of the decade. By the beginning of the 1930s Moten's group included a roster of intensely talented musicians and arrangers. Those who later acquired fame as independent artists included singer Jimmy Rushing, tenor saxophonist Ben Webster, trumpeter Oran "Hot Lips" Page, and pianist and bandleader Count Basie.

Key early Moten recordings, such as *"Elephant's Wobble"* and *"Crawdad Blues"* (1923), showcased his band's tight ensemble playing and heavy, percussive beat. The band's characteristic sound wed stellar solo passages and instrumental riffs to a distinctive underlying flow. Important later recordings included *"Moten Stomp"* (1927), *"Kansas City Breakdown"* (1928), *"Lafayette"* (1932), and *"Prince of Wails"* (1932).

Moten died in 1935 during an operation to remove his tonsils. Members of his band regrouped as the Count Basie Orchestra in 1936.

North America
___

Motown,

black-owned record company that became the most commercially successful and culturally influential record company of the 1960s, producing a distinct musical style that appealed to audiences across racial boundaries.

The Supremes, the Temptations, the Four Tops, Smokey Robinson and the Miracles, Martha and the Vandellas, the Contours, and the Jackson 5, as well as solo artists Mary Wells, Marvin Gaye, and Stevie Wonder were some of Motown's leading popular acts. This collection of musical talent produced scores of hits, including *"My Girl," "Stop! In the Name of Love," "Shop Around," "I Heard It Through the Grapevine," "Baby, I Need Your Loving,"* and *"Dancing in the Street."* These songs captured the spirit of an era and became—as the company motto promised—the "Sound of Young America."

Berry Gordy Jr. founded the company in Detroit, Michigan, in 1959 with the support of a family loan of $800. Gordy, who worked briefly at the Ford Motor Company, named the company Motown after Detroit's "Motor Town" nickname. He believed that the efficiency of the automobile assembly line could be applied to the music industry.

Gordy designed his "hit factory" in a modest two-story home on West Grand Boulevard in Detroit. His concept involved finding young talent from local neighborhoods and transforming these amateur musicians and singers into professional artists. Gordy set up a separate Artist Development Department, which was often referred to as the company "charm school," to teach performers how to sing, dance, and comport themselves in the public spotlight. Legendary bandleader Maurice King led the musical instruction. Cholly Atkins, a veteran choreographer, taught the synchronized black dance steps that became an integral part of Motown's signature style. Maxine Powell instructed performers on the etiquette of celebrity life— including how to dress, greet dignitaries, and behave on stage. With this schooling, Gordy's young artists, many of whom were just out of high school, exuded the confidence of seasoned entertainers.

The "Motown Sound" has always been difficult to define yet easy to recognize. Motown songs often combine strong bass lines and a gritty back beat with call-and-response vocals and clever lyrics about the trials and joys of teenage romance. The music's magic resulted from the combined efforts of skilled songwriters, producers, and musicians. Gordy, a talented songwriter, gained early fame writing songs for Jackie Wilson, including

"*Reet Petite*" (1957) and "*Lonely Teardrops*" (1958). He mentored other Motown writers and producers in the art of romantic storytelling through popular song.

In 1959 Gordy signed a new group, the Miracles, to the label. In February 1961 their song "*Shop Around*" became the company's first million seller. Smokey Robinson, the lead singer, quickly became one of Motown's most prolific songwriters. He composed top hits, including "*My Girl*," "*The Way You Do the Things You Do*," and "*You've Really Got a Hold on Me*." Motown's innovative studio musicians, also known as the Funk Brothers, created the company's unique "sound." The original members included James Jamerson on bass, Earl Van Dyke on keyboards, Benny "Papa Zita" Benjamin on drums, Robert White on guitar, and Thomas "Beans" Bowles on saxophone.

With such a powerful array of creative talent, the Motown recording studio soon lived up to its ambitious nickname: "Hitsville, U.S.A." Early hits included Barrett Strong's "*Money (That's What I Want)*" (1959) and the Marvelettes' "*Please Mr. Postman*" (1961). In 1962 Motown developed enough new acts to send its own road show, the Motortown Revue, on a national tour. The tour, the first sponsored solely by a black-owned record company, was a music industry first. The Revue's roster, which included Mary Wells, the Contours, Martha and the Vandellas, the Supremes, the Miracles, "Little" Stevie Wonder, Marvin Gaye, and the Marvelettes, testified to the company's rich potential. From 1961 to 1972 Motown performers sent over 100 songs to the Top Ten of the popular music charts, including 31 number-one hits.

The key to Motown's success was the company's ability to produce music that appealed to audiences across racial boundaries. No Motown group exemplified this skill more than the Supremes, the company's most commercially successful group. The Supremes first reached number one on the pop charts with their song "*Where Did Our Love Go?*" in the summer of 1964. A string of hits followed, including "*Baby Love*," "*Come See About Me*," "*Stop! In the Name of Love*," and "*I Hear a Symphony*." The songwriting team of Eddie Holland, Lamont Dozier, and Brian Holland—known as Holland-Dozier-Holland—masterminded the Supremes' unique sound. Diana Ross, Florence Ballard, and Mary Wilson became international celebrities through national television appearances and world tours. Ross left the group in 1970 to pursue a solo singing career and film acting.

By the late 1960s and early 1970s Motown music had moved beyond carefree teenage themes to address the political and social struggles of the Civil Rights Movement and the Vietnam War. Stevie Wonder was the first Motown artist to address social issues through song in 1966, when he recorded a cover version of Bob Dylan's song "*Blowin' in the Wind*." Wonder's moving interpretation spoke to the challenges of the Civil Rights campaign. The Supremes recorded "*Love Child*" (1968) and "*I'm Livin' in Shame*" (1969), both of which depicted the problems of urban ghetto life. The Temptations also recorded a series of "message" songs, including "*Ball of Confusion (That's What the World Is Today)*" (1970) and "*Papa was a Rollin'*

Stone" (1972). Edwin Starr's song *"War!"* (1970) became one of the strongest anti-Vietnam War anthems on the airwaves.

In 1971 Marvin Gaye produced his groundbreaking album *What's Going On*, which commented not only on the Vietnam War but also on ecology, racism, and urban violence. Motown Records also founded the Black Forum label, which produced spoken-word recordings on political and literary subjects. Black Forum releases included *Free Huey!* (1970), *Writers of the Revolution* (1970), *The Congressional Black Caucus* (1972), and Martin Luther King Jr.'s speech *Why I Oppose the War in Vietnam*, which won a Grammy Award in 1970 for Best Spoken-Word Recording.

In 1972 the Motown Record Company announced its plans to relocate its headquarters from Detroit to Los Angeles, California. Gordy wanted to expand into filmmaking as well as record producing. Motown's first feature film was *Lady Sings the Blues* (1973), starring Diana Ross. Ross's moving portrayal of Billie Holiday won her an Academy Award Best Actress nomination. Other Motown feature films include *Mahogany* (1975) and *The Bingo Long and the Travelling All-Star and Motor Kings* (1976). In the early 1980s Motown produced television specials, including *"Motown 25: Yesterday, Today, Forever"* (1983), which first featured Michael Jackson's famous "moonwalk" dance. In 1988 Gordy sold Motown to MCA, Inc., for $61.9 million. The Motown label is currently owned by Polygram Records and features groups such as Boyz II Men.

North America

Murphy, Eddie

(b. April 3, 1961, Brooklyn, N.Y.), African American comedian and actor.

Eddie Murphy first achieved fame in the United States in 1980 as a featured performer on the popular television show *Saturday Night Live* (SNL) at age 20. He was already a veteran of comedy clubs, where he had been performing since age 15. *SNL's* sketch comedy format proved the perfect vehicle for Murphy's hard-edged comedic characterizations and at times unflattering celebrity impersonations. Murphy became *SNL's* biggest star.

In 1982 Murphy released *Eddie Murphy*, an album of his standup material, which earned a Grammy nomination. Murphy capitalized on his popularity, taking his first film role later that year in *48 Hours*, which was well received critically and commercially. The success of *48 Hours* led to a costarring role with former *SNL* cast member Dan Ackroyd in *Trading Places*, which was among the top ten earning films of 1983. *Eddie Murphy: Comedian*, another comedy album, won a Grammy. By 1984, when he left *SNL* to pursue a film career full-time, Murphy was considered one of Hollywood's leading box office attractions.

Murphy has often achieved box-office success at the expense of critical acclaim. *Beverly Hills Cop* (1987) broke box-office records, which prompted Paramount Pictures to sign him to a $25 million six-film contract. Sequels to *48 Hours* and *Beverly Hills* Cop, on the other hand, were poorly received critically and enjoyed only modest commercial success. Critics panned Murphy's first attempt at writing and directing, *Harlem Nights* (1989). In addition, the success of *Coming to America* (1988) was diminished when in 1990 writer Art Buchwald successfully sued Murphy and Paramount Pictures for stealing his idea for the screenplay. Murphy's career rebounded in the 1990s with such films as *Boomerang* (1992) and a remake of *The Nutty Professor* (1996), which earned Murphy critical and popular acclaim.

North America
_____

Murray, Pauli

(b. November 20, 1910, Baltimore, Md.; d. July 1, 1985, Pittsburgh, Pa.), African American lawyer, teacher, poet, women's rights advocate; first African American woman Episcopal priest.

A pioneer in fields previously inaccessible to women and African Americans, Pauli Murray was the first African American to be awarded a doctorate in juridical science from Yale University. A freedom rider in the 1940s who later led student sit-ins in Washington, D.C. restaurants, Murray graduated at the top of her class at Howard University. Nominated by the National Council of Negro Women as one of the 12 outstanding women in Negro life in 1945, she was the recipient of many honorary degrees and was a founding member of the National Organization for Women. In 1977 she was the first African American woman to be ordained as a priest of the Episcopal Church.

The daughter of a racially mixed, middle-class family, Murray was the fourth of six children born to Agnes Georgianna Fitzgerald Murray and William Henry Murray. When Murray was 3 years old, her mother died as a result of a cerebral hemorrhage. Three years later, while Murray and her siblings were in the care of their aunt, their father was committed to a mental institution, where he died in 1923.

Murray received an A.B. at Hunter College in 1933 as one of four black students in a class of 247 women. Unsuccessful in breaking the color line at the University of North Carolina at Chapel Hill (where she was later awarded an honorary degree and honored with a scholarship in her name), she was accepted at the Howard University Law School, where she was the only female in the class of 1944. Murray completed an LL.M. at the University of California at Berkeley in 1945, after she was denied entrance to the all-male Harvard Law School. In 1976 she graduated from the General Theological Seminary with an M.Div. degree.

A writer since her early adolescence, Murray was a resident of the MacDowell Colony at the same time as James Baldwin in the early 1950s. In 1956 she documented her interracial family history in *Proud Shoes: The Story of an American Family*. Her collection of poetry, *Dark Testament and Other Poems*, appeared in 1970.

While teaching in Accra, Ghana, Murray co-authored the first textbook on law in Africa, titled *The Constitution and Government in Africa*. Thurgood Marshall lauded her book *States' Law on Race and Color* (1951) as a bible for lawyers battling segregation.

Murray died of cancer in 1985. Her autobiography, *Song in a Weary Throat: An American Pilgrimage*, appeared posthumously in 1987 and received the Robert F. Kennedy Book Award and the Christopher Award.

Latin America and the Caribbean

Mutabaruka (Allan Hope)

(b. 1952, Kingston, Jamaica), poet and producer best known for recording his poetry, influenced by Rastafarian and Black Power ideologies, to reggae rhythm tracks.

Mutabaruka's literary and musical career began when he became affiliated with Rastafarianism in the 1970s. He published three poetry collections during that decade, all marked by his imaginative handling of Jamaican colloquial speech patterns, his praise of Africanisms in Jamaican culture, and his fiery condemnations of Western politics and materialism. The release of his first recordings in 1982 signaled the start of a new career as a "dub poet" (a poet writing and performing poetry within the context of reggae instrumental music). Inspired by the example of poet Linton Kwesi Johnson, Mutabaruka sought to arouse his audiences to take political action to counter what he perceived as the destructive actions of hypocritical authorities. But his recording of *"Revolutionary Poets"* revealed a self-critical examination of that stance ("revolutionary poets/have all gone to the/creative art centre/ to watch/the sufferin/of the people"), and, although sympathetic to Rastafarianism, he has emphasized feminist themes and produced recordings of feminist dub poets antagonistic to Rastafarianism's traditional patriarchalism.

His albums blend a "Back to Africa" vision with a pantheistic "Back to Nature" sensibility; his reggae-anchored poems attack aspects of Western civilization, such as processed foods and other things that are antithetical to what in his perception belong to ancient and indigenous African civilization. A comprehensive overview of his recording career is offered on a compact disk, *Mutabaruka: The Ultimate Collection* (Shanachie Records).

N

Navarro, Theodore "Fats"

(b. September 24, 1923, Key West, Fla. ; d. July 7, 1950), African American jazz trumpeter who helped pioneer the genre of jazz known as bebop during the 1940s.

Theodore "Fats" Navarro was considered one of the foremost jazz trumpeters of the 1940s, helping to pioneer the new style of jazz known as bebop, which featured quick tempos and highly complex musical phrasing. Navarro, with the help of Dizzy Gillespie, toured with several famous musicians in his career, including Billy Eckstine, Lionel Hampton, and Coleman Hawkins. Navarro was a big man who at one point weighed more than 136 kg (300 lb), earning him the nickname "Fat Girl." Despite an addiction to heroin and a severe case of tuberculosis, Navarro continued to record until his 1950 death.

Naylor, Gloria

(b. January 25, 1950, New York, N.Y.), African American writer whose novels depict different African American communities and often incorporate elements of magical realism.

Gloria Naylor, recalling the influence that Toni Morrison's work has had on her own life, remembers discovering that for "a young black woman, struggling to find a mirror to her worth in this society, not only is your story worth telling but it can be told in words so painstakingly eloquent that it becomes a song." The realization was a turning point for Naylor, who, at age 27, began "gathering the authority within" to write her own stories.

Naylor's stories draw upon the legacy of her parents, former cotton sharecroppers in Mississippi who had migrated north; her father found a job as a transit worker and her mother as a telephone operator. After graduating from high school in 1968, Naylor traveled as a missionary for the Jehovah's Witnesses in New York City, North Carolina, and Florida. She returned to New York after seven years, completing a bachelor's degree in English at Brooklyn College in 1981 and a master's degree at Yale University in Afro-American Studies in 1983.

While she was still an undergraduate, Naylor began to write about the many different black communities to which her parents' stories and her own travels had brought her. Her first short story, "A Life on Beekman Place," was published in *Essence* magazine in 1980 and became a cornerstone for the novel she developed as her master's thesis, *The Women of Brewster Place* (1982). The novel portrays a disparate group of African American women who, having found themselves on a dead-end street in the inner city, explore their differences and draw upon their shared strength to survive. "All the good men are either dead or waiting to be born," one character comments, and with an unswerving gaze, Naylor looks at the brutality of relationships forged in the wake of oppression. *The Women of Brewster Place* received the American Book Award for best first novel of 1983.

Naylor's next novel, *Linden Hills* (1985), also derives narrative from place, this time an affluent community set on a hillside. As two young men, Willie and Lester, explore the sloping spiral of streets descending from Linden Hills, Naylor uses the structure of Dante's *Inferno* to portray a middle-class community obsessed with material gain. Wealth flows toward the bottom of the hill, and the successive line of identical sons, undertakers named Luther and Nedeed, rules from the house at the base. Naylor's novel is not only a critique of materialism, but also a feminist story of women's unwritten history, as Nedeed's wife, Willa, banished to the basement for producing an unidentical son, garners strength from the dusty testimonies of her predecessors.

Naylor develops the theme of spirituality in her third novel, *Mama Day* (1988), which explores the composition of individual belief. Again, Naylor juxtaposes disparate African American experiences, as George travels with his wife, Cocoa, from New York to the island of Willow Springs, the home of healer Mama Day. Naylor relies on the legacy of African American healers and conjurers to create an ambiguous narrative in which both the characters and the readers are left to grapple with the notions of the real, the magical, and the process of fiction itself.

Naylor's fourth novel, *Bailey's Café* (1992), brings magic to New York City, where it enters the lives of a group of people who gather in a café. With a narrative that resonates with the blues, Naylor depicts the hard lives of the café patrons. As in Mama Day, Naylor blurs the line between the real and the magical, placing a magical dock behind the real café.

Naylor has taught at numerous colleges, including George Washington, New York, Princeton, Cornell, and Boston Universities. She won a Guggenheim Fellowship in 1988.

North America

Neal, Larry

(b. September 5, 1937, Atlanta, Ga.; d. January 6, 1981, Hamilton, N.Y.), African American poet, essayist, and editor who helped develop the aesthetic theory of the Black Arts Movement.

An important contributor to the development of the Black Arts Movement, Larry Neal received his B.A. from Lincoln University (1961) and his M.A. from the University of Pennsylvania (1963). Using bebop and the blues as aesthetic references, he published the books *Black Boogaloo: Notes on Black Liberation* (1969) and *Hoodoo Hollerin' Bebop Ghosts* (1971). In addition to founding several journals, Neal, with Amiri Baraka, founded Harlem's Black Arts Repertory Theater and edited the seminal nationalist anthology *Black Fire* (1968).

Cross Cultural

Négritude,

neologism coined by Martinican poet and statesman Aimé Césaire in Paris in the 1930s in discussions with fellow students Léopold Sédar Senghor and Léon-Gontran Damas.

The concept of *Négritude* represents a historic development in the formulation of African diasporic identity and culture in this century. The term marks a revalorization of Africa on the part of New World blacks, affirming an overwhelming pride in black heritage and culture, and asserting, in Marcus Garvey's words, that blacks are "descendants of the greatest and proudest race who ever peopled the earth." The concept finds its roots in the thought of Martin Delany, Edward Wilmot Blyden, and W. E. B. Du Bois, each of whom sought to erase the stigma attached to the black world through their intellectual and political efforts on behalf of the African diaspora. Early in this century French Caribbean politicians such as Hégésippe Légitimus, René Boisneuf, and Gratien Candace affirmed the right and necessity of blacks to enter into the global community as equals, while historians such as Oruno Lara strove to "edify a more beautiful past, drawing upon our heritage of sacrifice and probity." The inspiration for Césaire's term comes most directly, however, from the example of the Harlem Renaissance, in which writers such as Langston Hughes and Claude McKay explored and revindicated the richness of black culture. Léopold Senghor himself referred to McKay as "the true inventor of [the values of] Négritude . . . . Far from seeing in one's blackness an inferiority, one accepts it, one lays claim to it with pride, one cultivates it lovingly." Like the evolution of the term "black" in the United States, Négritude took a stigmatized term and turned it into a point of pride.

As a historical movement, Négritude received two competing interpretations. Césaire's original conception sees the specificity and unity of black existence as a historically developing phenomenon that arose through the highly contingent events of the African slave trade and New World plantation system. This formulation was gradually displaced in intellectual debate by Senghor's essentialist interpretation of Négritude, which argues for an unchanging core or essence to black existence. As this later formulation gained currency, it was widely attacked, all the more so as Senghor, then president of an independent Senegal, came to use the term ideologically to justify his own political platform. Senghor's Négritude nonetheless served to reverse the system of values that had informed Western perception of blacks since the earliest voyages of discovery to Africa. Césaire's developmental model of Négritude, on the other hand, continues to offer a model for the ongoing project of black liberation in all its fullness, at once spiritual and political.

First used by Césaire in his 1939 poem "Cahier d'un retour au pays natal" (Notebook of a Return to My Native Land), Négritude refers to a collective identity of the African diaspora born of a common historico-cultural experience of subjugation. Césaire writes, "Négritude, not a cephalic index, or a plasma, or a soma, but measured by the compass of suffering." Both the term and the subsequent literary and cultural movement that developed equally emphasized the possible negation of that subjugation via concerted actions of racial affirmation, of which the Haitian Revolution (1791–1804) is the prototype. In succeeding decades the term became a focus for ideological disputes among the black intelligentsia of a Francophone world in the process of decolonization, and writers such as Senghor, Frantz Fanon, and the Anglophone Wole Soyinka each weighed in with his own reformulations and critiques of Césaire's concept. Négritude as a concept encompassed and distilled a wide range of previous historical moments, in turn generating a diverse field of debate that has, in its use of the term, extended, and at times even contradicted, Césaire's original intervention.

Origins of Négritude

The historical origins of Négritude can be traced to the various forms of cultural expression in the French Caribbean that find their roots in the African continent, practices that were transmogrified by the experience of the Middle Passage and slavery. Like the North American spirituals first championed in *The Souls of Black Folk*, by W. E. B. Du Bois, a variety of arts and practices served as refuges for Afro-Caribbean pride and African culture: the dances called *calenda*, *bamboula*, and *laghia*, the drumming and songs of the *bel-air*, *Gwoka*, and *léwoz*; Creole culinary arts; the *Kric-Krac* folktales; and the multitude of practices arising from Haitian Vodou.

Forced underground by the violence and racism of slavery, this proto-Négritude manifested itself less as overt, self-proclaimed affirmation than through the concrete, positive production of cultural, religious, and aesthetic practices. In addition, black slaves at times responded to the threat of annihilation with self-affirmation in the form of overt resistance: feigned laziness, ignorance, or incompetence; theft; poisoning of animals and burning of buildings; escape into maroon communities, and organized revolts.

The social dynamics of a Caribbean society created through the institution of slavery and its vehicle, the plantation (in its French variant, *l'habitation*), resulted in a powerful ideological valorization of and identification with a highly centralized metropolitan French culture. For commentators such as Edouard Glissant, this identification explains the success and longevity of a French colonial project that, in his estimation, continues to this day in the very Martinique that Aimé Césaire helped to integrate juridically in 1945. This overwhelming cultural identification points to the radicality of Césaire's revalorization of African, rather than French, culture. The Franco-centric cultural reference also explains why literary models for Négritude must be sought elsewhere in the African diaspora. No equivalent of Olaudah Equiano's 1789 slave narrative, *Interesting Narrative of the Life of Olaudah Equiano . . .* , or the various autobiographical narratives of Anglophone authors such as Phillis Wheatley, Ottobah Cugoano, and Frederick Douglass, appears to have survived in French Antillean letters. The French Code Noir of 1685 had forbidden blacks to read or write, and remained in effect through 1848. The authors Patrick Chamoiseau and Raphaël Confiant have described how, in a century and a half of literary production preceding Césaire, Martinican writing was characterized by a triple rupture. "From oral to written [production], a rupture of enunciation; from the Creole language to French, a rupture of language; from the storyteller to the writer, a temporal-spatial rupture." The result was a literature entirely subordinated to a "French cultural superego," mimetically echoing succeeding French literary fashions (Romantic, Parnassian, then Symbolist poetry), mired in the tradition of literary exoticism (*doudouisme*).

Despite the fundamental importance of the German philosopher Hegel for both Césaire and subsequent participants in the Négritude debate such as Fanon, Richard Wright, and Jean-Paul Sartre, an insidious aspect of Hegel's philosophy decisively marked the development of proto-Négritude thought in the nineteenth century. Hegel notoriously exempted blacks from the processes of historical development in his *Philosophy of History*, stating that their "condition is capable of no development of Culture, and as we see them at this day, such they have always been." Hegel's thesis participated in the development of a biological racism, whose main proponents in the French tradition were the doctor J. J. Virey, the biologist Georges Cuvier, and the writer Joseph-Arthur de Gobineau. This field of thought articulated a belief in the inferiority of blacks based on supposed physical and intellectual traits, furthermore presupposing the existence of discrete "races" that modern genetics has repeatedly disproved. In response, writers such as Alexander Crummell, Martin Robison Delany, and Edward Wilmot Blyden sought to rescue the image of Africa for New World blacks. Delany organized the first scientific expedition to Africa from the Western Hemisphere and is acknowledged as the founder of Black Nationalism in America, while

Blyden undertook the revalorization of African history after Hegel's blanket condemnation, developing as well an early form of Pan-Africanist thought that prefigures the championing of African culture enacted in Césaire's Négritude. Du Bois continued this turn to Africa and initiated reflection upon the formal continuities of African diasporic culture. The fruits of that more general reflection informed Du Bois's critique of North American racism in works such as *The Souls of Black Folk* in ways strikingly similar to Césaire's later critique of the specific forms of French racism as found in Martinique and Paris. Though not well known to Césaire in 1939, intellectual forerunners like Du Bois, Delany, and Blyden thus anticipated that aspect of Négritude that strives for the revalorization of Africa in French Caribbean culture.

Certain lone figures in the French Caribbean also participated in the affirmation of black culture. The early years of the French Third Republic (1871–1940) witnessed profound changes in Martinican and Guadeloupean culture. Economies previously based on the production of sugar cane were thrown into a long decline that would continue into this century, after the introduction of cheaply produced sugar beets undercut global sugar prices, making competition impossible. This recession, combined with the presence of a black proletariat and nascent middle class following the abolition of slavery in the French colonies in 1848, paved the way for the novel success of black socialist politicians such as Légitimus of Guadeloupe. Martinican politics remained dominated through this period by members of the white land-owning *béké* class, such as Ernest Deproge and Osman Duquesnay. In contrast, a relatively small *béké* population in Guadeloupe led that island's elected positions to be filled by representatives of the mulatto bourgeoisie, such as Gerville-Réache, Sarlat, Auguste Isaac, and Emile Réaux. The electoral defeat of the mulatto Isaac by Légitimus in 1898 signals the triumph of black electoral politics in the region, foreshadowing Césaire's 50-year dominance of Martinican politics as both mayor of Fort-de-France and Martinican representative in the French General Assembly. If Légitimus's early affirmation of racial pride and solidarity predated the Négritude movement by three decades, his recourse to race baiting in electoral politics soon reduced him to inflammatory diatribes against mulatto politicians, whom he referred to as "parasites" and "yellow politicians." Other black Guadeloupean politicians, such as René Boisneuf and Gratien Candace, continued the processes initiated by Légitimus in the years before the emergence of Négritude. Candace, along with Césaire one of the leading black political figures in French politics of the twentieth century, was one of the first black colonial leaders to begin questioning French racial and colonial hegemony.

World War I had brought blacks from the French Caribbean colonies of Martinique, Guadeloupe, and French Guiana to Europe. Already benefiting from full French citizenship since 1848, they, along with Senegalese blacks, fought beside metropolitan and black American soldiers and sent representatives to the French parliament following the war. Blaise Diagne of Senegal and Candace organized the first Pan-African Congress with Du Bois in 1919, immediately following the armistice. Though only tentative steps were taken in condemning colonialism at the congress, it nonetheless marked the beginnings of a truly international solidarity among members of the African diaspora.

In addition, a series of journals, publications, and organizations appeared that prefigure the Négritude of Aimé Césaire. In 1924 Kojo Tovalou Houénou of Benin founded the Ligue universelle de défense de la race noire, which two years later would change its name to the Comité de défense de la race nègre. The league's journal, *La Voix des Nègres*, quotes Légitimus's revindication of black pride: "We honor and glorify ourselves in using the word 'Black' [Nègre] with a capital B." In 1927 Lenis Blanche founded an Association des étudiants guadeloupéens, while the Comité de défense confusingly changed its name again to become the Ligue de défense de la race nègre, arguing in its journal, *La Race Nègre*, for collaboration between (Francophone) black intellectuals and workers and calling for a student-led Pan-Africanism. In 1928 the Internationale Syndicale Rouge published in Moscow *L'Ouvrier Nègre*, in defense of "the disinherited son of the proletarian family." In 1931 the Ligue split, and Tiémoko Garan Kouyaté founded, with the Martinican communist Trissot, the journal *Le Cri des Nègres*. This black communist journal vigorously defended Antillean workers, and its circulation was severely limited by the French authorities.

In the realm of black cultural production, *La Dépêche africaine*, published from 1928 to 1930 with the participation of René Maran and the Nardal sisters, saw its mission as forming a "juncture between Negroes of the entire world" via the valorization of black aesthetic and intellectual production. In 1928 the publication of Jean Price-Mars's *Ainsi parla l'oncle* (So Spoke the Uncle) was the first overt condemnation of the colonial identification with French culture, which had led, in Price-Mars's famous formulation, to a "collective boveryism," or romanticized yearning for French cultural products and the denigration of African-derived culture such as Haitian Vodou. In 1931 the *Revue du monde noir* valorized black cultural production, positioning itself as a moderate, pro-assimilationist voice. Far more radical, the revue *Légitime Défense*, founded in 1932 by the Martinican Etienne Léro, combined in its single published issue discourses of Surrealism, Hegelian Marxism, and Freudianism in its vehement condemnation of French colonialism, racism, and capitalist exploitation. Despite a certain lack of depth in its analysis and the immaturity of its poetic texts, it marked a fundamental step in the assertion of black identity in the Francophone world. In 1934 the 21-year-old student Césaire, along with Gilbert Gratiant, Léonard Sainville, Paulette Nardal, and Césaire's fellow student Senghor, founded the review *L'Etudiant Noir*. More moderate in tone than *Légitime Défense*, it nonetheless contains Césaire's first published text, the poem "Nègreries," in which he clearly prefigures Négritude in his forceful, affirmative use of the stigmatized term "nègre," refusing the assimilation of blacks into French society in favor of "emancipation."

Throughout the 1920s the triumph of Russian Bolshevism was followed closely throughout the African diaspora. Though the French Communist Party long regarded colonialism as strictly subsidiary to the triumph of

European proletarian revolution, journals such as *Les Continents* (founded in 1924 by René Maran and Kodjo Touvalou) and, in particular, *L'Action coloniale* (founded in 1918 by Maurice Boursaud) were fundamental in articulating a preliminary Marxist condemnation of colonialism. An increasing social and juridical permeability between colonized and colonizer helped make possible the rapid changes in black consciousness that occurred through the 1920s and 1930s.

The Harlem Renaissance was also central to Césaire's concept of Négritude. Césaire wrote a dissertation on the movement in the 1930s, and Langston Hughes, Claude McKay, James Weldon Johnson, Jean Toomer, and Countee Cullen were already well known among the Paris-based Antillean intelligentsia when Césaire arrived there in 1931. The Jamaican McKay in particular, in works such as *Banjo*, expressed a keen perception of the fractures dividing black cultures along lines of pigmentation and class. Indeed, Senghor has gone so far as to cite McKay as the spiritual founder of Négritude: "Claude McKay can rightfully be considered the true inventor of Négritude. I speak not of the word, but of the values of Négritude . . . . Far from seeing in one's blackness an inferiority, one accepts it, one lays claim to it with pride, one cultivates it lovingly." Léon-Gontran Damas's 1930 collection of poems, *Pigments*, powerfully appropriated many of McKay's insights, its violent condemnation of racial division and colonialist assimilation serving as the most immediate spur to Césaire's invention of Négritude. In Haiti a similar renaissance occurred during the 1920s and 1930s, as journals like the *Revue indigène* and writers such as Jacques Roumain, Emile Roumer, and Jacques Stéphen Aléxis developed the racial revindication articulated in Price-Mars's *Ainsi parla l'oncle*.

The work of another Caribbean, Marcus Garvey, though unknown to Césaire in 1939, prefigures the concept of Négritude in more than one respect. Garvey's critique of an assimilationist black middle class announces that of French Antilleans such as Léro and Césaire, while his revalorization of African culture is similar to both Césaire's and Senghor's subsequent development of Négritude. "Negroes," Garvey implored, "teach your children that they are direct descendants of the greatest and proudest race who ever peopled the earth." In 1933 the Jamaican Leonard Percival Howell founded the Rastafarian movement, striving to "construct the black race economically, the better to serve God." Elsewhere in the Caribbean, Cuban poets allied with the *Revista de Estudios Afrocubanos*, while Nicolas Guillén in particular, and the Cuban painter Wifredo Lam, sought to explore and valorize their African heritage.

Certain European intellectuals were central to the elaboration of Négritude. The fashionable interest in African art and culture that arose in 1920s Paris in the work of Pablo Picasso, the writers Jean Cocteau, Blaise Cendrars, and André Gide, and the composer Darius Milhaud made reference to an often vague amalgam known as "l'art nègre." Too often, little effort was made to differentiate between the cultural traditions of regions as diverse as Dakar, Senegal, Bahia, Brazil, and Harlem, New York, in deference to a putative "black soul." Nonetheless, this movement created a climate of receptivity in which intellectuals such as André Breton and Sartre would quickly recognize the importance of Négritude in the 1940s. Anthropologists also turned to Africa and its diaspora in these years. Maurice Delafosse, in his 1927 work *Les Nègres*, applied to African culture the methods of ethnographic analysis. The German Leo Frobenius's History of African Civilization was translated into French in 1936 and avidly read by both Césaire and Senghor. "We knew by heart chapter II of the first book of the History," Senghor has written, "entitled 'What does Africa mean to us?' a chapter adorned with lapidary phrases such as this: 'The idea of the "barbarous Negro" is a European invention, which in turn dominated Europe until the beginning of this century.'" Frobenius's work, along with Oswald Spengler's *The Decline of the West* (1918), provided Césaire and Senghor with a conception of history in which a tired, defeated West might be superseded by more vital African diasporic cultures.

Césaire's revindication of the term "nègre," though mirroring parallel processes occurring in the North American adoption first of "black," then "African American" as self-designations, occurred in a specific historical and linguistic environment. In 1939, when Césaire's poem appeared, the term "noir" ("black") roughly corresponded to the socially valorized North American "negro." The traditional French Caribbean identification with metropolitan French culture also meant, in the view of commentators like Frantz Fanon, that black Antilleans were largely alienated from their African roots. In Fanon's words, the Antillean black until 1939 conceived of Africa as "a country of savages, of barbarians, of natives, of 'boys' . . . . The African was a nigger [nègre] and the Antillean a European." In France during the 1920s and 1930s, "nègre," particularly in its adjectival form, was used more or less interchangeably with "noir" ("l'art nègre," "la musique nègre"). In Martinique, however, the term "nègre" shared a functional similarity with the racist North American epithet "nigger." A. James Arnold credits Césaire with being the first black intellectual outside Africa to have taken the humiliating term "nigger" and boldly transformed it into the proud term "black." The specificity of Césaire's intervention and affirmation arises from this highly specific historical conjuncture of self-alienation, in which, Fanon states, "haunted by impurity, overwhelmed by sin, ridden by guilt, [the Antillean] lives the drama of being neither white nor black [nègre]."

In addition to its historical importance, Césaire's coining of the term "Négritude" possesses a philosophical dimension later developed in the work of Fanon (1952) and Sartre. Theoretically, and in contradistinction to the uses and abuses that the term would undergo in succeeding decades, Négritude in Césaire's poem possesses a decidedly objective status, as the poet refuses to affirm the unity of black identity. Previous articulations of black identity in the Francophone world opted uniformly for the latter. Earlier in the century—to cite two relevant examples—Hégésippe Légitimus had affirmed with pride his status as "nègre," while Oruno Lara in his 1921 *History of Guadeloupe* proclaimed his pride to be a "writer of the black race." Lara states that his book—a little-known precursor to Négritude—is "the image of the painful and formidable creation of an American continent wrought with African tears and blood," written to serve "our advancement." The first black historian of the region and author of the 1923 novel *Questions de couleur: Blanches et noires* went on to affirm that "If, born yesterday, we seem to have neither a past, nor civil status, it was up to one of us to edify a more beautiful past, drawing upon our heritage of sacrifice and probity."

Césaire's concept of Négritude, in contrast to these and many other postulations of black identity that came before it, objectifies the self-alienation of colonized black subjects through an act of creation: the neologism. In Césaire's usage, an alienated black identity is forced to confront itself as a reified object:

> *ma négritude n'est pas une pierre,*
> * sa surdité ruée contre la clameur du jour*
> *ma négritude n'est pas une taie d'eau*
> * morte sur l'œil*
> *mort de la terre*
> *ma négritude n'est ni une tour ni une cathédrale*
> *elle plonge dans la chair rouge du sol*
> *elle plonge dans la chair ardente du ciel*
> *elle troue l'accablement opaque de sa*
> *droite patience.*
>
> (my Négritude is not a stone, its deafness dashed against / the clamor of the day / my Négritude is not an opaque spot of dead water / on the dead eye of the earth / my Négritude is neither a tower nor a cathedral / it plunges into the red flesh of the soil / it plunges into the ardent flesh of the sky / it pierces opaque prostration with its upright patience.)

This conception postulates Négritude as self-estrangement, a fact or quality that confronts the black subject as an object. Such a gesture initiates a movement in Césaire's poem toward a self-consciousness that breaks the bonds of subjugation through a grappling with negativity in the form of self-alienation. Négritude "is not" the lifeless object society has reduced it to (stone, spot, or even tower). Instead, it is active, creative, and liberatory ("plunging," "piercing" through the world that had enchained it in subjection). Césaire applies to the realm of black subjectivity Hegel's insight that "alienation" is in fact a transformational process in which the individual's so-called "natural" existence—in this case the ideological subjugation of blacks—is concretely negated for an artificial, self-created one: "[The self's] actuality consists solely in the setting-aside of its natural self . . . . The self knows itself as actual only as a transcended self." Césaire's neologism is at once the naming and active instantiation of the very process it describes, tracing the liberation of black subjectivity through a confrontation with racism and colonialism. Négritude is thus for Césaire the self-created object that negates the very objectivity of black existence itself—where humans are reduced to pure animal-objects (slaves)—in a becoming-human. Humans, following Marx's articulation of Hegel, "distinguish themselves from animals as soon as they begin to produce . . . . " In the concept of Négritude, Aimé Césaire produced the material, textual objectification of black self-consciousness, a program for self-understanding and liberation.

The Growth of Négritude as a Movement

When Aimé Césaire returned to Martinique in 1939, the term "Négritude" was known and used only by the small circle of black intellectuals who had surrounded Césaire in Paris, in particular Senghor and Damas. Césaire's "Cahier" was itself virtually unknown, having appeared only in an obscure Parisian review, Volontés. During the occupation of Martinique by the Nazi-controlled Vichy government, Césaire, along with his wife, Suzanne, René Menil, and Aristide Maugée, edited from 1941 to 1945 the journal Tropiques. The journal enacted a profound refusal of white European cultural values and references in favor of those of the African diaspora. Unlike Césaire's earlier historicizing use of the term "Négritude," articles such as "What Does Africa Mean to Us?" argued for a biologically based notion of black identity inherited from Frobenius, in which a black "biological reality" is invoked to account for black identity. During this period, as A. James Arnold has argued, both Césaire's and Senghor's uncritical reliance upon a sanguinary ideology of African "blood" resonates disturbingly with fascist doctrine of the era. At the same time Tropiques appealed non-dogmatically to a heterogeneous field of influences, invoking those elements of a European aesthetic heritage (surrealism, the French poets Rimbaud and Lautréamont) whose iconoclastic work could be appropriated as a tool in refashioning black Caribbean culture.

In 1947 Damas published an anthology of poetry from the French colonies, and in the following year Senghor published a similar collection, Anthologie de la nouvelle poésie nègre et malgache. In addition to Césaire, Damas, and Senghor, a number of black Francophone poets and writers produced works that participated indirectly in the project of Négritude, reflecting upon the vicissitudes of black existence. Paul Niger, David Diop, and Guy Tirollien all explored diasporic psyches damaged by colonialism and the contradictions of a dual African and European heritage. The novels of Cheikh Hamadou Kane (L'Aventure ambiguë), Mongo Béti (Pauvre Christ de Bomba), and Ousmane Sembène (La Femme noire) articulated the various forms of alienation encountered by colonized African subjects.

Senghor's 1948 anthology featured a preface by Jean-Paul Sartre, "Black Orpheus," that is largely responsible for establishing the concept of Négritude at the center of postwar Francophone debate regarding black identity. Sartre's position as the dominant postwar Francophone intellectual caused

the Négritude debate to focus on his articulation of the concept, with subsequent participants often defining their use of the term in relation to his
analysis. Sartre's text develops the Hegelian category of negativity in relation to black consciousness, building on the Russian philosopher Alexandre
Kojève's influential lectures on Hegel's master/slave dialectic. Sartre
endorses the notion of a racial essence ("The black soul is an Africa from
which the black [nègre] is exiled amidst the cold buildings of white culture
and technology"), grounding this conception within the undeniable visibility
of skin color: "A Jew, a white among whites, can deny that he is a Jew,
declaring himself a man among men. The black cannot deny that he is black
nor claim for himself an abstract, colorless humanity: he is black. Thus he is
driven to authenticity: insulted, enslaved, he raises himself up. He picks up
the word 'black' [nègre] that they had thrown at him like a stone, he asserts
his blackness, facing the white man, with pride."

Fanon critiques Senghor's famous statement "Emotion is black as Reason
is Hellenic," indicting Césaire and Senghor's glorification of the irrational as
a "regressive process" in his 1952 study *Black Skin, White Masks*. He then
proceeds to attack Sartre's interpretation of Négritude as what the latter
termed an "antiracist racism." Fanon critiques Sartre's reduction of Négritude to "the weak pole (or antithesis) of a dialectical progression" from
within the very Hegelian perspective Sartre invokes: "For once, this born
Hegelian [Sartre] had forgotten that consciousness needs to lose itself in
absolute night, this being the only requirement for the attainment of self-
consciousness." Fanon violently refuses Sartre's vision of an instrumentalized
black identity dissolved in the Hegelian *aufhebung* (sublation) of a "raceless
society," asserting: "I am not a potentiality for something. I am fully that
which I am."

In 1947 Alioune Diop of Senegal began in Paris the journal *Présence
Africaine* with the backing of the Parisian and colonial intelligentsia,
including Gide, Sartre, Albert Camus, Césaire, and many others. The
journal was fundamental in articulating the parameters of African diasporic
culture, addressing a global audience of English and French speakers in more
than a half century of publication. In addition, *Présence Africaine* sponsored
a series of celebrated conferences uniting black scholars of the world, at the
Sorbonne in 1956 and in Rome in 1959. In 1966 *Présence Africaine* also
sponsored the First World Festival of Negro Arts in Dakar, Senegal. By the
time Senghor organized the Colloquium on Négritude in 1971, Négritude
had itself become a highly contested term, whose interpretation had rigidi-
fied into a largely ideological concept.

During the postwar period the concept of Négritude developed along
two opposing lines of interpretation. The first sustains the notion as a cultural, historically developing process. This, we have seen, was implicit in
Césaire's original conception of the term, and he increasingly abandoned
any notion of Négritude as based on a genetic or "blood" inheritance: "My
Négritude has a ground. It is a fact that there is a black culture: it is historical, there is nothing biological about it." Similarly, recent interpretations of
Fanon's work have underlined its historical dimensions; in this view, the

author of *The Wretched of the Earth*, following Hegel's 1804 *Phenomenology of Spirit*, undertakes a veritable phenomenology of black consciousness as it moves from immersion in the immediacy of experience to self-consciousness and fully historical, human existence. In contrast, Senghor's notion of Négritude, and the general reception and critique of the concept in West Africa following Senghor, focused on the putatively "African" characteristics of emotion, intuition, and artistic creativity as opposed to a Western, or "Hellenic," rationality.

Senghor elaborates his conception of Négritude in various texts collected in the five-volume work *Liberté*. Dismissing without engaging the scientific invalidation of races, Senghor constructs a typology of an "eternal . . . black soul" based on the categories of "emotion," "rhythmic attitude," "humor," and "anthropopsychism." This last trait refers to the unmediated relation of the "black soul" to the phenomenological world, the "eternal . . . essential" trait, Senghor affirms, of the black soul. Though this early formulation dates from 1939, Senghor continued to defend and develop this conception of an "african personality" in the 1966 text "Négritude is a Humanism of the Twentieth Century," arguing tautologically for the objective existence of such a category [the "african personality"], since it had been accepted as a given over "60 years" of ethnological and sociological investigation. In this text Senghor further elaborates his articulation of an immediate black apprehension of phenomena, invoking the philosophers Henri Bergson and Pierre Teilhard de Chardin. Senghor's Négritude is, to use his own term, an ontology, or study of the being of blacks in the world, a fundamentally ahistorical, transcultural determination of the constituents and commonalities of "blackness" in African diasporic societies. In 1969 he refers to it as a modification of the Hedeggerian Dasein, a "Neger-sein" or "black being." As Senghor himself pointed out in 1993, this ontological definition of Négritude has become the accepted one: in the standard French *Robert* dictionary, we find the definition "The ensemble of characteristics, of manners of thinking, of feeling, proper to the black race; belonging to the black race." There follows a quotation of Senghor. No mention is made of Césaire's act of neologism. Senghor's Négritude reverses the stigmatization of blacks derived from the nineteenth-century racialism of Gobineau, Lucien Lévy-Bruhl's concept of a prelogical "primitive mentality," and fictional works such as Paul Morand's stereotype-laden novel, *Magie noire* (1928). Senghor's postulation of an African ontology is echoed in works such as Placied Tempel's *La Philosophie bantoue* (1949). In turn, philosophers such as Marcien Towa (*Essai sur la problématique philosophique dans l'Afrique actuelle*, 1971) and Paulin Hountondji (*Sur la "Philosophie africaine,"* 1977) have questioned whether traditional African philosophies can truly sustain such ontological interpretations.

Due to Senghor's overwhelming cultural and political influence in West Africa (he was president of Senegal from its independence in 1960 till 1979), it is precisely this ontological conception of Négritude that fueled attacks by writers such as Stanislas Adotevi. Adotevi's 1972 study *Négritude et négrologues* argues against a Senghorian racial explanation for African suffering in deference to a Marxist model of global capitalist exploitation. The Anglophone African nations received Négritude primarily as a politicized, ideological movement. Writers such as Es'kia Mphahlele, in *The African Image* (1962), and Wole Soyinka, in *Myth, Literature, and the African World* (1976), attacked a perceived cultural imperialism on the part of Francophone African intellectuals, the latter stating that "the tiger does not stalk about crying his tigritude." Senghor, responding to these attacks in 1969, points to the Anglophone historical derivation of Négritude from the African American writers of the Harlem Renaissance.

In the French Caribbean, Césaire's notion of Négritude has been developed and extended by another of his students, the writer Edouard Glissant. Glissant's notion of "antillanité," developed in works such as the 1981 *Caribbean Discourse*, envisages an opening of black experience to the entirety of global culture. Like Césaire's earlier critique of cultural assimilation, Glissant argues against subsuming or dissolving an African and Creole Martinican identity in the economic and cultural imperialism of a North American-led "New World Order," without, on the other hand, limiting that region to a stifling provincialism. Other Antilleans have been more critical of aspects of Césaire's concept. The Guadeloupean author Maryse Condé critiques the notion of a return to Africa by black Antilleans in novels such as *Heremakonon* (1976). Her 1974 article "Négritude césairienne, Négritude senghorienne," while drawing attention to Césaire's neologism, offers a trenchant warning against the fetishization of blackness: "The Black (Nègre) does not exist . . . . [Négritude] is a sentimental and empty trap. Starting from an illusory 'racial' community founded upon a heritage of suffering, it obliterates the true problems that have always been of a political, social, and economic nature . . . . Our liberation will come through the knowledge that there will never be any Blacks (Nègres). There has only ever been human exploitation." Condé's critique implies that Césaire's Négritude cannot remain a mere invocation to black identity politics; instead, the shock of its alienating gesture must serve to illuminate the very constructedness of "blackness" itself.

More recently, Jean Bernabé, Patrick Chamoiseau, and Raphaël Confiant attacked what they see as the mythologization of Africa in Césaire's Négritude, affirming instead the heterogeneous status of Antillean culture, with its French, Hindu, Chinese, Amerindian, and African elements. This attack reaches its apex in Confiant's 1993 polemic against Césaire, *Une traversée paradoxale du siècle*.

The concept of Négritude represents a fundamental development in notions of African diasporic identity and culture in this century. The African and Antillean controversies around the term's reception and its rigidification into a politicized, ideological category initiated one of the fundamental debates in postwar global black thought, while Senghor's elaboration of the term itself constituted a radical reversal of dominant racialist discourse in the West. Finally, Césaire's historicizing phenomenological use of the term remains largely unexplored, implying for the black subject a developmental model of enlightenment that sustains and advances the transformational project of black liberation, pointing beyond the circularity of identity politics toward the elusive instantiation of a fully realized utopian freedom.

North America

Negro Ensemble Company,
longest-running black theater company in the United States.

The Negro Ensemble Company was founded in New York City in 1967 by actor-director-playwright Douglas Turner Ward, actor Robert Hooks, and white manager Gerald Krone. Their intent was to provide a space where black playwrights "could communicate with an audience of other Negroes, better informed through commonly shared experience to readily understand, confirm, or reject the truth or paucity of [their] creative explorations." This was during the height of the Black Arts Movement, and many other companies shared the vision of creating theater by black people for black people. But while others were committed to theater with strong nationalistic and political messages, the Negro Ensemble Company produced a much wider spectrum of plays, including family dramas, folk musicals, and plays from African and Caribbean perspectives.

The company was criticized by more militant artists for its less political messages and for its early support from mainstream white sources such as the Ford Foundation. Its broader appeal, however, gave it staying power. In addition to producing plays, the company also offered actor training programs and playwrights' workshops. The Negro Ensemble Company's most successful productions included Joseph Walker's *The River Niger* (1972), which went to Broadway and won a Tony Award for Best Play of the Year; Charles Fuller's Pulitzer-Prize winning *A Soldier's Play* (1982); and Samm-Art Williams's *Home* (1979), which also became a Broadway success.

North America

Negro National Anthem,
the African American national hymn.

"Lift Ev'ry Voice and Sing," popularly considered the Negro national anthem, was composed in 1900 at the Colored High School in Jacksonville, Florida, by James Weldon Johnson and his brother, J. Rosamond Johnson. It is a 34-line poem that expresses the difficulty African Americans have experienced in reaching the present, exemplified in such lines as "Stony the road we trod." Despite acknowledging the pain and disappointment faced by black Americans, the song is essentially a hymn of faith in God, to whom it says, "Thou has brought us thus far on the way," and the Johnsons' lyrics express both hope for the future and American patriotism.

Nicholas Brothers

(Fayard, b. 1918, and Harold, b. 1924, Philadelphia, Pa.), African American tap dancers who performed in Hollywood musicals in the 1930s and 1940s.

Fayard and Harold Nicholas began dancing in Philadelphia in the 1930s. Rising to stardom as a tap-dancing duo, they appeared in the musicals *Tin Pan Alley*, *Stormy Weather*, *Down Argentine Way*, and *The Big Broadcast of 1936*. The pair performed with such contemporary stars as Josephine Baker, Lena Horne, Gene Kelly, Bill ("Bojangles") Robinson, and Cab Calloway. In the late 1940s, with tap dance's popularity waning in the United States, the Nicholas Brothers moved to Europe. They gave a royal command performance for the king of England in 1948 and performed at the inauguration of United States president Dwight D. Eisenhower in 1955.

Niger, Paul (Albert Beville)

(b. December 21, 1915, Basse-Terre, Guadeloupe; d. June 22, 1962, Sainte-Rose, Guadeloupe), one of the most powerful writers of the Négritude movement and an outspoken critic of French colonialism.

Paul Niger completed his primary schooling at the Lycée Carnot in the French Caribbean island of Guadeloupe. He then traveled to Paris, France, where he studied at the Lycée Louis-le-Grand and the Ecole Nationale de la France d'outre-mer. While in Paris, he became part of a circle of black intellectuals such as Aimé Césaire and Léopold Sédar Senghor before the war. He also fought for the French resistance following the installation of the Nazi-supported Vichy regime.

Niger subsequently began a career as a colonial administrator in Dahomey (now Benin), Mali, and Niger in 1944. This experience led him to an increasingly violent condemnation of French colonialism. In turn, he celebrated a somewhat mythical, essentialized Africa in poems such as "Or j'avais renoncé à prononcer ton nom" (1959). Niger was a frequent contributor to the journal *Présence Africaine* in the postwar years. In 1954 he published a collection of poems entitled *Initiation*, in which his violent condemnation of colonialism announces the coming explosion of African independence of the late 1950s:

> *L'Afrique va parler,*
> *J'entends chanter la sève au coeur du flamboyant*
> (Africa is going to speak, / I hear the sap sing from the heart of the flame tree)

Niger fought for the decolonization and independence of the French Overseas Departments (French Guiana, Martinique, and Guadeloupe) during the late 1950s as part of the Front des Antilles-Guyane organization. France's De Gaulle government banned him from Guadeloupe in the early 1960s. Niger was one of the authors of the pro-independence text produced by the Congress for the Independence of the Antilles, held April 22 and 23, 1961. In 1962, while attempting to return to Guadeloupe clandestinely, Niger died in a plane crash in Sainte-Rose, Guadeloupe.

Niger's last writings (*Les puissants* [1956] and *Les grenouilles du Mont Kimbo* [1964]) describe both his experience of colonialism and his vision of a future liberation from the domination of colonialist exploitation.

North America

Niggaz with Attitude,

Los Angeles rap group that brought "gangsta rap" to a mass audience.

Niggaz with Attitude (N.W.A.) was formed in Compton, California, in 1987 and included Eazy-E (Eric Wright), MC Ren (Lorenzo Patterson), Ice Cube (O'Shea Jackson), Dr. Dre (Andre Young), and Yella (Antoine Carraby). Recording for Eazy-E's own Ruthless Records, N.W.A. made its debut with one of the most important albums in rap history. *Straight Outta Compton* (1988) was powered by the innovative production of Dr. Dre (whose career in rap had started with the World Class Wreckin' Cru, a synthesizer-oriented dance group), which emphasized the heavy, loping beats of 1970s soul and funk.

The group's rhymes—especially those of Ice Cube—helped reinvent rap lyrics through the unflinching portraits of gang life that they created. While rap lyrics had traditionally been built around ebullient (if violent) boasts, songs like "*Dopeman*" told graphic stories of drugs and gangs and "bitches and ho's" without apology. "*F—tha Police*"—a block party anthem during the summer of 1989—was condemned by law enforcement officials nationwide, including the Federal Bureau of Investigation (FBI). Despite receiving scant radio play, *Straight Outta Compton* sold more than 2 million copies, and N.W.A.'s gangsta rap style made Los Angeles the capital of the hip hop world for years to come.

Soon after the release of the band's debut album, Ice Cube quit the group, and N.W.A. became even more reliant on Dr. Dre's production skills. But despite being ignored by commercial radio and many critics, the band's next album, *Efil4zaggin* (1991)—the title was written backward—went immediately to the top of the album charts.

After N.W.A. disbanded in 1992, each of its members pursued solo careers. Despite several attempts, MC Ren and Yella never achieved much success on their own. But Eazy-E, embroiled in an explosive public feud with Dr. Dre, found success with an anti-Dre album titled *It's On (Dr. Dre) 187um Killa* (1993). Eazy-E continued to release albums and run Ruthless Records (which found huge success with Cleveland's Bone Thugs-N-Harmony); he died of acquired immune deficiency syndrome (AIDS) in 1995. Dr. Dre went on to co-found Death Row Records, where he released his

wildly successful solo debut, *The Chronic* (1992); Dre's menacing yet accessible beats also powered the meteoric rise of Death Row's young stars
Tupac Shakur and Snoop Doggy Dogg.

Ice Cube established himself as one of hip hop's most important voices
with *Amerikkka's Most Wanted* (1990); his success continued with solo and
collaborative albums throughout the 1990s. He has acted as well, starring in
John Singleton's *Boyz N the Hood* (1991) and F. Gary Gray's *Friday* (1995),
for which he was also the screenwriter. *The Player's Club* (1998) was Cube's
directorial debut.

North America

Noone, Jimmie

(b. April 23, 1894, New Orleans, La; d. April 19, 1944, Los Angeles, Calif.),
African American musician who was considered one of the great first-generation jazz clarinetists and who was influential in the development of swing
music.

Jimmie Noone began playing clarinet around 1910 in New Orleans, taking
lessons from Lorenzo Tio Jr. and Sidney Bechet (who was himself only 13
years old at the time). In 1915 Noone got his first professional job playing
in Buddy Petit's Young Olympia Band. During his stint with Petit's band,
Noone befriended Freddie Keppard, whose band, the Original Creole
Orchestra in Chicago, he joined in 1917. From 1920 to 1926 he played
with Doc Cooke's Dreamland Orchestra, at the same time studying classical
clarinet. Noone led his own bands in Chicago between 1927 and 1931, the
most famous of which was Jimmie Noone's Apex Club Orchestra, which
performed at the Apex Club on Chicago's South Side.

Noone's style differed from that of Johnny Dodds and Bechet, two other
great New Orleans clarinetists, in that it was smoother and more romantic.
His style had a major influence on the swing music that was popular in the
1930s, in particular the music of fellow clarinetists Bennie Goodman and
Jimmy Dorsey.

Between 1927 and 1931 Noone and his bands recorded many songs that
are considered classic examples of Noone's clarinet virtuosity. Noone led
several bands in Chicago throughout the 1930s. In the early 1940s he
moved to southern California, where he played on several famous radio
programs, recordings of which are available. He was playing in a band led by
"Kid" Ory when he died of a heart attack.

North America

Northrup, Solomon

(b. 1808?, Minerva, N.Y.; d. 1863?, Glens Falls, N.Y.), author of a best-selling
story of his kidnapping and years of slavery.

In 1841 Solomon Northrup, a free black, was kidnapped in New York and sold to slave traders. He spent the next 12 years as a slave in Louisiana. In 1852 he met Samuel Bass, a Canadian carpenter. Bass contacted the former owner of Northrup's father, who traveled to Louisiana to free him. Inspired by *Uncle Tom's Cabin,* Northrup wrote the story of his enslavement, with the help of David Wilson. *Twelve Years a Slave: Narrative of Solomon Northrup,* published in 1853, was an immediate success. His book described the daily acts of resistance that most slaves directed against their owners.

North America

Notorious B.I.G. ("Biggie Smalls") (Christopher Wallace)

(b. 1972, New York, N.Y.; d. March 9, 1997, Los Angeles, Calif.), African American rap artist murdered in 1997.

Notorious B.I.G.'s debut album, *Ready to Die,* appeared on Sean "Puffy" Combs's Bad Boy Entertainment music label in 1995. The record was a critical and commercial success, exhibiting the rapper's lyrical talents through a series of taut, first-person narratives chronicling life as a hustler on the streets of New York's Bedford-Stuyvesant neighborhood. The grim humor of B.I.G.'s lyrics emphasized the claustrophobia of his ghetto universe; on *"Warning,"* he raps, "There's gonna be a lot of slow singing / and flower bringing / If my burglar alarm starts ringing." Songs like *"Suicidal Thoughts"* and *"Things Done Changed"* helped create one of "gangsta rap's" most sophisticated personas, a strange brew of subdued self-loathing and energetic violence. In B.I.G.'s world, the sexual boasting typical of hip hop became an occasion for self-parody, as on *"#!*@ Me (Interlude),"* a skit describing a sexual encounter complicated by the rapper's prodigious girth.

Soon after the success of his debut album, B.I.G. found himself immersed in a simmering feud with Los Angeles gangsta rap label Death Row Records, in a manifestation of hip hop's growing coastal animosity. Death Row star Tupac Shakur claimed that B.I.G. and Combs were behind a 1994 robbery in which Shakur was shot five times in the chest. The violent climate turned fatal in September 1996, when Shakur was murdered in a mysterious Las Vegas drive-by shooting; some suggested that the Bad Boy Entertainment crew was involved. Soon after, in March 1997, Notorious B.I.G. was gunned down while making an appearance in Los Angeles.

B.I.G.'s posthumously released double album, *Life After Death* (1997), topped the Billboard album charts and sold more than 7 million copies, thanks to radio-friendly songs like *"Mo Money Mo Problems"* and *"Hypnotize."* Death has only enhanced B.I.G.'s legend: Sean "Puffy" Combs's *"I'll Be Missing You,"* a tribute to his fallen friend, was one of the best-selling singles of 1997.

Oliver, Joseph ("King")

(b. May 11, 1885, Donaldsville, La.; d. April 8, 1938, Savannah, Ga.), African American cornetist and bandleader; pioneering figure in New Orleans- and Chicago-style jazz.

Joseph Oliver was born in Donaldsville, Louisiana. After his family moved to New Orleans he learned to play the trombone from local street musicians. He soon switched to the cornet and trumpet, and by 1907 Oliver had begun to play professionally with various local brass bands.

From 1916 to 1919 Oliver played in Edward "Kid" Ory's band. Ory gave him the moniker "King" because he was the best cornetist in the most popular jazz band in New Orleans. In 1918 Oliver was courted by bassist/banjoist Bill Johnson to join his band in Chicago, Illinois. A year later Oliver moved to Chicago, where he became first cornetist in Johnson's Creole Jazz Band. Oliver soon assumed the leadership of the band, taking the group to California from 1920 to 1921.

Returning to Chicago, Oliver solidified the Creole Jazz Band with powerful new members, creating one of the most important ensembles in the history of jazz. From 1922 to 1924 the band included Louis Armstrong on cornet, Honore Dutrey on trombone, Johnny Dodds on clarinet, his brother Baby Dodds on drums, Lil Hardin (Armstrong) on piano, and Bill Johnson on bass and banjo. Featuring a "wa-wa" cornet sound and polyphonic four-to-the-beat rhythmic attack, such performances as *"Dipper Mouth Blues,"* *"Riverside Blues,"* and *"Snake Rag"* influenced a new generation of jazz musicians that included many aspiring white performers.

The Creole Jazz Band disbanded after Armstrong left. Oliver then recorded several duos with the great Jelly Roll Morton during 1924. From 1924 through 1927 Oliver led the Dixie Syncopators, made up of former Creole Jazz Band members along with trombonist "Kid" Ory and clarinetist and saxophonist Barney Bigard. From 1930 until 1937 he led several bands on tours of the Midwest and the South, but did not play after 1931 due to painful gum disease. Oliver retired from music in 1937.

Opera,

musical theater that originated in seventeenth-century Florence, Italy; numerous African Americans have risen to prominence within the genre.

Early nineteenth-century African American opera singers and performers were crossover artists. Barred from all major American stages, they transgressed the boundaries between high and low culture by playing the marginal American concert stages and opera houses that permitted them, as well as minstrel and vaudeville shows. Careers were short lived, usually lasting only two or three years – the length of time it typically took for the novelty of seeing a black singer to wear off on white audiences. Europe often proved a more hospitable climate for African American artists.

Nonetheless, a number of black performers rose to prominence in the American opera scene. Elizabeth Taylor Greenfield—"The Black Swan"— toured North America and England with an African American troupe in the 1850s and 1860s. During the same period the multitalented Luca family included opera in their performances, as did the Hyers Sisters—renowned for their renditions of the works of Verdi and Donizetti. Sissieretta Joyner Jones was the most celebrated opera performer of the time. Known as "the Black Patti" after white soprano Adelina Patti, she gave a recital at the White House for President Benjamin Harrison. Jones outlasted her contemporaries—extending her career to 15 years—by forming, in 1896, the Black Patti Troubadours, which mixed opera with musical theater and offered a vehicle to showcase her talents. Similarly, soprano Nellie Brown Mitchell's career lasted almost ten years, thanks to her creation of the Nellie Brown Mitchell Concert Company.

Until the color bar that prevented African Americans from performing on America's greatest stages was lifted, recitals were the quickest way to success for black performers. In 1955 contralto Marian Anderson, thanks to her unmatched talent and the breadth of her repertoire, became the first African American to perform at New York City's Metropolitan Opera, after years of dazzling audiences on recital stages. Anderson's performances, like those of her predecessor, the tenor recitalist Roland Hayes, opened the stages to other opera singers. Both Anderson and Hayes incorporated the concert spiritual—an indigenous African American contribution that fused European art music with black spirituals—into their recitals.

Throughout the mid-twentieth century blacks were usually cast in secondary roles, confined to playing marginal dark-skinned characters. This began to change in 1966. The era of the African American diva began when

Mississippi-born soprano Leontyne Price performed at the opening of the new Metropolitan Opera House at New York City's Lincoln Center. By the 1980s the concept of the African American diva had been well established by the glamorous sopranos Jessye Norman and Kathleen Battle.

African American opera companies have developed alongside individual artists. Organizations such as the Colored American Opera Company and the Theodore Drury Opera Company staged productions in the early twentieth century. This work was followed by productions by the Imperial Company, the National Negro Opera Company, the DraMu Opera Company, and the Harlem Opera Company. With the establishment of Opera/South and the National Ebony Opera in the 1970s, black productions flourished. Their mandate was to create opportunities for professionals working in the field.

By the early 1990s mainstream American stages began to reconsider early compositions written by African Americans and to stage productions that conveyed the tragedy and triumph of the black experience. Duke Ellington's *Queenie Pie* and Leroy Jenkins's *The Mother of Three Sons* were among the first to take part in this mainstream revival. These compositions are part of a body of African American work that includes long-neglected pieces by composers like Harry Laurence Freeman, writer of 14 grand-style operas including the *Octoroon* and the early Jazz opera, *The Flapper*, and ragtime innovator Scott Joplin, who attempted to create an indigenous African American opera in *Treemonisha*. Anthony Davis, founder of the instrumental group Episteme, is the dominant figure in late twentieth-century African American opera composition. His *X: The Life and Times of Malcolm X*, *Under the Double Moon*, and *Amistad* have all reached well-known United States halls, bringing a contemporary flavor to traditional opera.

North America

Ory, Edward ("Kid")

(b. 1889, St. John Baptist Parish, La.; d. January 23, 1973, Hawaii), African American musician, jazz trombonist, and bandleader; pioneer of New Orleans-style jazz.

Born on a farm near New Orleans, Edward "Kid" Ory arrived on the music scene of New Orleans in 1917. Joining up with cornetist Joe "King" Oliver and clarinetist Johnny Dodds, he led several prominent bands in New Orleans. He carried the tradition of New Orleans-style jazz to California in 1919, leading Kid Ory's Brownskinned Babies and Kid Ory's Original Creole Jazz Band in the Los Angeles and San Francisco Bay Area.

Ory's Sunshine Orchestra recorded such hits as *"Ory's Creole Trombone"* and *"Society Blues"* in June 1922. With these recordings, Ory's band became the first African American group to make all-instrumental jazz records. Ory

moved to Chicago in 1925, where he participated in some of the most significant sound recordings of the period, alongside Louis Armstrong in
"Muskrat Ramble" (1926), with "Jelly Roll" Morton in *"Doctor Jazz"* (1926),
and with King Oliver in *"Every Tub"* (1927).

Ory's style was distinctive: expressive and highly rhythmic, incorporating glissando runs of the early tailgate trombone style. With his recorded
compositions, including *"Muskrat Ramble,"* he left the sounds of New
Orleans-style jazz as his legacy to music history. In 1930 Ory left the music
scene for ten years, returning to California to work on a poultry farm and in
a railroad office. He regained some prominence when he performed on an
Orson Welles radio broadcast in 1944. He toured until 1966, when he
retired to Hawaii.

P

Pace, Harry Hubert

(b. January 6, 1884, Covington, Ga.; d. July 26, 1943, Chicago, Ill.), music publisher and founder of the first African American recording company.

Harry Pace began his printing and business career in 1903, opening a company in Memphis with former teacher W. E. B. Du Bois. Together they
produced *Moon Illustrated Weekly* (1905), the first illustrated African
American journal. Pace met composer W. C. Handy in 1908, and they
formed one of the most enduring African American music companies, Pace
and Handy Music Co. (1909). Pace went on to establish Pace Phonograph
Company, issuing records by such artists as Alberta Hunter and Ethel
Waters under the label of Black Swan. With the bankruptcy of the company in 1923, Pace returned to insurance work, expanding Chicago's
Supreme Liberty Life Insurance Co. into the largest black-owned business
in the North.

Parker, Charles Christopher ("Bird")

(b. August 29, 1920, Kansas City, Kans.; d. March 12, 1955, New York, N.Y.),
masterful alto saxophonist who, along with Dizzy Gillespie, founded bebop, or
modern jazz.

Together with trumpeter John Birks "Dizzy" Gillespie, Charlie Parker was
the primary creator of bebop, or modern jazz. His musical innovations profoundly influenced other alto saxophonists, as is evident in the playing of
Julian "Cannonball" Adderley, Eric Dolphy, Lou Donaldson, Charles
McPherson, and Frank Morgan. Indeed, Parker's influence extended well
beyond jazz to popular music and film and television scores. Despite his
musical brilliance, however, Parker led a troubled life that included the use

of heroin at an early age, an addiction that contributed materially to his death and was deeply intertwined with his musical mystique.

Parker was born in Kansas City, Kansas, across the Kaw River from the much larger Kansas City, Missouri. His father, Charles Parker Sr., was a singer and dancer from Mississippi and Tennessee who abandoned the family when his son was about 11 years old. His mother, Adelaide Bailey Parker, was originally from Oklahoma. Between 1927 and 1931 the family moved to Kansas City, Missouri, the jazz capital of the Southwest.

Under the corrupt reign of Democratic boss Thomas Pendergast, Kansas City was a wide-open town, and its bars, honky-tonks, and night-clubs remained open until dawn, featuring live music and often no-holds-barred jam sessions. Kansas City gave birth to a freewheeling, stripped-down form of swing music that was deeply grounded in the blues and was epitomized by the Count Basie Band. Parker soon developed an interest in music. Lawrence Keyes, a musician and friend of Parker's at Lincoln High School remarked, "If he had been as conscientious about his school work as he was about music, he would have become a professor, but he was a terrible truant."

During 1935 and 1936, when Parker was about 15, his life changed dramatically. He dropped out of school, married Rebecca Ruffin, began playing with the Deans of Swing—a band led by Keyes—and had his first experience with heroin. Within a year he was addicted. Periodically throughout his life Parker would try to limit his heroin use, generally by substituting large quantities of alcohol, which was no less debilitating. In 1938 his first son, Francis Leon Parker, was born. Over the next few years Parker concentrated on his music and learned from older musicians in Kansas City and at resorts in the Ozarks. In 1939 Parker decided to hazard a trip to New York City, the nation's jazz center. There he took part in jam sessions, most notably at two Harlem nightspots, Clark Monroe's Uptown House and Dan Wall's Chili House.

While jamming at the Chili House one night in December 1939, Parker had a profound musical breakthrough. He recalled: "I'd been getting bored with the stereotyped changes that were being used at the time, and I kept thinking there's bound to be something else. I could hear it sometimes, but I couldn't play it. Well, that night I was working over 'Cherokee,' and as I did I found that by using the higher intervals of a chord as a melody line and backing them with appropriately related changes, I could play the thing I heard. I came alive." Although it took Parker several years to consolidate the full implications of this discovery, his achievement heralded a new era in jazz.

In early 1940, however, Parker left New York for Kansas City to join Jay McShann's big band. Parker would stay with McShann about two and a half years. During the swing era big bands provided the majority of job opportunities for jazzmen, but musicians such as Parker and Dizzy Gillespie, then playing in Cab Calloway's orchestra, rankled at their lack of artistic freedom. Parker's job with McShann did bring him back to New York City in late 1941 or 1942. Soon he began collaborating with Gillespie, who had independently achieved comparable harmonic breakthroughs.

The musical sparks Parker and Gillespie struck while playing together created modern jazz, initially known as *bebop* or simply *bop*. Parker clearly recognized the musical symbiosis between the two and regarded Gillespie as "the other half of my heartbeat." They worked together during 1943 and 1944 in Earl Hines's big band, an important bop incubator. But they perfected their music in jam sessions, especially at Monroe's Uptown House and Minton's. The new music offered richer harmonic textures with more varied tempos—both much faster and, on ballads, much slower than typical swing-era jazz—and a subtler rhythmic pulse.

Besides his advanced harmonic approach, Parker attained a previously unheard of rhythmic subtlety with his elliptical and fluid melodic lines. His technical mastery allowed him continuously to reinvent melodies, including rapid double-time passages, over the chord sequence of a given song. He was also at ease playing in every key, at a time when many jazz musicians were far more limited.

In 1943, while in Washington, D.C., with the Hines band, Parker married Geraldine Scott without bothering to divorce his first wife. Parker's heroin habit worsened, and fellow musicians pressured him to quit hard drugs. Instead Parker quit the band and returned to Kansas City, ending his relationship with Geraldine. The Hines band broke up soon after, and a number of its more modernist players regrouped around a new leader, singer Billy Eckstine, with Gillespie as musical director. The Eckstine band was the first bop big band and included, besides Gillespie, drummer Art Blakey, vocalist Sarah Vaughan, and, soon, Parker. Yet once again Parker quickly left an environment he found stifling. With few exceptions, the rest of his career involved playing in small groups.

Parker's first significant recording sessions came in late 1944 and 1945 for Savoy and, under Gillespie's leadership, for Musicraft. The latter produced a number of particularly fine recordings, including "*Salt Peanuts*" and "*Shaw 'Nuff.*" Gillespie and Parker also played an extended gig at the Three Deuces, which Gillespie later described as the "height of perfection of our music." But Parker's subsequent career was increasingly erratic. Gillespie asked Parker to join him on a trip to California to play at Billy Berg's, a Los Angeles nightclub. For Parker, the decision to go was a fateful one.

In California Parker made his first classic Dial recordings—including "*Moose the Mooche*," "*Yardbird Suite*," and "*Ornithology.*" Yet the arrest of his drug dealer, Emery "Moose the Mooche" Byrd, resulted in Parker's having a nervous breakdown on July 29, 1946, while recording "*Lover Man.*" Parker spent several months in Camarillo State Hospital, and Ross Russell, the owner of Dial Records, released his tortured "*Lover Man.*" Although the record was acclaimed by Parker's many followers, Parker insisted that it was "a horrible thing that should never have been released."

Beginning in 1947 Parker made New York City his home base. There he formed his great quintet, which included Miles Davis and Max Roach, and recorded a number of sessions for Dial, highlighted by the superb ballads *"My Old Flame," "Embraceable You,"* and *"Don't Blame Me."* In 1948 Parker began recording with Norman Granz's Verve label, including ground-breaking sessions with strings. However, the greatest moments of his later career took place in concert. Two of these were recorded, a 1949 appearance at Carnegie Hall and a 1953 reunion with Gillespie at Toronto's Massey Hall. During these years Parker regularly won the annual *Downbeat* magazine readers' poll as best alto player, and his fame extended to Europe, taking him to Paris in 1949 and to Scandinavia the following year.

But Parker's personal life became increasingly troubled. In 1948 he married his third wife, Doris Sydnor, but left her two years later to enter a relationship with Chan Richardson, with whom he had a daughter, Pree, and a son, Baird. Due to a drug conviction he lost his "cabaret card," required of all musicians playing in New York City nightclubs from 1951 to 1953, seriously limiting his ability to work.

The physical cost of Parker's heroin and alcohol abuse was also clearly mounting. Besides making his performances increasingly erratic, it gave him stomach ulcers, liver problems, and at least one heart attack. When he died in 1955, the attending physician estimated Parker's age at between 50 and 60 years. In fact, he was only 34. Yet despite his early death, Parker's uncompromising and innovative musicianship have assured his immortality. Indeed soon after his funeral, graffiti began appearing around New York City proclaiming, "Bird Lives!"

North America

Parks, Gordon, Jr.

(b. December 7, 1934, Minneapolis, Minn.; d. April 3, 1979, Nairobi, Kenya), African American filmmaker who inaugurated the blaxploitation film genre.

The son of Sally Alvis and director, writer, and photographer Gordon Parks Sr., Gordon Parks Jr. worked to define his own creative expression independently of his famous father. He even used the name Gordon Rogers early in his career to forge his own identity. After spending his early years at the American School in Paris, Parks graduated from White Plains High School in 1952, worked in New York City's garment district, and joined the army in 1956. In the 1960s he began his career in entertainment as a café folksinger in New York's Greenwich Village.

Parks entered the field of cinematography as a cameraman on his father's film *The Learning Tree* (1969) and as a still photographer for *Burn* (1969) and *The Godfather* (1972). In 1972 Parks took the director's chair with *Superfly*, which has often been cited as the defining example of a new genre of African American film: *blaxploitation*. Set in a dense urban landscape, the film chronicles a conflict between a black criminal and the white organized crime establishment, a symbolic representation of African American male self-determination in the face of an oppressive system. Enhancing this new cinematic form was Curtis Mayfield's memorable score. Despite controversy sparked by its uncritical depiction of a "heroic" drug dealer, *Superfly* was remarkably popular among black audiences hungry for powerful black images in film, and grossed more than $24.8 million. Parks quickly followed *Superfly*'s success with three new feature films: *Thomasine and Bushrod* (1974), the action film *Three the Hard Way* (1974), and the teen love story *Aaron Loves Angela* (1975).

Parks moved to Kenya in 1979, where he started the Africa International Productions/Panther Film Company and died in a Nairobi plane crash a short time later.

North America

Parks, Gordon, Sr.

(b. November 30, 1912, Fort Scott, Kans.), African American photographer famous for his portrait photography; first African American director of a major Hollywood film.

The youngest of 15 children, Gordon Parks, the son of a dirt farmer, left home when he was 16, shortly after his mother's death. After an unhappy attempt to move in with a married sister in Minneapolis, Parks ended up spending a frigid winter homeless, an experience that sensitized him to the plight of the poor and that he would draw on in later photography and films. At the time his hunger and loneliness nearly led him to a life of crime, but he managed to struggle through high school, working odd jobs herding cattle, carrying bricks, and even touring with a semipro basketball team.

Working as a waiter on the Northern Pacific Railroad, Parks saw magazine photos produced by the Farm Security Administration, a federally funded project chronicling the Great Depression in rural and urban America. Later, after watching a World War II newsreel by documentary filmmaker Norman Alley, Parks resolved to become a photographer.

Based in St. Paul, Minnesota, the self-taught Parks immediately showed an original eye for his subjects, even if he lacked the technical training at the time to capture them flawlessly. Once, after finally getting the big break of a fashion shoot, he double-exposed all but one photo. Yet even the results of these mishaps captivated his viewers, and Parks soon had established himself as a much-in-demand fashion photographer in St. Paul. His work eventually was discovered by Marva Louis, the wife of boxer Joe Louis, who helped him set up shop as a fashion photographer in a bigger market, Chicago.

In his spare time Parks turned his camera from the fantasy world of fashion to the destitute streets of the South Side of Chicago. These pictures, exhibited at the South Side Community Art Center, won him a Julius

Rosenwald Fellowship in 1941 and an opportunity to work at the Farm Security Administration, where he took on the assignment of showing the "face of America." Under the tutelage of Roy Stryker, the director of the staff photographers, Parks found that he could express himself more powerfully with the camera than with words. "I learned that photography would enable me to show what was right and wrong about America, the world and life," he said.

With the closing of the Farm Security Administration, Parks went to work at the Office of War Information in 1943, and then for the Standard Oil Company of New Jersey as a documentary photographer. Continuing his work in fashion photography, he published two books, *Flash Photography* (1947) and *Camera Portraits: The Techniques and Principles of Documentary Portraiture* (1948). In 1948 Parks was hired by *Life* magazine, then one of America's leading pictorial publications, and spent two years based in Paris. His work in the United States in the 1950s and early 1960s, and a highly acclaimed series on the slums of Rio de Janeiro won Parks international recognition as a photojournalist. His photographs in the United States dealt with many arenas, from politics to entertainment to the daily routines of ordinary men and women. Particularly noteworthy were his chronicles of the political activities of African Americans: the Civil Rights Movement (later collected into the 1971 anthology *Born Black*), the Black Power movement, and the growth of the Nation of Islam.

With photographs driven by a strong sense of narrative, it is no surprise that Parks found another calling in writing. In 1963 he published *The Learning Tree*, the saga of a farm family in the 1920s very much like Parks's own. *The Learning Tree* was the first in a trilogy of autobiographical novels, followed three years later by *A Choice of Weapons* and *To Smile in Autumn, A Memoir* in 1979. Parks combined his literary and visual talents in a 1969 movie version of *The Learning Tree*, becoming the first African American director of a major Hollywood movie. His hit movie *Shaft*, often cited as a forerunner of the blaxploitation genre, was released in 1971, followed by *Leadbelly* (1976) and *The Odyssey of Solomon Northup* (1984), the story of a free black sold into slavery. Parks, also a poet and composer, wrote the music for a ballet about the life of Dr. Martin Luther King Jr.

Parks received the Spingarn Medal from the National Association for the Advancement of Colored People in 1972, and the National Medal for the Arts in 1986. He is the father of the late filmmaker Gordon Parks Jr., whose credits include *Superfly* (1972).

North America

Petry, Ann Lane

(b. October 12, 1908, Saybrook, Conn.; d. April 28, 1997, Old Saybrook, Conn.), African American writer of adult novels and children's literature who chronicled the urban black female experience.

Ann Petry was born and raised in the predominantly white, middle-class community of Saybrook, Connecticut. The daughter of a pharmacist, she worked in her father's drugstore as a teenager and went on to major in pharmacology at the University of Connecticut. After graduating she worked at and managed the family drugstore in Old Saybrook. Her pharmacological endeavors notwithstanding, Petry wrote short stories while working, none of which have been published. After marrying George Petry, a mystery writer, in 1939, she moved to New York City and dropped pharmacy altogether, choosing instead to develop her career as a writer.

Her first job in New York was at a Harlem newspaper, the *Amsterdam News*, where she worked for four years. Petry moved on to the *People's Voice*, where she wrote a column on Harlem society in the women's section of the paper. Her first published work of fiction, a short story titled "Marie of the Cabin Club," was a romantic drama that she published under a pseudonym, preferring to save her real name for more serious works. In addition to writing Petry became involved in community issues. Her activities included the formation of a black women's consumer advocacy group and the establishment of a program in a Harlem school to help children living in crime-ridden neighborhoods.

During this period Petry joined writing workshops and creative writing classes at Columbia University. She wrote a few short stories, one of which, "On Saturday Night, the Sirens Sound," foreshadowed her first novel, *The Street*, which was to become her first literary coup. This short story, along with a few more she wrote, ran in the National Association for the Advancement of Colored People publication, *Crisis*, where it caught the attention of editors at Houghton Mifflin. Petry was urged to apply for a writer's fellowship awarded by the publishing company. She did, and won a $2,400 grant and a book contract in 1945.

The Street (1946) was a resounding success, eventually selling more than 2 million copies, the first book by a black woman to do so. An unsentimental tale of a single mother's fruitless efforts to secure a livelihood and shelter her child from the danger that the street represents, the book launched Petry's career as an author of considerable renown. She went on to publish two more novels, *Country Place* in 1947 and *The Narrows* in 1988. Neither work achieved the level of success that *The Street* had enjoyed, but in later years both were acknowledged as works of great literary merit.

In addition to her novels Petry authored works of adolescent nonfiction chronicling the lives of historical black figures, including *Harriet Tubman: Conductor on the Underground Railroad* (1955) and *Tituba of Salem Village* (1964). She also wrote two children's books, *The Drugstore Cat* (1949) and *Legend of the Saints* (1970), and penned numerous essays on a variety of topics.

Petry received numerous awards and honors in recognition of her contributions to the black literary canon, both juvenile and adult. A visionary and pioneer of multiculturalism and black feminism, Petry died on April 28, 1997, in Old Saybrook, Connecticut.

Pettiford, Oscar

(b. September 30, 1922, Okmulgee, Okla.; d. September 8, 1960), jazz bassist, bandleader, and bebop innovator.

Oscar Pettiford helped to invent and popularize the bass solo in jazz, significantly expanding the vocabulary and syntax of the language of the bass. Pettiford drew inspiration from the playing style of Jimmy Blanton, a bassist with Duke Ellington's band. Blanton had emphasized the melodic possibilities of the instrument at a time when the bass was most often relegated to the rhythm section of an ensemble. Pettiford, following Blanton's lead, plucked his strings with the length, rather than the width, of his index finger, thus extending the tonal and temporal possibilities for individual notes. At his best Pettiford produced a melodic clarity and complexity that echoed that of jazz guitar, and this bravura lent itself to a solo playing style. Pettiford was considered one of the top three bassists of his time, rivaling as well as influencing his contemporaries Ray Brown and Charles Mingus.

Born in Okmulgee, Oklahoma, to parents of Chocktaw, Cherokee, and African extraction, Pettiford moved with his family to Minneapolis when he was three years old. Pettiford came from a show-business family, and he contributed to the family's musical act as it toured the Minnesota vaudeville circuit. He demonstrated precocious musicality and by age 14 was devoting almost all of his attention to the string bass.

In 1943 Pettiford joined Charlie Barnet's big band and followed the group to New York, where he began working with other musicians. During his early New York years Pettiford collaborated with Roy Eldridge, Thelonious Monk, and Dizzy Gillespie. Pettiford participated in the legendary jam sessions at Minton's Playhouse, helping to establish the roots of bebop, a frenetic, hard-driving, and heavily improvisational style of jazz that broke away from the sweetness and set arrangements of swing. In 1944 Pettiford and Gillespie headed the first working bebop combo at the Onyx Club on 52nd Street, but the two parted within a year because of personal differences.

After a brief stint with the legendary tenor saxophonist Coleman Hawkins, Pettiford performed with his childhood idol, Duke Ellington, with whose band he remained for three years. Despite a long-running alcohol problem, Pettiford continued to be active on the club and concert circuit both in the United States and abroad. In the early 1950s he returned to New York full time to lead the Café Bohemia's house band, and in 1958 Pettiford immigrated to Copenhagen, where he remained until his death in 1960.

In addition to helping invent bebop and elevating the status of the bass in jazz, Pettiford won many music industry awards for his recordings and contributed a number of memorable songs to the jazz repertory, including "Tricrotism," "Bohemia After Dark," and "Swingin' Till the Girls Come Home."

North America

Pickett, Wilson

(b. March 18, 1941, Prattville, Ala.), African American soul singer.

Known for his dynamic stage presence and hard-rocking hits such as *"Mustang Sally," "Land of 1,000 Dances,"* and *"In the Midnight Hour,"* Wilson Pickett was one of the biggest stars of the 1960s. Influenced by the gospel music he sang as a child, along with the rhythm and blues then in vogue, Pickett began singing with a band, the Falcons, in 1959. Pickett, who had moved to Detroit, Michigan, at age 15, also wrote some of the band's songs, one of which, *"I Found a Love,"* became a Top Ten hit in 1962.

In 1964 Atlantic Records signed Pickett, sending him to Memphis, Tennessee, to record his first album. Working with Booker T and the MG's—the house band from the Stax record label—Pickett produced some of his most popular songs during this era, which lasted until 1967. Pickett's screams, growls, and moans punctuated the funky beat and powerful horn section that characterized these recordings, which not only defined the Southern soul sound but became some of the most played dance music ever.

Recording both at Stax and Muscle Shoals (the Atlantic studio famous as the birthplace of Aretha Franklin's most soulful music), Pickett also toured heavily. Billing himself as "Wicked Pickett," he was known as the king of the dance floor, one of soul's most thrilling performers. Throughout the 1970s and 1980s Pickett played concerts worldwide, though he ceased to produce noteworthy hits after leaving Atlantic in the early 1970s. In 1991, the same year he was elected to the Rock and Roll Hall of Fame, Pickett announced his retirement.

North America

Pippin, Horace

(b. February 22, 1888, West Chester, Pa.; d. July 6, 1946, West Chester, Pa.), African American painter who became famous for his nonacademic approach to art and superimposition of historical events and personal experiences.

Horace Pippin was discovered at a time in art history when such artists as Pablo Picasso were breaking away from academic painting standards to define a modern aesthetic. Art critics and dealers became particularly interested in self-taught artists whose works had not been influenced by traditional approaches to painting. One such artist was Henri Rousseau, a French painter hailed by Picasso for his indifference to perspective, use of strong color, and unorthodox, dreamlike subject matter. Pippin was compared to Rousseau because of his tendency to ignore concepts of realism, such as perspective and shadowing.

Another aspect of Pippin's work that intrigued art critics and dealers was the way in which Pippin interpreted historical events in terms of his own personal experiences. His painting *Abraham Lincoln and His Father Building Their Cabin on Pigeon Creek*, for example, is cast in the mold of his childhood memories from Goshen, New York, as reflected in the structure and fixtures of the house. The personal dimension in *John Brown Going to His Hanging* (1942) stems from Pippin's inclusion of his grandmother, who actually witnessed the event in 1859. These personal details lend to Pippin's depictions of historical events a sense of immediacy and intimacy.

Art critic and historian Christian Brinton discovered Pippin after seeing his *Cabin in the Cotton* on display in a barbershop window in 1936. Brinton sought Pippin out and arranged for ten of his works to be displayed at the West Chester Community Center on June 9, 1937. Within a year four of Pippin's works were included in an exhibition of self-taught French and American painters, "Masters of Popular Painting," at the Museum of Modern Art. In 1940 artist-turned-dealer Robert Carlen mounted Pippin's first gallery show in Philadelphia, Pennsylvania. During the 1940s Pippin's paintings were purchased by several major American museums, and galleries throughout the country mounted exhibitions featuring his works.

Part of the reason Pippin began to paint was to rehabilitate his right arm following a World War I injury. Pippin had taken an interest in drawing at an early age. As a boy he won a box of crayons and a set of watercolors for his entry in an art supply company's advertising contest. Pippin used the crayons and watercolors to decorate doilies, which were sold in a Sunday school festival. During his childhood and early adulthood he spent much of his free time drawing.

When the United States declared war in 1917, he enlisted and served as a corporal in what would become known as the 369th Colored Infantry Regiment of the United States Army. Pippin continued to sketch while in the service. Only six of the drawings documenting Pippin's war experiences survive, since he was made to destroy the others for security reasons. He was honorably discharged in October 1918 after a German sniper's shot seriously wounded his right shoulder. Pippin, who was very proud of his frontline service, was awarded a French Croix de Guerre in 1919 and a retroactive Purple Heart in 1945.

Upon returning to the United States from France, Pippin met Jennie Ora Featherstone, a widow with a young son living in West Chester, Pennsylvania; the couple married on November 21, 1920. Pippin's disability check was not enough to support the two of them, and he did his best with his good left arm to assist his wife at her laundry service. In 1925 he began to make pictures by burning images onto wood panels with a hot poker. This endeavor was intended to serve as therapy for his injured arm, which he rested across his knee. It also allowed him to work out the war memories that continued to trouble him.

Pyrography, burning drawings into wood, was a challenging way for Pippin to resume creating. Pyrography's laborious process allows no erasure and required that he work out the entire composition in his head before beginning. Toward the end of the 1920s, his right arm gaining strength, he attempted his first easel painting, supporting his disabled arm at the wrist with his left hand. He spent three years of his life painting and repainting his first work in oil, *The End of the War: Starting Home* (1930), which ambivalently depicts the surrender of German soldiers against a background of violence and chaos. Although his output was slow and exhausting during the early 1930s, he continued to reconstruct his personal past, particularly childhood and war memories, through painting.

Pippin's growing popularity in the 1940s led to some changes in his work. Collector Albert Barnes, who wrote two catalogue essays on the artist, invited Pippin to see his world-famous collection of paintings, to which he added two of Pippin's works. After seeing Barnes's collection, Pippin brightened his palette (influenced by Renoir's colors) and began creating still-life compositions (meticulously rendered flowers). The impact of other artists is also seen in Pippin's *John Brown* paintings, a narrative group of works inspired by Jacob Lawrence's *Toussaint L'Ouverture* series. In spite of these influences and Barnes's unsuccessful attempt to get Pippin to take art classes at the Barnes Foundation's art school, Pippin maintained his philosophy about art. He said, "My opinion of art is that a man should have a love for it, because it is my idea that he paints from his heart and mind. To me it seems impossible for another to teach one of art."

Pippin worked with increasing productivity until his death on July 6, 1946, creating more than 75 of his 137 known works in the last six years of his life. Unlike other important self-taught artists who tended to repeat themselves, Pippin explored a variety of subjects (American history, biblical themes, winter landscapes, portraits, and scenes of everyday black communal life) on a variety of mediums (fabric, paper, and wood). In attempting to be direct and true to reality as he understood it, Pippin created works with some of modern art's fundamental characteristics—unmodulated, sharply delineated colors and flat, shadowless forms—which makes him one of the twentieth century's most remarkable artists.

Africa

Plaatje, Solomon Tshekisho

(b. 1876, South Africa; d. 1932, South Africa), South African writer and journalist and one of the founders of the African National Congress (ANC), who served as its first secretary-general.

Although ethnically a Tswana of the Rolong branch, Solomon Tshekisho took the Dutch name Plaatje from a nickname used by his father. Following some schooling in the 1880s, Plaatje took a job as a postal clerk at Kimberley in Northern Cape Province, South Africa. During the Boer War (1899–1902) he reported the siege of Mafeking (now Mafikeng) and kept a diary of the period. In 1904 he launched the first newspaper in the Tswana language, *Koranta ea Bechuana* (Newspaper of the Tswana), and began opposing white violations of black rights.

In 1912 he became the secretary-general of what was at first known as the South African Native National Congress, later the ANC, with John Langalibalele Dube as president. Plaatje was a fine orator and in 1913 went with Dube and a delegation to Great Britain to oppose the 1913 Natives Land Act, which had drastically curtailed the right of blacks to purchase or own land. He remained in Great Britain during World War I (1914–1918), where he wrote and published several books. In *Native Life in South Africa* (1916) he outlined the reasons for black opposition to the Land Act. At the end of the war he was part of another black delegation that attended the Versailles peace conference but that was not allowed to participate. He also attended the Pan-African Congress, which was held in Paris at the same time, and was among the first South African black leaders to make contact with other African black leaders. Plaatje traveled back to Great Britain and went with delegations to see Prime Minister David Lloyd George and the Archbishop of Canterbury, but failed to obtain help for the black cause in South Africa. From there he traveled to Canada and the United States. He wrote poetry and translated five of Shakespeare's plays into Tswana. His novel *Mhudi: An Epic of Native Life 100 Years Ago* (1930) was one of the first novels in English by a black African.

North America
Plato, Ann

(b. 1820?; d. ?, Hartford, Conn.), African American poet and essayist who was the second African American woman to publish a book in the United States.

Although little is known about the life of Ann Plato, her legacy holds an important place in African American literature. Plato's sole book, *Essays: Including Biographies and Miscellaneous Pieces in Prose and Poetry*, published in 1841, represents the only book of essays issued by a black American between 1840 and 1865. Following that of Phillis Wheatley, it was also only the second book published by an African American woman.

Based on information garnered primarily from her writings, scholars have determined that Plato probably was born about 1820. Her poem "The Infant Class," for example, suggests that Plato began to teach young children when she herself was only 15 years old. Her poem "The Natives of America" links her to her paternal Native American heritage, and another poem, "I Have No Brother," indicates that she had a brother named Henry, who died when she was very young. Plato probably joined the Congregational Church at age 13. As she was not a slave, her writing provides unusual insight into the life of a mid-nineteenth-century, middle-class, free black woman.

The introduction to Plato's book was written by James W. C. Pennington, minister of the Colored Congregational Church in Hartford. Pennington presents Plato's work by emphasizing first her color, then her age and sex, and finally the literary tradition from which she drew. Pennington was reluctant, but felt obliged to stress that Plato was black: "I am not in the habit of introducing myself or others to notice by the adjective 'colored,' . . . but it seems proper that I should . . . say here that my authoress is a colored lady." He also emphasized Plato's "large heart full of chaste and pious affection for those of her own age and sex . . . . " He compares her to Phillis Wheatley, the eighteenth-century black poet: "She, as Phillis Wheatley was, is passionately fond of reading and delights in searching the Holy Scriptures; and is now rapidly improving her knowledge."

In her book Plato eulogizes four other black women, all of whom died at an early age: Louisa Sebury, Julia Ann Pell, Eliza Loomis Sherman, and Elizabeth Low. Eleven of Plato's twenty published poems have death as their themes, suggesting Plato's concern with the grim lives often led even by free blacks.

Some scholars have criticized Plato's writing, including one who described it as "the pious, moralistic effusions of a Puritan girl." Many of her poems are juvenile, her verse uneven. She almost always wrote in iambic tetrameter, and her language often reflected her puritanical environment. Still, Plato occasionally branches out to topics outside her personal experience, shedding her moral, florid tone in favor of more politically charged themes. Her poem "To the First of August" hailed the end of slavery in the West Indies in 1838.

Most of Plato's works elucidate events and sentiments drawn from her own life. In "Written upon Being Examined in School Studies for the Preparation of a Teacher" she demands, "Learn me the way to teach the word of love / For that's the pure intelligence above." While Plato's contribution to American literature is often regarded as insignificant, the circumstances in which she wrote elevate her achievements and place her at the head of the canon of esteemed African American poets.

North America

Platters, The,

the most successful African American vocal group of the 1950s, who played a key role in popularizing the rhythm-and-blues (R&B) vocal harmony group style that has since become known as *doo wop*.

The Platters were a popular vocal quintet and a consistent hit-maker for Mercury Records. But at the outset Mercury was more interested in acquiring the Penguins, another West Coast vocal group that had scored a major hit with *"Earth Angel,"* recorded for the small Dootone label. The Platters, on the other hand, had found little success after several early releases on Federal Records. Mercury, one of the six major record companies of the day, wanted the Penguins in order to strengthen its rhythm and blues (R&B) catalogue and thus gain more of the African American market. But arranger Buck Ram, who served as manager for both groups, insisted that if Mercury wanted the Penguins, it would have to sign the Platters as well.

In late 1954 Mercury reluctantly agreed. Ironically, the Penguins never had another Top Ten hit, whereas the Platters quickly rose to become the most successful vocal group of the decade. Although they recorded numerous up-tempo R&B numbers, the Platters were above all a ballad group. Their most successful recordings featured the smooth and romantic lead of Tony Williams. Williams ranks as one of the greatest lead tenors of the so-called *doo wop* era and—along with Sonny Til of the Orioles, Willie Winfield of the Harptones, and Nate Nelson of the Flamingos—one of the great ballad interpreters of the 1950s.

The Platters were a product of the new African American culture created by the Great Migration of blacks out of the South—in particular, those who came to Los Angeles, a city with a black community that had tripled in size during the 1940s as a result of the booming wartime economy. Los Angeles was home to the Platters, the Penguins, the Hollywood Flames, the Olympic Games, and many other African American vocal groups whose members had often begun singing together in informal groups while still in high school.

The Platters began as a quartet in 1952, performing at amateur night competitions at Los Angeles's Club Alabam and more informal settings. Herbert Reed, who had sung bass in a gospel group during his stint in the United States Air Force, suggested the name the Platters. "I remember . . . thinking to myself, on the radio they always say, 'Here's the latest platter by so-and-so,'" Reed recalled. The group experienced several changes in membership over its first two years, including the addition of Williams and Zola Taylor, a 14-year-old alto who became known as "the dish of the Platters." In 1954, not long before signing with Mercury, the group coalesced. Between 1955 and 1960, the years of its greatest success, the Platters consisted of Williams (tenor lead), Taylor (alto), David Lynch (tenor), Paul Robi (baritone), and Reed (bass).

The most demanding fans of African American vocal harmony singing dismissed the Platters for taking a simplistic approach to R&B group harmony singing. The Platters displayed little of the sophisticated voicings or complex harmonies found in the ballads performed by the Flamingos or the Harptones. Yet the Platters attained far greater commercial success, in large part because their singing was direct and emotionally engaging but also because they had the backing of a major record company. The group's first Mercury release, the haunting "*Only You,*" hit the charts and clearly revealed the group's crossover potential, reaching not only Number One on the R&B chart, but a striking Number Five on the white popular music chart.

Six months later Mercury released "*The Great Pretender,*" and the Platters became the first African American group to have a Number One hit on the white pop charts. Over the next six years the group enjoyed phenomenal success. During 1956 the Platters were second only to rock 'n' roller Elvis Presley in popularity. By 1962 the group had given Mercury Records 35 songs on *Billboard* magazine's Pop Hot 100 chart. A number of Platters hits, including the memorable *"Smoke Gets in Your Eyes"* (1958) and *"Harbor Lights"* (1959), actually ranked higher on the white pop charts than on R&B listings.

Success swept up the five African American singers in a whirlwind of travel and performances. The Platters were particularly significant for their crossing of racial barriers in popular music. They performed in Las Vegas and at the Olympia Theater in Paris with bandleader Quincy Jones, as well as for Pope Pius XII at the Vatican and for Queen Elizabeth II of England. In 1959 they became the first African American group to appear in the Eastern bloc, serving as goodwill ambassadors and performing in Poland.

The group's fall from success came suddenly. On August 10, 1959, Cincinnati police arrested the four men in the group for allegedly consorting with prostitutes. The case was eventually dismissed, and *Billboard* magazine published a charge that the arrests were a result of racism. But for several months the Platters discovered that their concert dates were canceled and radio disc jockeys refused to give them airplay.

The Platters returned to popularity with *"Harbor Lights"* (1959), which reached the Pop Top Ten, but their success was short-lived. Tony Williams left the group in 1960 to begin what proved to be a rather unsuccessful solo career. Other personnel changes followed, with Herbert Reed, the last of the original group members, departing in 1969. By the mid-1960s the Platters had become less a group than a franchise. During the 1980s and 1990s as many as ten different groups calling themselves the "Platters" toured and performed throughout the United States, but most had no relationship to the musicians of the original group.

On the other hand, during the years of their greatest successes the Platters had a powerful impact on popular music. Their importance was belatedly acknowledged by the popular music industry in 1990, when the Platters were inducted into the Rock and Roll Hall of Fame. Herbert Reed, one of the original members of the group, eloquently summed up the Platters' significance. "[B]ecause of our music," he declared, "white kids had a sense of fair play about blacks long before the Civil Rights Movement . . . . It opened a lot of doors to a better understanding. And it gave us, five kids from Watts, a taste of a better life . . . . "

North America

Pointer Sisters, The,
African American singing group.

The Pointer Sisters—Ruth (b. March 19, 1946), Anita (b. January 23, 1948), Bonnie (b. July 11, 1950), and June (b. November 20, 1954)— gained fame in the 1970s and 1980s with catchy pop songs that successfully spanned the country and rhythm and blues genres. Born and raised in Oakland, California, as children the Pointers sang in the choir of the West Oakland Church of God, where their parents were ministers. Although they performed gospel music, they grew up listening to the broad range of secular music that abounded in the Bay Area in the 1960s—jazz, soul, country, and everything in between. The Pointers quickly made contacts in the music industry, and by 1969 they were singing backup for several San Francisco-based musicians, including Elvin Bishop, Taj Mahal, Boz Scaggs, and Tower of Power.

The Pointer Sisters' self-titled debut, issued in 1973 on ABC/Blue Thumb Records, drew from blues and soul and enjoyed popular success: the single "Yes We Can Can" climbed to number 11 on the Billboard pop chart. Their sudden popularity led to a number of television appearances in which the sisters were featured wearing their trademark 1940s-style outfits that were reminiscent of the Andrews Sisters.

The Pointers' success continued in 1974 with the release of their second album, That's a Plenty, which featured the hit single "Fairytale," a song that garnered the group's first Grammy Award. The quartet was reduced to a trio when Bonnie Pointer embarked on a solo career with Motown Records in 1977, but the group remained popular, earning acclaim for its versatility. The Pointers experimented with rock on 1978's Energy, an album that included the hits "Happiness" and "Fire" (a cover of a Bruce Springsteen song), but focused on rhythm and blues in the 1980s, recording such hits as "Slow Hand" (1981), "What a Surprise" (1981), "Excited" (1982), "I Need You" (1983), and the Grammy Award-winning "Jump" (1983) and "Automatic" (1984). The group had its heyday in the mid-1980s, but continued to perform and record into the 1990s, switching to RCA Records in 1985 and to Motown in 1991, and starring in the musical Ain't Misbehavin' in 1995.

Though usually regarded as a pop or rhythm and blues group, the Pointer Sisters earned some of their highest accolades for their country performances. In 1974 they performed at the legendary Grand Ole Opry in Nashville, Tennessee, the first African American female group to do so. They were also the first black women to grace the top of Billboard's country and western charts. In honor of their country roots the Pointers collaborated with Clint Black to cover "Chain of Fools" for the Rhythm, Country and Blues collection in 1994.

North America

Poitier, Sidney

(b. February 20, 1927, Miami, Fla.), African American actor, director, and filmmaker, leading post-World War II African American movie star.

Sidney Poitier was raised in the Bahamas and returned to the United States as a teenager. He served in the United States Army during World War II and moved to New York in 1945 to study acting. At his first audition for the American Negro Theater, Poitier was rejected because of his strong Caribbean accent. After only six months he perfected a mainstream American accent by imitating radio announcers and was accepted on his second audition.

Poitier's first film role was in *No Way Out* (1950). Many leading roles followed, and in 1963 he became the first African American to win the Oscar for Best Actor for his performance in *Lilies of the Field*. Poitier's other films include *Blackboard Jungle* (1955), *The Defiant Ones* (1958), *In the Heat of the Night*, *To Sir with Love*, and *Guess Who's Coming to Dinner* (all 1967). He also originated the role of Walter Lee Younger in the 1959 Broadway production of Lorraine Hansberry's *A Raisin in the Sun*.

Poitier was the first African American to become a major Hollywood star with mainstream audiences. In the process he was criticized by some members of the black community for portraying stereotypical "noble Negroes." In response, as the 1960s ended, Poitier began to play more diverse roles. He also began to produce and direct films, and directed several hit films in the 1970s and 1980s. In 1993 Poitier won the National Association for the Advancement of Colored People's first Thurgood Marshall Lifetime Achievement Award.

North America

Polk, Prentice Herman

(b. November 25, 1898, Bessemar, Ala.; d. December 29, 1984, Tuskegee, Ala.), photographer and documentarian of the Tuskegee Institute community as well as the everyday lives of slaves and sharecroppers.

Prentice Herman Polk became interested in photography at a young age. He began studying through a correspondence course that he paid for with $10 he was mistakenly given as change after buying a candy bar at a local store.

Polk attended Tuskegee Institute from 1916 to 1920 and was appointed to the faculty of the photography department in 1928. He served as department head from 1933 to 1938. Between 1933 and 1982 he was the official school photographer, taking pictures of members of the Tuskegee community and of visitors such as Henry Ford and Eleanor Roosevelt. He also chronicled the experiences of George Washington Carver. Polk retired in 1982.

North America

Powell, Earl ("Bud")

(b. September 27, 1924, New York, N.Y.; d. August 1, 1966, New York, N.Y.), African American jazz pianist, often regarded as the most important bebop pianist of the 1940s.

In 1940 Powell began playing at Minton's Playhouse in New York and became a student of Thelonious Monk. From 1942 to 1944 he frequently played with his other mentor, Cootie Williams. Under the guidance of these two masters he developed his distinctive style and made a significant impact on the piano playing of the emerging bebop movement. Mike Baillie has written of Powell that "his total emotional commitment, at times quite ferocious, with an unrelenting sense of urgency . . . comes through on every recording he ever made." Powell, often in the trio format, has played with such jazz greats as Dizzy Gillespie, Charlie Parker, and Max Roach. Among his better-known jazz compositions are *Hallucinations*, recorded by Miles Davis as *Budo, Dance of the Infidels, Tempus Fugue-it*, and *Bouncing with Bud*.

Powell suffered a head injury in 1945 during a racial incident, after which he experienced several nervous breakdowns. His composition *The Glass Enclosure* is a musical expression of his numerous stays in mental institutions. His playing appearances began to decline in the late 1940s.

In 1959 Powell moved to Paris, where he led a trio with Kenny Clarke until 1962. There he enjoyed a brief renewal of his celebrity status. He returned to America in 1964. After performing a poorly received concert at Carnegie Hall in 1965, he abandoned music altogether.

North America

Price, Florence Beatrice Smith

(b. April 9, 1887, Little Rock, Ark.; d. June 3, 1953, Chicago, Ill.), composer and pianist who was one of the first African American women to achieve national recognition as a composer.

The third child of Little Rock's first black dentist, Florence Price had already published musical compositions as a high school student. She graduated as an organist and teacher from the New England Conservatory of Music in 1906, and in 1912 she married the attorney Thomas J. Price. Florence Price won the Wanamaker Prize in 1932 for her *Symphony in E minor*, which the Chicago Symphony Orchestra premiered at the 1933 Chicago World's Fair. She thus became the first African American woman to create a score played by a leading American orchestra. Price composed more than 300 works, and her songs and arrangements were performed by some of the most admired voices of her day, including Marian Anderson. Her symphonies and chamber works were famous for incorporating melodies from Negro spirituals, and her work is considered an important part of the New Negro Arts Movement.

North America

Pride, Charley Frank

(b. March 18, 1938, Sledge, Miss.), first African American country music superstar.

The son of sharecroppers in rural Mississippi, Charley Pride spent his early years surrounded by blues music, but chose to pursue country music professionally. Pride began his bid to be the first black to mount the Grand Ole Opry stage (the apex of country music performance) unconventionally—as a baseball player in the late 1950s. In between innings and on the tour bus as an outfielder for several Negro League teams, Pride displayed his sinewy voice and self-taught mastery of the guitar. Eventually, his nightclub singing was noticed and encouraged by Nashville producers. He gave up baseball for music in 1963. The popularity of his first hits, "*Snakes Crawl at Night*" (1965) and "*Just Between You and Me*" (1966), earned him invitations to perform at the Opry, making him the first black country music star to appear there.

Success in music and business followed. He is a superstar singer/composer of more than 50 Top Ten hits, the winner of three Grammy Awards, *Cash Box* magazine's Top Male Country Singer of the Decade (1970s), and the 1971 Country Music Association Entertainer of the Year. He is second only to Elvis Presley in records sold for the RCA label. In addition to owning other businesses whose profits have made him a multimillionaire, Pride owns First Texas Bank in Dallas, Texas.

While Pride's rise to fame was meteoric, he faced criticism from within the black community, which perceived country music to be a white arena. Also, early in his career, the Nashville music industry hid Pride's race by issuing publicity material without his photo. In order to help others avoid such discrimination, Pride has been active in a new Nashville organization, the Minority Country Music Association.

North America

Prince (born Prince Rogers Nelson)

(b. June 7, 1958, Minneapolis, Minn.), virtuoso pop musician known for his provocative musical and personal style.

Born Prince Rogers Nelson, Prince had many transformations on the journey from his childhood nickname, "Skipper," to ♀, an unpronounceable glyph that he assumed in 1993 that is representative of male and female principles. Deliberately frustrating efforts to characterize his image and his music, Prince announced a new persona with his 1996 album, *Emancipation*, which was a hoped-for return to his commercial and artistic success of the 1980s.

Notoriously private about his personal life, Prince is the biracial son of jazz musicians Mattie Shaw Nelson and John Nelson. Self-taught on the guitar, piano, and drums, he received a recording contract at age 20. His first album, 1978's *For You*, blends funk, rock, pop, and jazz; like those albums that follow, it evidences the eclectic musical influences of James Brown, George Clinton, Jimi Hendrix, and the Beatles.

Like his idol, Little Richard, Prince is flamboyant in dress and personality. After *For You*, his next few albums brought him notoriety as a result of their explicitly sexual lyrics and his own provocative androgyny.

Neither black nor white, his music neither rock nor funk, Prince appealed to all, a fact that helped him crossover onto MTV. He created a virtual cult following with the 1982 album 1999, which went triple platinum, and with 1984's *Purple Rain*, which won three Grammy Awards, Prince starred in and produced the semi-autobiographical film *Purple Rain*, for which he earned an Oscar for best score. His other films include the modestly successful *Under the Cherry Moon* (1986) and *Graffiti Bridge* (1990).

Prince took a brief retirement in 1993 and was then involved in a court battle with his former record label, Warner Brothers. He reemerged with his own label in 1996, no longer what he referred to as a "slave" to music industry commercialism or his own former reputation. He credits his "emancipation" to the influence of former dancer and backup singer Mayte Garcia, whom he married on Valentine's Day, 1996.

Europe

Prince, Mary

(b. 1788, Bermuda; d. ?, Great Britain), first black woman to publish a slave narrative.

The History of Mary Prince, A West Indian Slave, Related by Herself (1831) was the earliest account that gave a firsthand description of the brutality women suffered under slavery. Prince's autobiography became very popular and stirred debate on slavery and the treatment of slaves in the West Indies. Describing the harsh conditions she faced in the West Indies, Prince countered biased white conclusions that "slaves don't want to get out of slavery." As she explained, "They [whites] put a cloak about the truth. It is not so. All slaves want to be free . . . . I have been a slave myself—and I know what slaves feel—I can tell by myself what other slaves feel, and by what they have told me." With these words she became the first black woman to challenge whites on behalf of all black people.

Born a slave in Bermuda around 1788, Prince was separated from family members when they were sold to different West Indian plantation owners. Prince herself worked on various estates as a domestic servant and in the fields. Not only did she experience sexual exploitation, but she was left with severe scarring from beatings, and her labor on a salt plantation deformed her feet because of long exposure to the harsh chemicals. Prince married a free black man in 1826, but according to West Indian law she was still the property of her masters, John Wood and his wife, who often beat her in full view of her husband. Rheumatism further disabled Prince, which angered the Woods, who increasingly threatened to evict her. Finally, while traveling in England with the Woods in 1828, Prince escaped.

Having joined the Moravian Church in the West Indies, Prince now sought shelter at the church's branch in London. She obtained financial and legal aid from the British Anti-Slavery Society. One member, Thomas Pringle, hired her, and offered to purchase her freedom from Wood. Wood rebuffed his offer and insisted that she return to the West Indies. Prince refused, even though this meant she would be separated from her husband.

Prince was determined to fight for her freedom in the English courts, Parliament, and press. She recounted her slave narrative to a female member of the Anti-Slavery Society; it was then edited by Thomas Pringle, who took pains to keep to the original wording. Despite the publicity she received from the popularity of her book, she seems to have lost her celebrity status soon after. It is known that she remained legally a slave until 1834, when slavery was abolished in England and its colonies.

North America

Professor Longhair (Henry Byrd)
(b. December 19, 1918, Bogalusa, La.; d. January 30, 1980, New Orleans, La.), African American rhythm and blues artist, regarded as the progenitor of post-World War II New Orleans R&B sound.

Henry Byrd was born to James L. and Ella Mae Byrd, both musicians, but was reared in New Orleans, Louisiana, solely by his mother. Impoverished, Byrd left school to work on the streets as a musical performer and dancer. At the age of eight he was working for the CJK Medicine Show as a stuntman, while remaining a street performer.

Despite the fact that Byrd could play the guitar and the piano, dancing provided his main source of work even into the 1930s, most notably with singer Champion Jack Dupree at the Cotton Club in New Orleans. From 1937 to 1942 Byrd worked mostly outside of entertainment in the Civilian Conservation Corps and as a cook, in addition to gambling professionally throughout Louisiana.

After World War II Byrd focused on music as his source of livelihood, developing his patented style of "flamboyant . . . strutting and riffing barrel-house piano style." Before heading his own band, Professor Longhair and the Four Hairs, in 1949 Byrd played piano with several local bands. Under the names Professor Longhair and his Shuffling Hungarians and Roy Byrd, he recorded several hit records including "*Baldhead (a.k.a. 'She Ain't Got No Hair')*," "*Tipitina*," and "*Go to the Mardi Gras*," known as the "unofficial anthem" of New Orleans. These hits were popular due to Byrd's distinctively hoarse, semi-yodelling singing style, as well as his infectious piano rhythms. From the early 1960s until about 1970 Byrd faded from the musical world, but he regained wide renown after appearing in the 1971 New Orleans Jazz and Heritage Festival.

Professor Longhair's resurgent popularity continued even after his death in 1980; he was posthumously inducted into the Rock and Roll Hall of Fame in 1992. Leaving his mark on pianists from Fats Domino and Allen Toussaint to Harry Connick Jr., Professor Longhair, according to *Downbeat* magazine, "is the most influential pianist to emerge from the New Orleans milieu since Jelly Roll Morton."

North America

Prophet, Nancy Elizabeth

(b. March 19, 1890, Warwick, R.I.; d. December 1960, Providence, R.I.), African American sculptor who was active in the Harlem Renaissance and in Paris through the 1930s.

A classically trained sculptor lauded for her sensitive and dignified busts of people of color, Nancy Elizabeth Prophet was born into humble circumstances. At an early age she was recognized as having unusual artistic skill. Earnings from work as a domestic enabled her to take a degree in painting and portraiture from the Rhode Island School of Design (RISD) in 1918.

A teaching job in Harlem brought Prophet to New York during the Harlem Renaissance. The atmosphere ignited her creativity, and she left New York for Paris's Ecole des Beaux Arts, where she studied from 1922 to 1925. Prophet's next 12 years in Paris were marked by a high level of artistic achievement, during which she produced her well-known sculpture *Congolaise* (1930). Even though her work was exhibited at Paris salons between 1924 and 1927 and in the United States (at RISD and in Boston, 1928), Prophet had great difficulty supporting herself as an artist. In fact, her poverty, malnutrition, and near starvation were so obvious to other artists in Paris that Henry O. Tanner nominated her for the Harmon Foundation Prize in 1928, hoping to gain her some financial relief. Prophet won the Harmon's Otto Kahn Prize in 1929 for *Head of a Negro* and later won the 1932 Newport Art Association prize for her portrait *Discontent*.

Prophet moved back to the United States, at the suggestion of her admirer W. E. B. Du Bois, to take a teaching job at Spelman College in 1934. With painter Hale Woodruff, she taught art at Atlanta University and Spelman College (1934–1944). Frustrated by a lack of materials, space, and time in which to produce her own art, as well as the prejudices of Atlanta's art community, she returned to Providence in 1944.

Prophet produced little sculpture in her later years, and she was again forced to support herself as a domestic servant. In the last 20 years of her life she destroyed many of her sculptures and watched her wood and metal artworks rot and rust for lack of money for storage space. Once a producer of "stark, aggressive, naturalistic and non-sentimental" sculpted portraits, she died penniless at age 70.

Pryor, Richard Franklin Lenox Thomas

(b. December 1, 1940, Peoria, Ill.), African American comedian known for his
free-flowing, uncensored brand of humor.

Considered by many to be the most influential comedian since 1970,
Richard Pryor was born to Gertrude Thomas and Leroy Pryor, who met in a
brothel managed by Marie Carter, Leroy's mother. Raised in the brothel primarily by Carter, Pryor gravitated to humor early on to cope with his
chaotic family life. A disruptive student, Pryor left school at age 14 and
joined a community drama group, which he quit two years later. After
serving in the army for two years Pryor began his stand-up comedy career.
He performed successfully in Peoria nightclubs, giving him the confidence
to go to the more competitive nightclub scene of New York City. Pryor
modeled his first performances in New York closely on the comedy of Bill
Cosby and Dick Gregory.

By the late 1960s, however, Pryor had decided to present "the real side"
of himself, replacing a more refined persona with a raw, unglossy funkiness.
His recognition grew as he recorded stand-up routines and appeared in several films, including *Lady Sings the Blues* and *Uptown Saturday Night*,
Pryor's classic explorations of black life. In 1974 Pryor appeared on the
cover of *Rolling Stone* magazine because of his gold-selling album, *That
Nigger's Crazy*. Despite his overwhelming success Pryor was plagued with
financial and drug problems. In 1980, at the time of the release of his first
self-produced film, *Bustin' Loose*, he had a near fatal accident while free-
basing cocaine. Throughout his turbulent life Pryor retained his sense of
humor, as he demonstrated in his autobiographical film *Jo Jo Dancer, Your
Life is Calling* (1986). Diagnosed with multiple sclerosis in 1986, Pryor continued to appear in several films, notably in *Harlem Nights* (1989).

Public Enemy,

one of the premier African American rap music groups of the 1980s and 1990s.
Public Enemy infused a funk- and soul-based sound with sound samples (electronic snippets of prerecorded music) and other sound fragments, such as
traffic noise and police sirens. A political consciousness pervaded this multi-
layered sound, through rap texts and through physical appearance: group
members held fake automatic weapons and wore army fatigues and boots,
projecting an image of black militancy. Public Enemy's strident lyrics were
highly controversial, striking responsive chords with many people while
drawing critical responses from many others.

Public Enemy formed in Long Island, New York, in 1987 out of collaborations among lead rappers Chuck D. (Carlton Ridenhour) and Flavor Flav

(William Drayton), disk jockey (DJ) Terminator X (Norman Rogers), and the group's so-called minister of information, Professor Griff (Richard Griffin). The group's producers, Hank Shocklee, Eric "Vietnam" Sadler, and Chuck D., were collectively known as the Bomb Squad. The group took its name from *"Public Enemy Number One,"* a popular rap written by Chuck D. along with DJs Hank and Keith Shocklee.

Public Enemy's first release, *Yo! Bum Rush the Show* (1987), relied upon the rhythms of funk music to create an aggressive sound. The group's second release, *It Takes a Nation of Millions to Hold Us Back* (1988), was layered with additional samples to form a more complex sound. As the group perfected its production and sampling techniques, the content grew more politicized and Public Enemy grew more popular. Chuck D.'s strong vocals were countered by Flavor Flav's rasping voice, with dance steps by the militaristic quartet known as the S1W (Security of the First World). With this combination the group advocated black nationalist activism and opposed what it felt was mindless American consumerism. This world-view in combination with Public Enemy's occasional invectives against whites, women, gays, and Jews elicited strong reactions from listeners—both positive and negative.

In 1989 Public Enemy's song *"Fight the Power"* was part of the soundtrack for the motion picture *Do the Right Thing,* directed by African American filmmaker Spike Lee. Shortly thereafter Professor Griff made some anti-Semitic statements to the American press, and the group temporarily disbanded. It soon returned, without Griff, and released the commercially successful and critically acclaimed albums *Fear of a Black Planet* (1990) and *Apocalypse 91 . . . The Enemy Strikes Black* (1991). Other albums by Public Enemy include *Greatest Misses* (1992) and *Muse Sick-N-Hour Mess Age* (1994).

Latin America and the Caribbean

Puente, Ernesto Antonio (Tito)

(b. April 20, 1923, New York, N.Y.; d. May 31, 2000, New York, N.Y.), bandleader, composer, multi-instrumentalist—accomplished on timbales, conga, bongos, vibraphone, piano, and saxophone—and last of the great originators of Afro-Latin jazz.

With the death of Mario Bauza in 1993, Tito Puente became the last of the early innovators of Afro-Latin jazz who continued to be musically active. Although best known as a bandleader and timbales player, Puente is a multi-instrumentalist, performing on a wide range of percussion instruments as well as on piano and saxophone. For over half a century he has been a dynamic entertainer, emerging in the 1980s as a pop-culture celebrity.

Puente was born in New York City's Spanish Harlem. He had hoped to become a dancer, but an ankle injury led him to choose a career of instrumental performance. As a youth he played percussion and piano in the local

Tito Puente, composer, bandleader, percussionist, outstanding *timbales* player, and an originator of Afro-Latin jazz, performs at the Monterey Jazz Festival. *CORBIS/Craig Lovell*

band Los Happy Boys. He performed with Machito, Fernando Alvarez, and others while a teenager. He served three years in the United States Navy during World War II, and received his first informal lessons in composition and orchestration from white bandleader Charlie Spivak aboard the USS Santee. After his discharge in 1945 Puente studied music theory, orchestration, and conducting at the Juilliard School of Music in New York City.

During the late 1940s and early 1950s Puente played a key role in the merging of Latin American rhythms with contemporary jazz that produced Afro-Latin jazz. In the late 1940s he formed the Piccadilly Boys, which became the Tito Puente Orchestra. The group played a major role in promoting the mambo craze of the late 1940s. A decade later Puente helped popularize the *chachachá* sound. He produced swinging and danceable style by transforming the music of *charanga* bands, which feature violin and flute, and arranging it for a Latin jazz big band with saxes, trumpets, and trombones. In the 1970s, when salsa became popular, he gained a new and younger audience.

Since 1949 Puente has released more than 100 albums as a leader, an accomplishment rivaled by few musicians of any genre. His recording "*Abaniquito*" (1949) was a hit single and an early crossover success. In the 1970s Carlos Santana covered two of Puente's compositions: "*Para los rumberos*" (1956) and a hugely popular rendition of "*Oye como va*" (1963). Puente's various bands have featured many musicians who went on to prominence in Afro-Latin jazz, including percussionists Ray Barreto, Mongo Santamaría, and Willie Bobo; Fania Records founder Johnny Pacheco; and, more recently, saxophonist Mario Rivera, pianist Hilton Ruiz, trumpeter

Charlie Sepúlveda, and drummer Ignacio Berroa. Outside of the world of jazz Puente has performed with various Latin music stars, including the Fania All Stars, Celia Cruz, and Carlos "Patato" Valdez.

Since the late 1970s Puente has also gained wider exposure in American popular culture. In the 1980s he appeared on *The Cosby Show* and in a stylish and well-received Coca-Cola commercial. He was in Jeremy Marre's television film *Salsa '79* (1979), and seven years later made his feature film debut with cameos in *Radio Days* (1986) and *Armed and Dangerous* (1986). Puente's most significant film role was in *The Mambo Kings* (1991), playing a Latin jazz bandleader; he also arranged and performed much of the music on the film's soundtrack. He received Grammy Awards for *A Tribute to Benny Moré* (1979), *On Broadway* (1983), *Mambo Diablo* (1985), and *Goza mi timbal* (1989).

Europe

Pushkin, Alexander

(b. June 6, 1799, Moscow; d. February 10, 1837, St. Petersburg, Russia), Russian poet and author of plays, novels, and short stories, considered the founder of modern Russian literature; his maternal great-grandfather was African.

This undated illustration by Vasily Tropinin shows the poet Alexander Pushkin (1799-1837), whose work reflected both his love of Russian folktales and his fascination with his partially African heritage. His great-grandfather, Abram Hannibal, was a slave who had become a major general in the Russian army. *CORBIS/Bettmann*

Alexander Pushkin was of high birth: his father came from a long line of Russian aristocracy, and his mother was the granddaughter of Abram Hannibal, who proclaimed himself to be an African prince. Sold into slavery in the early eighteenth century, Hannibal became an engineer and major general in the Russian army and was a favorite of Tsar Peter I (Peter the Great).

Enchanted with his African ancestry, Pushkin often employed the subject in his poetry, to the point of exaggeration and obsession, according to his critics. In 1830 Faddey Bulgarin berated Pushkin for bragging about a nobility stemming from a "Negro" who had been "acquired" by a skipper in exchange for a bottle of rum. Pushkin replied sharply to

"Figliarin" (which translates roughly into "buffoon") in a poem entitled "My Genealogy": "Postscriptum / Figliarin, snug at home, decided / That my black grandsire, Hannibal, / Was for a bottle of rum acquired / And fell into a skipper's hands. / This skipper was the glorious skipper / Through whom our country was advanced / Who to our native vessel's helm / Gave mightily a sovereign course. / This skipper was accessible / To my grandsire: the black-amoor, / Bought at a bargain, grew up stanch and loyal / The emperor's bosom friend, not slave."

Pushkin was deeply influenced by the Russian folklore and stories his maternal grandmother told him as a child, and he searched out similar stories from Russian villagers throughout his life. As were many Russian aristocrats, he was also well versed in French language and literature. Educated at the Imperial Lyceum at Tsarkoye Selo, Pushkin demonstrated an early poetic genius in works such as "To My Friend the Poet" (1820), which demonstrated his allegiance to Romantic literary styles.

Pushkin diverged from this style in later works. In *Ruslan and Liudmila* (1820) he espoused a literary manner characterized by ample use of Russian folklore in the form of a narrative poem. Because this work rejected established rules and genres, he was criticized by the main literary schools of the day, classicism and sentimentalism. Still, *Ruslan and Liudmila* earned him a reputation as one of Russia's most promising poetic talents.

In 1817 Pushkin accepted a position in the Ministry of Foreign Affairs in St. Petersburg. He participated in the city's social life and belonged to an underground branch of the revolutionary group Union of Welfare. The radical fervor he expressed through his verse made him an inspiring spokesman for the revolutionaries who fought in the 1825 Decembrist uprising for a constitutional monarchy. They were violently suppressed. It was during this period that Pushkin wrote "Ode to Liberty" (1820), for which he was exiled to the Caucasus.

Pushkin's works written in exile, called his "southern cycle," were clearly influenced by the English poet Lord Byron. He demonstrates the love for liberty typical of his contemporaries in the romantic narrative poems *The Prisoner of the Caucasus* (1822), *The Fountain of Bakhchisarai* (1824), and *The Gypsies* (1824). In 1823 he began *Eugene Onegin* (1831), known to be the first of the great Russian novels (although in verse). Though a Byronic love story, *Eugene Onegin* treats the Russian historical setting realistically and the characters objectively.

Pushkin was transferred to Odessa in 1823, but after a series of incidents, including an affair with a superior's wife, he was dismissed from government service in 1824. He was banished to his mother's estate near Pskov, where he wrote *Boris Godunov* (1931), a Russian historical tragedy in the Shakespearean tradition. In *Boris Godunov*, Pushkin emphasizes the moral and political importance of "the judgment of the people" toward their rulers, and proved that he could, as he felt poet-prophets should, "fire the hearts of men with his words."

In 1826 Tsar Nicholas I, recognizing Pushkin's enormous popularity, pardoned him. On his return to the capital Pushkin continued to evoke

Russian nationalist themes in two long poems, *Poltava* (1828) and *The Bronze Horseman* (1833), as well as in his novel of the Pugachev rebellion, *The Captain's Daughter* (1836). He also wrote short stories including "The Queen of Spades" (1834) and a fictionalized biography of his great-grandfather, *The Negro of Peter the Great* (unfinished version published in 1837). In this biography Pushkin represented Hannibal in a completely positive manner, making the novel one of the earliest to promote the "Negro as hero" in world literature.

Pushkin died tragically on February 10, 1837, from wounds that he suffered in a duel he fought in St. Petersburg. Allison Blakely, author of *Russia and the Negro* (1986), argues that Pushkin had been experiencing emotional stress regarding his nominal position at the court as "Gentlemen of the Chamber." Pushkin had been given this title, which was usually reserved for aristocratic youths, primarily because it allowed his beautiful—and notoriously flirtatious—wife to attend social functions. Not only was Pushkin humiliated by his position, but he may have been insulted by the presence of colorfully attired African slaves at the court. The fateful duel, Blakely asserts, was fought not only on behalf of the Pushkins, but also to defend the honor of his Hannibal ancestry.

Quarles, Benjamin

(b. January 23, 1904, Boston, Mass.; d. November 17, 1996, Cheverly, Md.),
African American historian, author, and editor, key figure in the emergence of
African American history as an academic discipline.

Benjamin Quarles was the son of a subway porter. He earned a B.A. in 1931
from Shaw University, in Raleigh, North Carolina, an M.A. in 1933, and a
Ph.D. in 1940, both from the University of Wisconsin. Quarles taught at
Shaw, was the dean of Dillard University in New Orleans, Louisiana, and
served as chair of the history department at Morgan State University in Baltimore, Maryland.

One of the focuses of Quarles's historical research and writing was race
relations. His first published journal article was "The Breach Between Douglass and Garrison," which appeared in the *Journal of Negro History* in 1938.
Many of his other scholarly articles and monographs developed the same
theme. However, Quarles has also focused on the black contribution during
two major American crises in *The Negro in the American Revolution* (1961)
and *The Negro in the Civil War* (1953).

Early in Quarles's career, two popular misconceptions existed
regarding African American history. The first was that African Americans
could not write objective history. The second was that few documentary
sources existed for research and writing in African American history.
Quarles's scholarship did much to dispel these notions. He was the first
African American to publish essays in the *Mississippi Valley Historical
Review* (now the *Journal of American History*), in 1945 and 1959. He
served as a contributing editor to the journal *Phylon* and as an associate
editor of the *Journal of Negro History*. Quarles also wrote two textbooks,
The Negro in the Making of America and *The Negro American: A Documen-
tary History*.

Queen Latifah (Owens, Dana)

(b. March 18, 1970, Newark, N.J.), African American rap artist, actress, entertainment executive, and entrepreneur.

Queen Latifah, born Dana Owens in Newark, New Jersey, was nicknamed "Latifah" (which means "delicate" and "sensitive" in Arabic) at age eight by a black Muslim cousin. Soon afterward her parents separated, and Latifah moved with her mother, Rita, and older brother, Lance Jr., into a housing project in East Newark.

Determined to offer her children a better life, Rita Owens worked two jobs while attending community college. She eventually took a position as an art teacher at Irvington High School and the family moved to Newark.

In the second grade Latifah was found to be intellectually gifted. Her mother stretched the family finances so that she could attend Saint Anne's parochial school, where Latifah first performed as Dorothy in her school's production of *The Wiz*.

In high school Latifah played power forward on the school's basketball team. During her sophomore year she began rapping with two friends in an all-women's group called Ladies Fresh. Encouraged by her mother, she began recording and performing, and added "Queen" to her nickname.

Latifah was attending the Borough of Manhattan Community College in Manhattan when a demo tape featuring her rap *"Princess of the Posse"* made its way to Tommy Boy Records, based in New York City. She was quickly signed by the label, and in 1988 she released two singles, *"Wrath of My Madness"* and *"Dance for Me."* In 1989 she toured Europe, appeared at the Apollo Theater in Harlem, and issued her first album, *All Hail the Queen*, to wide acclaim. The album earned her the Best New Artist Award for 1990 from the New Music Seminar of Manhattan, and subsequently went platinum. Its second single, *"Ladies First,"* celebrated black women's contributions to the struggle for black liberation in America, Africa, and around the world. It became a rap classic, eventually named by the Rock and Roll Hall of Fame as one of the 500 Songs That Shaped Rock 'n' Roll.

By the time her second album *Nature of a Sista'* came out in 1991, Latifah had begun investing in small businesses in her neighborhood and acting both in television and movies (including Spike Lee's *Jungle Fever*, 1992). These successes were marred by contract conflicts that caused her to leave Tommy Boy, and by her brother's tragic death in a motorcycle accident in 1992.

After signing with Motown in 1993, Latifah released her third album, *Black Reign*, and with her newfound clout founded Flavor Unit Records and Management, which primarily handles rap and new-style rhythm and blues groups. *"U.N.I.T.Y.,"* the album's first single, denounced sexist attitudes and violence against women. Latifah also landed a regular spot on the highly rated television sitcom *Living Single*, which lasted five seasons.

Over the next few years Latifah went on to more film roles, including the critically acclaimed portrayal of Cleo, a lesbian bank robber, in *Set It Off* (1996). She also produced and guest-starred on various musical projects, managed Flavor Unit artists, and worked for numerous causes, including anti-drug campaigns.

In 1997 Queen Latifah was awarded the Aretha Franklin Award for Entertainer of the Year at the Soul Train Lady of Soul Awards. She released her fourth album, *Order in the Court*, in 1998.

R

Ragtime,

a late nineteenth-century African American musical genre that influenced strongly an emerging American popular music and that provided a major impetus in the development of jazz.

Although *ragtime* has come to connote a particular form of piano music associated with composer Scott Joplin, the term originally applied to a larger body of instrumental music and song. Emerging in the 1890s, ragtime thrived for two decades, as millions of middle-class whites bought sheet music, pianos, and piano rolls. Through its immense commercial success, ragtime gave birth to the American music industry, and through its rhythmic and melodic innovations, it signaled the end of America's dependency on Western European music. Ragtime ushered in a new style of concert music that built upon Afrodiasporic musical traditions.

Because ragtime emerged from African American folk music, its precise origins remain undocumented and obscure. Yet the roots of ragtime undoubtedly lie in the music of itinerant black pianists who played in bordellos and saloons. Ironically, ragtime's quick acceptance was due in part to the minstrel tradition that portrayed African Americans as exotic, lazy, and funny. Primed by these stereotypes as well as bastardized versions of black songs, middle-class audiences readily accepted real African American music.

The origin of the word "ragtime" also remains obscure. Some historians suspect it derives from the "ragged," or syncopated, playing style that characterized black music in the late nineteenth century. Others cite the use of "rag" as a name for a short African American folk tune. Evidence such as an early piece by Joplin, *"Original Rags,"* suggests that ragtime piano originally anthologized folk melodies. Bordello pianists probably collected and blended familiar strains. Nevertheless, "rag" soon came to designate the larger structure instead of the fragments that composed it.

Joplin, along with black composer James Scott and white composer

Joseph Lamb, established the conventions of ragtime piano and influenced a generation of black composers that included Arthur Marshall, Louis Chauvin, and Artie Matthews, all of whom, like Joplin and Scott, came from Missouri. Joplin, Scott, and Lamb also influenced white composers such as Paul Pratt and J. Russell Robinson.

Classic ragtime followed a number of formal conventions. First, it combined march-like bass notes with a heavily syncopated melody. Second, it comprised self-contained sections of 16 bars that each repeated once before giving way to a change; a typical pattern was AA BB A CC DD, where each letter represented a separate 16-measure section. Finally, it usually employed Western European harmonies, beginning and ending on a tonic key, while changing in the middle to the subdominant: for instance, a piece that began in C would alternate to F and return to conclude in C.

Joplin and Scott had defined these elements by 1897, just as sales of ragtime sheet music began to boom. Later innovations such as shifted accents and dotted rhythms added to the body of "hot," or syncopated, ragtime sounds, but were not in fact syncopated. Ragtime also influenced other African American styles such as blues and jazz. Jazz, in fact, probably grew out of ragtime, a lineage apparent in the career of the great musician and composer Jelly Roll Morton.

White bandleader William Krell published the first ragtime piano music, a piece called "*Mississippi Rag*," in 1897. Between 1897 and 1899 more than 150 "rags," written by both blacks and whites, supplied popular demand. Joplin's "*Maple Leaf Rag*," released in 1899, sold a million copies of sheet music alone. Indeed, ragtime sold so well that New York music companies hurried to mass-produce it, slapping the name "ragtime" on a wide range of music. Hack writers churned out "ragtime" vocal music, which often contained little or no syncopation at all.

Although many listeners considered Irving Berlin's 1911 hit "*Alexander's Ragtime Band*" the crowning accomplishment of the ragtime era, the majority of innovation and the best composition had occurred ten years before. Nevertheless, public enthusiasm continued until the early 1920s, reflected in high piano and sheet-music sales and the sheer volume of mediocre ragtime-style songs produced by New York's Tin Pan Alley.

The popularity of ragtime provoked much criticism from both musical and moral conservatives. Because ragtime's new rhythms inspired lively dancing, many older people found it threatening, and its syncopation sometimes caused musicians trained in simple European rhythms to find it cacophonous. The controversy reflected ragtime's revolutionary significance. By ushering in the jazz age and establishing African American rhythms as viable roots for classical music, ragtime challenged the old order, socially as well as musically. J. B. Priestly wrote, "Out of this ragtime came the fragmentary outlines of the menace to old Europe, the domination of America, the emergence of Africa, the end of confidence and any feeling of security, the nervous excitement, the feeling of modern times."

Rainey, Gertrude Pridgett ("Ma")

(b. April 26, 1886, Columbus, Ga.; d. December 22, 1939, Columbus, Ga.),
African American classic blues singer and vaudeville performer.

Born to minstrels Thomas and Ella Pridgett, Gertrude Pridgett entered
show business at age 14 as a member of the traveling stage show the "Bunch
of Blackberries." In 1904 she married showman William "Pa" Rainey, and the
two formed a song and dance act called "Rainey and Rainey: The Assassina-
tors of the Blues" that lasted until 1916. While touring mostly in the South
during that period, and subsequently as a soloist with the Rabbit Foot Minstrels on the Theater Owners' Booking Association circuit, Ma Rainey
developed her "classic blues" style of rough-edged reality moans and
humorous shouts.

In 1923 Ma Rainey began a brief but prolific recording career with
Chicago-based Paramount Records with "*Moonshine Blues.*" By 1928 she
had recorded 93 songs, many of which she wrote herself. As a result of
the wide circulation of these records, Rainey gained enormous popularity
with African Americans. Her contract was rescinded by Paramount, however, because it was felt that her style could not compete with the new
male acts such as "Big Bill" Broonzy and "Leadbelly," nor with her friend
Bessie Smith's growing status and stature. Rainey's once appealing raw
style was believed to be out of vogue with the African American record-
buying public.

Ma Rainey maintained a loyal fan base, however, and continued to perform throughout the country until 1935, when both her sister Malissa and
her mother died. Returning to her home in Columbus, she owned and managed two theaters until her death four years later. Rainey's significance
within African American popular culture is exemplified not only by her
impact on musical heirs such as singer Koko Taylor, but also by her appearance in the writing of poet Sterling Brown ("Ma Rainey") and playwright
August Wilson (*Ma Rainey's Black Bottom*). In 1990 Ma Rainey was
inducted into the Rock and Roll Hall of Fame.

Randall, Dudley Felker

(b. January 14, 1914, Washington, D.C.), African American poet and publisher
who was instrumental in promoting poetry of the Black Arts Movement.

Dudley Randall was the son of a teacher, Ada Viola Bradley Randall, and a
Congregational minister, Arthur George Clyde Randall. In 1923 the family
moved from Washington, D.C., to Detroit, Michigan, where Randall has
since spent most of his life.

After completing high school Randall worked for the Ford Motor Company and served in the army during World War II. He was unable to attend college until his early 30s. In 1949 Randall received a B.A. in English from Wayne University (now Wayne State University). He then earned a master of library science from the University of Michigan in 1951, providing him with credentials to work as a reference librarian at several colleges, including Morgan State College (now University) and the University of Detroit. In addition, he taught poetry at the University of Michigan and was poet-in-residence at the University of Detroit from 1969 to 1977.

In 1965 Randall established Broadside Press. He published his own poems and other important works by such writers as Gwendolyn Brooks, Sonia Sanchez, Haki Madhubuti (Don L. Lee), and Audre Lorde. These artists viewed African American creativity as the essence of their culture and contributed to the Black Arts Movement of the late 1960s and early 1970s. Randall's poetry collections include *Cities Burning* (1968), *Love You* (1970), and *A Litany of Friends: New and Selected Poems* (1981).

Randall's major contribution to African American literature has been to offer access to a liberating voice in print, where one had not existed on a mass scale since the Harlem Renaissance. According to poet Addison Gayle, he has "bridged the gap between poets of the 20s and those of the 60s and 70s."

North America

Rap,

an urban music that emerged from the hip hop movement of the South Bronx, New York, in the 1970s and that still thrives today.

Rap music combines rhythmic instrumental tracks created by a disc jockey, or DJ, with the spoken, rhyming bravura of a master of ceremonies, or MC. DJs often "sample" pieces of other recorded music in the creation of songs. MCs frequently rap about politics, sexual exploits, the conditions of daily life, and their own (sometimes exaggerated) personal attributes. MCs and DJs appropriate pop culture through lyrical allusions as well as rhythmic sound bites, leading many critics to consider rap the preeminent example of postmodern music. Writer John Pareles suggests, "In its structure and its content rap is the music of the television age, and the first truly popular music to adapt the fast, fractured rhythms, the bizarre juxtapositions, and the ceaseless self-promotion that are as much a part of television as logos and laugh tracks."

Unlike television, however, rap gives some African Americans a powerful voice. Its esoteric lyrical form provides ample space for political dissent, and the fact that rap music seems recondite and frightening to some white listeners adds to rap's political sting. In a talk-show discussion, rap activist Harry Allen argued that "[b]lack people are attempting to compensate for their lack of power under white supremacy, and it comes out in our art, it comes out in our music. They're trying to make up for what's missing.

What's missing is order. What's missing is power." The eager embrace of rap by young whites, however, complicates the dynamic. Rap reflects racial confusion as well as cultural innovation in an age of cable television, digital technology, and marked class stratification.

Origin

Popular lore attributes the birth of rap to Jamaican immigrant Clive Campbell, who performed under the name DJ Kool Herc. In Jamaica Herc had frequented backyard dance parties that were hosted by sound-systems operator King George, powered by booming speakers, and attended by working-class youth. When Herc DJed his first dance party in New York City in 1973, he joined the Bronx tradition of "mobile DJs," mixing up the music of James Brown, Sly Stone, and Rare Earth for kids on the street. In addition, however, Herc introduced the art of Jamaican toasting, in which DJs speak with humor and syncopation over remixed instrumental versions of records. Herc and other Bronx DJs combined old songs into new, danceable collages, which contained "break beats"—the rhythmic figures that gave rise to break-dancing.

Herc's popularity grew rapidly and inspired others to imitate his act. Soon a few popular DJs divided the Bronx into competing territories. Friendly rivalries arose between Herc in the west, Afrika Bambaataa in the east, Breakout in the north, and Grandmaster Flash in the South and Central Bronx. Competition spawned innovation. Grandmaster Flash invented backspinning, in which he played one record while turning a second one backward, repeating phrases and beats in a stuttering, rhythmic manner. Grandwizard Theodore invented scratching, a technique in which he shimmied a record back and forth beneath the needle of a turntable. Other DJs soon adopted these innovations, which became standards of the rap sound.

DJs first gained popularity by providing a soundtrack for other facets of the hip hop movement, namely dance, graffiti art, and fashion. By the late 1970s, however, artful mixing became a spectacle unto itself, and crowds ceased dancing in order to watch DJs spin. To keep people on the move, DJs recruited MCs, who led call-and-response sessions and fired up the crowd with shouts of "get up," and "jam to the beat," in the fashion of James Brown. Such oratory had precedent in gospel music, the covert rituals of slave religion, and the traditions of West Africa. Grandmaster Flash MCs the Furious Five—Melle Mel, Cowboy, Raheim, Kid Creole, and Mr. Ness—completed the genesis of rap when they began speaking to the rhythm of the music, trading rhymes in synch with each other and the DJ.

Rappers often tried to out-rhyme each other, and watching MCs became a major pastime. Independent labels such as Enjoy, Winley, and Sugar Hill Records began to record rap, and the music soon spread to other parts of New York City. In the fall of 1979 a group of rappers from Brooklyn called the Sugarhill Gang released the hit single "*Rapper's Delight*." Because it came from Brooklyn, many Bronx residents flouted it as derivative. The song, however, catapulted rap into the public eye, topping the R&B charts and reaching Number 36 on *Billboard's* Top 40.

The Golden Age

When the rap group Run-D.M.C. fused rap and hard rock on their epony-mous album in 1984, rap completed its break into the mainstream. The album sold more than 500,000 copies, becoming the first rap LP to go gold. Run-D.M.C.'s label, Def Jam Records, became the most successful indepen-dent record company in the business. Def Jam released hit music by rap star LL Cool J and, in 1985, signed a major distribution agreement with Columbia Records. Run-D.M.C.'s success among white audiences as well as their contract with a white-owned label reflected the mainstream appropri-ation of the new black form.

This appropriation prompted many to speculate about underlying issues of race. To some black critics, white listeners appeared to be seeking thrills from racially motivated fantasies. Writer David Samuels suggests that "the ways in which rap has been consumed and popularized speak not of cross-cultural understanding, musical or otherwise, but of a voyeurism and toler-ance of racism in which blacks and whites are both complicit."

Throughout the 1980s and 1990s, however, the popularity of white rap-pers like Vanilla Ice, the Beastie Boys, Third Bass, and House of Pain demonstrated that more than race was at play. Latino rappers began per-forming in Spanish (Mellow Man Ace, Kid Frost, and Gerardo), while Cypress Hill, with its mixed black and Hispanic membership, suggested that the integration of rap was happening at all levels.

Although rap began as a predominantly male activity, a number of suc-cessful female performers punctuated its history. Hit acts included MC Lyte, the Real Roxanne, Roxanne Shante, and Yo-Yo. In the 1990s women rappers often followed the male model, however, portraying men in the same derogatory way that men portrayed women. Sister Souljah broke this limited mold by addressing drug abuse, black-on-black violence, and national politics, while Queen Latifah and Salt 'n' Pepa both addressed female self-empowerment. The successful rap arranger, writer, and producer Missy "Misdemeanor" Elliott gained fame as a performer with the 1997 release of her solo debut album, *Supa Dupa Fly*.

Gangsta Rap and its Alternatives

In the late 1980s a more brutal brand of rap developed, which described drugs, sex, and violence in detail. Tremendous white consumption of such music made the grim, lurid, and angry lyrics profitable. "Gansta" rap, as per-formed by the Geto Boys, N.W.A., Ice Cube, Ice-T, and Too Short, supplied this demand. David Samuels writes that "rap's appeal to whites rested in its evocation of an age-old image of blackness: a foreign, sexually charged and criminal underworld against which the norms of white society are defined . . . ."

The glorification of misogyny and violence had ardent critics in both the black and white establishments. In 1990 a Florida district court declared the album *Nasty as They Wanna Be*, recorded by the Miami group 2 Live Crew, to be legally obscene—a ruling that outlawed the sale of the record. When

Members of the "gangsta rap" group Niggaz with Attitude included, *left to right,* Eazy-E, Dr. Dre, MC Ren, and Yella. Ice Cube, not pictured, was an early member of the group before launching a solo career. *CORBIS*

Ice-T released *Cop-Killer* in 1991, policemen organized a boycott against Time Warner, the company that distributed the album. In addition, police started blaming crimes on rap songs, as criminals cited the influence of gansta rap as part of their defense.

Many black critics declared white anger hypocritical, however, by pointing to the uncensored obscenity of popular white comedian Andrew Dice Clay as well as anti-police messages in songs by Eric Clapton, Bob Dylan, and Woody Guthrie. Commenting on *Nasty as They Wanna Be,* Henry Louis Gates Jr. likened the ribaldry of 2 Live Crew to the street tradition of playing the dozens: "In the face of racist stereotypes about black sexuality, you can do two things: you can disavow them or explode them with exaggeration. 2 Live Crew, like many 'hip hop' groups, is engaged in sexual Carnivalesque. Parody reigns supreme . . . . their off-color nursery rhymes are part of a venerable Western tradition."

Other African American leaders, however, dissented. Although most opposition reflected nothing more than a generation gap—parents scorning rap as their parents had scorned R&B—some of the criticism was grounded in ethical and political concern. On a talk show in 1993 Rev. Jesse Jackson railed against the rhetoric of gangsta rap. In the same year Rev. Calvin O. Butts III held a rally in New York to run over certain rap albums with a steamroller. Both men thought that the hyperbolic language of gansta rappers and groups like 2 Live Crew only hurt African Americans in their struggle against racism. Some events in the 1990s led critics to question the lifestyle of gansta rappers as well as the culpability of the media in celebrity-related crime. These events included the death of rapper Eazy-E from AIDS, and the murders of East Coast-West Coast rivals Chris Wallace, a.k.a. Biggie Smalls (The Notorious B.I.G.), and Tupac Shakur, a.k.a. 2PAC.

An increasingly popular and gentrified form of rap developed concurrently with gangsta rap. In the late 1980s lighthearted songs, more in the spirit of early Bronx rap, garnered popularity. Performers such as Young MC, MC Rob Base & DJ EZ Rock, and DJ Jazzy Jeff & the Fresh Prince recorded clean hits filled with playful braggadocio. Rap-based Saturday morning cartoons appeared in the wake of such songs. In 1990 rap reached prime-time television in the form of *The Fresh Prince of Bel-Air,* a situation comedy. Even the more serious rappers often found themselves in the thick of popular culture. LL Cool J landed a sitcom, while Tone Loc, Ice-T, Ice Cube, and Queen Latifah appeared in Hollywood films. Will Smith, a.k.a.

the Fresh Prince, went furthest in this direction, starring in two summer blockbusters, *Independence Day* (1996) and *Men In Black* (1997).

Meanwhile, however, most rappers neither perpetrated gangsta lyrics nor appeared in cartoons. Rappers who were dubbed "alternative" disavowed rap's violence while trying to preserve its edge. They included Me Phi Me, Disposable Heroes of Hiphoprisy, and Arrested Development. KRS-One of Boogie Down Productions initiated the Stop the Violence movement, and the West Coast Rap All-Stars began the Human Education Against Lies (H.E.A.L.) program, both of which pitted rap's influence against social ills. More bohemian acts, such as A Tribe Called Quest and De La Soul, concentrated on musical innovations, developing the art, rather than the politics, of rap.

In the late 1990s the widespread popularity of the Fugees reflected the new, international direction of rap. The Fugees addressed problems both within and outside the United States, and one of the group's members, Haitian Wyclef Jean, released material performed in Creole. Wu Tang Clan, a group of nine rappers from the East Coast, rejected R&B influences, adhering instead to global sensibilities and trends. At the end of the century rap scenes were burgeoning in most major European cities: MC Solar of France drew an international following while Japanese youth began to emulate the rap culture of the West.

Rap had begun as a homemade music, and its commercialization did not steal it from the streets. In the late 1990s amateurs across the United Ststes and the world continued to create innovative hip hop sounds, generating a culture far larger than that reflected by the recording industry. "Famous" rap became famous by virtue of mainstream listeners and media, while fresher sounds often remained local and undiscovered. Such new rap continues to prosper as a living art, always outdistancing its commercialized, pop-chart predecessors.

Latin America and the Caribbean

Rastafarians,

members of a social movement established in Jamaica around 1930 that combines elements of religious prophecy, specifically the idea of a black God and Messiah; the Pan-Africanist philosophy of Marcus Garvey; the ideas of Black Power Movement leader Walter Rodney; and the defiance of reggae music.

Religion has been the principal form of resistance in Jamaica since colonial times. As scholar of Rastafarianism Barry Chevannes affirms: "Whether resistance through the use of force, or resistance through symbolic forms such as language, folk-tales and proverbs . . . religion was the main driving force among the Jamaican peasants." During the early twentieth century resistance in Jamaica reached its pinnacle with the birth of Rastafarianism—as much an Afrocentric world-view and form of black nationalism as it was a new religion, inspired by the independent, anti-colonial Christian tradition of the Ethiopian Orthodox Church. As Horace Campell notes, "Rastafari culture combines the histories of the children of slaves in different societies. Within it are both the negative and the positive—the idealist and the ideological—responses of an exploited and racially humiliated people."

North America

Rawls, Louis Allen (Lou)

(b. December 1, 1936, Chicago, Ill.), African American fusion singer and a founder of the Lou Rawls Parade of Stars in support of the United Negro College Fund.

Raised by his grandmother on the South Side of Chicago, Lou Rawls began singing in his church choir at age seven. In the mid-1950s Rawls and friend Sam Cooke joined with two other vocalists and formed the Pilgrim Travelers, a gospel group. After the group disbanded in 1959, Rawls sang in blues clubs and cafes around Los Angeles. At one show a producer from Capitol Records asked him to submit an audition tape. His debut album, *Stormy Monday* (1962), was soon released. Lou Rawls Live followed in 1966, achieving gold status on the strength of its single, *"Love is a Hurtin' Thing,"* which reached Number One on the rhythm-and-blues charts. In 1967 Rawls won his first Grammy Award for Best Male R&B Vocals for the song *"Dead End Street."* He won again in 1971 for *"A Natural Man."* Rawls's success continued with his first platinum album, *All Things in Time* (1977), and the Grammy Award-winning album *Unmistakably Lou* (1977).

In 1979 Rawls and Anheuser-Busch founded the Lou Rawls Parade of Stars, an annual telethon for the United Negro College Fund (UNCF). By 1998 Rawls's telethon had raised an estimated $175 million for the UNCF and had featured such entertainers as Bill Cosby, Whoopi Goldberg, and Stevie Wonder. Rawls released two albums in 1993, *Portrait of the Blues* and *Christmas Is The Time*. He has also acted in television and film, from the late 1950s show *77 Sunset Strip* to the 1995 film *Leaving Las Vegas*.

North America

Redding, Otis

(b. September 9, 1941, Dawson, Ga.; d. December 10, 1967, Madison, Wis.), African American singer and songwriter who played a key role in the rise of soul music during the 1960s, but who attained his greatest success only after his premature death.

Otis Redding's life is the stuff of pop-music tragedy. From an early age he clearly had musical talent, first as a drummer, then as a singer. But his family was poor, and he had to endure a series of odd jobs and struggle to make ends meet before he got his big break in 1963, an opportunity to record for Memphis, Tennessee-based Stax Records. His career unfolded in a steep upward arc, culminating with a triumphant performance at the 1967 Monterey Pop Festival. Then—in an instant—it was over. Redding died in

December of that year when his chartered plane crashed near Madison, Wisconsin. Since his death Redding has been hailed as perhaps the quintessential male soul singer. But fame proved far more elusive during his lifetime.

Redding was born to a poor Georgia family and learned to play drums in school. On Sundays he played behind the various gospel groups that performed on local radio station WIBB. In 1957 he dropped out of high school in order to support his family, taking a variety of menial jobs and occasional gigs as a musician. He began to concentrate on his singing and entered a number of local amateur contests. Redding's early singing style was in the tradition of such rock 'n' roll shouters as Little Richard. In 1961 he made his recording debut, on a small Macon, Georgia, label.

But his big break did not come until two years later, when he was working in the band of guitarist Johnny Jenkins—and serving as the band's chauffeur. During a recording session at Stax Records he had the chance to record a featured vocal, the ballad "These Arms of Mine," which became a rhythm and blues (R&B) hit and earned Redding a Stax recording contract. Redding's vocals matured from his earlier shouting style to one that conveyed the emotion behind his lyrics by means of an expressive, hoarse singing voice that was grounded in gospel sonorities.

To black listeners, Redding was one of the definitive examples of the Memphis Soul sound. His live performances were legendary for their intensity and emotional fervor. During 1965 and 1966 Redding scored several R&B hits—including "Mr. Pitiful," "I've Been Loving You Too Long," a version of the Rolling Stones's hit "(I Can't Get No) Satisfaction," and his now-famous rendition of "Try a Little Tenderness"—but none "crossed over" to the white popular-music charts. According to Norm N. Nite's Rock On Almanac (1989), Redding only appeared on the American pop charts once in his lifetime—in October 1966, with his now little-remembered recording "Fa-Fa-Fa-Fa-Fa (Sad Song)."

In 1967, however, Redding's incandescent appearance at the Monterey Pop Festival put him on a trajectory for pop-music stardom. His musical promise is evident in many of his compositions—including "Respect," which became a much bigger hit in the hands of Aretha Franklin, and "(Sittin' on) The Dock of the Bay," which he recorded just three days before his death at age 26. Four members of the Bar-Kays, Redding's backup band, also died in the crash. With the posthumous release of "(Sittin' on) The Dock of the Bay," Redding charted his first Number One pop single.

Reggae,

a style of music that originated in the musically diverse and politically charged climate of Jamaica during the late 1960s.

Reggae combined the Zionistic beliefs of Rastafarians with loping rhythms and rich melodic textures. Reggae's freshness appealed to both casual listeners and dedicated ideologues worldwide, generating a fan base that included Indonesians and Moroccans, Parisians and Brazilians, Irish schoolchildren and American teens. Michael Manley, former Prime Minister of Jamaica, favored a political explanation of reggae's appeal: "Among other things, reggae is the spontaneous sound of a local revolutionary impulse. But revolution is a universal category. It is this, possibly, which sets reggae apart, even to the international ear."

Since the "discovery" of Jamaica by Christopher Columbus in 1494, a range of foreign influences—African, European, and American—have defined the culture and ethnic composition of the island. Reggae's forefathers spoke in numerous musical dialects, including Caribbean calypso, English balladic form, and African rhythms. While Jamaica's history led to reggae's musical synthesis, it also provided reggae with its content: the new music often protested the colonialism and exploitation that characterized the last 500 years of the island's history.

Reggae grew most directly from the rhythm and blues (R&B) music of the United States. In the 1950s Jamaicans often listened to R&B songs that were broadcast from Miami, Florida. Local musicians soon covered songs by acts such as Fats Domino and Louis Jordan and wrote new tunes in a similar style. The fusion of R&B with Jamaican music, or *mento*, yielded a new form called *ska*. Jamaican promoters such as Duke Reid and Clement Dodd recorded local acts, broadcasting ska over large sound systems at outdoor

Rastafarian bands like this one represent far more than the reggae music well known to many non-Jamaicans. Rastafarianism blends religious, political, and social philosophies to express opposition to the historic degradation of Africans in the Caribbean and worldwide.
CORBIS/Daniel Lainé

dance parties. Unlike R&B, which emphasized the first and third beats of a measure, ska hit the second and fourth, or "back" beats. In the early 1960s ska evolved into *rocksteady*, a slower, more bass-driven form.

The apocalyptic vision of Rastafarians appealed to disillusioned immigrants, who had not found the bounty they expected in Kingston. Rural newcomers adopted the religion; the religion, in turn, adopted rocksteady as a voice. Since many of the rural immigrants introduced African musical traditions that had survived in the countryside—and since rocksteady, like ska, invited musical experimentation—reggae soon emerged. The importation of new recording technology from England as well as increased overcrowding in the ghettoes of Kingston also contributed to the synthesis of reggae. In 1968 a band called Toots and the Maytals recorded *"Do the Reggay,"* giving name to the emerging style.

Reggae slowed rocksteady as rocksteady had slowed ska. The languorous new form included a more robust and driving bass sound that gave the drummer freedom to "play around the beat." In reggae, pianists and guitarists often emphasized beats in unison, producing sparser melodies but richer tones and rhythms. And in reggae the lyrical message had changed. Rocksteady's romantic lyrics, which often derived from local proverbs, gave way to frontal descriptions of ghetto life and biting indictments of economic and political oppression. Reggae retained some of rocksteady's romance, however. In addition to singing about street toughs or "rude boys," reggae artists described Rastafarian religious rapture and earthly despair in a manner analogous to American blues and spirituals.

Jamaican disc jockeys quickly adopted the new music, blasting local recordings over impressive sound systems at outdoor dances. By separating parts of the recorded mix, adding echo effects, and speaking or "toasting" along with the music, DJs assumed an active role in the development of reggae's sound. Toasting became a reggae convention that pointed toward the advent of rap in the United States.

In the 1970s reggae garnered international attention, largely due to the stirring riffs, powerful lyrics, and riveting performances of Bob Marley and the Wailers. In the eyes of many Marley became emblematic of reggae and its Rastafarian influences. A 1972 film about the reggae lifestyle, *The Harder They Come*, added to reggae's popularity. *The Harder They Come* starred musician Jimmy Cliff as an outlaw and pop star and featured a driving reggae soundtrack. The film became a mainstay of bohemian movie theaters in the United States, adding vibrant visuals to the captivating aural picture that Bob Marley created through his music.

Like rock 'n' roll and rap, reggae was soon appropriated by white musicians and adored by white fans. In the mid-1970s its influence appeared in the songs of Paul Simon and Eric Clapton; in the late 1970s and early 1980s it flavored new wave and punk. Rastafarianism's apocalyptic ideology attracted punk rockers, who adopted the rhythmic emphasis of ska-based music in many of their frenzied compositions.

Meanwhile, African American fans of reggae—many of whom came from the West Indies themselves—took the music in other directions. DJs toasted faster and faster until the resulting "dancehall" reggae seemed an analog of rap. Reggae fans soon globalized a provincial sound, and in the 1980s and 1990s the international music of "world beat" followed the formula of reggae's wide success.

Since the genesis of reggae was grounded so thoroughly in the Rastafarian movement—and since its portrayal of alienation captivated white Americans in the Nixon era—the music's relevance lessened with the passing of time. While reggae continues to influence the vocabulary of other musical styles, its politico-religious aspect, as epitomized by Bob Marley, has become a historical—rather than living—form. Many fans, however, celebrate this history and laud the staying power of reggae's message. Writers Steven Davis and Peter Simon proclaim: "Reggae is a philosophy that heals. The mini-trance produced by good roots reggae is Jamaican psychic hygiene for our apocalyptic era."

North America

Rhythm and Blues,

an African American musical style developed after World War II that both reflected the growing confidence of urban African Americans and introduced a greater emotional depth to American popular music.

Rhythm and blues (R&B) is the general term for African American popular music since World War II. R&B melded earlier musical styles of blues, jazz, boogie woogie, and gospel music. It matured in the late 1940s and between 1954 and 1960 broke through racial barriers and achieved unprecedented visibility in white-oriented popular music. In launching R&B, however, African Americans lost control over their own musical creation as white performers backed by major record companies and playing watered-down versions of R&B effectively hijacked the form.

R&B thus reflects complex relationships between the races, as well as the constraints placed on black cultural expression. Yet despite these constraints, R&B transformed American popular culture. It challenged the vapidity of white pop music, and its propulsive beat and sexual overtones catalyzed rock 'n' roll. Most significant, however, R&B expressed the pride and vitality of a new urban black culture that emerged as a product of the Great Migration out of the rural South.

The Musical Sources of R&B

R&B developed out of various earlier styles of black music, especially blues, jazz, and gospel and harmony singing. Chicago blues, epitomized by the searing electric guitar of Muddy Waters and the raspy, acid-etched singing of Howlin' Wolf, emerged almost simultaneously with R&B and was a major component of the R&B sound. Southwestern blues shouters such as Big Joe Turner were also important. The driving, eight-to-the-bar rhythm of boogie woogie also influenced many piano players, including Amos Mil-

burn and Little Richard, and provided the underlying rhythm that characterized much R&B.

Jazz contributed to R&B through jump bands like Louis Jordan and His
Tympany Five. Jordan's rhythmic approach, using a heavy backbeat that
placed the stress on the second and fourth beats of each measure, was particularly important. R&B's gruff, blustery tenor saxophones drew inspiration
from jazz players Illinois Jacquet and Arnett Cobb. Indeed, many jazz musicians played on R&B recording sessions or toured in R&B bands, as did John
Coltrane and Clifford Brown.

Harmony singing contributed the last key ingredient in R&B. African
Americans have a tradition of a cappella group singing that reaches back at
least to the ragtime quartets of the late nineteenth century. Many R&B
vocal groups began by modeling themselves on such popular singing groups
of the 1930s as the Mills Brothers and especially the Ink Spots. Even more
important was the influence of gospel music. Gospel quartets, from the
jazzed-up harmonies of the Golden Gate Quartet to the more soulful
approach of the Soul Stirrers and the Dixie Hummingbirds, gained popularity in the 1930s and 1940s and offered encouragement to many later
R&B singers.

An equally strong influence came out of the nondenominational, sanctified churches with their fervent and freewheeling vocal approach. This style
of singing uses complex improvised embellishment (*melisma*), including
dips, slides, and blue notes, as seen in the singing of Clyde McPhatter, Jerry
Butler, and Otis Redding. But the greatest exemplar of the secularized
gospel sound is the music of pianist and singer Ray Charles.

R&B and Rock 'n' Roll

R&B was a music of transgression, challenging the boundaries of segregation. In the mid-1950s many black R&B performers adopted a harder beat
and ascended the pop charts as increasing numbers of white teenagers discovered the more visceral R&B sound. Many first heard this music through
the broadcasts of black-format radio stations like Memphis's WDIA or the
rare white R&B DJs such as Alan Freed. Historian Robert Pruter noted that
package tours of leading R&B acts were also "instrumental in helping break
rhythm and blues into the white market as rock 'n' roll music." In 1952
Freed began hosting racially integrated R&B concerts, and in Los Angeles
concerts produced by R&B performer Johnny Otis brought together blacks,
whites, and Mexican Americans.

Older whites responded by condemning R&B, allegedly on musical
grounds, but also because it violated racial boundaries. Some blacks, especially those who identified with middle-class values, criticized the music
because it was rough and did not project what they considered to be a suitable image of the race. In 1953 the entertainment magazine Variety concluded that "100 percent rhythm and blues platters sell only in the colored
market, although diluted interpretations have been seeping into the pop
field with increasing frequency."

In 1954, however, Nat King Cole found his crossover success challenged by such rowdy R&B acts as Ruth Brown, Ray Charles, B. B. King, Big Joe Turner, Muddy Waters, the Clovers, and Hank Ballard and the Midnighters. In the following year Chuck Berry, Little Richard, Etta James, and Bo Diddley all made their recording debuts. The mid-1950s were also the golden era of R&B vocal groups. Some, like the Clovers, Hank Ballard and the Midnighters, and the Robins (which gave rise to the Coasters), took a raucous and bluesy approach. Other groups—including the Moonglows, the Harptones, the Orioles, and the Flamingos—emphasized complex voicings and greater interplay between the lead singer and the rest of the group, in a style that the *Chicago Defender*, an African American newspaper, labeled "doo wop."

For the first time, R&B performers began charting songs among the year's Top Ten. Such successful releases including the following:

1956—The Platters, *"My Prayer"*

1957—Sam Cooke, *"You Send Me"*

1959—Wilbert Harrison, *"Kansas City"*; The Platters, *"Smoke Gets in Your Eyes"*; Lloyd Price, *"Stagger Lee"*

1960—The Drifters, *"Save the Last Dance for Me"*; Chubby Checker, *"The Twist"*

The major record companies responded by turning to "covers," recordings made by white groups with the intention of preempting the hit songs of black performers.

Since the major labels had far greater resources behind their versions, covers often crowded out the black originals. For example, the hit songs of two black groups—*"Sh-Boom"* (1954), a novelty number by the Chords, and *"A Story Untold"* (1955), a ballad by the Nutmegs—were successfully covered by Mercury's slick white group, the Crewcuts. On the other hand, the McGuire Sisters' cover of the Moonglows' *"Sincerely"* (1954) could not keep the original out of the Top Twenty. In the mid-1950s Elvis Presley launched his career through covers of R&B hits like Roy Brown's *"Good Rockin' Tonight"* (1948) and Big Mama Thornton's *"Hound Dog"* (1953).

The End of the R&B Era

By the early 1960s the R&B era was over. Indeed, on November 30, 1963, *Billboard* stopped publishing a separate R&B chart because the music had effectively been absorbed into the pop music mainstream. African American performers either adapted to fit prevailing white tastes or else they created new musical forms that were more expressly grounded in black culture. In the 1960s these contrasting approaches were exemplified in Motown's smooth pop stylings versus the harder edge of soul music, and during the 1970s in the wide appeal of disco versus funk music's largely black audience.

Although in later years *Billboard* reintroduced an R&B chart, it has generally served as a residual category for black music that is not rap, reggae, or blues—in a sense, black middle-of-the-road. In its golden age, however,

R&B was by no means middle-of-the-road. It broke down racial barriers that had long divided American music, furthering a process of cross-fertilization that reaches from the Fisk Jubilee Singers, through jazz artists like Louis Armstrong, Cab Calloway, and Duke Ellington, up to the present. In its heyday R&B offered a high-spirited affirmation of black life. Most of all, it was the musical voice of a generation of African Americans who would no longer tolerate second-class citizenship or balcony-seat tickets to the American dream.

North America

Richards, Lloyd George

(b. June 29, 1919, Toronto, Ontario), Canadian theater director and educator who directed the award-winning play A Raisin in the Sun.

Lloyd Richards was born in Canada to Jamaican immigrants Albert and Rose Richards. His father died when he was young and the family moved to Detroit, Michigan. Richards graduated from Wayne State University in 1943 and went on to serve in the United States Air Force as a pilot during World War II. After the war he returned to Detroit, where he began working in theater and radio drama. Richards moved to New York City in the 1950s and studied with Paul Mann, a teacher of the Stanislavsky acting method.

Richards's first major directorial assignment was Lorraine Hansberry's *A Raisin in the Sun*, which won the 1959 New York Critics Circle Award. After this success he directed four other Broadway productions during the 1960s. Beginning in the mid-1960s Richards held positions at the New York University School of Arts, the Eugene O'Neill Theater Center, Hunter College, and the Yale School of Drama, where he was appointed dean in 1979. He retired from that position in 1991 and continued to write and direct.

Richards is also known for his collaborations with playwright August Wilson, starting with a 1982 production of *Ma Rainey's Black Bottom*. Richards directed all of Wilson's plays and received a Tony Award in 1986 for his direction of Wilson's *Fences*. The following year Richards received the Pioneer Award, the Frederick Douglass Award, and the Golden Plate Award for his accomplishments in drama.

North America

Riggs, Marlon Troy

(b. February 3, 1957, Fort Worth, Tex.; d. April 5, 1994, Oakland, Calif.), documentary filmmaker and educator who used video to oppose racism and homophobia.

Reflecting on the death of Marlon Riggs from acquired immune deficiency syndrome (AIDS), cultural theorist Kobena Mercer observed, "Independent cinema lost the voice and vision of an important artist at the very moment that he was coming into his own." At the time of his death Riggs was at work on *Black Is . . . . Black Ain't*. This feature-length film, completed by Riggs's collaborators in 1995, chronicled the variety of American identities seen as "black."

Riggs grew up in a military family, moving from Texas to Georgia to Germany before returning to the United States to attend Harvard University. As an undergraduate he began to explore connections between black and gay identities; his research culminated in a senior thesis on the treatment of male homosexuality in literature. After graduating magna cum laude in 1978, Riggs worked briefly at a Texas television station before moving to the San Francisco Bay Area. He received a master's degree from the Graduate School of Journalism at the University of California at Berkeley in 1981 and joined the Berkeley faculty six years later.

Ethnic Notions (1986), the first film Riggs wrote, directed, and produced, won an Emmy Award in 1988 for its investigation of racial stereotypes in American society. That same year Riggs began work on his most famous film, *Tongues Untied* (1989). A work that interweaves poetry, personal reflections, and scenes from the lives of black gay men, *Tongues Untied* challenged the marginalization of gayness in the black community. It also inspired outraged attacks from conservatives such as North Carolina senator Jesse Helms and religious fundamentalist Patrick Buchanan, who included footage from the film in his 1992 presidential campaign.

Despite deteriorating health, Riggs remained active as a lecturer, teacher, and filmmaker until his death. *Anthem* (1990) and *Non, Je Ne Regrette Rien/No Regret* (1991) continued the work of *Tongues Untied* in examining black gay men's experiences. *Color Adjustment* (1991), which earned him a Peabody Award, documented the representation of African Americans on television.

North America

Ringgold, Faith

(b. October 8, 1934, New York, N.Y.), African American artist who has spent her artistic career breaking boundaries and clearing spaces for African American creativity, especially that of women.

Born in 1934 and raised in Harlem, Faith Ringgold earned a B.A. in art and education in 1955 and an M.F.A. in 1959 at City College, New York. Dissatisfied with the traditional high art training that she received in New York and later in Europe, Ringgold reeducated herself by studying African art, reading the work of Black Arts Movement authors, and participating in the growing protest for a civil rights revolution in America. Ringgold's paintings from this period, *The Flag is Bleeding* (1967), *US Postage Stamp Commemorating the Advent of Black Power* (1967), and *Die* (1967), blend an African-inspired aesthetic of geometric shapes and flat, shadowless perspective with potent political and social protest.

Ringgold has been an outspoken critic of racial and gender prejudice in the art world. In the early 1970s she organized protests against the Whitney Museum of American Art and other major museums for excluding the works of blacks and women. In response to the museum world's exclusionary policies, Ringgold and other black women artists formed a collective and organized an exhibit of their own, whose title, *Where We At*, announced their visibility.

Ringgold's art focuses on black women and black women's issues. Diverse works—a mural in the Women's House of Detention in Riker's Island, New York (1971–1972) and a performance piece using soft cloth sculptures, *The Wake and Resurrection of the Bicentennial Negro* (1976)—focused on women's ability to heal and brought her work to a wider audience.

Since the 1970s Ringgold has documented her local community and national events in life-size soft sculptures, representing everyone from ordinary Harlem denizens to Rev. Martin Luther King Jr. and the young victims of the Atlanta child murders (1979–80). Ringgold's latest chosen medium, fabric, is traditionally associated with women.

Ringgold's expression of black women's experience is perhaps best captured in her "storyquilts." A combination of quilting and narrative text, quilts like *Who's Afraid of Aunt Jemima?* (1982) and the series *Women on a Bridge* (1988) tell stories of pain and survival in a medium that Ringgold finds essentially female and empowering. She transformed one of her quilts into a children's book, *Tar Beach*, that won the 1992 Caldecott Honor Book Award and the Coretta Scott King award.

North America

Robeson, Eslanda Cardozo Goode

(b. December 15, 1896, Washington, D.C.; d. December 13, 1965, New York, N.Y.), African American activist and writer who advocated African independence and managed the singing and acting career of her husband, Paul Robeson.

Eslanda Robeson's father died when she was six years old, and the family moved to New York City. In 1921 she married Paul Robeson. Eslanda ("Essie") Robeson received a B.S. in chemistry from Columbia University and, in 1945, a Ph.D. in anthropology from the Hartford Seminary Foundation. She co-founded the Council for African Affairs in 1941 and participated in many left-wing causes. Robeson was the author of two books: *Paul Robeson, Negro* (1930) and *African Journey* (1945).

North America

Robeson, Paul

(b. April 9, 1898, Princeton, N. J.; d. January 23, 1976, Philadelphia, Pa.), African American dramatic actor, singer of spirituals, civil rights activist, and political radical.

Paul Robeson was one of the most gifted men of this century. His resonant bass and commanding presence made him a world-renowned singer and actor and proved equally valuable when he spoke out against bigotry and injustice. By the 1930s Robeson was active in a wide range of causes, but his radicalism led to a long period of political harassment that culminated in his blacklisting during the McCarthy era. Although he resumed public performances in the late 1950s, this return to active life was brief. In the 1960s serious health problems sidelined him definitively.

Stage, Concert, and Film Career

While in law school Robeson had occasionally taken parts in amateur theatrical productions, leading in 1922 to his first professional roles—a lead in the short-lived Broadway play *Taboo* and as a replacement cast member in Eubie Blake and Noble Sissle's pioneering all-black musical, *Shuffle Along*. Robeson's career-making opportunity came when he was asked to join the Provincetown Players, an influential Greenwich Village theater company that included the playwright Eugene O'Neill among its three associate directors. In 1924 Robeson appeared in a revival of O'Neill's *The Emperor Jones* and premiered in the playwright's *All God's Chillun Got Wings*. In reviewing the latter, the American Mercury drama critic George Jean Nathan praised Robeson as "one of the most thoroughly eloquent, impressive, and convincing actors that I have looked at and listened to in almost twenty years of professional theater-going." Soon Robeson was offered other roles, most notably in a 1930 London production of *Othello* opposite Peggy Ashcroft; in a 1932 Broadway revival of Oscar Hammerstein II and Jerome Kern's musical, *Showboat*, which featured Robeson's dramatic rendition of "*Ol' Man River*"; and in a long-running, critically acclaimed 1943 production of *Othello* on Broadway.

Equally significant were Robeson's musical contributions. Robeson and his longtime pianist and arranger Lawrence Brown played a pivotal role in bringing spirituals into the classical music repertory. Robeson's 1925 recital at the Greenwich Village Theater was the first in which a black soloist sang an entire program of spirituals. The concert garnered superlative reviews, propelling Robeson into a new career as a concert singer and inspiring similar recitals by other black artists. Robeson also signed a recording contract with the Victor Talking Machine Company, which released his first recorded spirituals later that same year. Although Robeson would sing a wide range of material—including sentimental pop-

Singer, actor, and activist Paul Robeson played Othello in 1943 on Broadway. Here Robeson rehearses his part. *CORBIS/Hulton-Deutsch Collection*

ular tunes, work songs, political ballads, and folk music from many different lands—he made his mark as an interpreter of spirituals.

During the 1930s Robeson also emerged as a film star. His first role was in the black director Oscar Micheaux's *Body and Soul* (1925), but he was most active on the screen between 1933 and 1942, a period in which he was prominently featured in Hollywood versions of *The Emperor Jones* (1933) and *Show Boat* (1936), *Tales of Manhattan* (1942), and several British films. Robeson, however, was dissatisfied with his work in motion pictures. He came to believe that—with the exceptions of his roles in *Song of Freedom* (1936) and *The Proud Valley* (1940)—his characters reflected current racial stereotypes, or what Robeson derided as "Stepin Fetchit comics and savages with leopard skin and spear." Working in films like *Sanders of the River* (1935), which sang the praises of British imperialism, became particularly distasteful as Robeson discovered his African heritage.

The Final Years

Robeson fought his lonely battle at great personal cost. In 1955 he began to show the first clear signs of the emotional difficulties—probably bipolar disorder, a condition once known as manic-depression—that would eventually halt his public activities. It is ironic that he should pay so dearly for his alleged Communism. In truth, what lay at the heart of Robeson's political convictions was not Marxism so much as an empathy for African culture and an identification with common people, the poor, and the oppressed.

By the end of the decade the worst years of the cold war had passed, and Robeson's troubles began to ease. In 1958 he gave his first commercial concerts in several years, appearing in Chicago, Portland, and several California cities. He published *Here I Stand*, a trenchant autobiography written with Lloyd Brown. And a Supreme Court decision once again permitted him to travel abroad. The next few years were busy ones, with American concerts and recording sessions for Vanguard; concert tours of Europe, Australia, and New Zealand; visits to the Soviet Union; and in 1959 another London production of *Othello*. But on March 27, 1961, Robeson suffered a nervous breakdown and attempted suicide. For the rest of his life he would struggle with severe depression, and his public appearances would be extremely rare. Robeson dropped out of public awareness and was largely ignored by the leadership of the Civil Rights Movement, except for the militant young leaders of the Student Nonviolent Coordinating Committee (SNCC). At a gala celebration for his 67th birthday, Robeson was deeply moved when keynote speaker John Lewis, then the chairman of SNCC, proclaimed, "We of SNCC are Paul Robeson's spiritual children. We too have rejected gradualism and moderation." Yet there was more to Robeson than this. Beneath his militancy—and intertwined with it—was a profound compassion and a deep bond with Africa best seen in a passage he wrote in 1936: "I am a singer and an actor. I am primarily an artist. Had I been born in Africa, I would have belonged, I hope, to that family which sings and chants the glories and legends of the tribe. I would have liked in my mature years to have been a wise elder, for I worship wisdom and knowledge of the ways of men."

Robeson's final public appearance was at a 1966 benefit dinner for SNCC.

Robinson, Bill ("Bojangles")

(b. May 25, 1878, Richmond, Va.; d. November 15, 1949, New York, N.Y.), African American vaudeville performer, tap dancer, and movie star, considered the most famous African American entertainer of the early twentieth century.

Bill "Bojangles" Robinson was born Luther Robinson, the son of Maxwell Robinson, a machinist, and Maria Robinson, a singer. Robinson and his brother Bill, whose name he would later appropriate, were orphaned when their parents died in 1885. Following this the brothers lived with their paternal grandmother, Bedilia Robinson, and Robinson worked as a bootblack and danced on street corners for money. He began to use the nickname "Bojangles," which was possibly derived from "jangle," a slang term for fighting, and supposedly invented the expression "Everything's copacetic," which meant "life is great." At age 12 Robinson ran away to Washington, D.C., where he worked as a street dancer and at a racetrack.

His first professional job came in 1892 as a member of the "pickaninny" chorus—a group of African American children who sang backup for the main performer—in the revue *The South Before the War*. After a two-year stint in the army, Robinson moved to New York in 1900, where he emerged as one of the first black stars of vaudeville. At the time black roles normally were performed by whites in blackface, but from 1902 to 1914 Robinson toured the vaudeville circuit as the partner of the black comedian George W. Cooper. Cooper played the straight man to Robinson's clown. Although theirs was not a dance team, when the duo broke up Robinson persuaded his manager, Marty Forkins, to book him performances as a solo dancer. In 1917 Robinson performed for American serviceman ordered to Europe to fight in World War I, and in 1918 he premiered at New York's legendary Palace Theater, where he first performed his trademark "stair dance," a rapid tap dance up and down a five-step staircase, to a standing ovation. Robinson was one of the first black performers to star at the Palace, where audiences were amazed by his dancing. His footwork was complex, graceful, and often improvised. Often bedecked in tails and a top hat tilted to one side, Robinson charmed audiences with his irresistible smile. His career as a vaudeville star culminated in a European tour in 1926.

Robinson became one of the first black Broadway stars, debuting as the lead in the all-black revue Blackbirds of 1928. Newspaper reviews hailed him as the best tap dancer ever. Robinson's other notable Broadway starring appearances include *Brown Buddies* (1930), *Blackbirds of 1933*, *The Hot Mikado* (1939), *All in Fun* (1940), and *Memphis Bound* (1945). Because of his Broadway success, Robinson was crowned the honorary "Mayor of Harlem" in 1933.

Robinson began to make Hollywood films in the 1930s, at a time when the industry offered few opportunities to blacks. His films include *Dixiana* (1930), *Harlem is Heaven* (1933), and *Hooray for Love* (1935). His most popular films, however, were the four he made with white child star Shirley Temple: *The Littlest Colonel* (1935), *The Littlest Rebel* (1935), *Just Around the Corner* (1938), and *Rebecca of Sunnybrook Farm* (1938).

Throughout his career Robinson donated money and benefit performances to many causes and to organizations, including the National Association for the Advancement of Colored People. In recognition for his achievements and philanthropy, the Negro Actors Guild named Robinson its honorary president in 1937.

During his lifetime Robinson was married three times. In 1907 he married Lena Chase; that relationship ended in 1922. He next married his business manager Fannie Clay, divorcing her in 1943. He married the dancer Elaine Paines in 1944.

Robinson performed ceaselessly, keeping a hectic dancing schedule well into his 60s. His show business career spanned 50 years. He died of a heart attack backstage, after performing with Milton Berle, a month before his 70th birthday. Robinson is remembered as one of the greatest entertainers of our century. Dance historian Rusty E. Frank wrote of him, "They said that Bill Robinson could do the easiest routine in the world and get away with it because of his charm and charisma. They said that he could drive a dancer crazy with the complexity of a step that looked so easy. But when tap dancers talk about Bill Robinson, they talk about the greatest tap dancer of all time."

North America

Robinson, William ("Smokey")

(b. 1940?, Detroit, Mich.), popular rhythm and blues (R&B) singer and songwriter known for his romantic lyrics and his passionate, high-reaching voice. A leading member of the Motown vocal group the Miracles from 1958 to 1971, Robinson was one of the most influential singers and songwriters in popular music during the 1960s and 1970s.

William "Smokey" Robinson was born in Detroit, Michigan. At age 18, he formed a vocal group, which later became known as the Miracles, with high school friends Ronnie White, Pete Moore, Bobby Rogers, and Rogers's sister Claudette, whom Robinson later married. The group so impressed Motown owner Berry Gordy that he signed them to a recording contract in 1960.

The Miracles' first hit record was "*Shop Around*" (1961), an R&B song recorded for Tamla, one of the Motown Record Company labels. It was a phenomenal success, reaching Number One on the *Billboard* magazine R&B

charts and Number Two on the *Billboard* pop music charts, and helping to launch Gordy's fledgling music studio. In the decade that followed the Miracles produced a highly popular body of work, including the song "*You Really Got a Hold on Me*" (1962); hard-edged dance tunes such as "*Mickey's Monkey*" (1963) and "*Going to Go-Go*" (1965); and the dreamy songs "*More Love*" (1967) and "*I Second That Emotion*" (1967). Perhaps even more enduring are the ballads "*Ooo Baby Baby*" (1965), "*The Tracks of My Tears*" (1965), and "*Baby, Baby Don't Cry*" (1969). In 1967 the group became known as Smokey Robinson and the Miracles.

During the 1960s Robinson also wrote and produced classics for other Motown artists. "*My Girl*" was written for the vocal group the Temptations. Robinson's "*You Beat Me to the Punch*" (1962) and "*My Guy*" (1964) were written for soul singer Mary Wells, and he wrote "*Ain't That Peculiar*" (1965) for soul singer Marvin Gaye. Robinson's songwriting skills were admired by many popular musicians, including folk-rock artist Bob Dylan. Robinson's songs have endured, and many were later recorded by pop artists, including British rock group the Beatles, soul singers Aretha Franklin and Luther Vandross, and popular singers Linda Ronstadt and Kim Carnes.

Robinson left the Miracles in 1972 to pursue a solo music career. He released the highly regarded album *Quiet Storm* in 1975. In the 1980s Robinson continued to release a stream of dreamy romantic songs, including "*Cruisin'*" (1979), written with longtime collaborator and guitarist Marv Tarplin. Robinson's other notable hits include "*Being with You*" (1981) and "*Just to See Her*" (1987; Grammy Award, 1988). Robinson won a 1990 Grammy Legends Award. He was inducted into the Rock and Roll Hall of Fame in 1987.

North America

Rosewood Case,

one of the worst race riots in American history, in which hundreds of angry whites killed an undetermined number of blacks and burned down their entire Florida community.

In 1922 Rosewood, Florida, was a small, predominantly black town. During the winter of 1922 two events in the vicinity of Rosewood aggravated local race relations: the murder of a white schoolteacher in nearby Perry, which led to the murder of three blacks, and a Ku Klux Klan rally in Gainesville on New Year's Eve.

On New Year's Day of 1923, Fannie Taylor, a young white woman living in Sumner, claimed that a black man sexually assaulted her in her home. A small group of whites began searching for a recently escaped black convict named Jesse Hunter, whom they believed to be responsible. They incarcerated one suspected accomplice, Aaron Carrier, and lynched another, Sam Carter. The men then targeted Aaron's cousin Sylvester Carrier, a fur trapper and private music instructor who was rumored to be harboring Jesse Hunter.

A group of 20 to 30 white men came to Sylvester Carrier's house to confront him. They shot his dog, and when his mother, Sarah, stepped outside to talk with the men, they shot her. Carrier killed two men and wounded four in the shootout that ensued. After the men left, the women and children, who prior to this had gathered in Carrier's house for protection, fled to the swamp where the majority of Rosewood's residents had already sought refuge.

The white men returned to Carrier's house the following evening. After a brief shootout they entered the house, found the bodies of Sarah Carrier and a black man whom they believed to be Sylvester Carrier, and set the residence on fire. The men then proceeded on a rampage through Rosewood, torching other buildings and slaughtering animals. They were joined by a mob of approximately 200 whites who converged on Rosewood after finding out that a black man had killed two whites.

That night two local white train conductors, John and William Bryce, who knew all of Rosewood's residents, picked up the black women and children and took them to Gainesville. John Wright, a white general-store owner who hid a number of black women and children in his home during the riot, planned and helped carry out this evacuation effort. The African Americans who escaped by foot headed for Gainesville or for other cities in the northern United States.

By the end of the weekend all of Rosewood, except the Wright house and general store, was leveled. Although the state of Florida claimed that only eight people died in the Rosewood riot—two whites and six blacks—survivors' testimonies suggest that more African Americans perished. No one was charged with the Rosewood murders. After the riot the town was deserted, and even blacks living in surrounding communities moved out.

Though the Rosewood riot received national coverage in the *New York Times* and *Washington Post* as it unfolded, it was neglected by historians. Survivors of Rosewood did not come forward to tell their stories because of the shame they felt for having been connected with the riot and their fear of being persecuted or killed. In 1993 the Florida Department of Law Enforcement conducted an investigation into the case, which led to the drafting of a bill to compensate the survivors of the massacre.

After an extended debate and several hearings, the Rosewood Bill, which awarded $150,000 to each of the riot's nine eligible black survivors, was passed in April 1994. In spite of the state's financial compensation, the survivors remained frightened. When asked if he would go back to Rosewood, survivor Wilson Hall said, "No, . . . They still don't want me down there."

The director John Singleton, best known for his film *Boyz 'N the Hood*, released a fictionalized account of the massacre based on survivors' testimony, called *Rosewood*, in 1997.

North America

Ross, Diana

(b. March 26, 1944, Detroit, Mich.), African American singer and actress; lead vocalist of the Supremes, whose songs topped the *Billboard* charts throughout the 1960s, 1970s, and 1980s.

Diana Ross was born Diane Ross, the second of six children, to Fred and Ernestine Ross. She grew up in a poor district of Detroit, Michigan. As a child Ross sang with her siblings and parents in the choir at the Olivet Baptist Church and collaborated with neighborhood friends on renditions of the most popular songs of the day. She showcased her talent by performing on street corners, in school talent shows, and at dances. In 1959, while still in high school, Ross joined Mary Wilson, Florence Ballard, and Betty McGlown in a vocal group called the Primettes, the "sister act" for a group of male singers that later became the Temptations. In 1961, after both McGlown and her replacement Barbara Martin left the group, the Primettes signed a recording contract with Motown Records as a trio and changed their name to the Supremes.

The Supremes did not enjoy immediate recognition and success. Initially they sang as backup vocalists or served as handclappers for other Motown acts, including Mary Wells, Marvin Gaye, and the Shirelles. After three years as a group, the Supremes achieved their first Number-One hit in July 1964 with *"Where Did Our Love Go,"* their ninth release. A string of Number-One recordings followed: *"Baby Love"* (1964), *"Come See About Me"* (1964), *"Stop! In the Name of Love"* (1965), and *"Back in My Arms Again"* (1965). In 1967 Cindy Birdsong replaced Florence Ballard, and the group changed its name to Diana Ross and the Supremes. In 1970 Ross left the Supremes to pursue a solo career in singing and acting, but not before issuing one more group hit, *"Someday We'll Be Together."* A series of female singers assumed the lead vocals of the Supremes before the group's breakup in 1977.

Ross launched her career as a soloist with the Number-One single *"Ain't No Mountain High Enough"* (1970). She then turned her attention to film. In 1972 Ross's portrayal of Billie Holiday in *Lady Sings the Blues,* in which the actress costarred with Billy Dee Williams, earned her an Academy Award nomination. Ross starred in *Mahogany* (1975), singing the hit theme song, *"Do You Know Where You're Going To?,"* and later in *The Wiz* (1978). After recording two disco sensations, *"Love Hangover"* (1976) and *"Upside Down"* (1980), Ross collaborated with Lionel Richie on the ballad *"Endless Love"* (1981). Ross left Motown Records in 1981 but returned in 1989 to work as a recording artist, an equity partner, and a director of the company.

The Supremes were inducted into the Rock and Roll Hall of Fame in 1988, confirming their status as the most famous black performing group and the most famous female recording group in American music history. As the lead vocalist for the Supremes, Ross had 12 Number-One singles and sold more than 50 million records. Between 1970 and 1984 she recorded 31 albums and more than 50 singles, 6 of which reached the top spot on the *Billboard* chart. Ross is considered to be one of the most influential and versatile recording artists of the twentieth century.

North America

Rowan, Carl Thomas

(b. August 11, 1925, Ravenscroft, Tenn.), African American journalist, head of the United States Information Agency (USIA).

A veteran officer of the then segregated U.S. Navy, Carl Rowan entered into his career as a journalist at the white-owned newspaper *Minneapolis Tribune*. One of the first African American reporters for a large urban daily newspaper, Rowan captured the racial struggles of the 1950s with a series on discrimination in the South and articles on the U.S. Supreme Court school desegregation case *Brown v. Board of Education*. He entered government in 1961 as Deputy Assistant Secretary of State to President John F. Kennedy and was appointed ambassador to Finland in 1963, making him one of the first African Americans to serve in a predominantly white nation. As head of the USIA in 1963, he reached the highest executive branch position held thus far by an African American. He has remained visible with a nationally syndicated column, as well as radio and television broadcasts. Rowan's writings tend to espouse mainstream liberal politics, and he has drawn the fire of both conservatives and black nationalists.

North America

Run-DMC,

an early and influential rap music group from New York City. The group was known during the 1980s for its aggressive "raps" (spoken rhymes) on top of strong beats. Run-DMC distinguished its sound by incorporating elements of rock music, specifically heavy-metal guitar, which helped popularize black rap among many white listeners. By bringing the hip hop street look to the stage, Run-DMC changed the image of rap, wearing black leather in winter, athletic warm-up suits in summer, and always wearing their signature Adidas sneakers. The first rap group to be broadcast regularly on Music Television (MTV), Run-DMC in 1985 became the first rap group to appear on the television program *American Bandstand*, hosted by media personality Dick Clark.

Run-DMC was formed in 1983 by three friends from New York City's borough of Queens. Rapper Joseph "Run" Simmons recorded as a solo artist in 1982 for his older brother, rap producer Russell "Rush" Simmons, before teaming with rapper Darryl "D.M.C." McDaniels to record two minor singles. The two then brought in disc jockey (DJ) Jason "Jam Master Jay" Mizell, and the trio soon became known as Run-DMC. The group released its first album in 1984, *Run-D.M.C.* On the strength of one song, "*Sucker*

M.C.'s," the album became the best-selling rap album to that time. The album gained attention for its tough-sounding lyrics and its spare, clean sound; the group used only a drum machine and scratchy turntable noises for accompaniment. Another single from the album, "*Rock Box*," was one of the first rap pieces to include tracks of heavy-metal electric guitar, and was also distributed as a video.

In 1985 Run-DMC released its second album, *King of Rock*, and acted and performed in the motion picture *Krush Groove*, a fictionalized account of Run-DMC and the development of rap-music record label Def Jam. Also in 1985, a number of violent incidents at rap concerts caused the national media to focus on rap as a reflection of violence and drug abuse among young black males. Run-DMC and other rap groups found themselves caught between this negative image and the acceptance of rap by MTV and *American Bandstand*.

The group's third album, *Raising Hell* (1986), featured a remake of "*Walk This Way*," a song first performed by the hard-rock group Aerosmith in 1976. The remake, which included new performances by Aerosmith members Steven Tyler and Joe Perry, was a popular success and was hailed by critics as a breakthrough that masterfully fused white rock music with black rap. In 1988 the group starred in *Tougher Than Leather*, a film produced by Def Jam's Rick Rubin. Other albums from Run-DMC include *Back from Hell* (1990) and *Down with the King* (1993).

North America

RuPaul (Charles, RuPaul Andre)

(b. November 17, 1960, New Orleans, La.), African American singer, entertainer, actor, and the first openly gay cross-dresser to become a supermodel and mainstream celebrity.

Since the release of his debut album *Supermodel of the World* in 1992, RuPaul has become a nationally recognized celebrity. Although best known as a drag queen, he also enjoys surprising audiences by appearing as a man. "Drag queens are like the shamans of our society, reminding people of what's funny and what's a stereotype," he told *People Weekly* writer Tim Allis in 1993. "I feel very powerful when I'm in drag, and when I'm out of drag I observe our culture." RuPaul is 2 m (6 ft 7 in) tall (in heels). He is painfully aware of the contradictions of being a black man who wears a platinum wig and platform shoes. "When I'm dressed up as this goddess," he told Allis, "people trip over themselves to give me things. But as an African American male, I can walk into an elevator and have people clutch their handbags."

Born RuPaul Andre Charles, RuPaul grew up in San Diego, California, one of four children of Irving Charles, the operator of a beauty supply store, and Ernestine Charles, a college clerk. His parents divorced when he was six. At age 15 he moved with his sister Renetta to Atlanta, Georgia, where he studied at the Northside High School of the Performing Arts. "In school I was kind of alien to every group," he told Guy Trebay of the *New Yorker*. "I was perpetually an outsider . . . until the day I decided to get into drag." Inspired by images of Diana Ross, he began performing at Atlanta cabarets and comedy clubs in wigs and high heels. He also sang in various rock groups, including RuPaul and the U-Hauls.

In 1987 he moved to New York City, where he sang with the band Now Explosion, at the Pyramid, a popular East Village gay club. In 1991 he received a contract with Tommy Boy Records. Three songs from his debut album reached Number One on the *Billboard* chart, propelling RuPaul to national celebrity. Since then he has contributed to Elton John's *Duets* album, released a Christmas single, "*The Little Drummer Boy*," and recorded a second album, *Foxy Lady* (1996). In 1995 he won a contract with M.A.C. Cosmetics and was made co-chair of the company's acquired immune deficiency syndrome (AIDS) fund.

In 1996 RuPaul began hosting a television talk show, whose guests have included Dennis Rodman, Whoopi Goldberg, and Cher. He has appeared in numerous films, including Spike Lee's *Crooklyn* (1994) and Wayne Wang's *Blue in the Face* (1995).

North America

Rushing, Jimmy

(b. August 26, 1903, Oklahoma City, Okla.; d. June 8, 1972), African American jazz vocalist.

Jimmy Rushing was reared in a musical family and studied piano, violin, and voice from childhood. In 1927 he began his singing career with Walter Page's Blue Devils, moving to Bennie Moten's Kansas City Orchestra two years later. Rushing's career predated the microphone, and his rich and bellowing tenor voice carried over the sound of the band without mechanical amplification. Rushing performed as a vocalist with the Count Basie Orchestra from 1935 to 1950, producing such songs as "*Goin' to Chicago*," "*How Long, How Long*," and the self-descriptive "*Mr. Five by Five*."

North America

Russell, Nipsey

(b. October 13, 1923, Atlanta, Ga.), American comedian who was the first African American to appear as a host of a national television show.

Nipsey Russell began his career in 1948 when he moved to New York City to try his hand at stand-up comedy. Eschewing Black Vernacular English and racial references, Russell moved from Harlem nightclubs, like the Apollo Theater, Smalls Paradise, and the Baby Grand, to mainstream clubs and television appearances. He was one of the first African Americans to appear on talk shows and was a frequent guest of Jack Paar on *The Tonight Show*. He had a serial role on the television show *Car 54 Where Are You?*, and won critical acclaim as the Tin Man in the movie *The Wiz*.

North America

Russwurm, John Brown

(b. October 1, 1799, Port Antonio, Jamaica; d. June 9, 1851, Harper, Liberia), African American publisher of the first black newspaper in the United States, emigrationist, and Liberian government official.

Born John Brown to a Jamaican slave mother and a white American merchant father, he became John Russwurm when his stepmother demanded that his father acknowledge paternity by name. Sent to Quebec for schooling, Russwurm was taken by his father to Portland, Maine, in 1812. He attended Hebron Academy in Hebron, Maine, and graduated in 1826 from Bowdoin College, making Russwurm one of the first black graduates of an American college. In his graduation speech he advocated the resettlement of American blacks to Haiti.

Moving to New York City in 1827, Russwurm helped found *Freedom's Journal* with Samuel E. Cornish. It was the first black-owned and black-printed newspaper in the United States. The paper employed itinerant black abolitionists and urged an end to Southern slavery and Northern inequality. In February 1829 he stopped publishing the paper and accepted a position as the superintendent of education in Liberia. He left for Liberia having given up hope that African Americans would have any future equality or prosperity in the United States.

In Liberia, in addition to his government position, he edited the *Liberia Herald* and served as a Liberian agent, recruiting American blacks to return to Africa. Russwurm became the first black governor of the Maryland area of Liberia in 1836 and worked to enhance the country's economic and diplomatic position.

S

Salt 'n' Pepa,

the first female rap group to produce a platinum album.

Cheryl "Salt" James, Sandi "Pepa" Denton, and Dee Dee "Spinderella" Roper make up the female rap trio Salt 'n' Pepa. Since 1985 the group has released five award-winning albums (one gold, two platinum, and one triple platinum), and earned the honor of being the first female rap group to produce an album that sold more than 1 million copies. After more than 12 years in the male-dominated rap music industry, Salt 'n' Pepa have sold more than 4 million records and released eight singles that ranked in Billboard's Top 40, two of which climbed to the Number Three and Four positions on Billboard's Top Ten. In their fifth album, *Brand New*, Salt 'n' Pepa continue to blend thought-provoking lyrics with upbeat hip hop tempos.

Cheryl James and Sandi Denton first met in the mid-1980s when both were attending nursing school in Queens, New York. While working part-time at a department store, James and Denton met Hurby Azor, who had just finished composing a song titled "The Showstopper." Azor's song was a lyrical response to the 1985 hit "The Show," released by rappers Doug E. Fresh and Slick Rick. James and Denton performed "Showstopper" later that year.

Taking the name "Super Nature," James and Denton caught the eye of Next Plateau Records, which quickly signed them. After fans picked up on a line in "Showstopper" in which James and Denton refer to themselves as "the salt and pepa MCs," the duo became known as Salt 'n' Pepa. In 1986 the group's name was officially changed, just in time for the release of its second single, "I'll Take Your Man." That year the group also released its first album, Hot, Cool, and Vicious. Featuring such hits as "Tramp," "Beauty and the Beat," and "Push It," Hot, Cool, and Vicious was an instant success and sold more than 1 million copies, making Salt 'n' Pepa the first female rap group with a platinum album.

In 1987 the group replaced DJ Latoya Hanson with Dee Dee "Spin-derella" Roper. With Hurby Azor as its producer, Salt 'n' Pepa released its second album, *A Salt with a Deadly Pepa*. Filled with contemporary remixes of Isley Brothers classics, including "Twist and Shout" and "It's Your Thang," the album received a mixed reaction. It sold 500,000 copies before the group announced plans for another album.

In 1990 members of Salt 'n' Pepa took more control of the writing, composing, and production of their work and released *Blacks' Magic*. Hits such as "Independent" and "Expression" encouraged listeners not to follow the crowd and reminded young women to stand tall with pride. Their message and hard work were rewarded when the album went platinum. A single from the album, "Let's Talk About Sex," captured the attention of ABC News journalist Peter Jennings, who asked Salt 'n' Pepa to rewrite the song for a public service announcement about acquired immune deficiency syndrome (AIDS). The new song, titled "Let's Talk About AIDS," was released in 1992 and earned the group national acclaim.

A year later Salt 'n' Pepa delivered their fourth album, *Very Necessary*. With Top-Ten hits such as "Shoop" and "Whatta Man," the album went triple platinum. The single "None of Your Business" earned the group a Grammy Award in 1994 for Best Rap Vocal by a Group or Duo. At the height of their career, Salt 'n' Pepa have toured the world promoting female pride and social consciousness. They have won three MTV Video Music Awards, produced an all-female charity album called *Ain't Nuthin' But A She Thang*, and performed the song "Freedom" for the movie Panther. In 1995 Salt 'n' Pepa signed a multi-million-dollar contract with MCA Records and in 1997 they released their fifth album, *Brand New*. As leaders and innovators in the hip hop generation, they remain at the forefront of rap music.

Europe

Sancho, Ignatius

(b. 1729, slave ship; d. December 14, 1780, England), an educated African ex-slave in Britain whose published letters formed an early and important slave narrative.

Ignatius Sancho was born on a slave ship en route to the West Indies; both of his parents died during the journey, casualties of the Middle Passage. Never having lived in Africa, Sancho was in many ways a product of Western civilization. His letters, written between 1768 and 1780, and published post-humously in 1782, proved to the English public that an African could not only master the language and literature of England but become a discriminating reader and a discerning critic.

Upon arriving in Britain, Sancho was bought by three sisters in Greenwich who treated him poorly and denied him education. But the sisters' neighbors, the duke and duchess of Montague, were impressed by Sancho's curiosity about books and his quick mind and secretly lent him materials to read. In 1749, when the sisters threatened to sell him into American slavery, Sancho fled to the Montague household.

The duke and duchess died a few years later, leaving an inheritance to Sancho, who soon left Greenwich for the literary and artistic circles of London. There he wrote music and befriended musicians and artists, including the famous actor David Garrick. After a brief period of reckless living and gambling, Sancho returned to serve the new duke of Montague. But gout and a weight problem led him to retire in 1773, and he subsequently opened his own London grocery store, which became popular less for Sancho's produce than for his counsel. The duchess of Queensbury sought his help with her favored but troublemaking servant Julius Soubise. Other patrons included the artist Joseph Nollekens and the painter John Hamilton Mortimer, who consulted Sancho for his artistic sensibilities.

Sancho proved skillful in cultivating friendship and came to have many correspondents, including English novelist Laurence Sterne. Though Sancho praised Sterne's words against slavery, he wrote little on the subject himself, except to place it within the wider context of the greed for money and lust for power of the Christian East Indian traders. Sancho held a deep faith that the conditions blacks and the poor faced in this life would be resolved in "our next habitation," where, "there will be no care—love will possess our souls—and praise and harmony—and ever fresh rays of knowledge, wonder, and mutual commu-nication will be our employ." He advocated patience to one black correspondent, and advised him to "tread as cautiously as the strictest rectitude can guide ye—yet must you suffer from this—but armed with truth—honesty—and conscious integrity—you will be sure of the plaudit and countenance of the good." In this conviction, and in his words of affection for his West Indian wife, Anne, and their six children, Sancho's writing displays the sentimentalism of this era.

Although Sancho supported such liberal causes as a more equitable distribution of wealth, as a businessman, his interests lay in the proliferation of commerce, and, as a patriot, he denounced radicalism. Unlike black radicals such as Ottobah Cugoano or Robert Wedderburn, he preferred to use moral persuasion and his own example to convince the English people that Africans deserve equal treatment. Scholar Lloyd Brown explains that Sancho's background as a culturally assimilated outsider "subvert[ed] the standard images of the uncivilized Negro." Although he did not write anti-slavery appeals, Sancho's published letters testified to the humanity of Africans, thus strengthening the arguments of English abolitionists.

North America

Savoy Ballroom,

"Home of the Happy Feet," the most famous dance hall in Harlem, New York; birthplace of the dance style called the Lindy hop.

Inspired by the success of the segregated Roseland and Arcadia Ballrooms downtown on Broadway, white businessmen Moe Gale and Jay Faggen opened a dance hall for African Americans on Lenox Avenue in Harlem. The two white entrepreneurs bought an entire block of property and oversaw the construction of the palatial ballroom, which boasted marble staircases, thick carpets, two bandstands, a soda fountain, and room for 7000 patrons. Gale and Faggen hired Charles Buchanan, an African American, to manage the Savoy, which he did for the ballroom's 30 years of operation. Opening on Friday, March 12, 1926, to the music of Fletcher Henderson's Orchestra, the venture achieved instant success. The Savoy was the first elegant and spacious ballroom in a neighborhood of cramped and poorly ventilated clubs.

During the 1920s and 1930s the Savoy attracted crowds of Harlem residents—as well as white celebrities—to hear the biggest names in big-band music, including Duke Ellington and Louis Armstrong. Bennie Moten's band introduced Kansas City swing to New York at the Savoy in 1932, and the dance hall featured Chick Webb's Orchestra, backing Ella Fitzgerald, from 1932 to 1939. The Savoy also showcased its own house bands, like Fess Williams and his Royal Flush Orchestra, the Charleston Bearcats, and Al Cooper's Savoy Sultans. Arranger and saxophonist Edgar Sampson composed "Stompin' at the Savoy," in 1934, which became the ballroom's anthem.

White as well as black dancers at the Savoy pioneered the Lindy hop, a fast and free style of swing dancing that broke from conventions of popular dance. Since the crowd at the Savoy placed an unspoken premium on innovative dancing, every dancer tried something new. Each generation of Lindy hoppers kept hopping upward, and airborne movements in the 1930s superseded the "floor steps" of the 1920s.

While the harmonious integration of the Savoy was one of its exceptional qualities—black and white bands played, black and white dancers danced—the mingling also caused trouble. Provoked by the written testimony of a white police officer who claimed he had contracted syphilis from an African American prostitute, city officials harassed the Savoy's management and revoked its operating license in April 1943. The ballroom was closed until the following October, a suspension that reflected the heightened racial tension of Harlem during World War II.

After its reopening, the ballroom flourished once more, but when rock 'n' roll displaced big-band jazz as America's favorite music, the management found it difficult to book bands. The ballroom closed in 1958 and was demolished to make room for a housing project.

In its 32 years of operation, the Savoy Ballroom featured more than 250 bands and many of the biggest names in jazz. During those years the mixed audiences of working-class blacks and white celebrities danced together, peacefully if acrobatically.

North America
___

Schomburg Library,

the largest collection in the world of materials by and about people of African descent.

In 1925 the New York Public Library opened a Negro Division at its 135th Street branch, off Lenox Avenue in Harlem. The following year the

Carnegie Corporation purchased Arthur Schomburg's vast collection of African American books, manuscripts, and art, and donated it to the library. Schomburg, an Afro-Puerto Rican bibliophile who had amassed these works in an effort to prove the depth and richness of black history and culture, became the collection's curator in 1932, a post he held until his death in 1938. The collection has borne his name since 1940.

The collection grew rapidly, and today it houses more than 5 million items relating to the history and culture of the people of Africa and the African diapsora. In 1972 the New York Public Library transferred the collection from the neighborhood branch system to make it part of its research libraries. Now officially called the Schomburg Center for Research in Black Culture, the collection encompasses five divisions. The art and artifacts division collects objects from the seventeenth century to the present, including masks, weapons, statues, and rare items from such places as the Gold Coast of Africa (present-day Ghana). The general research and reference division possesses flyers, newspapers, magazine clippings, pamphlets, and monographs in English, French, Spanish, Portuguese, German, Russian, and all African languages, as well as indigenous languages such as Creole. The manuscripts, archives, and rare books division houses materials relating to history, literature, politics, and culture. The moving image and recorded sound division features the center's oral history and video documentation programs. The photographs and prints division holds the works of many famous photographers, including Gordon Parks Sr., Coreen Simpson, Aaron Siskind, James VanDerZee, and Carl Van Vechten.

Africa

Schreiner, Olive

(b. 1855, Wittebergen, South Africa; d. 1920, South Africa), South African novelist and political activist most famous for her *book The Story of an African Farm* (1883). Schreiner was a pioneer in her treatment of women in fiction and made many perceptive observations on the political future of South Africa, particularly the situation of blacks under apartheid.

Born Olive Emilie Albertina Schreiner in Wittebergen, South Africa (then Cape Colony), Schreiner had no formal education but was taught at home by her mother. She began writing two of her novels while supporting herself as a governess from 1874 to 1881, after which she went to England, hoping to study. *The Story of an African Farm* was published under the pseudonym Ralph Iron while Schreiner was in England. The story of a young girl growing up on a farm in the grasslands of southern Africa, trying to attain her independence in the face of a rigid, repressive society, the book met with immediate success. In England Schreiner came to be accepted in literary and political circles and became a supporter of women's rights. She was a friend of Cecil Rhodes, a British statesman and major proponent for British rule in southern Africa, but parted company with him for political reasons. Schreiner caused controversy in relation to

Rhodes's activities with her book *Trooper Halkett of Mashonaland* (1897), which criticized the way Rhodesia (which became Zimbabwe in 1980) was colonized. She returned to South Africa in 1899 and worked on behalf of the Boers, a local, white Afrikaner group that refused to live under British rule, during the Boer War (1899-1902). Schreiner also met and married a politician, Samuel Cronwright—he changed his name to Cronwright-Schreiner—and the two worked for a variety of political causes. In 1911 Schreiner wrote *Women and Labour*, a feminist novel criticizing the relations between men and women. Schreiner spent her last years in England, separated from her husband, but returned to South Africa in 1920 shortly before she died. Her other novels, both with feminist themes, are *From Man to Man* (1927) and *Undine* (1929). They were published posthumously.

North America

Schuyler, George S.

(b. 1895, Providence, R.I.; d. 1977, New York, N.Y.), African American journalist and novelist known for his conservative political views who was the first African American to be recognized primarily as a satirist.

George S. Schuyler was raised in Syracuse, New York. He had what he considered an ideal childhood in which he grew up believing that the United States, even with its considerable racial problems, was the best place for African Americans to live. He dropped out of high school to enlist in the United States Army and spent seven years in the service. During World War I he saw action in France and attained the rank of first lieutenant.

After returning to the United States after the war, Schuyler worked in menial jobs and lived with hobos in New York's Bowery before becoming a staff writer for A. Philip Randolph's the *Messenger* in 1923. Soon after joining the paper, he had his own column, "Shafts and Darts: A Page of Calumny and Satire." Later he became the paper's managing editor. Under Schuyler, the publication was considered so inflammatory that Southern members of the U.S. House of Representatives investigated it.

Schuyler's satire focused on the obsession in the United States with race, a subject he addressed in *Black No More* (1931). In this novel African Americans are able to become white by means of a surgical process. After treatment they disappear from Harlem and appear as whites in other places. Americans initially believe the race problem is solved. However, the blacks who have received the treatment are discovered to be three shades lighter than the original whites, who then begin adding pigmentation to their skin to differentiate themselves from the new whites. The race problem begins anew.

Black No More was critically well received. However, critics soon began to pay more attention to African American protest novels, and

Black No More was eventually forgotten. Adding to this problem was Schuyler's conservatism, which often put him in opposition to his more liberal colleagues and left him alienated from the mainstream African American intelligentsia.

Schuyler continued to publish columns and fiction. In addition to *Black No More*, he wrote *Slaves Today: A Story of Liberia* (1931), which exposed the slavelike conditions many laborers experienced in Liberia. A third novel, *Black Empire*, which Schuyler wrote under the pen name Samuel I. Brooks, was published posthumously in 1991 and is a compilation of a serial that was published in the Pittsburgh Courier from 1936 to 1937.

Schuyler's journalistic contributions were considerable. From 1927 to 1931 Schuyler contributed nine essays to H. L. Mencken's American Mercury. In addition to maintaining a 40-year association with the *Courier*, where he was a columnist and a special correspondent in Latin America, the West Indies, and West Africa, he contributed to several white-owned journals, the *Nation*, *Plain Talk*, and *Common Ground* among them.

Schuyler also published nonfiction, including *Racial Intermarriage in the United States* (1929) and his autobiography, *Black and Conservative: The Autobiography of George S. Schuyler*, which was published in 1966.

Schuyler was married to Josephine Cogdell, a white artist who, like Schuyler, believed that the children of interracial marriages would be genetically superior by virtue of "hybrid vigor" and would thus end racial problems in the United States. The couple had one daughter, Phillipa Duke Schuyler, who became a concert pianist.

North America

Scott, Hazel

(b. June 11, 1920, Port of Spain, Trinidad; d. October 2, 1981, New York, N.Y.), Caribbean-American jazz musician and political activist; the first black woman to host her own television show.

Hazel Scott made her debut as a pianist in Trinidad at age three. By her eighth birthday she had performed in New York City and won a scholarship to the Juilliard School of Music. Scott became a star of radio and Broadway in the 1930s and appeared in several movies in the 1940s. Her marriage in 1945 to Harlem minister and congressman Adam Clayton Powell Jr. was one of the year's major social events; the two divorced in 1956.

In the late 1940s Scott became the first black woman to host her own television show. She lost this job in 1950 when she was accused of being a Communist sympathizer. She refused to perform in segregated theaters and became an outspoken critic of both McCarthyism and racial injustice. After living abroad for five years in the 1960s, she returned to the United States and to her television and nightclub career. Called a "musical chameleon" for her ability to shift from jazz to classical to blues, Scott continued to perform until her death.

Scurlock, Addison

(b. June 19, 1883, Fayetteville, N.C.; d. 1964, Washington, D.C.), African American photographer known for his portraits of African American leaders and of Washington, D.C., luminaries.

The son of George Clay Scurlock, a Washington, D.C., lawyer who had moved his family from Fayetteville in 1900, Addison Scurlock began his career in photography as an assistant to Moses P. Rice in the same year. After four years of apprenticeship, Scurlock started his first studio at home, and in 1911 he opened the Scurlock Studio.

While employed as the official Howard University photographer, Scurlock produced newsreels in Washington, in addition to a portrait series sponsored by Carter G. Woodson for United States schools. He died at age 81, after passing the management of his business on to his son.

Senghor, Léopold Sédar

(b. August 15, 1906, Ndjitor, Senegal), scholar, poet, philosopher, and statesman; founder of the cultural and political movement known as Négritude, and president of Senegal (1960-1980).

Demonstrating a rare combination of intellectual, artistic, and political talent, Léopold Sédar Senghor has towered over modern Senegal unlike any other figure in that country's history. Senghor's lifelong quest to find a synthesis, artistically and politically, between two seemingly opposing ways of life—African and European—inspired his lifelong record of creative achievement. Although as a youth he immersed himself in French culture, his ultimate inability to become "a black-skinned Frenchman" led him to cultivate his "Africanness." He helped to define two of the key political and intellectual movements of twentieth-century Africa: African socialism and Négritude.

Born to a Serer father and a Fulani mother, Senghor has striven to represent all of Senegal's peoples in his writing and politics. He attended Roman Catholic mission schools in what was then French West Africa and, in 1922, entered the Collège Libermann, a seminary in Dakar, where he intended to study for the priesthood. He was forced to leave the seminary after participating in a protest against racism. After graduating from secondary school in 1928, Senghor won a scholarship to study in France.

While at the prestigious Ecole Normale Supérieure in Paris, Senghor studied contemporary French literature, including the work of Charles Baudelaire, on whom Senghor wrote his thesis. Senghor also studied the intellectual underpinnings of French political thought between the two world wars. Georges Pompidou, who later became the French president, was a classmate and a friend. Senghor was drafted into the French army at the start of World War II, after teaching classics at schools in Tours and Paris.

Outside class Senghor absorbed the intellectual ferment of Paris in the 1930s. Black students, writers, and artists from Africa, North America, and the Caribbean were discovering their common roots and defining their identities in opposition to colonial rule. The Pan-African Congress and the writings of W. E. B. Du Bois and the Harlem Renaissance all recognized and celebrated a growing black confidence and self-awareness, and this intellectual awakening deeply influenced Senghor and his contemporaries. In 1932 Senghor met Aimé Césaire, a writer from Martinique who would become an influential literary figure. Césaire and Senghor cofounded a newspaper, *L'Etudiant noir* (The Black Student), and founded a new artistic and intellectual movement, Négritude. The movement went beyond opposition to colonialism to attack white racism. Négritude sought to explore the common experience of peoples of African descent and to formulate a new black identity. Senghor would later say that the philosophy embodies the "sum total of African values of civilization."

The years after World War II were the high point of Senghor's political career. In 1945 and 1946 Senghor, along with his political mentor, Lamine Guèye, was elected to represent Senegal in the French Constituent Assembly (later the National Assembly). He won reelection and served in the National Assembly until 1958. Meanwhile, in 1948, he became a professor at the Ecole Nationale de la France d'Outre mer. Senghor became president of the parliament of the Mali Federation, comprising present-day Senegal and Mali, when it became independent in April 1960. Several months later the federation collapsed, and Senghor was elected the first president of Senegal. As a Serer Christian leading a predominantly Muslim and Wolof country, Senghor's political career can itself be considered an expression of Négritude, in that his African cultural background enabled him to serve and lead his people despite these differences.

Senghor also launched his literary career in earnest in 1945 with the publication of his first book of poetry, *Songs of the Shadow*. Two years later, in collaboration with fellow Senegalese Alioune Diop, he helped launch the journal *Présence Africaine*, which showcased African literature, including Senghor's writing. Torn between two very different worlds, Senghor dramatized the identity crisis of the Westernized African. He pushed French poetry past its preoccupation with the exotic, implying a detachment from the "other." Instead, Senghor's poetry presents a personal confrontation with the African past and present. "Black Woman,"one of his most famous poems, uses classical Western themes to describe the figure of an African woman and, by extension, black humanity.

Throughout the next two decades a number of other poetry volumes followed and received critical acclaim both for their vivid language and imagery and for their broader themes. While he was president (1960-1980) Senghor published less. However, he won the Apollinaire Prize for Poetry in 1974, and he published volumes of poetry in 1979 and 1980.

As Senegalese president during the 1960s and 1970s, Senghor implemented a moderate (pro-Western) form of African socialism, in which the state played a major role in the economy in alliance with the established indigenous elite. He also replaced Senegal's multiparty democracy in the early 1960s with a one-party authoritarian state. However, in the so-called passive revolution of 1976, Senghor responded to economic and political stagnation by introducing greater political and economic freedom. However, Senegal's economic crisis persisted and, bowing to popular discontent, Senghor retired from office in 1980, one of the few African rulers to relinquish power voluntarily. He left a legacy of relative stability and freedom of expression in Senegal. However, Senghor had also monopolized power and discouraged debate and opposition, and thus contributed to the stagnation of Senegalese politics.

Since his retirement Senghor has resettled in Verson, France, the hometown of his wife. In 1988 he published a philosophical memoir titled *Ce que je crois* (What I Believe). During the 1990s he published poetry and cultivated a quiet seclusion.

North America

Shakur, Tupac (2Pac)

(b. June 16, 1971, New York, N.Y.; d. September 13, 1996, Las Vegas, Nev.), African American rap star praised for his thought-provoking lyrics and criticized for his violent lifestyle; one of the most popular rap artists in the world when he was shot and killed at age 25.

Tupac Shakur was one of the most influential and controversial voices to emerge from hip hop's much maligned club of so-called gangster rappers. Criticized for their violent lyrics and misogynistic claims, gangster rappers became symbols of the best and worst of American musical creativity. Over a six-year period in the early 1990s Shakur became the voice for a generation of young, often frustrated, African Americans.

Through his music and his life Shakur embodied many of the harsh realities of "ghetto life." His raps addressed the difficulties of being young, black, and poor in the United States, and as a promising actor he captured those realities on the screen. True to the thuggish lifestyle that he rapped about, Shakur was arrested and served time in jail on more than one occasion, and often foreshadowed his own death in his songs and videos. Shakur's predictions of his violent death came true on September 13, 1996, when he was murdered shortly after attending a professional boxing match in Las Vegas, Nevada.

Shakur was born in New York City on June 16, 1971, to black activists Afeni Shakur and Billy Garland. Garland interacted infrequently with Tupac, but Shakur exposed her son to many of the activities and philosophies of the Black Panther Party. At times destitute, Shakur and his mother moved often between apartments in New York City. As a young teenager in Harlem, he explored his desire to act by joining the 127th Street Ensemble theater group and was cast as Travis in Lorraine Hansberry's play *A Raisin in the Sun*.

By 1988 the Shakurs had moved several times, finally settling in Marin, California. While in Marin Shakur pursued his interest in music, leaving home in 1988 to join the rap group Strictly Dope. Three years later he left Strictly Dope and joined forces with friends from Oakland, California, who had formed the successful rap group Digital Underground. Shakur initially served as a background dancer for the group, but he was given an opportunity to rap on the group's 1991 single, "Same Song." His powerful delivery and stage charisma made an immediate impression, and friends were soon urging him to go solo.

In late 1991 Shakur released his first solo album, *2Pacalypse Now*, which sold more than 500,000 copies and featured the acclaimed hit "Brenda's Got a Baby." Heralded for its compelling portrayals of the hardships faced by single black mothers and rebuked for its vivid depictions of violence, 2Pacalypse Now marked powerful contradictions within Shakur's music and life. These contradictions would also be manifest on the silver screen.

Shakur's portrayal of the aggressive, unbalanced character Bishop in the movie *Juice* (1992) and his role as Lucky in the film *Poetic Justice* (1993) mirrored many of the problems in his private life. In 1993 Shakur was arrested for using drugs, and he was later sentenced to ten days in jail for brutally beating another rapper with a baseball bat. In October 1993 Shakur was once again arrested, for allegedly shooting two off-duty Atlanta police officers. Although the charges were later dropped, Shakur's failure to draw a distinction between his public and private personas earned him public criticism.

Among those to criticize Shakur's music and behavior was C. Delores Tucker, chair of the National Political Congress of Black Women. Tucker objected to Shakur's glorification of what he referred to as "thug life" and urged him to use his podium in more positive ways. Shakur's response to Tucker and other critics was often hostile and bitter. Shakur claimed that in his music he was reflecting a lifestyle inspired by a poverty and despair that many Americans wished to ignore. He argued that his music represented the voices of those in America's most marginalized communities, and that to vilify his music simply vilified the realities facing those communities.

By 1994 Shakur's life was a blurred reflection of his art. In March Shakur lost his temper when he was cut from a film and was arrested when he assaulted the film's director, Allen Hughes. After Shakur spent 15 days in jail, his career received a boost when his third film, *Above the Rim*, was released. But eight months later Shakur was back in court defending himself against charges by a 19-year-old woman of sexual assault.

Shakur's troubles climaxed in 1995 when he was robbed and shot five times in the lobby of a recording studio in New York City. Like many of the characters in his movies and songs, Shakur managed to defy death. Although it is unclear who was involved in the attempt on Shakur's life, he blamed the shooting on rival rappers from New York, the Notorious B.I.G. and Sean "Puffy" Combs. At the time Shakur and B.I.G. were leading figures in a fierce rivalry between West Coast and East Coast rappers. When Shakur emerged from the hospital, a jury convicted him of sexual abuse and sentenced him to four and a half years in prison.

While in prison Shakur released his third album, *Me Against the World*, which debuted at Number One on the Billboard charts and earned him a Grammy Award nomination for Best Rap Album. *Me Against the World* went on to sell more than 2 million copies in seven months. On the album Shakur talked about his own mortality in the songs "If I Die 2Nite" and "Death Around the Corner," two of many songs that foreshadowed his violent death. Also featured on the album is the song "Dear Mama," which earned Shakur a second Grammy nomination for Best Rap Solo Performance.

After eight months in prison Shakur was released when Suge Knight, head of Death Row Records, paid his $1 million bail. Shakur joined Knight's recording label, and in 1996 he released the double album *All Eyez on Me*. The album has sold 5 million copies and con-tains Shakur's biggest hit to date, "California Love." While at Death Row Shakur was part of a team that featured many of the most prominent rappers/producers on the West Coast, including Dr. Dre and Snoop Doggy Dogg. By all accounts, Shakur's future seemed very promising.

But that promise ended on September 13, 1996, when Shakur was cut down in a barrage of bullets. Shakur and Knight were in Las Vegas, Nevada, attending the championship fight of boxer Mike Tyson. After the fight Shakur and Knight were driving along the Las Vegas strip when a car pulled up next to theirs and unloaded several rounds. While attempting to flee into the car's back seat, Shakur was shot several times. Knight sustained minor injuries, but Shakur was placed in intensive care. After six days in the hospital he was pronounced dead.

Since the rapper's death Shakur's estate has been plagued by lawsuits, including one by C. Delores Tucker. Tucker claims that Shakur's derogatory references to her in several of his songs caused damage to her marriage. Lawsuits by Shakur's biological father and by a fan injured during a rap concert in which Shakur allegedly taunted the crowd into rioting have been filed. Also, Shakur's mother has filed a lawsuit against Death Row Records for control of her son's unreleased songs.

Shakur's final video, filmed a month before his death, depicts his violent demise. Titled "I Aint Mad At Cha,'" the video and its song aired publicly just a few days after his death. Altogether, Shakur starred in six movies (three of which—*Bullet*, *Gridlock'd*, and *Gang-Related*—were released in 1997, after Shakur's death) and released six albums, two post-humously. He earned two Grammy Award nominations and sold millions of albums around the world. Shakur's voice echoed the concerns and the rage of many young African Americans who are left to face the challenges of the ghetto alone. But his music also spoke to young adults—many of them middle-class blacks and whites—who understood and valued Shakur's ability to bring the hardships of the marginalized to the surface of American culture.

North America

Shange, Ntozake

(b. October 18, 1948, Trenton, N.J.), African American writer known for innovative, experimental drama, poetry, and fiction.

As prolific as she is provocative, Ntozake Shange pushes the limits of literary form as she questions the social and political limitations imposed on people of color, especially women and children. Inventing her own dramatic medium, Shange created the choreo-poem, a combination of narrative text, dance, and music. Her music opens up as many avenues as possible to the exploration of the diverse experiences of the oppressed.

Born Paulette Williams, the daughter of a surgeon and psychiatric social worker, Shange spent her early years in Trenton, New Jersey, in privileged circumstances. Her parents' friends, including Josephine Baker, Miles Davis, and W. E. B. Du Bois, provided a culturally affirming black atmosphere. The family moved to St. Louis, Missouri, when Shange was eight. There she was one of the first students to integrate a school.

Depressed by a failed teenage marriage and the limitations she encountered as a talented black woman, Shange attempted suicide several times during her years at Barnard College (1966-1970). She began a new chapter of her life during graduate study at the University of Southern California (USC) in 1973, when she changed her name to the Zulu words Ntozake, "she who comes with her own things," and Shange, "who walks like a lion." After taking an M.A. from USC, Shange moved to the San Francisco Bay Area, where she taught women's studies and writing at area colleges and universities while performing her own poetry and dance. Her best-known work, *for colored girls who have considered suicide, when the rainbow is enuf*, originated in poems from this period.

In 1975 a move to New York saw the performance of *for colored girls* and the beginning of Shange's success. The Broadway production earned a 1977 Obie Award, and Tony, Emmy, and Grammy nominations. Her other plays include *Three Pieces* (1981), *Mother Courage and Her Children* (1980), and a collaboration with South African musicians Ladysmith Black Mambazo, *Nomathemba* (1996). Her other work includes poetry collections such as *Nappy Edges* (1978) and the novels *Sassafras, Cypress and Indigo* (1982), the autobiographical *Betsy Brown* (1985), and *Liliane: Resurrection of the Daughter* (1994).

Married to jazz musician David Murray in 1977, Shange lives with the couple's daughter Savannah in Philadelphia, Pennsylvania, where Shange teaches at Villanova University.

Short, Bobby

(b. September 15, 1924, Danville, Ill.), African American cabaret singer and pianist known for suave nightclub performances.

Bobby Short became a recognized talent in the New York cabaret world as early as 1937, the year he was acclaimed in Variety magazine. During the 1940s and 1950s he toured the United States, establishing himself as a premier nightclub act with his elegant stage personality and singing style. Short then settled in New York City, where he played in several Broadway shows and at well-known "café society" nightclubs. Dividing his time between France and the United States, Short performed four months out of the year at Cafe Carlyle in New York City beginning in 1968.

Simone, Nina

(b. February 21, 1933, Tryon, N.C.), African American vocalist known for her musical versatility and emotionally charged singing.

Nina Simone is widely known as "the high priestess of soul"—less for her interpretation of soul music than for the soulful intensity she brings to her highly eclectic repertoire. Since the late 1950s Simone has recorded extensively in the jazz, blues, soul, gospel, and pop idioms, interpreting both standard and original songs. During the 1960s her vocal career took on a powerfully political dimension. Indeed, "more than any other popular performer of the day, she has captured the essence of the black revolution and sings of it without biting her tongue," noted Ebony magazine in 1969.

The All Music Guide to Jazz (1996) has described Simone's voice as "moody-yet-elegant . . . presenting a fiercely independent soul who harbors enormous (if somewhat hard-bitten) tenderness." The quotation also reflects her struggle to succeed as a black female musician. She had originally dreamed of becoming a classical pianist and, during the 1950s, studied at New York's prestigious Juilliard School of Music. Yet black musicians met with considerable discrimination in the mostly white and exclusive realm of classical music, and Simone soon found herself performing at an Atlantic City nightclub. Asked to sing in addition to play piano, she began her career as a jazz vocalist. In 1959 she achieved a Top Twenty hit single with her recording of George Gershwin's "I Love You Porgy."

Simone has since recorded more than 40 albums. Her songs range from ballad interpretations of Billie Holiday and Jacques Brel to her own fiercely political pieces, "Old Jim Crow" and "Mississippi Goddam"—responses to the burgeoning violence committed against American blacks during the early 1960s. During the 1970s and 1980s she recorded rarely but experienced a career comeback in the United States with her 1993 album, A Single Woman.

Singleton, Arthur James ("Zutty")

(b. May 14, 1898, Bunkie, La.; d. July 14, 1975, New York, N.Y.), African American musician and bandleader responsible for innovations in jazz percussion accompaniment.

Raised in New Orleans, Louisiana, Arthur James "Zutty" Singleton began his professional musical career at age 15 as a drummer for silent film theater orchestras. He served in the United States Navy during World War I. Returning to New Orleans, he worked as a freelance drummer with several popular local bands, including Papa Celestin's, Louis "Big Eye" Nelson's, and Luis Russell's, in addition to forming his own band around 1920.

In 1924 Singleton recorded his first song, "Frankie and Johnny," with the Fate Marable riverboat band, with which he had performed since 1921. After playing in St. Louis, Missouri, with Charlie Creath in 1925, Singleton became an integral part of the burgeoning Chicago School of jazz, which placed soloists such as Louis Armstrong in the spotlight. However, he continued to play long stints in other cities, including New York and Los Angeles from the 1930s to the 1950s.

It was Singleton's introduction of sock cymbals and wire brushes, along with new accenting techniques, that secured his place as an accompanist for such musical giants as Louis Armstrong, "Jelly Roll" Morton, "Fats" Waller, "Dizzy" Gillespie, and Charlie Parker, as well as appearances on television and in films. Spanning several decades, Singleton's career was marked by an ability to play flexibly with all types of jazz. In 1953 he settled in New York. He continued to tour internationally until he accepted a permanent position at Jimmy Ryan's, the jazz club on West 57th Street, in 1963. A stroke forced Singleton to retire in 1970, and he died in New York City five years later.

Sissle, Noble

(b. July 10, 1889, Indianapolis, Ind.; d. December 17, 1975, Tampa, Fla.), African American musician and composer who participated in Shuffle Along, the most successful musical comedy created by African Americans.

Noble Sissle first sang in his father's Methodist church, and he was a soloist at his Cleveland, Ohio, high school's glee club. After serving in World War I as a drum major, Sissle had enormous success in the vaudeville theater, teaming up with "Eubie" Blake as the Dixie Duo. In 1921 the two created *Shuffle Along*, starring Florence Mills. *Shuffle Along* changed Broadway musical theater by introducing a jazz dancing chorus line and the vitality and style of African American music to a more "refined" mainstream theater. Sissle and Blake wrote songs, including the well-known "I'm Just Wild About Harry." They also produced *Runnin' Wild* (1924) and *Chocolate*

Dandies (1924). In 1937 Sissle was the cofounder and first president of the Negro Actors' Guild. In 1945 and 1946 Sissle toured Europe with a United Service Organizations (USO) show, performing a restaged *Shuffle Along*.

Slave Narratives,

written autobiographies and oral testimonies by escaped or freed slaves.

At the conclusion of her Pulitzer-Prize-winning novel *Beloved*, Toni Morrison sums up her retelling of one slave family's experience: "It was not a story to pass on." There are certainly logical reasons why the story of slavery might never have been passed on. One, the reason Morrison suggests, was its sheer horror and trauma—those who lived through slavery may not have wanted to remember their experiences. A second is more practical: it was illegal to teach slaves to read and write, which meant that the act of putting a story on paper was generally denied them. But neither of these reasons kept former slaves from passing on their stories and leaving a record about what living as a piece of property had been like. Slave narratives set the standard for a tradition of African American autobiography that continues today.

Historians estimate that there are approximately 6000 published narratives by African American slaves. This number includes both book-length autobiographies and shorter accounts published in newspapers or transcribed from interviews, and it spans 170 years' worth of testimonies from ex-slaves. Most of these narratives were published or collected after slavery was abolished in 1865, as slaves who had been emancipated looked back on their experiences. The most famous slave narratives are autobiographies by fugitive slaves that were published before 1865.

The best-known slave narrative is Frederick Douglass's *Narrative of the Life of Frederick Douglass, an American Slave, Written by Himself* (1845). In it Douglass describes his childhood separation from his mother, his struggle to teach himself to read and write, the brutal whippings he witnessed and received, and his determination to be free—all the while stressing his own humanity and the inhumanity of the system that kept him a slave. Douglass's autobiography was an international bestseller. After its publication Douglass traveled the world as a lecturer, implicitly providing a model for just how "civilized" blacks could be, and went on to become the most famous and respected black individual of the nineteenth century. His narrative's patterns and images were repeated not only in many later slave narratives, but also in such diverse works of African American literature as Zora Neale Hurston's *Their Eyes Were Watching God* (1937) and Ralph Ellison's *Invisible Man* (1952).

Other famous slave narrators from this period include William Wells Brown and Harriet Jacobs. Brown was one of the earliest African American novelists. Jacobs, whose *Incidents in the Life of a Slave Girl* is the best example of a woman's slave narrative, discusses the sexual intimidation and

NARRATIVE

OF THE

LIFE

OF

FREDERICK DOUGLASS,

AN

AMERICAN SLAVE.

WRITTEN BY HIMSELF.

BOSTON:
PUBLISHED AT THE ANTI-SLAVERY OFFICE,
No. 25 CORNHILL.
1845.

Frederick Douglass

The portrait of Frederick Douglass shown here appeared facing the title page of *Narrative of the Life of Frederick Douglass, an American Slave, Written by Himself,* which was published in Boston in 1845. *CORBIS/Bettmann*

abuse and the agony of being a slave mother that made slavery a different experience for women than for men.

After Emancipation the tone of many slave narratives changed. Authors continued to portray their experiences as slaves, but for many the new purpose in writing was to prove that slavery had been a testing ground from which African Americans had successfully emerged, ready to participate in the larger American society. Booker T. Washington's 1901 autobiography *Up From Slavery* is the best-known example of this new type of slave narrative. Washington uses many of the same conventions found in Douglass's slave narrative, but he turns them around so that in his autobiography slavery becomes the foundation for a classic rags-to-riches American success story.

In the late twentieth century the slave narratives' presence is still felt throughout African American literature in both form and function. Many authors have written contemporary retellings of slave narratives, in books as varied as Morrison's lyrical *Beloved* (1987), Octavia Butler's science fiction novel *Kindred* (1979), and Ishmael Reed's parody *Flight to Canada* (1976). Other novels, such as *Invisible Man,* use the narratives' themes and structure with very different subject matter. And throughout the history of African American literature, autobiography has remained a dominant genre. Many African Americans still identify with the need to write about themselves as a means of sharing their common humanity. Langston Hughes, Zora Neale Hurston, Richard Wright, Malcolm X, and Maya Angelou are among recent black writers who continued this tradition of using the written word to pass their stories on.

Sleet, Moneta J., Jr.

(b. February 14, 1926, Owensboro, Ky.; d. September 30, 1996, New York, N.Y.), photojournalist and the first African American man to win a Pulitzer Prize, his photographs chronicled pivotal moments in contemporary black history, such as Martin Luther King Jr.'s 1968 funeral and Ghana's independence in 1957.

Aspiring to become a photographer since early childhood, Moneta Sleet Jr. studied photography and business at Kentucky State College. In 1955 he became a staff photographer for *Ebony* magazine. On assignment he met Martin Luther King Jr. in 1956, and the two remained friends until King's assassination. During this period Sleet photographed the marches and rallies of the Civil Rights Movement, and won critical acclaim for his sensitive and vivid photos of both famous and ordinary people.

Sly and the Family Stone,

an interracial musical group formed in the late 1960s by African American singer Sly Stone (Sylvester Stewart); Sly and the Family Stone, together with singer James Brown, helped create the funk music style.

Sly and the Family Stone played a key role in the genesis of funk, a musical fusion combining gospel-inspired soul music with the guitar-driven sound and performance style of 1960s psychedelic rock. Sly Stone was born Sylvester Stewart in 1944 and moved in the 1950s with his family from Texas to San Francisco.

After playing in several area bands, Stone became a rhythm and blues (R&B) disc jockey for stations KSOL and later KDIA. As a record producer for Autumn Records, he recorded with such local bands as the Beau Brummels and the Mojo Men. In 1967 he organized Sly and the Family Stone, which was unique among 1960s rock or funk bands in including both blacks and whites, and women as well as men.

The group featured punchy horn riffs and wild guitar solos played over a deep funk rhythm. It soon had two hits, "Everyday People" (1968) and "Hot Fun in the Summertime" (1969), and appeared at the 1969 Woodstock Festival. The group's songs often displayed a racial militancy reminiscent of the Black Power movement, as in "Don't Call Me Nigger, Whitey" (1969). The album *There's a Riot Going On* (1971) combined social commentary with highly danceable music, setting the pattern for funk music in the 1970s.

By the early 1970s Sly and the Family Stone's music had turned darkly pessimistic as Stone began to fall apart. He became addicted to narcotics and acquired a reputation for unreliability after repeated no-shows at concerts. Sly and the Family Stone produced one more exceptional album, *Fresh* (1973), but changing musical tastes and Stone's mounting personal problems ended the group's national visibility.

In the early 1980s Stone joined George Clinton on Funkadelic's *The Electric Spanking of War Babies* (1981) and toured with the P-Funk All-Stars. During the 1980s Stone was repeatedly in trouble with the law and spent time in prison for cocaine possession.

In 1993, the year that he was inducted into the Rock and Roll Hall of Fame, Stone was reportedly living in a sheltered-housing complex. Yet despite his difficulties, Stone made a lasting contribution. In the 1990s urban soul, funk, and rap all reveal a debt to the music of Sly and the Family Stone.

North America

Smith, Anna Deveare

(b. September 18, 1950, Baltimore, Md.), African American actor, playwright, and educator.

Born in Baltimore, Maryland, Anna Deveare Smith was the oldest of Deveare and Anna Smith's five children. Her father owned a coffee and tea business, while her mother was an elementary school principal. In 1971, after receiving a bachelor's degree in linguistics from Beaver College, Smith left for San Francisco, California, where her acting talent earned her a place at the American Conservatory Theater and enabled her to work as an actor and director. She received a master of fine arts degree in 1976, and left for New York City in the same year. There, Smith played minor roles in soap operas and worked for KLM Airlines before becoming a drama teacher at Carnegie-Mellon University in Pittsburgh, Pennsylvania.

Though a casting agent had once told her she was too pale to convincingly portray black characters, Smith launched a one-woman performance, *On the Road: A Search for American Character* (1983), beginning a quest to represent dramatically America's multiple voices and identities. In 1992 Smith produced the 26-character, one-woman performance, *Fires in the Mirror*, which dealt with the riots that erupted in Crown Heights, Brooklyn, after an African American child was accidentally killed by a Jewish motorist, and a Jewish scholar was stabbed in apparent retaliation. Based on interviews with more than 50 people connected to the riots, the performance was described by Smith as an exploration of the incident's causes and impact, and of "the place where language fails, where people have to struggle to find words."

Fires in the Mirror received an Obie Award, a Drama Desk Award, the Lucille Lortel Award, the $10,000 Kesselring Prize, and the George and

Elizabeth Marton Award. It was a runner-up for a Pulitzer Prize. This success led directly to a commission that resulted in *Twilight: Los Angeles 1992*,
a performance that examined the five days of rioting in L.A. that followed
the acquittal of four policeman accused of severely beating a black motorist,
Rodney King. *Twilight* opened in 1993 in Los Angeles and then moved to
New York City, where it was the first nonmusical show by a black woman
to open on Broadway in ten years. *Twilight* won two Tony Award nominations, an Obie Award, a Drama Desk Award, and an Outer Circle Critics
Special Achievement Award. Because *Twilight*, like *Fires*, was dependent on
Smith's verbatim portrayals of the people she interviewed (a "documentary"
work rather than a "theater" work), the Pulitzer board decided to withdraw
her nomination for the Pulitzer Prize.

Other works by Smith include the plays *A Birthday Card and Aunt
Julia's Shoes* (1983) and *Aye, Aye, Aye, I'm Integrated* (1984). She appeared
in minor roles in the motion pictures *Dave* (1993) and *Philadelphia* (1993).
Smith has taught at New York University, Yale University, and the Univer-
sity of Southern California at Los Angeles, and is now a tenured professor at
Stanford University.

North America

Smith, Bessie

(b. April 15, 1894?, Chattanooga, Tenn.; d. September 26, 1937, Clarksdale,
Miss.), greatest blues vocalist of the 1920s, known as the Empress of the
Blues.

Bessie Smith was the greatest of the classic blues singers of the 1920s; she
laid the foundation for all subsequent women's blues and jazz singing. Her
singing combined an array of vocal embellishments, including scoops, slides,
and blue notes, and a rhythmic freedom that heightened the emotional effect of her lyrics. African American audiences loved her, especially those in
the South and those in the North made up of recent southern migrants,
who appreciated her rough, down-home style. "She could bring about mass
hypnotism," New Orleans guitarist Danny Barker recalled. "When she was
performing you could hear a pin drop." In part, this was due to her musical
artistry and showmanship; in part, it was because many identified with her
success. Smith had risen from poverty to comparative wealth on her own
terms and by her own talent. Many African Americans also admired her attitude toward white people—Smith made no effort to befriend whites and
never altered her performing style to appeal to them.

Smith was born around 1894 in a poor section of Chattanooga, Tennessee. One of seven children and orphaned young, she was singing on
street corners by age nine. Smith grew to be a large-boned woman with a
powerful and expressive voice. In 1912, while still a teenager, she joined a
traveling vaudeville show. Surprisingly, she was hired as a dancer rather than
as a singer, joining her dancer and comedian brother Clarence, who was al-

ready in the show. The troupe also included blues singer Gertrude "Ma" Rainey, who reportedly took Smith under her wing.

Smith settled in Atlanta, Georgia, where she performed regularly at the 81 Theater, part of the black nationwide Theater Owners Booking Association (TOBA) circuit. She began touring on the TOBA circuit, performing in the North as well as in the Southeast, and by the end of World War I she was TOBA's star attraction. During these years Smith also had a brief marriage to Jack Gee and began a lifetime of hard drinking. She did not enter a recording studio until she was nearly 30 years old and fully formed as an artist.

With the phenomenal success of "Crazy Blues," recorded in 1920 by Mamie Smith (no relation), record companies began to make "race records" for African American listeners, and began seeking black talent. At least two companies turned down Bessie Smith before Columbia Record Company brought her to its New York studios in 1923. Unlike many classic blues vocalists whose singing backgrounds were in vaudeville or popular music, Smith was primarily grounded in the blues. Consequently, as pianist Clarence Williams later explained, a number of record companies "said that her voice was too rough."

African American listeners did not agree. In less than six months her first record, "Downhearted Blues," sold an astonishing 780,000 copies. In fact, Smith played a direct role in rescuing Columbia, then nearly in receivership, and putting it on a firm financial basis. Columbia proclaimed its new star the Empress of the Blues, but Smith received no royalties, only a flat fee for each recording. During the 1920s she recorded prolifically with a wide range of accompanists, including cornetist Louis Armstrong, clarinet player Sidney Bechet, pianist Fletcher Henderson, and her two favorite musicians, trumpeter Joe Smith and trombone player Charlie Green.

In addressing what made Smith "such a superior singer," musicologist Gunther Schuller stressed the importance of her "remarkable ear for and control of intonation . . . [her] perfectly centered, naturally produced voice . . . [her] extreme sensitivity to word meaning and the sensory, almost physical, feeling of a word; and related to this, superb diction and what singers call projection."

Among Smith's important recordings are "Jailhouse Blues" (1923); "Cold in Hand Blues," "J. C. Holmes Blues," "You've Been a Good Old Wagon" (all 1925); "Gin House Blues," "Young Woman's Blues" (both 1926); and "Nobody Knows You When You're Down and Out" (1929). Throughout her career she also recorded popular songs and standards that were not blues based, including "After You've Gone" (1927) and "Gimme a Pigfoot" (1933).

Smith toured extensively. During the winter she appeared at black theaters and at occasional whites-only venues such as Nashville's Orpheum Theater. In warm weather she headlined her own big-tent variety show, with the entire cast traveling from performance to performance in her private Pullman car. In 1924 she made her first radio broadcast on WMC in Memphis, Tennessee, singing a set that included "Mistreatin' Papa" and

"Chicago Bound." Five years later she starred in a black-and-white short, *St. Louis Blues*, singing the title song; this short provides the only film footage of Smith performing. Although her Northern audiences declined when the blues craze passed in the late 1920s, Smith remained popular throughout the South, where the blues was indigenous. After the Depression put an end to her recording career in 1931, she continued performing before appreciative Southern audiences.

During the 1930s Smith made the transition from a heavier blues style to the more lightly swinging jazz of the Swing Era. She was featured at Harlem's renowned Apollo Theater during 1935 and a short time later substituted for Billie Holiday in the Broadway show *Stars over Broadway*. Smith appeared to be on the verge of a comeback when she was killed in a 1937 automobile accident. Record producer John Hammond, writing in *Downbeat* magazine five years after her death, and playwright Edward Albee, in *The Death of Bessie Smith* (1960), popularized the idea that the singer died because a whites-only hospital refused to admit her. However, her biographer Chris Albertson concluded that Smith died at the scene of the accident, and, given the extent of her injuries, she could not have been saved.

North America

Smith, Clara

(b. 1894?, Spartanburg, S.C.; d. February 2, 1935, Detroit, Mich.), African American blues singer and pianist during the 1920s, known as the Queen of the Moaners.

Clara Smith began performing around 1910, working the Southern black vaudeville circuit. By 1918 she was a star in the Theater Owners Booking Association (TOBA), which managed acts for black theater. Smith settled in Harlem in 1923, where she played in cellar clubs, speakeasies, and revues.

One of Smith's biggest recorded hits was "Every Woman's Blues" (1923). On her recordings Smith performed with Louis Armstrong, Fletcher Henderson, and Don Redman, and sang duets with Bessie Smith (no relation). Her style was dramatic and comic, and she is best remembered for expressive performances of songs like "Whip It to a Jelly" that played with sexual double entendres. Smith also managed her own revues, including the Clara Smith Theatrical Club.

North America

Smith, Clarence ("Pine Top")

(b. June 11, 1904, Troy, Ala.; d. March 15, 1929, Chicago, Ill.), African American jazz pianist who originated the boogie-woogie style.

Clarence "Pine Top" Smith began to play piano professionally in 1918, working at clubs in Birmingham, Alabama, before touring on the vaudeville and black Theater Owners Booking Association circuit. He was discovered by Charles "Cow Cow" Davenport in the mid-1920s, and began recording in 1928. With "Pine Top's Boogie Woogie" (1928) he coined the term "boogie woogie." The boogie-woogie style, marked by lively, improvised melodies on the right hand and rolling eight-to-the-bar figures on the left, developed as one of the most important strains of jazz piano. Smith recorded 20 songs in all, including "Pine Top's Blues." He died at 25 during a brawl in a Chicago dance hall.

North America

Smith, Mamie

(b. May 26, 1883, Cincinnati, Ohio; d. September 16, 1946, New York, N.Y.), singer who was the first African American woman to record the blues.

Mamie Smith began performing in vaudeville shows at age ten and came to New York in 1913 with the Smart Set Revue. After Smith appeared in Perry Bradford's musical *Made in Harlem*, Bradford helped her get a recording contract at OKeh Records for "That Thing Called Love" (1920) and "You Can't Keep a Good Man Down" (1920). That same year she recorded "Crazy Blues" with a backup band including Willie "the Lion" Smith. "Crazy Blues" sold close to a million copies. Its success energized the "race music" industry, which marketed blues and jazz recordings specifically to an African American audience. Smith continued to tour as a singer and actress throughout the 1930s and 1940s, appearing in films such as *Paradise in Harlem* (1939), and on stage with Billie Holiday.

North America

Smith, Marvin and Morgan

(Marvin: b. February 16, 1910, Nicholsville, Ky. / Morgan: b. February 16, 1910, Nichols-ville, Ky.; d. February 17, 1993?), African American photographers who depicted Harlem in the 1930s.

The twin sons of tenant farmers, Marvin and Morgan Smith grew up in Lexington, Kentucky, where they began painting and drawing. After moving to New York, they studied art under Augusta Savage and painted murals with the Works Progress Administration (WPA), a federal employment assistance program during the Depression. The Smiths realistically captured Harlem in the 1930s on film with photographs of Savoy Ballroom Lindy hoppers, street-corner preachers, and bread lines. In 1937 they were hired by New York's *Amsterdam News* as staff photographers. After a brief period in France the Smiths opened their M&M studio near the Apollo Theater. Their photographs continued to appear in prominent African American newspapers and magazines such as *Ebony*, *Crisis*, and the *Pittsburgh Courier*.

Smith, William Gardner

(b. February 6, 1927, Philadelphia, Pa.; d. November 6, 1974, France), African American novelist whose work posits a uniquely black artistry as part of the larger community.

William Gardner Smith spent much of his adult life as an exile, living in Paris and, for a time, Ghana. While writing for black periodicals in the United States and France, he wrote four novels, *Last of the Conquerors* (1948); *Anger at Innocence* (1950); *South Street* (1954); *The Stone Face* (1963); and one African American work, *Return to Black America* (1970), all of which attempt to resolve African Americans' tensions with the hostile larger society. Smith's project for himself and other black writers was two-fold: to harness deep empathy for suffering in the service of expressing profound truth and to resist a persistent artistic victimization of blacks that ended only in artistic ineffectiveness. Smith's work resembles that of other black writers of the 1940s and 1950s, including Richard Wright, James Baldwin, and Ann Petry, who depicted the conflicts between the artist and his society, and specifically between the black artist trying to establish a name in a largely white society hostile to recognizing black artistic achievements. Although Smith's own work found only a relatively small audience, his concerns anticipate more recent developments in African American literature.

Smith, Willie Mae Ford

(b. 1906?, Rolling Fort, Miss.; d. February 2, 1994, St. Louis, Mo.), African American gospel singer and preacher who contributed to the organized growth and development of gospel music.

Willie Mae Ford Smith's involvement with the world of gospel music started early; the daughter of the deacon of a Baptist church, she sang in church as a child. As a teen she was the lead vocalist in a gospel quartet she formed with her sisters. The group performed to great acclaim at the National Baptist Convention of 1922.

Smith was ordained as a minister in 1926, but as a woman was forbidden to preach in the Baptist church. This edict prompted her departure from that church in later years. In 1932, along with Thomas A. Dorsey and Sallie Martin, Smith formed the National Convention of Gospel Choirs and Choruses, an establishment credited with the nationwide popularization and development of gospel music. She then became the director of the National Convention Soloists Bureau where she was charged with teaching and mentoring young gospel singers.

Departing from the Baptist Church in 1939, Smith joined the Holiness

Church of God Apostolic and began to make fewer stage performances, focusing instead on singing principally at religious gatherings. It was at these performances that Smith's trademark "sermonnette," a short spoken statement preceding the song, gained fame.

In spite of the fact that she never focused on developing a professional recording career, Smith had an impact on the world of gospel music that remains unparalleled. Her protégés include Mahalia Jackson, the O'Neal twins, Martha Bass, and Delois Barret Campbell. The documentary *Say Amen, Somebody* celebrated Smith's life and contributions to gospel music. Willie Mae Ford Smith died in St. Louis in 1994.

North America

Smith, Willie ("the Lion")

(b. November 25, 1897, Goshen, N.Y.; d. April 18, 1973, New York, N.Y.), African American jazz pianist and composer who was an innovator in the "stride" style of jazz piano.

Willie "the Lion" Smith was raised in Newark, New Jersey, by his mother and his stepfather. By age 15 he was playing the piano professionally in local clubs and parties. Smith was a innovator in the "stride" style of jazz piano, which features a strong pumping line in the left hand. As early as 1921 Smith was making records, having performed in the backup band for Mamie Smith's "Crazy Blues." Although less well known than his contemporaries James P. Johnson and Fats Waller, Smith influenced musicians, most notably Duke Ellington. Smith's career surged in the 1950s and 1960s, and he recorded extensively. He published his autobiography, *Music on My Mind*, in 1964.

North America

Snoop Doggy Dogg (Calvin Broadus)

(b. 1972, Los Angeles, Calif.), the best-known figure in gangsta rap, a genre that chronicles in explicit detail life in and around the gangs of urban America.

Snoop Doggy Dogg's career began suddenly, when Dr. Dre, recently retired from NWA, asked Snoop to rap on the title song from the soundtrack to the film *Deep Cover*. The track, which described the murder of an undercover cop, was an underground hit, and Snoop joined the roster of Dre's Death Row Records.

In 1992 Dr. Dre released his solo debut, *The Chronic*, which featured Snoop's slow, nasal drawl on tracks like "Nuthin' but a 'G' Thang." *The Chronic* album achieved multi-platinum success, and Snoop capitalized on his sudden fame with *Doggystyle* (1993)—the most highly anticipated debut in hip hop history. Tracks like "Doggy Dogg World" and "Gin and

Juice" exemplified the feel-good side of Snoop's Long Beach Sound, while "Murder Was the Case" prefigured Snoop's subsequent trial (and acquittal) in a murder case.

In 1996 Dr. Dre quit Death Row, leaving Marion "Suge" Knight to run the label. Snoop appeared on tracks by label mates Tha Dogg Pound and Tupac Shakur, but the absence of his mentor, Dre, was sorely felt: *Tha Dog-gfather* (1996), Snoop's sophomore effort, garnered respectable sales but lousy reviews. On the eve of the album's release Shakur was murdered; a few months later Knight was indicted for probation violations. With Death Row in disarray, Snoop made an acrimonious public split; he currently records with the New Orleans-based No Limit Records.

North America
___

Soul Music,

a style of African American popular music, heavily influenced by gospel music, that emerged in the 1960s from rhythm and blues (R&B) and had a powerful impact on American vernacular culture.

During the soul music era of the 1960s African American music—for the first time in American history—gained popularity in an undiluted and culturally black form. Black music has long exerted a significant influence on American popular culture. Turn-of-the-century ragtime, classic jazz in the 1920s, 1930s big-band swing, and 1950s doo wop vocal groups each served to shape the musical tastes of mainstream America. But in the 1960s white Americans heard a genre of black music performed almost exclusively by African American artists, rather than a watered-down imitation sung by white performers. The new genre became known as soul music.

The soul music style was rooted in earlier forms of African American popular music. It was a direct extension of R&B but drew its primary influences from gospel music rather than from the blues. Important precursors to the soul style appeared during the 1950s, including Ray Charles's sanctified sound introduced on "I've Got a Woman" (1955); James Brown's "Please, Please, Please" (1956); Sam Cooke's "You Send Me" (1957); and the rich gospel sonorities heard in Arlene Smith and the Chantels' "Maybe" (1957) and Jerry Butler and the Impressions' "For Your Precious Love" (1958).

The soul aesthetic crystallized in the 1960s. Many elements of the new style are evident in Gladys Knight and the Pips' recording of "Every Beat of My Heart" (1960), especially in Knight's emotional lead singing, the prominent church-like organ, and the emphasis on the back beats, two and four—in this case by percussive guitar chords. There were a number of distinct styles or approaches to soul. Most significant were the harder-edged "Memphis sound," associated with Stax Records (1960-1975) of Memphis, Tennessee, and the slicker, more pop-oriented "Motown sound," of Berry Gordy's Detroit-based Motown Records (founded in 1959). In addition, James Brown had a rhythmic and danceable style all his own.

The hard soul of Stax – and of New York City's Atlantic Records—featured stripped-down production values and gritty small ensembles, such as Stax's Booker T. and the MGs or the Bar-Kays, that provided a powerful rhythmic drive and tightly riffing horns behind the gospel- and blues-tinged vocals of such singers as Otis Redding, Sam and Dave (Sam Moore and David Prater), Carla Thomas, the Staple Singers, Wilson Pickett, and Aretha Franklin. Gordy's Motown recordings employed more lavish production values, including the use of string sections, and achieved a sweeter sound that appealed to whites as well as blacks. Among Motown's most influential artists were Diana Ross and the Supremes, Smokey Robinson and the Miracles, Stevie Wonder, the Jackson Five, and the Temptations.

In the 1960s, during the height of the Civil Rights Movement, a historic process of racial integration began in the previously segregated realm of American popular music. Black artists achieved significant crossover success, producing hit records that sold in significant numbers to both whites and blacks. During the 1950s the popularity of black performers such as Nat "King" Cole, Dinah Washington, Chuck Berry, and the Platters revealed the beginnings of integration in American pop music. But prior to the soul music era black musicians had gained success primarily by appealing to the musical tastes of white listeners. During the 1960s an unparalleled number of black artists scored hits that made few concessions to white tastes, including Booker T. and the MGs' "Green Onions" (1962), Brown's "Papa's Got a Brand New Bag" (1965) and "I Got You (I Feel Good)" (1966), Pickett's "In the Midnight Hour" (1965), Sam and Dave's "Hold On! I'm Comin'" (1966), Percy Sledge's "When a Man Loves a Woman" (1966), and Franklin's "R-E-S-P-E-C-T" (1967). Soul music also inspired a "white soul" counterpart, exemplified in the early 1970s by such white pop singers as Carole King and Van Morrison.

Unlike R&B artists of the 1940s and 1950s who emphasized good-time music and made little effort to confront social issues, soul musicians engaged in cultural politics. Soul music—like R&B—concentrated mainly on themes of love and its discontents. But in the hands of a soul singer like Franklin, the frustrated lover's complaint in "R-E-S-P-E-C-T" became a sweeping anthem to freedom and empowerment. By the late 1960s a number of soul musicians gained popularity with songs that addressed a wide range of social issues and expressed black pride, exemplified by Brown's Top Ten hit "Say It Loud, I'm Black and I'm Proud" (1969). At the height of the Vietnam conflict Edwin Starr's "War" (1970) delivered an impassioned antiwar message. Marvin Gaye's "Mercy Mercy Me" (1971) was a gentler but no less earnest form of protest music, informed by ecological concerns.

Curtis Mayfield and Stevie Wonder in particular invested their music with a strong social conscience. As part of the Impressions in the 1960s and as a solo artist in the 1970s, Mayfield wrote many examples of soul music with a message, including "If There's a Hell Below We're All Going to Go" (1970) and "We People Who Are Darker Than Blue" (1970). Wonder proved equally adept at addressing issues of social injustice or spiritual uplift in songs such as "Living for the City" and "Higher Ground," from his album *Innervisions* (1973). Along with Isaac Hayes and Gaye, Mayfield and Wonder experimented with ambitious musical forms, for example the artistically unified "concept album," examples of which include Wonder's *Music of My Mind* (1972) and Mayfield's *There's No Place Like America Today* (1975).

Soul music retained an undiminished vigor into the 1970s and remained popular with black listeners. But by the late 1960s the larger white public had become less receptive. This change in musical tastes was part of a larger shift in white attitudes that was reflected in the waning of white support for the Civil Rights Movement, in the nation's growing political conservatism, and in a general heightening of racial tensions. In popular culture white and black musical styles seemed once more to retreat from each other. White pop music returned to the spotlight through the "British invasion" of such hit-making rock 'n' roll bands as the Beatles and the Rolling Stones, and black musicians found fewer opportunities. Although some African American artists, such as Donna Summer and the Commodores, had hits during the 1970s disco craze, black listeners preferred the contemporaneous but harder-edged funk style. As soul music became increasingly marginal and record sales dropped, Stax Records folded in the mid-1970s.

Both Motown and Atlantic have continued to be major forces in American popular music, as have Franklin, Mayfield, and Wonder. But the distinctive sound and aesthetic of soul music appears to have been lost. Subsequent developments in black popular music—most notably rap—reflect a general distancing from the gospel overtones and broad, quasi-religious themes of affirmation that lay at the heart of soul music.

North America

Soul Train,

one of the first nationally successful television shows conceived and produced by African Americans.

Don Cornelius, *Soul Train's* creator, envisioned the show as a black analogue to *American Bandstand*, a popular dance and music show. After gaining popularity in the early 1970s on a local channel in Chicago, *Soul Train* was adopted by stations nationwide. The show appealed to a far broader audience than the black teenagers for whom Cornelius had designed it. *Soul Train* returned season after season in the 1980s and 1990s, charting the evolving trends of pop music by showcasing rhythm and blues, soul, and eventually rap.

Soul Train was among the few major television programs of the 1970s that did not portray blacks by drawing on formulas and stereotypes. After the major civil rights victories of the 1960s—which redressed overt legal injustices—African Americans faced the equally formidable obstacle of ingrained cultural discrimination, expressed both on and off screen. The National Black Media Coalition, an organization that protested such racism, criticized the larger broadcasting networks, while some African Americans fought racial prejudice on the local level. Soul Train was the most successful among regional programs whose content was engineered by African Americans for African Americans.

Soyinka, Wole

(b. July 13, 1934, Abeokuta, Nigeria), internationally acclaimed Nigerian writer.

In 1986 Wole Soyinka (pronounced Sho-yin-ka), born Akinwande Oluwole Soyinka, was the first African writer to receive the Nobel Prize for Literature. The committee conferring the prize described the creator of more than 20 major works as "one of the finest poetical playwrights that have written in English," and also remarked that his writing was "full of life and urgency." Soyinka is the recipient of numerous other prestigious awards, including several honorary doctorates from universities all over the world. Apart from his stature as a pioneer in African drama written in English, Soyinka has produced a vast body of work—as poet, dramatist, theater director, novelist, essayist, autobiographer, political commentator, critic, and theorist of art and culture. Above all, he has remained a responsible citizen committed to the values of human freedom, truth, and justice. "Social commitment," he remarks, "is a citizen's commitment and embraces equally the carpenter, the mason, the banker, the farmer, the customs officer, etc., not forgetting the critic. I accept a general citizen's commitment which only happens to express itself through art and words." Through his entire career spanning more than 40 years, Soyinka has retained a remarkable consistency of vision in his dedication as an artist and as a socially responsible citizen.

Soyinka's vast creative talent is expressed in some 16 published plays—comedies, tragedies, and satires. His early play, *A Dance of the Forests* (1960), was written on the occasion of Nigeria's independence and includes his characteristic watchful irony and a warning to the Nigerian people and leaders not to romanticize the past as they forge a future for the new nation. *Death and the King's Horseman* (1975) typifies his imaginative engagement with tradition. *Priority Projects* (1982) are satirical agitprop sketches, written and performed with the Unife Guerrilla Theatre. Soyinka's play, *The Beatification of Area Boy: A Lagosian Kaleidoscope* (1996), is about the survival of the underclass in a deteriorating urban landscape around Lagos. Soyinka has created dramatic and memorable characters, including Elesin Oba, Iyaloja, Eman, Kongi, Sidi, and Sadiku, as well as the autobiographically inspired figures of his mother (The Wild Christian) and his father (Essay) in *Ake: The Years of Childhood* (1981). He has published four volumes of poetry, the most recent titled *Mandela's Earth and Other Poems*

(1988). That collection begins with the striking opening lines, "Your logic frightens me, Mandela . . . . Your bounty . . . that taut / Drumskin on your heart on which our millions / dance." Soyinka's three collec-tions of essays include *Myth, Literature and the African World* (1976); *Art, Dialogue and Outrage: Essays on Literature and Culture* (1988); and most recently, *The Open Sore of a Continent: Personal Narrative of the Nigerian Crisis* (1996). Soyinka has also written lyrics and musical compositions for a record album, *Unlimited Liability Company*. Songs such as "Ethike Revolution" and "I Love My Country" are, like his newspaper articles, topical, hard-hitting, and re-sponsive to particular situations.

An artist to the core—indeed, a cultural worker in the best tradition—Soyinka is deeply rooted in the African tradition of an artist who functions as the voice of vision of his times. He is not afraid to take action when nec-essary; he is never merely a commentator from the sidelines and never un-true to the demands of his craft, whether his work is in the form of a poem, an essay, or a play. Indeed, in Soyinka we discover the remark-able fusing of the creative and the political; he invents new ways (often misunderstood by his critics) of linking the mythic and political, of forging imaginative links between harsh political realities and cosmological, spiritual realms.

A biographical overview of this manifold artist must emphasize his Yoruba heritage and his roots in the Yoruba culture and world-view. (The Yoruba are among the three largest ethnic groups in Nigeria, along with the Igbo and the Hausa.) Although his parents, Ayo and Eniola, had converted to Christianity, Soyinka himself never embraced the Christian religion; he feels more at home with traditional Yoruba religion and is a personal devotee of the Yoruba god Ogun, who also figures prominently in his writ-ings. Soyinka describes Ogun as "god of creativity, guardian of the road, god of metallic lore and artistry. Explorer, hunter, god of war . . . custodian of the sacred oath." Changing historical times enable creative redefinitions of roles played by anthropomorphized deities like Ogun; today Ogun, as god of metal and of the road, is worshiped not only by blacksmiths, but also by truck drivers and airline pilots—all workers in metal.

In addition to his Yoruba-Christian upbringing, Soyinka received a Western academic education. Born in Abeokuta, Soyinka began his Western schooling in the Nigeria of the 1930s and 1940s, when it was still ruled by British colonizers. Next he spent two years (1952-1954) at the newly estab-lished University College in Ibadan, where his classmates included Chinua Achebe, Christopher Okigbo, and John Pepper Clark, all of whom made their marks later in Nigerian literature. Soyinka then earned a B.A. from the University of Leeds (1954-1957) in Great Britain. He spent a year as play reader at the Royal Court Theatre in London (1958-1959) and returned to Nigeria in 1960 on a Rockefeller Fellowship for the study of Nigerian tradi-tions and culture.

Through his education Soyinka imbibed the Western intellectual tradi-tion, but in his writing he comes across first and foremost as a Yoruba, and it is from a base in Yoruba culture—his inspiration—that he responds to other literary and cultural traditions. His art is eclectic, a successful blend of African themes with Western forms and techniques. In his hands African traditions assume meanings that are much wider than the ones accepted within their geographical location. "We must not think that traditionalism means raffia skirts," Soyinka has remarked. "It's no longer possible for a purist literature for the simple reason that even our most traditional literature has never been purist."

Just as he confronts African "traditionalism" in the narrow sense, Soyinka also recognizes the irony of using the English language—a lingering legacy of colonialism. However, he is never apologetic about this matter; rather, he proudly accepts the challenge of making the English language "carry the weight," as Achebe puts it, "of [his] African experience. But it will have to be a new English, still in full communion with its ancestral home, but altered to suit its new African surroundings . . . . The price a world language must be prepared to pay is submission to many different kinds of use." The role of English as a link language among people with various indigenous languages is certainly a historical reality in postcolonial societies. Language itself becomes a weapon for writers like Achebe, Soyinka, and others from the Third World to confront the disruptive remnants of colonialism and the negative continuities of neocolonialism in contemporary times.

Along with adapting the English language to his African experience, Soyinka optimally uses his education to transform literary forms from their European origins—often problem-atically considered universal—to suit his own cultural reality. In dramas such as *The Road* (1965) and *Death and the King's Horseman*, Soyinka presents a new form: Yoruba tragedy that departs in significant ways from Western dramatic forms, such as Shakespearean or Greek tragedy. In this form ritual, masquerade, dance, music, and mythopoeic language all work toward the very purpose of Yoruba tragedy, which is communal benefit.

Soyinka's contribution to Nigerian drama has gone beyond his considerable achievement as a playwright to his key role in professionalizing the English-language theater in Nigeria, forming companies such as the 1960 Masks and the Orisun Theater. The history of English-language professional theater in Nigeria is related integrally to Soyinka's dramatic career. There is a clear correspondence between the timing of his plays and the prevalent political climate. Biting satirical plays such as *The Trials of Brother Jero* (1963), *Opera Wonyosi* (1981), *Kongi's Harvest* (1967), and *A Play of Giants: A Fantasia on the Aminian Theme* (1984) indict African presidents-for-life (such as Idi Amin) as a "parade of monsters." Most recently, *The Beatification of Area Boy: A Lagosian Kaleidoscope* theatrically enacts the survival of the urban under-class under Sani Abacha's military regime.

Soyinka has the unique capacity not simply to write about social injustice in his creative work, but to meet the challenge and be an activist whenever necessary. There is no contradiction between Soyinka the artist, imaginatively exploring metaphysical matters in his creative work, and

Soyinka the engaged citizen, commenting on Nigerian sociopolitical issues. He is concerned with the quality of public life and speaks openly as the conscience of his nation. (An example of Soyinka's civic activism and his attempt to improve the safety of road travel in Nigeria was his establishment of the Oyo Road Safety Corps in 1980.) His incarceration for nearly two years (although he was never formally charged or tried) during the Nigerian civil war was a painful result of his attempt to redress "the colossal moral failure" in the nation. "The man dies in all who keep silent in the face of tyranny," he remarks in his prison notes, titled *The Man Died* (1972). Soyinka considers "justice . . . the first condition of humanity" and recognizes that "books and all forms of writing have always been objects of terror to those who seek to suppress truth."

Soyinka's deep and energetic concern for his country has remained unflagging over the past 40 years of his literary career. He has always been a stern and uncompromising critic of social injustice, regardless of its source. He roundly criticized Yakubu Gowon's military government in *The Man Died*, just as he criticized Shehu Shagari's "civilian" government in *Priority Projects* and Abacha's military rule in *The Open Sore of a Continent*.

Soyinka's artistic vision, even as it engages with Nigeria, encompasses a universal scope. "A historic vision is of necessity universal," Soyinka remarked in "The Writer in an African State," a 1967 essay. In *The Open Sore of a Continent*, even as he explores the troubled notion of the nation in Nigeria, he makes links to similar crises of nationhood in Yugoslavia and the Soviet Union. He asks directly and poignantly, "What price a nation?" especially when atrocities are committed in the name of "national protection, sovereignty, [and] development." His personal voice—bitter, angry, anguished—recognizes the traps of nationhood when the state acts as a repressive force crushing those who dissent.

Like Ogun, god of the road, Soyinka's creativity and courage blaze paths toward democratic ideals and social justice in Nigeria. "I have one abiding religion, human liberty," he has remarked. With his passion for freedom, with his deep concern for the quality of human life, Soyinka's work has profound significance in contemporary world literature.

North America
___

Spencer, Anne

(b. February 6, 1882, Henry County, Va.; d. July 12, 1975, Lynchburg, Va.), African American writer, Harlem Renaissance poet whose work combined nineteenth-century and modernist literary traditions.

Anne Bethel Bannister spent her early years with a foster family while her mother Sarah Scales, separated from her husband Joel Bannister, worked nearby as a cook. At age 11 she began formal schooling in the Virginia Seminary in Lynchburg under the name Annie Scales. With her first poem,

"The Skeptic" (1896), Scales revealed the independent thinking that would characterize her life and work. She graduated in 1899, taught for two years in West Virginia, and then returned to Lynchburg to marry Edward Spencer and raise their children, Bethel Calloway, Alroy Sarah, and Chauncey Edward.

During this time Spencer cultivated her poetry as well as her famous garden. When National Association for the Advancement of Colored People (NAACP) activist James Weldon Johnson visited her in 1917, he convinced her that she ought to publish, and "Before the Feast of Shushan" appeared in the February 1920 issue of Crisis. For the next 20 years her voice was heard in every collection of African American poetry.

Spencer's poetry invokes biblical and mythological allusions to speak of beauty in a decaying world. Her writing has been described as depicting a private vision, and she often employed images of the natural world. Despite the apparent influences of literary romanticism, Spencer has often been characterized as modernist, both for her complex style and her contemporary feminist concerns. She worked powerfully with detailed, focused images: a woman's hand, "Twisted, awry, like crumpled roots,/ bleached poor white in a sudsy tub," portrays the condition of women in "Lady, Lady."

Spencer's political activism in Lynchburg attested to her commitment to African American equality. She agitated for the hiring of African American teachers at the local segregated high school, she refused to ride segregated public transportation, and she initiated an African American library, where she worked from 1923 to 1945. Her garden home became a Southern locus for prominent African Americans that was visited regularly by such guests as W. E. B. Du Bois, Paul Robeson, and Langston Hughes. In the mid-1930s Spencer moved out of public life and lived as a recluse until her death in 1975.

North America

Spivey, Victoria Regina

(b. October 6, 1906, Houston, Tex.; d. October 3, 1976, New York, N.Y.), urban blues singer and the first African American woman to found a record label.

Known to many as "Queen Victoria," Spivey learned the piano while singing with her father's band in Dallas, Texas. After her father died, she performed wherever she could find work. In 1926 Spivey moved to St. Louis, Missouri, where she wrote and recorded songs, including her best-known, "T.B. Blues," for the St. Louis Music Company and for Okeh Records. Leaving Okeh but continuing to record, between 1929 and 1952 she also appeared in several stage shows, including Hellzapoppin' and in an all-black movie, Hallelujah. Her signature vocal sound was a nasal type of evocative moan that she termed her "tiger squall."

After a brief retirement Spivey returned to music with the revival of the blues in the 1960s. In 1961 she formed Queen Vee Records, changing the name to Spivey Records the following year. She died in 1976, the same year she released her last album, *The Blues Is Life*.

Staple Singers,

a well-known African American family music group that has performed and recorded gospel, folk, and soul music since the early 1950s.

The Staple Singers, composed of various members of the Staples family of Chicago, Illinois, made significant contributions to gospel and soul music as well as to the folk music revival. Even after leaving the realm of religious music, the group has continued to perform songs with an inspirational or uplifting message. At the heart of the four-person group was Roebuck "Pop" Staples, whose lead vocals and Delta blues-influenced guitar playing helped give the Staple Singers their distinctive sound. His youngest daughter, Mavis Staples, added an exhilarating contralto. Over time as various family members joined or left the group, the Staple Singers gradually altered its style. During the group's first decade the Staple Singers performed gospel music, but in the early 1960s the group took its increasingly secular repertoire on the folk music circuit. In 1968 the Staple Singers signed with Stax Records, perhaps the most important soul music record company, and soon emerged as one of the country's top soul groups.

Pop Staples was born in 1915 in Winona, Mississippi, where he came under the influence of the guitar style of such legendary Delta bluesmen as Robert Johnson, Bukka White, and "Big Bill" Broonzy. In 1935 Staples moved to Chicago with his wife Oceola and two children, Pervis and Cleotha. In Chicago the family grew with the addition of Yvonne and Mavis. The elder Staples sang in gospel quartets during the 1930s and began teaching his children music when they were quite young in the hope of forming a group. In the early 1950s Pervis, Cleotha, and Mavis joined him in performances at local churches.

Although the Staple Singers first recorded in 1953, the group did not gain recognition until it moved in 1955 to Chicago's black-owned Vee Jay Records, which released five notable gospel albums by the group over the next five years. But the Staple Singers achieved their greatest popularity with a series of more elaborately produced recordings for Stax, that featured a fuller instrumentation, including horn sections and synthesizers, exemplified by the hits "Respect Yourself" (1971), "I'll Take You There" (1972), and "If You're Ready (Come Go with Me)" (1973), as well as by their 1975 album for Curtis Mayfield's Custom label, *Let's Do It Again*, the group's all-time bestseller. The Staple Singers became less visible as soul music lost its popular appeal in the late 1970s, although the group briefly returned to prominence in the mid-1980s when it backed actor Bruce Willis's cover of "Respect Yourself," which gained considerable airplay on MTV.

North America

Stax Records,

an American recording studio based in Memphis, Tennessee, that played a key role in defining soul music and in popularizing the horn-driven "Memphis sound" during the 1960s.

Stax Record Company of Memphis, Tennessee, helped define the soul music era of the mid-1960s with what came to be known as its "Memphis sound," which combined gospel and blues-tinged vocals, tightly riffing horn sections, and a powerful rhythmic drive. Important Stax performers included Otis Redding, Booker T. and the MGs, Carla and Rufus Thomas, Sam and Dave (Sam Moore and David Prater), and the Staple Singers. Stax recordings also benefited from talented songwriters, especially the team of Isaac Hayes and David Porter, responsible for such hits as Sam and Dave's "Hold On, I'm Comin'" and Carla Thomas's "B-A-B-Y."

White siblings Jim Stewart and Estelle Axton opened the recording studio that would become Stax in 1960. They named their company Satellite Records, but in order to avoid confusion with another record company of the same name, they changed their label to Stax, derived from the first two letters of their last names. The Stax studio was located in a former movie theater whose marquee soon proclaimed: "SOULSVILLE USA." After a regional rhythm and blues hit in 1960—a Rufus and Carla Thomas duet titled "'Cause I Love You"—the fledgling company reached a long-term agreement with Atlantic Records to distribute that and future Stax recordings.

In search of the Memphis magic, Atlantic executive Jerry Wexler also began to bring his own artists to Stax, most notably Wilson Pickett. After several unsuccessful Atlantic recordings with large orchestras and elaborate arrangements, Pickett found his key to success in the leaner Stax approach, utilizing a small R&B band and simple riff-based accompaniments. His career-making Stax sessions of May and December 1965 yielded the hits "In the Midnight Hour," "634-5789," and "Ninety-Nine and One-Half Won't Do" and introduced what would be Pickett's signature sound.

One of the keys to Stax's success was the hiring in 1965 of Al Bell, a black disc jockey who had previously founded his own record label, to manage national promotion and sales. Bell was the first African American in the otherwise all-white Stax management. In 1968 he bought out Axton's share of the company and became a co-owner. The combination of Bell's vision and energy and the company's compelling music propelled Stax into a period of rapid growth and expansion. Stax—its management and musicians alike—began to view their studio as an alternative to Detroit's far larger Motown Records.

In contrast to Motown—which took a sweeter and slicker approach, often using lush string sections and producing music that seemed to emulate white pop songs—Stax brought an earthier, more hard-driving sound to American popular music. Al Jackson Jr., drummer for Booker T. and the

MGs as well as for many other Stax recording sessions, dismissed Motown recordings as being "made from the switchboard." Daily operations at Stax were marked by a closeness and informality that cut across racial barriers and seemed to draw everyone—musicians, engineers, and principal partners—together. Regular Stax session players included both blacks, such as Jackson, keyboards player Booker T. Jones, and sax player Andrew Love, and whites, including guitarist Steve Cropper, bass player Donald "Duck" Dunn, and trumpeter Wayne Jackson.

Yet despite numerous hits in the 1960s and early 1970s the company's success was shortlived. A combination of economic and political factors—including the consequences of the company's own sudden success and a deteriorating racial climate, particularly following the assassination of Martin Luther King Jr. in 1968—resulted in growing internal frictions that contributed to the bankruptcy that put Stax out of business in 1975.

North America

Still, William

(b. 1821, Burlington County, N.J.; d. July 14, 1902, Philadelphia, Pa.), African American abolitionist and author who documented the experience of fugitive slaves in the book *The Underground Railroad*.

The last of 18 children born to former slaves Levin and Charity Still, William Still spent most of his life in Philadelphia, Pennsylvania, where he had moved in 1844. By 1847 Still began his involvement in the antislavery movement while working for the Pennsylvania Society for the Abolition of Slavery. Until the Civil War he headed the Society's Philadelphia Vigilance Committee harboring fugitive slaves and directing them to Canada. Still would later compile the first detailed account of the Underground Railroad, as told by its participants. Published in 1872, *The Underground Railroad* remains an important text.

Leaving the Society in 1861, Still advocated for the economic development of the Philadelphia African American community, exemplified by the founding of his own coal business during the Civil War. Still remained attached to civil rights organizations as a researcher, writer, and activist until his death in 1902.

North America

Still, William Grant

(b. May 11, 1895, Woodville, Miss.; d. December 3, 1978, Los Angeles, Calif.), African American composer whose musical works included African American themes and spanned jazz, popular, opera, and classical genres.

William Grant Still grew up in Little Rock, Arkansas where, as a boy, he played the violin. He dropped out of Wilberforce University, where he had been studying to become a medical doctor, in order to pursue music. He studied music for two years at Oberlin Conservatory, and in 1921 he became a student of George Chadwick at the New England Conservatory in Boston. Still received a scholarship to study composition with Edgar Varese in New York as well as a Guggenheim and a Rosenwald fellowship.

Early in his career Still gained experience playing the oboe, violin, and cello for dance and theater orchestras. He toured the South with W.C. Handy's band, then went to New York, where he worked as a songwriter, arranger, and director of the black-owned recording company Black Swan Records. In 1921 Still performed in Noble Sissle and Eubie Blake's path-breaking show Shuffle Along, playing oboe in the pit orchestra. In the late 1920s Still turned to composing classical music. He created more than 150 musical works, including a series of five symphonies, four ballets, and nine operas. Two of his best-known compositions are *Afro-American Symphony* (1930) and *A Bayou Legend* (1941).

After studying the works of European masters, Still developed his own compositional style that incorporated African American folk and Native American songs. He was the first black composer to have a work performed by a major orchestra, to have an opera performed by a major company, and to conduct a major orchestra.

North America

Strayhorn, Billy

(b. November 29, 1915, Dayton, Ohio; d. May 31, 1967, New York, N.Y.), African American jazz composer, arranger, pianist; associate of the Duke Ellington Orchestra from 1939 to 1967.

Billy Strayhorn was born into a family that relocated from his birthplace in Dayton, Ohio, to Hillsborough, North Carolina, and finally to Pittsburgh, Pennsylvania. In Pittsburgh Strayhorn received private piano instruction in the classics. A technically accomplished student, he coupled his classical music training with an inventive approach to his playing, working out his own chromatic harmonies.

In December 1938 Strayhorn showed some of his own compositions to Duke Ellington, hoping to impress him enough to be taken on as a lyricist. Three months later Ellington recorded Strayhorn's "Something to Live For." As Ellington later recounted in his memoir, "Billy Strayhorn successfully married melody, words, and harmony, equating the fitting with happiness." "Something to Live For" was followed by four more recordings with Ellington's orchestra in 1939.

For the next 30 years Strayhorn worked with Ellington as an associate arranger and second pianist. The two collaborated so closely that it is difficult to assess the contribution of each on such arrangements as "Lush Life," "Satin Drill," and the orchestra's theme song, "Take the A Train," which Strayhorn composed. Ellington recalled that he and Strayhorn were so like-minded that once, when composing separately on a given mood, they chose the same first and last notes.

Strayhorn produced an album in his own name, the 1950 *Billy Strayhorn Trio*, and also participated in small group recordings with Ellington sidemen. His main work continued to be collaborative, creating such compositions as "Such Sweet Thunder," "Suite Thursday, and "Far East Suite" for Ellington's orchestra, before his death in 1967.

North America

Sugarhill Gang,

African American musical group whose "Rapper's Delight" was the first rap song to achieve commercial success.

With the phenomenal success of their 1979 single "Rapper's Delight," the Sugarhill Gang became the first rap group to break out of the dance clubs of New York and Los Angeles and achieve international fame. Ironically, the group did not originate in the post-disco DJ scene of other rap innovators, like Afrika Bambaataa and Grandmaster Flash. Instead, the Sugarhill Gang was the creation of Sugar Hill Records, a black-owned label that was the first to bring rap to a commercial audience.

The Sugarhill Gang consisted of three relatively unknown rappers—Big Bank Hank (Henry Jackson), Master Gee (Guy O'Brien), and Wonder Mike (Michael Wright)—whom Sylvia Robinson of Sugar Hill Records approached in early 1979. Backed by a track sampled from the disco group Chic's hit song "Good Times," the group's hit single exemplified the playful, positive, dance-oriented feel of early rap (which later fans have dubbed "old school"). Accused by veteran rappers of appropriating their trademark lyrics, the Sugarhill Gang popularized, rather than created, the sound for which they be-came famous. Despite the issues surrounding the group's authenticity, their work spawned a host of imitators and brought rap music into the American mainstream.

After the success of "Rapper's Delight," which was the first rap record to break into Top Forty radio play, the group dropped out of the public eye, though they continue to play (with manager Joey Robinson Jr. replacing Master Gee). In 1997 Rhino Records re-released the Sugarhill Gang's first record, now considered a classic of old school rap.

North America

Sun Ra

(b. May 22, 1914, Birmingham, Ala.; d. May 30, 1993, Birmingham, Ala.), African American jazz bandleader, arranger, and pianist, pioneer of collective improvisation and electric instruments who mounted multimedia, futuristic concerts from the 1950s through the early 1990s.

Sun Ra was born Herman "Sonny" Blount and grew up in Birmingham, Alabama, before moving to Chicago, Illinois during his teenage years. He played the piano as a boy, led his own band while in high school, and studied music education at Alabama A&M (now Alabama University). After touring with John "Fess" Whatley's band during the mid-1930s, Blount played piano and arranged songs for Fletcher Henderson in Chicago.

In the late 1940s Blount adopted the name Sun Ra, began calling Saturn his birthplace, and sported the motto "Space is the Place." His characteristic flowing Egyptian clothes reflected his new spiritual outlook. In 1953 Ra formed a musical ensemble called the Arkestra, which fused Afro-Cuban, avant-garde jazz, big-band, and hard bop styles. At the same time Ra founded Saturn Records, which released the Arkestra's albums during the following four decades. In the late 1970s the group moved its base from New York City to Philadelphia. Over the course of the Arkestra's 40 years, they recorded numerous albums, toured the United States, Europe, and Asia, and won international acclaim.

Sun Ra's music is characterized by a cosmic consciousness and outer space overtones. His performances incorporated dance, film, lighting effects, and music and featured many notable soloists, including John Coltrane's mentor, tenor saxophone player John Gilmore. Three documentaries were produced about Sun Ra: *The Cry of Jazz* (1959), *Space is the Place* (1971), and *Sun Ra: A Joyful Noise* (1980).

North America

Supremes, The,

African American female Motown popular music group that achieved commercial success in the 1960s by bringing African American singing style to a national audience.

From their first number one hit, "Where Did Our Love Go?" (1964) to later chart-toppers such as "Reflections" (1968) and "Someday We Will Be Together" (1969), the Supremes stand as the most commercially successful female group in 1960s popular music. They emerged as the top "model" in Berry Gordy Jr.'s "fleet" of acts at the Motown Record Company in Detroit, Michigan. Gordy, who worked briefly at Ford Motor Company, sought to produce and market his artists with an assembly-line technique. He wanted Motown music to appeal to audiences across racial boundaries. The Supremes achieved this goal and transformed American popular music.

The group's original members, Diana Ross, Florence Ballard, and Mary Wilson first began singing together in the late 1950s. They called themselves the Primettes—the sister group to the Primes, who eventually became known as The Temptations. After they won a local talent show the women secured an audition at Motown Records. They signed a contract in January 1961 and changed their name to The Supremes. Their first few records—"I Want A Guy" and "Buttered Popcorn"—were only modest successes and by 1963 the group earned the nickname, the "no-hit" Supremes. In 1964, however, the group's fate changed dramatically when "Where Did Our Love Go?" raced to the top of the charts. "Baby Love" and "Come See About Me" quickly followed and the Supremes were a national sensation.

The Supremes' success exemplified Motown's ability to market African American music to the baby boomer teenagers of the 1960s. The skillful songwriting team of Eddie Holland, Lamont Dozier, and Brian Holland—also known as Holland-Dozier-Holland—was responsible for the group's unique sound. The company's in-house charm school groomed the young women for the public spotlight. They learned choreography, manners, and fashion tips from entertainment veterans. As the group's fame grew, they became regulars on top television shows and toured around the world. For many, the Supremes epitomized elegance and glamour—a refreshingly new public image of black womanhood.

By the late 1960s the Supremes faced several professional and political challenges. In 1967 Cindy Birdsong replaced Florence Ballard, who struggled with the pressures of celebrity life, and Motown changed the group's name to Diana Ross and the Supremes. The group's music began to reflect the social turmoil of the times. Songs including "Love Child" (1968) and "I'm Living in Shame" (1969) spoke of the trials of life in an urban ghetto.

In January 1970 Diana Ross performed her last show as a Supreme at the Frontier Hotel in Las Vegas. She went on to pursue a solo singing and film career and received an Academy Award nomination for her portrayal of Billie Holiday in *Lady Sings the Blues* (1972). Jean Terrell replaced Diana Ross and the new Supremes were successful with songs such as "Stoned Love" (1970). The group never regained the popularity it attained throughout the 1960s, however, and disbanded in the late 1970s. In 1981 the musical *Dreamgirls*, which was largely based on the Supremes' story, became a hit on Broadway.

North America
___

Sweet Honey in the Rock (est. 1973),

African American female a cappella group that addresses global issues of social injustice through its music.

Sweet Honey in the Rock draws upon a wide range of styles, including the blues, spirituals, gospel, jazz, rap, and African traditional songs. Though an a cappella group, hand clapping, foot stomping, and light percussive African instruments such as *shekeres* sometimes accompany their harmonious vocal arrangements.

Struggle is a major theme in the music of Sweet Honey in the Rock, and their songs have consistently aimed to raise social consciousness. The group's founder and vocal director, Bernice Johnson Reagon, was a civil rights activist during the 1960s with the Student Nonviolent Coordinating Committee (SNCC) and a member of the SNCC Freedom Singers. Reagon has preserved a socially and politically responsible vision in her ongoing work with Sweet Honey in the Rock. Acquired immune deficiency syndrome (AIDS), worker and environmental exploitation, and racism are just a few of the issues addressed by the group.

Sweet Honey in the Rock refers to a land described in a religious parable as being so rich that if you crack open a rock, honey will flow. Bernice Johnson Reagon also relates the name to the legacy of African American women in the United States: "So, too, we, black women, have had to have the standing power of rocks and of mountains—cold and hard, strong and stationary. That quality has often obscured the fact that inside the strength, partnering the sturdiness, we are as honey." The group has witnessed some 20 personnel changes during the past 25 years and currently includes Ysaye Maria Barnwell, Nitanju Bolade Casel, Shirley Childress Johnson (a sign language interpreter), Aisha Kahlil, Carol Maillard, and Bernice Johnson Reagon. Sweet Honey in the Rock has recorded some ten albums, toured extensively within and beyond the United States, and won a Grammy Award in 1988 for their album *A Vision Shared: A Tribute to Woody Guthrie and Leadbelly*.

T

Tampa Red (Hudson Whittaker)

(b. December 25, 1900, Smithville, Ga.; d. December 19, 1981, Chicago, Ill.), African American blues guitarist and singer who helped define the urban blues sound in Chicago.

Hudson Whittaker, born Hudson Woodbridge, took the last name of the grandmother who raised him. He adopted the stage name Tampa Red after moving to Chicago in the 1920s. Initially, he played bottleneck slide guitar on recordings for Ma Rainey and Memphis Minnie. Whittaker wrote and performed his first hit, *"It's Tight Like That"* (1928), with gospel composer and impresario Thomas Dorsey. He formed a quintet in 1932 and continued to perform and record until 1953 when his wife died. In the early 1960s, he made an unsuccessful comeback attempt.

Tanner, Henry Ossawa

(b. June 21, 1859, Pittsburgh, Pa; d. May 25, 1937, Paris, France), African American painter who was called "the first genius among Negro artists" by art historian James A. Porter.

The son of a bishop of the African Methodist Episcopal Church, Henry Ossawa Tanner was named after Osawatomie, the site of John Brown's anti-slavery raid in Kansas. Tanner began painting at age 13, and beginning in 1880 was a student at the Philadelphia Academy of Fine Arts, where he studied with Thomas Eakins. Tanner taught at Clark College in Atlanta, Georgia, from 1889 to 1891, when he relocated to Paris, largely to escape racial prejudice in America. In Paris Tanner took courses at the Académie Julien and, with the exception of two brief visits home in 1893 and 1896, continued to live and paint there until his death in 1937.

While at the Pennsylvania Academy of Design and through 1890, Tanner painted traditional European subjects such as landscapes and animals. In the 1890s, however, Tanner began painting genre scenes of African American life, including his well-known works *The Banjo Lesson* (1893) and *The Thankful Poor* (1894). He is best known, though, for his paintings of biblical subjects, a theme Tanner began exploring in the mid-1890s, most famously in his 1896 painting *The Raising of Lazarus*. From 1894 to 1914 Tanner regularly exhibited his work at the Salon de la Société des Artistes Français in Paris, and after 1900 he also exhibited widely in the United States as well. In 1923 the French government named Tanner a chevalier of the French Legion of Honor.

North America

Tatum, Art

(b. October 13, 1909, Toledo, Ohio; d. November 5, 1956, Los Angeles, Calif.), African American jazz pianist whose harmonic and technical innovations set new standards in jazz music during the 1930s, 1940s, and 1950s.

Art Tatum was born partially blind, his vision impaired by cataracts in both eyes. He began playing the piano as a child, using his keen ear to imitate songs he heard on the radio. Encouraged by his musically inclined parents, Tatum also learned to play accordion, guitar, and violin at a young age. He further developed himself as a musician at the Cousino School for the Blind in Columbus, Ohio, and at the Toledo School of Music.

Tatum's career took off in 1929 when he began to play regularly for a Toledo radio station. After being hired by singer Adelaide Hall in 1932, Tatum went to New York City, where he performed at 52nd Street nightclubs. Over the course of the following decade he toured the United States and England, electrifying audiences with his virtuosity. As a member of a jazz trio featuring guitarist Tiny Grimes and bassist Slam Stewart, he enjoyed continued success from 1944 until his death in 1956. Tatum's bold exploration of extended harmonies deeply influenced the birth of bebop.

Tatum first recorded in 1933, after his arrival in New York City. While he intermittently collaborated with other jazz musicians on recordings, he is best known for his solo performances, of which he recorded more than 100 between 1953 and 1955. Two of his outstanding renditions of popular songs are *"Tea for Two"* (1933) and *"Rosetta"* (1944). Tatum's dexterity was so refined that he could play the piano just as effectively with the backs of his fingers, palms up, as with the tips of his fingers, palms down.

North America

Taylor, Koko (Cora Walton)

(b. September 28, 1935, Memphis, Tenn.), African American blues singer and a master of the electric Chicago blues style, known as the "Queen of the Blues."

The youngest of six children, Koko Taylor—whose name was originally Cora Walton—was born in Memphis, Tennessee. Her sharecropper father brought the children up after their mother's death in 1939. Taylor's father raised cotton, and she and her siblings worked in the fields. Taylor began singing gospel music in church, but she listened to the blues and rhythm and blues (R&B) broadcasts of B. B. King and Rufus Thomas (b. 1917) on Memphis's black radio station, WDIA. "The first blues record I ever heard," she recalled, "was 'Me and My Memphis Blues,' by Memphis Minnie [Douglas (1897–1973)]. I was 12 or 13, and just loved it."

At age 18 Taylor met truck driver Robert "Pops" Taylor. When he decided to leave Tennessee to work in a Chicago slaughterhouse, Taylor married him and moved north. In 1953 Taylor arrived in Chicago, part of a vast migration of African Americans leaving the South for greater opportunities in the urban North and West. She arrived in Chicago at the height of the new Chicago blues style, which featured electric guitars in small combos and used heavier, more driving rhythms than traditional rural blues. During the week she worked cleaning suburban homes, but she spent her weekends in Chicago's South Side blues bars.

During the mid-1950s Chicago's South Side nightspots featured such blues musicians as guitarist and singer Muddy Waters, the person most responsible for creating the Chicago blues style; harmonica player and vocalist Howlin' Wolf; guitarist and vocalist Buddy Guy (b. 1936); and guitarist, harmonica player, and vocalist Jimmy Reed (1925–1976). Taylor began sitting in with various performers, joining them on the stand to sing. Her powerful and rough-edged singing—in particular, her use of growling, raspy effects—quickly attracted attention. Taylor's singing reflected the influence not only of female blues singers Big Mama Thornton and Bessie Smith, but also bluesmen Muddy Waters and Howlin' Wolf, but she quickly forged her own distinctive style.

One evening in 1962, bass player and composer Willie Dixon, a prominent figure in the Chicago blues community, heard Taylor perform. Dixon took Taylor under his wing, and her career took off. In 1963 she made her recording debut, recording her own "Honky Tonky" for the small record label USA, but she soon signed a contract with Chess Records, Chicago's leading blues recording company. Taylor's 1966 rendition of Dixon's "Wang Dang Doodle" became a million-selling recording and gave Chess Records its last Top Ten R&B hit.

During the early 1970s interest in blues music waned, and Taylor dropped from sight until signing with Alligator Records in 1974. The first of her six albums for Alligator, I Got What It Takes (1975), was nominated for a Grammy Award. There were many more Grammy nominations in the following years. During the 1980s Taylor gained widespread recognition, including a Grammy Award for the album Blues Explosion (1984) and, between 1983 and 1992, a total of ten Handy Awards, the blues music equivalent of the Grammy, which is named for blues composer W.C. Handy.

While on tour in 1988 Taylor experienced a profound personal tragedy when her tour van was involved in an accident. Two band members and her husband, Pops Taylor, were seriously injured; six months later Taylor died of his injuries. Koko Taylor suffered a fractured shoulder, collarbone and ribs, which kept her from performing for several months. But she resolved to return to music, and soon resumed an active touring schedule, including appearances at many blues and folk music festivals.

Taylor, Susie Baker King

(b. August 6, 1848, Liberty County, Ga.; d. 1912), African American teacher, nurse, and writer; the only black woman to write of her experiences in the Civil War.

Born a Georgia slave, Susie Baker was quite young when an arrangement was made to send her to live with her grandmother in Savannah. She learned to read and write from two white children, even though this was illegal prior to the Civil War. When war broke out she moved with her uncle's family to the Sea Islands of South Carolina. The Union army, fighting for these islands, pressed her into service as a teacher of freed slave children and adults. Soon after, the men in her family joined the Union's First South Carolina Infantry, and she traveled with them as a nurse and laundress. In 1862 she married one of the regiment's sergeants, Edward King who died in 1866. In her memoir, *A Black Woman's Civil War Memoirs*, she recounted the events of her life in camp with the regiment. She is the only black woman known to have written of her life during the war.

After the war she remained in Georgia. At different times she began and ran schools for black children and adults. In 1879 she married Russell Taylor and moved to Boston, Massachusetts. She returned south in 1898 to care for her dying son in Louisiana; en route she rode in a segregated rail car and witnessed a lynching. Her memoir, published in 1902, not only spoke of the war, but of life after the war, ending with hopeful memories of the "wonderful revolution" that had taken place in 1861.

Temptations, The,

an African American vocal group that enjoyed its greatest successes during the 1960s and 1970s with a repertoire encompassing romantic ballads and hard-edged soul music.

The Temptations was one of the most successful groups in the history of black music. Over the course of 25 years the group had 43 Top Ten singles and by the early 1980s had sold more than 20 million records. The vocal quintet, initially called the Elgins, was founded in Detroit in 1961 by members of two local rhythm and blues (R&B) groups: Eddie Kendricks and Paul Williams sang with the Primes; Melvin Franklin, Eldridge Bryant, and Otis

Williams came from the Distants. In that year Berry Gordy signed them to his Detroit-based Motown Records and renamed them the Temptations. The group attained its classic lineup in 1963, when Bryant was replaced by David Ruffin. Many of the group's hits featured the contrasting leads of Ruffin's gritty baritone and Kendricks's crystalline high tenor and falsetto.

In conjunction with two gifted Motown producers—Smokey Robinson, 1962–1966, and Norman Whitfield, 1966–1975—the Temptations created memorable pop music. Robinson, a songwriter as well as a record producer, provided the group with several hits during 1965–1966. He co-wrote the group's first Number-One pop hit, *"My Girl"* (1965), an irresistible confection that set the Temptations' shimmering harmonies against a pungent electric-guitar line, with lush orchestral accompaniment that suggested classical music.

Whitfield continued the Temptations' success, encouraging performances of raw urgency that made it the only Motown group to match the harder soul music produced by Stax and Atlantic Records. The group also recorded "psychedelic soul music"—such as *"Cloud Nine"* (1968)—that reflected the influence of Sly and the Family Stone. On occasion the Temptations even performed protest music such as *"Stop the War Now"* (1970). The group's most significant hit with Whitfield was the soulful and funky *"Papa Was a Rolling Stone"* (1972), which won Motown its first Grammy Award.

By the mid-1970s, however, the Temptations had fallen from prominence. Between 1976 and 1980 the group left Motown for an unsuccessful stint with Atlantic Records before returning to Berry Gordy's label. Personnel changes undermined the group's identity. Ruffin left in 1968; Kendricks and Paul Williams followed three years later. Although Otis Williams and Franklin continued with the group for more than 30 years, the Temptations became less a band and more a brand name.

By the late 1990s all of the original, hit-making Temptations had died, except for Otis Williams. Paul Williams shot himself in 1973. Ruffin died of a drug overdose in 1991. In the following year Kendricks succumbed to lung cancer. Franklin died in 1995 of a heart attack. Following Franklin's death, Otis Williams told the *Chicago Tribune*, "I almost see us like a football franchise or a baseball franchise. People come and go, but [the group] still goes on."

North America

Tharpe, "Sister" Rosetta

(b. March 20, 1915, Cotton Plant, Ark.; d. October 9, 1973, Philadelphia, Pa.), gospel singer who paved the way for gospel's golden age in the 1940s and 1950s.

Born to Katie (Bell) Nubin, a singing and mandolin-playing evangelist for the Church of God in Christ (COGIC), the leading Pentecostal denomination, Sister Rosetta Tharpe (born Rosetta Nubin) made her gospel debut at age five, singing *"I Looked Down the Line and I Wondered,"* in front of an audience of 1,000 people. She became known as "Little Sister" as she traveled with her mother between 1923 and 1934, and she gained a reputation among Pentecostal Holiness people as a singer and guitar player. Tharpe's style was influenced by the sanctified blind pianist, Arizona Dranes, also a member of COGIC. Both Tharpe and Dranes traveled with Rev. F. W. McGee on the tent-meeting revival circuit.

In 1938 Thorne made national headlines, including a feature in *Life* magazine, when she performed her sacred music with Cab Calloway at the Cotton Club in New York City. That same year Tharpe became the first gospel performer to sign with a major record label when Decca Records offered her a recording contract. Her subsequent recording of Thomas A. Dorsey's composition *"Hide Me in Thy Bosom"* under the title *"Rock Me,"* became a hit. Also in 1938 Tharpe performed in John Hammond's legendary Carnegie Hall concert, *"Spirituals to Swing."*

By 1940 Tharpe had become very popular and toured America and Europe, performing in nightclubs, concert halls, and jazz festivals. Her success in these secular spaces created a controversy among the Holiness Churches. In spite of the controversy, Tharpe teamed with Marie Knight and the two made the Billboard charts with their song *"Up Above My Head."* She and Knight later recorded and performed the blues. This action caused a rift between Tharpe and the Holiness people that never completely healed. Tharpe continued to perform in secular venues throughout the 1940s, 1950s, and 1960s. She toured with secular performers such as Roy Acuff, Mary Lou Williams and Lucky Millender, as well as with gospel groups like the James Cleveland Singers, the Golden Gate Quartet, and the Dixie Hummingbirds.

Tharpe generally sang solo while accompanying herself on the guitar. Her style of playing placed her in a category with bluesmen Big Bill Broonzy and Lonnie Johnson. She used the guitar to respond to her vocal melodies, playing single note lines that were improvised variations of the vocal melody. Her biggest hits came from her upbeat and syncopated renditions of songs like *"I Looked Down the Line,"* *"That's All,"* and *"This Train."*

By the late 1960s Tharpe's popularity had waned, but she continued to tour the country on the "chitlin circuit," playing in backwoods bars and small-town theaters. She suffered a stroke in 1973 and died in Philadelphia, Pennsylvania, one day before an anticipated recording session.

North America
_____

Thornton, Willie Mae ("Big Mama")

(b. December 11, 1926, Montgomery, Ala.; d. July 25, 1984, Los Angeles, Calif.), African American blues singer, songwriter, and musician known for boisterous stage performances, shouting vocals, outspoken lyrics, and an eccentric lifestyle that influenced a later generation of popular musicians.

Willie Mae Thornton sang gospel music as a child in her minister father's church. Shortly after her mother's death, when Thornton was age 14, she joined Sammy Green's Hot Harlem Revue, traveling throughout the South's "chitlin circuit," singing and teaching herself the harmonica, guitar, and drums.

In 1948 Thornton moved to Houston, Texas, and signed an exclusive contract with Peacock Records. Thornton's 1.83 m (6 ft) tall and 114-kg (250-lb) frame earned her the nickname Big Mama, which she celebrated in *"They Call Me Big Mama."* Her recording sessions with the Johnny Otis rhythm-and-blues Caravan yielded *"Hound Dog,"* which reached Number One on the rhythm-and-blues charts and was made famous in the 1950s by Elvis Presley, and *"Ball and Chain,"* which became Janis Joplin's signature song in the late 1960s. Though both songs earned Thornton enough fame to tour nationally, she had signed away her royalty rights and saw little of the money that Presley and Joplin later did.

In the early 1960s, her career declining, Thornton moved to San Francisco in an attempt to revitalize her career. Because of the blues revival occurring in the late 1960s, Thornton's career rebounded. Through the 1960s and 1970s she played jazz and blues festivals in the United States and Europe, and recorded several albums.

Thornton suffered from alcohol-related problems, and she died of a heart attack poor and little known. A benefit concert was given to raise burial money. Though popular acclaim eluded Thornton, she influenced many later musicians, including Joplin, Aretha Franklin, Grace Slick, Stevie Nicks, and Angela Strehli.

North America

Thrash, Dox

(b. March 22, 1893, Griffin, Ga.; d. 1965, Philadelphia, Pa.), African American artist and printer; also co-inventor of the carborundum print-process.

Having studied for several years at the school at the Art Institute of Chicago, Dox Thrash settled in Philadelphia, Pennsylvania. Once there he painted signs and worked on the Federal Arts Project (FAP) to earn a living. Working with the FAP in the Graphic Division, he helped invent a new lithographic process, called the carborundum print-process. This method of printing created prints with more expressive tones and variation. His carbographs explored the portraits of African Americans, landscapes, and scenes of slum life. *My Neighbor* (1937) and the landscape *Deserted Cabin* (1939) are examples of Thrash's carbographs. In the late 1930s and through the 1940s Thrash's work was shown in many prominent places, including a 1942 solo exhibition at the Philadelphia Museum of Art.

Thurman, Wallace

(b. August 16, 1902, Salt Lake City, Utah; d. December 22, 1934, New York, N.Y.), African American writer of the Harlem Renaissance who espoused a frank and sometimes stark assessment of African American life in America.

In 1925 Wallace Thurman began his writing career at the University of Southern California, where he started and edited the short-lived *Outlet*, a literary magazine that discussed many ideas of the Harlem Renaissance. Leaving school for Harlem that same year, Thurman became a part of the cultural outpouring that he had been observing. He began working in New York as an editorial assistant at a small magazine called *Looking Glass*, followed by positions at other publications, such as the white magazine *The World Tomorrow*. At the left-wing *Messenger*, where he was temporary editor, Thurman became associated with other writers in Harlem, including Langston Hughes and Zora Neale Hurston.

In 1926 Thurman helped found *Fire!!*, a journal intended to expose the new thinking of the Harlem Renaissance and publish writing about African Americans who broke free from mainstream American culture. Unfortunately, the journal, which Thurman edited, was plagued with financial problems, and an actual fire in a basement where many issues of *Fire!!* were stored secured the downfall of the publication after only one issue. Thurman started a similar magazine in 1928, *Harlem, a Forum of Negro Life*, which failed after one issue.

Despite his failures as a publisher, Thurman wrote three books, a play, and several articles and editorials for numerous magazines. His writing often satirized African American life and the Harlem Renaissance, depicting the contradictions within black thought of the time, especially in his novels *The Blacker the Berry* (1929) and *Infants of the Spring* (1932). His play Harlem was originally produced at the Apollo Theater in 1929 and may have been his largest success. His final novel, *The Interne* (1932), exposed the injustices at City Hospital on Welfare Island (now Roosevelt Island). He died at that hospital in 1934, of tuberculosis and consumption, related to chronic alcoholism.

Tindley, Charles Albert

(b. July 7, 1851, Berlin, Md.; d. July 26, 1933, Philadelphia, Pa.), African American minister and gospel musician whose hymns became a basis of twentieth-century African American church music.

In 1916 Tindley published *New Songs of Paradise*, a collection of 37 gospel songs. By 1941 the collection had run to its seventh edition. Among his best-known songs are *"A Better Home," "Stand by Me," "What Are They Doing in Heaven Tonight?," "We'll Understand it Better By and By,"* and *"I'll Over-*

come Some Day." Many of them and others of his works are now standards in African American churches. His work inspired the gospel songs of Thomas A. Dorsey and Rev. Herbert Brewster.

Tlali, Miriam

(b. 1933, Johannesburg, South Africa), South African writer, many of whose works were banned under apartheid.

Born to educated parents, as a child Miriam Tlali was encouraged to study and write. But as a black South African she found her educational opportunities limited. After attending local elementary schools and studying art in high school, she won a scholarship to the University of Witwatersrand, but her hopes of studying medicine were dashed by the university's quotas for black students, which would allow her to study only administration. Tlali later pursued pre-medical training at Roma University in Lesotho but ran out of money after a year and never finished her medical training.

Back in Johannesburg, Tlali drew on her experiences working as a furniture store bookkeeper to write her autobiographical first novel, *Muriel at Metropolitan*. Written in 1969, the book was not published in South Africa until 1975, partly because of its subtle but scathing portrayal of white insensitivity and everyday cruelty toward black people. In the 1970s Tlali also began writing articles and stories that appeared in South African magazines such as the *Rand Daily Mail* and *Staffrider*.

Leaving Africa for the first time, Tlali attended the International Writers Program at the University of Iowa in 1978–1979. Her second novel, *Amandla* (1980), told the story of a black family living in Soweto during the 1976 uprising and was, like Tlali's first novel, banned in South Africa. (Tlali herself was banned from political activity for many years.) In the 1980s Tlali, by then a wife and mother, wrote an interview series for *Staffrider* called *Soweto Speaking*. She also published three books in 1989 alone: *Mihloti* and *Soweto Stories*, both collections of Tlali's journalism, and *Footprints in the Quag: Stories and Dialogues from Soweto*. Declining to describe herself as a feminist in "the narrow, Western" sense, Tlali has become an important proponent of womanism, the theory that black women living in a racially oppressive society must empower their community's men while at the same time supporting their sisters. As one of Tlali's female characters says to another in one of her short stories, "We're all alike; we're women. We need each other when things are difficult."

Tolson, Melvin Beaunorus

(b. February 6, 1898, Moberly, Mo.; d. August 29, 1966, Guthrie, Okla.), African American poet, chronicler of the cultural scene in Harlem.

Melvin Tolson attended Fisk University before transferring to Lincoln University, where he received his bachelor's degree in 1922. He took positions teaching English literature and coaching the debate team at Wiley College in Marshall, Texas, but was inspired to develop his talent for poetry after attending Columbia University on a Rockefeller Foundation scholarship from 1931 to 1932. Tolson's year at Columbia put him in Harlem at the end of the Harlem Renaissance, and he became friendly with many writers associated with it, most notably Langston Hughes. In several poems over the next two decades, Tolson would revisit the atmosphere of 1930s Harlem.

Tolson's first major work, *Rendezvous with America*, was published in 1944. Throughout the 1940s, his poems, characterized by their allusive, complex, modernist style and their long poetic sequences, were published in such magazines and journals as the *Atlantic Monthly*, the *Modern Quarterly*, the *Arts Quarterly*, and *Poetry*. In 1947 the government of Liberia named Tolson its poet laureate and commissioned him to write a piece for the country's centennial; the result was Libretto for the Republic of Liberia (1953). Tolson's best-known piece, the poetic sequence *Harlem Gallery*, was published in 1965. In 1966 he won the Arts and Letters Award in literature from the American Academy and Institute of Arts and Letters. *A Gallery of Harlem Portraits*, an extended work Tolson had begun with a single sonnet in 1932, was published posthumously in 1979.

North America

Toomer, Jean

(b. December 26, 1894, Washington, D.C.; d. March 30, 1967), African American writer whose experimental novel of Southern life, Cane, profoundly influenced twentieth-century black writers.

Jean Toomer's position in the canon of African American literature rests on his haunting narrative of Southern life, *Cane*. Since its original publication in 1923, the novel has been rediscovered by successive generations of black writers, despite Toomer's later ambivalence toward his racial identity. Toomer, racially mixed but able to pass for white, sought a unifying thesis that would resolve the conflicts of his identity. He spent his life trying to evade the categories of American racial and ethnic identification, which he felt constricted the complexity of a lineage like his.

As a writer Toomer was nurtured in the 1910s and 1920s by Greenwich Village progressive aesthetes like Waldo Frank and Hart Crane, but *Cane* was inspired by his two-month stint as a substitute principal at the black Sparta Agricultural and Industrial Institute in Georgia in 1921. Entranced by Georgia's rural geography and its black folk traditions, he saw in Southern life the harmony that escaped him, although he believed the culture to be disappearing through migration to the North and its encounter with modernity.

Cane is a series of vignettes whose narrative structure moves from the South to the North and back to the South, forming a troubled synthesis of the two regions. The book was a commercial failure on its first publication, but critics initiated a chorus of praise that has spanned the generations. Members of the Harlem Renaissance and the Black Arts Movement, as well as later African American women writers like Toni Morrison and Alice Walker, have cited its influence and acclaimed the author's sensitive treatment of black folk life, his formal elegance, and his progressive, uninhibited approach to sexuality and gender.

Cane was Toomer's only work that explicitly treated the lives of African Americans; after its publication he disappeared from literary circles. In 1924 the restless author made the first of several pilgrimages to Fontainebleau, France, to study with the mystic and psychologist Georges Ivanovich Gurdjieff at the Institute for the Harmonious Development of Man. Gurdjieff believed that a transcendent "essence," obscured by a socially determined "personality," could be recovered through his teachings. Through Gurdjieff, Toomer found a way to express his attempts at defining a holistic identity. He taught Gurdjieff's philosophy in Harlem and Chicago until his break with the mystic in the mid-1930s.

Toomer wrote voluminously until his death, and although much of his writing received occasional praise for its experimentation, it was largely dismissed by African American critics, who saw it not only as propaganda for Gurdjieff's teachings, but as being white-identified. Indeed, in 1930 Toomer declined to be included in James Weldon Johnson's *Book of American Negro Poetry*, on the grounds that he was not a Negro. Toomer continued to strive for a sense of wholeness, however, and for a definition of what Henry Louis Gates Jr. has described as a "remarkably fluid notion of race." He found this in the potential of an "American" race, described in the 1936 long poem "Blue Meridian"—the last work published while he was alive—as a hybrid, "blue," comprising the black, the white, and the red races.

Author Jean Toomer's 1923 novel, *Cane*, influenced generations of African American writers. The author is shown here in 1934.
CORBIS/Bettmann

Tosh, Peter (Peter McIntosh)

(b. 1944; d. 1987, Westmoreland, Jamaica), Jamaican singer and songwriter, best known as an original member of the Wailers, the singing trio that also included Bob Marley and Bunny Wailer (Neville O'Riley Livingston), and as an internationally popular solo artist with an emphatic political and prophetic bent.

Peter Tosh's entrance into music began during his teenage years in the Trenchtown ghetto of Kingston, where he and his friends Bob Marley and Bunny Wailer imitated the vocal harmonies of Curtis Mayfield. Tosh's early recordings as part of a ska/reggae trio with Marley and Wailer (who became known as the Wailers) made clear that his singing and song-writing talents were strongly flavored by rage against hypocritical individuals and institutions. Songs like "*400 Years*" and "*Downpressor*" are prime examples of his mastery of political protest songwriting. His first recordings as a solo artist in the early 1960s include a wry commentary on sexual mores ("*Shame and Scandal*") and a boastful declaration of Rastafarian identity ("*Rasta Shook Them Up*").

After quitting the Wailers in 1972, Tosh pursued a performing and recording career as a solo artist, marked by the cultivation of a persona of supreme toughness and righteous wrath, sentiments encapsulated in the song that became his anthem, "*I'm the Toughest.*" This stance was reinforced during a Jamaican concert when Tosh lectured Jamaica's prime minister, sitting in the audience, about the errors of the minister's ways. An overview of his recording career is available on CD as *Peter Tosh: Honorary Citizen* (Columbia). His murder by armed robbers silenced reggae's most politically inspired artist.

Tribe Called Quest, A,

an African American rap group whose innovative sound helped stretch the sonic parameters of hip hop.

The members of A Tribe Called Quest—DJ Ali Shaheed Muhammad and MCs Phife (or Malik Taylor) and Q-Tip (or Jonathan Davis)—were friends from high school in New York City. The group came together in 1988 and released its debut album, *People's Instinctive Travels and the Paths of Rhythm*, in 1990. It was a wild critical success, a playfully Afrocentric album full of wit ("*I Left My Wallet in El Segundo*") and verve ("*Bonita Applebum*"), and it garnered a rare five-microphone review from the hip hop magazine of record, *The Source. People's Instinctive Travels and the Paths of Rhythm* also helped define the "Native Tongues" posse, an informal group of like-minded rap bands that also included De La Soul, Jungle Brothers, and Black Sheep.

On their second album, *The Low End Theory* (1991), A Tribe Called Quest further pared down their already sparse sound. Tribe set its casual rhymes against deceptively simple jazz samples on tracks ranging from the thumping, kinetic "*Scenario*," with future rap star Busta Rhymes, to the more contemplative "*Verses from the Abstract*," featuring an original groove by renowned jazz bassist Ron Carter. Perhaps more important, *The Low End Theory* marked the creative peak of the jazz-rap movement that also included Guru's *Jazzmatazz* (1993) and Digable Planets' *Reachin' (A New Refutation of Time and Space)* (1993).

Midnight Marauders (1993) confirmed A Tribe Called Quest's reputation as consistently original performers, although after *Beats, Rhymes, and Life* (1996) some critics complained that the band was running low on inspiration. Q-Tip, the highest-profile member of the group, has made memorable guest appearances on Deee-Lite's "*Groove is in the Heart*," the Beastie Boys' "*Get it Together*," and Janet Jackson's "*Got 'Til It's Gone*". A Tribe Called Quest released *The Love Movement* in 1998 and disbanded the same year.

Latin America and the Caribbean

Tubby, King

(b. Osbourne Ruddock, Kingston, Jamaica, 1941; d. Kingston, Jamaica, 1989), a skilled sound engineer who pioneered dub reggae in Jamaica.

King Tubby gained prominence in 1968 for playing his instrumental mixes accompanied by the crowd-pleasing "talk-over" deejaying of U-Roy (Ewart Beckford). The duo was known as Tubby's Hi-Fi and became highly popular in the impoverished Watertown section of Kingston where Tubby lived. U-Roy's verbal wordplay provided a perfect compliment to Tubby's increasingly experimental song versions. Using homemade and modified studio equipment, Tubby started dropping in vocal snippets, adding ghostly layers of echo and reverberation, soloing various instruments, inserting sudden silences, and employing unusual equalization and other studio effects. Crowds loved the soulful roots reggae mutated by technical wizardry and avant-garde mixing approaches. Following Tubby's lead, many musicians and engineers began dubbing.

By 1972 dub fever had arrived. Fierce competition between sound systems kept creative pressures high, although King Tubby remained on top. In 1976 police attempted to shut down a dance at Tubby's Hi-Fi by shooting and axing his speakers on claims that his music attracted a hostile crowd. Dub's largest buying audience was the urban poor, and middle- and upper-class Jamaicans sought to suppress the form for being "rough" and "uncouth."

King Tubby turned to training studio apprentices in the 1980s as dub's popularity waned. Tubby's ideas and techniques have influenced a new generation of electronic musicians who value dub's aggressive reinvention and studio science. Dozens of dub albums feature King Tubby's mixing skills, and contemporary interest has fueled a steady stream of re-releases, such as the superlative *Glen Brown and King Tubby: Termination Dub and King Tubby* and *Soul Syndicate: Freedom Sounds in Dub.*

Turner, Lorenzo Dow

(b. January 1895, Elizabeth City, N.C.; d. February 10, 1972, Chicago, Ill.), African American linguist and ethnologist who identified and analyzed African survivals in African American language.

Lorenzo Dow Turner received a bachelor's degree from Howard University in 1914, a master's degree from Harvard University in 1917, and a doctoral degree from the University of Chicago in 1926. He taught English at several black colleges, and initially became interested in linguistics after hearing the black Gullah language.

In 1931 Turner became the first African-American member of the Linguistics Society. His research on Gullah, Creole, and the Niger-Kordofanian language family established connections between African languages and African American dialects, and helped rebut the common Western belief that African culture had not influenced the New World.

Turner, Tina

(b. November 26, 1939, Brownsville, Tenn.), African American pop singer and actress who made one of the biggest comebacks in recording history.

Tina Turner was born Anna Mae Bullock. As a child she sang and danced with a local trombonist named Bootsie Whitelaw. After her parents separated in 1950, she lived with her maternal grandmother. Six years later Turner moved to St. Louis, Missouri, to live with her mother and older sister. The same year she met guitarist Ike Turner after spontaneously performing a song with his group, the Kings of Rhythm, in an East St. Louis nightclub. Turner joined the group in 1957 and changed her name to Tina in 1960, at which time the Kings of Rhythm became the Ike and Tina Turner Revue. Ike and Tina Turner married in 1962, and they toured throughout the United States and Europe. Their biggest hit, *"Proud Mary,"* won a Grammy in 1971. Driven away by Ike's emotional and physical abuse, Tina Turner left the group in 1976.

After finalizing her divorce from Ike in 1978, Turner embarked on a solo career in Europe with the help of David Bowie, Mick Jagger, and Rod Stewart. She secured a recording contract with Capitol Records in 1983 and released the successful single *"Let's Stay Together,"* originally recorded by Al Green in 1971. Turner's 1984 album *Private Dancer*, featuring the hit single *"What's Love Got to Do with It,"* won three Grammy Awards and sold over 25 million copies worldwide. Both of Turner's next two albums,

Break Every Rule (1986) and *Tina Live in Europe* (1988), received a Grammy. She played leading roles in *Tommy* (1975) and *Mad Max: Beyond the Thunderdome* (1985), and was the subject of the film *What's Love Got to Do with It* (1993). Turner was inducted into the Rock and Roll Hall of Fame in January 1991.

North America

Tyson, Cicely

(b. December 19, 1933, New York City, N.Y.), African American stage, motion-picture, and television actor known for portraying strong female characters.

Cicely Tyson was educated at New York University and at the Actors Studio. After working as a successful fashion model, Tyson acted in Harlem and in off-Broadway productions in New York City in the late 1950s. She had a small role in the motion picture *Odds Against Tomorrow* (1959) and later became widely known as a regular cast member on the critically praised television drama series *East Side, West Side* (1963–1964). After appearing in supporting parts in the motion pictures *A Man Called Adam* (1966), *The Comedians* (1967), and *The Heart Is a Lonely Hunter* (1968), she costarred in *Sounder* (1972), about a black American sharecropper family in the 1930s. Tyson received a 1972 Academy Award nomination for best actress for her performance in *Sounder*. She is best known for her role in the television movie *The Autobiography of Miss Jane Pittman* (1974), for which she won an Emmy Award for best actress, and for her work in the television miniseries *Roots* (1977), which was adapted from the book of the same title by African American author Alex Haley. Her other motion-picture performances include roles in *The River Niger* (1976), *A Hero Ain't Nothin' but a Sandwich* (1978), *Fried Green Tomatoes* (1991), *Riot* (1996), and *Hoodlum* (1997). In 1994 she returned to television drama as a costar in the series *Equal Justice*.

Uncle Tom's Cabin,

best-selling but controversial 1852 American novel that increased worldwide sentiment against slavery.

When Harriet Beecher Stowe's antislavery novel *Uncle Tom's Cabin* was published in 1852, it was an immediate bestseller and became the most sensational and best-selling book of the nineteenth century. French writer George Sand described the international phenomenon: "This book is in all hands and in all journals. It has, and will have, editions in every form; people devour it, they cover it with tears." Today the novel has been criticized for its stereotypical depictions of black characters, as well as for its sentimentalism and moralism. But as problematic as some of the book's language and descriptions are, in the 1850s *Uncle Tom's Cabin* evoked international sympathy for African American slaves.

Harriet Beecher Stowe was born in Connecticut in 1811, the daughter of Lyman Beecher, a prominent Congregational minister. The Beechers, who were white, had never owned slaves, but in 1832 they moved to Cincinnati, just across the Ohio River from slaveholding Kentucky. There Stowe taught at a school for ex-slave children and saw firsthand race riots, terrified runaway slaves, bounty hunters, and suffering freed people. Upon returning to New England in 1850, she decided to write a book about her insights, one of the only forms of protest available to her: "My heart was bursting with the anguish excited by the cruelty and injustice our nation was showing to the slave, and praying God to let me do a little and cause my cry for them to be heard."

Uncle Tom's Cabin's strong religious overtones appealed to its largely Christian, white, nineteenth-century audience. Its plot follows the story of Uncle Tom, a pious and faithful slave, as he is sold to several owners. His last owner beats him to death, but even as the Christ-like Uncle Tom is dying, he prays that his master will repent and be saved. A favorite character among readers was Little Eva, a white child who treats her slaves with angelic love and kindness and dies in the middle of the book surrounded by

543

This 1899 theater poster advertises a stage version of Harriet Beecher Stowe's *Uncle Tom's Cabin*, the antislavery novel first published in 1852. *CORBIS/Bettmann*

weeping servants. Stowe complements these melodramatic deathbed scenes with equally dramatic descriptions of beatings, sexual abuse, and family separations, all of which added to the novel's powerful effect on its readers.

Uncle Tom's Cabin has had its critics. The first were Southern slaveholders, who argued that the book was horribly exaggerated fiction; ownership of the book was made illegal in the South. In response Stowe published in 1853 *A Key to Uncle Tom's Cabin*, a collection of slave narratives, newspaper clippings, and other facts that verified the details in her novel. In more recent years many readers have criticized the condescending racist descriptions of the appearance, speech, and behavior of many of the book's black characters, and the excessive pietism of Uncle Tom.

Uncle Tom's Cabin was so widely read that its characters helped spread common stereotypes of African Americans. These included lazy, carefree Sam, an example of the "happy darky"; Eliza, Cassy, and Emmeline, beautiful light-skinned women who are the products and victims of sexual abuse and stereotypes of the tragic mulatto; and several affectionate, dark-skinned women house servants who are examples of the Mammy figure (including a character named Mammy, the cook at the St. Clare plantation).

The name "Uncle Tom" has itself become a stereotype for an African American who is too eager to please whites. Soon after the book was published, traveling "Tom shows" became popular throughout the United States. These were essentially minstrel shows loosely based on *Uncle Tom's Cabin*, and their grossly exaggerated caricatures further perpetuated some of the stereotypes that Stowe used.

These negative associations now sometimes overshadow Stowe's original intentions, as well as the historical impact of *Uncle Tom's Cabin* as a vital antislavery tool. At the time of its publication, though, the novel's impact was without question. Some have claimed that it so affected British readers that it kept England from joining the American Civil War on the side of the Confederacy, and when President Abraham Lincoln met Stowe in 1862, he reportedly called her "the little woman who wrote the book that started this great war!" The cry that Stowe had hoped to sound about African Americans was indeed heard, and while *Uncle Tom's Cabin* did perpetuate cultural stereotypes of African Americans, it also turned the tide of public opinion against slavery in the United States.

VanDerZee, James Augustus

(b. June 29, 1886, Lenox, Mass.; d. May 15, 1983, Washington, D.C.), African American photographer whose work recorded and contributed to the Harlem Renaissance.

James VanDerZee was born in Lenox, Massachussetts, and made his earliest photographs there in 1900, after he won a camera for peddling large amounts of sachet powder. He immediately embraced photography and by the time he moved to New York City in 1906 had mastered the rudiments of the craft. After a job as a waiter, a short stay in Virginia, and a job snapping portraits in a New Jersey department store, VanDerZee opened his own studio in Harlem. From 1916 to 1931 he kept shop at 135th Street and Lenox Avenue, serving as the neighborhood's preeminent photographer.

VanDerZee documented faces and facets of the Harlem Renaissance, as well as numerous weddings, funerals, business clubs, and sports teams. In 1924 Marcus Garvey contracted with him to be the official photographer of the Universal Negro Improvement Association (UNIA). In addition to making documentary photographs that were realistic in style, VanDerZee experimented with photographic techniques—such as doctoring negatives and creating double exposures—demonstrating his artistic as well as technical ability.

Although VanDerZee's business survived the Great Depression and World War II, it began to wane during the early 1950s. For a time he supported himself by running a mail-order restoration service, but in 1969 he was evicted from his studio. At the same time, however, he caught the public eye through his contributions to *Harlem on My Mind*, an exhibition at New York's Metropolitan Museum of Art. Soon afterward a group of young photographers, including Harlem curator Reginald McGhee, founded the James VanDerZee Institute (now defunct), which organized exhibitions of his work.

As public recognition of VanDerZee's work grew, the photographer regained the prosperity of his early career. The return to success was strengthened by his marriage to Donna Mussenden in 1978. Mussenden, 60 years his junior, took charge of him and his estate, helped win back copyrights, and transformed the VanDerZee legacy into a business. She also helped VanDerZee with his final project, a series of celebrity portraits shot in the early 1980s.

James VanDerZee died on May 15, 1983, at age 96. Over the course of his long career he photographed numerous African American celebrities, including Muhammad Ali, Bill Cosby, Miles Davis, Eubie Blake, Romare Bearden, Cicely Tyson, Jean-Michel Basquiat, Ossie Davis,and Ruby Dee. He received awards from many institutions, including an honorary doctorate from Howard University.

North America

Van Peebles, Melvin

(b. August 21, 1932, Chicago, Ill.), author, filmmaker, and playwright, perhaps best known for his groundbreaking 1971 independent film, *Sweet Sweetback's Baadasssss Song*.

Melvin Van Peebles has traded stocks on the floor of the American Stock Exchange, published numerous novels, and directed, produced, composed, and starred in American films and plays. He is an innovative and successful entrepreneur who has worked for more than four decades to offer new, and sometimes controversial, images of African Americans.

Van Peebles was born in 1932 on the South Side of Chicago, but spent most of his adolescent years with his father, a tailor in Phoenix, Illinois. After graduating from high school in 1949 and from Ohio Wesleyan University in 1953, Van Peebles served as a flight navigator for three and a half years in the United States Air Force. After leaving the military he spent brief periods in Mexico and San Francisco—where he was married—before moving to Europe. He studied at the Dutch National Theatre in the Netherlands, then moved to France in the early 1960s. During nearly a decade in Paris Van Peebles wrote and published several novels in French, including *La permission*, which he filmed under the title of *The Story of the Three-Day Pass* and which concerns a black U.S. serviceman. The film won critical acclaim and helped Van Peebles earn a studio contract with Columbia Pictures.

Van Peebles returned to the United States and in 1969 directed *Watermelon Man*, a comedy about a racist white insurance salesman who wakes up one day to find that he has become black. Van Peebles took the proceeds from the film and made *Sweet Sweetback's Baadasssss Song* (1971), one of the most successful and controversial independent films of the era. *Sweetback* pushed the limits of cinematic decorum, combining sex and violence in its depiction of a black sex worker who witnesses the murder of a young black revolutionary by two white police officers. It was one of the first "blaxploitation" films of the 1970s and its success opened doors for African American directors, camera operators, designers, and editors.

In the early 1970s Van Peebles staged two plays on Broadway: the musical *Ain't Supposed to Die a Natural Death*, and *Don't Play Us Cheap*, based on his novel *Don't Play Us Cheap: A Harlem Party*. Later in the decade he wrote scripts for two television productions, *Just an Old Sweet Song* and *Sophisticated Gents*. Van Peebles turned his attention to business in the early 1980s and became an options trader on the floor of the American Stock Exchange. Drawing on his success, he published two books on the options market. Since then he has written a novel and appeared in the 1993 movie *Posse*, an all-black Western by his son, Mario Van Peebles.

North America

Vaughan, Sarah

(b. March 27, 1924, Newark, N.J.; d. April 3, 1990, Hidden Hills, Calif.), African American jazz singer and pianist lauded for her ability to command pitch and dynamics across three vocal octaves, Vaughan's singing style was informed by the harmony and improvisation of jazz horn sections.

Sarah Vaughan's parents, both of whom were musicians, cultivated and nurtured her early interest in music. She began taking piano lessons at age 7 and organ lessons at 8. By age 12 she was playing the organ for the Mount Zion Baptist Church and singing in its choir. She later attended Arts High School in Newark, New Jersey.

In 1942 Vaughan entered and won an amateur-night contest in which she sang *"Body and Soul."* Her award was $10 and a week of performances at the Apollo Theater, an engagement that led to her being hired as a vocalist and second pianist in Earl "Fatha" Hines's big band. In 1944 she joined singer Billy Eckstine's band. She recorded the hit *"Lover Man"* (1945) with Charlie Parker and Dizzy Gillespie, also members of Eckstine's ensemble, before launching her solo career in 1946 at the New York Cafe Society. In 1949 she landed a five-year recording contract with Columbia Records. Vaughan sustained her success as a singer through the early 1980s, recording on numerous labels, performing with a variety of jazz artists, and touring several countries.

Nicknamed "Sassy" and the "Divine One," Vaughan repeatedly was voted the top female vocalist by Down Beat and Metronome jazz magazines between 1947 and 1952. Her 1982 album *Gershwin Live!* won a Grammy Award, and in 1989 she received the Grammy Lifetime Achievement Award. Vaughan was inducted into the Jazz Hall of Fame in 1990.

Vee Jay Records,

the most influential and successful African American-owned record company before the appearance of Motown Records.

Vee Jay Records was founded in Chicago in 1952–1953, and it quickly emerged as America's most successful black-owned record company. Vee Jay recorded gospel music, jazz, blues, rhythm and blues, and early soul, but it was unique in concentrating on vocal harmony groups. Like many small record companies, Vee Jay was a family affair, involving Vivian Carter Bracken, her husband James Bracken, and her brother Calvin Carter. Vivian was a disc jockey in Gary, Indiana, where she and James owned a record store. Carter suggested the name Vee Jay, based on the first initials of his sister's and his brother-in-law's first names.

Vee Jay's first vocal group was the Spaniels, which featured the cool lead of James "Pookie" Hudson and which had a major hit with *"Goodnight Sweetheart Goodnight"* (1954). Other important Vee Jay vocal group hits included the El Dorados' *"At My Front"* (1955); the Dells' *"Oh What a Nite"* (1957); a memorable *"For Your Precious Love"* (1958) by the original Impressions, featuring Jerry Butler and Curtis Mayfield; and *"Duke of Earl"* by the Dukays, credited solely to the group's lead singer, Gene Chandler.

Within two years of releasing its first Spaniels' single, Vee Jay owned a building on Chicago's Michigan Avenue directly across from the offices of Chess Records, which was a major producer of music for the African American market, featuring such best-selling artists as Muddy Waters, Chuck Berry, and the Moonglows. Besides vocal groups, Vee Jay recorded a number of other significant talents in the late 1950s and early 1960s, including bluesmen John Lee Hooker and Jimmy Reed, solo vocalists Jerry Butler, Dee Clark, and Betty Everett, and gospel singers such as the Staple Singers and Alex Bradford. The company also recorded jazz, including tenor saxophonist Wardell Gray's last recording session, in 1955.

During the early 1960s Vee Jay stood on a par not only with Berry Gordy's fast-growing Motown Records, but also with the independents that focused on the audience for African American R&B and soul music: Chess, Atlantic, and Stax Records. But rapid expansion, sloppy finances, and internal bickering forced the company to declare bankruptcy in 1965.

Ventura, Johnny

(b. March 8, 1940, Santo Domingo, Dominican Republic), Afro-Dominican politician and merengue musician who incorporates the issues of race, politics, and social change in his music.

Johnny Ventura, affectionately called "El Caballo" (The Horse), has been praised as one of the few artists to blend politics and music successfully. His achievements are facilitated by a strong sense of national identity and a connection with the masses. Ventura made merengue the country's main musical form and a symbol of national identity accessible to all social classes. Unlike most other politicians, Ventura expresses pride in his African heritage within a society that emphasizes its Spanish and indigenous ancestry. Ventura has used music not only as a source of entertainment but also as a medium through which meaningful issues like Dominican identity and concepts of race can be expressed.

Ventura began his musical career under his birth name, Juan de Dios Ventura Soriano. After winning a 1956 radio station singing competition that drew attention to his powerful, smoky voice, the singer changed his name to the stylish Johnny Ventura for artistic as well as political reasons. Ventura's singing career took off soon after his debut. He was well received by Dominican society because his lyrics criticized the country's political system and its denial of an African heritage. Ventura entered the music scene at a time when Dominicans were eager for a new beginning after experiencing the oppressive rule of dictator Rafael Trujillo.

Between 1930 and 1961 the Trujillo government chose merengue to symbolize national culture and identity. The music was used as a political tool, and its lyrics praised the dictator. Only upon Trujillo's death in 1961 was merengue able to regain the vitality it once had and to develop through foreign musical influences forbidden by the Trujillo government. Ventura led others in revolutionizing merengue, changing the musical instruments merengue artists used and incorporating elements inspired by salsa and rock music. These changes resulted in Ventura's first hit—*"La agarradera"* (The Handle)—which gained both national and international notice.

In 1964 the young artist formed a band called Johnny Ventura y su Combo-Show and became a model for other *merengueros* (merengue performers). Breaking traditional form, the band's music was livelier and less inhibited than previous forms of merengue. Johnny Ventura y su Combo-Show—the top merengue band of the 1960s—traveled throughout the Dominican Republic, taking merengue out of the ballrooms of the elite and performing it for the rest of society.

Inspired by Elvis Presley and James Brown, to whom he was later compared, Ventura choreographed dance moves for his band. The artist also created a flashy wardrobe and provocative stage presence for himself. Although Ventura's music and style were influenced by foreign cultures, his political views remained grounded in Dominican thought. During the civil war of 1965 he allied himself with the nationalist party, which once again used merengue as a political tool to promote patriotism and assert Dominican national identity against the invading United States forces.

As a social activist Ventura joined with friends and colleagues to create El Club de Los Monos (The Monkeys' Club), a group whose objective was to eliminate the concept of black racial inferiority in Dominican society. According to Ventura, the group wanted to "demonstrate the brilliance of men and women of our [black] race . . . strengthening the idea of a re-encounter with [Afro-Dominican] cultural values." Appropriating *monos*, a

derogatory name for blacks, the club gathered celebrities from various pro-
fessions to demonstrate the contributions Afro-Dominicans made to their
nation. Ventura's overall purpose in establishing the club reflected his personal goal of promoting awareness among a people who often disavow their
African heritage.

Ventura's involvement in politics was not limited to his musical lyrics
and social activism. His energy and drive carried over into a political career
as a congressman, deputy mayor, and finally mayor of Santo Domingo, the
nation's capital. This accomplishment in May 1998 followed the release of
Ventura's autobiography, titled *Un poco de mí* (A Little of Me). In his new
position Ventura hopes to take the Dominican Republic into a prosperous
era, effecting social change and promoting an all-inclusive concept of
Dominican identity. His contributions to music and politics in the
Dominican Republic continue to gain him international notice.

Walker, Aaron ("T-Bone")

(b. May 28, 1910, Linden, Tex.; d. March 16, 1975, Los Angeles, Calif.), African American blues guitarist, pioneer of the electric guitar, and key creator of modern blues.

As a boy growing up in Dallas, Aaron Thibeaux "T-Bone" Walker befriended blues legend Blind Lemon Jefferson by holding his tin can and collecting his tips. In return Jefferson taught Walker the basics of blues. In 1929 Walker recorded "*Wichita Falls Blues*" and "*Trinity River Blues*" under the name Oak Cliff T-Bone. (The nickname "T-Bone" is a corruption of "Thibeaux.") In the 1930s in Los Angeles, California, Walker introduced an early form of the electric guitar into his music. His innovative rhythmic playing influenced almost every major blues and rock 'n' roll guitarist after him, including B.B. King, Jimi Hendrix, and Otis Rush. Walker said that "You've got to feel the blues to make them right . . . . It's played from the heart and if the person listening, understands and is in the right mood, why, man, I've seen them bust out and cry like a baby." His signature songs include "*T-Bone Shuffle*" and "*Call It Stormy Monday*," which many consider to be the best blues song of all time.

Walker was also a first-rate singer and master showman, often playing the guitar behind his back or between his legs. His career continued until the 1970s, when he suffered a stroke. Walker died of bronchial pneumonia in 1975.

Walker, Aida Overton

(b. February 14, 1880, New York, N.Y.; d. October 1, 1914, New York, N.Y.), singer, dancer, actress, and choreographer regarded as the leading African American female performing artist at the turn of the century.

Aida Overton began her career as a teenage chorus member of Black Patti's Troubadours. While performing in Senegambian Carnival (1899) she met

George Walker, and the two were married on June 22, 1899. After the marriage Aida Walker worked as a choreographer for Williams and Walker, her husband's vaudevillian comedy duo. By presenting ragtime musicals with all-black casts, Williams and Walker helped bring authentic black songs and dances to a form of entertainment that had been dominated by demeaning minstrel shows. Walker played the female lead in *The Policy Players* (1899), *Sons of Ham* (1900), *In Dahomey* (1902), *In Abyssinia* (1906), and *Bandanna Land* (1908). A command performance at Buckingham Palace in 1903 transformed Walker into an international star.

In 1908 George Walker became ill and could not continue in the run of *Bandanna Land*. Wearing her husband's male costumes, Aida Walker performed both his role and her own. After her husband's death in 1911, Walker saw her own career fall into decline, although she was celebrated for her part in the spectacular *Salome* at Oscar Hammerstein's Victoria Theater in New York City. This was the last major performance of her career.

As one of the first international black stars, Aida Walker brought versatility to her performances and authenticity to ragtime songs and cakewalk dances. Her dancing and singing abilities have been compared to and sometimes applauded over that of her successors, Florence Mills and Josephine Baker.

North America

Walker, Alice

(b. February 9, 1944, Eatonton, Ga.), African American writer, essayist, and poet, and Pulitzer Prize-winning author of *The Color Purple*.

In a passage from her 1983 essay collection *In Search of Our Mothers' Gardens: Womanist Prose*, Alice Walker reflects that "one thing I try to have in my life and in my fiction is an awareness of and openness to mystery, which, to me, is deeper than any politics, race, or geographical location." Walker was the youngest of eight children of sharecropping parents Willie Lee Walker and Minnie Tallulah (Grant) Walker. Her childhood was colored by an accident at age eight: she lost sight in one eye when an older brother shot her with a BB gun. Socially outcast as a result of her disfigured appearance, Walker became absorbed in books and began to write poetry while young.

Walker has said that while she was in high school, her mother gave her three important gifts: a sewing machine, which gave her the independence to make her own clothes; a suitcase, which gave her permission to leave home and travel; and a typewriter, which gave her permission to write. Walker graduated from high school as class valedictorian, and from 1961 to 1963 attended Spelman College in Atlanta on a scholarship. But when the "puritanical atmosphere" at Spelman became oppressive, Walker transferred to Sarah Lawrence College, where she completed a B.A. in 1965.

Walker then spent time in Georgia and Mississippi, where she registered voters, and in New York City, where she worked at the welfare department. She also married white human rights lawyer and activist Mel Leventhal in 1967, and in 1969 she gave birth to their daughter, Rebecca. She was divorced in 1977. Through all this activity Walker continued to write.

Walker published her first novel, *The Third Life of Grange Copeland*, in 1970 at age 26. Two years later she published *In Love and Trouble*, a short story collection, and the poetry collection *Revolutionary Petunias and Other Poems*. In 1976 she published her second novel, *Meridian*. In 1983, however, she became internationally known with the publication of her third novel, *The Color Purple*.

The Color Purple portrays Celie, a rural black woman in an abusive marriage, as she struggles to find her self-worth. Told entirely in the form of letters—Celie's simple letters to God, her letters to her lost sister Nettie, and Nettie's letters to Celie—the powerful narrative won the 1983 Pulitzer Prize and established Walker as a major American novelist. In 1985 *The Color Purple* was made into a popular movie that was both praised for its portrayal of African American heroines and condemned for its portrayal of black men. Walker reflected on the complicated issues surrounding the film's production in her essay collection *The Same River Twice: Honoring the Difficult* (1996).

One year after *The Color Purple* Walker published *In Search of Our Mothers' Gardens*, an influential essay collection that introduced the new term womanism as a way of defining black women's feminism. In 1984 she co-founded Wild Tree Press in Novarro, California. Since then Walker's publications have included the novels *The Temple of My Familiar* (1989) and *Possessing the Secret of Joy* (1992), another essay collection, several volumes of poetry, and a children's book.

Walker's numerous honors and awards include a National Endowment for the Arts grant and fellowship, a Radcliffe Institute fellowship, an honorary Ph.D. from Russell Sage College, a National Book Award nomination, a Guggenheim Award, and an O'Henry Award. She is highly in demand as a lecturer, and is not only a writer but also an outspoken liberal political activist. Walker's *Anything We Love Can Be Saved: A Writer's Activism* was published in 1997.

North America

Walker, Margaret

(b. July 7, 1915, Birmingham, Ala.; d. September 15, 1998, Jackson, Miss.), poet, novelist, and university teacher; the first African American woman to win a prestigious literary prize.

Margaret Walker began writing poems at age 11. Langston Hughes read her poetry when she was 16 and persuaded her parents to take her out of the South so she could "develop into a writer." She matriculated at Northwestern University, where she was influenced by W. E. B. Du Bois, and graduated in 1935. She left Chicago in 1939 to enter the creative writing M.A. program at the University of Iowa. There she published in 1942 a collection of poems, *For My People*, which won the prestigious Yale Young Poets Award. The book's poems, like her work as a whole, display a pride in her African American heritage and interweave autobiographical elements with larger themes of black history. She also wrote a historical novel, *Jubilee*, not completed until 1966, which was based on the life of her grandmother, who lived during the Civil War. It is one of the first modern novels about slavery told from an African American perspective.

Walker published more than ten books, including poems, essays, and short stories. Among these are her *Ballad of the Free* (1966), *Prophets for a New Day* (1970), and *October Journey* (1973). In the 1960s she received her Ph.D. from the University of Iowa and began teaching creative writing at Jackson State College in Mississippi, where she retired in 1979. The books she published since then include a biography of Richard Wright, a volume of poetry that includes old and new works, and a collection of essays.

North America

Wallace, Sippie

(b. November 1, 1898, Houston, Tex.; d. November 1, 1986, Detroit, Mich.), African American blues singer who was famous in Chicago during the 1920s for her spirited, hard-edged singing.

Born Beulah Belle Thomas, one of 13 children, Sippie Wallace was first exposed to music through her father's Shiloh Baptist Church. As a child she received the nickname "Sippie" either because of her habit of sipping or a lisp. After singing for several years in Texas and New Orleans, Wallace moved with her brothers in 1923 to Chicago, where she quickly became a blues star with songs like "*Up the Country Blues*" and "*Shorty George.*" Her singing was a combination of the Chicago blues tradition and her Texas-style blues background, which had a rougher singing style and often racier lyrics. Other well-known songs she recorded include "*Special Delivery Blues*" (1926), "*I'm a Mighty Tight Woman*" (1920), and, with Louis Armstrong, "*Dead Drunk Blues*" (1927).

Wallace moved to Detroit in 1929, and her reputation as a recording star began to wane. Until the 1970s she was the organist at the Leland Baptist Church in Detroit. Long-time friend and blues singer Victoria Spivey persuaded her in 1966 to come out of retirement. Although she suffered a stroke in 1970, she continued her new recording career. Musician Bonnie Raitt, whom Wallace heavily influenced, helped sign Wallace to a contract with Atlantic Records in 1982. Wallace's 1983 album, *Sippie*, featuring Raitt on guitar, won the W. C. Handy Award for the best blues album of the year.

Waller, Thomas Wright ("Fats")

(b. May 21, 1904, New York, N.Y.; d. December 15, 1943, Kansas City, Mo.), African American jazz pianist, vocalist, organist, and composer whose combination of musical sophistication and lyrical humor made him one of the most popular entertainers of his day.

Fats Waller, born Thomas Wright Waller, was born and raised in New York City, where his father was a Baptist minister. As a boy he charmed his classmates with animated facial gestures while playing piano at school talent shows. During his teenage years he played the organ at various Harlem theaters to accompany silent films. In 1920, the year he left home, he married Edith Hatchett. They divorced three years later, and in 1926 Waller married Anita Rutherford.

Having learned the fundamentals of piano in his childhood, Waller later studied stride piano under Russell Brooks and James P. Johnson. In the 1920s Waller played at Harlem rent parties and nightclubs and composed music for shows and revues. He collaborated with songwriter Andy Razaf to produce some of his best-known numbers: "Honeysuckle Rose" (1928), "(What Did I Do to Be So) Black and Blue" (1929), and "Ain't Misbehavin'" (1929). During the 1930s Waller toured the United States and Europe with his own band, appeared on radio broadcasts and in Hollywood films, and recorded hundreds of songs on the Victor label.

On April 27, 1928, Waller became the first jazz soloist to perform at Carnegie Hall. He is also credited with being the first musician to record jazz music on a pipe organ. Ain't Misbehavin', a tribute to Waller, was voted best Broadway musical in 1978.

Warwick, Dionne

(b. December 12, 1940, East Orange, N.J.), African American popular and soul singer; one of the top non-Motown artists to emerge from the 1960s.

Born Marie Dionne Warwick, this enduring vocalist got her start singing in a Methodist church. In 1960 she met songwriters Burt Bacharach and Hal David, who asked her to start making demonstration records with them; in 1962 the threesome was offered a contract with Scepter Records.

Bacharach and David wrote songs for Warwick that highlighted her diction and mellow alto voice. She remained with Scepter until 1971 and had numerous hits, including the Number-One hit "Anyone Who Had a Heart" (1964). In the mid-1970s her career faltered amidst family troubles and the breakup of Bacharach and David. In 1979 she again achieved popularity with the Number-Five hit "I'll Never Love This Way Again." Other hits after her comeback include "Deja Vu" (1979) and "That's What Friends Are For" (1986).

Warwick has given her money and talent to support hunger relief and acquired immune deficiency syndrome (AIDS) research. In 1986 she was named Entertainer of the Year by the National Association for the Advancement of Colored People (NAACP) at the Image Awards.

North America

Washington, Denzel

(b. December 28, 1954, Mount Vernon, N.Y.), Academy Award-winning African American actor.

Denzel Washington grew up in the middle-class family of a Pentecostal minister and a beauty shop owner. Washington won a small role in the 1977 television movie *Wilma*, a film about Olympic star Wilma Rudolph, before he graduated from Fordham University in 1977 with a B.A. in journalism. After graduating, he pursued acting professionally, studying drama at the American Conservatory in San Francisco, California.

Washington first achieved recognition for his stage performances. His portrayals of Malcolm X in Chickens *Coming Home to Roost* and Private Peterson in the Obie Award-winning *A Soldier's Play* won Washington critical acclaim for carefully chosen roles that resisted Hollywood's stereotypical options for blacks. Washington's stage performances led to a role in the popular television drama *St. Elsewhere* from 1982 to 1988, in which he played the dedicated Dr. Philip Chandler. In 1984 he began his successful transition from television to film when critics praised his reprise of the Private Peterson role in *A Soldier's Story*, the screen adaptation of *A Soldier's Play*.

By the end of the 1980s Washington had become one of Hollywood's most critically and commercially successful actors. He has received three Academy Award nominations, two for Best Supporting Actor (*Cry Freedom*, 1987, and *Glory*, 1990, which he won) and one for Best Actor as Malcolm X in Spike Lee's film of the same name. In addition to collaborating with Lee (in *Malcolm X*, 1992, and *Mo' Better Blues*, 1990), Washington has worked with some of film's most respected directors, including Jonathan Demme (*Philadelphia*, 1993) and Kenneth Branagh (*Much Ado About Nothing*, 1993).

North America

Washington, Dinah

(b. August 29, 1924, Tuscaloosa, Ala.; d. December 14, 1963, Detroit, Mich.), African American singer and pianist whose music spanned blues, gospel, pop, and rhythm and blues, known for her clear diction, uninhibited character, and efforts to promote other musicians.

Dinah Washington was born Ruth Lee Jones to Alice Williams and Ollie Jones. With her parents and three siblings, in 1928 she moved to Chicago, where she attended the city's public schools, including Wendell Phillips High School.

Taught piano by her mother, Washington sang and played solos at St. Luke's Baptist Church while still in elementary school, and gave gospel recitals with her mother at various black churches. At age 15, she won an amateur contest at Chicago's Regal Theater with her rendition of "*I Can't Face the Music.*" Washington then began to sing without her mother's knowledge at local nightclubs.

In 1940 Washington was discovered by gospel singer Sallie Martin, who hired her as an accompanist and singer for the Sallie Martin Colored Ladies Quartet. Washington performed for two years with Martin's ensemble. It was with Martin's group that she took her professional name, before being hired by bandleader Lionel Hampton in 1943.

Washington's career as a soloist was boosted in 1946 when she secured a 16-year recording contract with Mercury Records. During this time she toured extensively and placed 45 songs on Billboard magazine's rhythm-and-blues charts. Her biggest hit was "*Baby, You've Got What It Takes*" (1960). Nicknamed the "Queen of the Blues," she died of an accidental overdose of sleeping pills.

North America

Washington, Fredi

(b. December 23, 1903, Savannah, Ga.; d. June 28, 1994, Stamford, Conn.), African American actor who worked for equal opportunity for African American performers.

A gifted performer, Fredi Washington's most famous role typified her Hollywood experience. In *Imitation of Life* (1934) she played a woman who passes for white. Although she won critical acclaim, she was typecast after that as the light-skinned "tragic mulatto." Her performance was so convincing that many African American journalists believed that she carried racial self-hatred. In fact, however, Washington was positive about her heritage and worked on behalf of African American performers by co-founding the Negro Actors Guild in 1937 and serving as its first executive secretary. In 1975 she was inducted into the Black Filmmakers Hall of Fame.

North America

Waters, Ethel

(b. October 31, 1896?, Chester, Pa.; d. September 1, 1977, Chatsworth, Calif.), African American singer and actress who brought black urban blues into the mainstream.

Ethel Waters was born to a 12-year-old mother, Louise Anderson, who had been raped by a white man, John Waters. Although she was raised by her maternal grandmother, she took her father's surname. Reared in poverty, she left school at age 13 in order to support herself through domestic housework.

Waters performed for the first time at age five in a children's church program. She was called Baby Star and later, performing on the black vaudeville circuit, became known as Sweet Mama Stringbean. After moving to New York City in 1919, at the start of the Harlem Renaissance, Waters recorded songs for Black Swan Records and then Colombia Records while playing in revues and performing on the white vaudeville circuit during the 1920s. Two of her more popular songs were "*Dinah*" (1925) and "*Stormy Weather*" (1933). By refining the genre's lyrics and performance, Waters introduced urban blues to a white audience. Her stylistic alterations created a niche for the black nightclub singers who gained popularity from the 1930s through the 1950s.

In 1927 Waters's career as an actress began with the musical *Africana*. She played singing roles in other Broadway productions: *Blackbirds* (1930), *Rhapsody in Black* (1931), *As Thousands Cheer* (1933), *At Home Abroad* (1936), and *Cabin in the Sky* (1940). Waters played more dramatic roles in *Mamba's Daughters* (1939) and *The Member of the Wedding* (1950). Appearing in nine films between 1929 and 1959, she received an Academy Award nomination as Best Supporting Actress in *Pinky* (1949). Through these roles Waters transformed the image of the older black woman from that of the servile "Mammy" to the self-sufficient Earth Mother. She toured with evangelist Billy Graham from 1957 to 1976. Waters is the author of two autobiographies: *His Eye Is on the Sparrow* (1951) and *To Me It's Wonderful* (1972).

North America

Waters, Muddy

(b. April 4, 1915, Rolling Fork, Miss.; d. April 30, 1983, Chicago, Ill.), African American musician, pioneer of postwar electric blues.

Muddy Waters's long life in music essentially encompasses the story of the blues in the twentieth century. He grew up as McKinley Morganfield in the Mississippi Delta, immersed in the rural blues tradition and particularly fond of Son House and Robert Johnson. He got his nickname from his hobby of fishing in a nearby creek. He was musically active, first playing harmonica and then guitar in small bands around the Delta, and briefly in St. Louis, Missouri.

In 1941 and 1942 the traveling folklorist Alan Lomax recorded Waters, revealing a talented but still imitative singer. In 1943 Waters moved to Chicago, Illinois, and got a job in a paper mill. A year later he bought his first electric guitar, and the impact of the instrument on his music was profound. This new musical technology effectively complemented his powerful voice, and he was soon a popular singer at house parties and clubs on the

South Side. He also began recording in 1946, although none of the songs from this period became hits, and he remained a local phenomenon.

In 1948 Waters signed with Chess Records and released his first single, "*Rollin' Stone*," from which the British rock band the Rolling Stones took its name in the 1960s. It was a hit, and many more followed, including "*I Can't Be Satisfied*" and "*I Feel Like Going Home*." These recordings from the late 1940s, with their primitive electric sound and Waters's barely controlled musical and vocal energy, helped to form the foundation of modern rock music.

Waters continued his pioneering work through the 1950s, enlarging his band to include piano and working with such talent as Otis Spann, Little Walter, Willie Dixon, and Buddy Guy. Waters helped to define an exciting new urban blues sound associated with Chicago music in the 1950s, reminiscent of the Delta blues but different from it. This was a mix that appealed strongly to the large population of blacks who had relocated from Mississippi to Chicago. Songs from this period include "*I'm Your Hoochie Coochie Man*," "*I Just Want to Make Love to You*," and "*Mannish Boy*." Though his records did little on the pop charts, Waters was consistently near the top of the rhythm-and-blues charts.

Although he failed to achieve mainstream success in the United States and was largely unknown to white Americans, Waters influenced later musicians, particularly the rising generation of English rock 'n' rollers in the 1960s who experienced Waters firsthand when he toured England in 1958, the first of many successful visits. Waters was honored late in his career with several Grammys and a role in the Band's film, *The Last Waltz*.

North America

Watts, André

(b. June 20, 1946, Nuremberg, Germany), African American concert pianist, the first black American instrumental superstar.

Since his rise to prominence in 1963, André Watts has been one of the world's leading classical pianists. At age 16, he became the first black instrumental soloist in more than 60 years to perform with the New York Philharmonic Orchestra, under conductor Leonard Bernstein. Within a decade he was renowned worldwide for his poetic style, technical brilliance, and fiery temperament. According to music critic Elyse Mach, "Watts is to a concert stage as lightning is to thunder. Explosive. More than any other pianist, his performances are reminiscent of what a Liszt concert must have been like: mesmerizing, theatrical, charged with energy."

Watts ascribes his career success largely to luck and what he calls "a combination of those funny, indefinable qualities that are in a person at birth." He also cites his mother as a critical influence: "I wouldn't be a pianist today if my mother hadn't made me practice." He was born in a United States Army camp in Nuremberg, Germany, the only child of Herman Watts, an African American career soldier, and Maria Alexandra

Gusmits, a Hungarian who had been displaced in Germany following World War II. When he was four he began playing a miniature violin and at age seven studied piano with his mother, an accomplished pianist. In 1954 his family moved to Philadelphia, Pennsylvania, where he received a private school education and studied at the Philadelphia Academy of Music.

Watts first performed publicly at age 9, playing the Haydn *Concerto in D Major* in a children's concert sponsored by the Philadelphia Orchestra. Several performances with other orchestras followed, and at age 16 he won an audition to perform in a nationally televised Young People's Concert with the New York Philharmonic, playing Liszt's *Piano Concerto no. 1*. His performance stunned audiences and music critics alike.

In late January 1963, a few weeks after the Liszt performance, Leonard Bernstein, who predicted "gianthood" for the young pianist, invited Watts to substitute as a soloist for ailing pianist Glenn Gould. Bernstein proved instrumental in Watts's success: the young artist's second New York Philharmonic performance won him a ten-minute standing ovation and invitations to perform with the world's major orchestras, which were usually closed to black instrumentalists without the backing of an eminent conductor or music manager. Spared the ordeals of competitive life, he focused on his artistry and academic education.

In 1969 Watts enrolled at Baltimore's Peabody Conservatory of Music, where he studied with pianist Leon Fleisher and, in 1972, obtained his Artist's Diploma. That same year he became the youngest person ever to receive an honorary doctorate from Yale University. Meanwhile, his international career flourished. In 1966 he made his European debut with the London Symphony Orchestra and also performed his first solo recital in New York. He recorded extensively and continued to tour throughout Europe, Asia, and the United States. During the late 1960s and 1970s he was often chosen to perform at important political occasions: he became the first American pianist to play in the People's Republic of China, as a soloist with the Philadelphia Orchestra. In 1973 he toured Russia.

Although the quality of Watts's playing has not been consistent throughout his career, his recent recordings and concerts have reaffirmed his musical brilliance. In 1995 he recorded Tchaikovsky's *Piano Concerto no. 1* and Saint-Saens's *Piano Concerto no. 2* with the Atlanta Symphony—his first concerto recording in more than ten years. "His playing is technically superb, fluent and melodious," wrote music critic Alexander Morin. "A concert always is an incredible exposition of one's daring and insides," said Watts of his own playing. "If you're not willing to do that . . . then there's a limit to what you can offer the people."

North America

Webb, Frank J.

(b. 1828, Philadelphia, Pa.; d. 1894?, Galveston, Tex.), African American author who wrote about interracial marriage and passing.

Little is known about Frank Webb's life. Raised in Philadelphia, Pennsylvania, he lived in England, France, and Kingston, Jamaica. Webb returned to the United States in 1870, publishing two novellas that year, *Two Wolves and a Lamb* and *Marvin Hayle*. Following this he moved to Galveston, Texas, where he edited a radical newspaper before running a school until his death. His one novel, *The Garies and Their Friends*, published in 1857, was the second of only four African American novels published before the Civil War. The first novel about free African Americans in the North, Webb's book explored interracial marriage and passing.

North America

W. E. B. Du Bois: An Interpretation (Excerpt)
Cornel West

W. E. B. Du Bois is the towering black scholar of the twentieth century. The scope of his interests, the depth of his insights, and the sheer majesty of his prolific writings bespeak a level of genius unequaled among modern black intellectuals. Yet, like all of us, Du Bois was a child of his age. He was shaped by the prevailing presuppositions and prejudices of modern Euro-American civilization. And despite his lifelong struggle—marked by great courage and sacrifice—against white supremacy and for the advancement of Africans around the world, he was, in style and substance, a proud black man of letters primarily influenced by nineteenth-century, Euro-American traditions.

For those interested in the relation of white supremacy to modernity (African slavery in the New World and European imperial domination of most of the rest of the world) or the consequences of the construct of "race" during the Age of Europe (1492–1945), the scholarly and literary works of Du Bois are indispensable. For those obsessed with alleviating black social misery, the political texts of Du Bois are insightful and inspiring. In this sense, Du Bois is the brook of fire through which we all must pass in order to gain access to the intellectual and political weaponry needed to sustain the radical democratic tradition in our time.

Du Bois was first and foremost a black New England Victorian seduced by the Enlightenment ethos and enchanted with the American Dream. His interpretation of the human condition—that is, in part, his idea of who he was and could be—was based on his experiences and, most important, on his understanding of those experiences through the medium of an Enlightenment world-view that promoted Victorian strategies in order to realize an American optimism; throughout this essay, I shall probe these three basic foundations of his perspective. Like many of the brilliant and ambitious young men of his time, he breathed the intoxicating fumes of "advanced" intellectual and political culture. Yet in the face of entrenched evil and demonic power, Du Bois often found himself either shipwrecked in the depths of his soul or barely afloat with less and less wind in his existential sails.

"One never feels his two-ness—W. E. B. Du Bois wrote in an 1897 article, an American; a Negro; two souls, two thoughts, two unreconciled strivings; two warring ideals in one dark body, whose dogged strength alone keeps it from being torn asunder. *CORBIS*

Du Bois's Enlightenment world-view—his first foundation—prohibited this kind of understanding. Instead, he adopted a mild elitism that underestimated the capacity of everyday people to "know" about life. In "The Talented Tenth," he claims, "knowledge of life and its wider meaning, has been the point of the Negro's deepest ignorance." In his classic book *The Souls of Black Folk* (1903), there are 18 references to "black, backward, and ungraceful" folk, including a statement of his intent "to scatter civilization among a people whose ignorance was not simply of letters, but of life itself."

Du Bois's principal intellectual response to the limits of his Enlightenment world-view was to incorporate certain insights of Marx and Freud. Yet Marx's powerful critique of the unequal relations of power between capitalists and the proletariat in the workplace and Freud's penetrating attempt to exercise rational control over the irrational forces at work in self and society only deepened Du Bois's commitment to the Enlightenment ethos. And though particular features of this ethos are essential to any kind of intellectual integrity and democratic vision—features such as self-criticism and self-development, suspicion of illegitimate authority and suffocating tradition—the Enlightenment world-view held by Du Bois is ultimately inadequate, and, in many ways, antiquated, for our time. The tragic plight and absurd predicament of Africans here and abroad requires a more profound interpretation of the human condition—one that goes far beyond the false dichotomies of expert knowledge versus mass ignorance, individual autonomy versus dogmatic authority, and self-mastery versus intolerant tradition. Our tragicomic times require more democratic concepts of knowledge and leadership which highlight human fallibility and mutual accountability; notions of individuality and contested authority which stress dynamic traditions; and ideals of self-realization within participatory communities.

After 95 years of the most courageous and unflagging devotion to black freedom witnessed in the twentieth century, W E. B. Du Bois not only left America for Africa but concluded, "I just cannot take any more of this country's treatment. We leave for Ghana October 5th and I set no date for return . . . . Chin up, and fight on, but realize that American Negroes can't win."

In the end Du Bois's Enlightenment world-view, Victorian strategies, and American optimism failed him. He left America in militant despair—the very despair he had avoided earlier—and mistakenly hoped for the rise of a strong postcolonial and united Africa. Echoing Tolstoy's claim that "it's intolerable to live in Russia . . . . I've decided to emigrate to England forever" (though he never followed through) and Kafka's dream to leave Prague and live in Palestine (though he died before he could do so), Du Bois concluded that black strivings in a twilight civilization were unbearable for him yet still imperative for others—even if he could not envision black freedom in America as realizable.

W. E. B. Du Bois is considered the greatest African American intellectual figure of the twentieth century. *CORBIS*

For those of us who stand on his broad shoulders, let us begin where he ended—with his militant despair; let us look candidly at the tragicomic and absurd character of black life in America in the spirit of John Coltrane and Toni Morrison; let us continue to strive with genuine compassion, personal integrity, and human decency to fight for radical democracy in the face of the frightening abyss—or terrifying inferno—of the twenty-first century, clinging to "a hope not hopeless but unhopeful."

North America

Weems, Carrie Mae

(b. April 20, 1953, Portland, Ore.), African American photographer, folklorist, and self-proclaimed "image-maker" whose provocative images depict gender and racial stereotypes.

Carrie Mae Weems grew up in a working-class family in the western United States. After studying at Cal Arts, she earned a master of fine arts degree in photography from the University of California, San Diego, in 1984. A self-proclaimed "image-maker," Weems deals with issues of history, gender, and class by combining photographic images and narrative text. Often achingly personal, Weems's images explore bigotry, self-presentation, and relationships by incorporating African American folklore and bigoted or stereotypical narratives into her work. Her early work focused on the themes of family and class and quite often featured Weems and members of her own family. As in portraits such as *Honey Coloured Boy*, *Chocolate Coloured Man*, *Golden Yella Girl*, and *Blue Black Boy*, taken with a Polaroid camera and then hand tinted, many of her photographs illustrate both real and unreal varieties of "black" skin, calling into question the category "black" itself.

Weems's *Sea Islands Series* explores aspects of African American folklore and history from the Georgia Sea Islands, featured in Julie Dash's film *Daughters of the Dust*. Weems's *Untitled (Kitchen Table Series)* features a sequence of posed photographs exploring relationships between black men and women. In her photographs of degrading and stereotypical bric-a-brac and her portraits and self-portraits exploring stereotypes of black people, Weems uses cultural symbols such as watermelons, fried chicken, jump rope, rhymes, folklore, and proverbs to interrogate existing stereotypes.

Weems has received numerous grants and awards and has been published extensively. Her first retrospective was held in 1993 at the National Museum of Women in the Arts in Washington, D.C., and featured her works from 1978 to 1992. She has participated in group exhibitions around the country, including the 1991 Biennial at the Whitney Museum of American Art in New York.

North America

West, Cornel

(b. June 2, 1953, Tulsa, Okla.), African American philosopher, theologian, and activist.

Cornel West was born in Oklahoma—a place once envisioned as a homeland for Native Americans displaced by European colonization, and for African Americans acting on the idea of freedom promised by emancipation. The grandson of a Baptist minister, he was reared in the Baptist Church, and the church has remained a profound presence in his life. Even as a child, West was articulate, outspoken, and politically engaged—in elementary school he convinced a group of his classmates to stop saluting the flag to protest the second-class citizenship afforded to African Americans.

West encountered the activities of the Black Panther Party while growing up in Sacramento, California. The Panthers informed his early thinking about democratic socialism and acquainted him with an internationalist vision for black enfranchisement. He was also inspired by the teachings of Martin Luther King Jr. and Malcolm X, as well as by the music of John Coltrane and James Brown. By the time he won a scholarship to

Harvard University in 1970, West was already well on his way to becoming an activist-scholar. "Owing to my family, church, and the black social movements of the 1960s," he recalled, "I arrived at Harvard unashamed of my African, Christian, and militant decolonized outlooks." While in Cambridge he worked with the Black Panther Party, volunteering at their children's breakfast program.

West thrived at Harvard, consuming the work of the black intellectual tradition, including that of W. E. B. Du Bois and St. Clair Drake, as well as European philosophers such as Max Weber, Karl Marx, and Friedrich Nietzsche. At the core of West's development as a scholar lay the belief in integrating a religious faith with both political engagement and an intellectually rigorous course of study. "For me there was always a vital spiritual dimension to politics," West has explained. "Issues of death, disease, and despair have always been the fundamental issues of being human, and you didn't get too much talk about these issues in political circles."

After three years at Harvard, West graduated magna cum laude in 1973 and chose to pursue graduate studies in philosophy at Princeton. In 1977 he began teaching at Union Theological Seminary in New York. His doctoral dissertation, completed in 1980, was later revised and republished as the *Ethical Dimensions of Marxist Thought* (1991).

In 1984 West left Union for Yale Divinity School, where he was granted a full professor-ship in religion and philosophy. He returned to Union in 1987, but shortly after was recruited to direct Princeton University's program in Afro-American studies. In 1988 West joined Princeton as professor of religion and, working with a community of scholars that included novelist Toni Morrison, he helped revitalize the Afro-American Studies Department.

Other universities were also eager to have West join their faculty. When Henry Louis Gates Jr. took leadership of Harvard University's Department of Afro-American Studies in 1991, he immediately began trying to lure to Harvard the man he called "the preëminent African-American intellectual of our generation." Excited by the possibilities of a group of scholars working across disciplines in the field of African American studies, West joined Harvard in 1993. In 1998 he was appointed the prestigious university professorship, becoming the first Alphonse Fletcher Jr. University Professor.

West's scholarly writing pursues philosophical inquiry into the realm of the political, exploring the existential dimension within the moral, spiritual, and political space. Moreover, he traces this relationship in the work of his philosophic forbears. In *The American Evasion of Philosophy* (1989) West explores the history of American pragmatism, reading the American philosophic tradition, from Ralph Waldo Emerson to Richard Rorty, as an ongoing cultural commentary that responds to American society itself. In *Keeping Faith: Philosophy and Race in America* (1993) he continues to engage with philosophy, spiritual tradition, and history.

Indeed, West has consistently placed a heavy emphasis on the conversational form as intellectual inquiry. The issues he takes up—sexism, anti-Semitism, homophobia, affirmative action—are timely ones for both the black community and the community at large. In 1991 West engaged in a lively conversation on race and gender with the feminist scholar bell hooks in breaking bread: insurgent black intellectual life (1991). He has also taken a particular interest in black-Jewish relations, publishing in 1995 a conversation with Jewish intellectual Michel Lerner titled *Jews and Blacks: Let the Healing Begin*. West has also participated in several discussions on the relationship between African Americans and Hispanics, including a conversation with scholar Jorge Klor de Alva and author Earl Shorris in "Our Next Race Question," published in *Harper's Magazine* in 1996. He and Gates co-published *The Future of the Race* in 1996; in 1998 he co-authored a book on parenting and family policy with Sylvia Ann Hewlett.

West, Dorothy

(b. June 2, 1907; d. August 16, 1998, Boston, Mass.), African American author and journalist, literary figure of the Harlem Renaissance who specialized in short stories.

The only child of Rachel Pease Benson and Isaac Christopher West, Dorothy West started her education at age two under the tutelage of Bessie Trotter, sister of the *Boston Guardian's* militant editor, William Monroe Trotter. After attending Farragut and Martin schools, she went to Girl's Latin High School, from which she graduated in 1923. West continued her education at Boston University and the Columbia University School of Journalism.

West's career as a writer began at age seven when the *Boston Globe* published her first short story, "Promise and Fulfillment." In 1926 West, then living in New York among the luminaries of the Harlem Renaissance, shared second-place honors with Zora Neale Hurston in a national writing competition organized by the National Urban League's *Opportunity*. Her interest in the arts was not only literary, and in 1927 she traveled to London as a cast member of the play *Porgy*. In the early 1930s she went to the Soviet Union to participate in the film *Black and White* and remained there for a year after the project was abandoned.

Returning to New York, West founded two short-lived literary journals: *Challenge* in 1934 (six issues) and *New Challenge* in 1937 (one issue). After working as a welfare investigator for a year and a half, West found employment with the federal government's Works Progress Administration's Federal Writers' Project through the early 1940s. She moved to Martha's Vineyard in Massachusetts in 1945 and wrote regularly for *Martha's Vineyard Gazette*. She published *The Living Is Easy* (1948) and *The Wedding* (1995), and more than 60 short stories. In 1997 television producer Oprah Winfrey made *The Wedding* into a popular television miniseries.

Wheatley, Phillis

(b.1753?, the Gambia, West Africa; d. December 5, 1784, Boston, Mass.), poet, the first African American to publish a book; considered the founder of the African American literary tradition.

> *Some view our sable race with scornful eye,*
> *"Their colour is a diabolic dye."*
> *Remember, Christians, Negroes, black as Cain,*
> *May be refined, and join the angelic train.*

So ends Phillis Wheatley's 1773 poem, "On Being Brought From Africa to America." The poem is remarkable not only for the honest way it speaks about color prejudice among white Christians—never a polite subject, and certainly not one in 1773—but for the singular achievements of the author. Wheatley wrote the original version of this poem in 1768, seven years after she had come to America as a seven-year-old child and as an African slave. At the time of its publication in 1773, she was just 19 years old, yet already an internationally celebrated poet whose admirers included Benjamin Franklin and George Washington. She had also become the first African American—and the second American woman—to publish a book.

Wheatley was born, probably in 1753, in the Gambia, West Africa, but in 1761 she was stolen from her parents and transported on a slave ship to Boston, Massachusetts. There she was sold to John and Susanna Wheatley, who named her after the ship that had transported her to slavery. They purchased her to be a domestic servant, but when Susanna realized that Phillis had a talent for learning, she allowed her daughter Mary to tutor Phillis in Latin, English, and the Bible. Wheatley soon began composing her own poetry, and her first published poem appeared in the *Newport Mercury* newspaper on December 21, 1767.

Over the next five years several more of Wheatley's poems were published in local papers. In

Just 19 when her first collection of poetry was published in 1773, Phillis Wheatley is pictured here in the frontispiece of that volume. This portrait of the poet is attributed to African American artist Scipio Moorhead.
CORBIS/Bettmann

October 1770 she wrote an elegy for the English evangelical minister George Whitefield that was so popular that it was also reprinted in England, bringing her international recognition. But when Wheatley tried in 1772 to publish her first volume of poetry, publishers still felt they needed to guarantee to skeptical readers that a black slave could have written the poems she said were hers. She underwent an oral examination by 18 of "the most respectable Characters in Boston," including the governor of Massachusetts, to prove that she was indeed literate and articulate enough to have composed the poems. Wheatley passed the exam but still could not secure a Boston publisher.

Wheatley found an ally across the Atlantic in Selina, countess of Huntingdon, an evangelical Englishwoman with ties to Whitefield who had read her poetry and who arranged for her book to be published in London. In 1773 *Poems on Various Subjects, Religious and Moral* appeared. The frontispiece of the original edition, requested by the countess, makes the author's identity—and ability—very clear: under the caption "Phillis Wheatley, Negro Servant to Mr. John Wheatley of Boston," there is an engraving of the young black woman at her desk, with a piece of paper in front of her, a book at one hand, and a pen in the other. The image is thought to be the work of Scipio Moorhead, a young African American slave artist.

Wheatley traveled to England to oversee the book's publication, but the trip served other purposes as well. She met many British dignitaries and intellectuals, all of whom celebrated her literary ability, and American diplomat Benjamin Franklin came to call on her in London. Shortly after her trip her owners decided to free her—according to Wheatley, "at the desire of my friends in England." The trip brought Wheatley fame as an author, and pressure from English abolitionists led to her freedom.

Wheatley's poetic subjects were often the people and places that made news around her. She wrote numerous elegies for friends and acquaintances and also several popular poems supporting the colonists in the Revolutionary War, even though the white Wheatleys were Tories. A poem she wrote in October 1775 in honor of George Washington so impressed him that he invited her to a private visit with him in his Cambridge, Massachusetts, military headquarters. Washington was himself a slaveholder, but some scholars have speculated that his conversation with Wheatley may have influenced his later discomfort with slavery.

Some readers have criticized Wheatley because her subject matter is not more distinctly African American, and especially because some of her poetry even appears to condone slavery. For example, in "To the University of Cambridge, in New-England," Wheatley refers to Africa as "the land of errors, and Egyptian gloom," and goes on to say that it was God's "gracious hand" that "brought [her] in safety from those dark abodes." But while this poem does reflect Wheatley's evangelical Christianity (she believed that the hidden blessing in her capture was that it allowed her to be exposed to the Bible and be saved), it does not capture the complexities of Wheatley's feelings about her enslavement, or her identification with other blacks.

In other poems Wheatley does affirm that her separation from her home was indeed traumatic. For example, in "To the Right Honourable William Legge, Earl of Dartmouth," Wheatley explains that she empathizes with the American colonists because of her own experience with oppression:

> *when seeming cruel Fate*
> *Me snatched from Afric's fancied happy seat,*
> *. . . Ah! What bitter pangs molest,*
> *What sorrows laboured in the parent's breast?*

And Wheatley's letters, recently recovered, show clearly that she was aware of racial prejudice and injustice, and that she identified with other people of African descent. Recent scholars agree with Wheatley's implication that her poems supporting the American colonists are part of a larger discourse on freedom from tyranny, a discourse that was inextricably linked to the question of slavery—but that she chose to couch in terms her immediate audience would receive best.

In 1778 Wheatley married a free black Bostonian, John Peters. The next year she circulated a proposal for a new collection of poetry, indicating she had written dozens of new poems since 1773. But in a country now at war, the interest that had attended the publication of her first book had waned. Wheatley could not find a publisher and retreated from the public eye. Her short marriage was unhappy, marred by the deaths in infancy of her first two children. On December 5, 1784, Wheatley died in childbirth along with her third child.

At the time of her death Wheatley was living in poverty and obscurity on the outskirts of Boston, but the memory of the famed "Ethiopian muse" was strong enough that her obituary was printed in the Boston papers. Since the early nineteenth century other African American writers have continually acknowledged their debt to her accomplishments. Wheatley is celebrated as the founder of the African American literary tradition, and contemporary readers continue to learn more about the complexities she brought to that role.

North America

Wideman, John Edgar

(b. June 14, 1941, Washington, D.C.), African American author and scholar hailed as one of the most gifted writers of his generation.

According to the title of one of John Edgar Wideman's collections of short stories, "all stories are true." Guided by that principle, Wideman has spent a career as a scholar and author in pursuit of a more truthful history or chronicle of his own experience and that of other African Americans.

Wideman went to the famed Iowa Writers' Workshop as a Kent Fellow in 1966–1967. There he wrote his first novel, *A Glance Away* (1967). This and his second novel, *Hurry Home* (1970), received critical accolades for their experimental language, form, and style. Although the novels focus on black characters, both black and white critics found them more akin to works by great American or European modernists such as James Joyce, T. S. Eliot, and William Faulkner than to a black literary tradition.

While teaching at the University of Pennsylvania in the early 1970s, Wideman had a transformative experience when he was asked by black students to teach a course on African American literature. Giving them at first what he called "the jive reply that it wasn't [his] field," he eventually accepted the challenge and re-educated himself. The discovery of an alternative literary tradition spurred Wideman to establish and direct the University of Pennsylvania's first Afro-American studies department from 1971 to 1973. After writing a more "black" novel, *The Lynchers*, in 1973, Wideman took a break from writing fiction and left Pennsylvania for a teaching position at the University of Wyoming, which he held until 1986.

In 1981 the first two installments of Wideman's *Homewood Trilogy*, *Hiding Place* and a short-story collection, *Damballah*, were published. These two books mark the maturation of Wideman's aesthetic philosophy. Deeply concerned with the importance of memory, history, and the interweaving of multiple cultural and historical traditions, the *Homewood* books explore Wideman's own African American roots. *Sent for You Yesterday* (1983), the third book in the trilogy, won the 1984 PEN/Faulkner Award for fiction.

Wideman's next book, *Brothers and Keepers* (1984), continued this autobiographical impulse. A series of letters or essays to his brother Robbie, who was serving a life sentence for murder, the book explored the two very different lives of the two brothers. *Brothers and Keepers* was nominated for the 1985 National Book Award. In 1986 Wideman's son Jacob, then 18, was convicted of murdering a camping companion and was also sentenced to life in prison. After this personal tragedy, Wideman returned to the East Coast and accepted a full professorship at the University of Massachusetts at Amherst. (Wideman has two other children: daughter Jamila, who followed her father's footsteps as an outstanding basketball player in high school and college; and son Danny, who is also a writer.)

Wideman's literary reputation has been secured with the publication of *Fever* (1989), a novel about the yellow fever epidemic in nineteenth-century Philadelphia; *Philadelphia Fire* (1990), a novel about the incidents surrounding the black radical group MOVE for which he won a PEN/Faulkner Award in 1991; the acclaimed memoir *Fatheralong: A Meditation on Fathers and Sons* (1994); and the novel *Cattle Killing* (1996). In 1993 Wideman received a MacArthur Foundation "genius grant."

North America

Williams, Bert

(b. December 12, 1874?, Antigua, West Indies?; d. March 4, 1922, New York, N.Y.), actor and comedian of the vaudeville team of Williams and Walker who elevated Negro caricature to an art form.

Bert Williams's exact date and place of birth in the Caribbean is unknown. It is known that he moved to Riverside, California, in 1885 with his parents, Fred and Julia Williams. After high school he lived in San Francisco, where he entertained audiences in saloons and restaurants before touring with a small minstrel company.

In 1893 Williams met George Walker. The two developed an act that soon brought them national recognition. They combined Negro comedy with ragtime music and cakewalk dancing. Williams played the unkempt, fumbling "darky" while Walker was the dapper, smooth-stepping "dandy." Williams's hit songs included *"I'm a Jonah Man"* and *"Nobody."* Before Walker fell ill and retired in 1909, they performed several of their ragtime musicals on Broadway: *Son of Ham* (1900), *In Dahomey* (1902), *Abyssinia* (1906), and *Bandanna Land* (1907). *In Dahomey* was performed for the British royal family on Buckingham Palace lawn. They also recorded a number of skits for the Victor Company.

Williams continued to perform, becoming in 1910 the first African American to appear in the *Ziegfeld Follies*, the leading variety extravaganza of the time. After leaving the Follies in 1919, Williams performed his own shows until his death in 1922 during a run of *Under the Bamboo Tree*. Wearing blackface and using a "darky" dialect, Williams played a racially stereotyped caricature throughout his entire career. Williams's friends reported that despite the actor's stage success, the discrimination and rejection he faced in everyday life drove him to deep depression.

North America
_____

Williams, Billy Dee

(b. April 6, 1937, New York, N.Y.), African American actor known for his suave character in stage productions, movies, and television shows during the 1960s, 1970s, and 1980s.

Billy Dee Williams was born William December to a Texan father and a West Indian mother in Harlem. His parents juggled several jobs while his maternal grandmother helped raise Williams and his twin sister, Loretta. With aspirations of becoming a painter, Williams attended New York's High School of Music and Art and the National Academy of Fine Arts and Design. While pursuing his art studies, Williams learned about the Stanislavsky method of natural acting through his acquaintance with Sidney Poitier and Paul Mann at the Actors Workshop in Harlem. He initially viewed acting as a way to earn money for art supplies, but by the early 1960s Williams had begun to devote all of his energy to acting.

Williams first appeared on stage at age seven in *The Firebrand of Florence* (1945). His first screen appearance was in *The Last Angry Man* (1959). *A Taste of Honey* (1960), which won the New York Drama Critic's 1961 award for best foreign play, featured him in one of his earliest stage performances. After the failure of two marriages, the first to Audrey Sellers and the second to Marlene Clark, Williams fell into a depression in 1964.

Williams made a triumphant return to acting in 1970 with his Emmy-nominated portrayal of Chicago Bears football player Gale Sayers in *Brian's Song*. His success earned him a seven-year film contract with Motown's Berry Gordy, and he costarred with Diana Ross in *Lady Sings the Blues* (1972) and *Mahogany* (1975). In the 1980s he was featured in the movies *The Empire Strikes Back* (1980) and *Return of the Jedi* (1983), as well as in the television programs *Dynasty* and *Star Trek*. In 1984 Williams was inducted into the Black Filmmakers Hall of Fame, and in 1985 he was awarded a star on the Hollywood Walk of Fame.

North America

Williams, George Washington

(b. October 16, 1849, Bedford Springs, Pa.; d. August 2, 1891, Blackpool, England), scholar and minister; considered the first major American historian of African descent.

George Washington Williams left school at age 14 and lied about his age in order to enlist in the Union army during the Civil War. He later enlisted in the Mexican Army, in which he quickly rose to the rank of lieutenant colonel, and then joined the United States Cavalry in 1867, through which he served in the Indian campaigns.

In 1868 he enrolled at Newton Theological Seminary in Cambridge, Massachusetts. Graduating in 1874, he became the school's first African American alumnus. Immediately upon graduation, Williams was ordained as pastor of the Twelfth Baptist Church in Boston. Fascinated with the church, he wrote an 80-page study of its history. He left, however, after one year, and in Washington, D.C., started an unsuccessful academic journal about African Americans. Williams became pastor of Union Baptist Church in Cincinnati, Ohio, where he became a regular contributor to the *Cincinnati Commercial* under the pen name "Aristides." He also passed the bar exam to practice law in Ohio (and he would later practice in Boston), and in 1879 he became the first African American elected to the Ohio legislature.

At this time Williams also began to make his mark as an historian. He was a staunch supporter of the view, current at that time, that history was an objective science, and he was determined to apply this approach to African American history. In Ohio he began the research for his comprehensive, two-volume *History of the Negro Race in America, 1619–1880* (1882), which was the first full-length study of African American history by a person of African descent. He dedicated himself to African American history because of his opinion that African Americans had "been the most vexatious problem in North America from the time of its discovery down to the present day . . . [and writing] such a history would give the world more correct ideas of the Colored people, and incite the latter to greater effort in the struggle of citizenship and manhood." Williams also later wrote a *History of Negro Troops in the War of Rebellion* (1887), which argued that African Americans were among the most gallant soldiers in the Civil War.

Williams's scholarship brought him renown as an African American historian and advocate. In 1885 he was appointed minister to Haiti by outgoing President Chester A. Arthur. However, the presidency was assumed by Grover Cleveland, who refused to give Williams his post.

Williams became frustrated with Washington politics and turned his attention to international affairs, particularly the colonization and exploitation of Africa. He attended a major antislavery conference in Brussels in 1889. Belgium then sent him to Congo to study conditions there. The country's abysmal poverty so distressed him that, along with his official report, he wrote for wider circulation *An Open Letter to His Serene Majesty, Leopold II, King of Belgium.* This was the first public critique of King Leopold for his savage oppression of the people of the Congo. After his survey Williams traveled widely throughout Africa, and apparently contracted a disease that killed him upon his return to England.

North America

Williams, Mary Lou

(b. May 8, 1910, Atlanta, Ga.; d. May 28, 1981, Durham, N.C.), African American pianist, composer, arranger, and educator known as the "First Lady of Jazz" and considered the most significant female instrumentalist in jazz history for contributing to the development of both the Kansas City swing style of the 1930s and the bebop style of the early 1940s.

Born Mary Elfrieda Scruggs, Mary Lou Williams began playing piano professionally at age six in Pittsburgh, Pennsylvania. Her early influences included Earl Hines, Jelly Roll Morton, and Lovie Austin. As an adolescent, Williams performed in the Theater Owners Booking Association (TOBA) black vaudeville circuit alongside such figures as Fats Waller, Duke Ellington, and Willie "The Lion" Smith. In 1926 she married John Williams, a saxophonist and bandleader.

Williams began arranging in 1929 after she joined the Andy Kirk Band, first based in Oklahoma City and later in Kansas City, composing blues-based works that influenced the development of 1930s swing. During the 1930s

Pianist and arranger Mary Lou Williams was the most influential woman instrumentalist in the history of jazz, influencing both Kansas City swing and bebop. *CORBIS/Bettmann*

she performed and arranged for Louis Armstrong, Cab Calloway, Ellington, and others. Williams moved to New York in 1942 and joined Ellington's band as principal arranger and pianist, composing such notable works as *"Trumpet No End"* (1942). In the 1940s she mentored and jammed with many of the young beboppers, including Charlie Parker, Thelonious Monk, Bud Powell, and Dizzy Gillespie. Her famous *Zodiac Suite*, written in 1945, was adapted and performed by the New York Philharmonic in Carnegie Hall the following year.

In the 1950s Williams converted to Roman Catholicism and began concentrating on charitable activities and composing religious pieces. In 1957 she resumed performing and also formed Mary Records, the first record company established by a woman. Her major religious work, *Mary Lou's Mass* (1969), was commissioned by the Vatican and adapted for ballet by Alvin Ailey two years later. Williams went on to receive numerous honorary doctorates and two Guggenheim Fellowships. She taught courses on jazz at a number of colleges and universities, including Duke University in Durham, North Carolina, where she died in 1981.

North America

Williamson, Johnny Lee ("Sonny Boy")

(b. March 30, 1914, Jackson, Tenn.; d. June 1, 1948, Chicago, Ill.), African American musician revered for transforming the blues harmonica from a novelty instrument to an integral component of Chicago-style blues.

Johnny Lee Williamson taught himself to play the harmonica as a child. In his teens he left home and traveled, hobo-style, throughout the South with mandolin player Yank Rachel and guitarist Sleepy John Estes. He moved to Chicago in 1937 and quickly became one of the city's most popular bluesmen, recording such hits as *"Good Morning Little School Girl"* and *"Sugar Man Blues."*

Williamson's imaginative style and stunning virtuosity brought the harmonica to the forefront of blues, and they have influenced virtually every major blues harmonicist after him. Williamson pioneered numerous playing techniques that are now considered standard. Among them are manipulating the sound of the harmonica by cupping the hands, and "crossed key" playing, in which one tunes the harmonica a fourth below the key of the song. This allows the musician to play in the right key by inhaling rather than exhaling, affording him a greater ability to "bend" the notes.

Williamson was known for his distinctive "mumbling" singing style. One sign of his renown is that harmonicist Aleck "Rice" Miller began recording under the name Sonny Boy Williamson and came to be known as Sonny Boy #2.

Williamson was murdered on the steps of his home at the height of his popularity. In 1980 he was inducted into the Blues Foundation's Hall of Fame.

Williams, Sherley

(b. August 25, 1944, Bakersfield, Calif.), African American poet, novelist, and scholar who emphasized the importance of history and folklore in shaping black identity.

In an introduction to her first novel, *Dessa Rose*, Sherley Anne Williams writes, "Afro-Americans, having survived by word of mouth—and made of that process a high art—remain at the mercy of literature and writing; often, these have betrayed us." Williams's awareness of skewed histories shaped her own writing. Her consistent ability to tell black stories truthfully through poetry and fiction has brought her prominence among contemporary black American writers.

Born and raised in low-income housing projects, Williams earned an A.B. in history at California State University. After a lengthy absence from school, she received a master's degree from Brown University. Subsequently, Williams returned to California to join the faculty of the University of California, San Diego, in 1975.

Although Williams began writing in 1967, it was not until 1972, following the publication of *Give Birth to Brightness: A Thematic Study in Neo-Black Literature*, that her theories about the value of black folklore in shaping racial identity were fully articulated. These principles took artistic form when her book, *The Peacock Poems*, was published in 1975 to critical and popular acclaim, ultimately winning a nomination for the National Book Award in poetry. Among her other writings were *Some One Sweet Angel Chile* (1982) and *Dessa Rose* (1986), which was named a notable book by the *New York Times*.

Williams, Spencer, Jr.

(b. 1893, Vidalia, La.; d. December 13, 1969, Los Angeles, Calif.), African American television and movie director, actor, and writer best known for his role on the *Amos 'n' Andy* television show.

Born in Louisiana, Spencer Williams attended the University of Minnesota, dropping out to join the army. Returning South after his 1923 discharge, he got his start in movies by writing for a series of short black films based on stories by Octavsus Roy Cohen. These films were made by an affiliate of Paramount Pictures, and Williams soon moved to an office on Paramount's lot in Hollywood.

A talented actor, Williams appeared in some of the first African American talking movies of the 1920s, including *The Lady Fare*, *Oft in the Silly Night*, and *Music Has Charms*. His work as a producer included silent films such as *Hot Biscuits* (1929) and the earliest black Westerns, *Bronze Buckaroo* (1938) and *Harlem Rides the Range* (1939). Films that Williams wrote, directed, and starred in range from the comedy *Juke Joint* (1947) to the allegory *The Blood of Jesus* (1941).

In 1951 Williams accepted the role for which he is most famous, Andy Brown on the television version of *Amos 'n' Andy*. The show used exaggeration and stereotypes as a comic motif, but, airing in a changing and turbulent political climate, it was denounced by the National Association for the Advancement of Colored People (NAACP). Suffering from lack of support, the show lasted three years. After its cancellation Williams supported himself on a veteran's pension and social security until his death from a kidney disorder in 1969.

North America

Williams, Vanessa L.

(b. March 18, 1963, Tarrytown, N.Y.), African American singer and actress, the first black woman to be crowned Miss America.

Vanessa Williams has enjoyed a successful and diverse career as a singer and actress. Since the release of her debut album in 1988, she has produced six albums and won lead roles in stage and film productions, including the critically acclaimed movie *Soul Food* in 1997.

Williams grew up in predominantly white Millwood, New York. Encouraged by her parents, both music teachers, she learned to play the piano, French horn, and violin, and pursued intensive dance training. While in high school she starred in plays and musicals, and received numerous scholastic and theatrical awards.

Aspiring to become a stage actress, in 1981 Williams enrolled at Syracuse University as a musical theater major. Prompted by a talent scout, she entered and won the Miss Syracuse beauty pageant, a victory that propelled her to the 1983 Miss America pageant, in which she made history as the first black woman ever to be crowned Miss America. While some black leaders attributed her victory to her "light skin" and "middle-class background," others compared her breakthrough to that of Jackie Robinson, who in 1947 became the first black since the 1890s to play major league baseball.

In July 1984 Williams again made history—this time as the first woman forced to resign her Miss America title—after *Penthouse* magazine published explicit photos of her, taken when she was 19 years old. For many observers, Williams's predicament revealed the tension between the pageant's moral code and its business of judging scantily dressed women. Prominent feminists such as Gloria Steinem and Susan Brownmiller rallied to her defense, as did black leaders Benjamin Hooks and Jesse Jackson.

Although Williams lost her crown and a $900,000 advertising contract with the Gillette Company, the setback only steeled her resolve; in 1987 she launched a singing career with Mercury Records. Her debut album, *The Right Stuff*, released in 1988, received three Grammy nominations and the Best New Female Artist Award from the National Association for the

Advancement of Colored People (NAACP). Her second album, *The Comfort Zone* (1991), which featured the hit singles *"Save the Best for Last"* and *"Work to Do,"* sold more than 2 million copies. In 1994 she won rave reviews for her lead role in the Broadway musical *Kiss of the Spider Woman*, and performed *"Colors of the Wind"* on the Academy Award-winning soundtrack to the Disney film *Pocahontas*.

Williams has also appeared in numerous television shows and Hollywood films; in 1996 she starred with Arnold Schwarzenegger in the action film *Eraser*. Divorced, Williams has three children: Melanie, Jillian, and Devin.

North America

Wilson, August

(b. April 27, 1945, Pittsburgh, Pa.), playwright and poet; two-time winner of the Pulitzer Prize for drama.

August Wilson was born Frederick August Kittel in a poor, mixed-race neighborhood of Pittsburgh, Pennsylvania, known as the Hill. His father, a white German baker, was rarely around; his mother held cleaning jobs and received welfare payments to support her six children. When Wilson was a young teenager, his mother remarried and the family moved to a mostly white neighborhood. Wilson's encounters with racism in his new home were more direct, including a pivotal incident in which a teacher wrongly accused him of plagiarizing a paper.

In 1960 Wilson dropped out of school but continued his education in the libraries of Pittsburgh, where he read black writers such as Richard Wright and Ralph Ellison. He received another sort of education in the barber shops, cafés, and street corners that were frequented by a wide range of blacks. In 1965 Wilson began to write poetry. He was heavily influenced by the lyricism of Welsh poet Dylan Thomas and, later, by the Black Nationalism of African American poet and playwright Amiri Baraka. Baraka and other activists of the late 1960s argued that blacks, especially black artists, needed to be more race-conscious. Wilson agreed and spent many of the following years bringing life to black history and culture. In 1968, with little previous experience in the theater, he and a friend founded the Black Horizon Theatre Company in his old neighborhood, the Hill. The company featured minor plays by and about blacks. Around this time he also discovered and immersed himself in the blues—the genre's pained, harmonic realism gave him the inspiration for many of his later plays. In a culminating act of symbolism, he rejected his last name, the name of his white father, and took his mother's maiden name, Wilson, in recognition of her black heritage.

Wilson still believed himself to be a poet, but in the early 1970s he began writing plays. In 1977 he wrote *Black Bart and the Sacred Hills*, a musical satire about an outlaw of the Old West that was produced four years later in St. Paul, Minnesota. He finished two more plays (one of which, *Jitney*, about jitney drivers in Pittsburgh, was produced regionally) before Lloyd Richards, dean of the Yale Drama School, noticed his play *Ma Rainey's Black Bottom* in 1982.

Set in Chicago in the 1920s, *Ma Rainey* presents a fictional day in the real life of blues legend Gertrude "Ma" Rainey. Using realistic dialogue, the play depicts black musicians being exploited by white record companies and directing their rage at other blacks instead of their white oppressors. Richards produced the play first at the Yale Repertory Theatre, then on Broadway, establishing a pattern that he and Wilson, working collabora- tively, used in Wilson's future plays. Although a few reviewers criticized *Ma Rainey* for over-emphasizing politics, others praised it for presenting a poignant account of the effect of racism.

Shortly after writing *Ma Rainey*, Wilson wrote *Fences*, which focuses on the frustrations and responsibilities of a former Negro League baseball player, now a garbage man, barred from playing in the major leagues. *Fences*, winner of the 1987 Pulitzer Prize for drama, strengthened the playwright's reputa- tion for deft presentation of the consequences of racism. His next play, *Joe Turner's Come and Gone* (1986), further distinguished Wilson by debuting on Broadway while *Fences* was still running there. Set in a Pittsburgh boarding house in 1911, *Joe Turner* chronicles the life of a black freedman who comes North to find his wife, who fled while he was enslaved. Mystical and metaphorical, the play explores assimilation by African Americans into American society and is at once bitter and optimistic.

The Piano Lesson, immensely popular with both critics and audiences, followed in 1987. Set in 1936, its main characters are descendants of a slave family whose father and grandmother were traded for a piano. The grieving grandfather carved likenesses of his wife and son in the piano, which is now in the family's possession. The family is divided between those who want to sell the piano to buy the land where their ancestors were slaves and those who want to preserve the piano as an heirloom. *The Piano Lesson* won both a Pulitzer Prize and a Tony Award for best play.

In 1990 Wilson wrote *Two Trains Running*, a portrayal of friendships and conflicts during the late 1960s; in 1995 he wrote *Seven Guitars*, a portrayal of relationships among a group of musicians set in Pittsburgh in 1948. Wilson has declared that he will write a drama about black American life in each decade of the twentieth century.

North America
___

Wilson, Cassandra

(b. December ?, 1955, Jackson, Miss.), African American jazz vocalist and songwriter acclaimed for her smoky contralto and musical versatility.

Hailed by *Time* magazine as "the most accomplished jazz vocalist of her generation," Cassandra Wilson has enjoyed a success and visibility usually reserved for pop singers. Her singing is eclectic and innovative: she performs both original and standard songs, drawing upon many musical influences, including jazz, blues, folk, hip hop, funk, and rock. According to critic Gene

Santoro, "she is the direct descendant of Billie Holiday and Dinah Washington, with their bluesy pop tunes and wicked jazz feel for the unexpected twist, and can rivet audiences with her languid, curling voice while lighting a room with simmering sexual energy."

Wilson grew up in Jackson, Mississippi, where her mother was an elementary school teacher and her father was a jazz bassist. Her father nurtured her passion for music, and as a child she studied classical piano and taught herself to play the acoustic guitar. Her mother and grandmother, both women of spirit and energy, were her role models: while Wilson admired her mother's strength of character, she found inspiration in her grandmother's religiosity and powerful, uninhibited singing in church. "I come from a long line of women who, against all odds, did what they wanted to do," she told *Ms.* magazine in 1997.

After graduating with a degree in communications from Jackson State University, Wilson worked at a New Orleans television station. She also performed as a singer in local nightclubs. Set on a musical career, in 1982 she moved to New York City. There she met avant-garde saxophonist Steve Coleman, who introduced her to M-BASE, a Brooklyn-based collective of musicians who fused rock, hip hop, funk, and jazz. Wilson became the group's main vocalist, and in collaboration with Coleman and M-BASE musician Jean-Paul Bourelly, she recorded her first album, *Point of View* (1985), on the German label JMT. Subsequent albums won her comparisons to jazz vocalist Betty Carter, and in 1989 her *Blue Skies* became the top-selling jazz album of the year.

In 1993 Wilson took a new direction when she signed with Blue Note Records, one of the world's greatest jazz labels. "Once a daredevil of the avant-garde, Wilson is drawing on the very fundamentals of black-music expression, which is in itself a classic avant-garde gesture," said *New York* magazine writer Chris Norris. Collaborating with producer Craig Street, she recorded the widely acclaimed, top-selling album *Blue Light 'til Dawn,* which featured fresh renditions of vintage blues and folk songs as well as songs written by Wilson.

Wilson's Grammy-nominated album *New Moon Daughter* (1996) was praised by the *New York Times* as one of the best albums of the decade. It appealed to a wide audience, from jazz aficionados to mainstream listeners, and propelled her into the limelight as the jazz diva of the 1990s. She has since recorded *Rendezvous* (1997), with jazz pianist Jacky Terrasson, and is the featured vocalist on *Blood on the Fields* (1997), an epic oratorio about slavery in the United States, composed by Wynton Marsalis.

North America

Wilson, Harriet E. Adams

(b. 1828?, Milford, N.H.; d. 1870?), American writer whose book, *Our Nig*, published in 1859, is considered the first novel published by an African American woman and the first novel published by an African American in the United States.

Little is known about the life of Harriet E. Adams Wilson. The 1850 federal census lists a 22-year-old "Black" woman named Harriet Adams living with the Samuel Boyles family in the town of Milford, which suggests that she was born around 1828. In 1851 she married Thomas Wilson, a free man who pretended to be a fugitive slave from Virginia so he could lecture on the horrors of slavery. Shortly after the birth of the couple's son, George Mason Wilson, in May or June 1852, Thomas Wilson abandoned the family. Wilson, who was unable to work because of the physical and emotional abuse inflicted by her employers, lost custody of her son. She began writing to earn enough money to reclaim him. He died five and one-half months after her book's Boston publication in 1859. Neither the date nor the location of Wilson's death is known.

Our Nig; or, Sketches from the Life of a Free Black, in a Two-Story White House, North. Showing That Slavery's Shadows Fall Even There, is a largely autobiographical novel that explicitly compares the racist conditions suffered by a black indentured servant to slavery in the South. Using the slave narrative as a model, Wilson indicts Northern treatment of blacks. Possibly because of its controversial stand, the book was published at the author's own expense and sold poorly.

The story is told mostly through the eyes of a young girl, the novel's protagonist, Alfrado, a mulatto who is abandoned by her white mother after her black father dies. Left with a white family, she is severely mistreated by the mother and one of the daughters. Although the men of the family are absentmindedly fond of her, they are unable to protect her from the hunger, beatings, and scolding that she constantly endures. Misfortune continues into Alfrado's adulthood when the husband, who she thought would save her, leaves her and her young child. The novel ends with Alfrado, broken in body but not in spirit, expressing her contempt for a society that allowed her virtual slavery.

North America
Winfrey, Oprah Gail

(b. January 29, 1954, Kosciusko, Miss.), African American talk show host, Academy Award-nominated actress, and producer whose syndicated television show, *The Oprah Winfrey Show*, is the most popular talk show ever.

Oprah Winfrey was born on a Mississippi farm and raised by her paternal grandmother until she was six years old, when she moved to Milwaukee to live with her mother, Vernita Lee. Though Winfrey did well in school, she was allegedly sexually abused by male relatives and became increasingly troubled as a teenager. Her mother, a maid who was busy raising two other children, eventually sent Winfrey to live with her disciplinarian father, a barber and businessman in Nashville, Tennessee. Winfrey flowered under Vernon Winfrey's strict supervision, excelling academically and as a public speaker. At age 16 she won a partial scholarship to the Tennessee State University in a public speaking contest sponsored by the Elks Club.

As a freshman at Tennessee State University, Winfrey worked briefly as a radio newscaster before victories in two local beauty pageants helped land her a news anchor position at WTVF-TV in Nashville. In 1976, only a few months shy of her bachelor's degree at Tennessee State University, Winfrey landed a job as a reporter and evening news co-anchor at WJZ-TV in Baltimore. Although she did not succeed in that position, the station management realized that Winfrey, who had no formal journalistic training, was better suited to co-hosting WJZ's morning talk show, *People Are Talking*. Winfrey helped turn the show into a ratings success with her personable interviewing style and charismatic presence.

After eight years as the cohost of *People Are Talking*, Winfrey was offered a job as the host of *A.M. Chicago*, a Chicago talk show that aired opposite Phil Donahue's popular morning show and lagged behind it in the ratings. In one month Winfrey's ratings equaled Donahue's, and in three, surpassed them. Donahue acknowledged Winfrey's ratings supremacy by moving his show to New York in 1985. In 1985 *A.M. Chicago* was renamed *The Oprah Winfrey Show*, and it was syndicated in 1986. It eventually became the highest-rated talk show in television history. By 1997, 15 to 20 million viewers watched it daily in the United States, and it was seen in more than 132 countries. The show has received 25 Emmy Awards, 6 of them for best host. In 1996 *Time* magazine named Winfrey one of the 25 most influential people in the world.

Also a talented actress, in 1985 Winfrey earned Golden Globe and Academy Award nominations for her portrayal of Sofia in the film *The Color Purple*, based on Alice Walker's book of the same name. In 1986 Winfrey founded HARPO Productions, becoming only the third woman to own her own television and film studios. Based in Chicago, HARPO (Oprah spelled backwards) owns and produces *The Oprah Winfrey Show* as well as such dramatic miniseries as *The Women of Brewster Place* (1988), based on the book by Gloria Naylor, and *The Wedding* (1998), based on the book by Dorothy West. In addition to supporting African American literature through her television movies, Winfrey presents an on-air book club that has brought new readers to such writers as Toni Morrison.

A political activist as well as an entertainer, Winfrey testified before the United States Senate Judiciary Committee, describing the sexual abuse she suffered as a child, and worked for the passage of the National Child Protection Act in 1991, which provides for the establishment of a nationwide database of convicted child abusers. In December 1993 President Bill Clinton signed "Oprah's Bill" into law. Her many philanthropic ventures include donations of time and money to efforts aimed at protecting children and to the establishment of educational scholarships.

North America

Wings Over Jordan,

African American choir and radio program popular in the 1930s and 1940s for its performances of traditional black choral music.

The choir Wings Over Jordan debuted in 1937 in Cleveland, Ohio, on a radio show called "The National Negro Hour." The group was formed by Rev. Glenn T. Settle of the Gethsemane Church. Aired every Sunday morning on Cleveland's WGAR station, the choir swiftly gained popularity and, in 1939, attracted a national audience when "Wings Over Jordan"—now a national radio program—was broadcast weekly on Sunday mornings on the CBS national radio network.

During the next 15 years Wings Over Jordan gained fame throughout the United States and abroad. Under the direction of various conductors, including Thomas King, the choir toured nationally and recorded on major labels. In 1945 it toured with the United Services Organization throughout Europe, performing powerfully rendered gospel songs and spirituals for military personnel during World War II.

Wings Over Jordan paved the way for other black college choirs to appear on radio, and by 1950 the ABC network hosted a regular Sunday morning program called "Negro College Choirs." After concluding its own radio program in 1949, Wings Over Jordan continued to perform publicly until 1965.

North America
Wonder, Stevie
(b. May 13, 1950, Saginaw, Mich.), African American singer, songwriter, and musician.

Stevie Wonder, born Steveland Morris, is one of the most prolific and inventive artists in American popular music and rhythm and blues. Blind from birth, Wonder was first introduced to music as a young child and quickly developed musical skills beyond his years. At age 12 he was discovered by Ronnie White of the Miracles and won an audition at the Motown Record Company in Detroit, Michigan. When Motown's founder, Berry Gordy, witnessed the young boy's startling talents, he dubbed him "Little Stevie Wonder." Wonder was quickly adopted into the Motown "family" at Hitsville Studios. He charmed everyone with his prodigious musical range and lively sense of humor. Although Wonder played the drums, piano, and organ, his first Number-One hit, "*Fingertips, Part 2*" (1963), featured his exceptional skill on the harmonica, which became a trademark of his early career. More hits followed, including "*Workout Stevie, Workout*" (1963), "*Hey Harmonica Man*" (1964), and "*Uptight (Everything's Alright)*" (1966).

In 1966 Wonder recorded a cover of Bob Dylan's antiwar song, "*Blowin' in the Wind*." Wonder's interpretation of the song became an anthem of the struggling Civil Rights Movement and foreshadowed his future involvement in political causes. Always an independent spirit, Wonder sought more creative control over his music as he grew into adulthood. He began producing his own albums in 1970, and in 1971 renegotiated his Motown contract to get complete artistic control over his recordings.

The new artistic freedom resulted in one of the most productive phases of Wonder's career, which included hits such as "*My Cherie Amour*" (1969), "*Signed, Sealed, Delivered I'm Yours*" (1970), "*Superstition*" (1972), and "*You Are the Sunshine of My Life*" (1973). A musical visionary, Wonder combined poetic lyrics with experimental electronic music that he developed through his mastery of the synthesizer. He also took the idea of a "concept" album—an album based on a central theme—to new heights. Albums including *Talking Book* (1972), *Innervisions* (1973), *Fulfillingness' First Finale* (1974), and *Songs in the Key of Life* (1976) reflected Wonder's spiritual style and won him more Grammy Awards than any other Motown artist.

Wonder's music and life have always engaged with social issues and political causes. Songs such as "*Living for the City*" (1973) offered commentary on urban poverty, and one of his later hits, "*Happy Birthday*" (1980), was instrumental in the campaign to recognize Martin Luther King Jr.'s birthday as a national holiday. Wonder also performed in the United States for Africa's fundraising song, "*We are the World*," and was a leader in the antiapartheid movement in the United States. Wonder's recent work includes the soundtrack for Spike Lee's film *Jungle Fever* (1991), and *Conversation Peace* (1995). Wonder has received many awards in recognition of his musical achievements. He was inducted into the Songwriter's Hall of Fame in 1982 and the Rock and Roll Hall of Fame in 1989, and in 1996, at age 46, Wonder received the Grammy's Lifetime Achievement Award.

North America

Woodruff, Hale Aspacio

(b. August 26, 1900, Cairo, Ill.; d. September 6, 1980, New York, N.Y.), African American painter and teacher who is best known for his *Amistad Murals*.

Hale Woodruff attended public schools in Nashville, Tennessee, where he was raised by his mother. In 1920 he moved to Indianapolis to study art at the John Herron Art Institute, supporting himself with part-time work as a political cartoonist. During this period he developed an interest in African art, which influenced his later work. In 1926 Woodruff won a Harmon Foundation Award to study at the Académie Moderne de la Grande Chaumière in Paris from 1927 to 1931.

Woodruff returned to the United States in 1931 and founded the art department at Atlanta University, where he helped to develop a cohesive national African American arts community. In addition to teaching, Woodruff brought exhibitions to Atlanta University that featured a wide range of African American artists who were often excluded from mainstream art exhibitions. To promote African American art and artists further, Woodruff organized the Atlanta University Annuals in 1942, a national juried exhibition that continued until 1970. Woodruff used the Annuals to promote the interests of his students, including Frederick Flemister, Eugene Grigsby, Wilmer Jennings, and Hayward Oubré, and independent artists such as Charles Alston, Elizabeth Catlett, Lois Mailou Jones, and William H. Johnson.

A gifted artist as well as teacher, Woodruff achieved his greatest fame with the *Amistad Murals*, painted for Talladega College's Savery Library. The work reflects the influence of Mexican muralist Diego Rivera, with whom Woodruff studied briefly in 1934, and depicts moments of "the Amistad Incident," the 1839 mutiny by kidnapped Africans aboard a slave ship against their captors. The first panel, *The Mutiny Aboard the Amistad, 1839*, shows the violent struggle that occurred when the enslaved Africans sought to capture the ship. The second panel, *The Amistad Slaves on Trial at New Haven, Connecticut, 1840*, depicts a scene from the trial, as a white sailor who survived the attack accuses the African Cinque of leading the mutiny. The third panel, *The Return to Africa, 1842*, portrays the mutineers after winning their court case and returning home.

Woodruff moved to New York in 1946 and began teaching at New York University (NYU). During this period he abandoned figurative painting and shifted to an abstract expressionist style. He adopted abstract expressionism's spontaneity but also included design components of the African art he became interested in as a student, including Asante gold weights, Dogon masks, and Yoruba Shango implements. Woodruff also continued to support other African American artists. In 1963 Woodruff cofounded *Spiral*, a group whose members sought to represent the Civil Rights Movement in the visual arts. Woodruff was awarded a Great Teacher Award by NYU in 1966, and in 1968 he became professor emeritus at NYU. In April 1980, shortly before his death, he was one of ten African American artists honored by President Jimmy Carter at a White House reception for the National Conference of Artists.

North America

Works Progress Administration,

a program implemented during the Great Depression as part of President Franklin D. Roosevelt's New Deal that provided jobs for many unemployed African Americans.

During the 1930s, as the United States struggled through the Great Depression, millions of people were left unemployed or underemployed. The Works Progress Administration (WPA)—established in 1935 and four years later renamed the Work Projects Administration—was a massive program to provide jobs for the unemployed. It was part of President Franklin D. Roosevelt's New Deal, a set of initiatives designed to revive the American economy. In March 1936, a year after its creation, the WPA had 3.6 million people on its rolls.

Between 1935 and the program's demise in 1943 the WPA constructed more than 1,046,025 km (650,000 mi) of streets and highways. It built or worked on more than 850 airports, 8,000 parks, 120,000 bridges, and

125,000 public buildings. African Americans, who accounted for less than 10 percent of the American population, particularly benefited from the WPA, making up 15 to 20 percent of its 8.5 million employees. Moreover, in 1935 Roosevelt signed an executive order forbidding discrimination in WPA projects, one of his strongest actions in support of equality for African Americans and other minorities.

Although mainly employing people to perform manual labor, the WPA also established a variety of educational and arts projects. Ella J. Baker, later instrumental in founding the Student Nonviolent Coordinating Committee (SNCC), taught literacy and consumer education classes—and learned about grassroots political organizing—under the auspices of the WPA. Similarly, future lawyer and civil rights activist Pauli Murray worked in the New York City public schools with the WPA's Remedial Reading Project as well as in the WPA Workers' Education Project. For Baker, Murray, and others, experience in the WPA played a role in their subsequent activism in the Civil Rights Movement.

The WPA supported the arts and sponsored cultural activities through the Federal Writers' Project (FWP), the WPA Dance Theater, the Federal Music Project, and the Federal Theater Project. The Federal Theater Project, which Congress abolished in 1939, supported touring theatrical companies and circuses that brought inexpensive entertainment, including an all-black production of William Shakespeare's *Macbeth*, to towns and cities across the country.

The FWP employed such noted black writers as Ralph Ellison, Claude McKay, Richard Wright, Zora Neale Hurston, and Arna Bontemps. Among its various activities the FWP undertook a large-scale oral history project to interview former African American slaves and collect narratives of their experiences under slavery. In most states the interviewers were white, but Virginia's FWP was notable for its extensive use of black interviewers.

In response to an apparent economic recovery in 1936, Roosevelt and Congress made sharp cuts in the WPA budget. The cutbacks resulted in many workers—including many African Americans—being dismissed from WPA projects and helped trigger an economic downturn between 1937 and 1939, known as the "Roosevelt Recession." WPA policies were the subject of controversy, as evidenced by such topical blues as Casey Bill Weldon's *"WPA Blues"* (1936) and Porter Grainger's *"Pink Slip Blues,"* recorded by singer Ida Cox in 1939. But the main opponents of the WPA were Republicans and white Southern Democrats, who constituted a conservative anti–New Deal coalition that in 1943 succeeded in abolishing the agency.

North America

Wright, Richard

(b. September 4, 1908, Roxie, Miss.; d. November 28, 1960, Paris, France), African American novelist, among the first to show the destructive effects of white racism on both blacks and whites.

Richard Wright was born in rural Mississippi near Natchez, where white hostility was all-pervasive. His mother was a former schoolteacher; his father was a farmer who drank heavily and abandoned the family in 1914. In the absence of her husband Wright's mother took a series of low-wage, unskilled jobs to support her two boys. Moving from town to town, the family settled in Memphis, then in rural Arkansas, often going hungry. After his mother suffered a debilitating stroke, Wright returned to Mississippi in the care of his stern religious grandmother, who disapproved of his literary inclinations. The experience left Wright eager to leave the area and disdainful of religion.

Upon completing the ninth grade, Wright went North, first to Memphis, then to Chicago. He discovered and read H. L. Mencken, whose journalism inspired Wright's later writing, as well as Fyodor Dostoyevsky, Sinclair Lewis, Sherwood Anderson, and Theodore Dreiser. In Chicago in the late 1920s and early 1930s he held odd jobs, eventually settling in the United States post office, which was nicknamed "the University" for its high density of radical intellectuals.

Wright attended meetings of the John Reed Club, an organization of leftist writers, and soon became active in the Communist Party. Encouraged by party members, Wright published poetry, short stories, and articles in Communist newspapers and other left-wing journals. He later said that he had hoped his writings would bridge the gap between party leaders and common people. Beginning in 1935, for several years he wrote travel guides for the Depression-era Federal Writers' Project, first in Chicago, then in Harlem. He also produced fiction—a collection of forceful short stories about racial oppression and a humorous novel about working-class blacks in Chicago. Some of these stories were published in leftist periodicals; the novel was published in 1963, after his death, as *Lawd Today*.

Wright's debut in mainstream publishing came in 1938 with the publication of *Uncle Tom's Children*, a collection of cruel novellas based on his Southern childhood. The book was widely read, and its accounts of the pernicious effects of racism moved and impressed reviewers. Still, Wright was disappointed. He had intended readers to see and feel the devastation of racism on all of society, not just on African Americans.

His next novel, *Native Son* (1940), was merciless. In the story, Bigger Thomas, a young black man hardened by racism and ignorance, accidentally kills a white woman and is condemned to death. Although Bigger's Communist lawyer argues that guilt belongs to the society that would not accept him and drove him to brutality, Bigger, in fact, has tasted his first freedom in the act of murder: for once in his alienated life he has brought about an event to which others must respond. Editors toned down the original manuscript (the restored original version was published only in 1992), but *Native Son* was still the most militant protest novel about American race relations of its time. It became a huge bestseller, a Book-of-the-Month Club selection, and was dramatized on Broadway in a production by Orson Welles. Many reviewers marveled that Wright could make Bigger Thomas an unsympathetic character yet nonetheless force white readers to see their own guilt in Bigger's crime. Other reviewers, while appreciative of the novel's power, criticized Wright for presenting a stereotype and a victim in Bigger Thomas.

In 1944 Wright wrote an essay for the *Atlantic Monthly* titled "I Tried to Be a Communist" in which he expressed his long disenchantment with the dogma of the Communist Party as well as its refusal to speak and act on black civil rights. Shortly thereafter he published *Black Boy* (1945), the autobiography of his youth in the South. Like his previous works, *Black Boy* was unrelenting in its depiction of the scarring effects of racism and poverty. A few critics complained that it gave a one-sided picture of the South, but most heralded it as searing and precise, even a masterpiece.

In the late 1940s Wright traveled to France at the invitation of American expatriate writer Gertrude Stein. He was warmly received in Paris, where he met many of the country's leading intellectuals, including Jean-Paul Sartre and Simone de Beauvoir. Feeling the tensions of racism on his return to New York and annoyed at being acclaimed only as a great black writer, he emigrated to France with his second wife—he had been briefly married at the beginning of the 1940s—and young daughter.

In France Wright was deeply influenced by existentialism, a philosophy emphasizing the isolation of the individual in a hostile or indifferent universe. He wrote three more novels, none of which was well received in America, partly because they over-intellectualized the question of race, partly because they were perceived as out of touch with recent developments in American race relations, and partly because many critics were upset with him for leaving the United States. Wright also wrote extensively about colonialism in Africa; in his last years he became an inter-national spokesman for Pan-Africanism. He died in Paris.

Among Wright's other works are the novels *The Outsider* (1953), *Savage Holiday* (1954), and *The Long Dream* (1958); the collection of stories *Eight Men* (1961); the nonfiction works *Black Power* (1954), *The Color Curtain* (1956), *Pagan Spain* (1957), and *White Man, Listen!* (1957); and the expanded autobiography, *American Hunger* (1977).

XYZ

Young, Lester Willis ("Prez")

(b. August 27, 1909, Woodville, Miss.; d. March 15, 1959, New York, N.Y.),
African American tenor saxophonist whose distinctive approach and tone
inspired many musicians during the 1940s and 1950s.

Singer Billie Holiday gave Lester Young his nickname "Prez," short for president, during the 1930s: it was an era of dukes, counts, and kings of swing, and she insisted that Young should hold the highest office in the land. Today he is most widely heard through his musical collaborations with Holiday. During and after the swing era he and Coleman Hawkins offered the major alternative approaches to the tenor saxophone in jazz.

As an improviser Hawkins relied upon arpeggios built over the harmonies of each chord in a song. Young's improvisations were linear—melodies stretched across the chord sequence. Hawkins aggressively pushed the beat; Young's playing was gentle, and consistently behind the beat. Hawkins's tone was full, even harsh; Young's was light.

Young came from a musical family that moved during his childhood from Mississippi to New Orleans to Minneapolis. He learned several instruments and played in the successful Young family band. In 1927, while playing with another group, he took up the tenor saxophone. Eventually he settled in Kansas City, then a booming jazz center. He joined Bennie Moten's band in 1933, then left for New York City to fill the saxophone chair recently vacated by Hawkins in Fletcher Henderson's band. The Henderson band, accustomed to Hawkins's style, ridiculed Young, and he soon returned to Kansas City. But while he was in New York City, a chance encounter in a Harlem jam session introduced him to Billie Holiday, with whom he would collaborate in a classic series of recordings in the late 1930s and early 1940s.

Young influenced few saxophonists during the 1930s. However, the musician upon whom he had the greatest impact—alto saxophonist Charlie Parker—became the key jazz soloist to arise between Louis Armstrong in the 1920s and John Coltrane in the 1960s. Parker, a creator of bop during the 1940s, extended Young's style and made it his own. Parker's early recordings reveal his deep debt to Young.

Young rejoined the Count Basie band in 1935, and in 1936 he made his recording debut with a quintet drawn from that band. Producer John Hammond later recalled it as "one of the only perfect sessions I ever had." Musicologist Gunther Schuller described Young's solo on *"Oh, Lady Be Good"* as "quintessential Lester Young: economical and lean . . . and masterful in its control of form." Young remained with Basie between 1935 and 1940, and returned in 1943 for a stint that ended when he was drafted. During the late 1930s he also recorded regularly with Holiday. His improvised fills and counter melodies behind her vocals define the interplay that is the essence of jazz.

After World War II Young did not fare well, although his musical star was clearly ascendant. A large number of saxophonists—including Wardell Gray, Paul Quinichette (nicknamed the Vice President), and numerous white saxophonists such as Stan Getz and Zoot Sims—modeled their playing on Young's. On the other hand, his recordings suggest his unhappiness, which some attributed to his traumatic military experience, and others to his heavy drinking.

Even in the 1950s Young occasionally recaptured the fragile beauty of his early playing. In a 1956 series of recordings—including *The Jazz Giants* and three albums recorded at a nightclub in Washington, D.C.—Young was in prime form. But when he performed with Holiday in the 1957 television special "The Sound of Jazz," their performance had an aura of tragic finality. Young and Holiday died in 1959 within four months of each other.

Latin America and the Caribbean

Zapata Olivella, Manuel

(b. March 17, 1920, Lorica, Colombia), Afro-Colombian writer, essayist, physician, anthropologist, diplomat, and leading intellectual and artist of twentieth-century Latin America. Zapata Olivella is one of the most intriguing voices to emanate from the diaspora and, together with Nancy Morejón and Quince Duncan, among its most admired Afro-Hispanic writers.

Manuel Zapata Olivella's frequent use of the word *mulatto* (a person of both African and European descent) to describe his background suggests a biological union as much as a cultural mixture. Focusing less on phenotype and more on what the Afro-Cuban poet Nicolás Guillén would term cultural *mulatez*, or the mixing of cultures that characterizes the Caribbean, Zapata Olivella has sought to uncover what unites peoples rather than what separates them. Both his parents are of African descent, and he frequently reflects on the constant racial and cultural dynamics that define Latin America. However, from the naming of one of his daughters Harlem to the writing of one of the most artistically accomplished novels about the diaspora, the 1983 *Changó, el gran putas* (Shango: The Greatest S.O.B.), Zapata

Olivella is a strong voice in the dialogue on the contribution of African culture to the world. He provides a telling case study for a cultivated sense of an African connection in Latin America.

Born in the small town of Lorica on the western Caribbean coast of Colombia, Zapata Olivella used the area's rich folklore in his first novel, *Tierra mojada* (1947, Wetlands), to explore the conflicting social relations of the region. The novel recounts in accessible language and a straightforward narrative the struggles between a soon-to-be landless, rice-growing community and a large landowner and political boss. Other central characters are the parish priest, with whom the boss works in cahoots, and the local schoolteacher, a communist sympathizer and a civil rights leader who tries to defend the peasant community. Though simplistic in its approach to issues of good and evil and social disparity, *Tierra mojada* contains many of the thematic characteristics that Zapata Olivella's works would share over the decades: concern for the downtrodden, a sense of history from the viewpoint of the dispossessed, and issues of racial and cultural identity.

Zapata Olivella worked on *Tierra mojada* while traveling from Colombia up through Central America to Mexico and then to the United States. His adventures throughout the Americas are delightfully retold in a series of travel narratives. Most noteworthy is *He visto la noche: Las raíces de la furia negra* (1949, I Have Seen the Night: The Roots of Black Fury), in which the impressionable young man seeks out his African American brothers in the United States in the aftermath of the Harlem Riots of 1943. It was at this time that Zapata Olivella developed a friendship with Langston Hughes that would last until Hughes's death in 1967.

Clearly, Olivella's experiences in the United States helped shape a black world-view that grew sharper with each decade. While several of his later works militantly pursue the theme of blackness, three works in particular stand out: the novel *Chambacú: Corral de negros* (1963; translated as Chambacú: Black Slum, 1989); the short story "Un extraño bajo mi piel" (1967, A Stranger Under My Skin); and the critically acclaimed *Changó, el gran putas*.

Chambacú: Corral de negros, awarded the prestigious Cuban Casa de las Américas literary prize in 1963, highlights the mistreatment of Afro-Colombians in the coastal city of Cartagena, Colombia. Set against the backdrop of the Korean War (1950–1953), a war many felt Colombians fought because of U.S. pressure, the action of the novel charts out the path of a black community in the small black town of Chambacú. As the war breaks out, the town is surrounded and occupied by the local military forces who try forcefully to recruit soldiers to man the battle lines. The move is resisted by the population, led by Máximo, a local political activist who is captured and tortured by the army. Translated by Jonathan Tittler in 1989, *Chambacú* has been cited as exemplary of Zapata Olivella's aesthetic of protest against the degradation and oppression of Afro-Colombians.

The story "A Stranger Under My Skin," published in the collection of short stories *¿Quién dió el fusil a Oswaldo?* (1967, Who Passed the Gun to Oswald?), is a humorous probe of one black man's self-loathing. A half-black, half-white mulatto, Leroy Elder, the main character in the story, regrets his black side so much that his life is forever altered. Translated by Brenda Frazier and published in the *Afro-Hispanic Review* in 1983, the story takes its cue from the Martinican political philosopher and revolutionary Frantz Fanon's *White Mask, Black Skin* (1952), and is one of the most powerful psychological explorations of pain and suffering available in fiction.

When *Changó, el gran putas* was first published in 1983, it constituted a significant breakthrough in Spanish American literature. For the first time the African cultural component was successfully integrated on its own terms as Spanish American and black history in the Americas was told by black narrators and viewed from an Afrocentric perspective. Further, *Changó, el gran putas* manages to accomplish what no other fictive work has: it provides a sense of the whole of the African diaspora in the Americas. The novel opens with an epic poem that recounts the fall from grace and exile of the orisha Changó, a deity in the Yoruba religion of Nigeria and in Yoruba-derived religious traditions in the African diaspora. As a consequence of his own exile, Changó expels the human race from Africa and condemns them to the Middle Passage and slavery. Similarly, the novel recounts the struggles for freedom during colonial times, the Haitian Revolution, the postcolonial fight for equality, and the civil rights struggles in the United States. Some of the best-known historical figures in black history appear as narrators or literary personae, among them Benkos Biohó, the sixteenth-century leader of a Colombian maroon community; Toussaint L'Ouverture, the Haitian Revolution's military leader; Aleijadinho, the eighteenth-century Brazilian sculptor; and the twentieth-century political thinker Malcolm X.

In addition to writing fiction, Zapata Olivella has been a leading interpreter of racial and cultural *mestizaje* (cultural mixing in Latin America). However, unlike the proponents of racial democracy (the belief that racial mixture dilutes social tension in Latin America), Zapata Olivella views *mestizaje* as the form that oppressed groups have used to resist assimilation and genocide. In his 1990 biography, *¡Levántate mulato!* (Rise Up, Mulatto!, originally in French in 1987), Zapata Olivella writes: "America was blackened by the importation of Africans, not because of their black skin, but because of their resistance, their struggles against slavery, their joining forces with native Americans to fight against the oppressors."

Zapata Olivella also coordinated—in conjunction with Abdias do Nascimento and other black Latin Americans—the first Congress of Black Culture of the Americas, which took place in 1977 in Cali, Colombia. His most recent published work, titled *La rebelión de los genes: El mestizaje americano en la sociedad futura* (1997, The Revolt of the Genes: Mestizaje in the Future of American Societies), is an extensive essay that presents a historical and political analysis of *mestizaje* and its consequences for an increasingly globalized world.

Select Bibliography

ABAJIAN, JAMES DE T. *Blacks and their Contributions to the American West* (1974).

ABBOTT, D. "Revolution by Other Means," interview with Angela Davis, *New Statesman* 114 (14 August 1987): 16–17.

ABBOTT, ELIZABETH. *Haiti: The Duvaliers and their Legacy* (1988).

ABDUL-JABBAR, KAREEM, WITH MIGNON MCCARTHY. *Kareem* (1990).

ABENON, LUCIEN. *Petite histoire de la Guadeloupe* (1992).

ABERNATHY, RALPH DAVID. *And the Walls Came Tumbling Down: An Autobiography* (1989).

ABRAHAMS, R. G. *The Nyamwezi Today: A Tanzanian People in the 1970s* (1981).

ABRAHAMS, ROGER D. *Deep Down in the Jungle: Negro Narrative Folklore from the Streets of Philadelphia* (1964).

——. *Singing the Master: The Emergence of African American Culture in the Plantation South* (1992).

——. *Talking Black* (1976).

ABRAHAMS, ROGER, AND JOHN SZWED. *After Africa: Extracts from British Travel Accounts and Journals of the Seventeenth, Eighteenth and Nineteenth Centuries Concerning the Slaves, their Manners, and Customs in the British West Indies* (1983).

ABREU, MAURICIO DE. *Evolução urbana do Rio de Janeiro* (1987).*****

ABU-LUGHOD, JANET L. *Rabat: Urban Apartheid in Morocco* (1980).

ABU-JAMAL, MUMIA. *Live from Death Row* (1996).

ACHEBE, CHINUA. *Hopes and Impediments: Selected Essays* (1988).

ADAIR, GENE. *George Washington Carver* (1989).

ADAMS, BARBARA ELEANOR. *John Henrik Clarke: The Early Years* (1992).

ADAMS, W. M., A. S. GOUDIE, AND A. R. ORME. *The Physical Geography of Africa* (1996).

ADÉLAÏDE-MERLANDE, JACQUES. *Delgrés, ou, la Guadeloupe en 1802* (1986).

ADENAIKE, CAROLYN KEYES, AND JAN VANSINA, EDS. *In Pursuit of History: Fieldwork in Africa* (1996).

ADJAYE, JOSEPH K., AND ADRIANNE R. ANDREWS, EDS. *Language, Rhythm, and Sound: Black Popular Cultures into the Twenty-First Century* (1997).

"African-American Quilts: Tracing the Aesthetic Principles." *Clarion* 14, no. 2 (Spring 1989): 44–54.

"African Symbolism in Afro-American Quilts." *African Arts* 20, no 1 (1986).

"Afro-Brazilian Religion." Special issue of *Callaloo* 18, no. 4 (1995).

AGRONSKY, JONATHAN. *Marion Barry: The Politics of Race* (1991).

AGORSAH, E. KOFI, ED. *Maroon Heritage: Archaeological, Ethnographic, and Historical Perspectives* (1994).

AGUIRRE BELTRÁN, GONZALO. *El negro esclavo en Nuevo España: La formación colonial, la medicina popular y otros ensayos* (1994).

ALAGOA, E. J., F. N. ANOZIE, AND NWANNA NZEWUNWA, EDS. *The Early History of the Niger Delta* (1988).

ALBERTSON, CHRIS. *Bessie* (1972).

ALGOO-BAKSH, STELLA. *Austin C. Clarke: A Biography* (1994).

ALIE, JOE A. D. *A New History of Sierra Leone* (1990).

ALLAN D. AUSTIN, ED. *African Muslims in Antebellum America: A Source Book* (1984).

ALLEN, PHILIP M. *Madagascar: Conflicts of Authority in the Great Island* (1995).

ALPERT, HOLLIS. *The Life and Times of Porgy and Bess* (1990).

ALVAREZ NAZARIO, MANUEL. *El elemento afronegroide en el español de Puerto Rico: Contribución al estudio del negro en América* (1974).

AL-AMIN, JAMIL. *See* Brown, H. Rap.

The Amistad Case: The Most Celebrated Slave Mutiny of the Nineteenth Century, 2 vols. (1968).

AMMONS, KEVIN. *Good Girl, Bad Girl: An Insider's Biography of Whitney Houston* (1996).

ANDERSON, JEAN BRADLEY. *Durham County: A History of Durham County, North Carolina* (1990).

ANDERSON, JERVIS. *A. Philip Randolph: A Biographical Portrait* (1973).

——. *Bayard Rustin: Troubles I've Seen: A Biography* (1997).

ANDERSON, MARIAN. *My Lord, What a Morning: An Autobiography* (1956).

ANDREWS, BENNY. *Between the Lines: 70 Drawings and 7 Essays* (1978).

ANDREWS, GEORGE REID. *Blacks and Whites in São Paulo, Brazil, 1888–1988* (1991). ****

ANDREWS, WILLIAM L. *The Literary Career of Charles W. Chesnutt* (1980).

——. *Sisters of the Spirit: Three Black Women's Autobiographies of the Nineteenth Century* (1986).

——. *To Tell a Free Story: The First Century of Afro-American Autobiography, 1760–1865* (1986).

ANDREWS, WILLIAM L., AND HENRY LOUIS GATES, JR., EDS. *The Civitas Anthology of African American Slave Narratives* (1999).

ANGELL, ROGER. *The Summer Game* (1972).

ANJOS, JOANA DOS. *Ouvindo historias na senzala* (1987).

ANTOINE, JACQUES CARMELEAU. *Jean Price-Mars and Haiti* (1981).

ANTOINE, RÉGIS. *La littérature franco-antillaise* (1992).

APARICIO, RAÚL. *Sondeos* (1983).

APPIAH, KWAME ANTHONY. *In My Father's House: Africa in the Philosophy of Culture* (1992).

APTHEKER, HERBERT. *American Negro Slave Revolts.* 6th ed. (1993).

——. *Nat Turner's Slave Rebellion* (1966).

——. *"One Continual Cry": David Walker's Appeal to the Colored Citizens of the World 1829–30: Its Setting and its Meaning, Together with the Full Text of the Third, and Last, Edition of the Appeal* (1965).

ARAUJO, EMANOEL, ED. *The Afro-Brazilian Touch: The Meaning of its Artistic and Historic Contribution.* Translated by Eric Drysdale (1988).

ARMAS, JOSÉ R. DE, AND CHARLES W. STEELE. *Cuban Consciousness in Literature: 1923–1974* (1978).

ARNOLD, A. JAMES. *Modernism and Negritude: The Poetry and Poetics of Aimé Césaire* (1981).

ASANTE, MOLEFI KETE. *The Afrocentric Idea* (1987).

——. *Afrocentricity* (1988).

——. *Kemet, Afrocentricity, and Knowledge* (1990).

ASCHENBRENNER, JOYCE. *Katherine Dunham: Reflections on the Social and Political Aspects of Afro-American Dance* (1981).

ASCHERSON, NEAL. *The King Incorporated: Leopold II in the Age of Trusts* (1963).

ASHBAUGH, CAROLYN. *Lucy Parsons: American Revolutionary* (1976).

ASHE, ARTHUR. *Days of Grace: A Memoir* (1993).

——. *A Hard Road to Glory: A History of the African-American Athlete* (1988).

AUSTERLITZ, PAUL. *Merengue: Dominican Music and Dominican Identity* (1997).

AUSTIN-BROOS, DIANE. *Jamaica Genesis: Religion and the Politics of Moral Orders* (1997).

AVERILL, GAGE. *A Day for the Hunter, A Day for the Prey* (1997).

AXELSON, ERIC. *Portuguese in South-East Africa, 1488–1600* (1973).

AYISI, RUTH A. "The Urban Influx." *Africa Report* (November-December 1989).

AYOT, H. OKELLO. *Historical Texts of the Lake Region of East Africa* (1977).

AZEVEDO, CELIA MARIA MARINHO DE. *Onda negra, medo branco: O negro no imaginario das elites, seculo XIX* (1987).

AZEVEDO, MARIO. *Historical Dictionary of Mozambique* (1991).

AZEVEDO, THALES. *Les élites de couleur dans une ville brésilienne* (1953).

BABB, VALERIE MELISSA. *Ernest Gaines* (1991).

BACELAR, JEFERSON AFONSO. *Etnicidade: Ser negro em Salvador* (1989).

BAER, HANS A., AND MERRIL SINGER. *African-American Religion in the Twentieth Century: Varieties of Protest and Accommodation* (1992).

BAILEY, PEARL. *Between You and Me: A Heartfelt Memoir of Learning, Loving, and Living* (1989).

——. *The Raw Pearl* (1968).

BAKER, DAVID. *The Jazz Style of Cannonball Adderley* (1980).

BAKER, HOUSTON A., JR. BLUES, *Ideology, and Afro-American Literature: A Vernacular Theory* (1980).

BALANDIER, GEORGES. *Daily Life in the Kingdom of the Kongo: From the Sixteenth to the Eighteenth Century* (1968).

BALL, WENDY, AND TONY MARTIN. *Rare Afro-Americana: A Reconstruction of the Adger Library* (1981).

BALUTANSKY, KATHLEEN M., AND MARIE-AGNÈS SOURIEAU, EDS. *Caribbean Creolization: Reflections on the Cultural Dynamics of Language, Literature, and Identity* (1998).

BANDEIRA, MARIA DE LOURDES. *Territorio negro em espaço branco: Estudo antropologico de Vila Bela* (1988).

BAQUERO, GASTON. *Indios, blancos y negros en el caldero de America* (1991).

BARAKA, AMIRI. *The Autobiography of LeRoi Jones* (1984).

BARBOSA DEL ROSARIO, PILAR. *La obra de José Celso Barbosa.* 4 vols. (1937).

BARBOUR, DOUGLAS. *Worlds Out of Words: The SF Novels of Samuel R. Delaney* (1979).

BARFIELD, THOMAS J. *The Nomadic Alternative* (1993).

BARKER, DANNY. *A Life in Jazz* (1986).

BARNES, STEVE. "The Crusade of Dr. Elders." *New York Times Magazine* (October 15, 1989): 38–41.

BARNETT, ALAN W. *Community Murals: The People's Art* (1984).

BARNWELL, P. J., AND AUGUSTE TOUSSAINT. *A Short History of Mauritius* (1949).

BARRADAS, EFRAÍN. PARA LEER EN PUERTORRIQUENO: *Acercamiento a la obra de Luis Rafael S·nchez* (1981).

BARREDA-TOM·S, PEDRO M. *The Black Protagonist in the Cuban Novel* (1979).

BARROW, STEVE, AND PETER DALTON. *Reggae: The Rough Guide* (1997).

BASH, BARBARA. *Tree of Life: The World of the African Baobab* (1994).

BASIE, WILLIAM JAMES ("COUNT"), AS TOLD TO ALBERT MURRAY. *Good Morning Blues: The Autobiography of Count Basie* (1985).

"A Basis for Interracial Cooperation and Development in the South: A Statement by Southern Negroes." *In Southern Conference on Race Relations* (1942).

BASS, CHARLOTTA SPEARS. Forty Years: Memoirs from the Pages of a Newspaper (1960).

BASTIDE, ROGER, AND FLORESTAN FERNANDES. *Relacoes raciais entre negros e brancos em Sao Paulo (1955).*

BAUM, ROBERT M. *Shrines of the Slave Trade: Diola Religion and Society in Precolonial Senegambia* (1999).

BEACH, DAVID. *The Shona and their Neighbours* (1994).

BEARDEN, JIM, AND LINDA BUTLER. *Shadd: The Life and Times of Mary Shadd Cary* (1977).

BEARDEN, ROMARE, AND HARRY HENDERSON. *A History of African-American Artists from 1792 to the Present* (1993).

BEAUFORD DELANEY: *A Retrospective* (1978).

BECHKEY, ALLEN. *Adventuring in East Africa* (1990).

BECKFORD, RUTH. *Katherine Dunham: A Biography* (1979).

BECKLES, HILARY. *Afro-Caribbean Women and Resistance to Slavery in Barbados* (1988).

——. *Black Masculinity in Caribbean Slavery* (1996).

——. *Black Rebellion in Barbados: The Struggle against Slavery, 1627–1838* (1984).

——. *A History of Barbados: Amerindian Settlement to Nation-State* (1990).

——. *Natural Rebels: A Social History of Enslaved Black Women in Barbados* (1989).

——. *White Servitude and Black Slavery in Barbados, 1627–1715* (1989).

——, ED. *Inside Slavery: Process and Legacy in the Caribbean Experience* (1996).

BECKWOURTH, JAMES P. *The Life and Adventures of James P. Beckwourth, Mountaineer, Scout and Pioneer and Chief of the Crow Nation of Indians.* Edited by T. D. Bonner (1965).

BEDINI, SILVIO. *The Life of Benjamin Banneker* (1971–1972).

BEETH, HOWARD, AND CARY WINTZ. *Black Dixie: Afro-Texan History and Culture in Houston* (1992).

BEGO, MARK. *Aretha Franklin* (1989).

BEHAGUE, GERARD H., ED. *Music and Black Ethnicity: The Caribbean and South America* (1994).

BELL, BERNARD. *The Afro-American Novel and its Tradition* (1987).

BELLEGARDE-SMITH, PATRICK. *In the Shadow of Powers: Dantès Bellegarde in Haitian Social Thought* (1985).

——. Race, Class and Ideology: Haitian Ideologies for Underdevelopment 1806–1934 (1985).

BELL, HOWARD H. *Search for a Place: Black Separatism and Africa, 1860* (1969).

BELL, MALCOM. *The Turkey Shoot: Tracking the Attica Cover-Up* (1985).

BENBERRY, CUESTA. *Always There: The African-American Presence in American Quilts* (1992).

BENNETT, LERONE, JR. *Before the Mayflower* (1962; revised ed., 1987).

BENNETT, NORMAN. *Arab versus European: Diplomacy and War in Nineteenth-Century East Central Africa* (1986).

BENNETT, ROBERT. "Black Episcopalians: A History from the Colonial Period to the Present." *Historical Magazine of the Protestant Episcopal Church 43*, no. 3 (September 1974): 231–45.

BENOIT, EDOUARD. "Biguine: Popular Music of Guadeloupe, 1940–1960." In *Zouk: World Music in the West Indies*, ed. Jocelyne Guilbault (1993).

BENSTON, KIMBERLY, ED. *Speaking for You: The Vision of Ralph Ellison* (1995).

BENTLY, GEORGE R. *A History of the Freedmen's Bureau* (1955).

BERENDT, JOACHIM. *The Jazz Book: From Rag-time to Fusion and Beyond.* 6th ed. (1992).

BERGER, PHIL. *Blood Season: Tyson and the World of Boxing* (1989).

BERLIN, IRA. *Slaves without Masters: The Free Negro in the Antebellum South* (1974).

BERNABÈ, JEAN, PATRICK CHAMOISEAU, AND RAPHAÎL CONFIANT. *Eloge de la creolite / In Praise of Creoleness.* Translated by M. B. Taleb-Khyar (1993).

BERND, ZILA. *Introducao a literatura negra* (1988).

BERNSEN, CHARLES. "The Fords of Memphis: A Family Saga." *Memphis Commercial Appeal* (July 1–4, 1990).

BERNSTEIN, IVER. *The New York City Draft Riots: Their Significance for American Society and Politics in the Age of the Civil War* (1990).

BERROU, RAPHAEL. *Histoire de la littérature haïtienne illustrée par les textes.* 3 vols. (1975–1977).

BERRY, CHUCK. *Chuck Berry: The Autobiography* (1987).

BERRY, JAMES. *Chain of Days* (1985).

BERRY, JASON. *Amazing Grace: With Charles Evers in Mississippi* (1973).

BERTLEY, LEO W. *Canada and its People of African Descent* (1977).

BEYAN, AMOS J. *The American Colonization Society and the Creation of the Liberian State: A Historical Perspective, 1822–1900* (1991).

BIANCO, DAVID. *Heat Wave: The Motown Fact Book* (1988).

BIBB, HENRY WALTON. *Narrative of the Life and Adventures of Henry Bibb, an American Slave* (1849).

BICKERTON, DEREK. "The Language Bioprogram Hypothesis." *Behavioral and Brain Sciences* 7 (1984): 173–221.

BIEBUYCK, DANIEL P., SUSAN KELLIHER, AND LINDA MCRAE. *African Ethnonyms: Index to Art-Producing Peoples of Africa* (1996).

BIRMINGHAM, DAVID, AND RICHARD GRAY. *Pre-Colonial African trade: Essays on Trade in Central and Eastern Africa before 1900* (1966).

BISHOP, JACK. *Ralph Ellison* (1988).

"Black Clout in Clinton Administration." *Ebony* 48, no. 7 (May 1993): 60.

BLACK, PATTI CARR, ED. *Something to Keep You Warm* (1981).

"Blacks in U.S. Foreign Policy: A Retrospective." *TransAfrica Forum* (1987).

"Black Women: Sisters Without Leaders." *Economist* (November 1, 1997): 31.

BLAKELY, ALLISON. *Blacks in the Dutch World: The Evolution of Racial Imagery in a Modern Society* (1993).

——. *Russia and the Negro: Blacks in Russian History and Thought* (1986).

BLANCHARD, PETER. *Slavery and Abolition in Early Republican Peru* (1992).

BLAND, RANDALL W. *Private Pressure on Public Law: The Legal Career of Justice Thurgood Marshall* (1973).

BLANCQ, C. C. *Sonny Rollins: The Journey of a Jazzman* (1983).

BLASSINGAME, JOHN W., ED. *The Frederick Douglass Papers.* 4 vols. (1979–1991).

——. *The Slave Community: Plantation Life in the Antebellum South.* Rev. ed. (1979).

BLASSINGAME, JOHN W., AND MAE G. HENDERSON, EDS. *Antislavery Newspapers and Periodicals.* 5 vols. (1980).

BLESH, RUDI, AND HARRIET JANIS. *They All Played Ragtime.* 4th ed. (1971).

BLIER, SUZANNE PRESTON. *African Vodun: Art, Psychology, and Power* (1995).

———. *The Royal Arts of Africa: The Majesty of Form* (1998).

BLIGHT, DAVID W. FREDERICK DOUGLASS' *Civil War: Keeping Faith in Jubilee* (1989).

BLOCH, HERMAN D. *The Circle of Discrimination: An Economic and Social Study of the Black Man in New York* (1969).

BLOCH, M. *Placing the Dead: Tombs, Ancestral Villages, and Kinship Organization in Madagascar* (1971).

BLY, NELLIE. *Oprah! Up Close and Down Home* (1993).

BOFF, C., AND L. BOFF. *Introducing Liberation Theology* (1987).

BOGGS, VICTOR. *Salsiology: Afro-Cuban Music and the Evolution of Salsa in New York City* (1992).

BOGLE, DONALD. *Blacks in American Films and Television: An Illustrated Encyclopedia* (1988).

———. *Dorothy Dandridge: A Biography* (1997).

———. *Toms, Coons, Mulattoes, Mammies, and Bucks : An Interpretive History of Blacks in American Films*. 3d ed. (1994).

BOLCOM, WILLIAM, AND ROBERT KIMBALL. *Reminiscing with Sissle and Blake* (1973).

BOLLAND, O. NIGEL. *A History of Belize: Nation in the Making* (1997).

BOLOUVI, LEBENE PHILIPPE. *Nouveau dictionnaire étymologique afro-brésilien: Afro-brasilérismes d'origine Ewe-Fon et Yoruba* (1994).

BONGIE, CHRIS. "The (Un)Exploded Volcano: Creolization and Intertextuality in the Novels of Daniel Maximin." *Callaloo* 17, no. 2 (Summer 1994): 627–42.

BONILLA, ADRIAN. "Conversación con Adalberto Ortiz." *Cultura: Revista del Banco Central del Ecuador* 6, no. 16 (1983): 189–96.

BOODOO, KEN I., ED. *Eric Williams: The Man and the Leader* (1986).

BOONE, GRAEME M., AND JAMES CLYDE SELLMAN, "The Jook Joint: An Historical Note." Liner essay to *Quincy Jones, Q's Jook Joint* (1995).

BORDERS, WILLIAM H. *Seven Minutes at the Mike in the Deep South* (1943).

BOSKIN, JOSEPH. *Sambo: The Rise and Demise of an American Jester* (1986).

BOURDILLON, M. F. C. *The Shona Peoples: An Ethnography of the Contemporary Shona, with Special Reference to their Religion* (1987).

BOURNE, M. "Bob, Baroque, the Blues: Modern Jazz Quartet." *Down Beat* 59, no.1 (January 1992): 24.

BOVILL, E. W. *The Niger Explored* (1968).

BOWMAN, J. WILSON. *America's Black Colleges: The Comprehensive Guide to Historically and Predominantly Black 4-Year Colleges and Universities* (1992).

BOWMAN, LARRY W. *Mauritius: Democracy and Development in the Indian Ocean* (1991).

BOWSER, FREDERICK P. *The African Slave in Colonial Peru 1524–1650* (1974).

BOXER, C.R. *The Dutch in Brazil, 1624–1654* (1957).

———. *The Portuguese Seaborne Empire, 1415–1825* (1969).

BOYER, JAY. *Ishmael Reed* (1993).

BOYKIN, KEITH. *One More River to Cross: Black & Gay in America* (1996).

BOZONGWANA, WALLACE. *Ndebele Religion and Customs* (1983).

BRACEY, JOHN H., JR., ET AL, EDS. *Black Nationalism in America* (1970).

BRAGG, GEORGE FREEMAN. *The History of the Afro-American Group of the Episcopal Church* (1968).

——. *The Story of the First Blacks: Absalom Jones* (1929).

BRANCH, TAYLOR. *Parting the Waters: America in the King Years: 1954–63* (1988).

BRANDSTRÖM, PER. "Who is Sukuma and Who is a Nyamwezi?: Ethnic Identity in West-Central Tanzania." In *Working Papers in African Studies* no. 27 (1986).

BRAND-WILLIAMS, ORALANDAR. "Million Woman March: Black Women Vow to 'Act on Power,'" *Detroit News* (October 26, 1997).

BRATHWAITE, EDWARD KAMAU. *Roots* (1993).

BRAUSCH, GEORGES. *Belgian Administration in the Congo* (1961).

BRIGHAM, DAVID R. "Bridging Identities (The Works of Dox Thrash, Afro-American Artist)." *Smithsonian Studies in American Art* (Spring 1990).

BRISBANE, ROBERT. *Black Activism: Racial Revolution in the U.S., 1954–70* (1974).

BRISTOW, PEGGY, ET AL. *We're Rooted Here and They Can't Pull Us Up: Essays in African Canadian Women's History* (1994)

BRITT, STAN. *Dexter Gordon: A Musical Biography* (1989).

BRODE, DOUGLAS. *Denzel Washington: His Films and Career* (1996).

BRODERICK, FRANCIS L., AUGUST MEIER, AND ELLIOTT M. RUDWICK. *Black Protest Thought in the Twentieth Century*. 2d ed. (1971).

BROOKSHAW, DAVID. *Race and Color in Brazilian Literature* (1986).

BROUGHTON, SIMON, MARK ELLINGHAM, DAVID MUDDYMAN, AND RICHARD TRILLO. *World Music: The Rough Guide* (1994).

BROUSSARD, ALBERT S. *Black San Francisco: The Struggle for Racial Equality in the West, 1900–1954* (1993).

BROWN, A. THEODORE, AND LYLE W. DORSETT. *K.C.: A History of Kansas City, Missouri* (1978).

BROWN, CLAUDE. *Manchild in the Promised Land* (1965).

BROWN, DIANA DEGROAT. *Umbanda: Religion and Politics in Urban Brazil* (1994).

BROWN, GEOFF, AND CHRIS CHARLESWORTH. *A Complete Guide to the Music of Prince* (1995).

BROWN-GUILLORY, ELIZABETH. "Alice Childress: A Pioneering Spirit," *Sage: A Scholarly Journal on Black Women* (Spring 1987): 104–9.

BROWN, HENRY. *Narrative of Henry Box Brown Who Escaped from Slavery Enclosed in a Box Three Feet Long and Two Wide, with Remarks upon the Remedy for Slavery* (1849).

BROWN, H. RAP. *Die, Nigger, Die!* (1969).

BROWNING, BARBARA. *Samba: Resistance in Motion* (1995).

BROWN, MERVYN. *A History of Madagascar* (1995).

——. Madagascar Rediscovered: A History from Early Times to Independence (1978).

BROWN, RUTH, WITH ANDREW YULE. *Miss Rhythm: The Autobiography of Ruth Brown, Rhythm & Blues Legend* (1996).

BROWN, SCOTT E. *James P. Johnson: A Case of Mistaken Identity* (1986).

BROWN, STERLING A. "A Century of Negro Portraiture in American Literature." In *Black Insights: Significant Literature by Black Americans-1760 to the Present*, ed. Nick Aaron Ford (1971): 66–78.

BROWN, TONY. *Black Lies, White Lies: The Truth According to Tony Brown* (1995).

BRUCE, DICKSON D., JR. *Black American Writing from the Nadir: The Evolution of a Literary Tradition, 1877–1915* (1989).

BRUNDAGE, W. FITZHUGH, ED. *Under Sentence of Death: Lynching in the South* (1997).

BRYAN, T. J. "The Published Poems of Helene Johnson," *Langston Hughes Review* 6 (Fall 1987): 11–21.

BRYANT-JACKSON, PAUL, AND LOIS MORE OVERBECK, EDS. *Intersecting Boundaries: The Theater of Adrienne Kennedy* (1992).

BUCKLER, HELEN. *Daniel Hale Williams: Negro Surgeon* (1968)

BUCKLEY, GAIL LUMET. *The Hornes: An American Family* (1986).

BUENO, EVA PAULINO. *Resisting Boundaries: The Subject of Naturalism in Brazil* (1995).

BUGNER, LADISLAS, ED. *The Image of the Black in Western Art* (1976–).

BUHLE, PAUL. *C. L. R. James: The Artist as Revolutionary* (1988).

BULHAN, HUSSEIN ABDILAHI. *Frantz Fanon and the Psychology of Oppression* (1985).

BULLOCK, PENELOPE L. *The Afro-American Periodical Press, 1838–1909* (1981).

BUNI, ANDREW. *The Negro in Virginia Politics, 1902–1965* (1967).

BUNWAREE, SHEILA S. *Mauritian Education in a Global Economy* (1994).

BURCKHARDT, TITUS. *Fez, City of Islam* (1992).

BURDICK, JOHN. *Blessed Anastacia: Women, Race and Popular Christianity in Brazil* (1998).

——. "The Spirit of Rebel and Docile Slaves: The Black Verson of Brazilian Umbanda." *Journal of Latin American Love* 18 (1992): 163–87.

BURNS, KHEPHRA. "A Love Supreme: Ruby Dee & Ossie Davis." *Essence* (December 1994).

BUSBY, MARK. *Ralph Ellison* (1991).

BUSH, MARTIN. *The Photographs of Gordon Parks* (1983).

BUSTIN, EDOUARD. *Lunda under Belgian Rule: The Politics of Ethnicity* (1975).

BUTLER, ADDIE LOUISE JOYNER. *The Distinctive Black College: Talladega, Tuskegee and Morehouse* (1977).

CAAMAÑO DE FERNÀNDEZ, VICENTA. *El negro en la poesïa dominicana* (1989).

CABRERA GOMEZ, JORGE. *El Baobab* (1996).

CABRERA, LYDIA. *Anaforuana: Ritual y simbolos de la iniciacion en la sociedad secreta* (1975).

——. Anago: *Vocabulario lucumi (el yoruba que se habla in Cuba)* (1957).

——. *Los animales en el folklore y la magia de Cuba* (1988).

——. *Cuentos negros de Cuba* (1972).

——. *Francisco y Francisca: Chascarrillos de negros viejos* (1976).

——. *La lengua sagrada de los nanigos* (1988).

——. *El monte, Igbo, Finda, Ewe orisha, vitti nfinda: (Notas sobre las religiones, la magia, las supersticiones y el folklore de los negros criollos y del pueblo de Cuba)* (1968).

——. *La Regla Kimbisa del Santo Cristo del Buen Viaje* (1977).

——. *Reglas de Congo: Palo Monte Mayombe* (1979).

——. *La sociedad secreta Abakua, narrada por viejos adeptos* (1959).

——. *Yemaya y Ochun* (1974).

CAGIN, SETH, AND PHILIP DRAY. *We Are Not Afraid: The Story of Goodman, Schwerner, and Chaney and the Civil Rights Campaign for Mississippi* (1988).

CALCAGNO, FRANCISCO. *Poetas de color* (1878).

CALLAGHAN, BARRY, ED. *The Austin Clarke Reader* (1996).

CALVO OSPINA, HERNANDO. *Salsa! Havana Heat, Bronx Beat.* (1992).

CAMARGO, OSWALDO. *A raz„o da chama: Antologia de poetas negros brasileiros* (1986).

CAMINHA, ADOLFO. *The Black Man and the Cabin Boy.* Translated by E. Lacey (1982).

CAMPBELL, ELAINE, AND PIERRETTE FRICKEY, EDS. *The Whistling Bird: Women Writers of the Caribbean* (1998).

CAMPBELL, JAMES T. *Songs of Zion: The African Methodist Episcopal Church in the United States and South Africa* (1995).

CAMPBELL, STANLEY W. *The Slave Catchers: Enforcement of the Fugitive Slave Law, 1850–1860* (1968).

CANNON, STEVE, TOM FINKELPEARL, AND KELLIE JONES. *David Hammons: Rousing the Rubble* (1991).

CANTAROW, ELLEN, AND SUSAN GUSHEE O'MALLEY. "Ella Baker: Organizing for Civil Rights." In *Moving the Mountain: Women Working for Social Change* (1980).

CAPECI, DOMINIC J., JR. *The Harlem Riot of 1943* (1977).

CARBY, HAZEL V. *Reconstructing Womanhood: The Emergence of the Afro-American Woman Novelist* (1987).

CAREW, JAN. *Fulcrums of Change: Origins of Racism in the Americas* (1988).

CARMICHAEL, STOKELY, AND CHARLES V. HAMILTON. *Black Power: The Politics of Liberation in America* (1992).

CARMICHAEL, TREVOR, ED. BARBADOS: *30 Years of Independence* (1996).

CARNER, GARY, ED. *The Miles Davis Companion: Four Decades of Commentary* (1996).

CARO, TIMOTHY M. *Cheetahs of the Serengeti Plains: Group Living in an Asocial Species* (1994).

CARPENTER, BILL. "Big Mama Thornton: 200 Pounds of Bugaloo." *Living Bluesletter* no. 106 (November 1992).

CARPENTIER, ALEJO. *La m´sica en Cuba* (1946).

——. *Obras Completas* (1983–).

CARR, IAN. *Miles Davis: A Biography* (1982).

CARROLL, PATRICK JAMES. *Blacks in Colonial Veracruz: Race, Ethnicity, and Regional Development* (1991).

CARSON, CLAYBORNE. *In Struggle: SNCC and the Black Awakening of the 1960s* (1981).

CARVALHO, JOSÉ JORGE DE, AND RITA LAURA SEGATO. *Shango Cult in Recife, Brazil* (1992).

CASH, EARL A. *John A. Williams: The Evolution of a Black Writer* (1975).

CASSIDY, FREDERIC G. *Jamaica Talk: Three Hundred Years of the English Language in Jamaica* (1961).

CASTELLANOS, JORGE, AND ISABEL CASTELLANOS. *Cultura afrocubana: Las religiones y las lenguas. 3 vols.* (1992).

CASTLEMAN, CRAIG. *Getting Up: Subway Graffiti in New York* (1984).

CASTOR, ELIE, AND RAYMOND TARCY. *Fèlix Ebouè: Gouverneur et philosophe* (1984).

CASTRO, RUY. *Chega de saudade : A história e as histórias da bossa nova* (1990).

CAYETANO, SEBASTIAN. *Garifuna History: Language and Culture of Belize, Central America and the Caribbean.* Rev. ed. (1997).

CENTRO DE ARTICULÇÁO DE POPULAÇÕES MARGINALIZADAS. *The Killing of Children and Adolescents in Brazil.* Translated by Joscelyne Vera Mello (1991).

CHAFETS, ZE'EV. *Devil's Night and Other True Tales of Detroit* (1990).

CHALLENOR, HERCHELLE SULLIVAN. "The Influence of Black Americans on U.S. Foreign Policy Toward Africa." *Ethnicity and U. S. Foreign Policy* (1981).

CHAMBERLAIN, HOPE. "Against the System: Shirley Chisholm." *In A Minority of Mem-bers: Women in the U. S. Congress* (1973).

CHAMBERLAIN, WILT. *The View From Above* (1991).

CHAMBERS, JACK. *Milestones.* 2 vols. (1983–1985).

CHAMBERS, VERONICA. "The Essence of Essence." *New York Times Magazine* (June 18, 1995).

CHANAN, MICHAEL. *The Cuban Image: Cinema and the Cultural Politics in Cuba* (1985).

CHANOCK, MARTIN. *Law, Custom and Social Order: The Colonial Experience in Malawi and Zambia* (1985).

CHAPELLE, TONY. "Vanessa's Comeback." *The Black Collegian* (February 1995).

CHAPPELL, KEVIN. "The 3 Mayors Who Made it Happen." *Ebony* (July 1996): 66.

Charte de la révolution socialiste Malagasy Tous Azimuts (1975).

CHARTERS, SAMUEL B. *The Bluesmen.* 2 vols. (1967–1977).

CHENEY, ANNE. *Lorraine Hansberry* (1984).

CHIGWEDERE, AENEAS S. *Birth of Bantu Africa* (1982).

CHILTON, JOHN. *The Song of the Hawk: The Life and Recordings of Coleman Hawkins* (1990).

CHISHOLM, SHIRLEY. *Unbought and Unbossed* (1970).

CHRISMAN, ROBERT, AND ROBERT L. ALLEN, EDS. *Court of Appeal: The Black Community Speaks Out on the Racial and Sexual Politics of Clarence Thomas vs. Anita Hill* (1992).

CHRISTIAN, BARBARA. *Black Feminist Criticism: Perspectives on Black Women Writers* (1985).

——. *Black Women Novelists: The Devel-opment of a Tradition, 1892–1976* (1980).

CHRISTIE, IAIN. *Samora Machel: A Biography* (1989).

CHRISTOPHER, A. J. *The Atlas of Apartheid* (1994).

CHUCHO GARCIA, JESUS. *La diaspora de los Kongos en las Americas y los Caribes* (1995).

CHURCH, ANNETTE, AND ROBERTA CHURCH. *The Robert Churches of Memphis* (1975).

CLANCY-SMITH, JULIA A. *Rebel and Saint: Muslim Notables, Populist Protest, Colonial Encounters: Algeria and Tunisia, 1800–1904* (1994).

CLAIRMONT, DONALD, AND DENNIS MAGILL. *Africville: The Life and Death of a Canadian Black Community. Rev. ed.* (1987).

CLARKE, A.M. *Sir Constantine and Sir Hugh Wooding* (1982).

CLARKE, DUNCAN. *The Art of African Textiles* (1997).

CLARKE, GEORGE ELLIOTT, ED. *Fire on the Water: An Anthology of Black Nova Scotian Writing.* 2 vols. (1991–1992).

CLARK, SEBASTIAN. *Jah Music* (1980).

CLARK, SEPTIMA. *Echo in My Soul* (1962).

CLARK, SEPTIMA, WITH CYNTHIA STOKES BROWN. *Ready from Within: Septima Clark and the Civil Rights Movement* (1986).

CLASH, M.G. *Benjamin Banneker, Astronomer and Scientist* (1971).

"Claude Albert Barnett." *New York Times* (August 3, 1967).

CLAYTON, ANTHONY. *The Zanzibar Revolution and its Aftermath* (1981).

CLAY, WILLIAM L. *Just Permanent Interests: Black Americans in Congress, 1870–1991* (1992).

COBB, W. MONTAGUE. *The First Negro Medical Society: A History of the Medico-Chirurgical Society of the District of Columbia* (1939).

COHEN, DAVID W., AND JACK P. GREENE. *Neither Slave nor Free: The Freedman of African Descent in the Slaves Societies of the New World Baltimore* (1972).

COHEN, RONALD, GORAN HYDEN, AND WINSTON P. NAGAN, EDS. *Human Rights and Governance in Africa* (1993).

COLE, HERBERT. *Christophe: King of Haiti* (1967).

COLEMAN, JAMES W. *Blackness and Modernism: The Literary Career of John Edgar Wideman* (1989).

COLEMAN, LUCRETIA NEWMAN. *Poor Ben: A Story of Real Life* (1890).

COLI, SUZANNE M. *George Washington Carver* (1990).

COLLIER, ALDORE. "Maxine Waters: Telling It Like It Is in L.A." *Ebony* (October 1992).

——. "Pointer Sisters Shed Old Look, Old Clothes to Reach New Heights." *Jet* (April 15, 1985): 58.

——. "Whatever Happened to the Nicholas Brothers?" *Ebony* (May 1985).

COLLIER, JAMES LINCOLN. *The Making of Jazz: A Comprehensive History* (1978).

COLLINS, L. M. *One Hundred Years of Fisk University Presidents* (1989).

COLLINS, R. *New Orleans Jazz: A Revised History: The Development of American Jazz from the Origin to the Big Bands* (1996).

COLLINS, ROBERT O. *The Waters of the Nile: Hydropolitics and the Jonglei Canal, 1900–1988* (1990).

CONDÉ, MARYSE, AND MADELAINE COTTENET-HAGE, EDS. *Penser la Créolité* (1995).

CONE, JAMES H. *Martin and Malcolm and America: A Dream or a Nightmare* (1991).

CONGRESS, RICK. *The Afro-Nicaraguans: The Revolution and Autonomy* (1987).

CONNIFF, MICHAEL L. *Black Labor on a White Canal: Panama 1904–1981* (1985).

CONNIFF, MICHAEL L., AND THOMAS J. DAVIS. *Africans in the Americas: The History of the Black Diaspora* (1994).

CONNOLLY, HAROLD X. *A Ghetto Grows in Brooklyn* (1977).

CONRAD, ROBERT EDGAR, ED. *Children of God's Fire: A Documentary of Black Slavery.* (1983).

——. *The Destruction of Brazilian Slavery, 1850–1888* (1993).

CONSENTINO, DONALD J., ED. *Sacred Arts of Haitian Vodou* (1995).

COOK, DAVID, AND MICHAEL Okenimpke. *Ngugi wa Thiong'o: An Exploration of His Writing*, 2d ed. (1997).

COOLIDGE, CHRISTOPHER R. "Reply: Tolerance of Racial, Ethnic Jokes." In *ADS-L Digest 22* (February 22, 1997).

COOPER, GARY. "Stage Coach Mary: Gun Toting Montanan Delivered U.S. Mail," as told to Marc Crawford in *Ebony* 14 (October 1959): 97–100.

COOPER, RALPH, WITH STEVE DOUGHERTY. *Amateur Night at the Apollo: Ralph Cooper Presents Five Decades of Great Entertainment* (1990).

COOPER, WAYNE F. *Claude McKay: A Rebel Sojourner in the Harlem Renaissance: A Biography* (1987).

COPPIN, FANNY JACKSON. *Reminiscences of School Life, and Hints on Teaching* (1913).

CORDOBA, AMIR SMITH, ED. *Vision sociocultural del negro en Colombia* (1986).

CORNELIUS, WAYNE A. "Spain: The Uneasy Transition from Labor Exporter to Labor Importer." In *Controlling Immigration: A Global Perspective*, ed. Wayne A. Cornelius, Philip L. Martin, and James F. Hollifield (1994).

CORNISH, DUDLEY T. *The Sable Arm: Negro Troops in the Union Army, 1861–1865* (1956).

CORTÉS LÓPEZ, JOSÉ LUIS. *La esclavitud negra en la España peninsular del siglo XVI* (1989).

Cortner, Richard C. *A Mob Intent on Death: The NAACP and the Arkansas Riot Cases* (1988).

CORY, HANS H. *Sukuma Law and Custom* (1953).

COUFFON, CLAUDE. *René Depestre* (1986).

COUNTER, S. ALLEN. *North Pole Legacy: Black, White and Eskimo* (1991).

COURTNEY-CLARKE, MARGARET. *Ndebele: The Art of an African Tribe* (1986).

COVELL, MAUREEN. *Historical Dictionary of Madagascar* (1995).

———. *Madagascar: Politics, Economics, and Society* (1987).

COX, HARVEY. *Fire From Heaven: The Rise of Pentecostal Spirituality and the Reshaping of Religion in the Twenty-First Century* (1995).

CRAFT, WILLIAM, AND ELLEN CRAFT. *Running a Thousand Miles for Freedom; or, The Escape of William and Ellen Craft from Slavery* (1860; reprint ed., 1991.).

CREEL, MARGARET WASHINGTON. *A Peculiar People: Slave Religion and Community-Culture Among the Gullahs* (1988).

CRESPO R., ALBERTO. *Esclavos negros en Bolivia* (1977).

CRIPPS, THOMAS. *Making Movies Black: The Hollywood Message Movie from World War II to the Civil Rights Era* (1993).

———. *Slow Fade to Black: The Negro in American Film 1900–1942* (1977).

CROUCHETT, LORRAINE J. *Delilah Leontium Beasley: Oakland's Crusading Journalist* (1990).

CRUISE O'BRIEN, DONALD. *The Mourides of Senegal: The Political and Economic Organization of an Islamic Brotherhood* (1971).

CUDJOE, SELWYN, ED. *Caribbean Women Writers: Essays from the First International Conference.* (1990).

———. *Resistance and Caribbean Literature* (1980).

CULLEN, COUNTEE. *My Soul's High Song: The Collected Writings of Countee Cullen, Voice of the Harlem Renaissance.* Edited by Gerald Early (1991).

CULLMAN, BRIAN. "Cheb Khaled and the Politics of Pleasure." *Antaeus* (Fall 1993).

CUNEY-HARE, MAUD. *Norris Wright Cuney: A Tribune of the Black People* (1995).

CUNNINGHAM, CAROL, AND JOEL BERGER. *Horn of Darkness: Rhinos on the Edge* (1997).

CURRY, LEONARD P. *The Free Black in Urban America, 1800–1850: The Shadow of the Dream* (1981).

CURTIN, PHILIP D. *The Atlantic Slave Trade: A Census* (1969).

CUTLER, JOHN HENRY. *Ed Brooke: Biography of a Senator* (1972).

DABNEY, VIRGINIUS. *Richmond: The Story of a City* (1976).

DABNEY, WENDELL P. *Cincinnati's Colored Citizens: Historical, Sociological, and Biographical* (1926).

DABYDEEN, DAVID. "On Not Being Milton: Nigger Talk in England Today." In *The Routledge Reader in Caribbean Literature*, ed. Alison Donnell and Sarah Lawson Welsh (1996).

DAHL, OTTO C. *Malgache et Maanjan: Une comparaison linguistique* (1951).

DALFIUME, RICHARD M. *Desegregation of the U. S. Armed Forces: Fighting on Two Fronts, 1939–1953* (1969).

DALTON, NARINE. "The Maestros: Black Symphony Conductors are Making a Name for Themselves." *Ebony* (February 1989): 54–57.

DALY, VERE T. *A Short History of the Guyanese People* (1975).

DANCE, DARYL C. *Shuckin' and Jivin': Folklore from Contemporary Black Americans* (1978).

DANIELS, DOUGLAS HENRY. "Lester Young: Master of Jive." *American Music* 3 (Fall 1985): 313–28.

———. *Pioneer Urbanites: A Social and Cul-tural History of Black San Francisco* (1980).

DANIEL, WALTER C. *Afro-American Journals, 1827–1980: A Reference Book* (1982).

DASH, J. MICHAEL. *Edouard Glissant* (1995).

DASH, JULIE. *Daughters of the Dust: The Making of an African American Woman's Film* (1992).

DATES, JANNETTE L., AND WILLIAM BARLOW, EDS. *Split Image: African Americans in the Mass Media* (1990).

DATT, NORMAN. CHEDDI B. JAGAN: *The Legend* (1997).

DAVENPORT, M. MARGUERITE. *Azalia: The Life of Madame E. Azalia Hackley* (1947).

DAVIES, CAROL BOYCE, AND ELAINE SAVORY FIDO, EDS. *Out of the Kumbla: Caribbean Women and Literature* (1990).

DAVIS, ARTHUR P. *From the Dark Tower: Afro-American Writers, 1900–1960* (1974).

DAVIS, BENJAMIN O., JR. *Benjamin O. Davis, Jr., American: An Autobiography* (1991).

DAVIS, CHARLES T., AND HENRY LOUIS GATES, JR., EDS. *The Slave's Narrative* (1985).

DAVIS, CYPRIAN. *The History of Black Catholics in the United States* (1990).

DAVIS, DARIÉN J., ED. *Slavery and Beyond: The African Impact on Latin America and the Caribbean.*

DAVIS, DAVID BRION. *The Problem of Slavery in the Age of Revolution, 1770–1823.* 2d ed. (1998).

———. *The Problem of Slavery in Western Culture* (1966).

———. *Slavery and Human Progress* (1984).

DAVIS, H. P. *Black Democracy: The Story of Haiti* (1967).

DAVIS, JAMES J. "Entrevista con el dominicano Norberto James Rawlings." *Afro-Hispanic Review* (May 1987):16–18.

DAVIS, MICHAEL D. *Black American Women in Olympic Track and Field: A Complete Illustrated Reference* (1992).

DAVIS, RUSSELL. *Black Americans in Cleveland from George Peake to Carl B. Stokes, 1796–1969* (1972).

DAVIS, STEPHEN, AND PETER SIMON. *Reggae International* (1983).

DAVIS, THOMAS J. *A Rumor of Revolt: The "Great Negro Plot" in Colonial New York* (1985).

DAWKINS, WAYNE. *Black Journalists: The NABJ Story* (1993).

DAYAN, JOAN. "France Reads Haiti: An Interview with René Depestre." *Yale French Studies* 83: 136–153.

DEERR, NOEL. *The History of Sugar.* 2 vols. (1949–1950).

DELERIS, FERDINAND. *Ratsiraka: Socialisme et misère à Madagascar* (1986).

DELIUS, PETER. *A Lion Amongst the Cattle: Reconstruction and Resistance in the Northern Transvaal* (1996).

DEREN, MAYA. DIVINE HORSEMEN: *The Living Gods of Haiti* (1953).

DERRICOTTE, TOI. *The Black Notebooks: An Interior Journey* (1997).

DESMANGLES, LESLIE G. *The Faces of the Gods: Vodou and Roman Catholicism in Haiti* (1992).

DE WILDE, LAURENT. *Monk* (1997).

DIAWARA, MANTHIA: *Politics and Culture* (1992).

——, ED. *Black American Cinema* (1993).

DÍAZ AYALA, CRISTOBAL. *Música cubana del areyto a la nueva trova* (1981).

DIEDHIOUS, DJIB. "Paulin S. Vieyra a rencontré le cinèma africain." *Le Soleil* (December 27, 1982).

DILLON, MERTON L. *Benjamin Lundy and the Struggle for Negro Freedom* (1966).

DIOP, CHEIKH ANTA. *Nations nègres et culture: De l'antiquité Nègre-Egyptienne aux problèmes culturels de l'Afrique noire d'a. ujourd'hui.* 2d ed. (1965).

DITTMER, JOHN. *Black Georgia in the Progressive Era, 1900–1920* (1977).

——. *Local People: The Struggle for Civil Rights in Mississippi* (1995).

DIXON, WILLIE. *I Am the Blues: The Willie Dixon Story* (1989).

DOMÍNGUEZ ORTIZ, ANTONIO. "La esclavitud en Castilla durante la Edad Moderna." In *Estudios de historia social de España*, ed. Carmelo Vióas y Mey. 2 vols. (1952). Vol. II, pp. 369–427.

DONOVAN, NANCY, AND LAST, JILL. *Ethiopian Costumes* (1980).

DORSEY, CAROLYN. "Despite Poor Health: Olivia Davidson Washington's Story." *Sage: A Scholarly Journal on Black Women* (Fall 1985).

DORSEY, DAVID. "The Art of Mari Evans." In *Black Women Writers* (1984): 170–89.

DORSEY, THOMAS ANDREW. *Say Amen, Somebody* (1983).

DORSINVILLE, ROGER. *Jacques Roumain* (1981).

D'ORSO, MICHAEL. *Like Judgement Day: The Ruin and Redemption of a Town Called Rosewood* (1996).

DOUGLASS, WILLIAM. *Annals of the First African Church in the United States of America, Now Styled the African Episcopal Church of St. Thomas, Philadelphia* (1862).

DRAGO, EDMUND L. *Initiative, Paternalism, and Race Relations: Charleston's Avery Normal Institute* (1990).

DRAKE, SANDRA E. *Wilson Harris and the Modern Tradition: A New Architecture of the World* (1986).

DRAKE, ST. CLAIR. *Black Folk Here and There: An Essay in History and Anthropology.* 2 vols. (1987–1990).

DRAKE, ST. CLAIR, AND HORACE R. CAYTON. *Black Metropolis: A Study of Negro Life in a Northern City* (1945).

DRESCHER, SEYMOUR, AND STANLEY L. ENGERMAN, EDS. *A Historical Guide to World Slavery* (1998).

DRISKELL, DAVID. *Hidden Heritage: Afro-American Art, 1800–1950* (1985).

"Dr. Lillie M. Jackson: Lifelong Freedom Fighter." *Crisis* 82 (1975).

DROT, JEAN-MARIE. *Peintures et dessins, vaudou d'Haïti* (1986).

DUANY, JORGE, AND PETER MANUEL. "Popular Music in Puerto Rico: Toward an Anthropology of Salsa." *Latin American Music Review* 5 (1984): 186–216.

DUBOFSKY, MELVYN, AND STEPHEN BURWOOD, EDS. *Women and Minorities During the Great Depression* (1990).

DU BOIS, SHIRLEY GRAHAM. *His Day is Marching On: A Memoir of W. E. B. Du Bois.* (1971).

DU BOIS, W. E. B. *Black Reconstruction in America* (1935).

——. *The Souls of Black Folk: Essays and Sketches* (1903).

DUFFY, SUSAN. "Shirley Chisholm." *American Orators of the Twentieth Century*, ed. Barnard K. Duffy and Halford R. Ryan (1987).

DUGGAN, WILLIAM, AND JOHN CIVILLE. *Tanzania and Nyerere: A Study of Ujamaa and Nationhood* (1976).

DUGGY, JOHN. PRINCE: *An Illustrated Biography* (1995).

DUMMETT, CLIFTON O., AND LOIS DOYLE DUMMETT. *Afro-Americans in Dentistry: Sequence and Consequence of Events* (1978).

DUNBAR-NELSON, ALICE. *Give Us This Day: The Diary of Alice Dunbar-Nelson*, ed. Gloria T. Hull (1984).

DUNCAN, JOHN. "Negro Composers of Opera." *Negro History Bulletin* (January 1966): 79–80, 93.

DUNCAN, QUINCE. *Cultura negra y teologia* (1986).

——. *Dos estudios sobre diaspora negra y racismo* (1987).

DUNDES, ALAN, ED. *Mother Wit From the Laughing Barrel: Readings in the Interpretation of Afro-American Folklore* (1990).

DUNN, RICHARD S. *Sugar and Slaves: The Rise of the Planter Class in the English West Indies, 1624–1713* (1972).

DUNNING, JAMES MORSE. *The Harvard School of Dental Medicine: Phase Two in the Development of a University Dental School* (1981).

DURHAM, PHILIP, AND EVERETT L. JONES. *The Negro Cowboys* (1965).

DURIX, JEAN-PIERRE. *Dictionary of Literary Biography* (1992).

DUSTER, ALFREDA, ED. *Crusade for Justice: The Autobiography of Ida B. Wells* (1970).

DUSTER, TROY. *Backdoor to Eugenics* (1990).

DYNES, WAYNE R., ED. *Encyclopedia of Homosexuality* (1990).

EDELMAN, MARIAN WRIGHT. *The Measure of Our Success: A Letter to My Children and Yours* (1992).

EDRERIA DE CABALLERO, ANGELINA. *Antonio Medina, el don Pepe de la raza de color* (1938).

EGERTON, DOUGLAS R. *Gabriel's Rebellion: The Virginia Slave Conspiracies of 1800 and 1802* (1993).

EHRET, CHRISTOPHER, AND M. POSNANSKY. *The Archaeological and Linguistic Reconstruction of African History* (1982).

EHRLICH, WALTER. *They Have No Rights: Dred Scott's Struggle for Freedom* (1979).

ELDERS, JOYCELYN. *Joycelyn Elders, M.D.: From Sharecropper's Daughter to Surgeon General of the United States of America* (1997).

ELIAS, JOÃO. *A impotencia da raca negra não tira da fraqueza dos brancos.* 2d ed. (1994).

ELLISON, RALPH. *Romare Bearden: Paintings and Projections* (1968).

——. *Shadow and Act* (1964).

ELLSWORTH, SCOTT. *Death in A Promised Land: The Tulsa Race Riot of 1921* (1982).

ELY, MELVIN PATRICK. *The Adventures of Amos 'n' Andy: A Social History of an American Phenomenon* (1991).

EMECHETA, BUCHI. *Head Above Water* (1986).

EMERY, LYNNE FAULEY. *Black Dance in the United States from 1619 to 1970* (1980).

ENCICLOPÉDIA DA MÚSICA BRASILEIRA: Erudita, folclórica, popular (1977).

EQUIANO, OLAUDAH. *Equiano's Travels: His Autobiography: The Interesting Narrative of the Life of Olaudah Equiano or Gustavus Vassa, the African.* Edited by Paul Edwards (1967).

ERLEWINE, MICHAEL, ET AL, EDS. *All Music Guide to Jazz: The Experts' Guide to the Best Jazz Recordings* (1996).

ERLMANN, VEIT, AND DEBORAH PACINI HERNANDEZ, EDS. "The Politics and Aesthetics of Transnational Musics." Special issue of *World of Music* 35, no. 2 (1993).

ERSTEIN, HAP. "Richards, Wilson Team Up on Prize Dramas." *Washington Times* (November 8, 1991): E1.

ESTES, J. WORTH. *The Medical Skills of Ancient Egypt* (1993).

ESTUPIÑAN TELLO, JULIO. *Historia de Esmeraldas* (1977).

EVANS, MARI. *Black Women Writers (1950–1980): A Critical Evaluation* (1984).

EVERS, CHARLES, AND GRACE HASKELL, EDS. *Evers* (1971).

EWERS, TRAUTE. *The Origin of American Black English: Be-Forms in the HOODOO Texts* (1996).

FABRE, MICHEL. "The Last Quest of Horace Cayton." *Black World* 19 (May 1970): 41–45.

——. *The Unfinished Quest of Richard Wright.* Translated by Isabel Barzun (1973).

FAIRCLOUGH, ADAM. *To Redeem the Soul of America: The Southern Christian Leadership Conference and Martin Luther King, Jr* (1987).

FAIR, LAURA. "Dressing Up: Clothing, Class and Gender in Post-Abolition Zanzibar." *Journal of African History* 39 (1998): 63–94.

FANON, FRANTZ. *Black Skin, White Masks.* Translation of *Peau noire, masques blancs* by Charles Lam Markmann (1967).

FARMER, JAMES. *Lay Bare the Heart: An Autobiography of the Civil Rights Movement* (1985).

FARNSWORTH, ROBERT M. *Melvin B. Tolson, 1898–1966: Plain Talk and Poetic Prophecy* (1984).

FARRISON, WILLIAM EDWARD. *William Wells Brown: Author and Reformer* (1969).

FEHRENBACHER, DON E. *The Dred Scott Case: Its Significance in American Law and Politics* (1978).

FELDMAN, LINDA. "Norton Biography." *Christian Science Monitor* (March 31, 1992): 14:1

FERGUSON, JAMES. *Papa Doc, Baby Doc: Haiti and the Duvaliers* (1987).

FERGUSON, MOIRA. *Jamaica Kincaid: Where the Land Meets the Body* (1994).

FERGUSON, SHEILA. *Soul Food: Classic Cuisine from the Deep South* (1989).

FERRIS, WILLIAM, ED. *Afro-American Folk Arts and Crafts* (1983).

FERRIS, WILLIAM, AND BRENDA MCCALLUM, EDS. *Local Color: A Sense of Place in Folk Art* (1982).

FIELDS, BARBARA JEANNE. *Slavery and Freedom on the Middle Ground: Maryland During the Nineteenth Century* (1985).

FILHO, LUÍS VIANA. *O Negro na Bahia* (1988).

FITZGERALD, MARY ANN, HENRY J. DREWAL, AND MAYO OKEDIJI. "Transformation through Cloth: An Egungun Costume of the Yoruba." *African Arts* 28 (1995).

FLASCH, JOY. *Melvin B. Tolson* (1972).

FLEISCHER, NAT. *Black Dynamite: The Story of the Negro in the Prize Ring from 1782 to 1838* (1938).

FLETCHER, MARVIN E. *America's First Black General: Benjamin O. Davis, Sr.* (1989).

——. *The Black Soldier and Officer in the United States Army, 1891–1917* (1974).

FLETCHER, TOM. *One-Hundred Years of the Negro in Show Business* (1984).

FLINT, J. E. "Zanzibar 1890–1950." *In History of East Africa*, ed. Vincent Harlow and E. M. Chilver (1965).

FLOMENHAFT, ELEANOR, ED. *FAITH RINGGOLD: A 25–Year Survey* (1990).

FLOYD, SAMUEL, ED. *Black Music in the Harlem Renaissance* (1990).

FLYNN, JOYCE, AND JOYCE OCCOMY STRICKLIN, EDS. *Frye Street and Environs: The Collected Works of Marita Bonner Occomy* (1987).

FOGEL, ROBERT W. *Without Consent or Contract: The Rise and Fall of American Slavery* (1989).

FOLEY, ALBERT S. *Bishop Healy: Beloved Outcaste* (1954).

FONER, ERIC. *Reconstruction: America's Unfinished Revolution, 1863–1877* (1988).

FONER, PHILIP. *Antonio Maceo* (1977).

——. *Black Panthers Speak* (1995).

——. *Blacks in the American Revolution* (1976).

——. *Organized Labor & the Black Worker 1619–1973* (1974).

——. *The Spanish-Cuban-American War and the Birth of U.S. Imperialism. Vol. I* (1962).

FONER, PHILIP, ED. *Black Socialist Preacher: The Teachings of Reverend George Washington Woodbey and his Disciple Reverend George W. Slater, Jr.* (1983).

FONER, PHILIP, AND RONALD LEWIS. *Black Workers: A Documentary History from Colonial Times to the Present* (1989).

FOOTE, JULIA. *A Brand Plucked From the Fire. In Spiritual Narratives*, ed. Henry Louis Gates Jr. (1988).

FORBES, JACK D. *Africans and Native Americans: The Language of Race and the Evolution of Red-Black Peoples* (1988).

FORBES, STEVEN. *The Baymen of Belize and How They Wrested British Honduras from the Spaniards* (1997).

FORMAN, JAMES. *The Making of Black Revolutionaries* (1985).

FOSTER, FRANCES SMITH. "Adding Color and Contour to Early American Self-Portraitures: Autobiographical Writings of Afro-Amer-ican Women." In *Conjuring: Black Women, Fiction and Literary Tradition*, ed. Marjorie Pryse and Hortense J. Spillers (1985).

———. *Written By Herself: Literary Production by African American Women, 1746–1892* (1993).

FOUCHET, MAX POL. *Wifredo Lam.* (1976).

FOWLER, VIRGINIA. *Nikki Giovanni* (1992).

FRADY, MARSHALL. *Jesse: The Life and Pilgrimage of Jesse Jackson* (1996).

FRANCO, JOSÉ LUCIANO. *Apuntes para una historia de su vida.* 3 vols. (1951–1957).

Franco Silva, Alfonso. *La esclavitud en Sevilla y su tierra a fines de la edad media* (1979).

FRANKLIN, CHARLES LIONEL. *The Negro Labor Unionist of New York: Problems and Conditions among Negroes in the Labor Unions in Manhattan with Special Reference to the N.R.A. and Post-N.R.A. Situations* (1936).

FRANKLIN, JOHN HOPE. *The Free Negro in North Carolina, 1790–1863* (1943).

———. *From Slavery to Freedom: A History of Negro Americans* (1988).

———. *Race and History: Selected Essays, 1938–1988* (1989).

FRANKLIN, JOHN HOPE, AND AUGUST MEIER, EDS. *Black Leaders of the Twentieth Century* (1982).

FRANKLIN, VINCENT P. *The Education of Black Philadelphia: The Social and Educational History of a Minority Community, 1900–1950* (1979).

FRANK, RUSTY E. *Tap! The Greatest Tap Dance Stars and Their Stories, 1900–1955* (1990).

FRAZIER, E. FRANKLIN. "Durham: Capital of the Black Middle Class." In Alain Locke, ed. *The New Negro* (1925).

———. *On Race Relations: Selected Writings*, ed. Gilbert Edwards (1968).

FRAZIER, JOE, AND PHIL BERGER. *Smokin' Joe: The Autobiography of a Heavyweight Champion of the World, Smokin' Joe Frazier* (1996).

FREEDBERG, SYDNEY P. *Brother Love: Money, Murder, and a Messiah* (1994).

FRENCH, WILLIAM P. "Black Studies: Getting Started in a Specialty." *AB: Bookmans Weekly* (February 22, 1988): 737–41.

FREYRE, GILBERTO. *O Brasil em face das Africas negras e mesticas* (1963).

———. *The Masters and the Slaves: A Study in the Development of Brazilian Civilization.* Translation of *Casa grande e senzala* by Samuel Putnam (1986).

FREY, SYLVIA. *Water From the Rock: Black Resistance in a Revolutionary Age* (1991).

FRIEDEMANN, NINA S. DE. *Lengua y sociedad en el palenque de San Basilio* (1983).

———. *Ma ngombe: Guerreros y ganaderos en Palenque.* 2d ed. (1987).

———. *La saga del Negro: Presencia africana en Colombia* (1993).

FRIEDEMANN, NINA S. DE., AND ALFREDO VANIN, COMP. *Entre la tierra y el cielo: Magia y leyendas del Chocó* (1995).

FRIEDMAN, LAWRENCE J. *Gregarious Saints: Self and Community in American Abolitionism, 1830–1870* (1982).

FINLAYSON, IAIN. *Tangier: City of the Dream* (1992).

FOX, STEPHEN R. *The Guardian of Boston: William Monroe Trotter* (1970).

FOX, TED. *Showtime at the Apollo* (1983).

FRY, GLADYS-MARIE. *Stitched from the Soul: Slave Quilts from the Ante-Bellum South* (1990).

FREDERICKS, MARCEL, JOHN LENNON ET AL. *Society and Health in Guyana* (1986).

FUNARI, PEDRO PAUL A., MARTIN HALL, AND SIAN JONES, EDS. *Historical Archaeology: Back from the Edge* (1999).

FUNDACÓ CASA DE RUI BARBOSA. *O Abolicionista Rui Barbosa* (1988).

FUNKE, LEWIS. *The Curtain Rises: The Story of Ossie Davis* (1971).

FYFE, CHRISTOPHER. *Sierra Leone Inheritance* (1964).

GABBARD, KRIN, ED. *Representing Jazz* (1995).

GABRIEL, TESHOME. *Third Cinema in the Third World: The Aestheties of Liberation* (1982).

GADELII, KARL ERLAND. *Lesser Antillean French Creole and Universal Grammar* (1997).

GAINES, ERNEST. *Porch Talk with Ernest Gaines: Conversations on the Writer's Craft*, ed. Marcia Gaudet and Carl Wooton (1990).

GALEANO, EDUARDO. *Football in Sun and Shadow* (1998).

GAMBINO, FERRUCCIO. "The Transgression of a Laborer: Malcolm X in the Wilderness of America." *Radical History Review* 55 (Winter 1993): 7–31.

GAMBLE, DAVID. *The Wolof of Senegambia, Together with Notes on the Lebu and the Serer* (1967).

GANDY, SAMUEL LUCIUS. *Human Possibilities: A Vernon Johns Reader* (1977).

GANGITANO, LIA AND STEVEN NELSON, EDS. *New Histories* (1996).

GARCÍA, HORACIO, ED. *Pensamiento revolucionario cubano*. Vol. I (1971).

GARCÍA, JUAN. *Cuentos y décimas afro-esmeraldeñas* (1988).

GARCÍA, JUAN MANUEL. *La Masacre de Palma Sola (Partidos, lucha política y el asesino del general): 1961–1963* (1986).

GARFINKEL, HERBERT. *When Negroes March: The March on Washington Movement in the Organizational Politics for FEPC* (1959).

GARROW, DAVID J. *Bearing the Cross: Martin Luther King, Jr., and the Southern Christian Leadership Conference* (1986).

——. *Protest at Selma: Martin Luther King, Jr., and the Voting Rights Act of 1965* (1978).

GASPAR, DAVID BARRY. *Bondmen and Rebels: A Study of Master-Slave Relations in Antigua* (1985).

GATES, HENRY LOUIS, JR. *Black Literature and Literary Theory* (1984).

——. *Colored People: A Memoir* (1994).

——. *Figures in Black: Words, Signs, and the Racial Self* (1992).

——. *Loose Canons: Notes on the Culture Wars* (1992).

——. *The Signifying Monkey: Towards A Theory of Afro-American Literary Criticism* (1988).

——. *Thirteen Ways of Looking at a Black Man* (1997): 155–79.

GATES, HENRY LOUIS, JR., ED. *Bearing Witness: Selections from African-American Autobiography in the Twentieth Century* (1991).

——, ed. *The Classic Slave Narratives* (1987).

——, ed. *Collected Black Women's Narratives: The Schomburg Library of Nineteenth-Century Black Women Writers* (1988).

GATES, HENRY LOUIS, JR., AND KWAME ANTHONY APPIAH, EDS. *Richard Wright: Critical Perspectives Past and Present* (1993).

——.Gloria Naylor: *Critical Perspectives Past and Present* (1993).

GATES, HENRY LOUIS, JR., AND NELLIE Y. MCKAY. *The Norton Anthology of African American Literature* (1997).

GATES, HENRY LOUIS, JR., AND CORNEL WEST. *The Future of the Race* (1996).

GATEWOOD, WILLARD B. *Aristocrats of Color: The Black Elite, 1880–1920* (1990).

GAVINS, RAYMOND. *The Perils and Prospects of Southern Black Leadership: Gordon Blaine Hancock, 1884–1970* (1977).

GAYLE, ADDISON, JR., ED. *The Black Aesthetic* (1971).

GAY, ROBERT. *Popular Organization and Democracy in Rio de Janeiro: A Tale of Two Favelas* (1994).

GEARY, LYNETTE G. "Jules Bledsoe: The Original 'Ol' Man River'." *Black Perspective in Music* 17, nos. 1, 2 (1989): 27–54.

GEIS, IMMANUEL. *The Pan-African Movement: A History of Pan-Africanism in America, Europe and Africa* (1974).

GELPÍ, JUAN. *Literatura y paternalismo en Puerto Rico* (1993).

GENOVESE, EUGENE D. *Roll, Jordan, Roll: The World the Slaves Made* (1974).

GEORGE, CAROL V. R. *Segregated Sabbaths: Richard Allen and the Emergence of Independent Black Churches 1760–1840* (1972).

GEORGE, NELSON. *Elevating the Game: Black Men and Basketball* (1992).

——. *Where Did Our Love Go?: The Rise and Fall of the Motown Sound* (1985).

GEORGE, NELSON, ET AL., EDS. *Fresh: Hip Hop Don't Stop* (1985).

GERBER, JANE S. *Jewish Society in Fez, 1450–1700: Studies in Communal and Economic Life* (1980).

GIBB, H.A.R. IBN BATTUTA: *Travels in Asia and Africa 1325–1354* (1929).

GIBSON, BOB. *From Ghetto to Glory: The Story of Bob Gibson* (1968).

GIDE, ANDRÈ. *Travels in the Congo* (1962).

GILARD, JACQUES. "Crescencio ou don Toba? Fausses questions et vraies rèponses sur le 'vallenato'." *Cahiers du monde hispanique et luso-brésilien, Caravelle* 48 (1987): 69–80.

GILL, GERALD R. "Win or Lose -We Win." *In The Afro-American Woman: Struggles and Images* (1978).

GILLESPIE, JOHN BIRKS ("DIZZY"), WITH AL FRASER. *Dizzy To BE, or Not . . . to BOP: The Autobiography of Dizzy Gillespie* (1979).

GILROY, PAUL. *There Ain't No Black in the Union Jack: The Cultural Politics of Race and Nation* (1991).

GIRAL, SERGIO. "Cuban Cinema and the Afro-Cuban Heritage." Interview by Julianne Burton and Gary Crowdus. *In Film and Politics in the Third World*, ed. John D. H. Downing (1987).

———. "Sergio Giral on Filmmaking in Cuba." Interview by Ana M. López and Nicholas Peter Humy. *In Cinemas of the Black Diaspora: Diversity, Dependence, and Oppositionality*, ed. Michael T. Martin (1995).

GIRVAN, NORMAN. *Poverty, Empowerment and Social Development in the Caribbean* (1997).

GLAZIER, STEPHEN D. MARCHIN' the Pilgrims Home (1983).

———,ED. *Perspectives on Pentecostalism: Case Studies from the Caribbean and Latin America* (1980).

GLEN, JOHN M. *Highlander: No Ordinary School, 1932–1962* (1988).

GLISSANT, EDOUARD. *Caribbean Discourse: Selected Essays*. Translated by J. Michael Dash (1989).

GOGGIN, JACQUELINE ANNE. *Carter G. Woodson: A Life in Black History* (1993).

GOINGS, KENNETH W. *Mammy and Uncle Mose: Black Collectibles and American Stereotyping* (1994).

GOLDBERG, JANE. "A Hoofer's Homage: John Bubbles." *Village Voice* (December 4, 1978).

GONZ·LEZ BUENO, GLADYS. "An Initia-tion Ceremony in Regla de Palo." *In AfroCuba: An Anthology of Cuban Writing on Race, Politics and Culture*, ed. Pedro Pèrez Sarduy and Jean Stubbs (1993).

GONZLEZ DÍAZ, ANTONIO MANUEL. *La esclavitud en Ayamonte durante el Antiguo Régimen (siglos XVI, XVII y XVIII)* (1997).

GONZ·LEZ ECHEVARRIA, ROBERTO. *Myth and Archive: A Theory of Latin American Narrative* (1998).

———. *The Pride of Havana: The History of Cuban Baseball* (1999).

GONZALEZ-PEREZ, ARMANDO. *Acercamiento a la literatura afrocubana: Ensayos de interpretación* (1994).

GONZALEZ-WHIPPLER, MIGENE. *The Santeria Experience: A Journey into the Miraculous*. Rev. and exp. ed. (1992).

GOODHEART, LAWRENCE B., ET AL., EDS. *Slavery in American Society*. 3d ed. (1993).

GOODWIN, ANDREW, AND JOE GORE. "World Beat and the Cultural Imperialism Debate." *Socialist Review* 20, no. 3 (1990): 63–80.

GORDON, ALLAN M. *Echoes of Our Past: The Narrative Artistry of Palmer C. Hayden* (1988).

GORDON, P. "The New Right, Race, and Education." *Race and Class* 29, no. 3 (Winter 1987).

GOSNELL, HAROLD F. *Negro Politicians: The Rise of Negro Politics in Chicago* (1967).

GOURAIGE, GHISLAIN. *Histoire de la littérature haïtienne (de l'indépendance à nos jours)* (1982).

GOUREVITCH, PHILIP. *We Wish to Inform You that Tomorrow We Will Be Killed with Our Families: Stories from Rwanda* (1998).

GOURSE, LESLIE. *Unforgettable: The Life and Mystique of Nat King Cole* (1991).

GRANDA GUTIERREZ, GERMAN DE. *Estudios sobre un area dialectal hispanoamericana de poblacion negra: Las tierras bajas occidentales de Colombia* (1977)

GRANT, JOANNE. *Fundi: The Story of Ella Baker* (1981).

GRATIANT, GILBERT. *Fables créoles et autres récits* (1995).

GRAY, JOHN MILNER. *History of Zanzibar from the Middle Ages to 1856* (1962).

GRAY, RICHARD. *Black Christians and White Missionaries* (1990).

GREENBAUM, SUSAN. "A Comparison Between African-American and Euro-American Mutual Aid Societies in 19th-Century America." *Journal of Ethnic Studies* 19 (Fall 1991): 95–119.

GREENBERG, CHERYL LYNN. *"Or Does It Explode?: Black Harlem in the Great Depression* (1991).

GREENBERG, JACK. *Crusaders in the Courts: How a Dedicated Band of Lawyers Fought for the Civil Rights Revolution* (1994).

GREENE, LORENZO JOHNSTON. *Selling Black History for Carter G. Woodson* (1996).

GREENE, LORENZO JOHNSTON, GARY R. KREMER, AND ANTONIO F. HOLLAND. *Missouri's Black Heritage* (1993).

GREEN, TIM. *The Dark Side of the Game: The Unauthorized NFL Playbook* (1996).

GREGORY, DICK, WITH MARK LANE. *Up From Nigger* (1976).

GREGORY, DICK, WITH MARTIN LIPSYTE. *Nigger: An Autobiography* (1964).

GREGORY, PAYNE J., AND SCOTT C. RATZAN. *Tom Bradley: The Impossible Dream: A Biography* (1986).

GRENARD, STEVE. *Handbook of Alligators and Crocodiles* (1991).

GRIAULE, MARCEL. *Conversations with Ogotemmeli: An Introduction to Dogon Religious Ideas* (1965).

GROIA, PHILIP. *They All Sang on the Corner: A Second Look at New York City's Rhythm and Blues Vocal Groups* (1983).

GROSSMAN, JAMES R. *Land of Hope: Chicago, Black Southerners and the Great Migration* (1989).

GRUDIN, EVA UNGAR. *Stitching Memories: African-American Story Quilts* (1990).

GUERRERO, EDWARD. *Framing Blackness: The African American Image in Film* (1993).

GUILBAULT, JOCELYNE, WITH GAGE AVERILL, EDOUARD BENOÎT, AND GREGORY RABESS. *Zouk: World Music in the West Indies* (1993).

GUILLÉN, NICOLAS. *Martín Morúa Delgado: ¿Quién fue?* (1984).

GURALNICK, PETER. *Searching for Robert Johnson* (1989).

——. *Sweet Soul Music: Rhythm and Blues and the Southern Dream of Freedom* (1986).

GUTMAN, BILL. *The Harlem Globetrotters* (1977).

GUTMAN, HERBERT G. *The Black Family in Slavery and Freedom, 1750–1925* (1976).

GUY-SHEFTALL, BEVERLY, AND JO MOORE STEWART. *Spelman: A Centennial Celebration* (1981).

GUZMAN, JESSIE P. *Crusade for Civic Democracy: The Story of the Tuskegee Civic Association, 1941–1970* (1985).

HABEKOST, CHRISTIAN. *Verbal Riddim: The Politics and Aesthetics of African-Caribbean Dub Poetry* (1993).

HACKETT, ROSALIND. *Art and Religion in Africa* (1996).

HAIR, WILLIAM IVY. *Carnival of Fury: Robert Charles and the New Orleans Race Riot of 1900* (1976).

HALE, LINDSAY, "Preto Velho: Resistance, Redemption and Engendered Representations of Slavery in a Brazilian Possession-Trance Religion." *American Ethnologist* 24, no. 2 (1997): 392–414.

HALL, JACQUELYN DOWD. *Revolt Against Chivalry: Jessie Daniel Ames and the Women's Campaign Against Lynching* (1979).

HALL, MARGARET, AND TOM YOUNG. *Confronting Leviathan: Mozambique Since Independence* (1997).

HALL, RICHARD. *Stanley: An Adventurer Explored* (1974).

HALL, STUART. "Racism and Reaction." *In Five Views on Multi-Racial Britain* (1978).

HALL, STUART, AND BRAM GIEBEN, EDS. *Formations of Modernity* (1992).

HALL, STUART, AND MARTIN JACQUES, EDS. *New Times: The Changing Face of Politics in the 1990s* (1990).

HAMER, MARY. *Signs of Cleopatra: History, Politics, Representation* (1993).

HAMILTON, CHARLES V. *Adam Clayton Powell, Jr.: The Political Biography of an American Dilemma* (1991).

HAMILTON, HOLMAN. *Prologue to Conflict: The Crisis and Compromise of 1850* (1964).

HAMILTON, KENNETH MARVIN. *Black Towns and Profit: Promotion and Development in the Trans-Applachian West, 1877–1915* (1991).

HAMNER, ROBERT D, ED. *Critical Perspectives on Derek Walcott* (1993).

HANCHARD, MICHAEL GEORGE. *Orpheus and Power: The Movimento Negro of Rio de Janeiro and São Paulo, Brazil, 1945–1988* (1994).

HANDY, D. ANTOINETTE. "Conversations with Mary Lou Williams: First Lady of the Jazz Keyboard." *Black Perspectives on Music* 8 (Fall 1980): 195–214.

HANDY, WILLIAM C. *Father of the Blues: An Autobiography*. Edited by Arna Bontemps (1941).

HANSEN, EMMANUEL. *Frantz Fanon: Social and Political Thought* (1977).

HARDESTY, VON, AND DOMINICK PISANO. *Black Wings: The American Black in Aviation* (1983).

HARDY, CHARLES, AND GAIL F. STERN, EDS. *Ethnic Images in the Comics* (1986).

HARDY, GAYLE J. *American Women Civil Rights Activists: Biobibliographies of 68 Leaders, 1825–1992* (1993).

HARLAN, LOUIS R. *Booker T. Washington: The Making of a Black Leader, 1856–1901* (1972).

HARPER, MICHAEL S., ET. AL., EDS. *Chant of Saints: A Gathering of Afro-American Literature, Art, and Scholarship* (1979).

HARRINGTON, OLIVER. *Why I Left America and Other Essays* (1993).

HARRIS, FRED R., AND ROGER WILKINS, EDS. *Quiet Riots: Race and Poverty in the United States* (1988).

HARRIS, JESSICA B. *Iron Pots and Wooden Spoons: Africa's Gifts to New World Cooking* (1989).

HARRIS, MICHAEL. *The Rise of the Gospel Blues: The Music of Thomas Andrew Dorsey in the Urban Church* (1992).

HARRISON, ALFERDTEEN, ED. *Black Exodus: The Great Migration from the American South* (1991).

HARRISON, EARL. *The Dream and the Dreamer* (1956).

HARRIS, ROBERT. "Early Black Benevolent Societies, 1780–1830." *Massachusetts Review* 20 (Autumn 1979): 603–28.

HARRIS, WILLIAM HAMILTON. *Keeping the Faith: A. Philip Randolph, Milton P. Webster, and the Brotherhood of Sleeping Car Porters, 1925–37* (1977).

HARRIS, WILLIAM J. *The Poetry and Poetics of Amiri Baraka: The Jazz Aesthetic* (1985).

HARRIS, WILSON. *History, Fable, and Myth in the Caribbean and the Guianas* (1970).

HART, DAVID. *The Volta River Project: A Case Study in Politics and Technology* (1980).

HASKINS, JAMES. *Black Dance in America: A History through its People* (1990).

——. *Bricktop* (1983).

——. *Mabel Mercer: A Life* (1987).

——. *Pinckney Benton Stewart Pinchback* (1973).

HASKINS, JAMES, AND N. R. MITGANG. *Mr. Bojangles: The Biography of Bill Robinson* (1988).

HAYDEN, DOLORES. "Biddy Mason's Los Angeles, 1856–1891." *California History* 68 (Fall 1989): 86–99.

HAYDEN, TOM. *Rebellion in Newark: Official Violence and Ghetto Response* (1967).

HAYES, DIANA L. *And Still We Rise: An Introduction to Black Liberation Theology* (1996).

HAYGOOD, WIL. *King of the Cats: The Life and Times of Adam Clayton Powell, Jr.* (1993).

HAYNES, KARIMA A. "Mae Jemison: Coming in from Outer Space." *Ebony* 48, no. 2 (Dec. 1992):118.

HAYWOOD, HARRY. *Black Bolshevik: Autobiography of an Afro-American Communist* (1978).

HAZAEL-MASSIEUX, MARIE-CHRISTINE. "Le Criole aux Antilles: Evolutions et Perspectives." In Yacou Alain, ed., *Creoles de la Caraïbe: Actes du Colloque universitaire en hommage á Guy Hazael-Massieux, Pointe-á-Pitre, le 27 mars 1995* (1996): 179–200.

HEDGEMAN, ANNA ARNOLD. *The Trumpet Sounds: A Memoir of Negro leadership* (1964).

HEDRICK, JOAN. *Harriet Beecher Stowe: A Life* (1994).

HEILBUT, ANTHONY. *The Gospel Sound: Good News and Bad Times* (1971).

HELDMAN, MARILYN E., STUART MUNRO-HAY, AND RODERICK GRIERSON. *African Zion: The Sacred Art of Ethiopia* (1993).

HELG, ALINE. *Our Rightful Share: The Afro-Cuban Struggle for Equality, 1886–1912* (1995).

HELLER, PETER. *Bad Intentions: The Mike Tyson Story* (1989).

HELM, MCKINLEY. *Angel Mo' and Her Son, Roland Hayes* (1942).

HEMENWAY, ROBERT. *Zora Neale Hurston: A Literary Biography* (1980).

HEMPHILL, ESSEX, ED. *Brother to Brother: New Writings by Black Gay Men* (1991).

HENDERSON, ALEXA BENSON. *Atlanta Life Insurance Company: Guardian of Black Economic Dignity* (1990).

HENDERSON, HARRY, AND GYLBERT GARVIN COKER. *Charles Alston: Artist and Teacher* (1990).

HENSON, MATTHEW A. *A Black Explorer at the North Pole 1866–1955* (1989).

HENZE, PAUL B. *The Defeat of the Derg and the Establishment of New Governments in Ethiopia and Eritrea* (1992).

HEUMAN, GAD, ED. *Out of the House of Bondage: Runaways, Resistance, and Marronage in Africa and the New World* (1986).

HEYMOUNT, GEORGE. "Blacks in Opera." *Ebony* (November 1981): 32–36.

HIDALGO ALZAMORA, LAURA. "Del ritmo al concepto en la poesía de Preciado." *Cultura, Revista del Banco Central del Ecuador 3*, no.7 (May-August 1980): 102–19.

HIGGINBOTHAM, A. LEON. *In the Matter of Color: The Colonial Period* (1978).

——. *Shades of Freedom: Racial Politics and Presumptions of the American Legal Process* (1996).

HIGGINBOTHAM, EVELYN BROOKS. *Righteous Discontent: The Women's Movement in the Black Baptist Church, 1880–1920* (1993).

HILL, DANIEL G. *The Freedom Seekers: Blacks in Early Canada* (1981).

HILL, DONALD. *Calypso Calaloo: Early Carnival Music in Trinidad* (1993).

HILL, ROBERT A., ED. *The Crusader.* 3 vols. (1987).

——. *The Marcus Garvey and Universal Negro Improvement Association Papers* (1983–1991).

HINE, DARLENE CLARK, ED. *Black Women in America: An Historical Encylopedia.* 2 vols. (1993).

HIRO, DILIP. *Desert Shield to Desert Storm: The Second Gulf War* (1992).

HIRSH, ARNOLD R., AND JOSEPH LOGSDON. *Creole New Orleans: Race and Americanization* (1992).

HIRSCHORN, H. H. "Botanical remedies of South and Central America and the Caribbean: An Archival Analysis." *Journal of Ethnopharmacology* 4, no. 2 (1981).

HOCHSCHILD, ADAM. *King Leopold's Ghost: A Story of Greed, Terror, and Heroism in Colonial Africa* (1998).

HODGES, LEROY. *Portrait of an Expatriate: William Gardner Smith, Writer* (1985).

HOFFMAN, FREDERICK J., CHARLES ALLEN, AND CAROLYN R. ULRICH. *The Little Magazine: A History and a Bibliography* (1946).

HOFFMAN, LARRY G. *Haitian Art: The Legend and Legacy of the Naïve Tradition* (1985).

HOFFMANN, LÈON-FRANÇOIS. *Littèrature d'Haïti* (1995).

HOFLER, ROBERT. "Minority View: Seeing White, Being Black: Interview with Lou Gossett Jr." *Life* (March 1989).

HOLANDA, AURÉLIO BUARQUE DE. "Teixeira e Souza." *In O Romance Brasileiro*, ed. Olivio Montenegro (1952).

HOLDREDGE, HELEN. *Mammy Pleasant* (1953).

HOLLOWAY, JOSEPH E., ED. *Africanisms in American Culture* (1990).

HOLM, JOHN. *Pidgins and Creoles*. 2 vols. (1988–1989).

HOLT, RACKMAN. *Mary McLeod Bethune: A Biography* (1964).

HOLWAY, JOHN B. *Josh and Satch: The Life and Times of Josh Gibson and Satchel Paige* (1991).

HOLYFIELD, EVANDER, AND BERNARD HOLYFIELD. *Holyfield: The Humble Warrior* (1996).

HOOKS, BELL, "Black is a Woman's Color." In *Bearing Witness: Selections from African-American Autobiography in the Twentieth Century*, ed. Henry Louis Gates Jr. (1991).

HOOKS, BELL, AND CORNEL WEST. *Breaking Bread: Insurgent Black Intellectual Life* (1991).

HOPE KING, RUBY. *Education in the Caribbean: Historical Perspectives* (1987).

HORACE, LILLIAN B. *"Crowned with Glory and Honor": The Life of Rev. Lacey Kirk Williams* (1978).

HORNE, GERALD. *Communist Front? The Civil Rights Congress 1946–56* (1988).

HORTON, AIMEE ISGRIG. *The Highlander Folk School: A History of its Major Programs, 1932–1961* (1989).

HOSHER, JOHN. *God in a Rolls Royce: The Rise of Father Divine: Madman, Menace, or Messiah* (1936).

HOSIASSON, JOSE. "Kid Ory." *New Grove Dictionary of Jazz* (1988).

HOUSE, ERNEST R. *Jesse Jackson and the Politics of Charisma: The Rise and Fall of the PUSH/Excel Program* (1988).

HOWAT, GERALD. *Learie Constantine* (1975).

HOWES, R. "The Literature of Outsiders: The Literature of the Gay Community in Latin America." In *Latin American Masses and Minorities: Their Images and Realities* (1987).

HOWE, STEPHEN. *Afrocentrism: Mythical Pasts and Imagined Homes* (1998).

HOYOS, F. A. *A History from the Amerindians to Independence* (1978).

HUCKABY, ELIZABETH. *Crisis at Central High School: Little Rock, 1957–58* (1980).

HUGGINS, NATHAN IRVIN. *Harlem Renaissance* (1971).

HUGHES, C. ALVIN. "We Demand Our Rights: The Southern Negro Youth Congress, 1937–1949." *Phylon* 48, no. 1 (Spring 1987): 38–50.

HULL, GLORIA T. *Color, Sex, and Poetry: Three Women Writers of the Harlem Renaissance* (1987).

HUNTER-GAULT, CHARLAYNE. *In My Place* (1992).

HUNTINGTON, RICHARD. *Gender and Social Structure in Madagascar* (1988).

HURD, MICHAEL. *Black College Football, 1892–1992: One Hundred Years of History, Education, and Pride* (1993).

HURLEY, DANIEL. *Cincinnati, The Queen City* (1982).

HURSTON, ZORA NEALE. "Hoodoo in America." *Journal of American Folklore* 44 (1931): 414.

——. *I Love Myself When I am Laughing . . . and Then Again When I am Looking Mean and Impressive: A Zora Neale Hurston Reader*, ed. Alice Walker (1979).

——. *Mules and Men* (1935).

HUTCHINSON, EARL OFARI. *Betrayed: A History of Presidential Failure to Protect Black Lives* (1996).

——. *Blacks and Reds: Race and Class in Conflict, 1919–1990* (1995).

IANNI, OCTÁVIO. *Escravidão e racismo*. 2d ed. (1988).

IHONVBERE, JULIUS O. *Economic Crisis, Civil Society, and Democratization: The Case of Zambia* (1996).

ILLINOIS STATE MUSEUM. *Healing Walls: Murals and Community, A Chicago History* (1996).

"Interview: Queen Mother Moore." *Black Scholar* 4 (March–April 1973): 47–55.

IOAKIMIDIS, DEMETRE. "Chu Berry." *Jazz Monthly* (March 1964).

IRVINE, CECILIA. "The Birth of the Kimbanguist Movement in Bas-Zaire, 1921." *Journal of Religion in Africa* 6, no. 1 (1974): 23–76.

ISICHEI, ELIZABETH. *A History of African Societies to 1870* (1997).

JACKSON, CARLTON. *Hattie: The Life of Hattie McDaniel* (1990).

JACKSON, KENNETH T., AND BARBARA B. JACKSON. "The Black Experience in Newark: The Growth of the Ghetto, 1870–1970." *In New Jersey Since 1860: New Findings and Interpretations*, ed. William C. Wright (1972).

JACKSON, LUTHER P. *Free Negro Labor and Property Holding in Virginia, 1830–1860* (1942).

JACKSON, REGINALD, WITH MIKE LUPICA. *Reggie* (1984).

JACKSON, RICHARD L. *Black Writers in Latin America* (1979).

JACOBS, DONALD M. *Antebellum Black Newspapers* (1976).

——. "David Walker: Boston Race Leader, 1825–1830." *Essex Institute Historical Collections* 107 (Jan. 1971): 94–107.

JACOBS, HARRIET. *Incidents in the Life of a Slave Girl, Written by Herself*, ed. Jean Fagan Yellin (1987).

JACOBSON, MARK. "When He Was King: Former Heavyweight Boxing Champ Larry Holmes." *New York* 30, no. 28 (July 28, 1997): 32–35.

JACQUES-GARVEY, AMY, ED. *Philosophy and Opinions of Marcus Garvey* (1923–1925).

JADIN, LOUIS. *Le Congo et la secte des Antoniens* (1961).

JAGAN, CHEDDI. *The West on Trial: My Fight for Guyana's Freedom* (1967).

JAMES, ADEOLA. *In Their Own Voices: African Women Writers Talk* (1990).

JAMES, C.L.R. *The Black Jacobins: Toussaint L' Ouverture and the San Domingo Revolution* (1963).

——. *A History of Pan-African Revolt* (1969).

JAMES, M. *Ten Modern Jazzmen: An Appraisal of the Recorded Work of Ten Modern Jazzmen* (1960).

"J. A. Rogers: Portrait of an Afro-American Historian." *Black Scholar* 6, no. 5 (January-February 1975): 32–39.

JASEN, DAVID A., AND TREBOR TICHENOR. *Rags and Ragtime: A Musical History* (1989).

JEFFREY, HENRY B., AND COLIN BABER. *Guyana: Politics, Economics, and Society: Beyond the Burnham Era* (1986).

JENKINS, MARK. *To Timbuktu* (1997).

JIMÉNEZ-ROMAN, MIRIAM. "Un hombre (negro) del pueblo: José Celso Barbosa and the Puerto Rican 'Race' towards Whiteness." *Centro de Estudios Puertorriqueños* (Spring 1996).

JIMENO, MYRIAM, AND MARÍA LUCIA SOTOMAYOR, LUZ MARÍA VALDERRAMA. *Chocó: Diversidad cultural y medio ambiente* (1995).

JOHNS, CHRIS. *Valley of Life: Africa's Great Rift* (1991).

JOHNSON, ABBY ARTHUR, AND RONALD MABERRY JOHNSON. "Charting a New Course: African American Literary Politics since 1976." In *The Black Columbiad: Defining Moments in African American Literature and Culture*, ed. Werner Sollors and Maria Diedrich (1994), pp. 369–81.

——. *Propaganda and Aesthetics: The Literary Politics of African-American Magazines in the Twentieth Century* (1991).

JOHNSON, CECIL, *Guts: Legendary Black Rodeo Cowboy Bill Pickett* (1994).

JOHNSON, DIANE. *Telling Tales: The Pedagogy and Promise of African American Literature for Youth* (1990).

JOHNSON, JOHN H., AND LERONE BENNETT, JR. *Succeeding Against the Odds* (1989).

JOHNSON, JAMES WELDON. *Black Manhattan* (1930).

——. Preface to *The Book of American Negro Poetry* (1922).

JOHNSON, RANDAL. *Cinema Novo x 5: Masters of Contemporary Brazilian Film* (1984).

JOHNSTON, J. H. "Luther Porter Jackson." *Journal of Negro History* (October 1950): 352–55.

JONAS, JOYCE. *Anancy in the Great House: Ways of Reading West Indian Fiction* (1991).

JONES, HOWARD. *Mutiny on the Amistad: The Saga of a Slave Revolt and its Impact on American Abolition, Law and Diplomacy* (1987).

———. "The Peculiar Institution and National Honor: The Case of the Creole Slave Revolt." *Civil War History* 21 (1975): 28–50.

JONES, JAMES H. *Bad Blood: The Tuskegee Syphilis Experiment* (1993).

JONES, JOYCE. "The Best Commerce Secretary Ever." *Black Enterprise* 26, no. 11 (1990).

JONES, RALPH H. *Charles Albert Tindley: Prince of Preachers* (1982).

JONES, TAD. "Professor Longhair." *Living Blues* 26 (March-April 1976): 16–29.

JORDAN, BARBARA, AND SHELBY HEARON. *Barbara Jordan: A Self-Portrait* (1979).

JOSEPH, CLIFTON. "Jump Up and Beg." *Toronto Life* (August 1996).

JOYCE, DONALD FRANKLIN. *Black Book Publishers in the United States: A Historical Dictionary of the Presses, 1817–1990* (1991).

———. *Gatekeepers of Black Culture: Black-Owned Book Publishing in the United States, 1817–1981* (1983).

JOYCE, PETER. *Anatomy of a Rebel: Smith of Rhodesia: A Biography* (1974).

JOYNER, CHARLES. *Down by the Riverside: A South Carolina Slave Community* (1989).

JULIEN, ISAAC. *Looking for Langston: A Meditation on Langston Hughes (1902–1967) and the Harlem Renaissance, with the Poetry of Essex Hemphill and Bruce Nugent (1906–1987)* (1992).

KAHAN, MITCHELL D. *Heavenly Visions: The Art of Minnie Evans* (1986).

KAPLAN, SIDNEY. "The Miscegenation Issue in the Election of 1864." In *American Studies in Black and White: Selected Essays, 1949–1989*, ed. Allan D. Austin (1991): 47–100.

KAPLAN, SIDNEY, AND EMMA NOGRADY KAPLAN. *The Black Presence in the Era of the American Revolution*. 2d ed. (1989).

KAPLAN, STEVEN. *The Beta Israel (Falasha) in Ethiopia: From Earliest Times to the Twentieth Century* (1992).

KARENGA, MAULANA. *The African American Holiday of Kwanzaa: A Celebration of Family, Community, and Culture* (1988).

———. *Introduction to Black Studies*. 2d ed. (1993).

KATZ, JONATHAN. *Resistance at Christiana: The Fugitive Slave Rebellion, Christiana, Pennsylvania, September 11, 1851: A Documentary Account* (1974).

KATZMAN, DAVID. *Before the Ghetto: Black Detroit in the Nineteenth Century* (1973).

KATZ, WILLIAM L. *Black People Who Made the Old West* (1992).

———. *The Black West* (1987).

KECKLEY, ELIZABETH. *Behind the Scenes; or, Thirty Years a Slave and Four Years in the White House* (1868).

KELLEY, ROBIN D. G. *Hammer and Hoe: Alabama Communists During the Great Depression* (1990).

KENNEDY, ADRIENNE. *People Who Led to My Plays* (1987).

KENNEDY, RANDALL. *Dred Scott and African American Citizenship* (1996).

——. *Race, Crime, and the Law* (1997).

KENNEY, WILLIAM HOWLAND. *Chicago Jazz: A Cultural History, 1904–1930* (1993).

——. "Jimmie Noone, Chicago's Classical Jazz Clarinetist." *American Music* 4 (1986): 145–58.

KENYATTA, JOMO. *Facing Mount Kenya: The Tribal Life of the Gikuyu* (1938).

KEPPEL, BEN. *The Work of Democracy: Ralph Bunche, Kenneth B. Clark, Lorraine Hansberry, and the Cultural Politics of Race* (1995).

KESSELMAN, LOUIS. *The Social Politics of FEPC: A Study in Reform Pressure Movements* (1948).

KESSLER, JAMES H. *Distinguished African American Scientists of the Twentieth Century* (1996).

KESTELOOT, LILYAN. *Black Writers in French: A Literary History of Negritude.* Translated by Ellen Conroy Kennedy (1991).

KEVLES, DANIEL. *In the Name of Eugenics: Genetics and the Uses of Human Heredity* (1985).

KHAZANOV, A. *Agostinho Neto* (1986).

KIM, AEHYUNG, AND BRUCE BENTON. *Cost-benefit Analysis of the Onchocerca Control Program (OCP)* (1995).

KINCAID, JAMAICA. *A Small Place* (1988).

KING, B. B., WITH DAVID RITZ. *Blues All Around Me: The Autobiography of B. B. King* (1996).

KING, BRUCE, ED. *West Indian Literature* (1979).

KING, CORETTA SCOTT. *My Life with Martin Luther King, Jr.* (1969).

KINGDON, ZACHARY, "Chanuo Maundu: Master of Makonde Blackwood Art." *African Arts* (Autumn 1996).

KIPLE, KENNETH F. *The Caribbean Slave: A Biological History* (1984).

KIRSH, ANDREA, AND SUSAN FISHER STERLING. *Carrie Mae Weems* (1992).

KIRWAN, ALBERT DENNIS. *John J. Crittenden: The Struggle for the Union* (1962).

KISKA, TIM. "CBS' Ed Bradley Recalls Childhood Days in Detroit." *Detroit News* (March 21, 1997) A, 2:2.

KITT, EARTHA. *Alone with Me* (1976).

——. *Thursday's Child* (1956).

KITWANA, BAKARI. *The Rap on Gangsta Rap: Who Run It? Gangsta Rap and Visions of Black Violence* (1994).

KLAPISCH, BOB. *High and Tight: The Rise and Fall of Dwight Gooden and Darryl Strawberry* (1996).

KLEHR, HARVEY. *The Heyday of American Communism: The Depression Decade* (1984).

KLEIN, HERBERT S. *African Slavery in Latin America and the Caribbean* (1986).

——. *The Middle Passage: Comparative Studies in the Atlantic Slave Trade* (1978).

——. *Slavery in the Americas: A Comparative Study of Virginia and Cuba* (1967).

KLEMENT, FRANK L. *The Copperheads of the Middle West* (1972).

KLEPPNER, PAUL. Chicago *Divided: The Making of a Black Mayor* (1985).

KLOTMAN, PHYLLIS RAUCH, ED. *Screenplays of the African American Experience* (1991).

KLOTS, STEVE. *Richard Allen* (1991).

KLUGER, RICHARD. *Simple Justice: The History of Brown v. Board of Education and Black America's Struggle for Equality* (1975).

KNAACK, TWILA. *Ethel Waters: I Touched a Sparrow* (1978).

KNIGHT, FRANKLIN. *The African Dimension in Latin American Societies* (1974).

——. *Slavery and the Transformation of Society in Cuba, 1511–1760: From Settler Society to Slave Society* (1988).

KNIGHT, GLADYS. *Between Each Line of Pain and Glory: My Life Story* (1997).

KOLCHIN, PETER. *American Slavery, 1619–1877* (1993).

KONCZACKI, Z. A. *The Economics of Pastoralism: A Case Study of Sub-Saharan Africa* (1978).

KOOK, HETTY, AND GORETTI NARAIN. "Papiamento." In *Community Languages in the Netherlands*, ed. Guus Extra and Ludo Verhoeven (1993): 69–91.

KORNWEIBEL, THEODORE, JR. *No Crystal Stair: Black Life and the Messenger, 1917–1928* (1975).

KOSTARAS, JAMES GEORGE. *Fez: Transformation of the Traditional Urban Environment* (1986).

KOSTARELOS, FRANCES. *Feeling the Spirit: Faith and Hope in an Evangelical Black Storefront Church* (1995).

KOTLOWITZ, ALEX. "A Bridge Too Far? Benjamin Chavis." *New York Times Magazine* (June 12, 1994).

KOTTAK, CONRAD P. *The Past and the Present: History, Ecology, and Cultural Variation in Highland Madagascar* (1980).

KOUSSER, J. MORGAN. *The Shaping of Southern Politics: Suffrage Restriction and the Establishment of the One-Party South, 1880–1910* (1974).

KRADITOR, AILEEN S. *Means and Ends in American Abolitionism: Garrison and his Critics on Strategy and Tactics, 1834–1850* (1989).

KREAMER, CHRISTINE M. *A Life Well Lived: Fantasy Coffins of Kane Quaye* (1994).

KREMER, GARY R., ED. *George Washington Carver in His Own Words* (1987).

KUREISHI, H. "Dirty Washing." *Time Out* (London) (November 14–20, 1985).

KUSMER, KENNETH. *A Ghetto Takes Shape: Black Cleveland, 1870–1930* (1976).

KUTZINKSI, VERA. *Sugar's Secrets: Race and the Erotics of Cuban Nationalism* (1993).

KWAMENAH-POH, M., J.TOSH, R. WALLER, AND M. TIDY, *African History in Maps* (1982).

LABELLE, MICHELINE. *Idéologie de couleur et classes sociales en Haïti.* 2d ed. (1987).

LABOV, WILLIAM. *Language in the Inner City: Studies in the Black English Vernacular* (1972).

LA GUERRE, JOHN GAFFAR. *Enemies of Empire* (1984).

LAMBERT, BRUCE. "Doxey Wilkerson is Dead at 88: Educator and Advocate for Rights." *New York Times* (June 18, 1993): D 16.

LANE, ANN J. *The Brownsville Affair: National Crisis and Black Reaction* (1971).

LANE, ROGER. *Roots of Violence in Black Philadelphia, 1860–1900* (1986).

LANNING, MICHAEL LEE, LT. COL. (RET.). *The African-American Soldier: From Crispus Attucks to Colin Powell* (1997).

LAPP, RUDOLPH M. *Blacks in Gold Rush California* (1977).

LAURINO, MARIA. "Sensitivity Comes From 'The Soles of the Feet.'" Interview with Anna Deveare Smith, *New York Newsday* (Feb. 23, 1994).

LAWLAH, JOHN W. "The President-Elect." *Journal of the National Medical Association* 55 (November 1963): 551–554.

LAWRENCE, ELIZABETH A. *Rodeo: An Anthropologist Looks at the Wild and the Tame* (1982).

LEAMAN, OLIVER. *Averroes and His Philosophy* (1988).

LEAVY, WALTER. "Howard University: A Unique Center of Excellence." *Ebony* (September 1985): 140–142.

——. "Is Tony Gwynn the Greatest Hitter in Baseball History?" *Ebony* (August 1997): 132.

LECKIE, WILLIAM. *The Buffalo Soldiers: A Narrative of the Negro Cavalry in the West* (1967).

LEEDS, ANTHONY, AND ELIZABETH LEEDS. *A Sociologia do Brasil Urbano (The Sociology of Urban Brazil)*. Translated by Maria Laura Viveiros de Castro (1977).

LEE, JARENA. *The Life and Religious Experience of Jarena Lee* (1849). Reprinted *in Sisters of the Spirit: Three Black Women's Autobiographies of the Nineteenth Century*. Edited by William L. Andrews (1986).

LEEMING, DAVID. *James Baldwin: A Biography* (1994).

LEES, GENE. *Oscar Peterson: The Will to Swing* (1988).

LEFEVER, ERNEST W. *Crisis in the Congo: A United Nations Force in Action* (1965).

LEGUM, COLIN, AND GEOFFREY MMARI. *Mwalimu: The Influence of Nyerere* (1995).

LEMANN, NICHOLAS. *The Promised Land: The Great Black Migration and How It Changed America* (1991).

LEMARCHAND, RENÈ. *Political Awakening in the Belgian Congo* (1964).

LEÓN, ARGELIERS. *Del canto y el tiempo* (1984).

LEON, ELI. *Who'd a Thought It: Improvisation in African-American Quiltmaking* (1987).

LEONS, WILLIAM, AND ALLYN MACLEON STEARMAN. *Anthropological Investigations in Bolivia* (1984).

LEREBOURS, MICHEL PHILIPPE. *Haïti et ses peintres*. 2 vols. (1989).

LERNER, GERDA, ED. *Black Women in White America: A Documentary History* (1972).

LERNER, MICHAEL, AND CORNEL WEST. *Jews and Blacks: Let the Healing Begin* (1995).

LESLAU, WOLF, TRANS. *Falasha Anthology* (1954).

LESLIE, WINESOME J. *Zaire: Continuity and Political Change in an Oppressive State* (1993).

LEVINE, DONALD N. *Greater Ethiopia: The Evolution of a Multi-Ethnic Society* (1974).

LEVINE, LAWRENCE W. *Black Culture and Black Consciousness* (1977).

LEVINE, ROBERT M., AND JOSÈ CARLOS SEBE BOM MEIHY. *The Life and Death of Carolina Maria de Jesus* (1995).

LEWIS, DAVID LEVERING. *W. E. B. Du Bois: Biography of a Race* (1993).

——. *When Harlem Was in Vogue* (1981).

LEWIS, GORDON K. *Main Currents in Caribbean Thought: The Historical Experience of Caribbean Society and its Ideological Aspects, 1492–1900* (1983).

LEWIS, LANCELOT S. *The West Indian in Panama: Black Labor in Panama, 1850–1914* (1980).

LEWIS, MARVÍN A. *Ethnicity and Identity in Contemporary Afro-Venezuelan Literature: A Culturalist Approach* (1992).

LEWIS, MARY L. "The White Rose Industrial Association: The Friend of the Strange Girl in New York." *Messenger* 7 (April 1925): 158.

LEWIS, SAMELLA. *African American Art and Artists* (1990).

——. *The Art of Elizabeth Catlett* (1984).

LEWIS, SAMELLA, AND RICHARD POWELL. *Elizabeth Catlett: Works on Paper, 1944–1992* (1993).

LHAYA, PEDRO. *Juan Pablo Sojo, pasión y acento de su tierra* (1968).

LIBBY, BILL. *Goliath: The Wilt Chamberlain Story* (1977).

LICHTENSTEIN, GRACE, AND LAURA DANKNER. *Musical Gumbo: The Music of New Orleans* (1993).

LIEBENOW, J. GUS. *Colonial Rule and Political Development in Tanzania: The Case of the Makonde* (1971).

LIEB, SANDRA. *Mother of the Blues: A Study of Ma Rainey* (1981).

LIGHT, ALAN. "Curtis Mayfield: An Interview." *Rolling Stone* (October 28, 1993).

LINARES, OLGA. *Power, Prayer, and Production: The Jola of Casamance, Senegal* (1992).

LINCOLN, C. ERIC, AND LAWRENCE MAMIYA. *The Black Church in the African American Experience* (1990).

LINSLEY, ROBERT. "Wifredo Lam: Painter of Negritude." *Art History* 2, no. 4 (1988): 527–544.

LIPSKI, JOHN M. *The Speech of the Negros Congos of Panama* (1989).

LIPZITZ, GEORGE. *A Life in the Struggle: Ivory Perry and the Culture of Opposition* (1988).

LITVIN, MARTIN. *Hiram Revels in Illinois: A Biographical Novel about a Lost Chapter in the Life of America's First Black U.S. Senator* (1974).

LITWACK, LEON F. *Been in the Storm So Long: The Aftermath of Slavery* (1979).

——. *Trouble in Mind: Black Southerners in the Age of Jim Crow* (1998).

LITWACK, LEON F., AND AUGUST MEIER, EDS. *Black Leaders of the Nineteenth Century* (1988).

LIVINGSTON, JANE, JOHN BEARDSLEY, AND REGINIA PERRY. *Black Folk Art in America, 1930–1980* (1982).

LLERENA VILLALOBOS, RITO. *Memoria cultural en el vallenato* (1985).

LLEWELYN-DAVIES, MELISSA. *Some Women of Marrakech*. Videotape, Granada Television (1981).

LOCKE, ALAIN. *The New Negro* (1925).

LOCKE, MARY. *Anti-Slavery in America from the Introduction of African slaves to the Prohibition of the Slave Trade (1619–1808)* (1901).

LOCKE, THERESA A. "Willa Brown-Chappell, Mother of Black Aviation." *Negro History Bulletin* 50 (January-June 1987): 5–6.

LOCKHART, JAMES. *Spanish Peru, 1532–1560: A Social History* (1994).

LODER, KURT. "Bo Diddley Interview." *Rolling Stone* (February 12, 1987).

LOFTON, JOHN. *Denmark Vesey's Revolt: The Slave Plot that Lit a Fuse to Fort Sumter* (1983).

LOGAN, RAYFORD. *Howard University: The First Hundred Years, 1867–1967* (1969).

LOGAN, RAYFORD, AND MICHAEL R. WINSTON. *Dictionary of American Negro Biography* (1982).

LOMAX, ALAN. *Mister Jelly Roll: The Fortunes of Jelly Roll Morton, New Orleans Creole and Inventor of Jazz* (1973).

——. *The Land Where the Blues Began* (1993).

LONG, RICHARD. *The Black Tradition in American Dance* (1989).

LOOS, DOROTHY SCOTT. *The Naturalistic Novel of Brazil* (1963).

LOPES, HELENA T. *Negro e cultura no Brasil* (1987).

LOPES, JOSÈ SERGIO LEITE. "Successes and Contradictions in 'Multiracial' Brazilian Football." In *Entering the Field: New Perspectives on World Football*, ed. Gary Armstrong and Richard Giulianotti (1997).

LOTZ, RAINER, AND IAN PEGG, EDS. *Under the Imperial Carpet: Essays in Black History, 1780–1950* (1990).

LOVE, NAT. *The Life and Adventures of Nat Love, Better Known in the Cattle Country as "Deadwood Dick"* (1907; reprint ed., 1995).

LOVE, SPENCIE. *One Blood: The Death and Resurrection of Charles Drew* (1996).

LOVETT, CHARLES C. *Olympic Marathon: A Centennial History of the Games' Most Storied Race* (1997).

LOZANO, WILFREDO, ED. *La cuestión haitiana en Santo Domingo* (1992).

LUIS, WILLIAM. *Literary Bondage : Slavery in Cuban Narrative* (1990).

——, ed. *Voices from Under: Black Narrative in Latin America and the Caribbean* (1984).

LUMDSEN, I. *Society and the State in Mexico* (1991).

LUNDY, ANNE. "Conversations with Three Symphonic Conductors: Dennis De Couteau, Tania Leon, Jon Robinson." *Black Perspective in Music*, no. 2 (Fall 1988): 213–25.

LYNCH, HOLLIS R. *Black American Radicals and the Liberation of Africa: The Council on African Affairs, 1937–1955* (1978).

LYNCH, JOHN ROY. *Reminiscences of an Active Life: The Autobiography of John Roy Lynch.* Edited by John Hope Franklin (1970).

LYONS, LEONARD. *The Great Jazz Pianists: Speaking of Their Lives and Music* (1983).

MACDONALD, J. FRED. *Blacks and White TV: African Americans in Television Since 1948.* Rev. ed. (1992).

MACEO, ANTONIO. *El pensamiento vivo de Maceo: Cartas, proclamas, articulos y documentas.* Edited by José Antonio Portuondo (1960).

MACGAFFEY, WYATT. *Religion and Society in Central Africa: The BaKongo of Lower Zaire* (1986).

MACHARIA, KINUTHIA. *Social and Political Dynamics of the Informal Economy in African Cities: Nairobi and Harare* (1997).

MACKEY, NATHANIEL, ED. "Wilson Harris Special Issue." *Callaloo* (1995).

MACROBERT, IAIN. *The Black Roots and White Racism of Early Pentecostalism in the U.S.A.* (1988).

MAES-JELINEK, HENA, ED. *Commonwealth Literature and the Modern World* (1975).

MAGALHÃES, R., JR. *A Vida Turbulenta de Josè do Patrocínio* (1972).

MAGUBANE, VUKANI. "Graca Machel." *Ebony* (May 1997).

MAIN, MICHAEL. *Kalahari: Life's Variety in Dune and Delta* (1987).

MAIO, MARCOS CHOR. *A História do Projeto UNESCO: Estudos raciais e ciÎncias sociais no Brasil* (1997).

MAIR, GEORGE. *Oprah Winfrey: The Real Story* (1994).

MAKEBA, MIRIAM, WITH JAMES HALL. *Makeba: My Story* (1988).

MALCOLM X, WITH ALEX HALEY. *The Autobiography of Malcolm X* (1964).

MALONE, JACQUI. *Steppin' on the Blues: The Visible Rhythms of African-American Dance* (1996).

MALTBY, MARC S. *The Origins and Early Development of Professional Football* (1997).

MANDELA, NELSON. *Long Walk to Freedom: The Autobiography of Nelson Mandela* (1994).

——. *The Struggle Is My Life: His Speeches and Writings Brought Together to Mark His 60th Birthday* (1978).

MANESS, LONNIE E. "The Fort Pillow Massacre: Fact or Fiction." *Tennessee Historical Quarterly* 48 (Winter 1986): 287–315.

MANGIONE, JERRE. *The Dream and the Deal: The Federal Writers' Project, 1935–1945* (1972).

MANLEY, ALBERT E. *A Legacy Continues: The Manley Years at Spelman College, 1953–1976* (1995).

MANNICK, A. R. *Mauritius: The Politics of Change* (1989).

MANUEL, PETER, ED. *Essays on Cuban Music: North American and Cuban Perspectives* (1991).

MANUEL, PETER, WITH KENNETH BILBY AND MICHAEL LARGEY. *Caribbean Currents: Caribbean Music from Rumba to Reggae* (1995).

MANUH, TAKYIWAA. "Diasporas, Unities, and the Marketplace: Tracing Changes in Ghanaian Fashion." *Journal of African Studies* 16, no.1 (Winter 1998).

MAPP, EDWARD. *Directory of Blacks in the Performing Arts* (1990).

MARCUS, HAROLD G. *A History of Ethiopia* (1994).

MARKMANN, CHARLES LAM. *The Noblest Cry: A History of the American Civil Liberties Union* (1965).

MARKOWITZ, GERALD E., AND DAVID ROSNER. *Children, Race, and Power: Kenneth and Mamie Clark's Northside Center* (1996).

MARQUIS, DONALD M. *In Search of Buddy Bolden: First Man of Jazz* (1978).

MARSHALL, RICHARD, ET. AL. *Jean-Michel Basquiat* (1992).

MARSH, J. B. T. *The Story of the Jubilee Singers with Their Songs* (1880; reprint ed., 1971).

MARTEENA, CONSTANCE HILL. *The Lengthening Shadow of a Woman: A Biography of Charlotte Hawkins Brown* (1977).

MARTÍ, JOSÈ. CUBA, *Nuestra Amèrica, los Estados Unidos* (1973).

——. *En los Estados Unidos* (1968).

MARTIN, ESMOND BRADLEY. *Zanzibar: Tradition and Revolution* (1978).

MARTIN, JAY, ED. *A Singer in the Dawn: Reinterpretations of Paul Laurence Dunbar* (1975).

MARTIN, MARIE-LOUISE. *Kimbangu: An African Prophet and His Church* (1975).

MARTIN, MICHAEL T., ED. *Cinemas of the Black Diaspora: Diversity, Dependence, and Oppositionality* (1995).

MARTIN, REGINALD. *Ishmael Reed and the New Black Aesthetic Critics* (1988).

——. "Total Life Is What We Want: The Progressive Stages of the New Black Aesthetic in Literature." *South Atlantic Review* (November 1986): 46–47.

MARTINS, LEDA MARIA. *A cena em sombras* (1995).

MARTIN, TONY. *Race First: The Ideological and Organizational Struggles of Marcus Garvey and the Universal Negro Improvement Association* (1986).

MASON, TONY. *Passion of the People? Football in South America* (1995).

MATORY, J. LORAND. *Sex and the Empire That Is No More: Gender and the Politics of Metaphor in Oyo Yoruba Religion* (1994).

MATTA, ROBERTO DA. CARNIVALS, *Rogues, and Heroes: An Interpretation of the Brazilian Dilemma*. Translated by John Drury (1991).

MATTHEWS, MARCIA M. *Henry Ossawa Tanner, American Artist* (1969).

MATTOSO, KATIA M. DE QUEIRÓS. *To Be a Slave in Brazil, 1550–1888*. Translated by Arthur Goldhammer (1994).

MAYNARD, OLGA. *Judith Jamison: Aspects of a Dancer* (1982).

MAZRUI, ALI A. *The Africans: A Triple Heritage* (1986).

MCADAM, DOUG. *Freedom Summer* (1988).

MCBROOME, DELORES NASON. *Parallel Communities: African Americans in California's East Bay, 1850–1963* (1993).

MCCABE, BRUCE. "Bringing the Streets to the Stage." *Boston Globe* (April 18, 1997): F 3.

McCORMICK, RICHARD P. "William Whipper: Moral Reformer." *Pennsylvania History* 43 (January 1976): 22–46.

McDONNELL, PATRICK, KAREN O'CONNELL, AND GEORGIA RILEY DE HAVENON. *Krazy Kat: The Comic Art of George Herriman* (1986).

McDOWELL, ROBERT. "The Assembling Vision of Rita Dove." *Callaloo* 9 (Winter 1986): 61–70.

McELVAINE, ROBERT S. *The Great Depression: America, 1929–1941* (1984).

McFEELY, WILLIAM S. *Frederick Douglass* (1991).

McGOWAN, CHRIS, AND RICARDO PESSANHA. *The Brazilian Sound: Samba, Bossa Nova, and the Popular Music of Brazil* (1991).

McKIBLE, ADAM. "'These Are the Facts of the Darky's History': Thinking History and Reading Names in Four African American Tests." *African American Review* 28 (1994): 223–35.

McKIVIGAN, JOHN R. *The War against Proslavery Religion: Abolitionism and the Northern Churches, 1830–1865* (1984).

McLARIN, KIMBERLY J. *Native Daughter* (1994).

McLENDON, JACQUELYN Y. *The Politics of Color in the Fiction of Jessie Fauset and Nella Larsen* (1995).

McMILLAN, DELLA E. *Sahel Visions: Planned Settlement and River Blindness Control in Burkina Faso* (1995).

McMURRY, LINDA O. *Recorder of the Black Experience: A Biography of Monroe Nathan Work* (1985).

McNEIL, GENNA RAE. *Groundwork: Charles Hamilton Houston and the Struggle for Civil Rights* (1983).

McPHERSON, JAMES M. *The Negro's Civil War: How American Negroes Felt and Acted During the War for the Union* (1965).

MEIER, AUGUST. "Introduction: Benjamin Quarles and the Historiography of Black America." In *Benjamin Quarles, Black Mosaic: Essays in Afro-American History and Historiography* (1989): 3–21.

——. *Negro Thought in America,1880–1915: Racial Ideologies in the Age of Booker T. Washington* (1963).

MEIER, AUGUST, AND JOHN H. BRACEY, JR. "The NAACP as a Reform Movement: 1909–1965." *Journal of Southern History* 49, no. 1 (February 1993).

MEIER, AUGUST, AND ELLIOTT RUDWICK. *Black History and the Historical Profession* (1986).

——. *CORE: A Study in the Civil Rights Movement, 1942–1968* (1973).

MELHEM, D.H. "Dudley Randall: A Humanist View." *Black American Literature Forum* 17 (1983).

MELLAFE R., ROLANDO. *La introducción de la esclavitud negra en Chile: Tráfico y rutas* (1984).

MENTON, SEYMOUR. *Prose Fiction of the Cuban Revolution* (1975).

MERCER, K. "Imagining the Black Man's Sex." In *Photography/Politics: Two*, ed. P. Holland et. al. (1987).

MÉRIAN, JEAN-YVES. *Aluísio Azevedo, Vida e Obra (1857–1913): O Verdadeiro Brasil do Século XIX* (1988).

METCALF, GEORGE R. *Black Profiles* (1968).

MÉTRAUX, ALFRED. "UNESCO and the Racial Problem." *International Social Science Bulletin* 2, no. 3 (1950): 384–90.

——. *Voodoo in Haiti* (1959).

MIDDLETON, JOHN, ED. *Encyclopedia of Africa South of the Sahara.* 4 vols. (1997).

MILES, ALEXANDER. *Devil's Island: Colony of the Damned* (1988).

MILLER, ERROL. *Education for all: Caribbean Perspectives and Imperatives* (1992).

MILLER, FLOYD J. *The Search for a Black Nationality: Black Colonization and Emigration, 1787–1863* (1975).

MILLER, RANDALL M., AND JOHN DAVID SMITH, EDS. *Dictionary of Afro-American Slavery.* 2d ed. (1997).

MILLS, KAY. "Maxine Waters: 'I Don't Pretend to Be Nice No Matter What . . . '." *The Progressive* (December 1993).

MINER, HORACE. *The Primitive City of Timbuctoo* (1954).

MINNICK-TAYLOR, KATHLEEN, AND CHARLES TAYLOR II. *Kwanzaa: How to Celebrate It in Your Own Home* (1994).

MINORITY RIGHTS GROUP, ED. *No Longer Invisible: Afro-Latin Americans Today* (1995).

MINTER, WILLIAM. *Apartheid's Contras: An Inquiry into the Roots of War in Angola and Mozambique* (1994).

MINTZ, SIDNEY. *Sweetness and Power* (1985).

MINTZ, SIDNEY, AND SALLY PRICE, EDS. *Caribbean Contours* (1985).

MIMANYARA, ALFRED M. *The Restatement of Bantu Origin and Meru History* (1992).

MOBERG, MARK. *Myths of Ethnicity and Nation: Immigration, Work, and Identity in the Belize Banana Industry* (1997).

Models in the Mind: African Prototypes in American Patchwork (1992).

MOISE, CLAUDE. *Constitutions et luttes de pouvoir en Haiti (1804–1987)* (1988–1990).

MOISÉS, MASSAUD. *História da literatura Brasileira. Vol. II* (1989).

MOON, ELAINE LATZMAN, ED. *Untold Tales, Unsung Heroes: An Oral History of Detroit's African American Community, 1918–1967* (1994).

MOOREHEAD, ALAN. *The White Nile* (1971).

MOORE, JESSE THOMAS. *A Search for Equality: The National Urban League, 1910–1961* (1981).

MOORE, JOSEPH THOMAS. *Pride Against Prejudice: The Biography of Larry Doby* (1988).

MOORE, ROBIN. *Nationalizing Blackness: Afrocubanismo and Artistic Revolution in Havana, 1920–40* (1997).

MOORE, ZELBERT L. "Solano Trindade Remembered, 1908–1974." *Luso-Brazilian Review* 16 (1979): 233–38.

MORALES, FLORENTINO. "El poeta esclavo." *Conceptos* 2, no. 27 (December 1989): 2–3.

MORAN, CHARLES. *Black Triumvirate: A Study of L'Ouverture, Dessalines, Christophe: The Men Who Made Haiti* (1957).

MORDECAI, PAMELA, AND BETTY WILSON, EDS. *Her True-True Name* (1989).

MORELL, VIRGINIA. *Ancestral Passions: The Leakey Family and the Quest for Humankind's Beginnings* (1995).

MORENO NAVARRO, ISIDORO. *Los cuadros del mestizaje americano: Estudio antropológico del mestizaje* (1973).

MORGAN, PHILIP D. *Slave Counterpoint: Black Culture in the Eighteenth-Century Chesapeake and Lowcountry* (1998).

MORGAN, THOMAS L., AND WILLIAM BARLOW. *From Cakewalks to Concert Halls: An Illustrated History of African American Popular Music from 1895–1930* (1992).

MORNA, COLLEEN. "Graca Machel: Interview." *Africa Report* (July-August 1988).

MORRIS, MERVYN. "Louise Bennett." In *Encyclopedia of Post-Colonial Literatures in English*. Vol. I, ed. Eugene Benson and L. W. Conolly (1994).

MORRIS, THOMAS D. *Free Men All: The Personal Liberty Laws of the North, 1780–1861* (1974).

MORRISON, TONI. *Playing in the Dark: Whiteness and the Literary Imagination* (1992).

———, ed. *Race-ing Justice, En-gendering Power: Essays on Anita Hill, Clarence Thomas, and the Construction of Social Reality* (1992).

MORROW, CURTIS. *What's A Commie Ever Done to Black People?: A Korean War Memoir of Fighting in the U.S. Army's Last All Negro Unit* (1997).

MORSE, STEPHEN S. *Emerging Viruses* (1993).

MORSHA, A. C. "Urban Planning in Tanzania at the Crossroads." *Review of Rural and Urban Planning in Southern and Eastern Africa* (1989): 79–91.

MOSBY, DEWEY F., DARRELL SEWELL, AND RAE ALEXANDER-MINTER. *Henry Ossawa Tanner* (1991).

MOSELEY, THOMAS ROBERT. "A History of the New York Manumission Society." Ph.D. Diss. University of Michigan, 1963.

MOSES, WILSON JEREMIAH. *Black Messiahs and Uncle Toms: Social and Literary Manipulation of a Religious Myth* (1982).

———. *The Golden Age of Black Nationalism: 1850–1925* (1978).

MOSQUERA, GERARDO. "Modernism from Afro-America: Wifredo Lam." *In Beyond the Fantastic: Contemporary Art Criticism from Latin America*, ed. Gerardo Mosquera (1996).

MOSS, ALFRED A., JR. *The American Negro Academy: Voice of the Talented Tenth* (1981).

MOTA, ANA MARITZA DE LA. "Palma Sola: 1962," *Boletín: Museo de hombre dominicano* 14 (1980): 197–223.

MOTT, LUIZ. ESCRAVID„O, *Homossexualidade e Demonologia* (1988).

MOUNTOUSSAMY-ASHE, JEANNE. *View-finders: Black Women Photographers* (1986).

MUDIMBE-BOYI, ELISABETH. *L'oeuvre romanesque de Jacques-Stèphen Alexis : Une ècriture poètique, un engagement politique* (1992).

MUDIMBE, VALENTIN. *The Invention of Africa: Gnosis, Philosophy, and the Order of Knowledge* (1988).

MUNFORD, CLARENCE. *Race and Reparations: A Black Perspective for the Twenty-First Century* (1996).

MUNRO-HAY, STUART. *Aksum: An African Civilization of Late Antiquity* (1991).

MUNRO-HAY, STUART, AND RICHARD PANKHURST. *Ethiopia* (1995).

MUNSLOW, BARRY, ED. *Samora Machel, An African Revolutionary: Selected Speeches and Writings* (1985).

MURPHY, JOSEPH M. *Working the Spirit: Ceremonies of the African Diaspora* (1994).

MURRAY, PAULI. *Dark Testament and Other Poems* (1970).

——. *Proud Shoes: The Story of an American Family* (1956).

——. *Song in a Weary Throat: An American Pilgrimage* (1987).

MUSICK, PHIL. *Reflections on Roberto* (1994).

MYRDAL, GUNNAR. *An American Dilemma: The Negro Problem and Modern Democracy* (1944).

NADEL, ALAN, ED. *May All of Your Fences Have Gates: Essays on the Drama of August Wilson* (1994).

NAISON, MARK. *Communists in Harlem During the Depression* (1983).

NALTY, BERNARD C. *Strength for the Fight: A History of Black Americans in the Military* (1986).

NASCIMENTO, ABDIAS DO. *Africans in Brazil: A Pan-African Perspective* (1992).

——. *Dramas para negros e prologo para brancos: Antologia de teatro negro-brasileiro.* (1961).

——. *Orixas: Os deuses vivos da Africa* (1995).

——. *O quilombismo: Documentos de uma militancia pan-africanista* (1980).

——. *Racial Democracy in Brazil, Myth or Reality?: A Dossier of Brazilian Racism.* Translated by Elisa Larkin do Nascimento; foreword by Wole Soyinka (1977).

——, ed. *O Negro revoltado* (1968).

NASH, GARY B. *Forging Freedom: The Formation of Philadelphia's Black Community, 1720–1840* (1988).

——. *Race and Revolution* (1990).

NAVARRETE, MARÍA CRISTINA. *Historia social del negro en la colonia: Cartagena, siglo XVII* (1995).

NAVARRO, DESIDERIO. *Ejercicios del criterio* (1988).

NEFT, DAVID S. *The Football Encyclopedia: The Complete History of Professional NFL Football, from 1892 to the Present* (1991).

NEWBY, I. A. *Black Carolinians: A History of Blacks in South Carolina from 1895 to 1968* (1973).

NEWFIELD, JACK. *Only in America: The Life and Crimes of Don King* (1995).

NEWMAN, RICHARD. *Words Like Freedom: Essays on African-American Culture and History* (1996).

——. *Lemuel Haynes: A Bio-bibliography* (1984).

——, comp. *Black Access: A Bibliography of Afro-American Bibliographies* (1984).

NEWTON, HUEY P. *To Die for the People: The Writings of Huey Newton* (1972).

——. *War Against the Panthers: A Study of Repression in America* (1997).

"New Voice of the NAACP." Interview in *Newsweek* 46 (November 22, 1976).

NGUGI WA THIONG'O. *Decolonising the Mind: The Politics of Language in African Literature* (1986).

——. *Moving the Centre: The Struggle for Cultural Freedoms* (1993).

NICOLAS, ARMAND. *Histoire de la Martinique*. 2 vols. (1996).

——. *La rèvolution antiesclavagiste de mai 1848 à la Martinique* (1967).

NINA RODRIGUES, RAIMUNDO. *Os Africanos no Brasil* (1977).

NKOMO, JOSHUA. *Nkomo: The Story of My Life* (1984).

——. *Zimbabwe Must and Shall be Totally Free* (1977).

NOBLE, PETER. *The Negro in Films* (1948).

NOBRE, CARLOS. *Mães de Acari: Uma história de luta contra a impunidade* (1994).

NOONAN, JOHN T. *The Antelope: The Ordeal of the Recaptured Africans in the Administrations of James Monroe and John Quincy Adams* (1977).

NORMENT, LYNN. "Vanessa L. Williams: On her Painful Divorce, the Pressures of Superstardom and her New Life as a Single Mom." *Ebony* (October 1997).

NORRIS, H. T. *The Berbers in Arabic Literature* (1982).

NORRIS, JERRIE. *Presenting Rosa Guy* (1988).

NORTHRUP, SOLOMON. *Twelve Years a Slave: Narrative of Solomon Northrup, a Citizen of New York, Kidnapped in Washington City in 1841, and Rescued in 1853, from a Cotton Plantation near the Red River, in Louisiana* (1853).

NOTCUTT, LESLIE A., AND GEORGE C. LANTHAM. *The African and the Cinema: An Account of the Bantu Educational Cinema Experiment During the Period March 1935 to May 1937* (1937).

NOTTEN, ELEONORE VAN. *Wallace Thurman's Harlem Renaissance* (1994).

NUGENT, JOHN PEER. *Black Eagle* (1971).

NUNN, JOHN F. *Ancient Egyptian Medicine* (1996).

NYERERE, JULIUS K. *The Arusha Declaration: Ten Years After* (1977).

——. *Freedom and Socialism: Uhuru na Ujamaa: A Selection from Writings and Speeches, 1965–1967* (1968).

——. *Ujamaa: Essays on Socialism* (1971).

OATES, STEPHEN B. *The Fires of Jubilee: Nat Turner's Fierce Rebellion* (1975).

——. *To Purge This Land with Blood: A Biography of John Brown*. 2d ed. (1984).

OBADELE, IMARI. *America the Nation State: The Politics of the United States from a State-Building Perspective* (1988).

OCHS, STEPHEN J. *Desegregating the Altar: The Josephites and the Struggle for Black Priests, 1871–1960* (1970).

OFCANSKY, THOMAS, AND RODGER YEAGER. *Historical Dictionary of Tanzania* (1997).

OGOT, BETHWELL A. *Africa and the Caribbean* (1997).

OÍLIAM, JOSÉ. *O Negro na Economia Mineira* (1993).

OLANIYAN, TEJUMOLA. *Scars of Conquest/Masks of Resistance: The Invention of Cultural Identities in African, African-American, and Caribbean Drama* (1995).

OLIVER, PAUL. *Songsters and Saints: Vocal Traditions on Race Records* (1984).

——, ed. *Black Music in Britain: Essays on the Afro-Asian Contribution to Popular Music* (1990).

OLSON, JAMES STUART. *The Peoples of Africa: An Ethnohistorical Dictionary* (1996).

OLSON, SHERRY. *Baltimore: The Building of an American City*. Rev. and exp. ed. (1997).

OLWIG, KAREN FOG. *Cultural Adaptation and Resistance on St. John: Three Centuries of Afro-Caribbean Life*.

O'MEALLY, ROBERT G. *The Craft of Ralph Ellison* (1980).

OODIAH, MALENN. *Mouvement militant mauritien: 20 ans d'histoire (1969–1989)* (1989).

O'REILLY, KENNETH. *Nixon's Piano: Presidents and Racial Politics from Washington to Clinton* (1995).

ORIARD, MICHAEL. *Reading Football: How the Popular Press Created an American Spectacle* (1993).

ORMOND, ROGER. *The Apartheid Handbook: A Guide to South Africa's Everyday Racial Policies* (1985).

OROVIO, HELIO. *Diccionario de la música cubana: Biográfico y técnico* (1992).

ORTIZ, FERNANDO. *Los bailes y le teatro de los negros en el folklore de cuba* (1951).

——. *Los instrumentos de la musica afrocubana*. 5 vols. (1952–1955).

——. *La música afrocubana* (1974).

——. *Los negros brujos* (1995).

——. *Wifredo Lam y su obra vista a traves de significados criticos* (1950).

ORTIZ, RENATO, "OGUM AND THE UMBANDISTA RELIGION." *In Africa's Ogun: Old World and New*, ed. Santra Barnes (1989): 90–102.

OSOFSKY, GILBERT. *Harlem: The Making of a Ghetto: Negro New York, 1890–1930* (1971; revised ed., 1996).

OSPINA, HERNANDO CALVO. *Salsa: Havana Beat, Bronx Beat* (1985).

OSSMAN, SUSAN. *Picturing Casablanca: Portraits of Power in a Modern City* (1994).

OTHAM, HAROUB. *Zanzibar's Political History: The Past Haunting the Present?* (1993).

OTIS, JOHNNY. *Upside Your Head!: Rhythm and Blues on Central Avenue* (1993).

OTTLEY, ROI. *The Lonely Warrior: The Life and Time of Robert S. Abbott* (1955).

OTTLEY, ROI AND WILLIAM WEATHERBY, EDS. *The Negro in New York: An Informal Social History* (1967).

OWENS, THOMAS. *Bebop: The Music and its Players* (1995).

PACINI HERN·NDEZ, DEBORAH. "The Picó Phenomenon in Cartagena, Colombia." *Amèrica Negra* 6 (December 1993): 69–115.

PAINTER, NELL IRVIN. *Exodusters: Black Migration to Kansas after Reconstruction* (1986).

——. "Martin R. Delany: Elitism and Black Nationalism." *In Black Leaders of the Nineteenth Century*, ed. Leon Litwack and August Meier (1988): 148–171.

——. *Sojourner Truth: A Life, A Symbol* (1996).

PAIVA, EDUARDO FRANCA. *Escravos e libertos nas Minas Gerais do século XVIII: Estratégias de resistência através dos testamentos* (1995).

PALMER, COLIN. *Slaves of the White God: Blacks in Mexico, 1570–1650* (1976).

PALMER, RICHARD. *Oscar Peterson* (1984).

PALMER, ROBERT. *Deep Blues* (1981).

PAQUET, SANDRA POUCHET. *The Novels of George Lamming* (1982).

PARIS, PETER. *Black Religious Leaders: Conflict in Unity* (1991).

PARK, THOMAS K. *Historical Dictionary of Morocco* (1996).

PATTERSON, JAMES T. *America's Struggle Against Poverty, 1900–1994* (1994).

PATTERSON, ORLANDO. *Freedom in the Making of Western Culture* (1991).

——. *The Ordeal of Integration: Progress and Resentment in America's "Racial" Crisis* (1997).

——. *Rituals of Blood: Consequences of Slavery in Two American Centuries* (1998).

PATTERSON, WILLIAM. *The Man Who Cried Genocide: An Autobiography* (1971).

PAUL, JOAN, RICHARD V. MCGHEE, AND HELEN FANT. "The Arrival and Ascendance of Black Athletes in the Southeastern Conference, 1966–1980." *Phylon* 45, no. 4 (1984): 284–97.

PAYNE, DANIEL A. *History of the African Methodist Episcopal Church*. Vol. I (1891; reprint ed., 1968).

PEASE, JANE H., AND WILLIAM H. PEASE. *They Who Would Be Free: Blacks' Search for Freedom, 1830–1861* (1974).

PENKOWER, MONTY NOAM. *The Federal Writers' Project: A Study in Government Patronage of the Arts* (1983).

PENVENNE, JEANNE. *African Workers and Colonial Racism: Mozambican Struggles in Lourenáo Marques, 1877–1962* (1997).

PÉREZ SANJURJO, Elena. *Historia de la m'sica cubana* (1986).

PERKINS, KENNETH J. *Historical Dictionary of Tunisia* (1997).

PERKINS, LINDA M. *Fanny Jackson Coppin and the Institute for Colored Youth: A Model of Nineteenth-Century Black Female Educational and Community Leadership, 1865–1902* (1978).

PERLMAN, JANICE. *The Myth of Marginality: Urban Poverty and Politics in Rio de Janeiro* (1973).

PERN, STEPHEN. *Another Land, Another Sea: Walking Round Lake Rudolph* (1979).

PERRY, BRUCE. *Malcolm: The Life of a Man Who Changed Black America* (1991).

PERRY, REGINA A. *Free Within Ourselves: African-American Artists in the Collection of the National Museum of American Art* (1992).

PETERSON, CARLA. *Doers of the Word: African-American Women Speakers and Writers in the North (1830–1880)* (1995).

PETERSON, KIRSTEN HOLST, AND ANNA RUTHERFORD. *Chinua Achebe: A Celebration* (1991).

PETERSON, ROBERT. *Only the Ball Was White: A History of Legendary Black Players and All-black Professional Teams* (1992).

PETERS, WALLACE, AND HERBERT M. GILLES. *Color Atlas of Tropical Medicine and Parasitology* (1995).

PFAFF, FRANÇOISE. *Conversations with Maryse Condè* (1996).

PHELPS, J. ALFRED. *Chappie: America's First Black Four-Star General: The Life and Times of Daniel James, Jr.* (1991).

PHELPS, TIMOTHY M., AND HELEN WINTERNITZ. *Capitol Games: The Inside Story of Clarence Thomas and Anita Hill, and a Supreme Court Nomination* (1993).

PHILLIPS, CHRISTOPHER. *Freedom's Port: The African American Community of Baltimore, 1790–1860* (1997).

PICTON, JOHN, AND JOHN MACK. *African Textiles* (1989).

PIMPÃO, ÁLVARO JÚLIO DA COSTA. "José Basilio da Gama. Edição Comemorativa do Segundo Centenário." *Brasília* 2 (1942): 777–80.

PINO, JULIO CESAR. *Family and Favela: The Reproduction of Poverty in Rio de Janeiro* (1997).

PINTO, LUIZ DE AGUIAR COSTA. *O Negro no Rio de Janeiro: Relações de raças numa sociedade em mudança* (1953).

PIVEN, FRANCES FOX, AND RICHARD A. CLOWARD. *Poor People's Movements: Why They Succeed, How They Fail* (1977).

PLACKSIN, SALLY. *American Women in Jazz: 1900 to the Present: Their Words, Lives, and Music* (1982).

PLACOLY, VINCENT. *Dessalines, ou, la passion de l'indépendance* (1983).

PLASTOW, JANE. *Ethiopia: The Creation of a Theater Culture* (1989).

PLATO, ANN. *Essays: Including Biographies and Miscellaneous Pieces, in Prose and Poetry* (1841).

PLATT, ANTHONY M. *E. Franklin Frazier Reconsidered* (1991).

PLOWDEN, MARTHA WARD. *Olympic Black Women* (1996).

PLUCHON, PIERRE, AND LOUIS ABENON, EDS. *Histoire des Antilles et de la Guyane* (1982).

POITIER, SIDNEY. *This Life* (1980).

POLAKOFF, CLAIRE. INTO *Indigo: African Textiles and Dyeing Techniques* (1980).

POLLAK-ELTZ, ANGELINA. *Black Culture and Society in Venezuela (La Negritud en Venezuela)* (1994).

——. *La medicina popular en Venezuela* (1987).

——. *La religiosidad popular en Venezuela* (1994).

PORTER, DAVID L., ED. *Biographical Dictionary of American Sports: Basketball and Other Indoor Sports* (1989).

PORTER, DOROTHY B. "Maria Baldwin." *Journal of Negro History* (Winter 1952): 94–96.

PORTER, JAMES AMOS. *Modern Negro Art* (1943).

POSADA, CONSUELO. *Canción vallenata y tradición oral* (1986).

POTASH, CHRIS, ED. *Reggae, Rasta, Revolution: Jamaican Music from Ska to Dub* (1997).

POTTER, DAVID M. *The Impending Crisis, 1848–1861* (1976).

POUPEYE, VEERLE. *Modern Jamaican Art* (1998).

POVOAS, RUY DO CARMO. *A linguagem do candomble: Niveis sociolinguisticos de integração afro-portuguesa* (1989).

POWELL, COLIN L. *My American Journey* (1995).

POWELL, IVOR. *Ndebele: A People and Their Art* (1995).

POWELL, RICHARD J. *Black Art and Culture in the Twentieth Century* (1997).

———. *Homecoming: The Art and Life of William H. Johnson* (1991).

POWLEDGE, FRED. *Free at Last? The Civil Rights Movement and the People Who Made It* (1991).

PRANDI, J. REGINALDO. *Herdeiras do axé: Sociologia das religiões afro-brasileiras* (1996).

PRATHER, H. LEON. *We Have Taken A City: Wilmington Racial Massacre and Coup of 1898* (1984).

PRESCOTT, LAURENCE E. *Candelario Obeso y la iniciación de la poesía negra en Colombia* (1985).

PRICE, JOE X. *Redd Foxx, B.S. (Before Sanford)* (1979).

PRICE-MARS, JEAN. *La Rep'blica de Haiti y la Rep'blica Dominicana* (1958).

PRICE, RICHARD, ED. *Maroon Societies: Rebel Slave Communities in the Americas.* 3d ed. (1996).

PRICE, SALLY, AND RICHARD PRICE. *Maroon Arts: Cultural Vitality in the African Diaspora* (1999).

PRIDE, CHARLEY. *Pride: The Charley Pride Story* (1994).

PRIMM, JAMES NEAL. *Lion of the Valley, St. Louis, Missouri* (1981).

PRUTER, ROBERT. *Doowop: The Chicago Scene* (1996).

PRYSE, MARJORIE. "'Patterns Against the Sky': Deism and the Motherhood in Ann Petry's The Street." In *Conjuring: Black Women, Fiction and Literary Traditions,* ed. Marjorie Pryse and Hortense Spillers (1985).

QUARLES, BENJAMIN. *Black Abolitionists* (1969).

———. *The Negro in the American Revolution* (1961).

———. *The Negro in the Civil War* (1953).

QUERINO, MANUEL. *The African Contribution to Brazilian Civilization.* Translated by E. Bradford Burns (1978).

———. *A Bahia de Outoura* (1955).

———. *Costumes africanos no Brasil* (1938).

———. *A raça africana e os seus costumes* (1955).

QUILLEN, FRANK U. *The Color Line in Ohio* (1913).

QUILOMBHOJE. *Criação crioula, nu elefante branco* (1987).

QUINN, CHARLOTTE. *Mandingo Kingdoms of the Senegambia: Traditionalism, Islam, and European Expansion* (1972).

QUIROZ OTERO, CIRO. *Vallenato: Hombre y canto* (1982).

RABINOWITZ, HOWARD N. *Race Relations in the Urban South, 1865–1890* (1996).

RAGAN, SANDRA L. ET AL, ED. *The Lynching of Language: Gender, Politics, and Power in the Hill-Thomas Hearings* (1996).

RAHIER, JEAN. *La décima: Poesía oral negra del Ecuador* (1987).

RAINWATER, LEE. *Behind Ghetto Walls: Black Families in a Federal Slum* (1970).

RAJOELINA, PATRICK. *Quarante années de la vie politique de Madagascar, 1947–1987* (1988).

RAKE, ALAN. *Who's Who in Africa: Leaders for the 1990s* (1992).

RAKODI, CAROLE. *Harare: Inheriting a Settler-Colonial City: Change or Continuity* (1995).

RAMOS, ARTHUR. *The Negro in Brazil* (1951).

RAMOS GUEDEZ, JOSÉ MARCIAL. *El negro en Venezuela: Aporte bibliografico* (1985).

RAMPERSAD, ARNOLD. *The Art and Imagination of W. E. B. Du Bois* (1990).

——. *Jackie Robinson: A Biography* (1997).

——. *The Life of Langston Hughes.* 2 vols. (1986–1988).

RANVAUD, DON. "Interview with Med Hondo." *Framework* (Spring 1978): 28–30.

Rap on Rap: Straight Up Talk on Hip Hop Culture. Compiled by Adam Sexton (1995).

RASKY, FRANK. "Harlem's Religious Zealots." *Tomorrow* (Nov. 1949): 11–17.

RAPER, ARTHUR F. *The Tragedy of Lynching* (1933).

RAWLEY, JAMES A. *The Transatlantic Slave Trade: A History* (1981).

RAY, BENJAMIN. *African Religions: Symbol, Ritual, and Community* (1976).

READER, JOHN. *Africa: A Biography of the Continent* (1998).

READ, FLORENCE. *The Story of Spelman College* (1961).

REDD, LAWRENCE N. *Rock Is Rhythm and Blues: The Impact of Mass Media* (1974).

REDKEY, EDWIN S. *Black Exodus: Black Nationalist and Back-to-Africa Movements, 1890–1910* (1969).

REDMON, COATES. *Come As You Are: The Peace Corps Story* (1986).

REGO, WALDELOIR. *Capoeira Angola: Ensaio socio-etnografico* (1968).

REID, CALVIN. "Caught in the Flux." *Transition* (Spring 1995).

REID, IRA DE AUGUSTINE. *The Negro Immigrant: His Background, Characteristics, and Social Adjustment, 1899–1937* (1939).

REIS, JOÃO JOSÉ. *Slave Rebellion in Brazil: The Muslim Uprising of 1835 in Bahia.* Translated by Arthur Brakel (1993).

"Religious Symbolism in African-American Quilts." *Clarion* 14, no. 3, (Summer 1989): 36–43.

Report of the National Advisory Commission on Civil Disorders (1968).

RENDER, SYLVIA LYONS. *Charles W. Chesnutt* (1980).

RESWICK, IRMTRAUD. *Traditional Textiles of Tunisia and Related North African Weavings* (1985).

REYNOLDS, MOIRA DAVIDSON. *"Uncle Tom's Cabin" and Mid-Nineteenth Century United States: Pen and Conscience* (1985).

RIBEIRO, RENÉ. *Religião e relações raciais* (1956).

RIBOWSKY, MARK. *Don't Look Back: Satchel Paige and the Shadows of Baseball* (1994).

RICHARDS, LEONARD L. *Gentleman of Property and Standing: Anti-Abolition Mobs in Jacksonian America* (1970).

RICHARDSON, JOE M. *A History of Fisk University, 1865–1946* (1980).

RICHARDSON, MICHAEL, ED. *Refusal of the Shadow: Surrealism and the Caribbean.* Translated by Krzysztof Fijalkowski and Michael Richardson (1996).

RICHMOND, MERLE. *Bid the Vassal Soar: Interpretative Essays on the Life and Poetry of Phillis Wheatley* (ca. 1753–1784) and George Moses Horton (ca. 1797–1883) (1974).

RICH, WILBUR C. *Black Mayors and School Politics: The Failure of Reform in Detroit, Gary, and Newark* (1996).

——. *The New Black Power* (1987).

RILEY, JAMES A. *The Biographical Encyclopedia of the Negro Baseball Leagues* (1994).

——. *Dandy, Day and the Devil* (1987).

RINGGOLD, FAITH. *We Flew Over the Bridge: The Memoirs of Faith Ringgold* (1995).

RISHELL, LYLE. *With A Black Platoon in Combat: A Year in Korea* (1993).

RITCHIE, CARSON. *Rock Art of Africa* (1979).

RITZ, DAVID. *Divided Soul: The Life of Marvin Gaye* (1985).

RIVLIN, BENJAMIN, ED. *Ralph Bunche: The Man and His Times* (1990).

RIVLIN, GARY. *Fire on the Prairie: Chicago's Harold Washington and the Politics of Race* (1993).

ROBERTS, JOHN STORM. *The Latin Tinge: The Impact of Latin American Music on the United States* (1979).

ROBERTS, A. D. "Tippu Tip, Livingstone, and the Chronology of Kazembe." *Azamoa* 2 (1967).

ROBERTS, ANDREW. *A History of Zambia* (1976).

ROBERTS, A. "Nyamwezi Trade." In *Pre-colonial African Trade*, ed. R. Gray and D. Birmingham (1970).

ROBERTS, MARTIN. "'World Music' and the Global Cultural Economy." *Diaspora* 2, no. 2 (1992): 229–41.

ROBERTS, RANDY. *Papa Jack: Jack Johnson and the Era of White Hopes* (1983).

ROBESON, PAUL. *Here I Stand* (1958).

ROBESON, SUSAN. *The Whole World in His Hands: A Pictorial Biography of Paul Robeson* (1981).

ROBINSON, DONALD. *Slavery in the Structure of American Politics, 1765–1820* (1971).

ROBINSON, JACKIE, WITH ALFRED DUCKETT. *I Never Had It Made* (1972).

ROBINSON, JO ANN GIBSON. *The Montgomery Bus Boycott and the Women Who Started It: The Memoir of Jo Ann Robinson* (1987).

ROBINSON, JONTYLE THERESA, AND WENDY GREENHOUSE. *The Art of Archibald J. Motley, Jr.* (1991).

ROBINSON, RAY, AND DAVE ANDERSON. *Sugar Ray* (1969).

ROBINSON, WILLIAM H. *Phillis Wheatley and her Writings* (1984).

RODMAN, SELDEN. *Renaissance in Haiti: Popular Painters in the Black Republic* (1948).

———. *Where Art is Joy: Haitian Art: The First Forty Years* (1988).

RODNEY, WALTER. *A History of the Guyanese Working People, 1881–1905.* (1981).

ROGERS, KIM LACY. *Righteous Lives: Narratives of the New Orleans Civil Rights Movement* (1993).

ROLLIN, FRANK A. *Life and Public Services of Martin R. Delany, Sub-assistant Commissioner, Bureau Relief of Refugees, Freedmen, and of Abandoned Lands, and Late Major 104th U.S. Colored Troops* (1868).

ROLLOCK, BARBARA. *Black Authors and Illustrators of Children's Books* (1988).

ROMAINE, SUZANNE. *Bilingualism* (1989).

RONDÓN, CÉSAR MIGUEL. *El libro de la salsa: Cronica de la m´sica del Caribe urbano* (1980).

RO, RONIN. *Gangsta: Merchandizing the Rhymes of Violence* (1996).

ROSE, AL. *Eubie Blake* (1979).

ROSELLO, MIREILLE. *Littérature et identité créole aux Antilles* (1992).

ROSE, TRICIA. *Black Noise: Rap Music and Black Culture in Contemporary America* (1994).

ROSE, WILLIE LEE, ED. *A Documentary History of Slavery in North America* (1976).

ROSS, B. JOYCE. *J. E. Spingarn and the Rise of the NAACP, 1911–1939* (1972).

ROTH, DAVID. *Sacred Honor: A Biography of Colin Powell* (1993).

ROULHE, NELLIE C. *Work, Play, and Commitment: A History of the First Fifty Years, Jack and Jill of America, Incorporated* (1989).

ROUT, LESLIE B. *The African Experience in Spanish America, 1502 to the Present Day* (1976).

ROVINE, VICTORIA. "Bogolanfini in Bamako: The Biography of a Malian Textile." *African Arts* 30 (1997).

ROWELL, CHARLES H., AND BRUCE WILLIS. "Interview with Afro-Brazilian playwright and poet Luiz Silva Cuti." *Callaloo* 18, no. 4 (Fall 1996): 729–33.

RUEDA NOVOA, ROCÍO. *Zambaje y autonomía: La historia de Esmeraldas siglos XVI-XIX* (1990).

RUEDY, JOHN. *Modern Algeria: The Origins and Development of a Nation* (1992).

RUDWICK, ELLIOTT M. *Race Riot at East St. Louis, July 2, 1917* (1964).

RUFF, SHAWN STEWART. *Go the Way Your Blood Beats: An Anthology of Lesbian and Gay Fiction by African-American Writers* (1996).

RULE, SHEILA. "Fredi Washington, 90, Actress; Broke Ground for Black Artists." *New York Times* (June 30, 1994): D21.

RUSSELL, ROSS. *Bird Lives: The High Life and Hard Times of Charlie (Yardbird) Parker* (1973).

———. *Jazz Style in Kansas City and the Southwest* (1971).

RUSSELL-WOOD, A. J. R. *The Black Man in Slavery and Freedom in Colonial Brazil* (1982).

SACK, KEVIN. "A Dynamic Farewell from a Longtime Rights Leader." *New York Times* (July 29, 1997).

——. "Ex-Charlotte Mayor Earns Helms Rematch." *New York Times* (May 8, 1996): B10.

SAGINI, MASHAK M. *The African and the African American University: A Historical and Sociological Analysis* (1996).

SALEM, NORMA. HABIB *Bourguiba, Islam and the Creation of Tunisia* (1984).

SALZMAN, JACK, DAVID LIONEL SMITH, AND CORNEL WEST, EDS. *Encyclopedia of African-American Culture and History.* 5 vols. (1996).

SAMKANGE, STANLAKE. *What Rhodes Really Said About Africans* (1982).

SAMMONS, JEFFREY T. *Beyond the Ring: The Role of Boxing in American Society* (1988).

SAMMONS, VIVIAN O. *Blacks in Science and Medicine* (1990).

SÁNCHEZ-BOUDY, JOSÉ. *Diccionario de cubanismos m·s usuales (Como habla el cubano).* 6 vols. (1978–1992).

SANDERSON, PETER. *Marvel Universe* (1995).

SANDOVAL, ALONSO DE. *De instauranda aethiopum salute - Un tratado sobre la esclavitud.* Translated by Enriqueta Vila Vilar (1987).

SAN MIGUEL, PEDRO. "The Dominican Peasantry and the Market Economy: The Peasants of the Cibao: 1880–1960." Ph.D. diss. Columbia University, 1987.

——. "The Making of a Peasantry: Dominican Agrarian History from the Sixteenth to the Twentieth Century." *Punto y Coma* 2, nos.1 and 2 (1990): 143–62.

SANTINO, JACK. *Miles of Smiles, Years of Struggle: Stories of Black Pullman Porters* (1989).

SANTOS, SYDNEY M. G. DOS. *André Rebouças e seu tempo* (1985).

SARTRE, JEAN-PAUL. "Orphée Noire." *Situations* 3 (1949): 227–86.

SATCHEL, LEROY. *Pitchin' Man: Satchel Paige's Own Story* (1992).

SATER, WILLIAM F. "The Black Experience in Chile." *In Slavery and Race Relations in Latin America,* ed. Robert Brent Toplin (1974).

SAUNDERS, A. C. *A Social History of Black Slaves and Freedmen in Portugal (1441–1555)* (1982).

SAVIANI, DERMEVAL, GERMAN RAMA, NORBERTO LAMARRA, INÉS AGUERRONDO, AND GREGÓRIO WEINBERG. *Desenvolvimento e educação na América Latina* (1987).

SAVOIA, RAFAEL. *Actas del Primer Congreso de Historia del Negro en el Ecuador y Sur de Colombia, Esmeraldas, 14–16 de octubre* (1988).

——, ed. *El Negro en la historia: Raices africanas in la nacionalidad ecuatorana* (1992).

SCARANO, JULITA. *Cotidiano e solidariedade: Vida di·ria da gente de cor nas Minas Gerais, século XVIII* (1994).

SCHAFFER, MATT, AND CHRISTINE COOPER. *Mandinko: The Ethnography of a West African Holy Land* (1980).

SCHARFMAN, RONNIE L. *"Engagement" and the Language of the Subject in the Poetry of Aimé Césaire* (1987).

SCHATZBERG, MICHAEL. *The Dialectics of Oppression in Zaire* (1988).

SCHEADER, CATHERINE. *Shirley Chisholm: Teacher and Congresswoman* (1990).

SCHIEFFELIN, BAMBI, AND RACHELLE DOUCET. "The 'Real' Haitian Creole: Ideology, Metalinguistics, and Orthographic Choices." *American Ethnologist* 21, no. 1 (1994): 176–200.

SCHNEIDER, JOHN J., AND D. STANLEY EITZEN. "Racial Segregation by Professional Football Positions,1960–1985." *Sociology and Social Research* 70, no. 4 (1986): 259–61.

SCHNEIDER, JOHN T. *Dictionary of African Borrowings in Brazilian Portuguese* (1991).

SCHREINER, CLAUS. *Música brasileira: A History of Popular Music and the People of Brazil.* Translated by Mark Weinstein (1993).

SCHUBERT, FRANK. *Black Valor: Buffalo Soldiers and the Medal of Honor, 1870–1898* (1997).

SCHULLER, GUNTHER. *Early Jazz: Its Roots and Musical Development* (1968).

——. *The Swing Era: The Development of Jazz, 1930–1945* (1989).

SCHWARTZMAN, MYRON. *Romare Bearden: His Life and Art* (1990).

SCHWARTZ-BART, SIMONE. *The Bridge of Beyond.* Translated by Barbara Bray. Introduction by Bridget Jones (1982).

SCHWARZ, ROBERTO. *Misplaced Ideas: Essays on Brazilian Culture* (1992).

SCOTT, KENNETH. "The Slave Insurrection in New York in 1712." *New York Historical Society Quarterly* 45 (January 1961).

SECRETAN, THIERRY. *Going into Darkness: Fantastic Coffins from Africa* (1995).

SENGHOR, LÉOPOLD SEDAR. *Liberté.* 5 vols. (1964–1993).

SERAILE, WILLIAM. *Voice of Dissent: Theophilus Gould Steward (1843–1924) and Black America* (1991).

SERELS, M. Mitchell. *A History of the Jews of Tangier in the Nineteenth and Twentieth Centuries* (1991).

SHARP, WILLIAM FREDERICK. *Slavery on the Spanish Frontier: The Colombian ChocÛ, 1680–1810* (1976).

SHANNON, SANDRA G. *The Dramatic Vision of August Wilson* (1995).

SHAW, ARNOLD. *Honkers and Shouters: The Golden Years of Rhythm and Blues* (1978).

SHAW, DONALD L. *Alejo Carpentier* (1985).

SHERMAN, JOAN. *Invisible Poets: Afro-Americans of the Nineteenth Century.* 2d ed. (1989).

SHERMAN, RICHARD B. *The Case of Odell Waller and Virginia Justice, 1940–1942* (1992).

SHIELDS, JOHN C. "Phillis Wheatley." In *African American Writers,* ed. Valerie Smith (1991).

SHOCKLEY, ANN ALLEN. *Afro-American Women Writers, 1746–1933: An Anthology and Critical Guide* (1988).

SHOGAN, ROBERT, AND TOM CRAIG. *The Detroit Race Riot: A Study in Violence* (1964).

SHOMAN, ASSAD. *13 Chapters of a History of Belize* (1994).

SHUCARD, ALAN R. *Countee Cullen* (1984).

Sierra Leone: Twelve Years of Economic Achievement and Political Consolidation under the APC and Dr. Siaka Stevens, 1968–1980 (1980).

SILL, ROBERT. *David Hammons in the Hood* (1994).

SILVA, J. ROMÃO DA. *Luís Gama e suas poesias satíricas* (1981).

SILVERA, MAKEDA, ED. *The Other Woman: Women of Colour in Contemporary Canadian Literature* (1994).

SILVESTER, PETER. *A Left Hand like God: A History of Boogie-Woogie Piano* (1988).

SIMKINS, CUTHBERT O. *Coltrane: A Musical Biography* (1975).

SIMMONS, DIANE. *Jamaica Kincaid* (1994).

SIMO, ANA MARÍA. *Lydia Cabrera: An Intimate Portrait* (1984).

SIMMS, PETER. *Trouble in Guyana: An Account of People, Personalities, and Politics as They Were in British Guiana* (1966).

SIMPSON, DAVID IAN H. *Marburg and Ebola Virus Infections: A Guide for Their Diagnosis, Management, and Control* (1977).

SIMPSON, GEORGE EATON. *Black Religions in the New World.* (1978).

——. *The Shango Cult in Trinidad* (1965).

SIMS, JANET L. *Marian Anderson: An Annotated Bibliography and Discography* (1981).

SIMS, LOWERY STOKES. *Robert Colescott, A Retrospective 1975–1986* (1987).

SIMS, RUDINE. *Shadow and Substance: Afro-American Experience in Contemporary Children's Fiction* (1982).

SINGER, BARRY. *Black and Blue: The Life and Lyrics of Andy Razaf* (1992).

SINNETTE, ELINOR DES VERNEY. *Arthur Alfonso Schomburg, Black Bibliophile & Collector: A Biography* (1989).

SINNETTE, ELINOR DES VERNEY, W. PAUL COATES, AND THOMAS C. BATTLE, EDS. *Black Bibliophiles and Collectors: Preservers of Black History* (1990).

SITKOFF, HARVARD. *A New Deal for Blacks: The Emergence of Civil Rights as a National Issue.* Vol. I, *The Depression Decade* (1978).

SKIDMORE, THOMAS E. *Black Into White: Race and Nationality in Brazilian Thought* (1974; revised ed., 1993).

SLATER, LES. "What is Mas? What is Carnival? Profiling Carnival and its Origins." *Black Diaspora: A Global Black Magazine* (August 1997).

SLAUGHTER, THOMAS PAUL. *Bloody Dawn: The Christiana Riot and Racial Violence in the Antebellum North* (1991).

SMITH, ANNA DEVEARE. *Fires in the Mirror: Crown Heights, Brooklyn and Other Identities* (1993).

SMITH, BARBARA, ED. *Home Girls: A Black Feminist Anthology* (1983).

SMITH, CHARLES MICHAEL. "Bruce Nugent: Bohemian of the Harlem Renaissance." In *In the Life: A Black Gay Anthology*, ed. Joseph Beam (1986).

SMITH CÓRDOBA, AMIR. *Vida y obra de Candelario Obeso* (1984).

SMITH, IAN DOUGLAS. *The Great Betrayal: The Memoirs of Ian Douglas Smith* (1997).

SMITH-IRVIN, JEANNETTE. *Footsoldiers of the Universal Negro Improvement Association: Their Own Words* (1988).

SMITH, JESSIE CARNEY. *Black Academic Libraries and Research Collections: An Historical Survey* (1977).

——, ed. *Notable Black American Women.* 2 vols. (1992–1996).

SMITH, KEITHLYN B. *No Easy Pushover: A History of the Working People of Antigua and Barbuda, 1836–1994* (1994).

SMITH, KEITHLYN B., AND FERNANDO C. *To Shoot Hard Labour: The Life and Times of Samuel Smith, an Antiguan Workingman, 1877–1982* (1986).

SMITH, ROBERTA. "A Forgotten Black Painter Is Saved from Obscurity." *New York Times* (June 12, 1992): C18.

SMITH, RONNA. "Vida de Adalberto Ortiz." *Cultura: Revista del Banco Central del Ecuador* 6, no. 16 (1983): 99–118.

SMITH, S. CLAY, JR. "Patricia Roberts Harris: A Champion in Pursuit of Excellence." *Howard Law Journal* 29, no. 3 (1986): 437–55.

SMITH, WILLIAM E. "Commandments Without Moses: Abandoning His Principles, Sullivan Wants U. S. Firms to Pull Out." *Time* (June 15, 1987).

SNOWDEN, FRANK M., JR. *Before Color Prejudice: The Ancient View of Blacks* (1983).

——. *Blacks in Antiquity; Ethiopians in the Greco-Roman Experience* (1970).

SOLLORS, WERNER. *Amiri Baraka/LeRoi Jones: The Quest for a "Populist Modernism"* (1978).

——. *Neither Black nor White, Yet Both: Thematic Explorations of Interracial Literature* (1997).

——, ed. *Multilingual America: Transnationalism, Ethnicity, and the Languages of American Literature* (1998).

SOLOW, BARBARA L., ED. *Slavery and the Rise of the Atlantic System* (1991).

SOMJEE, SULTAN. *Material Culture of Kenya* (1993).

SOMMER, DORIS, *Foundational Fictions : The National Romances of Latin America* (1991).

SOTO, SARA. *Magia e historia en los "Cuentos negros": "Por que" y "Ayapa" de Lydia Cabrera* (1988).

SOUTHERN, EILEEN. *The Music of Black Americans: A History* (1983).

SOYINKA, WOLE. *The Burden of Memory, the Muse of Forgiveness* (1999).

——. *Myth, Literature, and the African World* (1976).

——. *The Open Sore of a Continent: A Personal Narrative of the Nigerian Crisis* (1996).

SPELLMAN, A. B. *Black Music: Four Lives* (1970).

SPINNER, THOMAS J., JR. *A Political and Social History of Guyana, 1945–1983* (1984).

SPIVAK, GAYATRI CHAKTAVORTY. *In Other Worlds: Essays in Cultural Politics* (1987).

SPOFFORD, TIM. *Lynch Street: The May 1970 Slayings at Jackson State College* (1988).

STAMPP, KENNETH M. *The Peculiar Institution: Slavery in the Ante-Bellum South* (1956).

STAM, ROBERT. *Tropical Multiculturalism: A Comparative History of Race in Brazilian Cinema and Culture* (1997).

STAM, ROBERT, AND RANDAL JOHNSON. *Brazilian Cinema*. Rev. and exp. ed. (1995).

STANLEY, HENRY MORTON. *In Darkest Africa; or, The Quest, Rescue and Retreat of Emin, Governor of Equatoria* (1890).

——. *Through the Dark Continent; or The Sources of the Nile around the Great Lakes of Equatorial Africa and Down the Livingstone River to the Atlantic Ocean* (1878).

ST. BOURNE, CLAIR. "The African-American Image in American Cinema." *Black Scholar* 21, no.2 (March-May 1990): 12 (8).

STEARNS, MARSHALL, AND JEAN STEARNS. *Jazz Dance: The Story of American Vernacular Dance*. Rev. ed. (1979).

STEIN, JUDITH E., ET AL. I *Tell My Heart: The Art of Horace Pippin* (1993).

STEIN, STEVE J. "Visual Images of the Lower Classes in Early Twentieth-Century Peru: Soccer as a Window to Social Reality." *In Windows on Latin America: Understanding Society through Photographs*, ed. Robert M. Levine (1987).

STEPAN, NANCY. *The Idea of Race in Science* (1982).

STEPHENS, THOMAS M. *Dictionary of Latin American Racial and Ethnic Terminology* (1989).

STEPTO, ROBERT B. "After Modernism, After Hibernation: Michael Harper, Robert Hayden, and Jay Wright." In *Chant of Saints: A Gathering of Afro-American Literature, Art, and Scholarship* (1979).

——. *From Behind the Veil: A Study of Afro-American Narrative* (1979)

STERLING, DOROTHY. *Black Foremothers: Three Lives* (1988).

——. *The Making of an Afro-American: Martin Robison Delany 1812–1885* (1971).

——. *We Are Your Sisters: Black Women in the Nineteenth Century* (1984).

STERN, YVAN. "Interview: Souleymane Cissé." *Unir Cinema* 23–24 (March-June 1986): 44–45.

STEVENSON, BRENDA, ED. *The Journals of Charlotte Forten Grimké* (1988).

STEVENS, PHILLIPS, JR. "Magic" and "Sorcery and Witchcraft." *In Encyclopedia of Cultural Anthropology*, ed. Melvin Ember and David Levinson (1996).

STEVENS, SIAKA. *What Life Has Taught Me* (1984).

STEWART-BAXTER, DERRICK. *Ma Rainey and the Classic Blues Singers* (1970).

STILL, JUDITH ANNE. *William Grant Still: A Bio-bibliography* (1996).

STILL, WILLIAM. *The Underground Railroad: A Record of Facts, Authentic Narratives, Letters, &c., Narrating the Hardships, Hair-breadth Escapes, and Death Struggles of the Slaves in Their Efforts for Freedom, as Related by Themselves and Others or Witnessed By the Author: Together with Sketches of Some of the Largest Stockholders and Most Liberal Aiders and Advisers of the Road* (1872).

STINSON, SULEE JEAN. *The Dawn of Blaxploitation: Sweet Sweetback's Baadasssss Song and its Audience* (1992).

STORY, ROSALYN M. *And So I Sing: African American Divas of Opera and Concert* (1990).

STRAUSS, NEIL. "Curtis Mayfield" (interview). *New York Times* (February 28, 1996).

STRAUS, NOEL. "Dorthy Maynor Berkshire Soloist." *New York Times* (August 10, 1939).

STOWE, HARRIET BEECHER. *Uncle Tom's Cabin: Authoritative Text. Backgrounds and Contexts* (Norton Critical Edition) (1994).

STREICKER, JOEL. "Policing the Boundaries: Race, Class and Gender in Cartagena, Colombia." *American Ethnologist* 22, no. 1 (1995), 54–74.

STUART, CHRIS, AND TILDE STUART. *Africa's Vanishing Wildlife* (1996).

——. *Chris and Tilde Stuart's Field Guide to the Mammals of Southern Africa* (1994).

STUCKEY, STERLING. *Slave Culture: Nationalist Theory and the Foundations of Black America* (1987).

SUGGS, HENRY LEWIS. *P. B. YOUNG, Newspaper-man: Race, Politics, and Journalism in the New South, 1910–1962* (1988).

SULLIVAN, PATRICIA. *Days of Hope: Race and Democracy in the New Deal Era* (1996).

SUMMERVILLE, JAMES. *Educating Black Doctors: A History of Meharry Medical College* (1983).

SUPER, GEORGE LEE, MICHAEL GARDEN, AND NANCY MARSHALL, EDS. *P. H. Polk: Photographs* (1980).

SUTTON, JOHN E. G. *Dar es Salaam: City, Port, and Region* (1970).

SUZIGAN, GERALDO. *Bossa nova: música, política, educação no Brasil* (1990).

SWEETMAN, DAVID. *Women Leaders in African History* (1984).

SWENSON, JOHN. *Stevie Wonder* (1986).

SYLVANDER, CAROLYN WEDIN. *Jessie Redmon Fauset, Black American Writer* (1981).

TARRY, ELLEN. *The Other Toussaint: A Modern Biography of Pierre Toussaint, a Post-Revolutionary Black* (1981).

TATE, CLAUDIA. *Domestic Allegories of Political Desire: The Black Heroine's Text at the Turn of the Century* (1992).

TAYLOR, FRANK. *Alberta Hunter: A Celebration in Blues* (1987).

TAYLOR, PATRICK. *The Narrative of Liberation: Perspectives on Afro-Caribbean Literature, Popular Culture, and Politics* (1989).

TAYLOR, QUINTARD. *The Forging of a Black Community: Seattle's Central District from 1870 through the Civil Rights Era* (1994).

TEIXEIRA, IVAN. *Obras poéticas de Basílio da Gama* (1996).

TENENBAUM, BARBARA A., ED. *Encyclopedia of Latin American History and Culture.* 5 vols. (1996).

"The Ten Most Beautiful Black Women in America (A Wide Range of External and Internal Beauty)." *Ebony* (July 1987).

TERRY, DON. "Hatcher Begins Battle to Regain Spotlight in Gary." *New York Times.* (May 6, 1991): A12.

TERRY, WALLACE, ED. *Bloods: An Oral History of the Vietnam War, by Black Veterans* (1984).

THOBY-MARCELIN, PHILIPPE. *Panorama de l'art Haïtien* (1956).

THOMAS, ANTONY. *Rhodes* (1996).

THOMAS, BETTYE COLLIER. "Harvey Johnson and the Baltimore Mutual United Brother-hood of Liberty, 1885–1910." In *Black Communities and Urban Development in America, 1720–1990: From Reconstruction to the Great Migration, 1877–1917,* ed. Kenneth L. Kusmer. Vol. IV, part 1 (1991).

THOMAS, BROOK. *Plessy v. Ferguson: A Brief History with Documents* (1997).

THOMAS, DAVID S. G. *The Kalahari Environment* (1991).

THOMAS, HUGH. *Cuba: The Pursuit of Freedom* (1971).

THOMPSON, FRANCESCA. "Final Curtain for Anita Bush." *Black World* 23 (July 1974): 60–61.

THOMPSON, LESLIE. *An Autobiography* (1985).

THOMPSON, ROBERT FERRIS. *Flash of the Spirit: African and Afro-American Art and Philosophy* (1983).

——. *Jean-Michel Basquiat* (1985).

THORNTON, J. MILLS III. "Challenge and Response in the Montgomery Bus Boycott of 1955–1956." *Alabama Review* 33 (1980): 163–235.

THORNTON, JOHN. *Africa and Africans in the Making of the Atlantic World: 1400–1800* (1998).

THORPE, EDWARD. *Black Dance* (1990).

THURMAN, HOWARD. *With Head and Heart: The Autobiography of Howard Thurman* (1979).

TIBBLES, ANTHONY, ED. *Transatlantic Slavery: Against Human Dignity* (1994).

TILLERY, TYRONE. *Claude McKay: A Black Poet's Struggle for Identity* (1992).

TIMBERLAKE, LLOYD. *Africa in Crisis: The Causes, the Cures of Environmental Bankruptcy* (1985).

TINGAY, PAUL, AND DOUG SCOTT. *Handy Guide: Victoria Falls* (1996).

TINHORAO, RAMOS JOSÉ. *Os Negros em Portugal: Uma presença silenciosa* (1988).

TIPPU TIP. *Maisha ya Hamed bin Muhammed el Murjebi, Yaani Tippu Tip, kwa Maneno Yake Mwenyewe.* Translated by W. H. Whitely (1966).

TOBIAS, CHANNING. "Autobiography." In *Thirteen Americans: Their Spiritual Biographies* (1953).

TOMKINS, CALVIN, "A SENSE OF URGENCY." *New Yorker* (March 1989): 48–74.

TOOBIN, JEFFREY. *The Run of His Life: The People v. O. J. Simpson* (1996).

TOOP, DAVID. *Ocean of Sound: Aether Talk, Ambient Sound, and Imaginary Worlds* (1995).

TOPLIN, ROBERT BRENT. *The Abolition of Slavery in Brazil* (1972).

TORRENCE, RIDGELY. *The Story of John Hope* (1948).

TOUREH, FANTA. *L'imaginaire dans l'úuvre de Simone Schwartz-Bart: Approche d'une mythologie antillaise* (1986).

Toussaint, Auguste. *History of Mauritius* (1977).

Trexler, Harrison. *Slavery in Missouri, 1804–1865* (1914).

Trevisan, João Silverio. *Perverts in Paradise*. Translated by Martin Foreman (1986).

Truth, Sojourner, and Olive Gilbert, *Narrative of Sojourner Truth, a Northern Slave, Emancipated from Bodily Servitude by the State of New York, in 1828 (1850).*

Turnbull, Colin M. The Forest People (1961).

Turner, Frederick W. *Remembering Song: Encounters with the New Orleans Jazz Tradition*. Exp. ed. (1994).

Turner, Lorenzo Dow. *Africanisms in the Gullah Dialect* (1949).

Turner, Mary. *From Chattel Slaves to Wage Slaves: The Dynamics of Labour Bargaining in the Americas* (1995).

———. *Slaves and Missionaries: The Disintegration of Jamaican Slave Society* (1982).

Tushnet, Mark V. *The NAACP's Strategy Against Segregated Education, 1925–1950* (1987).

Tuttle, William M., Jr. *Race Riot: Chicago in the Red Summer of 1919* (1970).

———, ed. W. E. B. Du Bois (1973).

Tygiel, Jules. *Baseball's Great Experiment: Jackie Robinson and His Legacy* (1983).

Uche, Nena. "Textiles in Nigeria." *African Technology Forum* 7, no. 2 (1994).

Ullman, Michael. *Jazz Lives: Portraits in Words and Pictures* (1980).

Ullman, Victor. *Martin R. Delany: The Beginnings of Black Nationalism* (1971).

Unesco General History of Africa. 8 vols. (1981–1993).

Urban, W. J. *Black* Scholar: Horace Mann Bond 1904–1972 (1992).

Urquhart, Brian. *Ralph Bunche: An American Life* (1993).

Valdez Aguilar, Rafael. *Sinaloa: Negritud y olvido* (1993).

Van Deburg, William L. *New Day in Babylon: The Black Power Movement and American Culture, 1965–1975* (1992).

Vandercook, John W. *Black Majesty: The Life of Christophe, King of Haiti* (1934).

Van Sertima, Ivan. *Blacks in Science: Ancient and Modern* (1991).

———, ed. *African Presence in Early America* (1987).

———, ed. *African Presence in Early Europe* (1985).

———, ed. *Black Women in Antiquity* (1984).

Van Sertima, Ivan, and Runoko Rashidi, eds. *African Presence in Early Asia* (1988).

Vansina, Jan. *Les anciens royaumes de la savane: Les états des savanes méridionales de l'Afrique centrale des origines à l'occupation coloniale* (1965).

———. *Art History in Africa: An Introduction to Method* (1984).

———. *The Children of Woot: A History of the Kuba Peoples* (1978).

———. *Kingdoms of the Savanna* (1966).

———. *Oral Tradition as History* (1985).

——. *Paths in the Rainforests: Toward a History of Political Tradition in Equatorial Africa* (1990).

VAN TASSEL, DAVID D., AND JOHN J. GRABOWSKI. *Cleveland: A Tradition of Reform* (1986).

——. *The Encyclopedia of Cleveland History* (1987).

VARELA, BEATRIZ. *El español cubano-americano* (1992).

VASQUEZ DE URRUTIA, PATRICIA, ED. *La democracia en blanco y negro: Colombia en los anos ochenta* (1989).

VEDANA, HARDY. *Jazz em Porto Alegre* (1987).

VENET, WENDY HAMMOND. *Neither Ballots Nor Bullets: Women Abolitionists and the Civil War* (1991).

VERBEKEN, AUGUSTE. *Msiri, roi du Garenganze: L' homme rouge du Katanga* (1956).

VERGER, PIERRE. *Bahia Africa Bahia: Fotografias* (1996).

——. *Bahia and the West African Trade, 1549–1851* (1964).

——. *Dieux d'Afrique; Culte des Orishas et Vodouns à l' ancienne côte des esclaves en Afrique et à Bahia, la baie de tous les saints au Brésil.*

——. *Ewe: Le verbe et le pouvoir des plantes chez les Yoruba* (1997).

——. *Flux et reflux de la traite des nègres entre le Golfe de Bénin et Bahia de todos os Santos, du XVIIè au XIXè siècle* (1968).

——. *Orixas: Deuses iorubas na Africa e no Novo Mundo* (1981).

——. *Retratos da Bahia, 1946 a 1952* (1980).

VERGER, PIERRE, AND JORGE AMADO. *Iconografia dos deuses africanos no candomblé da Bahia* (1980).

VÉRIN, PIERRE. *The History of Civilization in North Madagascar.* Translated by David Smith (1986).

VÉRIN, PIERRE, C. P. KOTTACK, AND P. GORLIN. "The glottochronology of Malagasy speech communities." *Oceanic Linguistics* 8 (1970): 26–83.

VERÍSSIMO, INÁCIO JOSÉ. *André Rebouças através de sua auto-biografia* (1939).

VESTAL, STANLEY. *Mountain Men* (1937).

VICKERY, WALTER N. *Alexander Pushkin* (1970).

VINES, ALEX. *Renamo: Terrorism in Mozambique* (1991).

VITIER, CINTIO, AND FINA GARCÍA MARRUZ, EDS. *Flor oculta de poesía cubana* (1978).

——. Temas martianos (1981).

VLACH, JOHN MICHAEL. *The Afro-American Tradition in the Decorative Arts* (1978).

VOGEL, ARNO. *A galinha-d'Angola: Iniciacão e identidade na cultura afro-brasileira* (1993).

WADE, PETER. *Blackness and Race Mixture: The Dynamics of Racial Identity in Colombia* (1993).

——. *Race and Ethnicity in Latin America* (1997).

WAGLEY, CHARLES., ED. *Race and Class in Rural Brazil.* 2d ed. (1963).

WAHLMAN, MAUDE SOUTHWELL. *Contemporary African Arts* (1974).

——. *Signs and Symbols: African Images in African-American Quilts* (1993).

WAKHIST, TSI TSI. "Taking the Helm of the NAACP: The Ever-Ready Evers-Williams." *Crisis* 102 (May/June 1995): 14–19.

WALDMAN, GLORIA F. *Luis Rafael Sánchez: Pasión teatral.* (1988).

WALKER, ETHEL PITTS. "The American Negro Theater." In *The Theater of Black Americans,* ed. Errol Hill (1987).

WALKER, GEORGE E. *The Afro-American in New York City, 1827–1860* (1993).

WALKER, JAMES W. ST. G. *The Black Loyalists: The Search for a Promised Land in Nova Scotia and Sierra Leone, 1783–1870* (1992).

WALKER, MELISSA. *Down from the Mountaintop: Black Women's Novels in the Wake of the Civil Rights Movement, 1966–1989* (1991).

WALLS, WILLIAM J. *The African Methodist Episcopal Zion Church: Reality of the Black Church* (1974).

WARD, WILLIAM EDWARD. "Charles Lenox Remond: Black Abolitionist, 1838–1873." Ph.D. diss., Clark University, 1977.

WARE, GILBERT. *William Hastie: Grace Under Pressure* (1984).

WASHINGTON, BOOKER T. *Up From Slavery* (1901).

WASHINGTON, JAMES M. *Conversations with God* (1994).

WATKINS, MEL. *On The Real Side: Laughing, Lying, and Signifying. The Underground Tradition of African-American Humor* (1994).

WATSON, ALAN. *Slave Law in the Americas* (1989).

WATSON, DENTON L. *Lion in the Lobby: Clarence Mitchell, Jr.'s Struggle for the Passage of Civil Rights Laws* (1990).

WATTS, JILL. *God, Harlem U.S.A.: The Father Divine Story* (1992).

WEARE, WALTER B. *Black Business in the New South: A Social History of the North Carolina Mutual Life Insurance Company* (1973).

WEAVER, JOHN DOWNING. *The Brownsville Raid* (1970).

——. *The Senator and the Sharecropper's Son: Exoneration of the Brownsville Soldiers* (1997).

WEAVER, ROBERT C. "The Health Care of Our Cities." *National Medical Association Journal* (January 1968): 42–48.

WEBB, BARBARA J. *Myth and History in Caribbean Fiction: Alejo Carpentier, Wilson Harris, and Edouard Glissant* (1992).

WEBB, LILLIAN ASHCROFT. *About My Father's Business: The Life of Elder Michaux* (1981).

WEINBERG, KENNETH G. *Black Victory: Carl Stokes and the Winning of Cleveland* (1968).

WEINSTEIN, BRIAN. *Eboué* (1972).

WEINSTEIN, NORMAN. *A Night in Tunisia: Imaginings of Africa in Jazz* (1993).

WEISS, NANCY J. *Farewell to the Party of Lincoln: Black Politics in the Age of FDR* (1983).

——. *Whitney M. Young, Jr., and the Struggle for Civil Rights* (1989).

WELLS-BARNETT, IDA B. *On Lynchings: Southern Horrors; A Red Record; Mob Rule in New Orleans* (1969).

WESLEY, CHARLES H. *Charles H. Wesley: The Intellectual Tradition of a Black; Historian*, ed. James L. Conyers, Jr. (1997).

WESLEY, DOROTHY PORTER. "Integration Versus Separatism: William Cooper Nell's Role in the Struggle for Equality." In *Courage and Conscience: Black and White Abolitionists in Boston*, ed. Donald M. Jacobs (1993): 207–24.

WEST, CORNEL. *Beyond Eurocentrism and Multiculturalism* (1993).

———. *Black Theology and Marxist Thought* (1979).

———. *Keeping Faith: Philosophy and Race in America* (1993).

———. *Prophetic Reflections: Notes on Race and Power in America* (1993).

———. *Race Matters* (1993).

WEST, GUIDA. *The National Welfare Rights Movement: The Social Protest of Poor Women* (1981).

"What Martin Luther King Would Do Now about Drugs, Poverty and Black-Jewish Relations: Widow and Associates Tell How He Would Respond to Today's Burning Issues." *Ebony* (January 1991).

WHEAT, ELLEN HARKINS. *Jacob Lawrence, American Painter* (1986).

WHEELER, B. GORDON. *Black California: The History of African-Americans in the Golden State* (1993).

WHITE, ALVIN, "LET ME TELL YOU ABOUT MY LOVE AFFAIR WITH FLORENCE MILLS." *Sepia* 26, no. 11 (November 1977).

WHITE, TIMOTHY. *Catch a Fire: The Life of Bob Marley*. Rev. and enl. ed. (1998).

WHITE, WALTER F. *A Man Called White: The Autobiography of Walter White* (1948; reprint ed., 1995).

———. *Rope and Faggot: A Biography of Judge Lynch* (1929).

WHITFIELD, STEPHEN J. *A Death in the Delta: The Story of Emmett Till* (1988).

WHITING, ALBERT N. *Guardians of the Flame: Historically Black Colleges Yesterday, Today, and Tomorrow* (1991).

WHITMAN, MARK, ED. *Removing a Badge of Slavery: The Record of Brown v. Board of Education* (1993).

WHITTEN, NORMAN. *Black Frontiersmen: A South American Case* (1974).

———, ed. *Cultural Transformations and Ethnicity in Modern Ecuador* (1981).

WICKER, TOM. *A Time to Die* (1975).

WIENER, LEO. *Africa and the Discovery of America*. Vol. I (1920).

WIGG, DAVID. *And Then Forgot to Tell Us Why: A Look at the Campaign Against River Blindness in West Africa* (1993).

WIKRAMANAYAKE, MARINA. *A World in Shadow: The Free Black in Antebellum South Carolina* (1973).

WILKINS, ROY. *Standing Fast: The Autobiography of Roy Wilkins* (1982).

WILLIAMS, ELSIE A. *The Humor of Jackie Moms Mabley: An African American Comedic Tradition* (1995).

WILLIAMS, ERIC. *Capitalism and Slavery* (1944; reprint ed., 1994).

———. *Inward Hunger: The Education of a Prime Minister* (1969).

WILLIAMS, LORNA V. "Morˈa Delgado and the Cuban Slave Narrative." *Modern Language Notes* 108, no. 2 (March 1993): 302–13.

———. *The Representation of Slavery in Cuban Fiction.* (1994).

WILLIAMS, MICHAEL W. *Pan-Africanism: An Annotated Bibliography* (1992).

WILLIAMSON, JANICE. *Sounding Differences: Conversations with Seventeen Canadian Women Writers* (1993).

WILLIAMSON, JOEL. *After Slavery: The Negro in South Carolina During Reconstruction, 1861–1877* (1965; reprint ed., 1990).

———. *The Crucible of Race: Black-White Relations in the American South Since Emancipation* (1984).

———. *New People: Miscegenation and Mulattoes in the United States* (1980).

WILLIAMS, PONTHEOLLA T. *Robert Hayden: A Critical Analysis of His Poetry* (1987).

WILLIAMS, ROGER. *The Bonds: An American Family* (1971).

WILLIS, SUSAN. "Crushed Geraniums: Juan Francisco Manzano and the Language of Slavery." In *The Slave's Narrative,* ed. Charles T. Davis and Henry Louis Gates, Jr. (1985).

———. *Specifying: Black Women Writing the American Experience* (1987).

WILLIS-THOMAS, DEBORAH. *Black Photographers, 1840–1940: An Illustrated Bio-Bibliography* (1985).

———. *An Illustrated Bio-Bibliography of Black Photographers, 1940–1988* (1989).

WILMER, VALERIE. "'Blackamoors' and the British Beat." In *Views on Black American Music,* no. 3 (1985–1988): 60–64.

WILSON, CHARLES REAGAN, AND WILLIAM FERRIS, EDS. *Encyclopedia of Southern Culture* (1989).

WILSON, MARY, WITH PATRICIA ROMANOWSKI AND AHRGUS JULLIARD. *Dreamgirl: My Life as a Supreme* (1986).

WILSON, WILLIAM JULIUS. *The Bridge over the Racial Divide: Rising Inequality and Coalition Politics* (1999).

———. *When Work Disappears: The World of the New Urban Poor* (1996).

WINANT, HOWARD. "Rethinking Race in Brazil." *Journal of Latin American Studies* 24 (1992): 173–92.

WINCH, JULIE. *Philadelphia's Black Elite: Activism, Accommodation, and the Struggle for Autonomy, 1787–1848* (1988).

WINKS, ROBIN W. *The Blacks in Canada: A History* (1997).

WIPPLER, MIGENE GONZÁLEZ. *Santería: The Religion* (1982).

WOIDEK, CARL. *Charlie Parker: His Music and Life* (1996).

WOLFENSTEIN, EUGENE VICTOR. *The Victims of Democracy: Malcolm X and the Black Revolution* (1981).

WOLSELEY, ROLAND E. *The Black Press, U.S.A.* (1990).

WOODBRIDGE, HENSLEY C. "Glossary of Names Found in Colonial Latin America for Crosses Among Indians, Negroes, and Whites." *Journal of the Washington Academy of Sciences* 38 (1948): 353–62.

WOOD, JOE, ED. *Malcolm X: In Our Own Image* (1992).

WOOD, PETER H. *Black Majority: Negroes in Colonial South Carolina from 1670 through the Stono Rebellion* (1974).

WOOD, PETER H., AND KAREN C. C. DALTON. *Winslow Homer's Images of Blacks: The Civil War and Reconstruction Years* (1988).

WOODSON, CARTER G. "The Negroes of Cincinnati Prior to the Civil War." In *Free Blacks in America, 1800–1860*, ed. John Bracey, Jr. August Meier, and Elliot Rudwick (1971).

WOODS, SYLVIA. *Sylvia's Soul Food: Recipes from Harlem's World Famous Restaurant* (1992).

WOODWARD, C. VANN. *Origins of the New South: 1877–1913* (1951).

——. *Reunion and Reaction: The Compromise of 1877 and the End of Reconstruction* (1951; reprint ed. 1991).

——. *The Strange Career of Jim Crow* (1955).

Woolman, David S. *Stars in the Firmament: Tangier Characters, 1660–1960s* (1997).

WORCESTER, KENT. *C. L. R. James and the American Century, 1938–1953* (1980).

WORLD BANK. *Mauritius Country Report* 4 (1988).

WRIGHT, GILES R. *Afro-Americans in New Jersey: A Short History* (1988).

WRIGHT, LEE ALFRED. *Identity, Family, and Folklore in African American Literature* (1995).

WRIGHT, RICHARD R., JR. *The Negro in Pennsylvania, A Study in Economic History* (1969).

WUBBEN, HUBERT H. *Civil War Iowa and the Copperhead Movement* (1980).

WYNES, CHARLES E. *Charles Richard Drew: The Man and the Myth* (1988).

XAVIER, ISMAIL. *Allegories of Under-development: Aesthetics and Politics in Modern Brazilian Cinema* (1997).

YANCEY, DWAYNE. *When Hell Froze Over: The Untold Story of Doug Wilder: A Black Politician's Rise to Power in the South* (1988).

YAU, JOHN. "Please, Wait by the Coatroom: Wifredo Lam in the Museum of Modern Art." *Arts Magazine* 4 (1988): 56–59.

YELLIN, JEAN FAGAN, AND JOHN C. VAN HORNE, EDS. *The Abolitionist Sisterhood: Women's Political Culture in Antebellum America* (1994).

YOHE, KRISTINE A. "Gloria Naylor." In *The Oxford Companion to African American Literature*, ed. James David Hart and Phillip W. Leininger. 6th ed. (1995).

YOUNG, ANDREW. *An Easy Burden: The Civil Rights Movement and the Transformation of America* (1996).

——. *A Way Out of No Way: The Spiritual Memoirs of Andrew Young* (1994).

YOUNG, CRAWFORD. *Politics in the Congo: Decolonization and Independence* (1965).

ZANGRANDO, ROBERT. *The NAACP Crusade Against Lynching, 1909–1950* (1980).

ZENÓN CRUZ, ISABELO. *Narciso descubre su trasero: El negro en la cultura puertorriqueña*. 2d ed. (1975).

ZIELINA, MARIA CARMEN. *La africania en el cuento cubano y puertorriqueño* (1992).

ZINN, HOWARD. *SNCC: The New Abolitionists* (1965).